Schott's
Almanac

2009

All knowledge is of itself of some value.
There is nothing so minute or inconsiderable,
that I would not rather know it than not.
— SAMUEL JOHNSON (1709–84)

Schott's Almanac 2009 ™ · Schott's Almanac ™
Schott's Annual Astrometer ™ © 2008

© BEN SCHOTT 2008 · All rights reserved

Published by Bloomsbury Publishing Plc., 36 Soho Square, London, W1D 3QY, UK

www.benschott.com

1 2 3 4 5 6 7 8 9 10

Cover illustration by Alison Lang. © Ben Schott 2008. All rights reserved.
Portraits by Chris Lyon. © Ben Schott 2006, 2007, 2008. All rights reserved.
The surveys on pp.102–03, 228, 242–43, 290–91, 295, and 335 were undertaken by Ipsos MORI and first published in *The Times* in a more extended form; grateful thanks are extended to both.
The table of PMs on pp.252–53 was first published in *The Times*; grateful thanks are extended to *Facts About the British Prime Ministers*, Englefield, Seaton, & White (The H.W. Wilson Co., NY)
The oil trading pictures on pp.234–35 were first published in the *New York Times*.
Other illustrations © Ben Schott 2008. All rights reserved.

NOTE · Information included within is believed to be correct at the time of going to press. Neither the author nor the publisher can accept any responsibility for any error or subsequent changes.

The paper this book is
printed on is certified by the
© 1996 Forest Stewardship
Council A.C. (FSC).
It is ancient-forest friendly.
The printer holds FSC chain
of custody SGS-COC-2061

FSC
Mixed Sources
Product group from well-managed
forests and other controlled sources
Cert no. SGS-COC-2061
www.fsc.org
© 1996 Forest Stewardship Council

ISBN (hardback) 978-0-7475-9562-5
ISBN (paperback) 978-1-4088-0021-8
A CIP catalogue record for this book
is available from the British Library.
Designed & typeset by BEN SCHOTT
Printed in Great Britain by
CLAYS Ltd, ST IVES Plc.

Also by BEN SCHOTT

Schott's Original Miscellany
Schott's Food & Drink Miscellany
Schott's Sporting, Gaming, & Idling Miscellany
Schott's Miscellany Diary (with Smythson)
American and German editions of *Schott's Almanac 2009* are also available

Schott's
Almanac

2009

· *The book of things past and the song of the future* ·

Conceived, edited, and designed by

BEN SCHOTT

UK & Series Editor · Claire Cock-Starkey

US Editor · Bess Lovejoy
Assistant Editor · Victoria Kingston
German Editor · Alexander Weber
Researcher · Iona Macdonald

· BLOOMSBURY

Preface

A calendar, a calendar! look in the almanack;
find out moonshine, find out moonshine.
— A Midsummer Night's Dream, III i

Completely revised and updated, *Schott's Almanac 2009* picks up from where the 2008 edition left off, to create a seamless biography of the year. ❦ The celebrated wit James Thurber (1894–1961) once observed, 'So much has already been written about everything that you can't find out anything about it'. If this is true, and it seems increasingly so, then mechanisms for filtering news and opinion become ever more valuable. *Schott's Almanac* aspires to be one such filter – stepping back from the torrent of rolling news to offer an informative, selective, and entertaining analysis of the year. ❦ The C21st almanac is necessarily different from some of its distinguished predecessors [see p.6], which were published in times when the year was defined by considerations astronomical, ecclesiastical, or aristocratic. By exploring high art and pop culture, geopolitics and gossip, scientific discovery and sporting achievement, *Schott's Almanac* endeavours to describe the year as it is lived, in all its complexity.

— *Schott's* is an almanac written to be read.

―――――――――――― THE ALMANAC'S YEAR ――――――――――――

In order to be as inclusive as possible, the *Schott's Almanac* year runs until mid-September.

Data cited in *Schott's Almanac* are taken from the latest sources available at the time of writing.

―――――――――――― ERRORS & OMISSIONS ――――――――――――

Every effort has been made to ensure that the information contained within *Schott's Almanac* is both accurate and up-to-date, and grateful acknowledgement is made to the various sources used. However, as Goethe once said: 'error is to truth as sleep is to waking'. Consequently, the author would be pleased to be informed of any errors, inaccuracies, or omissions that might help improve future editions.

Please send all comments or suggestions to the author, care of:

Bloomsbury Publishing Plc, 36 Soho Square, London, W1D 3QY
or email *editor@schottsalmanac.com*

The author is grateful to the readers who sent in comments on the 2007 edition. Notable corrections and clarifications are included in the Errata section on p.352.

Contents

EARLY ALMANACS OF NOTE

Solomon Jarchi................. *c.*1150
Peter de Dacia.................. *c.*1300
Walter de Elvendene............ 1327
John Somers (Oxford) 1380
Nicholas de Lynna 1386
Purbach.................... 1150–1461
After the invention of printing
Gutenberg (at Mainz)........... 1457

Regiomontanus (at Nuremberg) . 1474
Zainer (at Ulm)................. 1478
Richard Pynson 1497
Stoffler (in Venice) 1499
Poor Robin's Almanack.......... 1652
Francis Moore's Almanack. 1698–1713
Almanach de Gotha.............. 1764
Whitaker's Almanack 1868

ALMANAC vs ALMANACK

The spelling and etymology of 'almanac' are the subject of some dispute. The *Oxford English Dictionary* notes the very early use of 'almanac' by Roger Bacon in 1267, though Chaucer used 'almenak' in *c.*1391; and Shakespeare, 'almanack' in 1590. Variations include almanach(e), amminick, almanacke, &c. A number of etymologies for *almanac* have been suggested: that it comes from the Arabic *al* [the] *mana(h)* [reckoning or diary]; that it comes from the Anglo-Saxon *al-moan-heed*, 'to wit, the regard or observations of all the moons', or from the Anglo-Saxon *al-monath* [all the months]; or that it is linked to the Latin for sundial, *manachus*. In 1838, *Murphy's Almanac* made the bold prediction that 20 January that year would be 'Fair, prob. lowest deg. of winter temp'. When, on the day, this actually turned out to be true, *Murphy's Almanac* became a bestseller.

SYMBOLS & ABBREVIATIONS

> ....greater than
≥ .... greater than or equal to
< .... less than
≤ ....less than or equal to
♂ ....male/men
♀ .... female/women
c...... *circa*, meaning around or roughly

km............................ kilometre
m .... metre
mi..................................mile
'/" ....feet/inches
C.................Century (e.g., C20th)
ONS ...... Office of National Statistics
Crown © ....Crown Copyright

Throughout the *Almanac*, some figures may not add to totals because of rounding.

'AVERAGES'

With the following list of values: 10, 10, 20, 30, 30, 30, 40, 50, 70, 100 = 390

MEAN or AVERAGE..... the sum divided by the number of values...............39
MODE................... the most popular value 30
MEDIAN................. the 'middle' value of a range, here: (30+30)/2 30
RANGE .... the difference between the highest & lowest values 90

Chronicle

*Time has too much credit ... It is not a great healer. It is an indifferent and
perfunctory one. Sometimes it does not heal at all. And sometimes when it seems to,
no healing has been necessary.* — IVY COMPTON-BURNETT (1884–1969)

———————————— SOME AWARDS OF NOTE ————————————

Time magazine Person of the Year [2007] · VLADIMIR PUTIN
*'At significant cost to the principles and ideas that free nations prize, he has performed
an extraordinary feat of leadership in imposing stability on a nation that has rarely
known it and brought Russia back to the table of world power'*

Tipperary International Peace Prize..........................Benazir Bhutto [see p.61]
Woodrow Wilson Award for Public Service..................Dr A.P.J. Abdul Kalam
Robert Burns Humanitarian Award................................ Jonathan Kaplan
Australian of the Year............................... Lee Kernaghan [country musician]
BP Portrait Award...Craig Wylie, for *K*
Car of the Year [*What Car?*] ....Jaguar XF
Prison Officer of the Year [HM Prison Service] ....David Wingfield [HMYOI Castington]
International Engine of the Year........... BMW 3-litre Twin Turbo [135, 335, X6]
Int. Wine Challenge · champion red..Wild Earth Central Otago Pinot Noir 2006
– champion white.....................Auvigue Pouilly Fuissé Vieilles Vignes 2006
Charity Awards · overall winner.......................... Excellent Development
GQ Woman of the Year....................................... Sam Taylor Wood
Barrister of the Year [*The Lawyer*]........Mark Howard QC, Brick Court Chambers
Annual Ernest Hemingway Look-Alike Award.................Tom Grizzard, USA
Slimming World Man of the Year..................... Brian Semple [lost 95kg · 15st]
Pet Slimmer of the Year .... Oscar the Labrador [lost 9·5kg · 1·5st]
Chess Club of the Year.................................... Mushrooms Chess Club
Rears of the Year .... ♂ Ryan Thomas · ♀ Jennifer Ellison
Pier of the Year.. Deal Pier
Airline of the Year [Skytrax] ....Singapore Airlines
Pantone Colour of the Year...Blue Iris
Celebrity Mum of the Year .... Suzanne Shaw
Best British Cuppa [UK Tea Council]..The Olde Bakery Tea Shoppe, Gloucestershire

———————————— PLAIN ENGLISH CAMPAIGN · 2007 ————————————

Ex-England manager, Steve McClaren, won the PEC's 'Foot in Mouth' award for:

*'He (Wayne Rooney) is inexperienced,
but he's experienced in terms of what he's been through.'*

——— MISC. LISTS OF 2008 ———

THE WORST GADGETS
*according to a poll by
reevoo.com*
Electric nail file
Laser guided scissors
Soda stream · Foot spa
Fondue set [fondon't]
Hair crimper · Egg boiler
Electric fluff remover
Electric carving knife
Trouser press
Face steamer · Teasmade
MiniDisc player
Facial tanner · Egg slicer
Electric tin opener
Yoghurt maker
Towel warmer
Back scratcher

**TREES MOST OFTEN
FOUND IN BRITISH
STREETS & PARKS**
*according to the Dept
for Communities &c.*
Leyland cypress
Hawthorn · Sycamore
Silver birch
Common ash
Lawson cypress
English oak
Japanese cherry
Beech · Holly

10 WITTIEST BRITONS
according to Dave TV
Oscar Wilde
Spike Milligan
Stephen Fry
Jeremy Clarkson
Winston Churchill
Paul Merton
Noël Coward
William Shakespeare
Brian Clough
Liam Gallagher
[Margaret Thatcher ranked 12th]

**NICKNAMES FOR
NICOLAS SARKOZY**
*according to Paris
correspondent for* The
Times, *Charles Bremner*
Super-Sarko
Speedy Sarko
L'Hyperprésident
L'Omniprésident
Le Petit Nicolas
Le Lapin Duracell
Le Président Bling Bling
Le Roi Sarko I
Also, for his government
Le Sarko Show
Le Sark-Opéra

**THE MOST BEAUTIFUL
WORDS IN ENGLISH**
*according to a British
Council survey of people
learning the language*
Mother · Passion
Smile · Love
Eternity · Fantastic
Destiny · Freedom
Liberty · Tranquillity

THE UGLIEST THINGS
according to The Ecologist
Bagged salad
Urban dogs · Kids' food
Bike lanes · Fake tans
The Rochdale Asda
Fireworks · Junk mail
New housing estates
Shrink-wrapped swedes

**KIDS' MOST HATED
VEGETABLES**
according to a Heinz poll
Aubergines .. *dislike* 39%
Sprouts 37%
Celeriac.............32%
Cabbage...........16%
Mangetout 12%

———2009 WORDS———

The following words
celebrate anniversaries
in 2009, based upon the
earliest cited use traced
by the venerable *Oxford
English Dictionary*:

{1509} *elocution*
(oratorical or literary style) ·
refulgent (resplendent with
light) · {1609} *baritone*
(male voice, from lower A
in the bass clef to lower F
in the treble) · *pipe office*
(humorous term for the
mouth) · *queen bee* (the
reproductive female in a
colony of social bees) ·
stateswoman (a female
statesman) · {1709} *blood
relation* (one related by
birth or consanguinity) ·
story-teller (one who ...)
· {1809} *ambulance* (a
movable [army] hospital) ·
ginger beer · *jollification*
(the act of making merry) ·
{1909} *air conditioning*
· *caravanner* [see p.215]
· *cinema* (abbreviation of
'cinematograph') · *gaffe*
(inadvertent error) · *oo-er*
(expression of surprise or
innuendo) · {1919} *ad
lib* (speaking extempore)
· {1929} *balls-up* (an
inch away from a cock-up)
· {1939} *dognapping*
(stealing dogs for a reward)
· *jitterbug* (the dance)
· {1949} *Big Brother*
(Orwell's leviathan) ·
tweenager (almost or
just a teenager) · {1959}
binge eating · {1969}
moonwalk (not the dance)

———————— SOME SURVEY RESULTS OF 2007–08 ————————

%	*of British adults, unless stated*	*source & month*
84	of 14–25s would remain friends with someone with HIV	[British Red Cross; Nov 07]
76	of women judge potential dates by analysing their text messaging style	[118118; Jun]
76	say depriving civilians of medicine, food, and water in war is wrong	[ICRC; Dec 07]
75	felt they belonged strongly to their neighbourhoods	[Dept Comm. & Local Gov.; Mar]
75	support stronger immigration controls	[Pew Global Attitudes Project; Oct 07]
73	claimed to have volunteered in the last 12 months	[Comm. and Local Gov.; Mar]
72	of women find a man wearing a cardigan 'sexy'	[Asda; Mar]
69	say parental income plays too large a part in a child's life chances	[Ipsos MORI; June]
67	of parents worry about the company their children keep	[ICM/Random House; Mar]
66	believe that religion and government should be kept separate	[Pew Global; Oct 07]
60	have bet on a horse in the past year	[The Brooke; June]
60	of children think people on TV drink too much	[Life Education; June]
59	saw passing their driving test as a life-changing event	[British Int. Motor Show; Feb]
57	believe that Jesus was crucified, buried, and rose from the dead	[Theos; Mar]
55	of women with children <5 work outside the home	[Children's Society; Jun]
52	regularly feel so tired at work they would like to go home	[The Sleep Council; Mar]
49	trust their housemates not to use their credit/debit cards	[So Protect Me; Nov 07]
42	pray outside of church or other religious services	[Tearfund; Nov 07]
41	claim they 'always cook from scratch'	[Mintel; May]
40	of men say their partner should not pay for anything on a date	[NS&I; Mar]
39	would rather enjoy a good standard of living than save for retirement	[ONS; Jan]
39	consider the environmental impact of a new TV, DVD player, or PC	[Ofcom; Aug]
39	say there is too much emphasis on convenience foods	[Mintel; Sept 08]
38	feel it is acceptable for a woman to sell sex to a man [see p.104]	[Ipsos MORI; June]
33	of women ≥16 have had their belly-button pierced	[BMJ; June]
31	agree 'our people are not perfect, but our culture is superior to others'	[Pew; Oct 07]
30	say they are 'very' or 'a little' biased against other races	[NatCen; Jan]
28	say the benefits of the London Olympics will outweigh the cost	[YouGov; Aug]
27	say Admiral Lord Nelson is the greatest British military hero	[UKNDA; Aug]
25	have put their personal details on a social networking site	[Microsoft/YouGov; Nov 07]
21	have considered adoption	[BAAF; Nov 07]
21	did not know that the square root of 64 is 8	[KPMG/YouGov; Mar]
20	of web users avoid shopping online because of safety fears	[GetSafeOnline.org; Dec 07]
20	of over-55s try activities abroad that they would not do at home	[FCO; Mar]
19	with children have cut back on food due to fuel costs [see p.17]	[Save the Children; Feb]
16	say their healthcare system works well	[Harris Interactive/*Intl Herald Tribune*; May]
13	of married internet users check on their partner's browsing history	[Oxford Uni.; Jul]
13	of ≤40s have cooked steak and kidney pie at least once	[Tesco; Mar]
13	of men eat 5 servings of fruit and vegetables each day	[Health Food Man. Assoc.; Feb]
12	agree 'we are leaving our children a better world than our parents left us'	[JWT; Jan]
11	of female workers have experienced sex discrimination at work	[Croner/YouGov; Apr]
9	are helping pay for the cost of their parents' retirement	[Engage Mutual Assurance; Mar]
6	of dental patients have resorted to self-treatment [see p.112]	[British Dental Assoc.; Oct]
5	are not on first-name terms with their next-door neighbours	[Full of Life; Aug]
1	believe God is female	[Populus/Movement for Reform Judaism; May]

WORDS OF THE YEAR

UNMENTIONABLES · Cherie Blair's euphemism for the items (including 'contraceptive equipment') she was too embarrassed to take to Balmoral, which led to the conception of her son, Leo.

DUMBLEGATE · brouhaha following J.K. Rowling's suggestion that Albus Dumbledore was homosexual.

TT · *Total Tosh* · Lady Amber Leighton's term for the rumours about (her son) Guy Ritchie's marriage to Madonna.

NOT FLASH, JUST GORDON · attempt to brand Brown as the anti-Blair; later mocked as CRASH GORDON.

TRAVOLTA MICAWBER STRATEGY · Brown's political plan: i.e., staying alive whilst hoping that something will turn up (coined by *The Times*'s Danny Finkelstein).

MILIPUTSCH · David Miliband's positioning to succeed Brown.

GST · *Good Ship Titanic* · nickname for the chaos inside Brown's government.

TINY LITTLE DOT · Mugabe's dismissive description of Gordon Brown.

THE INVISIBLE TRIP · Brown's ill-timed trip to the US, which was overshadowed by Pope Benedict XVI's visit.

NON DOM[iciled] · those who pay no tax on earnings made outside the UK.

FLOPSY BUNNY ISSUES · policies to which few object (alleviating poverty, &c.).

CARLA EFFECT · the boost in popularity of French President Nicolas Sarkozy after he divorced Cécilia and married the pop star model Carla Bruni.

PAY AS YOU THROW · the trend of 'charging at the point of refuse'.

PSYCHICS, VISIONS, DREAMS; NASTY; NUTTY; IDEAS; WELL WISHERS · some of the categories used by Kate & Gerry McCann to sort the letters sent to them after the disappearance of Madeleine.

LAMBETH LIST · the C of E's *Lambeth & Bishopthorpe Register* which lists those prevented from public ministry.

THE N.I.C.E. DECADE · in May 2008, the Governor of the Bank of England Mervyn King said: 'for the time being at least, the N.I.C.E. decade is behind us.' In this context, N.I.C.E. meant 'Non-Inflationary Consistent Expansion'.

NIGHT-TIME SPINACH · euphemism for illegal bushmeat traded and cooked (at night) by refugees in E Africa.

FATHER OF THE NATION · the deliberately vague description of Vladimir Putin's place in Russian politics after the March 2008 elections.

Mucca Chucksa Cuppa Water Over Macca's Lawyer Shacka · *Sun* headline alleging Heather Mills poured water over the head of Paul McCartney's divorce lawyer, Fiona Shackleton.

SHORT SELLING · legal (if currently unpopular) strategy of selling financial instruments one has borrowed in the hope of buying them back at a lower price and profiting from the difference. On 18/9/08, in response to the financial turmoil [see p.37], the British government halted the SHORTING of certain financial stocks for a limited time.

THRISIS · a thirtysomething crisis.

—————————— WORDS OF THE YEAR cont. ——————————

ANGEL FLIGHTS · US military term for flights repatriating dead soldiers.

ECONOMIC HIV · the severity and impact of Zimbabwe's unstoppable hyperinflation [see p.33]. *Also* MOLLAR · Zimbabwean slang for Z$1m. *Also* ZIMBABTHEM · sad allusion to the arrogance of Zimbabwe's rulers [i.e., not Zimbab-we]. *Also* MUGABE'S TSUNAMI · the mass of refugees fleeing Zimbabwe.

YAWNS · *Young & Wealthy but Normal* · billionaires who eschew ostentation and excess in favour of philanthropy.

MOMPRENEURS · mothers who combine child care with a home business.

ANDYMONIUM · Andy Murray equivalent of (Tim) Henmania.

MARMITE POLITICIAN · those, like Boris Johnson or Ken Livingstone, that voters either 'love' or 'hate'.

TERRORIST FIST JAB · DAP · see p.13.

SECULAR SABBATH · one day a week (more or less) when all electronic inputs (email, phone, &c.) are turned off.

PEAKNIKS · those who predict the end of oil, and with it the fall of capitalism.

WALL STREET GOT DRUNK · Bush's 'off the record' analysis of the economy.

RECESSIONISTA · one who predicts, talks up, or invests in expectation of a recession. *Also*, one who manages to maintain their lifestyle in a downturn.

SCRIMP & SPLURGE · the recessionary trend of saving on some items, while still being prepared to pay for luxury.

BLUE-SKY DAYS · low pollution target set for Beijing's air quality during the Olympics. [100μg/m³: twice the WHO level]

FLAME OF SHAME · demonstrators' term for the Olympic torch [see p.297].

BEIJINGOISM · China's Olympic pride.

PHELPS PHEVER · see p.24.

GREAT HAUL OF CHINA · description of GB's Olympic medal tally [see p.298].

IPOD GENERATION · Insecure, Pressurised, Overtaxed, Debt-ridden.

TIME HORIZON · new euphemism for the 'timetable' of withdrawal from Iraq.

KAROSHI · Japanese term for 'sudden death from overwork'.

DISTAVORE · one who (deliberately) sources food from far-flung places.

STOP LIST · the Kremlin's list of those banned from appearing in the media.

PROTESTIVALS · festivals with political or social agendas.

GREEN GOLD · valuable material that was previously given away for recycling.

ALLERGY BULLYING · exploiting food (or other) allergies to torment others.

BAITING · tactic of the US Army in Iraq of leaving items useful to the insurgency (explosives, ammo) and targeting with snipers those who collect them.

PIIGS · Portugal, Italy, Ireland, Greece, & Spain · The Eurozone countries most at risk from an economic downturn.

———————— WORDS OF THE YEAR cont. ————————

PRECAUTIONARY BUYING · political euphemism for panic buying.

HYPERMILING · using a variety of driving techniques (e.g., pre-emptive braking) to increase fuel efficiency.

BOREOUT · burnout by boredom.

AGFLATION · agricultural inflation. *Also* SILENT TSUNAMI · The UN's term for rising world food prices [see p.16].

TANOREXIA · addiction to (fake) tans.

NEAR ABROAD · Russian term for former Soviet areas [see p.23].

WIDOW SIX SEVEN · see p.273.

FAT, MUSCLE, BONE · supposedly the three stages of corporate redundancies, as the least talented are fired first.

CLEAN TEAMS · investigators untainted by any involvement in torture, selected to prosecute Guantánamo detainees.

TAXODUS · the relocation of firms or individuals to lower-taxed jurisdictions.

QUEASICAM · filmmaking that aspires to verisimilitude by mimicking raw, amateur footage from cell phones, &c. *Also* MUMBLECORE · emerging indie movie genre characterised by an awkward twentysomething slacker sensibility, low-key plots, and realistic, casual, and often improvised dialogue.

LKBC · those who combine a powerful influence with a low profile: the Least Known, Best Connected.

A SOLDIER OF IDEAS · Fidel Castro's self-defined role after resigning.

DRUNKOREXICS · those who starve or purge in order to mitigate the calories they later consume in alcohol.

UNFITNEY · a Britney Spears moniker.

DESKWICH · sandwich eaten '*al desko*'.

CHILD PROTECTION SPACES · areas set up to provide security for children orphaned after major disasters.

3Gs · households that, out of necessity, contain 3 generations of the same family.

BOOMTOWN BRATS · the daughters of Bob Geldof: Peaches and Pixie.

SEE-HEAR-BUY · near-instantaneous purchase and delivery of goods (e.g., music heard at Starbucks and downloaded there and then via iTunes, &c.).

PLAIN VANILLA · traders' term for the simplest forms of financial investment.

BEERBOARDING · extracting information by getting someone drunk.

SHOPDROPPING · placing items *onto* store shelves for the purpose of political activism, artistic expression, or self-promotion. *Also* DROPLIFTING.

DEFICTIONISE · actually manufacturing a hitherto fictional product, such as the real-life confectionery based upon sweets in the *Harry Potter* series.

LEANOVER · a mild hangover.

SPORNO · the heady convergence of sporting and sexual imagery; such as David Beckham's underwear ads.

STAYCATION · see p.221.

———————— OBJECT OF THE YEAR · THE HAND ————————

One of the year's most iconic images was of the ink-stained fingers of voters in Zimbabwe. Indelible ink has prevented voter fraud in undeveloped areas since at least the 1920s, and George W. Bush boasted of the ink-stain of freedom in Iraq's 2005 elections. But under Robert Mugabe's vicious regime, those who could not show ink-stained proof of voting risked assault by Zanu-PF thugs, since the only candidate in the presidential runoff was Mugabe himself [see p.33]. ❦ Superficially, few things could be less modern than the hand or its component fingers. In 1888, the anthropologist Frank Baker wrote, 'The hand is so intimately connected with the brain as the executor of its behests that the savage mind naturally ascribes to it a separate and distinct force independent of the rest of the body – makes it, in fact, a fetish'. The ancient Greeks, for example, 'cut from the body of a suicide the hand which had committed the deed and buried it in a separate place'. ❦ In 2008, hands and fingers linked the most fragile societies and the most modern technologies. As Zimbabweans struggled with democracy, so millions were getting to grips with Apple's iPhone which, for the first time, put multi-touch technology into the hands of the masses. Apple, Microsoft, and many others are now pioneering (and attempting to patent) a vocabulary of touch-screen 'tactile events' (*tap, swipe, drag, flick, pinch*), in the most significant innovation in gestural communication since the invention of sign language in 1775. ❦ Palmistry has long held that hands can foretell the future, and fingers have tracked the past since the clay fingerprint seals of the Han Dynasty (206 BC–AD 220).

Now security systems are bridging this divide by using biometric finger and palm scans, as well as techniques of gesture recognition and authentication by 'typing pattern'. ❦ In an increasingly mediated society, where computers 'handshake' across networks and Facebookers 'poke' one another, human touch remains resolutely significant. In 2008, the 'Harare handshake' between Mugabe and Morgan Tsvangirai proved almost as newsworthy as the 'fist bump' between Barack and Michelle Obama – sneered at by Fox News as a 'terrorist fist jab'. In Paris, Nicolas Sarkozy engineered a curious three-way handshake with Israel's Ehud Olmert and Palestine's Mahmoud Abbas, while in N Ireland, Gordon Brown was baffled by Bush's 'homeboy' handshake. Brown also drew a clumsy distinction between *receiving* the Olympic torch and refusing to *touch* it, and before the Games, the Chinese were told it was rude to shake hands for longer than 3 seconds. (The buttock-obscured hand signals of bikini-clad Olympic beach volleyballers proved irresistible to the media.) The hand also lingers as a tool in the communication of news [see p.234], and as a culprit in the transmission of disease. And, as ever, individual fingers hold their own significance: a photograph of Madonna's ringless fourth finger catalysed a wave of speculation about her marriage, while Conrad Black was snapped presenting a different digit to reporters outside his trial. ❦ But we could be forgiven for letting much of this pass us by. As the anatomist Charles Bell wrote in his 1833 monograph on the hand, 'Is it not the very perfection of the instrument which makes us insensible to its use?'

SIGNIFICA · 2008

Some (in)significa(nt) footnotes to the year. ❦ The US Navy was forced to spend $682,000 to alter a base in California that resembled a swastika when viewed from the air. Although building officials had been aware of the structure's shape, it did not become problematic until the invention of Google Earth. ❦ A disgruntled Belgian citizen put his entire country up for sale on eBay; bidding reached $14m before the auction was cancelled. ❦ Roads were closed, buildings sealed, and

an anti-terrorist chemical response team was dispatched to the Soho area of London after residents complained of a noxious smell. The cause turned out to be 9 pounds of chillis left roasting by a Thai cook. ❦ After the brutal 2007 Myanmarese crackdown on monk-led demonstrations, residents resorted to one of the few forms of protest open to them: switching off their lights and television sets during the evening news (i.e., propaganda) broadcasts. ❦ According to the European Tissue Symposium, the average Briton uses 110 rolls of toilet paper a

year; this compares with 98 rolls per year for Americans, and a restrained 73 rolls for Germans. ❦ A Tanzanian man requiring brain surgery was mistakenly given a knee operation after hospital staff confused him with another patient who shared the same first name. He later died, and the knee-surgery patient, who was given a brain operation, was left paralysed. ❦ The tree that comforted Anne Frank as she hid from the Nazis in Amsterdam was saved from felling after a Dutch judge ruled that authorities should find a way to preserve it, despite a bad fungal infection. ❦ In the middle of a severe drought, the governor of Georgia, USA, held a multidenominational service during which he asked the crowd to 'pray up a storm', and said the drought was God's way of bringing to our attention the need for resource conservation. ❦ An Italian retailers' association reported that 20% of Italian shops regularly pay money to the Mafia in order to carry on their business unhindered. The association also claimed that the Mafia rakes in $120bn a year – 7% of Italy's GDP. ❦ Researchers at the University of Copenhagen alleged that the furniture giant IKEA names its cheaper products (doormats, draught excluders, &c.) after Danish towns and its more expensive lines (chairs, beds, &c.) after Finnish, Norwegian, and Swedish towns. IKEA rejected the claim as 'nonsense'. ❦ As property prices collapsed in parts of America, some houses became less valuable than the copper pipes and wiring within them. As a result, there were reports of a crime wave of break-ins at foreclosed houses, where metal was stripped out to be sold on the black market. ❦ Mexico City opened a free outdoor ice-skating rink in the city's central square in December 2007; at 34,000 sq ft, it was said to be the world's largest. ❦ Sales of Neapolitan mozzarella fell by 30% in March 2008, amid fears that 15 years of trash dumping and burning in the city had contaminated local water buffalo milk with dioxin, a potent carcinogen. ❦ The record for the Trinity College, Cambridge, 'Great Court Run' was smashed in October 2007 by Sam Dobin, a 19-year-old undergraduate. Made famous by the 1981 film *Chariots of Fire*, the run involves circumcursitating Trinity's 367-metre quad within the *c.*43 seconds it takes the college clock to strike noon (including the preparatory chimes and the two sets of 12). Dobin's time of 42·77s narrowly beat the record of 43·1s set in 1927. ❦ In July, a New Zealand judge made a 9-year-old girl a ward of court so that

———————SIGNIFICA · 2008 cont.———————

the name she had been given by her parents could be changed: the girl had been called 'Talula Does the Hula from Hawaii'. ❦ Press reports revealed that a common nickname for the Thai Prime Minister, Samak Sundaravej, was 'Mr Rose Apple Nose', since his schnozzle is said to have a striking resemblance to the 'pear-shaped Asian fruit'. ❦ Officials in the English village of Lunt debated changing the name of their conurbation to thwart vandals who repeatedly defaced local signs with a single stroke of a pen. ❦ The French parliament introduced a bill to combat eating disorders that would punish (with fines and even prison sentences) websites, blogs, and other media that encourage 'excessive thinness'. ❦ Congolese police arrested 13 men accused of using black magic to steal or shrink other men's penises, in what was said to be an attempt to extort cash. ❦ Global Language Monitor predicted that the English language will celebrate its millionth word on 29 April, 2009. There are currently 995,844 official words in English. ❦ The mayor of a remote Australian mining town faced calls for his resignation after telling a local paper, 'May I suggest if there are five blokes to every girl, we should find out where there are beauty-disadvantaged women and ask them to proceed to Mount Isa'. ❦ The Vatican was forced to deny reports that Pope Benedict XVI wore Prada shoes. The pontiff's footwear is apparently made by Adriano Stefanelli from Novara, and repaired in the Borgo by Antonio Arellano. ❦ Jim Bob & Michelle Duggar, from Springdale, AR, have given all of their 17 children names that begin with the letter *J*: Joshua, Jana & John-David (twins), Jill, Jessa, Jinger, Joseph, Josiah, Joy-Anna, Jedidiah & Jeremiah (twins), Jason, James, Justin, Jackson, Johannah, Jennifer. In July, it was reported that Michelle was expecting another child in January 2009; the couple were said to be canvassing suitable names. ❦ A Finnish MP proposed that the country's employees be granted paid week-long 'love vacations' in order to connect 'both at an erotic and emotional level'. It was hoped such holidays would reduce the country's high divorce rate. ❦ A Swedish engineering firm plotted the most efficient Christmas Eve route for Father Christmas, and found that Kyrgyzstan was Santa's ideal delivery hub. Delighted, Kyrgi officials announced plans to make Kyrgyzstan 'the land of Santa Clauses', and to rename a local peak Mount Santa. ❦ A May 2008 survey by *Consumer Reports* revealed that Americans frequently exhibit 'risky mowing behaviour' while tending their lawns: 77,000 ER visits a year are caused by mowing accidents, and 12% of Americans admit to drinking beer while using a mower. ❦ A female voice-over artist who recorded safety announcements for the London Underground was fired after recording spoof messages for her website, including one that advised American tourists they were 'almost certainly' speaking too loudly. ❦ A teenager from Reykjavik prank-called the White House and was put through to George W. Bush's secretary after claiming to be the president of Iceland. He later faced questioning by the CIA. ❦ A *New York Times* report on dental problems in Kentucky noted that 1 in 10 residents of the state are missing all of their teeth. ❦ Officials in Hanover, Germany, were criticised for including a real-life serial killer in a cartoon advent calendar designed for children. Fritz 'the Butcher of Hanover' Haarman – responsible for at least 24 brutal murders between 1919–24 – was depicted lurking behind a tree and brandishing an enormous axe. ❦

──── WORLD FOOD CRISIS ────

After many years of relative food price stability, the cost of basic foodstuffs escalated alarmingly during 2007–08, resulting in severe food shortages, social unrest, and fears of hunger and starvation in many of the world's poorest regions. As of August 2008, riots and protests over food prices had erupted in *c.*30 countries – reflecting the fact that the UN's index of world food prices had more than doubled since 2000, as the chart [right] illustrates.

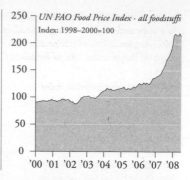

UN FAO Food Price Index · all foodstuffs
Index: 1998–2000=100

The causes of this agflation (agricultural inflation) were numerous and interrelated. Inevitably, the soaring price of oil touched almost every aspect of food production, processing, and transportation [see p.37]. And disasters like Cyclone Nargis skewed food's supply and demand. But much of the crisis was driven by the price of grain, which rose due to a confluence of events, including: six years of drought in Australia (a major wheat-producing nation); lower agricultural yields due to global warming; the expansion of the Indian and Chinese middle class, hungry for (grain-fed) meat; and a wave of panicked protectionism that cut food exports. The impact of biofuels was much debated. Diverting land from food to fuel crops necessarily cuts the supply of food, yet while America claimed its biofuel subsidies were responsible for only 2–3% of global agflation, the World Bank reckoned the impact at *c.*75% [see p.209]. ❦ Whatever the causes, the consequences were dramatic, and the World Bank estimated that 100m people were at risk of being driven into poverty. In June, the UN's World Food Programme announced $1·2bn in food aid for 60 struggling nations, and in August it announced a $214m plan for 16 'hunger hot spots' (including Somalia, Ethiopia, Haiti, Liberia, the Palestinian territories, and Mozambique). However, many argued that aid could only be a temporary measure and, as the world's population continues to grow, agricultural research is needed to find ways of producing more food on less land. ❦ Charted below is the rise in the price of various foods since 2006:

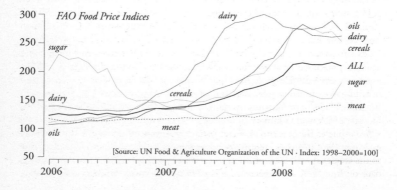

FAO Food Price Indices
[Source: UN Food & Agriculture Organization of the UN · Index: 1998–2000=100]

——————————— WORLD FOOD CRISIS cont. ———————————

In September 2008, the British Retail Consortium reported that – although the rises appeared to be slowing – food prices had risen by 10% between August 2007–August 2008, which presented a serious problem for those on low or fixed incomes. Below is the rate of food inflation, as calculated by the ONS, since 1996:

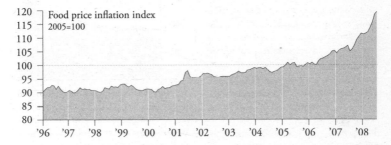

A BBC/Verdict Research survey indicated that between January–August 2008, food prices in UK supermarkets and shops rose by 8·3%; a breakdown is below:

Group	±%	Group	±%
Meat and fish	+22·9	Bakery/cereal	+6·0
Store cupboard/general	+15·0	Frozen food	+5·8
Fresh fruit/vegetables	+14·7	Household	+4·4
Laundry/washing/paper	+14·4	Health & beauty	+0·4
Drink	+6·8	Ready meals	–0·4
Pet food	+6·5	Dairy	–1·8
		Baby food	–2·5

Below are some revealing reports on the food crisis from countries around the world:
In March, Egyptian President Hosni Mubarak ordered his army to bake bread, after shortages of subsidised loaves led to riots in which at least a dozen 'bread martyrs' died. ❦ Frustrated by the pace of international relief, nations forged individual assistance deals: Ukraine agreed to allow Libya to grow wheat on 247,000 acres, in exchange for access to construction and gas deals; Uganda agreed to sell more coffee, milk, and bananas to India; and China signed a free-trade deal with New Zealand – China's first such agreement with a developed country. ❦ In April, food riots in Haiti killed >5 and forced out PM Jacques-Édouard Alexis. ❦ Also in April, US chains Sam's Club and Costco limited the quantity of rice their customers could purchase, despite official assurances that there was no US rice shortage. ❦ In May, the newly created Philippines Anti-Rice Hoarding Task Force accused 33 people of hoarding rice, diverting subsidised rice, and other illegal rice-related activities. ❦ In June, the US Dept of Agriculture reported that agflation in 2007 had caused a 14% increase in the world's hungry (an additional 122m people, roughly the population of Japan). ❦ According to the Stockholm Water Institute, 30% of all US food is thrown away each year [see p.105]. ❦ A Friends Provident survey in September reported that, due to the credit crunch, 56% of Britons were buying cheaper food, 15% were cutting back on fresh fruit and vegetables, and *c*.7% said they were drinking *more* alcohol.

——————————— AFGHANISTAN CONFLICT ———————————

As of 13/9/2008, 120 British Forces personnel or MOD civilians had been killed in operations in Afghanistan since 2001; 93 had been killed as a result of hostile action. Additionally, as of 31/8/08, 145 soldiers or civilians had been seriously or very seriously injured or wounded; 1,731 had been admitted to field hospitals; and 1,302 had been aeromedically evacuated. At the time of writing, the British forces in Afghanistan totalled *c*.7,800. ❦ According to the Brookings Institution, as of 8/9/08, the following troops from other coalition countries had been killed:

Australia........6	Finland 1	Lithuania.......1	Romania........8
Canada 97	France 22	Netherlands .. 16	S Korea.........1
Czech Rep......3	Germany 26	Norway.........3	Spain 23
Denmark.....17	Hungary........2	Poland..........8	Sweden 2
Estonia 3	Italy...........12	Portugal 2	USA.........584

Despite the presence of *c*.65,000 troops in Afghanistan – including *c*.34,000 from the United States – the UN Office on Drugs and Crime reported in 2008 that 'the area under opium poppy cultivation in Afghanistan increased 17% in 2007, with cultivation expanding to a record high of 193,000 hectares in 2007. Global opium poppy cultivation, as a result, rose 17% in 2007 to almost 234,000 hectares. Afghanistan's share of global cultivation remained 82%'. The chart below illustrates how Afghanistan's opium production has grown since 1990, despite the invasion:

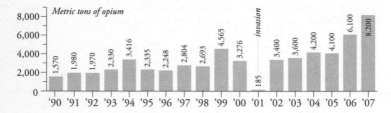

——————— US COMBAT EXPERIENCE IN IRAQ · 2007 ———————

A 2008 US Army report into the mental health of soldiers in Iraq surveyed the 'combat experience' of troops (rank E1–E4) during nine months 'in theatre' in 2007:

Receiving incoming artillery, rocket, or mortar fire .... *% experiencing* 78·4
Knowing someone seriously injured or killed.....................................72·1
Seeing destroyed homes and villages ....61·1
Seeing dead bodies or human remains ....60·2
Working in areas that were mined or had improvised explosive devices........59·8
Receiving small arms fire...57·7
Having a member of your unit become a casualty...............................55·6
Being attacked or ambushed...51·7
Seeing dead or seriously injured Americans.....................................48·7

─────────── IRAQ CONFLICT ───────────

As of 15/9/2008, 176 British Forces personnel or MOD civilians had been killed in operations in Iraq since 2003; 136 had been killed as a result of hostile action. Additionally, as of 31/8/08, 221 soldiers or civilians had been seriously or very seriously injured or wounded; 3,145 had been admitted to field hospitals; and 1,583 had been aeromedically evacuated. At the time of writing, the British forces in Iraq totalled *c.*4,000 – though *c.*6,500 personnel were deployed in total. ❦ As of 19/9/08, 4,168 US troops had been killed in Iraq – below is a breakdown:

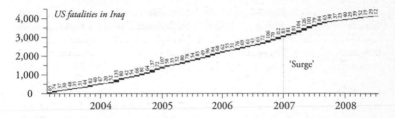

As of 16/9/08, 138 troops from other coalition forces had been killed in Iraq. ❦ As of August 2008, there were *c.*149,233 coalition troops in Iraq, of which *c.*140,000 were American; the remaining *c.*9,233 were from 4 countries. Below is the number of US and other troops since 05/03, and a breakdown of current coalition support:

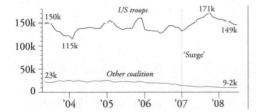

Country	approx. troops
UK	4,000
Poland	900
South Korea	650
Romania	600

On 10/8/08, *c.*2,000 Georgian troops were airlifted from Iraq to fight against Russia [see p.23]

The calculation of civilian deaths in Iraq is problematic and controversial, and opinions differ as to which estimates are most accurate. As of 14/8/08, the Iraq Body Count (IBC) estimated that the documented civilian death toll from violence in Iraq was 86,609–94,490. Below is the IBC's estimate of fatalities since 3/2003:

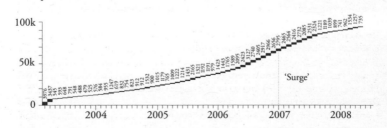

[Sources for the page: The Brooking Institution, *Iraq Index*; iCasualties.org; Iraq Body Count]

──────────── KEY UK ECONOMIC MEASURES ────────────

The September announcement by the OECD that Britain was likely to sink into recession came just days after the Chancellor, Alistair Darling, bluntly admitted that the country was facing 'arguably the worst' economic conditions in six decades – and a downturn that would be 'more profound and long-lasting' than people generally expected. Below are a range of economic indicators that illustrate the economic scene, but see also p.16 for food inflation, and the Money section on p.233. ❦ The number of individuals declared insolvent in England and Wales has increased in recent years. In part this is because of a 2004 change in the law which allows bankrupts to be discharged after 1 year (rather than 3), and protects their homes. However, recent rises also reflect higher inflation and tightening credit:

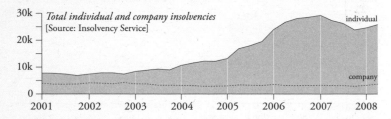

The global price of oil [see p.37] influences a host of other prices, including petrol:

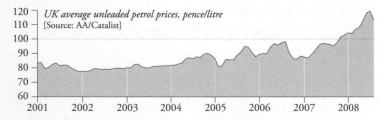

On 17/9/08, the ONS reported that the number of people out of work rose by 60,000 between May–July, to 1·72m, or 5·5%. In August, 904,900 were claiming jobseeker's allowance. In September, KPMG said that the number of permanent jobs available was the lowest since November 2001. The number unemployed is below:

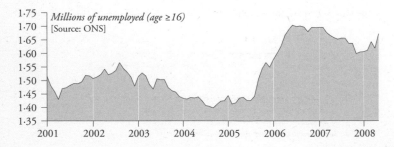

———————— KEY UK ECONOMIC MEASURES cont. ————————

The country's largest mortgage lender, the Halifax, reported in September that the average UK house had lost £25,434 in value between August 2007–August 2008. This 12·7% loss, the largest annual fall the Halifax had recorded since its survey began in 1983, came just days after Gordon Brown announced a number of measures to revivify the housing market. (These measures included temporarily raising the £125,000 stamp duty threshold to £175,000; loans to help first-time buyers purchase new homes; extending the powers of councils and housing associations to take over mortgages and charge tenants rent; and changing the rules on income support for mortgage interest.) At the time of writing, it was unclear how effective this (supposedly £1·6bn) package would be:

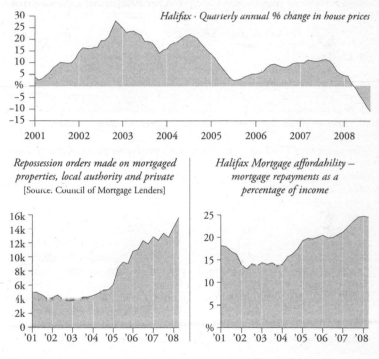

Halifax · Quarterly annual % change in house prices

Repossession orders made on mortgaged properties, local authority and private
[Source. Council of Mortgage Lenders]

Halifax Mortgage affordability – mortgage repayments as a percentage of income

The GfK NOP 'consumer confidence barometer' gives a sense of the public mood:

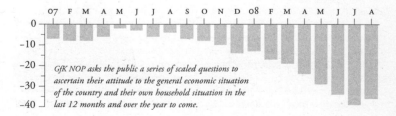

GfK NOP asks the public a series of scaled questions to ascertain their attitude to the general economic situation of the country and their own household situation in the last 12 months and over the year to come.

—BRITISH YOUTH · KNIFE CRIME, GANGS, & SUICIDES—

In February 2007, a Unicef report into the health and happiness of children ranked Britain last out of the 21 'rich countries' surveyed: 'the UK lags behind in terms of relative poverty and deprivation, quality of children's relationships with their parents and peers, child health and safety, behaviour and risk-taking and subjective well-being'. At the time, this report was described by experts in the field as 'shocking' and 'a wake-up call' – but the events of 2008 seem to indicate that little has changed:

KNIFE CRIME

Incidents of serious youth violence, especially those involving knives, dominated much of the news in 2008 as, week after week, teenage assaults and murders around the country hit the headlines. At the time of writing, 26 young people had been murdered in London alone during 2008: the majority were victims of knife crime, and most, though not all, were male and black. ❦ While some spoke of an 'epidemic' of knife attacks, the statistics were not clear-cut. In June, the Home Sec. said 'although we are very worried about [knife crime], it is not more serious than it has been previously'. But a Policy Exchange poll found that >80% of police officers said that knife crime was more of a problem in their area than 5 years ago. In July, Cherie Blair told a committee of MPs, 'the statistics do not acknowledge what is happening to young people under 16. We know younger people are carrying knives. This is almost a new phenomenon ... the statistics are not looking at the right areas'. ❦ The latest official data [see p.119] showed that 22,151 knife crimes (excluding murder and manslaughter) were reported in 2007–08 in England & Wales. Since this was the first time knife crime had been recorded separately, only when the 2008–09 data are released can trends be analysed and the success of various youth-crime initiatives assessed. (In 2009, the British Crime Survey will interview <16s for the first time.)

GANG CULTURE

In September, the government published the booklet *Gangs: You and Your Child* to educate parents about why children join gangs, what can be done to prevent it, and some of the ways to spot gang membership, including:

Has your child withdrawn from the family? · Has s/he dropped out of positive activities? · Has s/he started to use new/unknown slang words? · Does s/he hold unexplained money or possessions? · Does s/he have a new nickname? · Is s/he dressing in a particular style or 'uniform' (bandanas &c.) similar to that of the people s/he is hanging around with? · Does s/he have unexplained physical injuries?

BRIDGEND SUICIDES

On 9/8/08, 23-year-old Rhys Davies was found hanged in Bridgend – he was the 23rd youth to have committed suicide in the Welsh county since 2007. Although, by comparison, there were just 6 young suicides during 2005–06, the police denied there was any 'pact' or link between the recent spate of deaths. The director of the Bridgend Samaritans told the *Telegraph*, 'they are imitative suicides. The contagion happens through personal communication, with people talking to each other about the events that have happened, and through the media. ... It's as if a door has opened. If one suicide happens in the community, it is as if permission has been granted to commit suicide, and it becomes a viable option.'

—— GEORGIA, SOUTH OSSETIA, RUSSIA, & THE WEST ——

On 7/8/08, as the eyes of the world were on Beijing [see p.24], Georgia escalated low-level skirmishes by launching a surprise attack on South Ossetia – a Georgian province supported by Russia which for years had been agitating for independence. ❦ Tensions in the region, palpable since the Soviet Union's collapse, had worsened in 2008, as the newly re-elected (and not uncontroversial) Georgian President Mikhail Saakashvili sought closer ties with the US and the West, and NATO promised Georgia membership sometime in the future. Both of these moves dismayed Russia – already angered by Western interference in its 'sphere of influence' and by the perceived threat of America's 'defence shield'. ❦ On 8/8, Moscow reacted to the incursion by sending an overwhelming force of troops, tanks, and air power deep into Georgia. The ensuing fighting killed *c.*1,500, forced tens of thousands to flee, and spread into Georgia's northwestern breakaway province, Abkhazia. On 10/8, reeling from Russia's attack, Georgia declared a ceasefire and said its troops had withdrawn from S Ossetia. Moscow brushed aside these claims – and US condemnation – and continued its assault. Over the next few days, with France acting as EU mediator, Russia spun out the peace negotiations

while maintaining a strong military presence in Georgia. America attempted to exert pressure on Russia by flying *c.*2,000 Georgian soldiers home from Iraq and sending in humanitarian aid. Yet for all their words of support, it was evident that neither the US nor NATO was willing to engage the Russian military beyond salvos of condemnation. ❦ On 12/8 Russia and Georgia agreed in principle to a peace plan, yet almost immediately began accusing one another of violations. Russia finally signed the ceasefire on 16/8, and by 23/8, said all combat troops had withdrawn and that only 'peacekeepers' remained, a claim greeted with some scepticism. As fighting died down, diplomatic tensions were heightened on 26/8, when Russia formally recognised the independence of Abkhazia and S Ossetia. On 17/9, Russia signed 'friendship treaties' with the breakaway regions – binding the three together diplomatically and militarily. ❦ At the time of writing, Russia maintained a military presence in undisputed Georgia, and reportedly planned to keep *c.*7,600 troops total in Abkhazia and S Ossetia. The catastrophic fall in world stock markets [see p.37] temporarily shifted attention away from the region, but it was clear that Russia, its 'near abroad', and NATO were going to have to find a new balance of power.

OLYMPIC GAMES · BEIJING 2008

At 8·08pm on 08/08/08 the XXIX Olympics opened in Beijing. An unforgettable 4-hour ceremony of synchronised music and acrobatics set the scene for 16 days of sporting achievement. The creation of 38 world records and 85 Olympic records – in a series of stunning venues – would significantly, but not entirely, obscure China's problematic record on human rights, political oppression [see p.297], and pollution.

The undisputed star of the Games was the 23-year-old swimmer Michael Phelps, who shrugged off the frenzy of 'Phelps Phever' to break 7 world records while amassing 8 Olympic golds. In so doing, he beat both Mark Spitz's 1972 haul of 7, and all but 8 of the national squads. As headline writers ran short of superlatives, the 'People's Republic of Michael Phelps' vowed to add to his career tally of 14 Olympic golds at London 2012. ❦ Phelps's only rival for column inches was the Jamaican sprinter Usain Bolt. On 16/8, 'Lightning' Bolt stunned spectators by running the 100m in a world record time of 9·69s. That he achieved this feat after slowing down mid-race to celebrate (and with a loose shoelace) only added to his appeal. On 18/8, Bolt ran the 200m in 19·30s – shaving ·02s off Michael Johnson's 'unbreakable' best. Bolt's third gold and world record came in the 4×100m relay. ❦ Inevitably the Games were not without incident or accident. As the opening ceremony drew nearer, concern grew that Beijing's notoriously polluted air would not meet even the lowest standard of quality. To ensure 'blue sky days', authorities limited the use of private cars and temporarily shut down factories and building sites. And, in an attempt to improve standards of civility, campaigns were launched to encourage queuing and clapping and discourage swearing and spitting. More disturbingly, groups such as Amnesty reported that draconian security measures were used to sweep criminals, vagrants, and drug addicts, as well as dissidents and protesters, out of the media's sight. This desire for presentational perfection was also behind the use of a 'cute' 7-year-old girl to mime during the opening ceremony the singing of a child deemed less photogenic, and the broadcasting of computerised fireworks rather than the actual display. ❦ Rigorous testing ensured the Games were relatively free from doping scandals, although 5 athletes were expelled for drugs, including Ukrainian heptathlete Liudmyla Blonska, who was stripped of her silver after testing positive for an anabolic steroid. (Bizarrely, 4 horses were ejected from the show-jumping after testing positive for capsaicin – a substance rubbed onto a horse's legs to encourage it over the jumps.) Many attributed the breaking of 25 swimming world records to the popularity of the Speedo LZR Racer swimsuit – which employs NASA technology for improved aerodynamics. Although these suits are perfectly legal, some called the use of such high-tech equipment 'technological doping'.

The Chinese authorities had every right to be pleased with the Games, which were spectacular in scale and effect, and free from boycotts, podium protests, or serious diplomatic censure. It remains to be seen what the much-vaunted 'Olympic legacy' or the slogan 'One World One Dream' will mean for the ordinary Chinese citizen.

—— OLYMPIC GAMES · BEIJING 2008 · MEDALS TABLE ——

#	Country	Gd	Sv	Bz	All
1	China	51	21	28	100
2	United States	36	38	36	110
3	Russian Fed.	23	21	28	72
4	Great Britain	19	13	15	47
5	Germany	16	10	15	41
6	Australia	14	15	17	46
7	Korea	13	10	8	31
8	Japan	9	6	10	25
9	Italy	8	10	10	28
10	France	7	16	17	40
11	Ukraine	7	5	15	27
12	Netherlands	7	5	4	16
13	Jamaica	6	3	2	11
14	Spain	5	10	3	18
15	Kenya	5	5	4	14
16	Belarus	4	5	10	19
17	Romania	4	1	3	8
18	Ethiopia	4	1	2	7
19	Canada	3	9	6	18
20	Poland	3	6	1	10
21	Hungary	3	5	2	10
	Norway	3	5	2	10
23	Brazil	3	4	8	15
24	Czech Rep.	3	3	·	6
25	Slovakia	3	2	1	6
26	New Zealand	3	1	5	9
27	Georgia	3	·	3	6
28	Cuba	2	11	11	24
29	Kazakhstan	2	4	7	13
30	Denmark	2	2	3	7
31	Mongolia	2	2	·	4
	Thailand	2	2	·	4
33	DPR Korea	2	1	3	6
34	Argentina	2	·	4	6
	Switzerland	2	·	4	6
36	Mexico	2	·	1	3
37	Turkey	1	4	3	8
38	Zimbabwe	1	3	·	4
39	Azerbaijan	1	2	4	7
40	Uzbekistan	1	2	3	6
41	Slovenia	1	2	2	5
42	Bulgaria	1	1	3	5
	Indonesia	1	1	3	5
44	Finland	1	1	2	4
45	Latvia	1	1	1	3
46	Belgium	1	1	·	2
	Dominican Rep.	1	1	·	2
	Estonia	1	1	·	2
	Portugal	1	1	·	2
50	India	1	·	2	3
51	Iran	1	·	1	2

#	Country	Gd	Sv	Bz	All
52	Bahrain	1	·	·	1
	Cameroon	1	·	·	1
	Panama	1	·	·	1
	Tunisia	1	·	·	1
56	Sweden	·	4	1	5
57	Croatia	·	2	3	5
	Lithuania	·	2	3	5
59	Greece	·	2	2	4
60	Trinidad/Tobago	·	2	·	2
61	Nigeria	·	1	3	4
62	Austria	·	1	2	3
	Ireland	·	1	2	3
	Serbia	·	1	2	3
65	Algeria	·	1	1	2
	Bahamas	·	1	1	2
	Colombia	·	1	1	2
	Kyrgyzstan	·	1	1	2
	Morocco	·	1	1	2
	Tajikistan	·	1	1	2
71	Chile	·	1	·	1
	Ecuador	·	1	·	1
	Iceland	·	1	·	1
	Malaysia	·	1	·	1
	South Africa	·	1	·	1
	Singapore	·	1	·	1
	Sudan	·	1	·	1
	Vietnam	·	1	·	1
79	Armenia	·	·	6	6
80	Chinese Taipei	·	·	4	4
81	Afghanistan	·	·	1	1
	Egypt	·	·	1	1
	Israel	·	·	1	1
	Rep. of Moldova	·	·	1	1
	Mauritius	·	·	1	1
	Togo	·	·	1	1
	Venezuela	·	·	1	1

	Individuals	Gd	Sv	Bz	All
USA	Michael Phelps	8	·	·	8
JAM	Usain Bolt	3	·	·	3
GBR	Chris Hoy	3	·	·	3
AUS	Stephanie Rice	3	·	·	3
CHN	Kai Zou	3	·	·	3
AUS	Lisbeth Trickett	2	1	1	4
AUS	Leisel Jones	2	1	·	3
USA	Matt Grevers	2	1	·	3
CHN	Wei Yang	2	1	·	3
USA	Aaron Peirsol	2	1	·	3
USA	Ryan Lochte	2	·	2	4
USA	Jason Lezak	2	·	1	3
JAP	Kosuke Kitajima	2	·	1	3

—————————— ELECTIONS · 2008 ——————————

The convention of local election spin – when every party finds something to smile about – failed on 1 May 2008, when Labour suffered its worst electoral defeat for 40 years. In the English and Welsh council elections, Labour lost 331 councillors and 9 councils, winning just 24% of the national vote, behind the Lib Dems (25%) and the Tories (44%). In the London Assembly elections, although Labour's vote held up, the Tories enjoyed a 6·2% swing and took 2 seats. However, the nail in Labour's psephological coffin was the election of Boris Johnson as the first Tory London Mayor and the ousting of 2-term incumbent Ken Livingstone. Although the Lib Dems claimed to have 'confounded expectations' and 'regained momentum', their performance was of little comfort to recently elected leader Nick Clegg [see p.254].

ENGLAND & WALES ELECTIONS	COUNCILLORS		COUNCILS	
	net ±	*total*	*net ±*	*total*
Conservative	+257	3,155	+12	65
Labour	–334	2,365	–9	18
Liberal Democrats	+33	1,804	+1	12
Plaid Cymru	+31	205	–1	0
Other	+10	898	0	0
No Overall Control	NA	NA	–3	64

LONDON ASSEMBLY	*constituencies*	*top ups*	*total seats*	*change*
Conservative	8	3	11	+2
Labour	6	2	8	+1
Liberal Democrat	0	3	3	–2
Green	0	2	2	–
British National Party	0	1	1	+1

LONDON MAYOR	*party*	*1st pref.*	*2nd pref.*	*final*	*%*
Boris Johnson	Conservative	1,043,761	124,977	1,168,738	53
Ken Livingstone	Labour	893,877	135,089	1,028,966	47
Brian Paddick	Lib Dem	236,685			
Siân Berry	Green	77,374			

Many noted that these elections were the first chance anyone (even Labour MPs) had been given to vote on Gordon Brown's accession to PM after he sidestepped party selection in June 2007, and 'funked' a general election 4 months later. And although Livingstone took responsibility for his defeat in London, Labour's meltdown was near-universally blamed on the bad luck, mismanagement, and ill-judgement (not least over abolishing the 10p tax band [see p.237]) that had characterised Brown's short premiership. Brown could do little more than admit the results had been 'bad', and promise to 'listen and lead'. In contrast, David Cameron was upbeat, calling the Conservatives' performance 'a big moment' for his party, and promising to make London a test bed for a future Tory government. In victory, Boris Johnson was generous to Livingstone, ebullient about London, and realistic about himself: 'I know there will be many whose pencils hovered for an instant before putting an X in my box and I will work flat out to repay and to justify your confidence'.

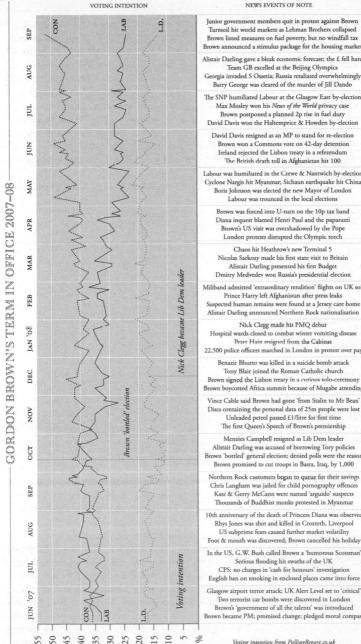

GORDON BROWN'S TERM IN OFFICE 2007–08

VOTING INTENTION

CON   LAB   L.D.

Brown 'bottled' election

Nick Clegg became Lib Dem leader

Voting intention

CON   LAB   L.D.

SEP · AUG · JUL · JUN · MAY · APR · MAR · FEB · JAN '08 · DEC · NOV · OCT · SEP · AUG · JUL · JUN '07

55 · 50 · 45 · 40 · 35 · 30 · 25 · 20 · 15 · 10 · 5 · %

NEWS EVENTS OF NOTE

Junior government members quit in protest against Brown
Turmoil hit world markets as Lehman Brothers collapsed
Brown listed measures on fuel poverty, but no windfall tax
Brown announced a stimulus package for the housing market

Alistair Darling gave a bleak economic forecast; the £ fell hard
Team GB excelled at the Beijing Olympics
Georgia invaded S Ossetia; Russia retaliated overwhelmingly
Barry George was cleared of the murder of Jill Dando

The SNP humiliated Labour at the Glasgow East by-election
Max Mosley won his *News of the World* privacy case
Brown postponed a planned 2p rise in fuel duty
David Davis won the Haltemprice & Howden by-election

David Davis resigned as an MP to stand for re-election
Brown won a Commons vote on 42-day detention
Ireland rejected the Lisbon treaty in a referendum
The British death toll in Afghanistan hit 100

Labour was humiliated in the Crewe & Nantwich by-election
Cyclone Nargis hit Myanmar; Sichaun earthquake hit China
Boris Johnson was elected the new Mayor of London
Labour was trounced in the local elections

Brown was forced into U-turn on the 10p tax band
Diana inquest blamed Henri Paul and the paparazzi
Brown's US visit was overshadowed by the Pope
London protests disrupted the Olympic torch

Chaos hit Heathrow's new Terminal 5
Nicolas Sarkozy made his first state visit to Britain
Alistair Darling presented his first Budget
Dmitry Medvedev won Russia's presidential election

Miliband admitted 'extraordinary rendition' flights on UK soil
Prince Harry left Afghanistan after press leaks
Suspected human remains were found at a Jersey care home
Alistair Darling announced Northern Rock nationalisation

Nick Clegg made his PMQ debut
Hospital wards closed to combat winter vomiting disease
Peter Hain resigned from the Cabinet
22,500 police officers marched in London in protest over pay

Benazir Bhutto was killed in a suicide bomb attack
Tony Blair joined the Roman Catholic church
Brown signed the Lisbon treaty in a curious solo-ceremony
Brown boycotted Africa summit because of Mugabe attending

Vince Cable said Brown had gone 'from Stalin to Mr Bean'
Discs containing the personal data of 25m people were lost
Unleaded petrol passed £1/litre for first time
The first Queen's Speech of Brown's premiership

Menzies Campbell resigned as Lib Dem leader
Alistair Darling was accused of borrowing Tory policies
Brown 'bottled' general election; denied polls were the reason
Brown promised to cut troops in Basra, Iraq, by 1,000

Northern Rock customers began to queue for their savings
Chris Langham was jailed for child pornography offences
Kate & Gerry McCann were named 'arguido' suspects
Thousands of Buddhist monks protested in Myanmar

10th anniversary of the death of Princess Diana was observed
Rhys Jones was shot and killed in Croxteth, Liverpool
US subprime fears caused further market volatility
Foot & mouth was discovered; Brown cancelled his holiday

In the US, G.W. Bush called Brown a 'humorous Scotsman'
Serious flooding hit swaths of the UK
CPS: no charges in 'cash for honours' investigation
English ban on smoking in enclosed places came into force

Glasgow airport terror attack; UK Alert Level set to 'critical'
Two terrorist car bombs were discovered in London
Brown's 'government of all the talents' was introduced
Brown became PM; promised change; pledged moral compass

Voting intention from PollingReport.co.uk

BY-ELECTIONS · 2008

CREWE & NANTWICH

The Crewe and Nantwich by-election, triggered by the death of Gwyneth Dunwoody [see p.62], was an acrimonious affair set against a backdrop of Gordon Brown's personal unpopularity and the 10p tax debacle [see p.237]. (To the dismay of some, Labour broke convention by moving the by-election writ before Dunwoody's funeral.) The campaign was marked by a bitter tussle between the Conservatives' Edward Timpson and Labour's Tamsin (daughter of Gwyneth) Dunwoody, in which Labour relentlessly played the 'class card'. Two Labour apparatchiks dogged Timpson's steps in top hat and tails, and Labour's leaflets portrayed the 34-year-old barrister as a 'Tory boy' 'toff'. [Ironically, the only candidate to appear in *Burke's Peerage & Gentry* was Tamsin Dunwoody.] On 22/5/2008, a 58·2% turnout turned Gwyneth Dunwoody's 7,078 majority into a Tory majority of 7,860 – a 17·6% swing:

Candidate [party]	votes	%
Edward Timpson [Con]	20,539	49·5
Tamsin Dunwoody [Lab]	12,679	30·6
Elizabeth Shenton [Lib D]	6,040	14·6

Conservative leader David Cameron described the first Tory by-election victory since 1982 as 'remarkable', and called the electorate's rejection of the 'class war' campaign, and Brown's leadership, the 'end of New Labour'.

HENLEY

The Henley by-election arose when Boris Johnson resigned as an MP after becoming Mayor of London [see p.26]. (He was not obliged to resign from the Commons, and could have held both posts.) Labour was never likely to do well in this safe Conservative seat – which had been held by Michael Heseltine

between 1974–2001. Yet the scale of Labour's defeat on 26/5/08 was another blow to Brown – not least as it marked his first anniversary as PM. Humiliatingly, with a share of just 3·07% (1,066 actual votes), the Labour candidate failed to pass the 5% threshold and lost his £500 deposit.

Candidate [party]	votes	%
John Howell [Con]	19,796	56·9
Stephen Kearney [Lib D]	9,680	27·9
Mark Stevenson [Green]	1,321	3·8
Timothy Rait [BNP]	1,243	3·6
Richard McKenzie [Lab]	1,066	3·1
Turnout	34,761	50·3

HALTEMPRICE & HOWDEN

One of the more curious by-elections in recent history came about when the Shadow Home Sec. David Davis resigned his seat to re-stand in protest against Labour's record on civil liberties, notably its policy of 42-day detention [see p.29]. Prior to quitting, Davis had been assured that the Lib Dems would not field a challenger, but his thunder was stolen somewhat when Labour followed suit, denying him a fight and exposing him to criticism that his 'vanity' would cost the taxpayer *c.*£80,000. On 10/7/08, as expected, Davis was returned as MP for Haltemprice & Howden: he secured an increased majority (15,355 compared to 5,116 in 2005), though his total number of votes fell (17,113 against 22,792), as did turnout (34·5% against 70·1%). The Green Party came second with just 1,758 votes. The by-election set a record for the greatest number of candidates: 25 people stood against Davis, including Gemma Garrett (Miss Great Britain), and idiosyncratic ex-footballer David Icke. 23 candidates lost their deposits.

—— BY-ELECTIONS cont. ——

GLASGOW EAST

If Brown thought his disastrous electoral run would end in Glasgow East – the 25th safest Labour seat in the UK and the 3rd safest in Scotland – he was wrong. The vote was triggered when David Marshall stepped down citing ill health, and although Labour moved the writ with alacrity, they struggled for some time to find a willing candidate. Every Labour MP (except Brown himself) was ordered to canvass in the constituency – which is blighted with unemployment of 10% for men and 25% for women and, in some parts, a life-expectancy 11 years lower than the UK average. Although the race was reported to be tough, most expected Labour to hold the seat, albeit with a reduced majority. However, in a dramatic upset, the SNP overturned Labour's safe majority of 13,507 to win by 365 votes – a swing of 22·5% that, if repeated, could endanger most of Labour's Cabinet, including Brown.

Candidate [party]	votes	%
John Mason [SNP]	11,277	43·1
Margaret Curran [Lab]	10,912	41·7
Davena Rankin [Con]	1,639	6·3
Ian Robertson [Lib D]	915	3·5
Turnout	26,219	42·0

In his acceptance address, the SNP's John Mason said, 'It is an epic win and the tremors will be felt all the way to Downing Street'. Brown could do little more than attempt to put the defeat into the context of the world economic downturn: 'We are looking at everything we can so that, in what is a global problem, we can in Britain help people through these difficult times'. David Cameron retorted, 'I think the PM should have his holiday, but then I think we need an election'.

—— 42-DAY DETENTION ——

On 11/6/08 the government narrowly won a Commons vote to extend the time suspects can be held without charge from 28 to 42 days. The controversial policy was attacked by some as a draconian measure designed primarily to present Gordon Brown as tough on security; it was defended by No.10 as a vital aid to police faced with increasingly complex terror plots. (Fearing a back-bench rebellion, the government had already conceded a range of safeguards, including parliamentary and judicial oversight.) The Counter-Terrorism Bill was passed by 315 votes to 306, after 9 Democratic Unionist MPs backed the government. Despite rumours of 'pork-barrel' concessions [see p.255] and personal favours to secure the vote, Brown maintained, 'There were no deals'. Notwithstanding the Commons victory, the Bill was expected to face a rough passage through the Lords, as well as legal challenges were it to become law. ❦ According to the campaign group Liberty, at 28 days the UK already has the 'longest pre-charge detention period in the western world'; below is their international comparison:

Country	days		
UK	28 (?42)	France	6
Turkey	7½	Russia	5
Ireland	7	USA	2
		Canada	1

On 12/6, Shadow Home Sec. David Davis announced that he would resign as an MP and force a by-election. His intention was to re-stand for his seat in order to argue against 'the slow strangulation of fundamental British freedoms by [the] government'. As expected, on 10/7 he easily won re-election [see p.28]. As predicted, he was not given a place in the Shadow Cabinet and he returned to the backbenches.

———— 2008 US PRIMARIES · VOCABULARY OF NOTE ————

Phrases, quotes, and bon mots from the interminable 2008 US presidential primaries:
PINGATE · Autumn 2007 non-scandal prompted by Obama's initial refusal to wear an American flag pin on his lapel. (In September, he said: 'I'm less concerned about what you're wearing on your lapel than what's in your heart.') ❦ SUPER-DUPER TUESDAY · 24 states voted on 5/2/08, the largest 'Super Tuesday' ever – *also* TSUNAMI TUESDAY *and* THE TUESDAY OF DESTINY. ❦ SNIPER FIRE · In March, Clinton said that during a 1996 trip to Bosnia, 'I remember landing under sniper fire ... we just ran with our heads down to get into the vehicles to get to our base'. (Later, after pictures revealed her to have walked calmly across the tarmac, she said she MISSPOKE.). ❦ UNITY TICKET · Hillary and Obama in some combination of POTUS and VP. ❦ 3 AM · A Clinton TV ad in February portrayed her as the candidate best able to handle a crisis. The (racially charged) ad began: 'It's 3 am, and your children are safe and asleep. But there's a phone in the White House, and it's ringing.' ❦ YES WE CAN! · Obama's relentless campaign slogan; in Spanish: SI SE PUEDE! ❦ LUCKY · In March, 1984 VP nominee Geraldine Ferraro resigned from Clinton's finance committee after arguing that Obama had benefited from being a black man: 'He happens to be very lucky to be who he is.' ❦ MONSTER · In March, Obama's foreign policy adviser Samantha Power resigned after saying, to the *Scotsman*, of Clinton: 'She is a monster, too – that is off the record – she is stooping to anything.' ❦ BITTER · At a San Francisco fund-raiser in April, Obama said, 'it's not surprising' that voters struggling financially 'get bitter ... they CLING to guns or religion or antipathy to people who aren't like them...' ❦ A NATION OF WHINERS · In July, McCain's (now former) economic adviser Phil Gramm told the *Washington Times*: 'You've heard of mental depression; this is a MENTAL RECESSION ... We have sort of become a nation of whiners.' ❦ NUTS · The part of Obama's anatomy Jesse Jackson said, in July, that he'd like to cut off. ❦ FIRST LAD · what Bill would have become had Hillary won. ❦ PUMAs · Hillary supporters who refused to back Obama, arguing 'Party Unity My Ass'. ❦ ENCYCLOPEDIA BARACKTANNICA · *Slate.com*'s compilation of >800 Obama-inspired neologisms – from the sublime (Nirbama) to the ridiculous (Dalai Lobama). ❦ OBAMANIAC, McCAINIAC · Passionate supporters of each. ❦ NOBAMA · Anti-Obama monicker. *Similarly*, McLAME; McSAME; McSHAME. ❦ D-AMTRAK · reference to Obama's VP pick, Joe 'RARE MIX' Biden, who invariably mentions that he takes the commuter train home each night instead of staying in Washington. ❦ The BIDEN GAFFE CLOCK · running count on the Republican National Committee website of the time since Biden's last 'Freudian slip' – notably his August introduction of Obama as 'BARACK AMERICA'. ❦ LIPSTICK · During her acceptance speech, Republican VP nominee Sarah Palin introduced herself as a HOCKEY MOM and then asked: 'What is the difference between a hockey mom and a pit bull? Lipstick.' Days later, Obama drew charges of sexism after dismissing Republican promises of 'change', saying: 'You can put lipstick on a pig, but it's still a pig.' ❦ CELEBRITY · In July, McCain ran an ad suggesting similarities between Obama, Britney Spears, and Paris Hilton. (In his August acceptance speech, Obama highlighted his family's early struggles and said, 'I don't know what kind of lives John McCain thinks that celebrities lead, but this has been mine'.) ❦ SARAH BARRACUDA · Palin's high school basketball nickname (according to the *Anchorage Daily News*, a reference to her 'aggressive play and ferocious defence').

STATE RESULTS

Paul	Romney	Huckabee	McCain		Obama %	Clinton	Edwards
3	18	41	37	AL	56	42	1
17	44	22	16	AK	75	25	.
4	35	9	47	AZ	42	50	5
5	14	60	20	AR	27	70	2
4	35	12	42	CA	43	51	4
8	60	13	18	CO	67	32	.
4	33	7	52	CT	51	47	1
4	33	15	45	DE	53	42	1
8	6	16	68	DC	75	24	.
3	31	13	36	FL	33	50	14
3	30	34	32	GA	66	31	2
.	.	.	.	HI	76	24	.
24	.	.	70	ID	80	17	1
5	29	16	47	IL	65	33	2
8	5	10	78	IN	49	51	.
10	25	34	13	IA	38	29	30
11	3	60	24	KS	74	26	.
7	5	8	72	KY	30	65	2
5	6	43	42	LA	57	36	3
18	52	6	21	ME	59	40	.
6	7	29	55	MD	61	36	1
3	51	4	41	MA	41	56	2
6	39	16	30	MI	.	55	.
16	41	20	22	MN	66	32	.
4	2	13	79	MS	61	37	1
4	29	32	33	MO	49	48	2
25	38	15	22	MT	56	41	.
13	.	.	87	NE	68	32	.
14	51	8	13	NV	45	51	4
8	32	11	37	NH	36	39	17
5	28	8	55	NJ	44	54	1
14	.	.	86	NM	48	49	1
6	28	11	52	NY	40	57	1
8	.	12	74	NC	56	42	.
21	36	20	23	ND	61	37	1
5	3	31	60	OH	44	54	2
3	25	33	37	OK	31	55	10
15			85	OR	59	41	.
16	.	11	73	PA	45	55	.
7	4	22	65	RI	40	58	1
4	15	30	33	SC	55	27	18
17	3	7	70	SD	45	55	.
6	24	34	32	TN	40	54	4
5	2	38	51	TX	47	51	1
3	89	1	5	UT	57	39	3
7	5	14	72	VT	59	39	1
4	4	41	50	VA	64	35	1
22	15	24	26	WA	68	31	.
5	4	10	76	WV	26	67	7
5	2	37	55	WI	58	41	1
.	67	.	.	WY	61	38	.
.	.	.	100	Am Sa	42	57	.
.	.	.	100	Guam	50	50	.
4	.	5	91	Pu Ri	32	68	.
3	19	.	31	Vi Is	90	8	.
.	.	.	.	DemAb	67	33	.

CONVENTIONS

Democratic National Convention
25–28 August · Denver, Colorado

Barack Hussein Obama was nominated for president by the Democratic party on 27/8/08, becoming the first African American nominee from a major party and bringing to an end a bitter 2-year campaign against Hillary Clinton – once the contest's clear favourite. Yet Obama's 28/8 acceptance speech (before *c.*75,000 at a Denver football stadium) made no mention of the historic nature of his win; instead he offered a series of vignettes about struggling citizens and declared, 'America … we are a better country than this'. Delaware Senator Joseph Robinette Biden Jr accepted his Vice Presidential nomination on 28/8 also. In a speech that drew upon his own middle-class background he tried to make the case against the Republicans: 'John McCain doesn't get it. Barack Obama gets it.'

Republican National Convention
1–4 Sept. · Minneapolis-St Paul, Minn.

John Sidney McCain III was chosen as the Republican presidential nominee on 3/9/08, ending a roller-coaster primary campaign amongst a crowded field of candidates. Yet the evening (and the convention) belonged to Alaska's governor Sarah Heath Palin, McCain's surprise VP pick. In her acceptance speech, Palin portrayed herself as a passionate conservative, launching scathing attacks and withering sarcasm at the 'Washington elite', community organisers (of which Omaba was one), and 'all those reporters'. In a weaker speech, McCain borrowed from Obama: 'an advance warning to the old, big-spending, do-nothing, me-first, country-second crowd: Change is coming.'

─────── MYANMAR & CYCLONE NARGIS ───────

On 2–3 May, 2008, Cyclone Nargis, which had developed in the Bay of Bengal, made landfall in Myanmar. By the time it hit coastal communities, Nargis had been upgraded from Category 1 to 3–4, and the >120mph winds wrought devastation across *c.*23,500km^2 of the low-lying Irrawaddy delta. To the south and west of the capital, Yangon [née Rangoon], coastal villages that stood just 5' above sea level were deluged by a 12' flood surge, which also threatened *c.*65% of Myanmar's rice production by contaminating the filigree of paddy fields with seawater and corpses.

As the death toll rose from hundreds to tens of thousands, the impact of Nargis was compared to the 2004 SE Asian tsunami. Yet if 2004's aid 'air bridge' was a model of cooperation, efforts post-Nargis were obstructed by the mistrust, superstition, xenophobia, and bureaucracy of Myanmar's idiosyncratic and secretive junta. After some days, aid trickled in from trusted neighbours, but charities complained that their staff were denied entry visas, and repeated offers of assistance, notably from US troops on exercise nearby, were rebuffed. Only on 8/5 were the first UN aid flights permitted to land but, within hours, these flights were suspended when the junta declared that it would accept aid to distribute itself, but would ban 'rescue and information teams from foreign countries'. As the military confiscated enough high-energy biscuits to feed 95,000, and refused to waive import duties on aid, charities warned of a 'second catastrophe' of 'apocalyptic proportions' as hunger, exposure, and disease threatened >1·5m. ❧ In a series of surreal photo-ops, Myanmar's generals were shown handing out TV sets and single bags of rice; press reports claimed that these leaders also affixed their names to foreign aid for pro-army propaganda. In the midst of the crisis, on 10/5, the junta forced a referendum on a constitution designed to secure its power and ban opposition leader Aung

San Suu Kyi from ever holding office. Although polling was delayed in the worst-hit areas, anger was voiced that a (plainly rigged) vote took precedence over the feeding of a people (opposing the constitution carried a 3-year prison sentence). On 12/5, a single unarmed C-130 transport plane carrying US aid was permitted to land in Yangon. On the same day, the UN Sec-General expressed 'immense frustration' at the delay, disclosing that he had been unable to contact Myanmar's military leaders. ❧ Frustration gave way to outrage after it was reported that Myanmar was exporting rice, and that the junta was selling foreign aid to its own people. Yet a French suggestion that the UN exercise its 'responsibility to protect' by air-dropping aid was blocked by China and Russia. ❧ Those who hoped that Nargis might force change on the junta were disappointed. On 27/5, Suu Kyi's house arrest was extended for another year, and in June the regime accused the media of fabricating stories about the disaster. In July, the UN stated that the cost of Nargis to Myanmar's assets was $4bn, and calculated that $1bn was required over 3 years to assist the survivors. In total, *c.*600,000 hectares of farmland were destroyed or damaged, along with *c.*800,000 houses; >800,000 people were displaced, and it was estimated that 84,537 people had died and a further 53,836 were presumed dead.

———————OTHER MAJOR STORIES IN BRIEF———————

John & Anne Darwin

On 1/12/07, 5½ years after disappearing whilst canoeing, a 'tanned and well-nourished' John Darwin walked into a London police station. Claiming to remember nothing of the past 5 years, he told officers, 'I think I am a missing person'. His wife Anne appeared astonished at her husband's reappearance. However, it soon emerged that her surprise was feigned, since just weeks after 'vanishing' in 2002, John Darwin had moved into a bedsit next door to his own home, where he lived in secret (and in disguise), visiting his wife via a hidden connecting door. In 2003, once a death certificate had been issued, Anne Darwin set about collecting *c*.£250,000 in life insurance and pensions. A year later, tired of their clandestine existence, the couple began to travel abroad and eventually decided to settle in Panama. But John missed his two sons, who knew nothing of the fraud, and returned to the UK hoping to fool the authorities with claims of amnesia. Within days, a member of the public had Googled a photograph of the couple taken 4 years after John's 'death', and the bizarre scam was exposed. ❦ In 2008, John and Anne Darwin were each jailed for >6 years for fraud; at the time of writing, both had lodged appeals.

Zimbabwe's elections and economy

On 29/3/08, in an environment of relative calm, Zimbabweans voted in parliamentary and presidential elections. After days of delay and allegations of corruption, it became clear that Morgan Tsvangirai's Movement for Democratic Change (MDC) had toppled Robert Mugabe's Zanu-PF parliamentary majority for the first time since independence in 1980. The official result of the presidential elections was even more delayed. On 2/5, Zimbabwe's Electoral Cmsn declared that Tsvangirai had won 47·9% of the vote: more than Mugabe's 43·2%, but short of the absolute majority required. On 10/5, despite the violent harassment of MDC supporters, Tsvangirai announced that he would stand in a run-off election, later set for 27/6. However, as the weeks passed, Zanu-PF's systematic campaign of intimidation, starvation, arrest, abduction, arson, torture, rape, and murder intensified. Mugabe even boasted, 'We are not going to give up our country for a mere X on a ballot. How can a ballpoint pen fight with a gun?' On 22/6, Tsvangirai withdrew his candidacy, refusing to participate in a 'violent, illegitimate sham', yet this halted neither the election nor Mugabe's campaign of terror. By election day, the MDC told its supporters to vote for Mugabe (the sole candidate) if only to stay alive. On 29/6, Mugabe was sworn in for his 6th presidential term, claiming to have won >85% of the vote. ❦ The backdrop to these events was the rapid collapse of Zimbabwe's economy and civil society. In May, the central bank issued Z$5bn, Z$25bn, and Z$50bn notes in rapid succession; and in July, the official inflation rate was 2·2m%, though 10m% was more realistic. On 1/8, days after issuing a Z$100bn note, Zimbabwe lopped 10 zeros off its currency, making Z$10bn=Z$1. This did nothing to curb inflation or unemployment (*c*.80%), or the acute shortages of water, power, fuel, medicine, and food. The flood of refugees into neighbouring countries only intensified. ❦ In July, soon after Mugabe's 'victory', encouraged by international pressure and the 'quiet diplomacy' of S Africa's President Thabo Mbeki, Mugabe and Tsvangirai met (and shook hands [see

————————— OTHER MAJOR STORIES IN BRIEF cont. —————————

p.13]) in Harare to discuss power-sharing. On 15/9, after weeks of difficult negotiation, an historic deal was signed in which Mugabe would remain president, chair the cabinet, and head the army, while Tsvangirai would become PM, chair the council of ministers, and head the police. Zanu-PF would have 15 cabinet seats, and the MDC 16. ❧ The people of Zimbabwe, as well as their African neighbours and the rest of the world, watched and waited for signs that power-sharing would work in principle and in detail. Yet, few were optimistic that the country's immediate needs had been met. The UN warned that in 2009, >5·1m would face hunger in what was once Africa's breadbasket.

The Sichuan earthquake

On 12/5/08, at 2:28pm local time, a 7·9 Richter earthquake hit the mountainous region near Chengdu, in the Sichuan province of W China. The quake was felt >1,000 miles away in Beijing and Shanghai. Within days, the death toll was *c*.20,000, and *c*.4m homes were said to have been destroyed. In some areas, 80% of all buildings were in ruins. ❧ Mindful surely of the upcoming Olympics (and the outrage at Myanmar's response to Nargis [see p.32]), the government reacted with uncharacteristic speed and transparency. *c*.130,000 soldiers, medics, engineers, &c., were ordered to the region; assistance was solicited from (selected) neighbours; and both the President and PM were filmed visiting the area. ❧ However, the inaccessibility of the region, the destruction of vital infrastructure, bad weather, and the scale of the devastation combined to hinder rescue efforts. As the death toll hit *c*.50,000, it was reported that >3m tents were urgently needed. Miraculous reports of people rescued

against all odds did little to ameliorate the tragedy. Soon, pride in China's resilience gave way to anger that many of the rural region's buildings, not least schools, appeared cheaply and corruptly built. The death of >10,000 children led local authorities to suspend China's one-child policy for parents who had lost their only child (though this was of no comfort to those who were too old to conceive or who had been sterilized). ❧ A series of aftershocks terrorised the area after the quake, and within days millions were placed in further jeopardy by *c*.34 'quake lakes' – vast, unstable, and fast-rising reservoirs formed after rivers had been dammed by landslides. Notably, >250,000 were forced to evacuate from the 'Tangjiashan Lake', whose waters threatened >1·3m people, before it was partially drained in June. ❧ At the time of writing, *c*.88,000 were reported dead or missing, *c*.5m were homeless, and many thousands had been left childless. Clearly, the psychological, political, and socio-economic consequences of the quake will emerge only in time. But, although not perfect, China's response to the tragedy marked a shift in the regime's relationship with the international community, the media, and its own people [see p.38].

The Lisbon treaty

The Lisbon treaty was the EU's response to the rejection of the EU constitution by French and Dutch voters in 2005. Amongst many other reforms designed to equip an enlarged and growing Union, the Lisbon treaty would: create the post of EU President, to be elected every 2½ years, and a new representative for foreign affairs; reduce the number of national vetoes in favour of adapted qualified majority voting; cut the size of the Commission; and give new

———————— OTHER MAJOR STORIES IN BRIEF cont. ————————

powers to the European Parliament and European Court of Justice. ❦ Even its advocates noted similarities between the treaty and the constitution; its critics stated that the former was merely a cynical repackaging of the latter, designed to avoid referenda. ❦ In December 2007, all but one of the heads of EU states signed the treaty in Lisbon's Jerónimos Monastery; Gordon Brown signed the document in a bizarre solo ceremony, having chosen to attend the Commons Liaison Committee instead. ❦ However, the process of parliamentary ratification was derailed on 12/6/08 when Ireland, the only member state obliged by domestic law to hold a referendum, rejected the treaty 53·4% to 46·6%. This result stunned Europhiles, delighted Eurosceptics, and threw into confusion the process of reform. ❦ At the time of writing, the Czech Republic, Germany, Poland, and Sweden had yet to ratify the treaty. And debate was under way as to whether the treaty was dead, whether Ireland would be asked to vote again, or whether a two-speed EU might be formed to cater for the less enthusiastic [see p.268].

North Korea's nuclear ambitions
In February 2007, N Korea agreed to end its nuclear programme in return for a thaw in diplomatic relations and much-needed economic aid. And, on 26/6/08, six months behind schedule, N Korea submitted a 60-page declaration of its nuclear programme to the Chinese, who, along with Japan, Russia, S Korea, and the US, are engaged in the '6-party process' to denuclearise the Korean peninsula. In return for this declaration, the US agreed to remove N Korea from its list of state sponsors of terrorism, lift some sanctions (including those imposed by the Trading with

the Enemy Act), and open the way for loans, aid, and increased trade. A day later, N Korea demolished the cooling tower at its nuclear reactor in Yongbyon, which had produced the plutonium for Pyongyang's first nuclear test in 2006. ❦ Some were critical that N Korea had neither fully disclosed its nuclear arsenal nor addressed the issues of proliferation or what nuclear assistance it had given Syria. Others saw the declaration and the tentative resumption of talks as a sign that progress, albeit slow, was being made to disarm one of the world's most secretive and paranoid countries.

Church of England & female bishops
On 7/7/08, a vote by the Church of England's ruling body, the General Synod, moved the church closer to the consecration of women bishops. The Synod rejected a number of 'safeguard' concessions to 'traditionalists', including the creation of 'super bishops' who would oversee parishes opposed to women bishops, and the establishment of 'men only' dioceses. Instead, it was agreed that a code of practice would be drafted to cater for those 'who as a matter of theological conviction will not be able to receive the ministry of women as bishops or priests'. The draft of this code is to be discussed by the Synod in February 2009 [see also p.295].

Radovan Karadžić
On 21/7/08, after more than 10 years as a fugitive, the wartime leader of the Bosnian Serbs, Radovan Karadžić, was arrested in Belgrade, Serbia. At the time of his capture he was using the alias Dragan Dabic and working in bearded and bespectacled disguise as a practitioner of alternative medicine. ❦ In 1995 Karadžić was indicted by the UN for the most horrific crimes, including 'the

──────────OTHER MAJOR STORIES IN BRIEF cont.──────────

unlawful confinement, murder, rape, sexual assault, torture, beating, robbery and inhumane treatment of civilians; the targeting of political leaders, intellectuals and professionals; the unlawful deportation and transfer of civilians; the unlawful shelling of civilians; the unlawful appropriation and plunder of real and personal property; the destruction of homes and businesses and the destruction of places of worship'. ❦ On 30/7, Karadžić was transferred to The Hague. On 29/8, rejecting the proceedings as 'a court of NATO whose aim is to liquidate me', Karadžić refused to enter a plea on 11 counts of war crimes, genocide, and crimes against humanity. The judge entered a plea of 'not guilty' on his behalf, and the case continues.

Max Mosley & The News of the World
On 24/7/08, Max Mosley – president of the Fédération Internationale de l'Automobile, and son of British fascist Oswald – won a significant privacy case against the *News of the World*. The paper alleged that Mosley and five prostitutes had enjoyed sado-masochistic sex with 'Nazi' overtones. Mosley admitted the S&M sex, but claimed he had a right to privacy and vigorously stated 'their Nazi lie was completely invented'. In his ruling, Mr Justice Eady agreed that there was no evidence to support the allegations of Nazism, and he ruled that Mosley 'had a reasonable expectation of privacy in relation to sexual activities (albeit unconventional) carried on between consenting adults on private property'. Mosley was awarded £60,000 in damages. A number of media outlets complained that this ruling would limit their ability to expose actual wrongdoing, protesting that a privacy law was being introduced by judges without parliamentary debate.

However, it seems that the right to privacy will increasingly be defined by the judicial application of the European Convention on Human Rights. ❦ At the time of writing, Mosley was reported to be considering further legal action against organisations that had repeated the *News of the World*'s erroneous claims.

Barry George
On 1/8/08, a retrial found Barry George not guilty of the murder of TV presenter Jill Dando outside her London home on 26/4/1999. ❦ George was arrested in May 2000, after one of Britain's largest manhunts; in July 2001 he was convicted of shooting Dando at point-blank range, and was sentenced to life; in 2002, he lost an appeal against his conviction and was refused permission to appeal to a higher court. However, in June 2007, the Criminal Cases Review Cmsn judged that too much weight had been placed on certain aspects of forensic evidence and, five months later, the Court of Appeal declared his conviction unsafe and ordered a retrial. ❦ At the time of writing, George was thought to be considering claiming compensation for the 8 years he spent in prison; the police were debating how best to reopen the hunt for Jill Dando's actual murderer.

Pervez Musharraf's resignation
Pakistan's President Pervez Musharraf resigned on 18/8/08 – days before he was due to face impeachment charges of corruption and violating the constitution, laid by the coalition government elected in February. ❦ Musharraf seized power in a bloodless coup in 1999 and for *c.*9 years ruled Pakistan as a military dictator (only on 11/07 did he resign as army chief to govern as a civilian). After 9/11, he

————OTHER MAJOR STORIES IN BRIEF cont.————

allied Pakistan with America and became a pivotal player in the 'war on terror', exchanging tough action against Islamic extremism for >$10bn in military aid. However, this stance was unpopular domestically, and was blamed for fuelling the Taliban insurgency and terrorist attacks across the country. ⚜ Musharraf's peaceful exit, though welcomed by many, left a power vacuum in Pakistan just when the country faced economic turmoil, judicial instability, violent terrorist attacks, growing sympathy for Islamic extremism, and further threats of militancy in the North West Frontier Province.

Large Hadron Collider

On 10/9/08, to the excitement of the scientists, the fascination of the media, and the bewilderment of most of the public, the Large Hadron Collider (LHC) was switched on. Built 330' below the French–Swiss border by the European Organisation for Nuclear Research (CERN), the LHC is designed to fire atomic particles around its 17-mile circumference 11,245 times a second before smashing them into each other. It is hoped that the *c*.£4·4bn project will re-create the conditions that existed just after the 'big bang' formed the cosmos *c*.14bn years ago, find the hitherto elusive Higgs boson (or 'God particle'), and revolutionise our understanding of physics. ⚜ CERN's LHC, possibly the largest and most expensive scientific experiment in history, was challenged in the courts as a risk to the safety of the planet, and criticised for its vast cost. Reassuringly, Professor Stephen Hawking said, 'the world will not come to an end when the LHC turns on', and he added, 'if the human race cannot afford this, then it doesn't deserve the epithet "human"'.

Oil prices

The soaring price of oil influenced many facets of life in 2008 – from the cost of food [see p.16] to the decision of where (or if) to holiday [see p.221]. At the time of writing, recent falls in oil prices had not yet been felt by most consumers.

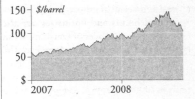

Meltdown Monday

On Monday 15/9/08, almost a year to the day after the British government nationalised Northern Rock, Lehman Brothers, the 4th largest US investment bank, filed for bankruptcy. At the same time, Merrill Lynch was snapped up by Bank of America at 'fire sale' prices. On 17/9, the US government effectively nationalised AIG – one of the world's largest insurance companies – for $85bn. These spectacular collapses came just weeks after the US government had 'bailed out' America's two mortgage monoliths, Fannie Mae and Freddie Mac, and JP Morgan had acquired Bear Stearns with Fed assistance. ⚜ The response on 'Meltdown Monday' was swift: the Dow fell by 4·4% (its steepest drop since 9/11); the FTSE and the Nikkei fell by *c*.5%. ⚜ US intervention failed to calm world markets and, on 18/9, the British government was forced to suspend competition rules to allow Lloyds TSB to take over the lending giant Halifax Bank of Scotland, whose share price had been crippled by uncertainty and (some said) speculative 'short selling'. At the time of writing, the only certainty was further uncertainty.

─── PERSON OF THE YEAR · HU JINTAO ───

Before his elevation in 2003, profiles of China's new president were often prefaced, 'Not much is known about Hu Jintao'. Five years on, we know only a little more about the man who leads the most populous nation on Earth. ❦ Two events intensified the world's gaze on China in 2008: the tragedy of the Sichuan earthquake and the triumph of the Beijing Olympics. Yet neither of these was clear-cut. For while the quake catalysed an unusually open (though not perfect) state response, it also exposed China's structural corruption and rural poverty. And while the Games were spectacular, their scale and security were premised on a firmly authoritarian grip. These tensions characterise both modern China and Hu himself. ❦ Hu Jintao was born in 1942 to a family of tea merchants. He grew up in Taizhou, Jiangsu, and in 1959 entered Beijing's Qinghua University, where he excelled in hydroelectric engineering. It was here he met his wife, with whom he has a son and daughter. In 1964, Hu joined the Communist Party and worked as a political instructor, before the Cultural Revolution banished him to the countryside for 're-education'. In 1968, he was sent to the desolate Gansu province, where he laboured for a year before he was promoted to technician. Hu worked assiduously, travelled extensively in the region, and formed powerful Party allies. In 1982, he was transferred to Beijing, and in 1984 he headed the Communist Youth League. A year later, political intrigue forced him back to the provinces as Party Secretary in Guizhou. Yet he shone in this role too, and in 1988 became the first civilian Party Secretary in Tibet. Interpretations differ as to Hu's role in the bloody suppression of the 1989 Tibetan unrest, but he proved himself no squeamish moderate, and after Tiananmen Square he did not hesitate to voice his support for the Party. ❦ In 1990, Hu returned to Beijing, where he was propelled by Deng Xiaoping, the author of China's reform era, to the top ranks of the political hierarchy. After a decade's tutelage, Hu succeeded Jiang Zemin as China's top party, government, and military leader between 2002 and 2005. ❦ Some were warily optimistic of Hu as China's paramount leader, considering him technocratic, pragmatic, and even reforming. His response to the 2003 SARS outbreak was initially secretive, but he responded to international criticism with greater transparency. Similarly, he reacted to protests in Hong Kong by shelving an anti-subversion law. Hu's ideological innovation is 'scientific development', whereby economic growth is tempered by social and ecological considerations for a 'harmonious society'. Yet while this 'people first' approach has ameliorated corruption, pollution, inequality, and incivility, Hu is unwavering over Tibet and Taiwan, and severe in his treatment of political dissidents, religious activists, and media critics. Hu is working to focus China's awesome potential so that the environment and the poor are not crushed in the stampede. But he is far from ushering in Western capitalist democracy. As he said in 2007, 'only socialism can save China and only reform and opening up can develop China, socialism, and Marxism'. ❦ Hu is expected to retire in 2012, the year London's Olympics will be compared to Beijing's. Expect profiles to begin: 'Not much is known about Hu's successor...'

SCHEMATIC · WORLD EVENTS OF NOTE · 2007–08

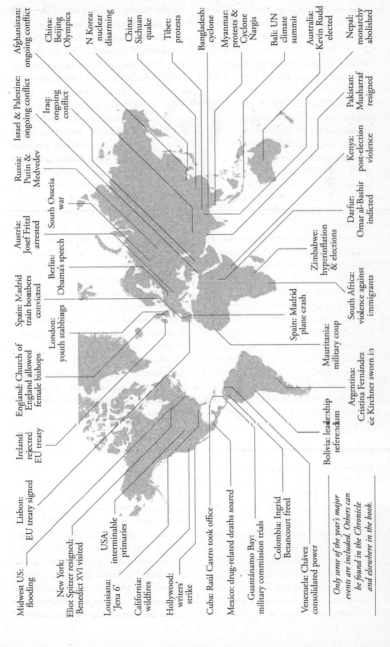

Afghanistan: ongoing conflict

China: Beijing Olympics

N Korea: nuclear disarming

China: Sichuan quake

Tibet: protests

Bangladesh: cyclone

Myanmar: protests & Cyclone Nargis

Bali: UN climate summit

Australia: Kevin Rudd elected

Nepal: monarchy abolished

Israel & Palestine: ongoing conflict

Iraq: ongoing conflict

Pakistan: Musharraf resigned

Russia: Putin & Medvedev

Kenya: post-election violence

South Ossetia war

Austria: Josef Fritzl arrested

Darfur: Omar al-Bashir indicted

Berlin: Obama's speech

Zimbabwe: hyperinflation & elections

Spain: Madrid train bombers convicted

South Africa: violence against immigrants

London: youth stabbings

Spain: Madrid plane crash

England: Church of England allowed female bishops

Mauritania: military coup

Ireland: rejected EU treaty

Argentina: Cristina Fernández ce Kirchner sworn in

Lisbon: EU treaty signed

Bolivia: leadership referendum

Midwest US: flooding

New York: Eliot Spitzer resigned; Benedict XVI visited

Cuba: Raúl Castro took office

USA: interminable primaries

Mexico: drug-related deaths soared

Louisiana: 'Jena 6'

Guantánamo Bay: military commission trials

California: wildfires

Colombia: Ingrid Betancourt freed

Hollywood: writers' strike

Venezuela: Chávez consolidated power

Only some of the year's major events are included. Others can be found in the Chronicle and elsewhere in the book.

——— IN BRIEF · SEPTEMBER 2007 ———

The daily chronicle below picks up from the 2008 edition of Schott's Almanac.

SEPTEMBER 2007 · {12} A new case of foot & mouth (F&M) disease was identified at a Surrey farm, 10 miles from the August outbreak. ❦ An 8·4 earthquake struck Sumatra, Indonesia, killing 9. {13} Police killed 2 alleged bank robbers during a foiled raid at a bank outside Southampton; a third man was taken into custody. {14} Shares in Northern Rock fell 32% after it asked for an emergency loan from the Bank of England. ❦ Actor Chris Langham was sentenced to 10 months in jail for downloading child pornography. ❦ A 2nd Surrey farm confirmed F&M. {15} Northern Rock customers began queuing outside branches across the country to withdraw their savings. ❦ RIP @ 39, rally driver Colin McRae. {16} >88 died after a plane crashed on a runway in Phuket, Thailand. {17} The government announced it would guarantee all money held in Northern Rock in an effort to stem the bank run. {19} Lebanese MP Antoine Ghanim, a well-known anti-Syrian activist, was murdered in Beirut. ❦ Thousands of Buddhist monks began protest marches across Myanmar against the military junta. {20} At the Lib Dem party conference, Menzies Campbell protested that he was not too old to lead the party. ❦ The BBC admitted that an internet vote to select a name for the Blue Peter cat had been rigged. ❦ José Mourinho left Chelsea by mutual consent. {22} A 4th case of F&M was confirmed on a Surrey farm. ❦ RIP @ 81, former Conservative minister Lord

M. Ahmadinejad

With age comes experience, and with experience comes judgement.
– SIR MENZIES CAMPBELL

Gilmour. ❦ RIP @ 84, Marcel Marceau [see p.61]. {23} The first UK case of bluetongue was discovered in a cow on a farm in Ipswich; the virus is spread by midges and can cause severe illness and death in cattle. ❦ >20,000 people, led by Buddhist monks, protested on the streets of Rangoon, Myanmar. {24} Gordon Brown extolled the virtues of Britishness in his speech to the Labour party conference; the media continued to speculate that he would call an early election. ❦ A 2nd cow in Suffolk was diagnosed with bluetongue. ❦ Iranian president Mahmoud Ahmadinejad caused controversy during a speech at New York's Columbia University by claiming there were no homosexuals in Iran. ❦ India beat Pakistan in the World Twenty20 final by 5 runs [see p.308]. {26} Myanmarese riot police attacked protesters; several deaths were reported. ❦ GMTV was fined a record £2m by Ofcom over a phone-in competition scandal. {27} Myanmarese soldiers fired shots into crowds of monks as protests in Rangoon continued; >9 were killed. {28} Myanmarese troops sealed off the 5 main monasteries in Rangoon in an effort to stem the 11th day of mass protests; international leaders condemned the junta's response; Brown questioned if death tolls might be higher than admitted. ❦ Bluetongue was confirmed as an outbreak; a protection zone was established in Suffolk. ❦ The Supreme Court in Pakistan ruled that President Musharraf could stand as a candidate in the country's elections. {29} UN special envoy Ibrahim Gambari arrived in Rangoon for talks as (muted) protests continued. ❦ 2 Britons, 2 Japanese, and 8 Chinese were hurt when a terrorist bomb

─────── IN BRIEF · SEPTEMBER – OCTOBER 2007 ───────

exploded in a park in Male, the Maldives. {30} >10 UN peacekeepers were killed and >50 were missing in Darfur after an attack by rebel forces. ✸ RIP @ 80, Lois Maxwell (aka Miss Moneypenny).

OCTOBER · {1} Vladimir Putin announced he might stand as a candidate for PM. ✸ RIP @ 76, Ned Sherrin [see p.61]. ✸ Britney Spears lost custody of her 2 young children to ex-husband Kevin Federline [see p.125]. {2} Brown made his first visit to Iraq as PM and announced troop numbers would be cut by 1,000. ✸ The leaders of N and S Korea met for a historic summit in Pyongyang. ✸ An inquest into the death of Princess Diana opened in London. {3} >3,000 workers were trapped down a mine in S Africa after a cable in the main lift broke. {4} After >40 hours, all of the S African miners were rescued. {5} Speculation mounted that Brown would call a snap election. ✸ BBC 1 controller Peter Fincham resigned after an inquiry into misleading documentary footage of the Queen. {6} As speculation reached fever pitch, Brown announced there would be no snap general election. ✸ England beat Australia 12–10 at the Rugby World Cup to reach the semi-finals. {8} Ann Widdecombe announced she would stand down at the next general election. ✸ A gunman killed 6 young people at a house party in Wisconsin, USA. ✸ Brown announced that troop numbers in Iraq would be reduced to 2,500 by spring. {9} Chancellor Alistair Darling was accused of purloining Tory ideas when he announced an increase to the inheritance tax threshold and taxes on non-domiciled

Vladimir Putin

The climate crisis is not a political issue, it is a moral and spiritual challenge to all of humanity. – AL GORE

foreign residents in his pre-Budget report. {11} The Healthcare Cmsn reported that 90 had died of *C. difficile* poisoning over 2½ years due to errors made by Maidstone & Tunbridge Wells NHS Trust. ✸ The jury in the Diana inquest was shown paparazzi shots taken as she lay dying; the images were not released to the media. ✸ 15 civilians were killed (including 9 children) after a US airstrike in the Lake Tharthar region of Iraq. {12} Al Gore and the UN's Intergovernmental Panel on Climate Change won the Nobel Prize for Peace [see p.70]. {14} The Russian secret service said they had warned Putin of a plot to assassinate him during a trip to Iran; Iran's Foreign Ministry denied the allegations. {15} Menzies Campbell resigned as Lib Dem leader [see p.254]. {16} In the latest in a series of official and unofficial walkouts, the Communication Workers Union called off a planned postal strike, to consider a new pay offer. {17} A wideranging government report concluded that sedentary modern life is contributory to obesity, and that less emphasis should be placed on individual responsibility for being overweight. ✸ A government report into migration welcomed the economic benefit of migrants but raised concerns that infrastructure was struggling to cope. ✸ Chris Huhne launched a bid for leadership of the Lib Dems. {18} Turkish MPs voted overwhelmingly for the right to take military action against Kurdish rebels in N Iraq who had launched rocket attacks on Turkey; America and Iraq urged caution. ✸ Former Pakistani PM Benazir Bhutto ended her self-imposed exile and returned to Pakistan; >130 were killed

--------- IN BRIEF · OCTOBER – NOVEMBER 2007 ---------

when a bomb struck her convoy in Karachi. ❦ The BBC announced that 1,800 staff would be made redundant to streamline the organisation. ❦ RIP @ 86, actress Deborah Kerr. ❦ ITV released a report uncovering more wrongdoings in the phone-in scandal; the company reportedly made £7·8m from uncounted phone votes. {19} A new EU Treaty was agreed in Lisbon; Brown said it protected Britain's national interests; the Tories called for a referendum. ❦ RIP @ 69, Alan Coren [see p.61]. ❦ The Serious Fraud Office announced it would examine irregularities relating to the GMTV phone-in scandal. ❦ Nick Clegg announced he would stand for leadership of the Lib Dems. {20} England were defeated by South Africa 6–15 in the Rugby World Cup Final [see p.303]. {21} Lewis Hamilton failed to win the Formula One world championship after engine problems; Ferrari's Kimi Räikkönen took the race and the championship. ❦ 12 Turkish soldiers were killed and 8 taken hostage after an attack by PKK rebels from Iraq; Turkey vowed to do whatever was necessary to prevent further attacks. ❦ RIP @ 74, American painter R.B. Kitaj. {23} 3 Britons and a German drowned off the Algarve coast attempting to save their children who had swum into difficulty. ❦ >500,000 people were evacuated from their California homes due to wildfires. {25} The Airbus A380 made its first commercial flight from Singapore to Sydney. ❦ America stepped up sanctions against the Iranian government, alleging support for terrorism. {26} Ministers announced that, from Sept 2008, all 12–13-year-old girls would be vaccinated against human papilloma virus

Jacqui Smith

(HPV), thought to cause most cases of cervical cancer. {29} Home Sec. Jacqui Smith apologised after it emerged the government had under-estimated by 300,000 the number of foreign workers in the UK since 1997. {30} Government figures revealed that >50% of new jobs (1·1m) created since 1997 were filled by foreign workers. ❦ Iraq announced that its soldiers would take full control of Basra from the British in December. ❦ RIP @ 64, Professor Anthony Clare. {31} >100 monks marched through Pakokku, Myanmar, for the first time since the regime cracked down on anti-government protests. ❦ A Spanish court found 21 people guilty of the 2004 Madrid train bombings in which >190 died.

NOVEMBER · {1} Turkey, Iraq, and the US united to curb the threat of PKK rebels in N Iraq; it was hoped that sanctions, extra patrols, &c. would ease tensions between Turkey and the PKK. ❦ There were calls for Met Police Commissioner Ian Blair to resign after an Old Bailey jury found the police guilty of endangering the public during the shooting of Jean Charles de Menezes. ❦ >700,000 were affected by severe flooding in Tabasco, Mexico. {3} 1 firefighter was confirmed dead and 3 missing after a vast fire at a Warwickshire vegetable warehouse. ❦ Pakistan's President Musharraf declared emergency rule to crack down on militant violence; >400 'preventative arrests' were made. ❦ A 21-year-old British student, Meredith Kercher, was found murdered in her apartment in Perugia, Italy. {5} Pakistani police broke up protests against

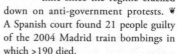

Who gets a say on the EU treaty?
Not you – just Gordon.
– CONSERVATIVE POSTER SLOGAN

IN BRIEF · NOVEMBER 2007

the imposition of emergency rule. ❦ 92 were arrested across Europe after police cracked an alleged paedophile network. {6} The first Queen's Speech of Gordon Brown's government was read. ❦ >40 died in a suicide attack in Baghlan province, Afghanistan. ❦ The bodies of 3 firemen missing after the Warwickshire warehouse fire were found. ❦ The Queen reopened the redeveloped St Pancras Station in London. ❦ 3 people were questioned in connection with the murder of Kercher; it was reported that she had been sexually assaulted before being stabbed. {7} A student at a

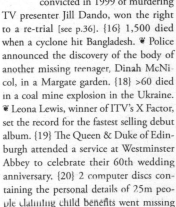

Benazir Bhutto

school in S Finland shot dead 8 people and injured >10. ❦ A state of emergency was declared in Georgia after days of opposition protests. ❦ The average price of UK unleaded petrol passed £1/litre for the first time. {8} An Independent Police Complaints Commission (IPCC) report into the 2005 shooting of Jean Charles de Menezes criticised the Met for bungling the operation; the London Assembly passed a vote of no confidence in Sir Ian Blair as calls for his resignation intensified. ❦ RIP @ 95, Chad Varah, founder of the Samaritans. {9} 23-year-old Samina Malik became the first woman to be convicted under the Terrorism Act for supporting martyrdom. ❦ Police stopped Pakistani opposition leader Benazir Bhutto from leaving her house to address a rally. ❦ Glasgow was selected to host the 2014 Commonwealth Games. {10} RIP @ 84 Norman Mailer [see p.61]. {11} Prince William laid a wreath at the Cenotaph for the first time, as part of the annual Remembrance Day ceremony. ❦ Cambodian police arrested 2 leading Khmer Rouge figures. ❦ The Home Of-

I was honoured to be the England head coach and for 18 months I've enjoyed every minute. – STEVE MCCLAREN

fice admitted 1000s of illegal immigrants had been cleared for jobs as security staff. {12} 6 died at a Gaza rally after clashes between Fatah supporters and Hamas-controlled police. {13} >6,500 birds were slaughtered after avian flu (later confirmed as H5N1) was found on a Suffolk poultry farm. ❦ Strikes swept France in protest at President Sarkozy's pension reforms. {14} Human remains found in the garden of a house in Margate, Kent, were confirmed as those of Vicky Hamilton, the 15-year-old who went missing in 1991. {15} Barry George, convicted in 1999 of murdering TV presenter Jill Dando, won the right to a re-trial [see p.36]. {16} 1,500 died when a cyclone hit Bangladesh. ❦ Police announced the discovery of the body of another missing teenager, Dinah McNicol, in a Margate garden. {18} >60 died in a coal mine explosion in the Ukraine. ❦ Leona Lewis, winner of ITV's X Factor, set the record for the fastest selling debut album. {19} The Queen & Duke of Edinburgh attended a service at Westminster Abbey to celebrate their 60th wedding anniversary. {20} 2 computer discs containing the personal details of 25m people claiming child benefits went missing from HM Revenue & Customs. ❦ RIP @ 88, Ian Smith, former PM of Rhodesia. {21} England failed to qualify for Euro 2008 after losing 2–3 to Croatia; England manager Steve McClaren was later sacked. {22} Pakistan was suspended from the Commonwealth for imposing emergency rule. ❦ Transport Sec. Ruth Kelly unveiled proposals for Heathrow's 3rd runway and 6th terminal. ❦ The government announced that from 14 December all properties sold in England &

——— IN BRIEF · NOVEMBER – DECEMBER 2007 ———

Wales would require Home Information Packs (HIPs). {23} 150 passengers and crew were rescued from a cruise ship after it hit ice in the Antarctic. {24} In the Australian general election, the Labour Party led by Kevin Rudd swept PM John Howard from power. ❦ England were drawn to play Croatia in the 2010 Football World Cup qualifiers, after recently losing to them in the Euro 2008 qualifiers. {26} Northern Rock named the Virgin Group as its preferred buyer. ❦ Labour General Sec. Peter Watt resigned in the wake of controversial donations to the party involving property developer David Abrahams. ❦ British teacher Gillian Gibbons was arrested in Sudan, and later jailed, for 'insulting' Islam after allowing pupils to name a teddy bear Muhammad. {27} At a Middle East peace conference in Annapolis, USA, Palestinian and Israeli leaders agreed to start talks aimed at reaching a peace deal by the end of 2008. ❦ >80 police officers were injured during rioting in Paris suburbs provoked by the death of 2 teenagers hit by a police car. {28} Police charged a man with the 1992 murder of Rachel Nickell on Wimbledon Common. ❦ Brown came under further pressure over Labour Party funding; at PMQs acting Lib Dem leader Vince Cable quipped that Brown had been transformed 'from Stalin to Mr Bean' [see p.254]. {29} The Electoral Cmsn referred some of Labour's donations to the police. {30} RIP @ 69, Evel Knievel [see p.61]. ❦ Christopher Biggins won 7th series of *I'm A Celebrity... Get Me Out of Here!* [see p.122] ❦ New Zealand police arrested a teenager alleged to have led a cyber-crime group that stole millions of dollars from bank accounts.

Gordon Brown

We are prepared to make a painful compromise rife with risks.
— EHUD OLMERT

December · {1} John Darwin, presumed dead after apparently disappearing during a 2002 canoeing trip, resurfaced at a London police station, claiming to have lost his memory. ❦ Events took place across the globe to mark the 20th World Aids Day. {3} Putin's United Russia party celebrated a resounding victory in Russian parliamentary elections; international observers described the election as unfair. ❦ Teacher Gillian Gibbons was released from Sudan and flown home. ❦ A US intelligence report concluded that Iran had halted its nuclear weapons programme in 2003. ❦ Mark Wallinger won the Turner Prize for his installation 'State Britain' [see p.171]. ❦ A UN summit opened in Bali to discuss a deal on climate change. ❦ John Darwin was reunited with his 2 sons. {4} Video footage was released of one of 5 British men taken hostage in Baghdad in May; their kidnappers threatened to kill one of the men unless British forces left Iraq. {5} Defence Sec. Des Browne apologised to families of 14 servicemen killed when a Nimrod plane exploded in Afghanistan in 2006, after an inquiry found a catalogue of MOD errors. ❦ John Darwin was arrested on suspicion of fraud, after a photo was published by a newspaper allegedly showing John and his wife Anne together in Panama in 2006. ❦ RIP @ 79, Karlheinz Stockhausen. {6} A gunman killed 8 people and himself in a shopping mall in Omaha, Nebraska. ❦ Home Sec. Jacqui Smith announced controversial plans to extend the period for which terror suspects can be held without charge to 42 days [see p.29]. ❦ The Bank of England cut interest rates from 5·75%

—————— IN BRIEF · DECEMBER 2007 ——————

to 5·5%. {7} Brown boycotted an EU–Africa summit in Lisbon because Zimbabwean leader Robert Mugabe was attending. {9} Boxer Joe Calzaghe won BBC Sports Personality of the Year [see p.315]. ❦ During a TV interview, the Archbishop of York, John Sentamu, cut up his dog collar and vowed not to wear one again until Mugabe had left office. ❦ Canadian pig farmer Robert Pickton was found guilty of murdering 6 women; he faced a further 20 murder charges. {10} Former media tycoon Conrad Black was sentenced to 6½ years in jail for fraud and obstructing justice.

Fabio Capello

❦ Brown visited British troops in Iraq and Afghanistan as Afghan and NATO troops captured the Taliban stronghold of Musa Qala. ❦ Putin backed Russian first deputy PM Dmitry Medvedev to replace him as president. {11} >30 were killed in al-Qaeda bomb attacks on UN and justice buildings in Algiers. {12} RIP @ 76, Ike Turner. {13} All but one of Europe's leaders signed the Lisbon Treaty [see p.34]; Brown claimed a diary clash was the reason he signed the treaty alone hours later. {14} Italian Fabio Capello was named as new England football manager. {15} 16-year-old David Nowak died after being stabbed outside a party in N London; 17-year-old Ahmed Hassan was stabbed to death in Dewsbury, W Yorkshire. ❦ The UN Bali Climate Change summit ended with agreement on a roadmap, starting 2 years of negotiations to agree emissions targets to replace those in the Kyoto Protocol. ❦ The Spice Girls gave their first UK concert in 9 years, at London's O2 arena. {17} British forces transferred control of Basra province to Iraqi authorities. {18} Nick

Why aren't we, as a world community, uniting against Mugabe?
– DR JOHN SENTAMU

Clegg was elected new Lib Dem leader [see p.254]. ❦ Jacob Zuma was elected new leader of S Africa's ruling ANC, making him front runner for the presidency in 2009. {19} 3 British residents released from US detention in Guantánamo Bay were detained on arrival in the UK. ❦ A tug capsized in heavy fog on the River Clyde; 3 of its 4 crew members died. {20} A N Irish man, Sean Hoey, was cleared of murdering 29 people in the 1998 Omagh bomb attack; the judge criticised police forensic techniques. {22} Tony Blair converted to Catholicism. {23} RIP @ 82, Oscar Peterson. {25} 2 high-ranking officials from the EU and UN were ordered to leave Afghanistan after being accused of making contact with the Taliban. ❦ An escaped Siberian tiger attacked 3 visitors at San Francisco zoo, killing one. {27} Former Pakistani PM Benazir Bhutto was killed in a suicide bomb attack at an election rally in Rawalpindi, aged 54; >20 others died in the attack [see p.61]. {28} One-year-old Archie-Lee Hirst was killed by a pet rottweiler at his grandparents' home in W Yorkshire. ❦ 6 French aid workers jailed in Chad for child abduction returned to France after the Chadian government agreed they could serve their sentences at home. {29} RIP @ 44, radio DJ Kevin Greening. ❦ RIP @ 79, Shu Uemura, Japanese make-up artist. {30} Benazir Bhutto's 19-year-old student son Bilawal was chosen to take over her Pakistan People's Party; his father Asif Ali Zardari was slated to run the party day-to-day. ❦ Kenya's President Mwai Kibaki was declared the winner of closely fought elections, triggering accusations of fraud, rioting, and ethnic violence.

IN BRIEF · JANUARY 2008

JANUARY · {1} >30 burned to death in a church in W Kenya, where they were seeking refuge from the escalating post-election violence. ❧ Malta and Cyprus joined the eurozone. {2} Oil traded at $100 a barrel in New York for the first time [see p.37]. ❧ A ban on smoking in France was extended to clubs, bars, restaurants, and cafés. ❧ RIP @ 82, George MacDonald Fraser, creator of Flashman. {3} Delays to engineering works on the West Coast mainline caused travel chaos. {4} Barack Obama and Mike Huckabee won the Democratic and Republican nominations respectively in the Iowa caucuses. ❧ >100 UK hospital wards closed to new patients in an attempt to halt the spread of norovirus ('winter vomiting disease'), which was infecting >100,000 a week. {6} The Right Rvd Dr Michael Nazir-Ali, Bishop of Rochester, caused controversy when he claimed that Islamic extremism had created 'no-go areas' for those of different faiths or race; he later apologised. {7} Kenny Richey was freed from US jail after 20 years on death row, following the overturning of his conviction last year. ❧ The US accused Iran of 'provocative and dangerous' behaviour, alleging Iranian speedboats harassed US navy vessels in the Strait of Hormuz. {8} The Golden Globes ceremony was cancelled due to a strike by the Writers Guild of America; it was replaced with a press conference [see p.163]. {9} George Bush made his first visit as president to Israel and the West Bank. ❧ Nick Clegg made his PMQ debut as Lib Dem leader; he urged Brown to help poorer families facing high fuel bills [see p.233]. ❧ RIP @ 83, Sir John Harvey-Jones. {10} The

Nick Clegg

I think we all ought to remember really that politics can be rough.
– RHODRI MORGAN on Peter Hain

government gave formal backing to a new generation of nuclear power stations. ❧ 3 swans were found dead from H5N1 bird flu in Dorset. ❧ Investment bank JP Morgan announced Tony Blair was to take up a part-time post. {11} RIP @ 88, Sir Edmund Hillary [see p.61]. ❧ Liverpool began its year as European Capital of Culture [see p.178]. {12} Work & Pensions and Welsh Sec. Peter Hain came under increased pressure over questions relating to donations made to his deputy leadership campaign. {14} A Taliban attack on a luxury hotel in Kabul killed >6. ❧ An Anglo-Russian diplomatic row intensified after Russia ordered the British Council to shut its offices in St Petersburg and Yekaterinburg. {15} >18 Palestinians were killed in an Israeli raid on the Gaza Strip, intended to halt rocket attacks on Israel. {16} A 2002 ceasefire between the government of Sri Lanka and Tamil Tiger rebels ended. ❧ Actress Leslie Ash won £5m compensation after contracting an infection at London's Chelsea & Westminster Hospital. {17} A BA passenger plane arriving from China crash-landed short of the runway at Heathrow; there were no serious casualties. ❧ RIP @ 64, Bobby Fischer [see p.62]. {18} A police investigation was launched after the theft of an MOD laptop containing personal details of 600,000 people interested in joining the forces. {20} It was announced that metal detectors would be installed in hundreds of English schools to cut knife crime. {21} The FTSE 100 dropped its furthest since 9/11. {22} The US Federal Reserve cut interest rates to 3·5%. ❧ RIP @ 28, Heath Ledger [see p.62]. {23} >22,000 police officers marched in London in a

——— IN BRIEF · JANUARY – FEBRUARY 2008 ———

protest over pay. {24} Peter Hain resigned after queries over donations to his deputy leadership campaign were referred to the police. ❦ A trader at French bank Société Générale lost his employer €4·9bn (£3·7bn). ❦ Italian PM Romano Prodi resigned after losing a Senate vote of confidence. {27} Barack Obama won the South Carolina primary. ❦ Holocaust Memorial Day was marked with a ceremony in Liverpool. ❦ RIP @ 86, former Indonesian President Suharto [see p.62]. ❦ RIP @ 97, Mormon leader Gordon Hinckley. ❦ Dozens died during violence in Kenya triggered by December's disputed elections. {29} 5 men were jailed for a £53m raid on a Securitas depot in Tonbridge, Kent in 2006. {30} Tory MP Derek Conway announced he would not fight the next election, after criticism of the amount he paid his son to work as his researcher [see p.265]. ❦ John Edwards quit the US presidential race. ❦ RIP @ 59, merry prankster Jeremy Beadle [see p.62]. ❦ RIP @ 66, journalist and writer Miles Kington. {31} Rudy Giuliani quit the US presidential race.

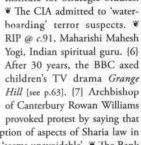

Carla Bruni

F EBRUARY · {1} HM Revenue and Customs extended the self assessment deadline for taxpayers after website problems. {2} Nicolas Sarkozy married model and singer Carla Bruni after weeks of speculation about their relationship. {3} Justice Sec. Jack Straw ordered an inquiry into press claims that police had bugged a Labour MP when he visited a constituent in jail. {4} The pro-Western president of Serbia, Boris Tadić, won the presidential election against a nationalist challenger. {5} On America's 'Super Tuesday', Rep.

I find that my conscience will not allow me to continue business as usual.
— STEVEN SPIELBERG

John McCain moved closer to his party's nomination; Dem. contenders Obama and Clinton both claimed victories. ❦ Baitullah Mahsud, a 'neo-Taliban' leader in Pakistan, replaced Osama bin Laden as the most deadly threat to the West, according to the International Institute for Strategic Studies. ❦ The CIA admitted to 'waterboarding' terror suspects. ❦ RIP @ *c*.91, Maharishi Mahesh Yogi, Indian spiritual guru. {6} After 30 years, the BBC axed children's TV drama *Grange Hill* [see p.63]. {7} Archbishop of Canterbury Rowan Williams provoked protest by saying that the adoption of aspects of Sharia law in the UK 'seems unavoidable'. ❦ The Bank of England cut interest rates from 5·5% to 5·25% [see p.240]. ❦ Mitt Romney suspended his presidential campaign. {9} A fire ravaged large parts of Camden Market, N London. {11} The Pentagon announced charges against 6 Guantánamo prisoners for alleged involvement in 9/11. ❦ 3 teenagers were jailed for life for kicking to death Garry Newlove outside his Warrington home in August 2007. ❦ Amy Winehouse won 5 Grammy Awards, but was absent from the ceremony due to US visa difficulties. ❦ RIP @ 75, *Jaws* star Roy Scheider. {12} Australian PM Kevin Rudd formally apologised to the Aboriginal population for wrongdoings by previous governments. ❦ Obama overtook Clinton in the race for the Democratic nomination, winning in Virginia, Maryland, and Washington, DC. {13} The Court of Appeal quashed the 2007 convictions of 5 young Muslims for downloading extremist literature. ❦ Steven Spielberg withdrew as artistic adviser to the 2008 Beijing Olympics in

————— IN BRIEF · FEBRUARY 2008 —————

protest at China's policy towards Sudan and Darfur. ❦ The Hollywood writers' strike ended [see p.163]. ❦ Top Hezbollah leader Imad Mughniyeh was killed by a bomb in Damascus. {14} The Court of Appeal ruled that Lotfi Raissi, a pilot falsely accused of training 9/11 hijackers, could claim damages. ❦ A gunman killed 6 at N Illinois University, near Chicago. {15} Cousins Nathaniel Pritchard, 15, and Kelly Stephenson, 20, were found hanged, bringing to 16 the number of apparent suicides amongst young people in the Bridgend area [see p.22]. {17} Chancellor Alistair Darling announced the temporary nationalisation of Northern Rock. ❦ Kosovo's parliament declared independence from Serbia. {18} Mohamed Fayed told the Princess Diana inquest that he believed Diana and his son Dodi had been murdered. ❦ Parviz Khan was jailed for life for plotting to kidnap and behead a Muslim soldier in the British army. {19} Cuba's 81-year-old leader Fidel Castro announced he would not accept another term as president, after 49 years in power; his brother Raúl was later confirmed as his successor. ❦ In Pakistan's elections, President Musharraf's party suffered heavy losses; the biggest winner, the late Benazir Bhutto's PPP, offered to form a coalition with the rival PML-N party. {20} An extensive search began after 9-year-old Shannon Matthews failed to return home from school in Dewsbury, W Yorkshire. ❦ At the Princess Diana inquest, former MI6 head Sir Richard Dearlove denied that the intelligence service was responsible for her death. {21} Foreign Sec. David Miliband admitted that 2 US 'extraordinary rendition' flights had landed on UK

Alistair Darling

I am fighting forces, dark forces.
— MOHAMED FAYED

territory in 2002, refuelling on the Pacific island of Diego Garcia; the government had previously denied any such involvement. {22} Steve Wright was sentenced to life for murdering 5 women, all working as prostitutes in Ipswich, in 2006 [see p.117]. ❦ Mark Dixie was sentenced to life for the murder of Sally Anne Bowman outside her Croydon home in 2005. ❦ Turkish troops crossed into N Iraq to target Kurdish rebels. ❦ Police released CCTV footage of Shannon Matthews leaving Dewsbury sports centre, and admitted they were 'gravely concerned' for her safety. {23} Police found what were said to be human remains at a former children's home in Jersey which was the focus of an alleged abuse inquiry. {24} The Coen brothers' *No Country For Old Men* dominated the Oscars [see p.156]. ❦ Ralph Nader announced his intention to run as an independent for the US presidency. {26} Levi Bellfield was sentenced to life for the murder of 2 young women and the attempted murder of a 3rd in SW London in 2003–04. ❦ Mohammed Hamid, said to be one of Britain's top recruiters for Islamic extremism, was found guilty of training men to fight abroad. ❦ Lib Dem foreign affairs spokesman Edward Davey was ordered out of the Commons, after repeated protests against a decision preventing MPs from debating a call for a referendum on the UK's EU membership. {27} A 5·2 earthquake – the strongest in the UK for *c.*25 years – was felt across large parts of the country. ❦ Art dealer Anthony d'Offay's £125m collection of modern art was secured for the nation at a cost of £26·5m. ❦ Campaigners from 'Plane Stupid' staged a protest on the roof of

─────── IN BRIEF · FEBRUARY – MARCH 2008 ───────

Parliament against Heathrow expansion. {28} The MOD confirmed Prince Harry had been serving in Afghanistan for the last 10 weeks, following the breach of a news embargo [see p.273]. ❦ President Mwai Kibaki and opposition leader Raila Odinga signed an agreement to end Kenya's post-election crisis. {29} Prince Harry was withdrawn from Afghanistan.

MARCH · {1} Karen Matthews made an emotional plea for her missing daughter Shannon to return home. {2} RIP @ 82, Paul Raymond, porn baron & property magnate. {3} Dmitry Medvedev, Vladimir Putin's chosen successor, won a landslide victory in Russian presidential elections. ❦ Nurse Colin Norris was found guilty of murdering 4 elderly patients in Leeds in 2002, by injecting them with insulin. ❦ The mother of Scarlett Keeling, a 15-year-old girl found dead in Goa in February, claimed that, contrary to Indian police reports, her daughter had been murdered. {4} N Ireland's first minister Ian Paisley announced he would stand down in May. ❦ RIP @ 69, Gary Gygax, American co-creator of Dungeons & Dragons. {5} MPs voted against a Tory proposal to hold a UK referendum on ratifying the EU Lisbon Treaty; 3 Lib Dem frontbenchers resigned after defying party orders to abstain and voting in favour. ❦ Hillary Clinton won the Democratic primaries in Ohio, Texas, and Rhode Island, reviving her campaign. {6} A Palestinian gunman killed 8 at a Jewish seminary in W Jerusalem. ❦ Pierre Williams received 3 life sentences for battering to death his former girlfriend Beverley Samuels and her children Fred &

Dmitry Medvedev

If you have Shannon will you please let her go.
– KAREN MATTHEWS

Kesha Wizzart at their Manchester home. {7} Mohammed Hamid, convicted as a leading Islamic extremism recruiter, was jailed indefinitely. ❦ RIP @ 86, Francis Pym, former Conservative Cabinet minister. ❦ RIP @ 97, Leon Greenman, the only Englishman to have been sent to Auschwitz. {8} RIP @ 63, Carol Barnes, TV journalist and newsreader. {9} A 2nd post-mortem on the body of Scarlett Keeling indicated that she had been murdered; 3 men were arrested in Goa. {10} The ruling Socialist Party won Spain's general election. {11} Michael Todd, Chief Constable of Greater Manchester Police, was found dead in Snowdonia, N Wales. ❦ The EU (Amendment) Bill to ratify the Lisbon Treaty was approved in the Commons. ❦ Admiral William Fallon, commander of US forces in Iraq & Afghanistan, announced he would retire early after speculation that he opposed the use of force against Iran. ❦ The *Sun* offered £20,000 for the safe return of Shannon Matthews; her mother Karen voiced fears that someone she knew had abducted her. {12} Darling set out his 1st Budget, announcing big increases in taxes on alcohol and 'gas-guzzling' cars [see p.236]. ❦ New York Governor Eliot Spitzer resigned amidst allegations he had paid for prostitutes. {13} A major security alert hit Heathrow after a man climbed a perimeter fence and ran into the path of an aircraft. ❦ Gold reached a record $1,000/ounce for the first time. ❦ Indian police revealed that Scarlett Keeling had been drugged and raped before being murdered in Goa. {14} Missing 9-year-old Shannon Matthews was found alive in a house a mile from her home in W Yorkshire. ❦

——— IN BRIEF · MARCH – APRIL 2008 ———

The Queen opened Heathrow's (£4·3bn) Terminal 5. ❧ Mass protests were held in the Tibetan capital Lhasa against Chinese rule. {15} It emerged that Michael Donovan, the uncle of Shannon Matthews' stepfather, had been arrested for her kidnap. ❧ Wales won the Rugby 6 Nations [see p.304]. {17} A female suicide bomber killed at least 42 people in Karbala, the Shia Iraqi holy city. {18} RIP @ 54, Anthony Minghella. ❧ RIP @ 90, Sir Arthur C. Clarke [see p.62]. {19} Express Newspapers agreed to pay £550,000 in libel damages to the parents of Madeleine McCann, for falsely suggesting they were responsible for their daughter's death. ❧ President Bush marked the 5th anniversary of the Iraq invasion with a speech proclaiming its success. ❧ RIP @ 86, actor Paul Schofield. {20} Chinese authorities admitted that police had opened fire on anti-Chinese protesters in a Tibetan area of Sichuan province. {22} RIP @ 89, Israel 'Cachao' López, Cuban-born jazz musician and inventor of the mambo. {24} RIP @ 65, Neil Aspinall, the Beatles' business manager. {25} Brown announced a free vote for Labour MPs on the most controversial parts of a new Embryology Bill, after warnings that some Catholic Labour MPs and Cabinet ministers would rebel. ❧ Hillary Clinton admitted she 'misspoke' in claiming she came under sniper fire on a trip to Bosnia in 1996 [see p.30]. ❧ RIP @ 89, Herb Peterson, US inventor of the Egg McMuffin. {26} Ford announced it was selling Jaguar and Land Rover to Indian company Tata. ❧ Heavy fighting continued in Basra, S Iraq, between government forces and Shia militias. ❧ Sarkozy began his first state visit to Britain; the press

Hillary Clinton

seemed more interested in his new wife Carla. ❧ David Beckham won his 100th cap for his country, but England lost 1–0 to France in a friendly in Paris. {27} Leona Lewis became the first British female to top the US charts for >20 years with the single *Bleeding Love*. {28} A woman was killed by a train after her foot became trapped on a level crossing near Colchester in Essex; a man was later charged with manslaughter. ❧ Problems with baggage-handling systems at Heathrow's new Terminal 5 led to the suspension of luggage check-in; BA was later forced to cancel more than 200 flights. {29} British forces were drawn into fighting between the Iraqi army and Shia militias in Basra, providing back-up for the government forces. ❧ RIP @ 41, artist Angus Fairhurst. {30} All 5 passengers of a small plane were killed when it crashed into a housing estate in Farnborough, Kent. ❧ RIP @ 65, Dith Pran, Cambodian journalist and inspiration for the film *The Killing Fields*. {31} The coroner at the Diana inquest said there was 'not a shred of evidence' that the Duke of Edinburgh ordered her death or that it was planned by MI6. ❧ Tory MP Boris Johnson launched his London Mayoral campaign.

Defeating this enemy in Iraq will make it less likely we will face this enemy here at home. – GEORGE BUSH

APRIL · {1} Newcastle University scientists created hybrid part-animal part-human embryos for the first time in Britain. ❧ Nick Clegg admitted he had slept with 'no more than 30' women in an interview for *GQ*, earning himself the nickname 'Cleggover'. {2} Official results showed that Mugabe's Zanu-PF had lost its parliamentary majority for the first time since Zimbabwean independence in

──────── IN BRIEF · APRIL 2008 ────────

1980 [see p.33]. ❦ Irish PM Bertie Ahern announced his resignation; Brian Cowen was later confirmed as his successor. {3} Mayor of London Ken Livingstone revealed he was the father of 3 publicly undisclosed children by 2 former girlfriends. {4} The Duke of Edinburgh was admitted to hospital with a chest infection. {5} RIP @ 83, Charlton Heston [see p.62]. {6} Pro-Tibet protesters and police clashed as the Olympic torch made its way through London [see p.297]. ❦ Snow caused the cancellation of 185 flights from Heathrow. {7} The jury at the Diana inquest found that Diana & Dodi Al Fayed were unlawfully killed because of the 'gross negligence' of the driver Henri Paul and the paparazzi. ❦ Social worker Philip Ellison was stabbed to death while working in Preston, Lancashire. ❦ The Paris leg of the Olympic torch relay was abandoned after anti-Chinese protests. {8} Mohamed Fayed announced he was abandoning his campaign to 'prove' that Dodi & Diana were murdered. ❦ TV presenter Mark Speight, whose fiancée had recently died after taking drugs, was reported missing. {9} Islamic preacher Abu Qatada (described as 'Osama bin Laden's right-hand man in Europe') won an appeal against deportation to Jordan. {10} The Bank of England cut interest rates from 5·25% to 5%. ❦ The High Court ruled that the Serious Fraud Office acted unlawfully when it dropped a corruption inquiry into a £43bn arms deal between BAE and Saudi Arabia. {12} Kenyan President Mwai Kibaki and opposition leader Raila Odinga agreed to form a cabinet, ending the crisis sparked by election results in December. ❦ In Zambia,

Robert Mugabe

southern African leaders held a summit to discuss the Zimbabwean electoral deadlock; Mugabe did not attend. {13} 5 British women (4 gap-year students and their guide) were killed in a bus crash in Ecuador. ❦ Mark Speight was found dead at Paddington Station, London. ❦ 2 members of the RAF were killed in Afghanistan; one, 51-year old Gary Thompson, was the oldest British serviceman to be killed in the conflict to date. {14} Richard Butler, a British CBS journalist held hostage in Iraq for >2 months, was rescued by Iraqi forces in Basra. ❦ Peter Robinson was elected new leader of the Democratic Unionist Party, replacing Ian Paisley. ❦ Silvio Berlusconi won Italy's general election. ❦ Zimbabwe's High Court ruled against an opposition demand for the release of last month's election results. {15} 13 people were arrested in Liverpool in connection with the shooting of 11-year-old Rhys Jones in August 2007; a 17-year-old was later charged with his murder. {16} Pope Benedict XVI arrived in America for his first official visit to the country. {17} RIP @ 77, MP Gwyneth Dunwoody [see p.62]. {18} 3 men were jailed for life for murdering Mark Witherall, 47, whilst burgling his house in Whitstable, Kent, in January 2007. {20} Former deputy PM John Prescott claimed

> *I found it difficult as a man like me to admit that I suffered from bulimia.*
> – JOHN PRESCOTT

to have suffered from bulimia during the 1980s–90s. ❦ 19-year-old Sean Rees became the 19th young person from Bridgend to commit suicide since January 2007. {21} A £50bn Bank of England scheme to help banks weather the credit crunch, by swapping mortgage debts for government bonds, was backed by Darling. {23} Brown was forced into a U-turn on a key measure of the 2007 Budget – the scrapping of the 10p tax rate – after the threat of a backbench rebellion [see p.237]. ❦ Hillary Clinton beat Barack Obama in the Pennsylvania primary. {24} The first national teachers' strike in 20 years had a varying impact across the country; it was called by the National Union of Teachers to protest at a below-inflation pay settlement. {25} RIP @ 86, Humphrey Lyttelton [see p.62]. {27} 1,200 workers at Scotland's Grangemouth Oil refinery began a strike over pensions; production ceased and additional fuel was imported from Europe to prevent shortages. {28} An Austrian man, Josef Fritzl, confessed to imprisoning his daughter in a cellar for 24 years and fathering her 7 children; DNA tests later confirmed his admission. ❦ 2 teenage boys were jailed for life for the 2007 murder of Sophie Lancaster, killed in a park in Lancashire for dressing as a Goth. {29} ❦ Defence Sec. Des Browne announced that 600 British troops would be sent to Kosovo for NATO peacekeeping. ❦ RIP @ 102, Albert Hofmann [see p.63]. {30} In a BBC interview, Brown admitted 'mistakes' in the way he abolished the 10p income tax rate [see p.237].

Boris Johnson

off [see p.33]. ❦ Brown admitted Labour had suffered 'disappointing' results in the local elections: they lost 331 councillors in the worst result for 40 years [see p.26]. {3} Boris Johnson was sworn in as the new Mayor of London. {4} >10,000 died after a cyclone lashed Myanmar [see p.32]. ❦ RIP @ 71, Lord Holme. ❦ Ronnie O'Sullivan won his 3rd World Snooker Championship, beating Ali Carter 18–8 at the Crucible [see p.317]. {6} Myanmar's state media announced that the death toll from Cyclone Nargis had risen to 22,000; *c.*41,000 remained missing. ❦ A gunman was shot dead by police during a siege in Chelsea, London. {7} The UN urged Myanmar to allow in aid agencies to prevent the death toll from spiralling. ❦ Hillary Clinton lost ground to Obama after losing in N Carolina and suffering a funding crisis. ❦ Dmitry Medvedev was sworn in as President of Russia. {8} The Iraqi defence ministry announced it had arrested Abu Ayyub al-Masri, al-Qaeda's leader in Iraq. ❦ ITV was fined a record £5·675m for running unfair premium-rate phone competitions. ❦ As expected, Putin was appointed Russia's new PM. {9} Myanmar announced it would accept foreign aid but not foreign aid workers, preferring to organise distribution itself. ❦ Hezbollah seized a large section of W Beirut after 3 days of fighting in which >15 died; the Lebanese government called it a 'bloody coup'. {10} Hezbollah agreed to withdraw from Beirut after talks with the Lebanese government. ❦ The first small shipments of aid arrived in Myanmar. {11} 16-year-old Jimmy Mizen was murdered in SE London. ❦ Manchester Utd took their 17th Premiership title [see

M AY · {1} Local elections were held in England and Wales [see p.26]. ❦ 5 died and 9 were injured after a collision between two boats in Sydney Harbour, Australia. ❦ America admitted carrying out a missile strike on Somalia that killed a militant target. {2} Zimbabwe finally announced that Morgan Tsvangirai had won the presidential election but with insufficient votes to become president, forcing a run-

The sheer survival of the affected people is at stake.
– BAN KI-MOON

IN BRIEF · MAY 2008

p.300]. {12} >10,000 were feared dead after a 7·9 Richter earthquake struck the Sichuan province in SW China [see p.34]. {13} The toll of the China quake was raised to 12,000, as a massive search and rescue operation began. ❦ Darling introduced measures to help those hit by the abolition of the 10p tax band [see p.237]. ❦ >60 died in a series of bomb blasts in Jaipur, India. {14} Chinese media reported that >15,000 had died and >25,000 were still trapped after the earthquake. ❦ The UN raised its estimate of those affected by Cyclone Nargis from 1·5m to 2·5m. ❦ John Edwards backed Obama. {15} Riot police were deployed in Manchester after Rangers fans rampaged when a big screen showing their UEFA cup final against Zenit St Petersburg failed. {16} The Nargis death toll rose to 78,000; 56,000 remained missing. ❦ The Chinese government reported that *c.*5m people had been left homeless by the recent earthquake. ❦ Teachers complained of communication problems and delays with the company responsible for marking Sats. {17} Britain and France strongly condemned Myanmar for not admitting aid workers. ❦ Portsmouth beat Cardiff 1–0 in the FA Cup Final [see p.301]. {18} China announced there would be 3 days of official mourning for the victims of the earthquake. ❦ >12 died in a series of attacks on immigrants in Johannesburg, S Africa. {19} After debates on the Human Fertilisation and Embryology Bill, MPs voted against an attempt to ban animal-human hybrid embryos and 'saviour siblings'. {20} MPs voted against lowering the time limit for abortions [see p.94]. {21} Manchester Utd beat Chelsea in the Champions League

Morgan Tsvangirai

The challenge is still severe, the task is still arduous, and the time is pressing.
– HU JINTAO on the Sichuan quake

Final [see p.301]. ❦ Police excavating the Haut de la Garenne children's home in Jersey found what were said to be human remains. {22} Voters went to the polls in the Crewe & Nantwich by-election [see p.28]. ❦ The S African government sent troops onto the streets to protect foreigners who had been targeted in recent unrest, in which 42 had died. {23} The Tories won the Crewe & Nantwich by-election in spectacular fashion [see p.28]. ❦ Ban Ki-moon announced that Myanmar's military leaders had agreed to let all foreign aid workers into the country. {23} Brown came under increased pressure as Cameron hailed the 'end of New Labour'. {24} An 18-year-old actor, Rob Knox, was killed and 3 others were injured after a knife attack in Sidcup, London [see p.22]. ❦ Russia triumphed at the Eurovision Song Contest in Belgrade [see p.146]. {25} 17-year-old Amar Aslam was found dead in a park in Dewsbury. {27} RIP @ 73, Sydney Pollack. ❦ Hundreds of lorry drivers converged on London to protest about the rising cost of fuel. ❦ Chinese state media announced that 420,000 homes had been destroyed in aftershocks from the recent earthquake. {28} Nepal became the world's newest republic, after the constituent assembly voted to abolish the monarchy. ❦ RIP @ 81, artist Beryl Cook. {29} 2 died after an army helicopter crashed in Devon. ❦ A 6·1 earthquake struck Iceland, causing damage to buildings. ❦ Torrential rain caused flash flooding in parts of Somerset. {31} A 5-year-old boy and his 4-year-old sister were stabbed to death in Carshalton, and their 6-month-old sister was taken to hospital with serious injuries; the chil-

─────── IN BRIEF · MAY – JUNE 2008 ───────

dren's parents were arrested in connection with the attack.

JUNE · {1} The mother of the children stabbed in Carshalton was detained under the Mental Health Act. ❦ Jamaican sprinter Usain Bolt broke the 100m world record, clocking a time of 9·72 [see p.24]. {2} Bradford and Bingley's shares fell by 24% after it announced a loss in profits. ❦ A 15-year-old girl, Arsema Dawit, was found stabbed to death in a lift in S London. ❦ RIP @ 79, Bo Diddley [see p.63]. ❦ RIP @ 71, Yves Saint Laurent [see p.63].

Barack Obama

{3} It emerged that the family of Arsema Dawit had reported to the police that she had been harassed by a young man in the weeks before her murder. ❦ Chickens on a farm in Oxfordshire tested positive for the H7 strain of bird flu. {4} Obama claimed victory in the race to become Democrat nominee; Clinton declined to concede. ❦ A 17-year-old boy died in Oxford after becoming trapped in a drain during flash flooding. {5} 5 men, including Khalid Sheikh Mohammed, appeared before a military tribunal in Guantánamo Bay, accused of masterminding 9/11. ❦ Zimbabwean police detained a group of US & UK diplomats investigating political violence in the country. ❦ Peter Robinson and Martin McGuinness were appointed First and Deputy First Ministers of the N Ireland Assembly. {6} Mugabe banned opposition rallies, citing security fears. ❦ 3 Britons were feared dead after they were reported missing with 2 other divers off the coast of Indonesia. {7} Hillary Clinton suspended her campaign and pledged her support for Obama. ❦ The 3 British divers feared

> *Tonight, I can stand before you and say that I will be the Democratic nominee.* – BARACK OBAMA

dead in Indonesia were found alive; they had been caught in a strong current and spent 2 nights on a remote island. ❦ The European Championships began as co-hosts Switzerland lost to the Czech Rep. [see p.299]. {8} 7 died and 10 were injured after a man went on a 'stabbing rampage' in Tokyo. ❦ 3 British soldiers were killed in Afghanistan, bringing to 100 the total killed there since 2001 [see p.18]. ❦ BBC reporter Abdul Samad Rohani was found dead after being kidnapped in Afghanistan. {9} A 32-year-old police officer died after being accidentally shot during training. ❦ The government agreed to allow congestion charging to begin in Manchester in 2013. {10} A civil servant was suspended after confidential files concerning al-Qaeda were left on a train. {11} Brown won a controversial vote on extending the maximum time police can hold a terror suspect to 42 days – the vote was passed 315 to 306 [see p.29]. ❦ Yeshi Girma, the 32-year-old wife of convicted 21/7 would-be bomber Hussain Osman, was convicted of failing to alert police of his intentions. {12} David Davis resigned as an MP over the issue of 42 days, prompting a by-election [see p.28]. {13} Shell tanker drivers began a 4-day strike over pay; motorists were urged not to panic-buy fuel. ❦ Irish voters rejected the Lisbon Treaty 53·4% to 46·6%, thereby placing the ratification process in doubt [see p.34]. ❦ >1,000 Taliban inmates were freed after a raid on a prison in Kandahar. {14} Petrol supplies ran low at a number of Shell garages affected by the tanker drivers' strike. {15} George W. Bush was greeted by protesters as he arrived in the UK for a farewell visit. ❦ A man and 2

———— IN BRIEF · JUNE – JULY 2008 ————

children were found dead in a car in N Wales; it later emerged that Brian Philcox had gassed himself and his children after an acrimonious split from his wife. {16} Des Browne announced that troop numbers in Afghanistan would increase by 230 to >8,000 by spring 2009. {17} The tanker drivers' union reached a pay agreement with Shell and further strikes were cancelled. ❦ The Bank of England warned that inflation could exceed 4% in 2008. ❦ Radical Islamist preacher Abu Qatada was released from jail under strict curfew conditions. {18} 4 British soldiers died in Afghanistan, including the first female soldier to die in the theatre. ❦ RIP @ 86, musical star Cyd Charisse. {19} A 6-month truce began between Hamas and Israel. ❦ It was reported that the number of girls under 16 having abortions rose by 10% in 2007 [see p.94]. ❦ Amid growing violence ahead of the presidential run-off in Zimbabwe, the corpses of 4 MDC activists were found outside Harare. {20} The *New York Times* reported that Israel had performed a military training exercise thought to be a practice attack on Iran's nuclear sites. {21} 5 coalition troops were killed in Afghanistan, marking an increase in violence in the region. {22} Morgan Tsvangirai pulled out of the presidential run-off vote, explaining that

Ingrid Betancourt

'We have resolved that we will no longer participate in this violent, illegitimate sham of an election process' [see p.33]. ❦ >700 went missing after a ferry capsized in the Philippines during Typhoon Fengshen. {25} The Queen stripped Robert Mugabe of his honorary knighthood. ❦ A US jury found Neil Entwistle guilty of murdering his wife and baby daughter.

{26} The Henley by-election was held [see p.28]. ❦ The price of crude oil hit $140 a barrel. {27} Voting went ahead in Zimbabwe's presidential run-off despite Mugabe being the only candidate; Tsvangirai told people to vote in order to protect themselves. ❦ Tory John Howell won the Henley by-election with a majority of 10,116; Labour came in 5th and lost its deposit [see p.28]. {28} Leader of the Scottish Labour party, Wendy Alexander, stood down after funding irregularities were alleged. {29} Archbishop Desmond Tutu called for the international community to intervene in Zimbabwe, using force if required. ❦ A 16-year-old boy, Ben Kinsella, was stabbed to death in Islington, N London. ❦ Spain beat Germany in the Euro 2008 final [see p.299]. {30} At a meeting of the African Union, Kenyan PM Raila Odinga called for Mugabe to be suspended until free and fair elections were held in Zimbabwe. ❦ The Bank of England announced that the number of mortgage approvals in May had dropped 28% since the previous month, and 64% since the same month last year.

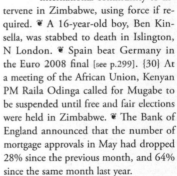

You are illegitimate, and we will not recognise your administration.
– DESMOND TUTU on Robert Mugabe

JULY · {1} Portuguese police announced they were closing the investigation into the disappearance of Madeleine McCann. ❦ Hundreds of young people staged an impromptu march in N London against knife crime, in response to the murder of Ben Kinsella. ❦ The Mongolian government called a 4-day state of emergency after violent protests over an alleged rigged election. {2} Politician Ingrid Betancourt and 14 other hostages held by rebel group FARC

———————— IN BRIEF · JULY 2008 ————————

for >6 years in the Colombian jungle were rescued by Colombian soldiers. ❦ Leader of the Lib Dems in Scotland, Nicol Stephen, stepped down, citing the pressures of the job. {3} 2 French research students, Laurent Bonomo and Gabriel Ferez, were found brutally murdered in a burnt-out flat in New Cross, SE London; the pair had been stabbed *c*.240 times before their bodies were set alight. ❦ 3 were charged with the murder of Ben Kinsella. {4} Zimbabwe announced it would not attend the Twenty20 Cricket World Cup in England in 2009 in a compromise with the ICC, which in turn agreed not to suspend the country. ❦ It was revealed that administrative failures meant that >1m 11- and 14-year-olds would get their Sats results late. {5} Venus Williams won her 5th Wimbledon final, beating her sister Serena 7–5 6–4; 14-year-old Laura Robson became the first Brit to take the girls' title since 1984 [see p.312]. {6} Rafael Nadal beat Roger Federer in an epic 5-set final at Wimbledon, bringing to an end Federer's 5-year domination of the competition [see p.312]. ❦ >20 died after coalition forces accidentally attacked a wedding in E Afghanistan. {7} The Church of England General Synod voted to allow the ordination of women bishops. ❦ Ruth Kelly announced the UK

David Davis

Are we heading for schism? Well, let's see.
– DR ROWAN WILLIAMS

would cut biofuel use, due to uncertainty over its impact on agriculture [see p.209]. ❦ Briton Simon Mann was sentenced to 34 years in jail for leading an attempted coup in Equatorial Guinea. ❦ 41 died in a suicide attack on the Indian embassy in Kabul. {8} The G8 said it did not accept the legitimacy of the Zimbabwean government and promised sanctions against those perpetrating violence. ❦ America signed a deal with the Czech Republic, allowing the US to base part of their controversial missile defence system there; Russia warned of a military response. ❦ British housebuilders Persimmon announced 2,000 redundancies as a consequence of the housing downturn. {9} Israel and the US condemned Iran for testing a missile capable of reaching Tel Aviv. ❦ A 33-year-old man was charged with the murders of Laurent Bonomo and Gabriel Ferez. ❦ UK housebuilders Bovis Homes and Redrow announced job cuts. ❦ Briton Mark Cavendish won stage 5 of the Tour de France [see p.306]. {10} The British government was ordered to pay >£3m in compensation to 10 Iraqis and their families who were tortured while in British custody. ❦ 9 British troops were injured by 'friendly fire' in Afghanistan. ❦ The Haltemprice & Howden by-election was held [see p.28]. ❦ Yorkshire were expelled from the Twenty20 Cup for fielding an ineligible player. ❦ Luton Town started the football season with an unprecedented minus 30 points, after the FA fined them for insolvency and paying agents via a third party. {11} David Davis won the Haltemprice & Howden by-election [see p.28]. ❦ China and Russia vetoed a UN resolution to impose sanctions on Zimbabwe. {12} A second man was charged with the murders of Laurent Bonomo and Gabriel Ferez. {13} 9 US troops were killed after Taliban fighters attacked a US base. ❦ A heckler interrupted a sermon by openly gay American Bishop Gene Robinson as he preached in W London, calling the bishop a 'heretic'. {14} The International Criminal Court accused

——— IN BRIEF · JULY 2008 ———

Sudanese President Omar al-Bashir of perpetrating war crimes in Darfur; the UN withdrew many of its staff in the region in case of unrest. ❦ The trial of Anne Darwin opened; she was accused of helping her husband John fake his own death and defrauding pensions and life insurance companies; she denied any wrongdoing [see p.33]. {15} June inflation hit 3·8%, an 11-year high. {16} 600,000 Unison and Unite union members began a 48-hour strike over pay. ❦ Brown announced that a planned 2p rise in fuel duty would be postponed until March 2009; Cameron accused him of timing the announcement to coincide with the Glasgow East by-election. ❦ Israel and Lebanon completed an exchange of prisoners; Israel received the remains of 2 soldiers in return for 5 Lebanese militants. ❦ The supermarket chain Co-op agreed to buy Somerfield for £1·57bn. {18} An 18-year-old was stabbed to death in SW London. ❦ Disgraced sprinter Dwain Chambers lost a court case regarding his bid to compete in Beijing 2008 [see p.311]. {19} One of the 5 British men held captive in Iraq for >1 year was reported to have committed suicide; the British government urged the kidnappers to release the remaining hostages. {20} Zimbabwe printed Z$100bn notes as hyperinflation spiralled [see p.33]. ❦ Padraig Harrington defended his Open title [see p.305]. {21} Portuguese police announced they were officially ending their investigation into the disappearance of Madeleine McCann. ❦ Mugabe and Tsvangirai agreed to hold power-sharing talks. {22} After ten years on the run, Radovan Karadžić was apprehended in Belgrade for committing

Radovan Karadžić

war crimes in Bosnia; he had disguised himself as a practitioner of alternative medicine [see p.35]. {23} John & Anne Darwin were jailed for >6 years [see p.33]. {24} Max Mosley won his privacy case against the *News of the World* [see p.36]. ❦ Voters went to the polls in the Glasgow East by-election. {25} The SNP stunned Labour and severely undermined the credibility of Brown by winning Glasgow East [see p.29]. ❦ A Qantas 747 was forced to make an emergency landing in Manila after a large hole appeared in the fuselage causing a loss of cabin pressure. ❦ A British soldier was killed in Helmand, Afghanistan. ❦ Barack Obama arrived in the UK and held (separate) talks with Brown and Cameron. {26} >38 died after a series of bombs were detonated in Ahmedabad, India. {27} >17 died and >150 were injured after 2 bombs went off in Istanbul. {28} Women suicide bombers in Iraq killed >53 Shia Muslim pilgrims in Baghdad and Kirkuk. ❦ A 31-year-old British doctor, Catherine Mullany, was shot dead on her honeymoon in Antigua; gunshot wounds left her husband Ben in a critical condition. ❦ Unease over Brown's leadership escalated as Labour MP Gordon Prentice called for his resignation. {29} World Trade Organisation talks, known as the 'Doha round', aimed at opening up Western markets to the developing world, collapsed. ❦ 14-year-old Sarika Singh won a discrimination claim against her school; she had been banned from wearing her Sikh *Kara* bracelet under the school's 'no jewellery' policy. ❦ At a pro-Karadžić rally in Belgrade, protesters clashed with police. ❦ British Airways and Spanish carrier Iberia entered merger talks. {30}

I fundamentally disagree with the suggestion that any of this is depraved. – MAX MOSLEY

───────── IN BRIEF · JULY – AUGUST 2008 ─────────

David Miliband wrote an article in the *Guardian* setting out his future vision for the Labour party; many interpreted the act as the beginning of a leadership challenge against Brown. ❦ British Gas announced it was raising prices by 35% [see p.233]. {31} Radovan Karadžić made his first appearance before the war crimes tribunal at The Hague. ❦ After months of uncertainty, Turkey's constitutional court narrowly voted not to ban the ruling AKP party over concerns they were too Islamist. ❦ Critically injured Ben Mullany was flown home to Wales from Antigua.

Pervez Musharraf

schools were published, even though 460 schools had yet to receive a full set of marks; the American company responsible for the marking, Educational Testing Service (ETS), was blamed for the chaos. ❦ 11 climbers died in an avalanche on K2, the world's second highest and most treacherous peak. {5} Northern Rock announced a loss of £585m. {6} The army in Mauritania launched a coup, overthrowing the first freely elected president, Sidi Ould Cheikh Abdallahi. ❦ A report claimed that many NHS hospitals were infested with rats, mice, and cockroaches. {7} Georgia launched an attack on the breakaway separatist state of South Ossetia [see p.23]. ❦ The first US military trial at Guantánamo Bay found Osama bin Laden's former driver, Salim Hamdan, guilty of supporting terrorism; he was sentenced to 5½ years in prison. ❦ Pakistan's ruling coalition voted to begin impeachment proceedings against President Musharraf. ❦ RIP @ 71, Simon Gray, author and playwright. {8} The Royal Bank of Scotland recorded a £691m loss, the second biggest loss in UK banking history. ❦ Russia retaliated against Georgia's attack on S Ossetia [see p.23]. ❦ Beijing hosted the opening ceremony of the 2008 Olympic Games [see p.24]. {9} Fighting continued to rage in South Ossetia, as Russian fighter jets bombed Georgian targets in support of Ossetian separatists. The UN failed to agree on the wording of a statement calling for a ceasefire, but the US and EU both called for peace. ❦ RIP @ 50, US comedian and actor Bernie Mac. {10} Georgia announced that they had withdrawn from South Ossetia and that Russian troops were now in control

A UGUST · {1} Barry George was cleared of the murder of Jill Dando after a re-trial; he had served 8 years in prison [see p.36]. {2} >9 died in Gaza after infighting between Fatah and Hamas; Israel allowed a number of Fatah members to cross the border into Israel. {3} Alistair Darling, John Denham, and Harriet Harman publicly backed Brown in an effort to stem speculation about party rifts and leadership challenges. ❦ >12 died after a truck bomb was detonated near a passport office in Baghdad. ❦ >140 were killed in a stampede during a Hindu festival in the N Indian state of Himachal Pradesh. ❦ RIP @ 89, Alexander Solzhenitsyn [see p.63]. ❦ Ben Mullany died in hospital, a week after the shooting in Antigua in which his wife was killed. ❦ Michael Vaughan resigned as England cricket captain. {4} 16 Chinese policemen were attacked and killed by militants in the Muslim region of Xinjiang. ❦ Kevin Pietersen was named as new England cricket captain. ❦ Sats results for primary

The odds are against us, no question. But I still believe we can win the next election. – DAVID MILIBAND

— IN BRIEF · AUGUST 2008 —

of the regional capital; reports of casualties varied, but Georgia said >1,500 South Ossetians had been killed. {11} Georgia announced they were holding to a ceasefire despite continued military action by Russia [see p.23]. ❦ Nicole Cooke won Britain's first gold medal of the Olympics in the women's cycling road race [see p.296]. ❦ A Chinese couple, Xi Zhou and Zhen Xing Yang, were found murdered in their flat in Newcastle. ❦ RIP @ 65, Isaac Hayes [see p.63]. {12} Bush strongly criticised Russia as incursions continued into Georgia. ❦ RIP @ 80, Bill Cotton, former BBC TV executive. {13} Georgia and Russia agreed to a Sarkozy-brokered ceasefire. {14} American aid arrived in Georgia amid reports that Russia was breaching the terms of the agreed ceasefire and continuing to occupy Gori. {15} President of Georgia Mikhail Saakashvili signed a ceasefire agreement; the US put pressure on Russia to do the same. ❦ The contract with Sats markers ETS was terminated by 'mutual consent'. ❦ Maoist leader Prachanda was elected PM of Nepal after the country abolished the monarchy. {16} Russia signed the ceasefire with Georgia but claimed it could not withdraw its troops until the security situation had improved. ❦ Jamaican Usain Bolt won the 100m in Beijing, setting a new world record of 9·69s [see p.24]. {17} After victory in the 4×100m medley, Michael Phelps won his 8th gold medal, beating Mark Spitz's 1972 record of 7. ❦ 5 died after 2 light aircraft collided outside Coventry airport. ❦ Mugabe and Tsvangirai failed to reach agreement at a power-sharing summit in S Africa. {18} 1 died and >70 were injured in a bus crash

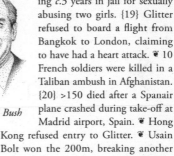

George W. Bush

With so many people saying it couldn't be done, all it takes is an imagination.
– MICHAEL PHELPS

near Alton Towers. ❦ Pakistan's President Pervez Musharraf stepped down after 9 years in power. ❦ A 20-year-old man and 17-year-old boy were charged with the murders of Catherine and Ben Mullany. ❦ Gary Glitter was released from prison in Vietnam after spending *c*.3 years in jail for sexually abusing two girls. {19} Glitter refused to board a flight from Bangkok to London, claiming to have had a heart attack. ❦ 10 French soldiers were killed in a Taliban ambush in Afghanistan. {20} >150 died after a Spanair plane crashed during take-off at Madrid airport, Spain. ❦ Hong Kong refused entry to Glitter. ❦ Usain Bolt won the 200m, breaking another world record [see p.24]. {21} Spain declared 3 days of national mourning for the 153 victims of Spanair flight JK5022; only 19 people were pulled alive from the burning wreckage, many of whom were in a critical condition. {22} Glitter arrived back in the UK. ❦ Russia claimed it had withdrawn all troops from Georgia but kept *c*.2,600 soldiers in 'buffer-zones' around Abkhazia and South Ossetia; the US called on Russia to withdraw completely. ❦ UK economic growth was reported to have been static between April–June, raising fears of a recession. {23} Obama announced Senator Joe Biden as his running mate. ❦ The widower of Benazir Bhutto, Asif Ali Zardari, announced he would stand for the presidency of Pakistan. {24} The Beijing Olympics closed [see p.297]. ❦ >70 died after a plane crashed shortly after take-off at Bishkek, Kyrgyzstan. ❦ >8 climbers were swept away by an avalanche on Mont Blanc. {25} Former Pakistani PM Nawaz Sharif pulled his PML-N party

————— IN BRIEF · AUGUST – SEPTEMBER 2008 —————

out of the ruling coalition in Pakistan in an ongoing dispute with the PPP. {26} Russia announced it was recognising the independence of Abkhazia and South Ossetia; the US and many European countries opposed the move. ❦ Anti-government protesters clashed with police in Bangkok, Thailand. ❦ 3 members of the Foster family were reported missing after a fire destroyed their Shropshire mansion. {28} 3 British Asians were charged in relation to an alleged plot to attack Gordon Brown and Tony Blair. {29} The budget transatlantic airline Zoom went bust, stranding thousands of customers; high fuel costs were blamed for its collapse. ❦ Chancellor Alistair Darling warned of a serious economic downturn [see p.20]. ❦ Radovan Karadžić refused to enter a plea at his trial in The Hague. {30} Hurricane Gustav hit Cuba as a category 4 storm after claiming >80 lives in the Caribbean. ❦ 2 bodies were found at the burnt-out mansion in Shropshire amid reports that the dogs and horses belonging to the family had been shot. {31} New Orleans mayor Ray Nagin ordered the evacuation of the city as Hurricane Gustav approached. ❦ A 14-year-old boy was stabbed to death in E London.

Andy Murray

shot dead his wife and daughter before setting fire to their Shropshire mansion and killing himself. {4} Brown confirmed that the government would not be giving one-off payments to families to help with their fuel bills [see p.233]. {5} Flood warnings were put in place across Britain as heavy storms rolled in. {6} The widower of Benazir Bhutto, Asif Ali Zardari, won the presidential election in Pakistan. ❦ Flash floods hit parts of the Midlands and N England. {7} Israeli police recommended that Prime Minister Ehud Olmert be indicted after a corruption investigation. ❦ RIP @ 98, Anita Page, silent movie star. {8} In the trial of 5 men suspected of plotting to blow up transatlantic flights, 3 were found guilty of conspiracy to murder, but the jury failed to reach a verdict over the bomb plot. ❦ Andy Murray was beaten by Roger Federer in the final of the US Open; Federer won the title for a record 5th time in a row. {9} President Bush announced the recall of 8,000 troops from Iraq, and the redeployment of 4,500 to Afghanistan. ❦ Speculation about the health of N Korean leader Kim Jong-il grew after his absence from a military parade. {10} The Large Hadron Collider was switched on [see p.37]. ❦ The CPS announced that the men accused of attempting to blow up transatlantic flights

S EPTEMBER · {1} A third body, thought to be that of 15-year-old Kirstie Foster, was found in Shropshire. {2} In an effort to bolster the housing market, the government announced a range of measures, including raising the 1% stamp duty threshold from £125k to £175k for 1 year [see p.21]. ❦ Hurricane Gustav weakened to a tropical storm as it passed over New Orleans. ❦ CCTV images confirmed that Christopher Foster

*African problems must be
solved by Africans.*
– ROBERT MUGABE

would face retrial. {12} The UK's 3rd-largest tour operator, XL, went bust, leaving tens of thousands of holidaymakers stranded abroad. ❦ Mugabe and Tsvangirai announced they had reached a deal to share power in Zimbabwe [see p.33].

*The daily chronicle will continue in the
2010 edition of Schott's Almanac*

——————SOME GREAT LIVES IN BRIEF——————

MARCEL MARCEAU
22·3·1923–22·9·2007 (84)

Undoubtedly the most famous mime artist in the world (few can name another), Marceau enchanted all ages and nationalities with a gift that transcended maturity and language. He will best be remembered for his creation 'Bip' (the shambolic white-faced clown with a flower in his hat) and for a host of routines, including 'Youth, Maturity, Old Age, Death', in which the ages of man are lived in just a few moving minutes.

NED SHERRIN
18·2·1931–1·10·2007 (76)

Sherrin made an early mark on the world of entertainment when, in his 30s, he devised and produced *That Was the Week that Was* – the show that ignited the satire boom and launched a thousand wits. Sherrin's subsequent career reads like a showbiz Roget's: producer, director, raconteur, radio host, quiz master, novelist, dramaturgist, and performer. In each role, his urbane, if sometimes waspish, wit shone through.

ALAN COREN
27·6·1938–18·10·2007 (69)

The 'Sage of Cricklewood' made a career (and thousands of devoted fans) by combining his idiosyncratic and generally genial world-view with an unfailing and abundant wit. His stock-in-trade was words, which he edited at *Punch*, wrote for a host of publications, collected into numerous books, launched as missiles in *The News Quiz*, and dissected with glee in *Call My Bluff*.

NORMAN MAILER
31·1·1923–10·11·2007 (84)

One of the giants of US letters, Mailer was celebrated as much for his Pulitzer-winning prose as his pugnacious personality and uncompromising private life (he had 9 children with 6 wives). Yet, like Hemingway, with whom he was often compared, while the legends of his life will live long, works such as *The Naked and the Dead* and *The Executioner's Song* are likely to live longer.

EVEL KNIEVEL
17·10·1938 30·11·2007 (69)

Undoubtedly the most famous daredevil motorcyclist in the world (few can name another), Knievel trod that well-worn path from insurance salesman to stuntman. In a series of ever more extreme stunts, Knievel broke most of the bones in his body, earning him fame, fortune, and female companionship. As he said: 'Bones heal, pain is temporary, chicks dig scars, but glory is forever'.

BENAZIR BHUTTO
21·6·1953–27·12·2007 (54)

The glamorous and populist daughter of a political dynasty, Bhutto became Pakistan's first female leader – and one of the first in the Muslim world. Yet she proved to be a divisive figure, and was dismissed on corruption charges from each of her 2 terms as PM. After a period of exile, she staged a triumphant return to Pakistan in 2007, only to be assassinated shortly thereafter.

EDMUND HILLARY
20·7·1919–11·1·2008 (88)

At 11:30 on 29/5/1953, Hillary became the first man to ascend Mount Everest, the planet's highest point. (Hillary later admitted that Sherpa Tenzing Norgay was 10' behind him.) The news of this Commonwealth triumph (Hillary was born in New Zealand) was broadcast on the morning of Elizabeth II's coronation, as was his famous boast – 'Well … we've knocked the bastard off'.

─────── SOME GREAT LIVES IN BRIEF cont. ───────

ROBERT 'BOBBY' FISCHER
9·3·1943–17·1·2008 (64)

The archetypal chess genius – eccentric, mercurial, arrogant, paranoid – Fischer made cold war history when he took the world title from Boris Spassky in 1972. After this, Fischer became ever more idiosyncratic: he forfeited his title, refusing to defend it; rejected his country, claiming persecution; and later praised the 9/11 attacks. Yet he will be remembered as one of the greatest-ever players (and popularisers) of chess.

HEATH LEDGER
4·4·1979–22·1·2008 (28)

Ledger's premature death from an accidental (it is assumed) overdose shocked a legion of fans – many of whom had been captivated by his Oscar-nominated role in *Brokeback Mountain*. His legendary status will be sealed by a bravura performance as the Joker in Christopher Nolan's Batman movie *The Dark Knight*, released after Ledger's death to critical acclaim and box-office fortune.

SUHARTO
8·6·1921–27·1·2008 (86)

From a peasant background, Suharto rose through the ranks of the army, mysteriously surviving a botched coup in 1965 to become Indonesia's president in 1968. For three decades Suharto (like many Indonesians he used one name) ruled his country repressively and corruptly, though he did transform its fortunes before the S Asian economy collapsed in 1997, and with it his regime.

JEREMY BEADLE
12·4·1948–30·1·2008 (59)

At the zenith of his popularity, Beadle was Britain's most famous practical joker and a staple of prime-time ITV. In *Game For a Laugh*, *Beadle's About*, and *You've Been Framed*, the bearded prankster revelled in 'watching us, watching you, watching us, watching you'. Yet his star waned as his antics became tired.

ARTHUR C. CLARKE
16·12·1917–18·3·2008 (90)

One of the most popular and influential sci-fi writers of the genre, Clarke entertained a global audience without losing the respect of scientific experts. He will best be remembered for collaborating with Stanley Kubrick on *2001: A Space Odyssey* (1968), though since his DNA was blasted up into space in 2001, clones of Clarke may yet one day return.

CHARLTON HESTON
4·10·1923–5·4·2008 (84)

Heston used his imposing presence and rugged good looks to dominate Hollywood's most monumental roles, including Ben Hur, Michelangelo, and Moses. At 75, he became president of the National Rifle Association – a position he held for >5 years until the symptoms of Alzheimer's took their toll. Famously, at the NRA's 2000 convention, he held a musket aloft and vowed it would only be taken 'From my cold, dead hands'.

GWYNETH DUNWOODY
12·12·1930–17·4·2008 (77)

As Labour member for Exeter (1966–70), and Crewe & Nantwich (1974–2008), Dunwoody was the longest-serving female MP. A doughty champion both of her constituents' rights and those of parliament, Dunwoody was invariably described as 'redoubtable', 'independent', and a 'battle axe' – yet she never lost the respect of MPs from all parties.

HUMPRHEY LYTTELTON
23·5·1921–25·4·2008 (86)

Humph gave new life to the bromide

—————————SOME GREAT LIVES IN BRIEF cont.—————————

'polymath'; he was a skilled writer and cartoonist, and one of the most significant pioneers of British jazz. Yet he will be remembered most fondly as the ever-exasperated host of *I'm Sorry I Haven't a Clue*, who managed, through a combination of erudition and innocence, to say the most outrageous things on radio.

ALBERT HOFMANN
11·1·1906–29·4·2008 (102)

Hofmann was a Swiss chemist who, in 1938, accidentally discovered lysergic acid diethylamide (LSD). In 1943, he deliberately ingested '0·5cc of ½ promil aqueous solution of diethylamide tartrate', and was so unnerved by its effects that he cycled home as his surroundings 'transformed themselves in more terrifying ways'. The anniversary of this first 'acid trip' is still celebrated by amp heads every 19 April, aka 'Bicycle Day'.

BERYL COOK
10·9·1926–28·5·2008 (81)

Instantly recognisable, Cook's busty and boisterous paintings were simultaneously larger than life and down to earth. Victoria Wood once described Cook's work as 'Rubens with jokes', and it is fitting that a woman who was once a seaside landlady seemed so at home with a dash of Donald McGill's sauce.

YVES SAINT LAURENT
1·8·1936–1·6·2008 (71)

YSL first made his mark on fashion when, aged just 21, he became chief designer of the House of Dior. From then, though his professional and personal life veered between triumph and despair, he dressed some of the world's most elegant women and changed the way the rest aspired to dress. Fashionista Diana Vreeland called YSL a 'genius', dubbing him 'the Pied Piper of fashion'.

BO DIDDLEY
30·12·1928–2·6·2008 (79)

Inspired by John Lee Hooker, Diddley himself inspired countless musicians with his trademark (and much copied) 'shave and a haircut' rhythm and grinding guitar. 'The Originator' had a series of hits, including *Road Runner*, but justifiably complained that the flattery of recognition and imitation 'didn't put no figures in my chequebook'.

ALEXANDER SOLZHENITSYN
11·12·1918–3·8·2008 (89)

Solzhenitsyn exposed the horror of Stalin's labour camps (in which he spent eight years) in a series of brutally honest books – one of which, *The Gulag Archipelago*, led to his exile from Russia in 1974. His legacy was encapsulated in 1970 by his Nobel Prize citation, which praised 'the ethical force with which he has pursued the indispensable traditions of Russian literature'.

ISAAC HAYES
20·8·1942–10·8·2008 (65)

Hayes's 1969 album *Hot Buttered Soul* and his soundtrack for the 1971 blaxploitation classic *Shaft* secured his reputation, in Aretha Franklin's words, as 'a shining example of soul at its best'. He acquired an unlikely new fan base in his 50s, voicing Chef on the cartoon *South Park* – before he quit the show after it mocked the Church of Scientology, which Hayes had joined in the 1990s.

GRANGE HILL
8·2·1978–15·9·2008 (30)

For many millions, the fictional school Grange Hill was almost as real as their own, and a host of characters – from Tucker Jenkins and 'Zammo' Maguire, to Mrs McClusky and Mr Bronson – still spark fond and fearful memories.

The World

The world is a severe schoolmaster, for its frowns are less dangerous than its smiles and flatteries, and it is a difficult task to keep in the path of wisdom.
— PHYLLIS WHEATLEY, 1774

CLOCK OF THE WORLD · 2008

Every 5 seconds, a child dies from hunger. [UN FAO] ❦ Every 5 seconds, a website is infected. [Sophos] ❦ Every 6 seconds, someone dies from tobacco use. [World Health Organization] ❦ Every 6 seconds, an Australian buys an item of clothing on eBay. [*The Age*] ❦ Every 7 seconds, the Irish Samaritans receive a phone call. [*Irish Times*] ❦ Every 20 seconds, someone in the world contracts tuberculosis. [*Pakistan Dawn*] ❦ Every 24 seconds, someone is murdered in South Africa. [*The Independent*] ❦ Every 26 seconds, a refrigerator is produced at the Mabe refrigerator factory in Celaya, Mexico. [*The Economist*] ❦ Every 30 seconds, someone in the world commits suicide. [World Health Organization] ❦ Every 30 seconds, a child with birth defects is born in China. [*China Daily*] ❦ Every 30 seconds, someone in the world loses a limb as a consequence of diabetes. [*US News & World Report*] ❦ Every 45 seconds, a plane takes off or lands at Heathrow. [*The Economist*] ❦ Every minute, 1,000 people around the world sign up for a cell phone. [*TheStar.com*] ❦ Every minute, 253 children are born. [US Census Bureau] ❦ Every 3 minutes, a newborn somewhere in the world dies of tetanus. [UNICEF] ❦ Every 4 minutes, someone in the UK is a victim of knife crime. [Home Office] ❦ Every 8 minutes, a woman in a developing country dies of complications from an abortion. [World Health Organization] ❦ Every 8 minutes, someone in the UK is deported. [*The Guardian*] ❦ Every 15 minutes, someone in Scotland has a heart attack. [British Heart Foundation] ❦ Every 35 minutes, a case of child abuse is reported to Australian authorities. [Wesley Mission] ❦ Every hour & 44 minutes, there is one case of 'dowry death' in India. [*The Guardian*] ❦ Every 2 hours, someone in New Zealand fractures a hip. [Osteoporosis New Zealand] ❦ Every day, 1·6m blog posts appear online. [Technorati] ❦ Every day, 6,800 people are infected with HIV. [United Nations] ❦ Every day, the average person in the UK uses 150 litres of water. [*The Telegraph*] ❦ Every 2 weeks, a language falls out of use. [*New York Times*; see p.78] ❦ Every month, 300 specialist nurses leave S Africa. [World Health Organization] ❦ Every month, the US government adds *c.*20,000 names to its terrorist watch lists. [ACLU] ❦ Every month, *c.*130m people ride the New York City subway. [Metropolitan Transportation Authority] ❦ Every 17 months, an Automated Transfer Vehicle carries cargo to the International Space Station. [*New Scientist*] ❦ Each year, 210,000 missing person reports are filed in the UK. [BBC] ❦ Each year, 13bn plastic bags are handed out to UK shoppers. [*The Independent*]

—————————— YEAR IN DISASTERS · 2007 ——————————

Although somewhat overshadowed by the events of 2008, 399 natural disasters hit worldwide in 2007, killing *c*.16,517 and costing *c*.$62·5bn, according to the UN International Strategy for Disaster Reduction. Below are 2007's worst disasters:

Disaster	deaths		
Cyclone Sidr (Nov, Bangladesh)	4,234	Heat wave (July, Hungary)	500
Flood (July–August, Bangladesh)	1,110	Cyclone Yemyin (June, Pakistan)	242
Flood (July–September, India)	1,103	Flood and landslides (June, Pakistan)	230
Flood (August, North Korea)	610	Flood (July, India)	225
Flood (June–July, China)	535		
Earthquake (August, Peru)	519		

8 of the worst disasters were in Asia – a pattern the UN says is consistent with climate change.

Below is a breakdown of 2007 disasters by disaster type, with the number killed:

Disaster type	no. in 2007	deaths			
Flood	206	8,382	Landslides	10	264
Wind storm	103	5,970	Wildfires	18	161
Extreme temperature	24	1,011	Wave/surge (incl. tsunamis)	3	64
Earthquake	19	654	Volcano	6	11
			Drought	10	N/A

According to Columbia University's Centre for Hazard and Risk Research, Taiwan is the country most exposed to natural hazards – 73% of its land area is exposed to some type of potential disaster.

—————————— AIDS & HIV ——————————

In 2007, 33·2m people around the world (0·8% of the world's population) were living with HIV, according to the UN. This figure represents a significant drop from the 39·5m estimated in 2006, a difference due almost entirely to improved research methodology that better extrapolates the total number of infections from sample populations. A breakdown of the global HIV population in 2007 is given below:

Region	No. infected with HIV	adult prevalence %	AIDS deaths
Sub-Saharan Africa	22·5m	5·0	1·6m
South & Southeast Asia	4m	0·3	270,000
Latin America	1·6m	0·5	58,000
Eastern Europe & Central Asia	1·6m	0·9	55,000
East Asia	800,000	0·1	32,000
Middle East & North Africa	380,000	0·3	25,000
North America	1·3m	0·6	21,000
Western and Central Europe	760,000	0·3	12,000
Caribbean	230,000	1·0	11,000
Oceania	75,000	0·4	1,200

The UN estimates that new HIV infections peaked in the late 1990s, at >3m new infections per year; *c*.2·5m people were infected in 2007. [For HIV rates by country, see the Gazetteer section, pp.88–89.]

NUCLEAR POWER WORLDWIDE

439 nuclear reactors were in operation worldwide as of November 2007, down from a record high of 444 in 2002, according to a report from European parliamentary group, the Greens. The World Nuclear Industry Status Report 2007 surveyed the state of reactors across the globe and concluded that predictions of a nuclear 'renaissance' (driven by increasing global energy needs and climate change concerns) were greatly exaggerated. According to the report, 338 new reactors would need to be built before 2030 to maintain the same number of plants as those operating in 2007, yet as of November 2007, only 32 reactors were listed as 'under construction' by the International Atomic Energy Agency. Tabulated on the right is the report's snapshot of nuclear power in some countries of note.

† The life span of a reactor is *c.*40 years, though the mean age of the 117 reactors closed thus far is 22 years. ‡ Share of electricity data is 2006.

	number of reactors	average reactor age†	under construction	new reactors planned	% share of electricity‡
Argentina	2	29	1	1	7
Brazil	2	16	0	1	3
Canada	18	23	0	4	1
China	11	7	5	30	2
Czech Rep	6	16	0	0	32
France	59	23	0	1	78
Germany	17	25	0	0	32
India	17	16	6	10	3
Iran	0	0	1	2	0
Japan	55	22	1	12	30
Mexico	2	16	0	0	5
Pakistan	2	22	1	2	3
Russia	31	25	7	8	16
S Africa	2	23	0	1	4
S Korea	20	14	2	6	39
Sweden	10	28	0	0	48
UK	19	26	0	0	18
Ukraine	15	19	2	2	48
USA	104	28	1	7	19
TOTAL	439	23	32	91	16

Although nowadays the 'peace sign' ☮ is usually considered synonymous with 1960s hippies, the symbol was actually created in 1958 as a logo for British anti-nuclear groups. According to *Peace: The Biography of a Symbol*, released in 2008 to celebrate the sign's 50th anniversary, the symbol was created by designer Gerald Holtom by combining the semaphore for 'N'(uclear) and 'D'(isarmament) [right] over a circle symbolising Earth. Since its debut at a 1958 anti-nuclear march in England, the sign has been used by civil rights, environmental, and counter-cultural movements, although it has also been dismissed as a 'chicken footprint' and reviled as a Satanic sign.

'D'

'N'

LANDMINE CASUALTIES

According to the most recent information from the International Campaign to Ban Landmines, casualties from landmines are declining: 1,367 people were killed and 4,296 injured in 2006, a 16% decrease from 2005. The 2006 casualties by region:

Asia-Pacific .... *casualties* 2,510
Sub-Saharan Africa 1,205
Americas 1,127
Middle East & North Africa 539

Commonwealth of Ind. States† 205
Europe 165

† Former Soviet states

──────IBRAHIM INDEX OF AFRICAN GOVERNANCE──────

The Ibrahim Index of African Governance was developed as a tool to assess governance in the 48 countries of sub-Saharan Africa. Released by the Mo Ibrahim Foundation, the index is designed to quantify the delivery of 'political goods' through measurable outcomes. For example, a country's safety is judged on the number of battle deaths, the level of violent crime, the number of refugees, and other quantifiable measures. Each country is scored in the following five categories: safety and security; rule of law, transparency, and corruption; participation and human rights; sustainable economic development; and human development. These category scores are then averaged to create an overall score. In 2007, the following countries were judged to have the best and worst all-round governance:

Best governance	Worst governance
1 ....Mauritius	48................................Somalia
2 ....Seychelles	47.........Democratic Rep. of Congo
3................................Botswana	46...................................Chad
4..........................Cape Verde	45..................................Sudan
5.........................South Africa	44.......................Guinea-Bissau

In November 2007, former Mozambican president Joaquim Chissano won the inaugural Mo Ibrahim Prize, which was created to encourage African leaders who promote development while improving the lives of their people. After taking office in 1986, as Mozambique was grappling with civil war and national disasters, Chissano brokered peace talks, launched a new constitution, and instituted an economic recovery programme. Reportedly the world's richest award, the Mo Ibrahim Prize includes $5m over 10 years, ≤$200,000 for the winner's causes, and $200,000 annually for life thereafter.

──────────CHILD SOLDIERS──────────

According to a 2008 report from the Coalition to Stop the Use of Child Soldiers, 2004–07 saw a decrease in the number of conflicts involving child soldiers following peace agreements in Afghanistan, the Democratic Republic of Congo, Liberia, and elsewhere. Yet *c*.200,000–300,000 children, some as young as 8, are still used as soldiers by government forces or armed rebel groups around the world. According to various human rights groups, child soldiers[†] are currently used in:

Africa	Burundi, Chad, Côte d'Ivoire, Democratic Republic of Congo, Rwanda, Somalia, Sudan, Uganda
Asia	Myanmar (Burma [see p.79]), Afghanistan, India, Indonesia, Laos, Philippines, Sri Lanka
Middle East	Iran, Iraq, Israel, Palestinian Territories, Yemen
Americas	Colombia
Europe	Chechen Republic of the Russian Federation

† In some reports, 'child' is defined as any person <18; some entries are disputed. ❦ In 2000, the UN adopted an Optional Protocol to the Convention on the Rights of the Child, prohibiting the forced recruitment of those <18, and their use in hostilities. [Sources: Human Rights Watch; CSUCS]

————————— ASYLUM LEVELS & TRENDS · 2007 —————————

Asylum applications rose 10% between 2006 and 2007, the first increase recorded by the UN High Commissioner for Refugees (UNHCR) in 5 years. This upsurge was largely due to applications from Iraqis, which nearly doubled in comparison to 2006. Below are the top countries of origin for asylum seekers (defined by the UN as those seeking international protection and formal refugee status) during 2007:

Origin	applications	'06–'07 ±%			
Iraq	45,247	+98	Somalia	11,487	+43
Russian Fed.	18,781	+19	Mexico	9,545	+41
China	17,141	–7	Afghanistan	9,309	+8
Serbia	15,366	–2	Iran	8,627	–19
Pakistan	14,262	+87	Sri Lanka	7,548	+31
			TOTAL	306,857	+10

The US was the top destination for asylum seekers in 2007, with 15% of applications, followed by Sweden (11%), France (9%), and Canada and the UK (both 8%).

————————— WORLD'S TEN WORST DICTATORS —————————

The weekly magazine *Parade* annually publishes a list of the world's worst dictators, based on their record of human rights abuse. The 2008 top ten [facial hair added, Ed.]:

No.	dictator	age	country	years' reign	facial hair?
1 (2)	Kim Jong-il	66	North Korea	14	none
2 (1)	Omar al-Bashir	64	Sudan	19	goatee
3 (6)	Than Shwe	75	Myanmar	16	none
4 (5)	King Abdullah	84	Saudi Arabia	13	cavalier beard
5 (4)	Hu Jintao	65	China	6	none
6 (7)	Robert Mugabe	83	Zimbabwe	28	Hitler-esque
7 (3)	Sayyid Ali Khamenei	68	Iran	19	bushy beard
8 (15)	Pervez Musharraf	64	Pakistan	9	moustache
9 (8)	Islam Karimov	70	Uzbekistan	19	none
10 (13)	Isayas Afewerki	62	Eritrea	17	full moustache

————————————— EXECUTIONS —————————————

1,252 people were executed in 2007, and at least 3,347 were sentenced to death, according to Amnesty International. China executed more people than any other country, although Saudi Arabia had the highest number of executions per capita. The countries in which the most people were executed during 2007 are listed below:

China........470	USA...........42	Afghanistan ... 15	[Source: Amnesty
Iran..........317	Iraq............33	Libya 9	Intl, 2008. Totals are
Saudi Arabia..143	Vietnam.......25	Japan 9	minimums, given
Pakistan 135	Yemen.........15	Syria............7	frequent state secrecy.]

—————————— STABLE & UNSTABLE COUNTRIES ——————————

The violent power struggles, crime, and paucity of border controls in the Palestinian Territories make them the most unstable place on the planet, according to an assessment by the intelligence firm Jane's Information Group released in March 2008. Jane's ranking was based on a yearlong investigation into the politics, society, economics, military, and threats facing 235 countries or territories around the world. The top 10 most stable and most unstable countries or territories were:

Most stable		*Most unstable*	
1 ....Vatican	6 ....San Marino	1 ...Palestin. Ter.	6 ....Haiti
2 ....Sweden	7 ..Liechtenstein	2 ....Somalia	7 .....Zimbabwe
3 ...Luxembourg	8 ....UK	3 ....Sudan	8 ....Chad
4 ....Monaco	9 ...Netherlands	4 ...Afghanistan	9 ....Congo
5 ....Gibraltar	10 ....Ireland	5 ..Côte d'Ivoire	10 ...C Afr. Rep.

—————————— INTERNATIONAL DEVELOPMENT & AID ——————————

The Organisation for Economic Cooperation & Development (OECD) stated that in 2007 development aid from the Development Assistance Committee (a group of the world's major donors) was $103·7bn: an 8·4% fall from 2006. The US was the largest donor in 2007, and, as before, only 5 of the 22 major donors gave in Overseas Development Aid the UN target of 0·7% of their Gross National Income:

Country	ODA $m	% GNI			
Australia	2,471	0·30	Luxembourg	365	0·90
Canada	3,922	0·28	Netherlands	6,215	0·81
Denmark	2,563	0·81	Norway	3,727	0·95
France	9,940	0·39	Spain	5,744	0·41
Germany	12,267	0·37	Sweden	4,334	0·93
Ireland	1,190	0·54	UK	9,921	0·36
Japan	7,691	0·17	US	21,753	0·16
			[Provisional figures, 2007]		

The top 10 beneficiaries of US aid, according to latest figures from the OECD:

Iraq $4,781m	Colombia.......$721m	[Source: OECD, 2006.
Afghanistan ...$1,403m	Pakistan $490m	In 2006, the US's total
DR Congo $818m	Egypt $407m	budget for aid to developing
Nigeria $787m	Zambia $380m	countries was $22,005m.]
Sudan............$739m	Ethiopia $316m	

Between 1990 and 2005, armed conflicts in Africa cost their countries' economies roughly the same amount as they received in development aid, according to a 2007 report by Oxfam, the International Action Network on Small Arms, and Saferworld. The report found that, during this period, the GDPs of African countries that had experienced armed conflict shrunk by 15% when compared with the GDPs of economically similar countries that did not experience conflict. These losses amounted to $284bn, about the same sum of aid given by OECD countries during these 15 years.

─────── NOBEL PEACE PRIZE ───────

The 2007 Nobel Peace Prize was awarded in equal parts to ALBERT GORE (1948–)
and the INTERGOVERNMENTAL PANEL ON CLIMATE CHANGE

for their efforts to build up and disseminate greater knowledge
about man-made climate change, and to lay the foundations for
the measures that are needed to counteract such change

Albert (Al) Arnold Gore Jr was born in 1948 in Washington, DC, the son of a prominent Tennessee congressman. After a childhood in Washington and Tennessee, he graduated from Harvard in 1969, after which he served in the army and fought in Vietnam. Gore was elected to the House in 1976, and the Senate in 1984. While in Congress, he co-sponsored hearings on toxic waste and the first congressional hearings on global warming. After being elected Vice President in 1992, he led the Clinton administration's environmental efforts, spearheading work on the Kyoto Protocol. Yet it was only after his controversial defeat in the 2000 presidential election that Gore became a full-time 'climate crusader', travelling the world to lecture on the dangers of climate change. In 2006, he released an eco-documentary based on his lectures; *An Inconvenient Truth* became one of the highest-grossing documentaries of all time, earning two Academy Awards in February 2007 and establishing Gore's place at the vanguard of the green movement. For some, Gore's Nobel Prize even raised hopes of another presidential run in 2008. Yet, the 'Goracle' has not been without critics – including those who argue his film is alarmist and exaggerated, those who criticise his personal energy consumption, and those who question whether awarding the prize to a 'celebrity' detracts from

Al Gore

the credibility of the Peace Prize. ❦ The award to the Intergovernmental Panel on Climate Change (IPCC) was less controversial. Founded in 1988 by the UN Environmental Programme and the World Meteorological Organization, the IPCC comprises *c.*2,000 scientists who assess the latest climate change data and produce summaries for policy-makers. IPCC reports are generally deemed the most authoritative word on climate change – though they are approved line by line by 113 governments. According to the Nobel committee, 'over the past two decades, the IPCC has created an ever-broader informed consensus about the connection between human activities and global warming'. Indeed, many saw 2007 as a turning point in the global opinion on climate change, thanks to IPCC reports. ❦ Inevitably, some questioned the link between climate change and peace. Yet as the Nobel committee noted, global warming 'may induce large-scale migration and lead to greater competition for the earth's resources', in turn leading to conflict and war. In June 2007, UN Secretary General Ban Ki-moon discussed the connections between drought caused by global warming and the atrocities in Darfur. It seems that climate change may present a uniquely global threat to world peace, one the Nobel committee felt needed to be addressed both by a popular leader and by rigorous science.

HIGHLY VIOLENT CONFLICTS

According to Germany's Heidelberg Institute for International Conflict Research, there were 328 conflicts around the globe in 2007, of which 31 were considered 'highly violent'. Of these, 6 were categorised as wars, and 25 as 'severe crises'. Listed below are these 31 highly violent conflicts:

Conflict issues

WARS		resources	secession	national power	ideology	autonomy	regional predominance
Country	*parties*						
Pakistan	*Waziristan militants, government*	·	·	·	·	·	×
Sri Lanka	*Tamil Tiger rebels, government*	·	×	·	·	·	·
Somalia	*Islamic Courts Union, transitional govt*	·	·	×	×	·	·
Sudan	*rebel groups, Sudanese govt in Darfur*	×	·	·	·	·	×
Afghanistan	*Taliban, government*	·	·	×	×	·	·
Iraq	*insurgents, government*	·	·	×	×	·	·

SEVERE CRISES		resources	secession	national power	ideology	autonomy	regional predominance
Central African Rep.	*rebels, government*	·	·	×	·	·	·
Chad	*rebel groups*	·	·	×	·	·	·
Chad	*Arab and African ethnic groups*	·	·	·	·	·	×
DR Congo	*rebels, militias, government*	·	·	×	·	·	·
Ethiopia	*separatist rebel group, government*	·	×	·	·	·	·
Kenya	*ethnic groups, government*	×	·	·	·	·	·
Nigeria	*ethnic groups, government*	×	·	·	·	·	×
Colombia	*FARC, ELN revolutionaries*	×	·	·	×	·	×
Colombia	*FARC revolutionaries*	×	·	·	×	·	×
Mexico	*drug cartels*	·	·	·	·	·	×
India	*Kashmiri, Pakistani separatists, govt*	·	×	·	·	·	·
India	*Naxalites, government*	·	·	·	×	·	·
Myanmar	*rebels, military groups, government*	·	×	·	·	·	·
Myanmar	*political opposition, government*	·	·	×	×	·	·
Pakistan	*Islamists, government*	·	·	·	×	·	·
Pakistan	*militant Sunnis, militant Shiites, govt*	·	·	·	×	·	×
Thailand	*Muslim separatists, government*	·	×	·	·	·	·
Algeria	*Islamist groups, government*	·	·	×	×	·	·
Iran	*Kurdish nationalist groups, government*	·	·	·	·	×	·
Iraq	*Moqtada al-Sadr militia, government*	·	·	×	×	·	·
Iraq	*Abu Musab al-Zarqawi militia, government*	·	·	×	×	·	·
Israel	*Fatah, Hamas*	·	·	·	×	·	×
Israel	*Fatah, Hamas, Pal. Auth., Israeli govt*	×	×	·	×	·	·
Lebanon	*Hezbollah, Fatah, government*	·	·	×	×	·	·
Turkey	*Kurdish militants, government*	·	·	·	·	×	·

According to the Institute, a SEVERE CRISIS is a conflict 'in which violent force is used repeatedly in an organised way'. The Institute defines a WAR, in part, as a conflict in which violent force is used 'in an organised and systematic way ... [and the] extent of destruction is massive and of long duration'.

LONGEST-SERVING LEADERS

When Fidel Alejandro Castro Ruz resigned as President of Cuba on 19 Feb, 2008, he also stepped down from his post as the world's longest-serving leader. Below are the longest-serving leaders (apart from kings and queens†) as of Feb 2008:

Leader	country	in power since
Omar Bongo	Gabon	1967
Muammar Gadhafi	Libya	1969
Maumoon Abdul Gayoom	Maldives	1978
Teodoro Obiang Nguema Mbasogo	Equatorial Guinea	1979
Jose Eduardo dos Santos	Angola	1979
Robert Mugabe [see p.33–34]	Zimbabwe	1980
Hosni Mubarak	Egypt	1981

[Source: Associated Press] † Thai King Bhumibol Adulyadej is the world's longest-reigning living monarch. Crowned in 1946, he is revered in his country as semi-divine. In November 2007, he inspired a Thai craze for pink shirts after he was seen leaving the hospital in a blush-coloured blazer (royal astrologers had recently divined that pink was an auspicious colour for the King's health). On 5 December, tens of thousands of Thais thronged the streets of Bangkok to celebrate his 80th birthday.

GLOBAL FREEDOM

The US pressure group Freedom House annually compiles a *Freedom in the World Survey*, classifying countries by the rights and civil liberties their citizens enjoy. Countries are judged to be: FREE, PARTLY FREE, or NOT FREE. In 2008, 47% of the world's countries were deemed FREE; 31% PARTLY FREE; and 22% NOT FREE. The following countries were classified by *freedomhouse.org* as being NOT FREE:

Algeria · Angola · Azerbaijan · Belarus · Bhutan · Brunei · Burma [see p.79] Cambodia · Cameroon · Chad · China · Congo (Brazzaville) · Congo (Kinshasa) Côte d'Ivoire · Cuba · Egypt · Equatorial Guinea · Eritrea · Guinea · Iran · Iraq Kazakhstan · Laos · Libya · Maldives · North Korea · Oman · Pakistan · Qatar Russia · Rwanda · Saudi Arabia · Somalia · Sudan · Swaziland · Syria · Tajikistan Tunisia · Turkmenistan · UAE · Uzbekistan · Vietnam · Zimbabwe [see p.33]

SAKHAROV PRIZE

Presented by the European Union since 1988, the Sakharov Prize for Freedom of Thought rewards individuals who challenge oppression and fight for human rights. The prize is named after Soviet physicist Andrei Sakharov (1921–89), who helped develop the hydrogen bomb but later won the Nobel Peace Prize for his work campaigning against nuclear weapons. In 2007, the €50,000 prize was awarded to human rights lawyer and Sudanese parliament member Salih Mahmoud Osman, who for over two decades has worked alongside the Sudan Organization Against Torture to provide free legal representation for victims of human rights abuses.

─────── CONTESTED LAND ───────

During 2008, a number of countries were preparing to submit claims for valuable underwater territory to the UN Commission on the Limits of the Continental Shelf. Under the UN Convention on the Law of the Sea, countries may submit claims for 'extended underwater territory rights' up to 350 miles from their shores within 10 years of ratifying the Convention. As global warming reshapes topography and technology improves access to oil and gas reserves, some of these regions have become even more valuable, and several major countries, including the UK, face a May 2009 deadline to submit their claims. Below are some of the contested areas:

Area	claimed by	significance
ANTARCTICA	*Argentina, UK, Norway, France, Chile, Australia, New Zealand*	iron, copper, gold, & other minerals; hydrocarbons
ARCTIC CIRCLE	*Russia, Canada, US, Denmark, Norway*	potential *c.*10bn tons oil & gas; fishing & shipping routes
ROCKALL BASIN	*Iceland, Ireland, Denmark, UK*	potential oil and natural gas
FALKLAND ISLANDS	*UK, Argentina*	possibly 60bn barrels of oil

Some worry that these claims could add to the world's list of long-simmering land disputes. Below is a sampling of such current conflicts between sovereign nations:

Area	claimed by	significance
ARUNACHAL PRADESH	*China, India*	historical border dispute
ATACAMA CORRIDOR	*Bolivia, Chile*	oil & gas, maritime access
AVES ISLAND	*Venezuela, Colombia*	territorial rights to large portion of E Caribbean
CHAGOS ARCHIPELAGO	*Mauritius, Seychelles, British Indian Ocean Territory*	uncertain status of inhabitants evicted for military base
CYPRUS	*Republic of Cyprus, Turkey, Greece*	Greek Cypriot Rep. of Cyprus claims island – Turks disagree
EAST CHINA SEA	*China, Japan*	vast reserves of natural gas
ERITREA–ETHIOPIA BORDER	*Eritrea, Ethiopia*	demarcation never resolved after Eritrean independence
GIBRALTAR	*Spain, UK*	gateway to Mediterranean
GREATER & LESSER TUNBS; ABU MASA	*Iran, United Arab Emirates*	strategic placement in Persian Gulf
GULF OF GUINEA	*9 West African nations*	potentially *c.*24bn barrels oil
KASHMIR	*China, India, Pakistan*	Hindu-Muslim strife &c.
NAGORNO-KARABAKH	*Armenia, Azerbaijan*	ethnic dispute
SPRATLY ISLANDS	*China, Malaysia, Philippines, Taiwan, Vietnam, Brunei*	potentially 17.7bn tons oil; shipping route; fishing rights
TIMOR SEA	*East Timor, Australia*	oil & gas reserves†
WESTERN SAHARA	*Morocco, Algeria*	phosphates, possible oil; rebels seek self-determination

† Australia and East Timor have signed a revenue-sharing agreement for Timor Sea oil and gas reserves but have deferred a decision on maritime boundaries. [Sources: *Foreign Policy*; CIA World Factbook]

─────────── MOST POLLUTING POWER SECTORS ───────────

A November 2007 survey of carbon dioxide (CO_2) emissions produced by the world's power plants concluded that the Australian power sector releases the most CO_2 per capita (11 tons per year), although American power plants weren't far behind (9 tons per year). The survey, released by the Carbon Monitoring for Action project, compiled data on CO_2 emissions from 50,000 power plants and 4,000 power companies to create a global inventory of carbon emissions produced by the power sector. Below are the countries whose power sectors annually produce the most CO_2:

annual power sector CO_2 emissions	
United States.............2·79bn *tons*	Japan 400m
China...........................2·68bn	Germany 356m
Russia...........................661m	Australia.......................226m
India............................583m	South Africa....................222m
	United Kingdom.................212m

─────────── EXPERT TIPS TO SAVE THE WORLD ───────────

In November 2007, the UK's Environment Agency asked 25 scientists, authors, and environmental experts to each recommend up to 5 ways of saving the planet. Their top 10 tips, ranked by the number of times each was recommended, are below:

1	*use less electricity: make products more efficient, say goodbye to standby* [see p.201]
2	*prioritise the environment as an issue for faith groups*
3	*employ solar energy on a much larger scale*
4	*ratify a tough and binding successor to the Kyoto Protocol*
5	*use micro-scale, decentralised methods of energy production*
6	*use 'green taxes' to make eco-goods cheaper and harmful goods more costly*
7	*discourage flying and halt airport expansion*
8	*kick the addiction to fossil fuels*
9	*discourage consumption and encourage responsible trade*
10	*transform transport by encouraging green alternatives*

─────────── MORE PLANETS NEEDED ───────────

The UN estimates that the world currently produces 29 gigatons of CO_2 per year, twice the target the UN considers a sustainable level of emission (14·5 gigatons). Thus, mankind effectively requires 'another Earth' if CO_2 production is to remain at current levels. If the entire world were to produce emissions at the same rate as the US, 9 Earths would be necessary. Below are the number of Earths that would be needed if the entire world produced CO_2 at the same rate as other OECD countries:

Earths needed	Germany 4	Spain 3
Australia............... 7	Italy.................... 3	United Kingdom...... 4
Canada 9	Japan 4	United States.......... 9
France 3	Netherlands 4	(World................ 2)

—PRIMATES IN PERIL—

29% of all primate species are in danger of becoming extinct, according to a 2007 report released by Conservation International, the Species Survival Commission, and the International Primatological Society. Below are some of the 25 species said to be most at risk:

Peruvian yellow-tailed woolly monkey (Peru) · *Horton Plains slender loris* (Sri Lanka) · *Miss Waldron's red colobus* (Ivory Coast, Ghana) · *Sahamalaza Peninsula sportive lemur* (Madagascar) *Grey-shanked douc* (Vietnam) · *Silky sifaka* (Madagascar) · *Brown-headed spider monkey* (Colombia, Ecuador) *Rondo dwarf galago* (Tanzania) *Kipunji* (Tanzania) · *Western Hoolock gibbon* (Bangladesh, India, Myanmar)

—AMPHIBIANS AT RISK—

London Zoo produced a list of the 100 most biologically valuable amphibians threatened with extinction, for the launch of the Evolutionarily Distinct and Globally Endangered (Edge) project in January 2008. Below are the top 10 amphibians most at risk:

Amphibian	location
Chinese giant salamander	China
Sagalla caecilian	Kenya
Purple frog	India
Ghost frog	South Africa
Olm salamander	S Europe
Lungless salamander	Mexico
Malagasy rainbow frog	Madagascar
Darwin's frog	Chile
Betic midwife toad	Spain
Gardiner's frog	Seychelles

—————THE RED LIST · 2007—————

The World Conservation Union (IUCN) publishes an annual 'Red List' of species that are under threat – classifying them from those considered to be at a minor risk of extinction ('Least Concern') to those that have already been rendered extinct:

Least Concern (LC) → *Near Threatened (NT)* → *Vulnerable (VU)* → *Endangered (EN)* → *Critically Endangered (CR)* → *Extinct in the Wild (EW)* → *Extinct (EX)*

41,415 species were included on the 2007 Red List, of which 16,306 were considered threatened (a rise from the 16,118 in 2006). The status of 76 species declined, the status of 74 improved, and one species was declared extinct[†]. Below are some of the species whose status declined, and the reasons these species are threatened:

Species	status change	threatened by
Speke's gazelle	VU→EN	hunting, drought, overgrazing
Yangtze River dolphin	CR→CR (PE)[‡]	pollution, development, fishing practices
Gharial crocodile	EN→CR	loss of habitat, fishing practices
Egyptian vulture	LC→EN	poisoning by veterinary drug Diclofenac
Western gorilla	EN→CR	commercial bushmeat trade, Ebola
Red-breasted goose	VU→EN	causes largely unknown

† The woolly-stalked begonia, a herb known only from C19th collections made in Malaysia, was declared extinct in 2007 after searches of nearby forests failed to find new specimens. ‡ Critically Endangered (Possibly Extinct). An August 2007 sighting was being investigated at the time of writing.

SLUM DWELLERS

Large-scale evictions and forced displacements caused by development, infrastructure projects, and 'mega' events such as the Olympics have led to an increase in the number of slum dwellers worldwide, according to a 2007 report by the UN Human Settlements Programme (UN-HABITAT). Although reliable data are difficult to come by, the UN estimates that *c.*31% of the world's urban population lives in slums – defined as areas in which tenants lack reliable, durable housing, clean water, and other basic necessities. Tabulated below are the slum populations around the world:

Total slum population (m)	1990	2001	2005 *(est.)*	2010 *(est.)*	2020 *(est.)*
World	715	913	998	1,246	1,392
Developed regions	42	45	47	48	52
Transitional countries	19	19	19	19	18
Developing regions	654	849	933	1,051	1,331

TATA'S NANO · THE WORLD'S CHEAPEST CAR

In January 2008, the Indian firm Tata Motors unveiled what it claimed would be the world's cheapest car. The Nano will cost just 100,000 rupees (£1,277), about half the annual pay of the average Indian accountant. The Nano will have 4 doors, 5 seats, and a top speed of 65mph, though no air-con or central locking (except in the 'deluxe' version). Tata hopes to sell 1m Nanos in a region where car sales are predicted to more than quadruple by 2016. Environmentalists have voiced concern at the ecological impact of so many Nanos – though, at the time of writing, the car's release had been delayed by local struggles over the plant's construction.

MOST POLLUTED PLACES

Six of the ten most polluted places on Earth are located in the developing economies of China, India, and Russia, according to a list released in September 2007 by the Blacksmith Institute, a US-based environmental watchdog, and Green Cross Switzerland. The ten most polluted sites in the world were assessed on the scale of their toxicity and the estimated number of people placed at risk – they are:

Location	pollutants & causes	*est. number of people affected*
Sumgayit, Azerbaijan	*petrochemical & industrial waste*	275,000
Linfen, China	*smog from industry & traffic*	3,000,000
Tianying, China	*heavy metals in air & soil from industry*	140,000
Sukinda, India	*waste from chromite mines*	2,600,000
Vapi, India	*chemical waste & other industrial effluents*	71,000
La Oroya, Peru	*lead contamination from mining*	35,000
Dzerzhinsk, Russia	*by-products from Cold War chemical weapons*	300,000
Norilsk, Russia	*smog and heavy metals from mining*	134,000
Chernobyl, Ukraine	*radioactive remains from 1986 explosion*	5,500,000
Kabwe, Zambia	*lead from mining and smelting*	255,000

WORLD PIRACY

Reports of pirate attacks rose by 20% during the first 3 months of 2008, following a rise of 10% for the whole of 2007, according to the International Maritime Bureau's Piracy Reporting Centre. Much of this rise was attributed to an increase in incidents reported in waters off Somalia and Nigeria. Somalia is one of the world's most unstable states, and pirates along its coastline are launching increasingly frequent and violent attacks on merchant vessels travelling between the Red Sea, the Mediterranean, and the Indian Ocean. In Nigeria, piracy has been encouraged by the political instability of the oil-rich Niger Delta region. ❦ Far from the buckle-swashing ruffians of *Pirates of the Caribbean* or *Treasure Island*, modern pirates tend to be poor dockworkers or fishermen who enlist in criminal syndicates equipped with global positioning systems and modern weaponry such as rocket-propelled grenades. Some have even broadcast distress signals to lure ships to their aid, before raiding them. ❦ As of 31 March, 2008, 49 actual and attempted pirate attacks had been reported, compared with 263 such attacks in all of 2007. However, it seems that many shipping companies decline to report piracy to prevent their insurance premiums from escalating, or to avoid ships being impounded for investigations. Below are the attacks in the worst-hit areas in 2008 (as of 31/3/08) and 2007:

Country/region	1/08–3/08	2007
Indonesia	4	43
Nigeria	10	42
Somalia	1	31
Bangladesh	2	15
Gulf of Aden/Red Sea	5	13
India	5	11
Tanzania	4	11
Malaysia	1	9
Malacca Straits†	0	7
Philippines	2	6
Peru	2	6

† Between Malaysia & Indonesia, and used by ⅓ of the world's shipping fleets. Piracy has declined after efforts by regional governments.

One of the more dramatic piracy attacks of 2008 began on 4 April, when Somali pirates attacked the French luxury yacht *Le Ponant* in the Gulf of Aden, and held the yacht's 30-strong crew captive for a week. Elite French commandos negotiated for the crew's release on 12 April, then chased the pirates through the Somali desert, capturing 6 and recovering part of the reported $2m ransom. In response to the attack, and others off Somalia's coast, the UN Security Council adopted in June 2008 a 6-month resolution allowing ships to use 'all means necessary' to repress attacks in Somalia's waters.

WORLD HUMAN RIGHTS

The 2008 Amnesty International *State of the World's Human Rights* report surveyed human rights issues in 150 countries around the world. Released to coincide with the 60th anniversary of the UN Universal Declaration of Human Rights, the report found persistent discrimination and repression across the globe in 2007, including:

Countries where ...	
People are tortured or ill-treated	81
People are denied free speech	77
Unfair trials are held	54
Prisoners of conscience are held	45
Laws discriminate against *women*	23
– against *migrants*	15
– against *minorities*	14

———————GLOBAL ENVIRONMENTAL CITIZEN AWARD———————

Kofi Annan and Alice Waters shared the 2007 Global Environmental Citizen Award, presented since 2001 by Harvard Medical School's Centre for Health and the Global Environment. Former UN Secretary General Annan was praised for his commitment to the environment during his term, and for his environmental advocacy since leaving the post in 2006. Restaurateur Alice Waters was honoured for her work founding the restaurant Chez Panisse in Berkeley, California, where she has been a vocal and passionate advocate for locally sourced and sustainable foods.

———————————ENDANGERED LANGUAGES———————————

Hundreds of languages across the globe are close to extinction, according to a September 2007 report in the *New York Times*, which estimated that a language dies each fortnight. Some languages vanish instantly when a sole surviving speaker dies, while others are replaced gradually by more dominant tongues like English, Spanish, or Portuguese. The *Enduring Voices* project, backed by the US National Geographic Society, has identified 5 'hotspots' where languages are vanishing most rapidly[†]:

Northern & Central Australia
nearly all 153 Aboriginal tongues in this area are endangered; in the rest of Australia most are extinct

Eastern & Central Siberia
government policies are forcing speakers of minority languages to speak regional/national ones

Central South America
high language diversity, little documentation of those languages

Southwestern US
only 40 Native American languages still spoken in Oklahoma, Texas, and New Mexico

US/Canadian Pacific Northwest
dominance of English is causing many to abandon the 54 native languages of the region

† Hotspots were identified by the diversity of languages spoken, the level of endangerment, and the scientific documentation available.

In January 2008, the BBC reported that three speakers of the Kusunda language of Nepal, previously thought extinct, had been found in two separate locations. The three were brought together, enabling one of them to converse in the language for the first time since she was 10 years old – in 1940.

———————————————MISS WORLD———————————————

Three years after China lifted a ban on beauty pageants, the country hosted Miss World and celebrated its first ever victory. Zhang Zilin, a 23-year-old secretary from Shijiazhaung in the northern Hebei province, beat 106 contestants to be crowned Miss World 2007. The ceremony was held at the Beauty Crown Theatre in the resort of Sanya, Hainan province. Zilin's hobbies include travel, reading, swimming, classical and folk dancing, and her favourite foods are fruit, chocolate, and ice cream. Zilin's inspiring personal motto is: 'Where there's a will, there's a way'.

———BURMA vs MYANMAR———

The monk-led protests in September 2007 and devastating Cyclone Nargis in April 2008 [see p.32] led to some confusion over the (politically) correct name of the country known as Burma and Myanmar. Below is a short attempt at clarification:

Historically, 'Burma' was used in informal conversation by Burmese people as a colloquial name for their country. The name 'Myanmar' was the high, formal, and literary title used during official ceremonies and matters of state. While both titles were and are still used inside the country, in English the country was called 'Burma' until 1989, when the ruling military junta changed the country's official title to Myanmar. According to the ruling junta, 'Mynamar' is more inclusive of the region's ethnic minorities, and its use was an attempt to break with the country's colonial past. However, because the decision was made unilaterally, and by a regime widely considered oppressive, many countries have chosen to continue using the name Burma. Both the US and UK governments call the country by that name, although the UN has chosen to recognise the name Myanmar.

According to linguists, though 'Burma' and 'Myanmar' sound quite distinct in English, in Burmese the two terms sound similar.

Thailand was called Siam until 1939, and again between 1945–49. Côte d'Ivoire is often called the Ivory Coast, but the country's government prefers the French. On the subject of cunning linguistics, in 2008, 3 natives of the island of Lesbos submitted a legal challenge to a Greek homosexual group prohibiting the use of the word 'lesbian' to mean those who share Sappho's sexual preference.

———SPAIN'S SHORT-LIVED ANTHEM———

Spain's Euro 2008 triumph [see p.299] was the country's first major football title since 1964. One theory blamed this long dry spell on the Spanish national anthem, which has no lyrics. While players from other nations can rely on an adrenalin-pumping sing-along, the Spanish are forced to stand in a sombre silence that can do little to energise them. For perhaps this reason (or possibly because merely humming along to an anthem became tiresome), in 2007 the Spanish Olympic Committee was inspired to invite members of the public to submit lyrics for the existing tune. In January 2008, the committee announced that the contest had been won by 52-year-old Paulino Cubero, who bested 7,000 budding lyricists with a hymn to Spain's 'green valleys' and 'vast sea'. However, some Spaniards were offended by the anthem's opening line – *Viva España!* – the rallying cry of Franco. After five days the lyrics were withdrawn, and Spain rejoined the ranks of countries with wordless anthems, including Bosnia and Herzegovina and the minuscule San Marino.

In January 2008, the Iraqi parliament voted to change the country's flag, removing the 3 stars that represented the Ba'ath Party in power under Saddam Hussein. The flag has been changed before: in 2004, a line of script allegedly in Hussein's handwriting was changed to Kufic script, an ancient calligraphy used to transcribe the Koran. Apropos of nothing, the flag of Mozambique currently sports an AK-47 machine gun, despite a 2005 attempt by some opposition members to have it removed.

THE MAFIA'S TEN COMMANDMENTS

In November 2007, Sicilian police announced that a Mafia 'code of behaviour' had been discovered in a raid at the home of a top Mafia boss. According to investigators, the document was unearthed among a cache of coded notes on mob administration. The following commandments were listed, under the title 'Rights and Duty':

[1] No one can present himself directly to another of our friends. There must be a third person to do it. [2] Never look at the wives of friends. [3] Never be seen with cops. [4] Don't go to pubs and clubs. [5] Always being available for Cosa Nostra is a duty – even if your wife's about to give birth. [6] Appointments must absolutely be respected. [7] Wives must be treated with respect. [8] When asked for any information, the answer must be the truth. [9] Money cannot be appropriated if it belongs to others or to other families. [10] People who can't be part of Cosa Nostra – anyone who has a close relative in the police, anyone with a two-timing relative in the family, anyone who behaves badly and doesn't hold to moral values. [Source: BBC]

THE FBI'S MOST WANTED

Fugitive [as at 26/8/2008]	*allegation*	*reward*
Osama bin Laden	terrorism	$25,000,000
James J. Bulger	murder; racketeering	$1,000,000
Victor Manuel Gerena	armed robbery	$1,000,000
Emigdio Preciado Jr	attempted murder; assault	$150,000
Jorge Alberto Lopez-Orozco	murder	$100,000
Jason Derek Brown	murder; robbery	$100,000
Robert William Fisher	murder	$100,000
Alexis Flores	kidnapping; murder	$100,000
Glen Stewart Godwin	murder; prison escape	$100,000
Michael Jason Registe	murder	$100,000

BRIBERY

A 2007 survey released by Transparency International found that bribery was most rampant in poor countries. The following nations reported the highest percent of respondents who said they'd paid a bribe in the past 12 months:

Cameroon	79%	Pakistan	44
Cambodia	72	Nigeria	40
Albania	71	Senegal	38
Kosovo	67	Romania	33
Macedonia	44	Philippines	32

ARMS SALES

The US sells significantly more arms than any other country, according to a 2007 report from the Congressional Research Service. The top arms sellers in 2006, the latest year of data available:

US	$16·9bn†	Sweden	1·1bn
Russia	8·7bn	Italy	900m
UK	3·1bn	China	800m
Germany	1·9bn		
Israel	1·7bn	† Value of arms	
Austria	1·5bn	transfer agreements	

THE PLANETS

Symbol	Name	Diameter km	No. of moons	Surface gravity m/s²	Rings?	Distance from Sun ×10⁶ km	Mean temp. °C	Day length hours
☿	Mercury	4,879	0	3·7	N	57·9	167	4,222·6
♀	Venus	12,104	0	8·9	N	108·2	457	2,802·0
⊕	Earth	12,756	1	9·8	N	149·6	15	24·0
♂	Mars	6,794	2	3·7	N	227·9	–63	24·6
♃	Jupiter	142,984	63	23·1	Y	778·4	–110	9·9
♄	Saturn	120,536	60	9·0	Y	1,426·7	–140	10·7
♅	Uranus	51,118	27	8·7	Y	2,871·0	–195	17·2
♆	Neptune	49,532	13	11·0	Y	4,498·3	–200	16·1

In June 2008, the International Astronomical Union announced a new class of heavenly bodies, Plutoids, for all near-spherical dwarf planets orbiting past Neptune. So far, only Pluto and Eris qualify.

PLANETARY MNEMONIC

Many **V**ery **E**ducated **M**en **J**ustify **S**tealing **U**nique **N**inth
Mercury Venus Earth Mars Jupiter Saturn Uranus Neptune

THE CONTINENTS

Continent	area km²	est. population	population density
Asia	44,579,000	3,959m	88·8
Africa	30,065,000	910m	30·3
North America	24,256,000	331m	13·6
South America	17,819,000	561m	31·5
Antarctica	13,209,000	(a scientist or two)	—
Europe	9,938,000	729m	73·4
Australia	7,687,000	33m	4·3

THE OCEANS

Oceans make up c.70% of the globe's surface. The five oceans are detailed below:

Ocean	area km²	greatest known depth at	depth
Pacific	155,557,000	Mariana Trench	11,033m
Atlantic	76,762,000	Puerto Rico Trench	8,605m
Indian	68,556,000	Java Trench	7,258m
Southern	20,327,000	South Sandwich Trench	7,235m
Arctic	14,056,000	Fram Basin	4,665m

———————— A WORLD OF SUPERLATIVES ————————

Highest capital city..............La Paz, Bolivia.............................. 3,636m
Highest mountain..............Everest, Nepal/Tibet...................... 8,850m
Highest volcano ....Ojos del Salado, Chile................ 6,908m
Highest dam ....Nurek, Tajikistan............................. 300m
Highest waterfall..............Angel Falls, Venezuela........................ 979m
Biggest waterfall (volume) ......Inga, Dem. Rep. of Congo.............43,000m³/s
Lowest point ....Dead Sea, Israel/Jordan *c.*–400m
Deepest point...................Challenger Deep, Mariana Trench......*c.*–11,033m
Deepest ocean ....Pacific........................average depth –4,300m
Deepest freshwater lake ....Baikal, Russia............................. 1,637m
Largest lake ....Caspian Sea............................370,886km²
Largest desert..................Sahara.............................9,065,000km²
Largest island ....Greenland............................2,166,086km²
Largest country.................Russia 17,075,200km²
Largest population ....China .... 1·3bn
Largest monolith................Uluru, Australia ....345m high; 9·4km base
Largest landmass...............Eurasia..........................*c.*54,000,000km²
Largest river (volume)..........Amazon...............................28bn gal/min
Largest peninsula ....Arabian...............................2,590,000km²
Largest rain forest..............Amazon, South America .... 1·2bn acres
Largest forest ....Northern Russia.................... 2·7bn acres
Largest atoll...................Kwajalein, Marshall Islands.................. 16km²
Largest glacier..................Lambert Glacier, Antarctica......*c.*1,000,000km²
Largest concrete artichoke .....Castroville, USA............................ 6m×4m
Largest archipelago.............Indonesia .... 17,508 islands
Largest lake in a lake ....Manitou, on an island in Lake Huron......104km²
Largest city by area.............Mount Isa, Australia.................. 40,977km²
Smallest country.................Vatican City .... 0·44km²
Smallest population ....Vatican City ....824 people
Smallest republic................Republic of Nauru 21km²
Longest coastline ....Canada.............................202,080km
Longest mountain range ....Andes *c.*8,900km
Longest suspension bridge ......Akashi-Kaikyo, Japan 1,990m
Longest rail tunnel..............Seikan, Japan .... 53·8km
Longest road tunnel.............Lærdal, Norway .... 24·5km
Longest river ....Nile 6,695km
Tallest inhabited building.......Burj Dubai, UAE [but see p.184] 688m
Tallest structure ....KVLY-TV Mast, USA...................... 629m
Most land borders..............China & Russia........................ 14 countries
Most populated urban area ....Tokyo, Japan......................... 35·2m
Most remote settlement..........Tristan da Cunha........... 2,334km from neighbours
Least populous capital city ......San Marino, San Marino................pop. 4,482
Warmest sea....................Red Sea........................Average temp. *c.*25°C
Longest bay ....Bay of Bengal......................... *c.*2,000km
Largest banknote................Brobdingnagian bills, Philippines..........14"×8½"

Unsurprisingly, a degree of uncertainty and debate surrounds some of these entries and their specifications.

—————————— POPULATION BY CONTINENT ——————————

Year	World	Africa	N America	S America	Asia	Europe	Oceania
Millions							
1980	4,447	472	371	242	2,645	694	23
1990	5,274	626	424	296	3,181	721	27
2000	6,073	801	486	348	3,678	730	31
2010	6,838	998	540	393	4,148	726	35
2020	7,608	1,220	594	431	4,610	715	38
2030	8,296	1,461	645	461	4,991	696	41
2040	8,897	1,719	692	481	5,291	671	43
2050	9,404	1,990	734	490	5,505	640	45
Percentage distribution							
1980	100%	10·6	8·4	5·4	59·5	15·6	0·5
2000	100%	13·2	8·0	5·7	60·6	12·0	0·5
2050	100%	21·2	7·8	5·2	58·5	6·8	0·5

—————————— WORLD BIRTH & DEATH RATES ——————————

Births	time unit	deaths	change
133,353,798	*per* YEAR	55,532,963	+77,820,835
11,112,817	*per* MONTH	4,627,747	+6,475,931
364,355	*per* DAY	151,729	+212,625
15,181	*per* HOUR	6,322	+ 8,859
253	*per* MINUTE	105	+148
4·2	*per* SECOND	1·8	+2·5

[Source: US Census Bureau, 2008 · Figures may not add up to totals because of rounding]

—————————— URBAN POPULATION ——————————

Tabulated below are the percentages of the urban population in various regions:

Region % of population in urban areas · 1975		2005	2030 (est.)
Africa	25·3	38·3	50·7
Asia	24·0	39·8	54·1
Europe	66·0	72·2	78·3
Latin America & Caribbean	61·2	77·4	84·3
North America	73·8	80·7	86·7
Oceania	71·7	70·8	73·8
World	37·3	48·7	59·9

[Source: United Nations Department of Economic and Social Affairs, 2005]

———————————— CHILD MORTALITY ————————————

9·7m children <5-years-old died around the world in 2006, the first time the global child death toll fell below 10m per year, according to UNICEF data. Officials attribute this fall to campaigns against measles and mumps, as well as economic improvements and efforts to encourage breast-feeding. Below are the 2006 rates of child mortality around the world, as well as the primary causes of child death:

Children <5 deaths per 1,000 live births	*Cause*	*% of global <5 deaths*
W and Central Africa.............. 186	Pneumonia........................... .29	
Sub-Saharan Africa................ 160	Neonatal causes† .... .27	
E and S Africa...................... 131	Diarrhoea............................ .17	
S Asia................................ .83	Malaria 8	
Middle East and N Africa .... .46	Measles 4	
E Asia and Pacific................... .29	AIDS................................. 3	
Latin America & Carib. .... .27	Other................................ .13	
Central & E Europe & CIS .... .27	† Including infections, premature birth,	
Industrialised countries.............. 6	asphyxia, and tetanus [Source: UNICEF]	

———————————— GLOBAL GENDER GAP ————————————

Nordic countries enjoy the most gender equality, according to the 2007 Gender Gap Index produced by the World Economic Forum. The index assessed 128 countries in 4 categories: economic participation and opportunity, educational attainment, political empowerment, and health and survival. Each country was given a score between 0 (inequality) and 1 (equality). Below are the top-ranked countries:

Rank	*country*	*overall score*			
1	.... Sweden	.... 0·8146	6	.... Philippines	.... 0·7629
2	.... Norway	.... 0·8059	7	.... Germany	.... 0·7618
3	.... Finland	.... 0·8044	8	.... Denmark	.... 0·7519
4	.... Iceland	.... 0·7836	9	.... Ireland	.... 0·7457
5	.... New Zealand	.... 0·7649	10	...... Spain	.... 0·7444
			11	...... UK†	.... 0·7441

† The UK fell from 9th place to 11th place in 2007, although its raw score actually improved.

———————————— WAIST MEASUREMENTS WORLDWIDE ————————————

Results from the International Day for the Evaluation of Abdominal Obesity (IDEA):

Mean waist circumference (cm)	♂	♀		♂	♀		♂	♀
NW Europe	97·8	88·3	S Africa	93·6	89·8	Latin Am.	96·4	89·7
S Europe	99·4	91·3	Mid. East	98·2	93·4	OVERALL	95·8	88·7
E Europe	96·9	89·7	E Asia	86·4	80·2			
N Africa	93·6	93·1	S Asia	89·3	84·1	[Based on measurements		
			Australia	99·1	89·0	of 168,000 people in 63		
			Canada	101·4	92·2	countries in May 2005]		

— DEVELOPMENT INDEX —

The UN Human Development Index annually ranks 177 countries by health, life expectancy, income, education, and environment. The 2007 ranking was:

Most developed	Least developed
1 .... Iceland	177 .... Sierra Leone
2 .... Norway	176 ... Burkina Faso
3 .... Australia	175 .. Guinea-Bissau
4 .... Canada	174 .... Niger
5 .... Ireland	173 .... Mali
6 .... Sweden	172 ... Mozambique
7 ...... Switzerland	171 .. C African Rep
8 .... Japan	170 .... Chad
9 ..... Netherlands	169 .... Ethiopia
10 .... France	168 .... Congo

— PEACE INDEX —

The Global Peace Index, produced by the Economist Intelligence Unit, ranks 140 countries on 24 qualitative and quantitative indicators, including military spending, homicide rates, jail populations, and international relations. According to the Index, the most and least peaceful countries in 2008 were:

Most peaceful	Least peaceful
1 .... Iceland	140 .... Iraq
2 .... Denmark	139 .... Somalia
3 .... Norway	138 .... Sudan
4 ..... New Zealand	137 .... Afghanistan
5 .... Japan	136 .... Israel
6 .... Ireland	135 .... Chad

— NOTES TO THE GAZETTEER —

Travelling is almost like talking with men of other centuries. – RENÉ DESCARTES

The gazetteer on the following pages is designed to allow comparisons to be made between countries around the world. As might be expected, some of the data are tentative and open to debate. A range of sources has been consulted, including the CIA's *World Factbook*, Amnesty International, HM Revenue and Customs, &c.

Size km²	*sum of all land and water areas delimited by international boundaries and coastlines*
Population	*July 2008 estimate*
GMT	*based on capital city; varies across some countries; varies with daylight saving*
Life expectancy at birth	*in years; 2008 estimate*
Infant mortality	*deaths of infants <1, per 1,000 live births, per year; 2008 estimate*
Median age	*in years; 2008 estimate*
Birth & death rates	*average per 1,000 persons in the population at mid-year; 2008 estimate*
Fertility rate	*average theoretical number of children per woman; 2008 estimate*
HIV rate	*percentage of adults (15–49) living with HIV/AIDS; mainly 2003 estimate*
Literacy rate	*%; definition (especially of target age) varies; mainly 2003 estimate*
Exchange rate	*Rate as at September 2008 (HM Revenue & Customs)*
GDP per capita	*($) GDP on purchasing power parity basis/population; from 2007*
Inflation	*annual % change in consumer prices; years vary, generally from 2007*
Unemployment	*% of labour force without jobs; years vary, generally from 2007*
Voting age	*voting age; (U)niversal; (C)ompulsory for at least one election; *=entitlement varies*
Military service	*age, length of service, sex and/or religion required to serve vary*
Death penalty	*(N) no death penalty; (N*) death penalty not used in practice;*
	(Y) death penalty for common crimes; (Y*) death penalty for exceptional crimes only
National Day	*some countries have more than one; not all are universally recognised*

—— GAZETTEER · ALGERIA – SOUTH KOREA · [1/4] ——

Country	Size (km²)	Population (m)	Capital city	Phone access code	Phone country code	Flying time (h)	GMT
United Kingdom	244,820	60·8	London	00	44	—	n/a
United States	9,826,630	301·1	Washington, DC	011	1	7h50	–5
Algeria	2,381,740	33·3	Algiers	00	213	2h45	+1
Argentina	2,766,890	40·3	Buenos Aires	00	54	15h45	–3
Australia	7,686,850	20·4	Canberra	0011	61	25h	+10
Austria	83,870	8·2	Vienna	00	43	2h20	+1
Belarus	207,600	9·7	Minsk	810	375	4h40	+2
Belgium	30,528	10·4	Brussels	00	32	1h	+1
Brazil	8,511,965	190·0	Brasilia	0014	55	16h	–3
Bulgaria	110,910	7·3	Sofia	00	359	3h	+2
Burma/Myanmar	678,500	47·4	Rangoon	00	95	13h	+6½
Cambodia	181,040	14·0	Phnom Penh	001	855	14h	+7
Canada	9,984,670	33·4	Ottawa	011	1	7h45	–5
Chile	756,950	16·3	Santiago	00	56	17h	–4
China	9,596,960	1·3bn	Beijing	00	86	10h	+8
Colombia	1,138,910	44·4	Bogota	009	57	13h	–5
Cuba	110,860	11·4	Havana	119	53	12h	–5
Czech Republic	78,866	10·2	Prague	00	420	1h50	+1
Denmark	43,094	5·5	Copenhagen	00	45	1h50	+1
Egypt	1,001,450	80·3	Cairo	00	20	4h45	+2
Estonia	45,226	1·3	Tallinn	00	372	4h	+2
Finland	338,145	5·2	Helsinki	00	358	3h	+2
France	547,030	60·9	Paris	00	33	50m	+1
Germany	357,021	82·4	Berlin	00	49	1h40	+1
Greece	131,940	10·7	Athens	00	30	3h45m	+2
Haiti	27,750	8·7	Port-au-Prince	00	509	20h30	–5
Hong Kong	1,092	7·0	—	001	852	12h	+8
Hungary	93,030	10·0	Budapest	00	36	2h25	+1
India	3,287,590	1·1bn	New Delhi	00	91	8h30	+5½
Indonesia	1,919,440	234·7	Jakarta	001	62	16h	+7
Iran	1,648,000	65·4	Tehran	00	98	6h	+3½
Iraq	437,072	27·5	Baghdad	00	964	14h30	+3
Ireland	70,280	4·1	Dublin	00	353	1h	0
Israel	20,770	6·4	Jerusalem/Tel Aviv	00	972	5h	+2
Italy	301,230	58·1	Rome	00	39	2h20	+1
Japan	377,835	127·4	Tokyo	010	81	11h30	+9
Jordan	92,300	6·1	Amman	00	962	6h	+2
Kazakhstan	2,717,300	15·3	Astana	810	7	8h15	+6
Kenya	582,650	36·9	Nairobi	000	254	8h20	+3
Korea, North	120,540	23·3	Pyongyang	00	850	13h45	+9
Korea, South	98,480	49·0	Seoul	001	82	11h	+9

────────── GAZETTEER · KUWAIT – ZIMBABWE · [1/4] ──────────

Country	Size (km²)	Population (m)	Capital city	Phone access code	Phone country code	Flying time (h)	GMT
United Kingdom	244,820	60·8	London	00	44	—	n/a
United States	9,826,630	301·1	Washington, DC	011	1	7h50	−5
Kuwait	17,820	2·5	Kuwait City	00	965	6h	+3
Latvia	64,589	2·3	Riga	00	371	2h45	+2
Lebanon	10,400	3·9	Beirut	00	961	4h45	+2
Liberia	111,370	3·2	Monrovia	00	231	12h	0
Lithuania	65,200	3·6	Vilnius	00	370	4h	+2
Malaysia	329,750	24·8	Kuala Lumpur	00	60	12h25	+8
Mexico	1,972,550	108·7	Mexico City	00	52	11h15	−6
Monaco	1·95	32·7k	Monaco	00	377	2h	+1
Morocco	446,550	33·8	Rabat	00	212	5h45	0
Netherlands	41,526	16·6	Amsterdam	00	31	1h15	+1
New Zealand	268,680	4·1	Wellington	00	64	28h	+12
Nigeria	923,768	135·0	Abuja	009	234	6h15	+1
Norway	323,802	4·6	Oslo	00	47	2h	+1
Pakistan	803,940	164·7	Islamabad	00	92	10h	+5
Peru	1,285,220	28·7	Lima	00	51	15h15	−5
Philippines	300,000	91·1	Manila	00	63	15h	+8
Poland	312,685	38·5	Warsaw	00	48	2h20	+1
Portugal	92,391	10·6	Lisbon	00	351	2h30	0
Romania	237,500	22·3	Bucharest	00	40	3h15	+2
Russia	17,075,200	141·4	Moscow	810	7	4h	+3
Rwanda	26,338	9·9	Kigali	00	250	11h20	+2
Saudi Arabia	2,149,690	27·6	Riyadh	00	966	6h15	+3
Singapore	692·7	4·6	Singapore	001	65	12h45	+8
Slovakia	48,845	5·4	Bratislava	00	421	3h30	+1
Slovenia	20,273	2·0	Ljubljana	00	386	3h30	+1
Somalia	637,657	9·1	Mogadishu	00	252	12h45	+3
South Africa	1,219,912	44·0	Pretoria/Tshwane	00	27	11h	+2
Spain	504,782	40·4	Madrid	00	34	2h20	+1
Sudan	2,505,810	39·4	Khartoum	00	249	12h	+3
Sweden	449,964	9·0	Stockholm	00	46	2h30	+1
Switzerland	41,290	7·6	Bern	00	41	2h	+1
Syria	185,180	19·3	Damascus	00	963	6h30	+2
Taiwan	35,980	22·9	Taipei	002	886	14h30	+8
Thailand	514,000	65·1	Bangkok	001	66	14h20	+7
Turkey	780,580	71·2	Ankara	00	90	5h15	+2
Ukraine	603,700	46·3	Kiev/Kyiv	810	380	3h25	+2
Venezuela	912,050	26·0	Caracas	00	58	11h30	−4
Vietnam	329,560	85·3	Hanoi	00	84	13h45	+7
Zimbabwe	390,580	12·3	Harare	00	263	12h50	+2

—— GAZETTEER · ALGERIA – SOUTH KOREA · [2/4] ——

Country	Male life expectancy	Female life expectancy	difference	Infant mortality	Median age	Birth rate	Death rate	Fertility rate	Adult HIV rate	Literacy
United Kingdom	76·4	81·5	−5·1	4·9	39·9	10·7	10·1	1·7	0·2	99
United States	75·3	81·1	−5·8	6·3	36·7	14·2	8·3	2·1	0·6	99
Algeria	72·1	75·5	−3·4	28·8	26·0	17·0	4·6	1·8	0·1	70
Argentina	72·8	80·4	−7·6	13·9	30·3	16·3	7·5	2·1	0·7	97
Australia	77·9	83·8	−5·9	4·5	37·4	11·9	7·6	1·8	0·1	99
Austria	76·5	82·4	−5·9	4·5	41·7	8·7	9·9	1·4	0·3	98
Belarus	64·6	76·4	−11·8	6·5	38·4	9·6	13·9	1·2	0·3	100
Belgium	75·9	82·4	−6·5	4·5	41·4	10·2	10·4	1·7	0·2	99
Brazil	68·6	76·6	−8·0	26·7	29·0	16·0	6·2	1·9	0·7	89
Bulgaria	69·2	76·7	−7·5	18·5	41·4	9·6	14·3	1·4	0·1	98
Burma/Myanmar	60·7	65·3	−4·6	49·1	27·8	17·2	9·2	1·9	1·2	90
Cambodia	59·7	63·8	−4·1	56·6	21·7	25·7	8·2	3·1	2·6	74
Canada	78·7	83·8	−5·1	5·1	40·1	10·3	7·6	1·6	0·3	99
Chile	73·9	80·6	−6·7	7·9	31·1	14·8	5·8	2·0	0·3	96
China	71·4	75·2	−3·8	21·2	33·6	13·7	7·0	1·8	0·1	91
Colombia	68·7	76·5	−7·8	19·5	26·8	19·9	5·5	2·5	0·7	93
Cuba	75·0	79·6	−4·6	5·9	36·8	11·3	7·2	1·6	0·1	100
Czech Republic	73·3	80·1	−6·8	3·8	39·8	8·9	10·7	1·2	0·1	99
Denmark	75·8	80·6	−4·8	4·4	40·3	10·7	10·3	1·7	0·2	99
Egypt	69·3	74·5	−5·2	28·4	24·5	22·1	5·1	2·7	0·1	71
Estonia	67·2	78·3	−11·1	7·5	39·6	10·3	13·4	1·4	1·1	100
Finland	75·3	82·5	−7·2	3·5	41·8	10·4	10·0	1·7	0·1	100
France	77·7	84·2	−6·5	3·4	39·2	12·7	8·5	2·0	0·4	99
Germany	76·1	82·3	−6·2	4·0	43·4	8·2	10·8	1·4	0·1	99
Greece	77·0	82·2	−5·2	5·3	41·5	9·5	10·4	1·4	0·2	96
Haiti	55·8	59·4	−3·6	62·3	18·5	35·7	10·2	4·8	5·6	53
Hong Kong	79·1	84·7	−5·6	2·9	41·7	7·4	6·6	1·0	0·1	94
Hungary	69·0	77·6	−8·6	8·0	39·1	9·6	13·0	1·3	0·1	99
India	66·9	71·9	−5·0	32·3	25·1	22·2	6·4	2·8	0·9	61
Indonesia	68·0	73·1	−5·1	31·0	27·2	19·2	6·2	2·3	0·1	90
Iran	69·4	72·4	−3·0	36·9	26·4	16·9	5·7	1·7	0·2	77
Iraq	68·3	71·0	−2·7	45·4	20·2	30·8	5·1	4·0	0·1	74
Ireland	75·4	80·9	−5·5	5·1	34·6	14·3	7·8	1·9	0·1	99
Israel	78·5	82·8	−4·3	4·3	28·9	20·0	5·4	2·8	0·1	97
Italy	77·1	83·2	−6·1	5·6	42·9	8·4	10·6	1·3	0·5	98
Japan	78·7	85·6	−6·9	2·8	43·8	7·9	9·3	1·2	0·1	99
Jordan	76·2	81·4	−5·2	15·6	23·9	20·1	2·7	2·5	0·1	90
Kazakhstan	62·2	73·2	−11·0	26·6	26·6	29·3	16·4	9·4	1·9	0·2	100
Kenya	56·4	56·9	−0·5	56·0	18·6	37·9	10·3	4·7	6·7	85
Korea, North	69·5	75·1	−5·6	21·9	32·7	14·6	7·3	2·0	—	99
Korea, South	74·0	81·1	−7·1	5·9	36·4	9·8	6·1	1·3	0·1	98

——— GAZETTEER · KUWAIT – ZIMBABWE · [2/4] ———

Country	Male life expectancy	Female life expectancy	difference	Infant mortality	Median age	Birth rate	Death rate	Fertility rate	Adult HIV rate	Literacy
United Kingdom	76·4	81·5	−5·1	4·9	39·9	10·7	10·1	1·7	0·2	99
United States	75·3	81·1	−5·8	6·3	36·7	14·2	8·3	2·1	0·6	99
Kuwait	76·4	78·7	−2·3	9·2	26·1	21·9	2·4	2·8	0·1	93
Latvia	66·7	77·4	−10·7	9·0	39·9	9·6	13·6	1·3	0·6	100
Lebanon	70·9	76·0	−5·1	22·6	28·8	17·6	6·1	1·9	0·1	87
Liberia	39·9	42·5	−2·6	143·9	18·0	42·9	21·5	5·9	5·9	58
Lithuania	69·7	79·9	−10·2	6·6	39·0	9·0	11·1	1·2	0·1	100
Malaysia	70·3	75·9	−5·6	16·4	24·6	22·4	5·0	3·0	0·4	89
Mexico	73·1	78·8	−5·7	19·0	26·0	20·0	4·8	2·4	0·3	91
Monaco	76·1	84·0	−7·9	5·2	45·5	9·1	13·0	1·8	—	99
Morocco	69·2	74·0	−4·8	38·2	24·7	21·3	5·5	2·6	0·1	52
Netherlands	76·7	82·0	−5·3	4·8	40·0	10·5	8·7	1·7	0·2	99
New Zealand	78·3	82·3	−4·0	5·0	36·3	14·1	7·0	2·1	0·1	99
Nigeria	47·2	48·5	−1·3	93·9	18·7	40·0	16·4	5·4	5·4	68
Norway	77·2	82·6	−5·4	3·6	39·0	11·1	9·3	1·8	0·1	100
Pakistan	63·1	65·2	−2·1	67·0	21·2	26·9	7·8	3·6	0·1	50
Peru	68·6	72·4	−3·8	29·5	25·8	19·8	6·2	2·4	0·5	88
Philippines	67·9	73·9	−6·0	21·5	23·0	24·1	5·3	3·0	0·1	93
Poland	71·4	79·7	−8·3	6·9	37·6	10·0	10·0	1·3	0·1	100
Portugal	74·8	81·5	−6·7	4·9	39·1	10·5	10·6	1·5	0·4	93
Romania	68·7	75·9	−7·2	23·7	37·3	10·6	11·8	1·4	0·1	97
Russia	59·2	73·1	−13·9	10·8	38·3	11·0	16·1	1·4	1·1	99
Rwanda	48·6	51·0	−2·4	83·4	18·7	40·0	14·5	5·3	5·1	70
Saudi Arabia	74·0	78·3	−4·3	12·0	21·5	28·8	2·5	3·9	0·01	79
Singapore	79·3	84·7	−5·4	2·3	38·4	9·0	4·5	1·1	0·2	93
Slovakia	71·2	79·3	−8·1	7·0	36·5	10·6	9·5	1·3	0·1	100
Slovenia	73·0	80·7	−7·7	4·3	41·4	9·0	10·3	1·3	0·1	100
Somalia	47·4	51·1	−3·7	111·0	17·5	44·1	15·9	6·6	1·0	38
South Africa	43·3	41·4	1·9	58·3	24·5	17·7	22·7	2·1	21·5	86
Spain	76·6	83·5	−6·9	4·3	40·7	9·9	9·9	1·3	0·7	98
Sudan	49·4	51·2	−1·8	87·0	18·9	34·3	13·6	4·6	2·3	61
Sweden	78·5	83·1	−4·6	2·8	41·3	10·2	10·2	1·7	0·1	99
Switzerland	77·9	83·7	−5·8	4·2	40·7	9·6	8·5	1·4	0·4	99
Syria	69·5	72·4	−2·9	26·8	21·4	26·6	4·7	3·2	0·1	80
Taiwan	74·9	80·9	−6·0	5·5	36·0	9·0	6·7	1·1	—	96
Thailand	70·5	75·3	−4·8	18·2	32·8	13·6	7·2	1·6	1·5	93
Turkey	70·7	75·7	−5·0	37·0	29·0	16·2	6·0	1·9	0·1	87
Ukraine	62·2	74·2	−12·0	9·2	39·4	9·6	15·9	1·3	1·4	99
Venezuela	70·4	76·7	−6·3	22·0	25·2	20·9	5·1	2·5	0·7	93
Vietnam	68·5	74·3	−5·8	23·6	26·9	16·5	6·2	1·9	0·4	90
Zimbabwe	40·9	38·6	2·3	50·6	20·3	27·4	21·7	3·0	24·6	91

—— GAZETTEER · ALGERIA – SOUTH KOREA · [3/4] ——

Country	Currency	Currency code	£1 =	GDP per capita $	Inflation %	Unemployment %	Fiscal year end
United Kingdom	Pound=100 Pence	GBP	—	35,100	2·3	5·4	5 Apr
United States	Dollar=100 Cents	USD	1·85	45,800	2·9	4·6	30 Sep
Algeria	Dinar=100 Centimes	DZD	113·9	6,500	3·7	13·0	31 Dec
Argentina	Peso=100 Centavos	ARS	5·6	13,300	8·8	14·1	31 Dec
Australia	Dollar=100 Cents	AUD	2·1	36,300	2·3	4·4	30 Jun
Austria	euro=100 cent	EUR	1·3	38,400	2·2	4·4	31 Dec
Belarus	Ruble=100 Kopecks	BYR	3,935·2	10,900	8·4	1·6	31 Dec
Belgium	euro=100 cent	EUR	1·3	35,300	1·8	7·5	31 Dec
Brazil	Real=100 Centavos	BRL	3·0	9,700	3·6	9·3	31 Dec
Bulgaria	Lev=100 Stotinki	BGN	2·5	11,300	7·6	7·7	31 Dec
Burma/Myanmar	Kyat=100 Pyas	MMK	12·0	1,900	34·4	10·2	31 Mar
Cambodia	Riel=100 Sen	KHR	7,593·0	1,800	5·9	2·5	31 Dec
Canada	Dollar=100 Cents	CAD	2·0	38,400	2·1	6·0	31 Mar
Chile	Peso=100 Centavos	CLP	960·4	13,900	4·4	7·0	31 Dec
China	Renminbi Yuan=100 Fen	CNY	12·8	5,300	4·8	4·0	31 Dec
Colombia	Peso=100 Centavos	COP	3,514·2	6,700	5·5	11·2	31 Dec
Cuba	Peso=100 Centavos	CUP/C	1·9	4,500	3·1	1·8	31 Dec
Czech Republic	Koruna=100 Haléru	CZK	31·2	24,200	2·8	6·6	31 Dec
Denmark	Krone=100 Øre	DKK	9·4	37,400	1·7	2·8	31 Dec
Egypt	Pound=100 Piastres	EGP	9·9	5,500	11·0	9·1	30 Jun
Estonia	Kroon=100 Sents	EEK	19·8	21,100	6·6	4·7	31 Dec
Finland	euro=100 cent	EUR	1·3	35,300	1·6	6·8	31 Dec
France	euro=100 cent	EUR	1·3	33,200	1·6	8·3	31 Dec
Germany	euro=100 cent	EUR	1·3	34,200	2·3	8·4	31 Dec
Greece	euro=100 cent	EUR	1·3	29,200	3·0	8·3	31 Dec
Haiti	Gourde=100 Centimes	HTG	72·6	1,300	9·0	c.65	30 Sep
Hong Kong	HK Dollar=100 Cents	HKD	14·5	42,000	2·0	4·1	31 Mar
Hungary	Forint=100 Fillér	HUF	303·3	19,000	7·9	7·3	31 Dec
India	Rupee=100 Paise	INR	81·2	2,700	6·4	7·2	31 Mar
Indonesia	Rupiah=100 Sen	IDR	17,123·3	3,700	6·4	9·6	31 Dec
Iran	Rial	IRR	17,734·4	10,600	17·5	12·0	20 Mar
Iraq	New Iraqi Dinar	NID	2,230·4	3,600	4·7	—	31 Dec
Ireland	euro=100 cent	EUR	1·3	43,100	3·0	4·6	31 Dec
Israel	Shekel=100 Agora	ILS	6·6	25,800	0·5	7·3	31 Dec
Italy	euro=100 cent	EUR	1·3	30,400	2·0	6·0	31 Dec
Japan	Yen=100 Sen	JPY	204·3	33,600	0·0	3·9	31 Mar
Jordan	Dinar=1,000 Fils	JOD	1·3	4,900	5·4	13·5	31 Dec
Kazakhstan	Tenge=100 Tiyn	KZT	223·9	11,100	10·8	7·3	31 Dec
Kenya	Shilling=100 Cents	KES	125·7	1,700	9·8	40·0	30 Jun
Korea, North	NK Won=100 Chon	KPW	248·1	1,900	—	—	31 Dec
Korea, South	SK Won=100 Chon	KRW	1,950·1	24,800	2·5	3·3	31 Dec

GAZETTEER · KUWAIT – ZIMBABWE · [3/4]

Country	Currency	Currency code	£1 =	GDP per capita $	Inflation %	Unemployment %	Fiscal year end
United Kingdom	Pound=100 Pence	GBP	—	35,100	2·3	5·4	5 Apr
United States	Dollar=100 Cents	USD	1·85	45,800	2·9	4·6	30 Sep
Kuwait	Dinar=1,000 Fils	KWD	0·5	39,300	5·0	2·2	31 Mar
Latvia	Lats=100 Santims	LVL	0·9	17,400	10·1	5·7	31 Dec
Lebanon	Pound=100 Piastres	LBP	2,808·9	11,300	4·1	20·0	31 Dec
Liberia	Dollar=100 Cents	LRD	—	400	11·2	85·0	31 Dec
Lithuania	Litas=100 Centas	LTL	4·4	17,700	5·8	3·5	31 Dec
Malaysia	Ringgit=100 Sen	MYR	6·2	13,300	2·1	3·2	31 Dec
Mexico	Peso=100 Centavos	MXN	18·8	12,800	4·0	3·7	31 Dec
Monaco	euro=100 cent	EUR	1·3	30,000	1·9	0·0	31 Dec
Morocco	Dirham=100 centimes	MAD	14·4	4,100	2·0	10·2	31 Dec
Netherlands	euro=100 cent	EUR	1·3	38,500	1·6	3·2	31 Dec
New Zealand	Dollar=100 Cents	NZD	2·6	26,400	2·4	3·6	31 Mar
Nigeria	Naira=100 Kobo	NGN	219·4	2,000	5·5	4·9	31 Dec
Norway	Krone=100 Øre	NOK	10·0	53,000	0·8	2·5	31 Dec
Pakistan	Rupee=100 Paisa	PKR	142·6	2,600	7·8	7·5	30 Jun
Peru	New Sol=100 Centimos	PEN	5·5	7,800	1·8	6·9	31 Dec
Philippines	Peso=100 Centavos	PHP	84·8	3,400	2·8	7·3	31 Dec
Poland	Zloty=100 Groszy	PLN	4·2	16,300	2·5	12·8	31 Dec
Portugal	euro=100 cent	EUR	1·3	21,700	2·4	7·7	31 Dec
Romania	New Leu=100 New Bani	RON	4·5	11,400	4·8	4·1	31 Dec
Russia	Ruble=100 Kopecks	RUB	45·8	14,700	11·9	6·2	31 Dec
Rwanda	Franc=100 Centimes	RWF	1,018·7	900	9·4	—	31 Dec
Saudi Arabia	Riyal=100 Halala	SAR	7·0	23,200	4·1	c.25	31 Dec
Singapore	Dollar=100 Cents	SGD	2·6	49,700	2·1	2·1	31 Mar
Slovakia	Koruna=100 Halierov	SKK	38·5	20,300	2·8	8·4	31 Dec
Slovenia	euro=100 cent	EUR	1·3	27,200	3·6	4·8	31 Dec
Somalia	Shilling=100 Cents	SOS	2,610·5	600	—	—	—
South Africa	Rand=100 Cents	ZAR	14·4	9,800	7·1	24·3	31 Mar
Spain	euro=100 cent	EUR	1·3	30,100	2·8	8·3	31 Dec
Sudan	Pound=100 Piastres	SDG	3·9	2,200	8·0	18·7	31 Dec
Sweden	Krona=100 Øre	SEK	11·9	36,500	1·7	6·1	31 Dec
Switzerland	Franc=100 Centimes	CHF	2·0	41,100	0·9	2·5	31 Dec
Syria	Pound=100 Piastres	SYP	95·1	4,500	7·0	9·0	31 Dec
Taiwan	Dollar=100 Cents	TWD	58·3	30,100	1·8	3·9	31 Dec
Thailand	Baht=100 Satang	THB	63·4	7,900	2·2	1·4	30 Sep
Turkey	New Lira=100 New Kurus	TRY	2·2	12,900	8·8	9·9	31 Dec
Ukraine	Hryvena=100 Kopiykas	UAH	8·6	6,900	12·8	c.7·0	31 Dec
Venezuela	Bolívar=100 Centimos	VEB	4·0	12,200	18·7	8·5	31 Dec
Vietnam	Dong=100 Xu	VND	30,930·0	2,600	8·3	5·3	31 Dec
Zimbabwe	Dollar=100 Cents	ZWD	—	200	p.33	80·0	31 Dec

—— GAZETTEER · ALGERIA – SOUTH KOREA · [4/4] ——

Country	Voting age	Driving side	UN vehicle code	Internet country code	Military service	Death penalty	National Day
United Kingdom	18 U	L	GB	.uk	N	N	—
United States	18 U	R	USA	.us	N	Y	4 Jul
Algeria	18 U	R	DZ	.dz	Y	N*	1 Nov
Argentina	18 UC	R	RA	.ar	N	Y*	25 May
Australia	18 UC	L	AUS	.au	N	N	26 Jan
Austria	16 U	R	A	.at	Y	N	26 Oct
Belarus	18 U	R	BY	.by	Y	Y	3 Jul
Belgium	18 UC	R	B	.be	N	N	21 Jul
Brazil	16 U*	R	BR	.br	Y	Y*	7 Sep
Bulgaria	18 U	R	BG	.bg	N	N	3 Mar
Burma/Myanmar	18 U	R	BUR	.mm	N	N*	4 Jan
Cambodia	18 U	R	K	.kh	Y	N	9 Nov
Canada	18 U	R	CDN	.ca	N	N	1 Jul
Chile	18 UC	R	RCH	.cl	N/Y	Y*	18 Sep
China	18 U	R	RC	.cn	Y	Y	1 Oct
Colombia	18 U	R	CO	.co	Y	N	20 Jul
Cuba	16 U	R	CU	.cu	Y	Y	1 Jan
Czech Republic	18 U	R	CZ	.cz	N	N	28 Oct
Denmark	18 U	R	DK	.dk	Y	N	5 Jun
Egypt	18 UC	R	ET	.eg	Y	Y	23 Jul
Estonia	18 U	R	EST	.ee	Y	N	24 Feb
Finland	18 U	R	FIN	.fi	Y	N	6 Dec
France	18 U	R	F	.fr	N	N	14 Jul
Germany	18 U	R	D	.de	Y	N	3 Oct
Greece	18 UC	R	GR	.gr	Y	N	25 Mar
Haiti	18 U	R	RH	.ht	—	N	1 Jan
Hong Kong	18 U*	L	—	.hk	N	N	1 Oct
Hungary	18 U	R	H	.hu	N	N	20 Aug
India	18 U	L	IND	.in	N	Y	26 Jan
Indonesia	17 U*	L	RI	.id	Y	Y	17 Aug
Iran	16 U	R	IR	.ir	Y	Y	1 Apr
Iraq	18 U	R	IRQ	.iq	N	Y	17 Jul
Ireland	18 U	L	IRL	.ie	N	N	17 Mar
Israel	18 U	R	IL	.il	Y	Y*	14 May
Italy	18 U*	R	I	.it	N	N	2 Jun
Japan	20 U	L	J	.jp	N	Y	23 Dec
Jordan	18 U	R	HKJ	.jo	N	Y	25 May
Kazakhstan	18 U	R	KZ	.kz	Y	Y*	16 Dec
Kenya	18 U	L	EAK	.ke	N	N*	12 Dec
Korea, North	17 U	R	—	.kp	Y?	Y	9 Sep
Korea, South	19 U	R	ROK	.kr	Y	N*	15 Aug

Country	Voting age	Driving side	UN vehicle code	Internet country code	Military service	Death penalty	National Day
United Kingdom	18 U	L	GB	.uk	N	N	—
United States	18 U	R	USA	.us	N	Y	4 Jul
Kuwait	?21 U*	R	KWT	.kw	Y	Y	25 Feb
Latvia	18 U	R	LV	.lv	N	Y*	18 Nov
Lebanon	21 C*	R	RL	.lb	N	Y	22 Nov
Liberia	18 U	R	LB	.lr	N	N*	26 Jul
Lithuania	18 U	R	LT	.lt	Y	N	16 Feb
Malaysia	21 U	L	MAL	.my	N	Y	31 Aug
Mexico	18 UC	R	MEX	.mx	Y	N	16 Sep
Monaco	18 U	R	MC	.mc	—	N	19 Nov
Morocco	18 U	R	MA	.ma	Y	N*	30 Jul
Netherlands	18 U	R	NL	.nl	N	N	30 Apr
New Zealand	18 U	L	NZ	.nz	N	N	6 Feb
Nigeria	18 U	R	WAN	.ng	N	Y	1 Oct
Norway	18 U	R	N	.no	Y	N	17 May
Pakistan	18 U	L	PK	.pk	N	Y	23 Mar
Peru	18 UC*	R	PE	.pe	N	Y*	28 Jul
Philippines	18 U	R	RP	.ph	Y	N	12 Jun
Poland	18 U	R	PL	.pl	Y	N	3 May
Portugal	18 U	R	P	.pt	N	N	10 Jun
Romania	18 U	R	RO	.ro	N	N	1 Dec
Russia	18 U	R	RUS	.ru	Y	N*	12 Jun
Rwanda	18 U	R	RWA	.rw	N	N	1 Jul
Saudi Arabia	21 ?	R	SA	.sa	N	Y	23 Sep
Singapore	21 UC	L	SGP	.sg	Y	Y	9 Aug
Slovakia	18 U	R	SK	.sk	N	N	1 Sep
Slovenia	18 U*	R	SLO	.si	N	N	25 Jun
Somalia	18 U	R	SO	.so	—	Y	1 Jul
South Africa	18 U	L	ZA	.za	N	N	27 Apr
Spain	18 U	R	E	.es	N	N	12 Oct
Sudan	17 U	R	SUD	.sd	Y	Y	1 Jan
Sweden	18 U	R	S	.se	Y	N	6 Jun
Switzerland	18 U	R	CH	.ch	Y	N	1 Aug
Syria	18 U	R	SYR	.sy	Y	Y	17 Apr
Taiwan	20 U	R	—	.tw	Y	Y	10 Oct
Thailand	18 UC	L	T	.th	Y	Y	5 Dec
Turkey	18 U	R	TR	.tr	Y	N	29 Oct
Ukraine	18 U	R	UA	.ua	Y	N	24 Aug
Venezuela	18 U	R	YV	.ve	Y	N	5 Jul
Vietnam	18 U	R	VN	.vn	Y	Y	2 Sep
Zimbabwe	18 U	L	ZW	.zw	Y	Y	18 Apr

Society & Health

Man is a social animal.
— BENEDICT SPINOZA (1632–77)

─────────────── ABORTION ───────────────

On 20 May 2008, MPs voted against a series of proposals to cut the upper time limit for abortions (to 12, 16, 20, or 22 weeks), ensuring that the 24-week limit (reduced from 28 weeks in 1990) remained in force. The parliamentary debate was widely praised for its non-partisan passion, though some questioned how free the free vote was after (denied) allegations of a whipping operation to protect the (Gordon Brown-supported) status quo. ❦ According to the Dept of Health, 198,500 abortions were performed on residents of England and Wales in 2007, of which 89% were NHS funded. (7,100 abortions were performed on non-residents: 19% of whom were from N Ireland; 66% from the Republic of Ireland.) Below are the gestations of 2007's abortions:

3–9 weeks............. 139,144 (70·1%)	20–21 weeks ....1,726 (0·9%)
10–12 weeks ....38,998 (19·6%)	22–23 weeks ....1,066 (0·5%)
13–19 weeks ....17,430 (8·8%)	>24 weeks .... 135 (0·1%)

32% of women undergoing abortions in 2007 had one or more previous abortion:

Previous abortions	total	age <18	18–24	25–29	≥30
0	134,269	18,824	58,433	24,939	32,073
1	49,484	1,378	18,220	12,530	17,356
2	11,136	74	3,223	3,145	4,694
3	2,605	[<10]	[<10]	787	1,214
4	740	[<10]	[<10]	225	379
5	184	[<10]	[<10]	47	119
6	52	[<10]	[<10]	[<10]	27
≥7	29	[<10]	[<10]	[<10]	15

Below is the abortion rate by age group (per 1,000 females), in England and Wales:

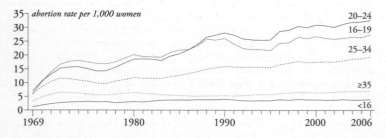

———————— UK POPULATION FIGURES ————————

(million)	1971	1981	1991	2001	2006	2011	2021	2031
England	46·4	46·8	47·9	49·5	50·8	52·7	56·8	60·4
Wales	2·7	2·8	2·9	2·9	3·0	3·0	3·2	3·3
Scotland	5·2	5·2	5·1	5·1	5·1	5·2	5·3	5·4
N Ireland	1·5	1·5	1·6	1·7	1·7	1·8	1·9	2·0
UK	55·9	56·4	57·4	59·1	60·6	62·8	67·2	71·1

[Mid-year estimates for 1971–2006; 2006-based projections for 2011–31 · Source: © ONS]

———— ENGLISH POPULATION BY ETHNIC GROUP & AGE ————

2005	% of	<16	16–64	≥65	number
White					
White British		19	64	17	42,753,000
White Irish		6	65	29	592,000
Other White		13	78	9	1,623,000
Mixed		46	51	3	791,000
Asian or Asian British					
Indian		19	74	7	1,215,000
Pakistani		32	64	5	826,000
Bangladeshi		34	62	4	324,000
Other Asian		21	74	5	310,000
Black or Black British					
Black Caribbean		18	69	13	590,000
Black African		26	72	3	659,000
Other Black		35	62	4	110,000
Chinese		13	82	4	347,000
Other ethnic group		15	82	3	325,000
All ethnic groups		19	65	16	50,466,000

[The Office of National Statistics cautions that these are experimental (and rounded) figures.]

———— CENTENARIANS & AN AGEING POPULATION ————

There were *c.*9,000 people over 100 years old in England and Wales in 2006, according to the Office for National Statistics. This is a 90-fold increase since 1911, when there were an *c.*100 centenarians. There are proportionally more female centenarians than male: in mid-2006 there were 7 women over 100 for every man. The main factors for this increase in the number of centenarians are improvements in hygiene, sanitation, diet, medical treatment, and living standards. ❦ The UK has an ageing population due to the fall in fertility rates and greater life expectancy. Since 1971 the population aged <16 has decreased from *c.*14·3m to 11·5m while that aged >65 has increased by 2·3m, making up 16% of the population in 2006. The number of people aged >65 is expected to exceed those aged <16 by 2021.

——— AVERAGE AGE OF MOTHER AT CHILDBIRTH ———

Average age of mother (years)	1971	1981	1991	2001	2008
All births					
all live births	26·2	26·8	27·7	29·2	29·5
all first births	23·6	24·6	25·7	27·2	27·6
Births inside marriage					
all births inside marriage	26·4	27·2	28·9	30·9	31·4
first births inside marriage	23·9	25·3	27·5	29·6	30·2
Births outside marriage					
all births outside marriage	23·7	23·4	24·8	26·7	27·0

England & Wales. The mean ages shown are not standardised and therefore take no account of the structure of the population by age, marital status or number of births. [Source: © ONS]

——————— TEENAGE CONCEPTION & PREGNANCY ———————

According to the 2008 *Social Trends*, there were 102,312 conceptions to females aged <20 in England and Wales in 2005. The rate of teenage pregnancy is influenced by a range of factors, but is 'considerably higher' in deprived areas, whereas teenagers from affluent areas are more likely to terminate their pregnancy – possibly because those in affluent areas see pregnancy as a barrier to education. Tabulated opposite are teenage conceptions in England and Wales in 2005.

Number	age	% aborted
327	<14	.60
1,830	14	.64
5,773	15	.55
7,930	all <16	.57
13,335	16	.46
21,060	17	.42
42,325	all <18	.46
28,044	18	.37
31,943	19	.35
102,312	all <20	.40

——————————— BIRTHS OUTSIDE MARRIAGE ———————————

Social Trends notes that 'births outside marriage became more commonplace during the 1960s and 1970s' – by 2006, 43·7% of all UK births were outside wedlock:

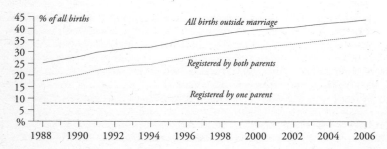

BULLYING

56% of British children have been bullied, and >71% have been bullies, according to 2008 research by charity Beatbullying. Below are the reasons given for bullying:

Anger...............13%	Self-defence 5%	Made them popular.....
Bullied themselves .10%	Their friends did it. .4%	2%

A separate British Council survey discovered that 48% of children in England (aged 12–18) thought bullying was a problem in their school; in Scotland 43% so thought; and in Wales, 32%. This survey also revealed that first-generation migrant children were 25% more likely to be bullied in British secondary schools than non-migrant children. Below are levels of bullying in these two groups, across Europe:

country	non-migrant	1st generation		non-migrant	1st generation
Germany	19%	20%	Netherlands	7%	5%
UK	12%	15%	Italy	5%	7%
Belgium	9%	21%	Portugal	4%	4%
			Spain	3%	4%

BEST ROLE MODELS

Richard Branson bested Jesus Christ as the best role model for children, according to a March 2008 survey of British parents. The top 10 best role models were:

A family member	Nelson Mandela	Martin Luther King
Richard Branson	Princess Diana	Bill Gates
Jesus Christ	Jamie Oliver	
A teacher	Winston Churchill	[Source: Opinium Research]

MOST POPULAR NAMES · 2007

Below are the most popular names of 2007, from the Office of National Statistics:

Jack (–)	*nickname for John*	1	*from the Latin Gratia*	(+1)	Grace
Thomas (–)	*Greek form of Aramaic for 'twin'*	2	*from the gemstone*	(+2)	Ruby
Oliver (+1)	*? from Latin for 'olive tree'*	3	*? feminine version of Oliver*	(-2)	Olivia
Joshua (-1)	*Jehova saves*	4	*from the Latin Aemilia*	(+1)	Emily
Harry (–)	*nickname for Henry*	5	*allegedly created by Shakespeare*	(-2)	Jessica
Charlie (+4)	*pet form of Charles*	6	*French form of Sophia*	(–)	Sophie
Daniel (+2)	*from Hebrew for 'God is my judge'*	7	*Greek for 'young green shoot'*	(–)	Chloe
William (–1)	*from German for 'protector'*	8	*flower, symbol of purity*	(+1)	Lily
James (-3)	*English form of Jacomus & Jacob*	9	*pet form of Ellen*	(+2)	Ella
Alfie (+6)	*pet form of Alfred*	10	*blend of medieval Emilia & Amalia*	(+6)	Amelia

Mohammed climbed five places to number 17 in 2007 – although, according to *The Times*, if all seven spelling variations of the name were combined, Mohammed would rank second.

———————————— SCHOOL CENSUS · 2008 ————————————

There are currently 7·3m pupils in state-funded education in England, according to the School Census conducted by the Department for Children, Schools and Families in January 2008. Of these, 23·3% of primary school pupils were classified as minority ethnic origin, an increase of 1·4% since 2007. In secondary schools 19·5% of pupils in 2008 were from an ethnic minority, up 1·5% since 2007. The table below shows the primary language of school children in England:

% pupils	primary schools	secondary schools	special schools
1st language is not English	14·4	10·8	9·9
1st language is English	85·5	88·9	89·8
Unclassified	0·1	0·3	0·2

The average class size in state-funded primary schools in January 2008 was 26·2; 10·8% of primary school classes had >30 pupils, a decrease of 11·5% since January 2007. In state-funded secondary schools, the average class size was 20·9, and 10·4% were taught in classes with >31 pupils. 8·1% of the primary school population were assessed to be in the 'gifted and talented cohort' (a classification aimed at targeting gifted children and removing 'barriers to learning'), which rose to 13·6% in secondary schools. In contrast, 2·8% of all pupils across England had a Statement of Special Educational Needs† (SEN), 56·7% of whom were placed in mainstream schools in 2008. Below is a table of the number and percentage of children with SEN by type of need, in English primary and secondary schools in 2008:

PRIMARY SCHOOLS		Type of need	SECONDARY SCHOOLS	
number	%		number	%
33,210	10·6	Specific learning difficulty	42,990	16·9
85,000	27·2	Moderate learning difficulty	66,610	26·2
5,390	1·7	Severe learning difficulty	2,730	1·1
1,270	0·4	Profound/multiple learning difficulties	350	0·1
58,140	18·6	Behaviour, emotional & social difficulties	77,610	30·6
74,570	23·8	Speech, lang. & communication	17,490	6·9
6,650	2·1	Hearing impairment	5,980	2·4
3,890	1·2	Visual impairment	3,330	1·3
530	0·2	Multi-sensory impairment	240	0·1
12,420	4·0	Physical disability	8,570	3·4
19,410	6·2	Autistic spectrum disorder	13,680	5·4
12,080	3·9	Other difficulty/disability	14,270	5·6
140	<0·1	Unclassified	190	0·1
312,700	100	TOTAL	254,040	100

† A child is classified as having learning difficulties if they have significantly greater difficulty in learning than the majority of children of the same age, or have a physical disability which hinders them from making use of the educational facilities provided for children of the same age. Those with a high level of learning difficulty may receive a Statutory Assessment that indicates whether the child needs extra educational provision. If so, a Statement of Special Educational Needs can be created, which describes the child's difficulties and outlines how they are to be addressed by the local authority.

——————————————TRUANCY——————————————

348,000 pupils in England were classified as being at risk of becoming 'persistent truants', according to official figures for autumn 2007, released in May 2008. Persistent truants are those that miss >63 school sessions in a year – 43,900 pupils fell into this category in 2007. A 2005 study by the Department for Children, Schools, and Families revealed some of the reasons why children played truant:

Reason for truancy	% boys	% girls	% all
Boredom	24	20	22
Dislike of a particular subject or lesson	18	24	21
Dislike of school	16	13	14
Dislike of a particular teacher or teachers	15	12	13
Bullying	4	8	6
Other reason/not sure/dunno	22	23	23

——————————————FAITH SCHOOLS——————————————

1·7m pupils attended a faith school in 2007 – 99% of which were of a Christian denomination. Below is a breakdown of English maintained schools, by faith:

School by faith	primary	secondary	all
Christian	6,221	573	6,794
Jewish	28	9	37
Muslim	4	3	7
Sikh	1	1	2
Other religious†	1	1	2
No religious character	11,106	2,756	13,862
Total	17,361	3,343	20,704

[Source: Department for Children, Schools and Families · 2007] † Seventh Day Adventist and Greek Orthodox. The construction of the UK's first Hindu State School, the Krishna-Avanti primary school in Edgware, London, began in June 2008 – ready to take pupils in September 2008.

——————————CHILDREN'S ATTITUDES TO SCHOOL——————————

%	strongly agree	agree	disagree	strongly disagree
School work is worth doing	40	46	7	5
I am happy at school	22	60	11	4
I work as hard as I can	21	54	19	2
I am bored in lessons	10	36	43	6
Work in lessons is interesting	9	62	20	3
I don't want to go to school	7	24	44	21
School is a waste of time	3	6	37	51

[Source: Longitudinal Study of Young People in England, 2005, Dept Children, Schools, & Families]

FORCED MARRIAGES & 'HONOUR' VIOLENCE

17,000 women each year may be the victim of forced marriage†, kidnap, assault, or murder by relatives claiming to uphold family 'honour', according to data from the Association of Chief Police Officers released in February 2008. This startling figure is 35× higher than previous estimates. While people of S Asian origin are most often affected, forced marriage is not limited to these communities, and is inextricably linked with so-called 'honour' violence. ❦ In April 2008, a national helpline – the Honour Network – was established for British victims of forced marriage and 'honour' violence. The helpline was created by the Forced Marriage Unit (FMU), which was formed in 2005 by the Foreign & Commonwealth Office and the Home Office. The FMU currently investigates *c.*400 cases of forced marriage each year (of which 85% involve female victims), and handles 5,000 enquiries. ❦ In the autumn of 2008, the Forced Marriage (Civil Protection) Act came into force, allowing courts to issue Forced Marriage Orders to halt coercive unions.

† Defined by the government as one 'conducted without the valid consent of both people, where pressure or abuse is used'. ❦ The fact that young British Asian women are 3x more likely to kill themselves than the national average is thought to be linked to 'honour' violence. [Source: *Independent*]

METHODS USED TO FIND A PARTNER

A 2007 YouGov survey asked people to reveal the methods they had used, at any time, to find a casual date or long-term partner; the most popular methods were:

Method	%
Going out to bars/clubs	70
Meeting through work	37
Dates organised by family/friends	22
Fellow members of club/assoc	21
Internet dating sites	19
Friends' dinner parties	13
Approaching in a public place	11
Classified newspaper ad	10
Singles parties/events	5
Fellow member of church	5
Introduction agency (offline)	3
Phone dating	2
Speed dating	2

WEDDING RINGS

According to *The Yearbook of Daily Recreation and Information* (1832), the wedding ring is worn on the fourth finger of the left hand because it was once thought that a vein ran directly from this finger to the heart. *The Yearbook* cites Dutch physician Levinus Lemnius (1505–68), who wrote that he would resuscitate those 'who are fallen in a swoon by pinching this joint, and by rubbing the ring of gold with a little saffron; for ... it passeth to the heart, and refresheth the fountain of life, unto which this finger is joined. Wherefore antiquity thought fit to compass it about with gold'.

The number of marriages fell by 4% to 236,980 in 2006, the lowest annual number of marriages since 1895, when there were 228,204. ❦ A National Wedding Show survey in Feb 2008 found that the average length of time between a couple meeting and getting engaged is 2yrs, 11 months, 8 days.

NUMBER OF SEXUAL PARTNERS

Partners (%)		16–19	20–24	25–34	35–44	45–49
♂	No partners	44	7	7	9	12
	1 partner	27	48	77	83	83
	2 or 3 partners	22	30	12	5	4
	≥4 partners	7	14	5	4	1
♀	No partners	34	6	7	9	16
	1 partner	35	74	83	86	83
	2 or 3 partners	23	17	8	3	1
	≥4 partners	8	3	2	1	–

[Self-reported number of sexual partners in the previous 12 months, 2006/2007;
Great Britain. Source: Omnibus Survey, Office of National Statistics]

'MR RIGHT'

A January 2008 survey of 40,000 women by UKdating.com proposed a 20-point guide to what British women were looking for in a man. Apparently, Mr Right must:

be at least 5' 10" tall	have had ≤3 prior serious relationships
be good looking	be clean-shaven
weigh 12½ stone	drive a silver Mercedes
earn >£30,000	like the cinema
have blue eyes	enjoy eating out
have short, dark brown hair†	have had <6 previous sexual partners
be of medium build	own a £300,000 home
have a BA degree	not smoke
never have been married	not be keen on football
have no children	be a pet lover‡

† 11% of women surveyed said they preferred ginger hair; 18% liked men with grey hair.
‡ Only 1% of women questioned for the survey said that their Mr Right could hate pets.

PROBABILITY OF DIVORCE

If current divorce rates continue, approximately 45% of all marriages will end in divorce, according to a study by the Office for National Statistics in March 2008. The research predicted that almost half of all divorces will occur before a couple has been married for ten years. If divorce and death rates remain unchanged from 2005, then just 10% of married couples would celebrate their 60th (diamond) wedding anniversary; 45% of marriages would end in divorce; and the remaining 45% will end due to death. For marriages that last over ten years, the probability of divorce falls to 31%. After 20 years of marriage, just 15% end in divorce. Those who have been previously divorced are statistically much more likely to divorce again, and those who marry young also have a higher probability of divorce.

———————————— ON CLASS ————————————

In March 2008, *Schott's Almanac* and Ipsos Mori analysed British attitudes on class:

Which of these best describes you, working class or middle class?

%	Working	Middle	?
All	52	44	4
Men	54	43	3
Women	51	44	5
Age: 16–34	50	46	4
· 35–54	57	40	3
· 55+	50	46	4
Parents: wrk. class	70	27	3
· middle class	16	82	2
Vote: Labour	52	45	3
· Conservative	42	55	3
· Lib Dem	42	56	2
· other	66	31	2
Radio 4 listener	39	56	5
· non-listener	65	32	3
Read: tabloid	62	36	2
· broadsheet	26	70	4

How often, if at all, do you feel uncomfortable when dealing with people of a different class to you?

%	all of the time	some of the time	rarely	never
All	2	12	24	62
Men	1	11	21	66
Women	2	12	27	59
Age: 16–34	3	16	22	58
· 35–54	1	7	27	65
· 55+	2	12	23	63
Radio 4 listener	1	11	28	60
· non-listener	2	12	20	64
Own a car	1	10	24	64
· do not	5	19	22	54

Is there a class system in Britain?

%	Yes	No	?
All	88	10	2
Age: 16–34	85	12	3
· 35–54	89	8	3
· 55+	88	11	1
Parents: wrk. class	89	8	3
· middle class	85	14	1

Have you ever been in a romantic relationship with someone of a different class to yourself?

%	Yes	No	?
All	34	63	3
Age: 16–34	39	60	1
· 35–54	40	58	2
· 55+	25	70	5
Class: working	27	71	2
· middle	43	54	3
Radio 4 listener	39	58	3
· non-listener	30	68	2

Which political party, if any, do you feel best represents the rights of each class?

Party %	working	middle	upper
Labour	39	19	7
Conservative	10	46	65
Lib Dem	8	7	2
Other	5	2	1
None	21	7	6
Don't know	17	19	19

Of those that said yes [=363]: Did you find the class difference to be…

How problematic	All	♂	♀
Very	5	6	4
Fairly	12	7	17
Not much	40	38	43
Not at all	42	48	35
Don't know	1	0	1

——————— ON CLASS cont. ———————

Who is most likely to engage in each of these activities:
a working-class person, a middle-class person, or an upper-class person?

Activity %	Working	Middle	Upper	Any	?
Watch *Coronation Street*	45	11	<½	40	4
Have an allotment	52	22	2	20	4
Holiday in Spain	37	16	4	41	2
Eat peas with a knife	35	6	13	25	21
Recycle	9	38	2	48	3
Eat in front of the television	48	9	1	40	2
Take the bus	62	9	<½	26	3
Go to university	3	40	12	44	1
Watch the news regularly	8	33	4	53	2
Own designer clothes	7	25	30	35	3
Buy organic food	2	52	19	25	2

Some people alter the way they behave in certain situations to make it appear as if they are in a different class. Have you ever done this?

%	Yes	No	?
All	16	84	<½
Men	17	83	<½
Women	14	85	1
Age: 16–34	20	79	1
· 35–54	19	81	1
· 55+	9	91	1
Class: working	14	86	<½
· middle	19	81	0

How often, if at all, do you think that other people can tell what class you are by the way you speak?

%	all of the time	some of the time	rarely	never
All	27	39	13	12
Male	27	41	12	12
Female	26	38	15	13
Age: 16–34	25	45	14	10
· 35–54	25	44	13	12
· 55+	29	30	14	15

% agreeing with the statement	1991	2008	±%
There will never be a 'classless society' in Britain	79	68	−11
Britain has too many barriers based on social class	76	55	−21
You are much more likely to get to the top in this country if you've been to a private school	69	63	−6
If you want to get ahead it is important to talk with the right accent	59	44	−15
In this country the best people get to the top whatever start they've had in life	49	49	0
It is easy for people to move up from one social class to another	37	35	−2
I would be happier if I belonged to a different class	9	4	−5

[See ipsos-mori.com for full details; some 'don't knows' have been excluded for reasons of space.]

──────── OFF-STREET PROSTITUTION IN LONDON ────────

The scale of London's off-street sex industry was explored in an August 2008 report by the Poppy Project. Male researchers phoned 921 brothels across London's 33 boroughs and enquired about the women available, the services offered, and the prices charged. As the report notes, 'prime-time documentaries and dramas, such as *Secret Diary of a Call Girl* ... and *Respectable* customarily depict a glamorous, fun, and victimless off-street sex industry, but what is really going on in London's brothels?' Below are some of the findings from this disturbing report:

85% of brothels contacted were in a residential setting with a discreet appearance; 63% were in private flats, and 22% were located in a house. ❦ The average age of women offered by brothels was 21; ages given ranged from 18–55; numerous establishments offered 'young' girls or 'babyface' girls but refused to specify ages. ❦ 77 different nationalities and ethnicities of women were cited by the brothels surveyed. The ethnic origin of women offered by brothels is tabulated below:

Ethnicity	%		
Asia	30	Africa	6
N/W Europe	31	S America/	
S/E Europe	24	Caribbean	5
		Other	4

79% of brothels readily admitted to providing full, penetrative sex on-site.

Prices for full sex ranged from £15 to £250; the average price was £61·93. Prices for penetrative sex (vaginal or anal) without a condom started at £10 extra, up to a maximum of £200; the average price was £71·25. Only 2% of brothels admitted to providing penetrative sex without a condom. ❦ 13% of brothels said they offered oral sex without a condom; prices for oral sex without a condom ranged from £10 extra to £240 inclusive; the average price was £58·20. ❦ Over one-fifth of brothels offered kissing [traditionally considered taboo]. Prices ranged from £10–£600; the average price was £42·43. 52% offered kissing for only £10; only 11% of brothels charged more than £100.

18% of brothels were happy for stag parties to book group visits in advance.

──────────── HOMELESSNESS ────────────

According to the Government, the number of homeless households in England peaked in 2003/04, 'and since then have more than halved, with year on year reductions'. The latest English data show that 15,680 applicants were accepted as homeless by local authorities during Apr–Jun 2008, and 74,690 households were in temporary accommodation on 30/6/08. Welsh data show that 1,694 households were accepted as homeless during Jan–Mar 2008, and 2,880 households were in temporary accommodation on 30/3/08. In Scotland, 28,376 applications of homelessness were made during Apr–Sep 2007, and 8,633 households were in temporary accommodation on 31/12/07. ❦ However, given recent economic conditions, these figures are likely to rise. In June 2008, Shelter reported that 6m householders in Britain are suffering stress or depression because of housing costs; 400,000 are falling behind with their rent or mortgage; 4·1m have used a credit card to pay their housing costs; and 1m households spend >66% of their income on housing.

———————— FOOD WASTE & EXCESS PACKAGING ————————

6·7m tonnes of food are wasted by UK households every year, at a cost to the average family of £420, according to a May 2008 study by environmental group WRAP. About one-third of the 21·7m tonnes of food we purchase each year ends up in the bin – an issue Gordon Brown picked up on in July 2008 when he urged Britons to waste less food. 61% of food thrown away is avoidable waste – i.e., food that would have been edible had it been stored properly. Unavoidable waste (e.g., tea bags, vegetable peelings, &c.) constitutes 19% of disposed food. Potatoes are the type of food (by weight) most likely to be wasted; 359,000 tonnes of the tuber are binned each year. Below are the top five foods thrown away by weight and cost:

Foods most wasted by weight	*Foods most wasted by cost*
[1] potatoes [2] bread slices [3] apples [4] meat or fish mixed meals [5] world breads (e.g., naan, ciabatta)	[1] meat or fish mixed meals [2] world breads [3] bread slices [4] apples [5] potatoes

It was also reported that 45% of all salad purchased, 31% of all bakery goods, and 26% of all fruits was binned. WRAP advised that better food management could prevent much of this waste. Below are the reasons given for throwing food away:

Reason for disposal	% weight of all food waste	% cost of all food waste	weight per year (tonnes)	cost £m/year
Inedible	36·5	34·7	2,445,600	5,020
Left on plate	15·7	17·1	1,051,900	2,480
Out of date	15·1	18·9	1,011,700	2,740
Mouldy	9·3	7·2	623,100	1,040
Looked bad	8·8	6·5	589,600	940
Smelt/tasted bad	4·5	4·9	301,500	710
Left over from cooking	4·0	3·7	268,000	540
Other	3·8	4·6	254,600	670
In fridge/cupboard too long	1·5	1·4	100,500	200
Not specified	0·5	0·5	33,500	70
Freezer burn	0·3	0·4	20,100	60
ALL FOOD WASTE	100	100	6,700,200	14,480

71% of people in England are recycling more than in 2001, and 65% are wasting less food, according to a 2007 Defra survey, suggesting that food and packaging are of high concern. However, a May 2008 report by the Local Government Association indicated that supermarkets are failing to curb excess packaging. Researchers bought the same selection of goods from six supermarkets, a local trader, and a market, and compared the weight of packaging and the proportion that could be recycled:

Retailer	weight (g)	% recyclable			
Lidl	813	62	Local shop	687	74
M&S	807	62	Tesco	667·5	65
Sainsbury	746	70	Asda	646	69
Morrisons	726	67	Market	617	76

[see also pp.16–17]

—————————————— A8 MIGRANTS ——————————————

Britain introduced the Worker Registration Scheme (WRS) after the 8 new Eastern European countries (A8) joined the EU in 2004. It was designed to ensure that migrating workers from these relatively poor states were self-sufficient and would not overwhelm the benefits system. 508,487 A8 workers registered under the WRS between May 2004 and December 2006. Registered workers can claim basic benefits, such as tax credits, but cannot access social security benefits until they have worked for at least 12 months. Below are National Statistics figures, released in October 2007, which illustrate the number of migrants from each A8 member state:

A8 country	number of migrants	% of all A8 migrants	top destination (local authority)
Poland	327,538	64·4	Gedling, East Midlands
Lithuania	54,529	10·7	Castle Morpeth, North-east
Slovakia	51,736	10·2	S Oxfordshire, South-east
Latvia	28,810	5·7	Eilean Siar, Scotland
Czech Republic	24,650	4·8	Orkney Islands, Scotland
Hungary	15,312	3·0	Great Yarmouth, East
Estonia	5,441	1·1	Nuneaton, West Midlands
Slovenia	450	0·1	Derbyshire Dales, East Mid.

[Source: Population Trends 129] In June 2008 the *Sun* produced a special Polish language edition of the paper for Euro 2008. The *Polski Sun* included Polish news, sports, and a Polish page 3 stunner.

————————— ATTITUDES TO IMMIGRATION —————————

59% of people thought there were too many immigrants in Britain, according to an April 2008 survey by Ipsos MORI. Other results from the immigration poll include:

Would you describe yourself as: %
Very racially prejudiced 3
A little racially prejudiced 17
Not prejudiced at all 79
Don't know/refused 1

Parts of this country don't feel like GB any more because of immigration: %
Agree 58
Disagree 38
Don't know/refused 4

Should govt. encourage immigrants to return to their country of origin? %
Should 49
Should not 43
Don't know/refused 8

There are too many immigrants in GB:
Strongly agree 33
Tend to agree 26
Neither agree/disagree 11
Tend to disagree 14
Strongly disagree 12
Don't know/refused 4

Is there tension in GB between people of different races & nationalities? %
A great deal 24
A fair amount 52
Not very much 18
None at all 4
Don't know/refused 2

[see ipsos-mori.com for further details]

———————————— PUBLIC TRUST ————————————

An Ipsos MORI/BBC survey in January 2008 found varying degrees of trust in a range of organisations, including the media, government, and the military:

% most trusted		least trusted %	
50	BBC	7	
47	National Health Service	15	
36	Church of England	15	

29	military	16	
14	media	44	
10	government	65	
9	big companies	35	

Newspaper readers were asked how much they trusted their paper of choice to tell them the truth; below are the levels of trust reported by readers of various titles:

Guardian	94%	*Express* (inc. *Sunday*)	62%
Telegraph (inc. *Sunday*)	93%	*Mirror* (inc. *Sunday*)	55%
Times (inc. *Sunday*)	89%	*News of the World*	31%
Daily Mail (inc. *Sunday*)	67%	*Sun*	29%

The survey revealed that 83% of people questioned *disagreed* with the statement 'In general, I tend to trust politicians', stating the following reasons for distrust:

Reason	%		
Don't tell the truth	31	Say what we want to hear	12
Don't deliver on promises	22	Evasive/no straight answers	10
Work for their own ends	17	Have own agenda	7
		Corrupt	6

The same survey found that 24% believed the death of Princess Diana was a conspiracy rather than an accident; 30% believed that evidence of UFO landings was being hidden from the public; and 6% believed that 'US radicals' rather than foreign terrorists were responsible for 9/11.

In another Ipsos MORI survey, commissioned by the Royal College of Physicians in March 2008, doctors topped the poll of most trusted professionals[†]. Those polled were asked whether they believed the following professions told the truth:

Profession (%)	Yes	No	d/k
Doctors	90	6	4
Teachers	86	9	5
Professors	78	10	12
Judges	78	14	8
Clergy/priests	73	17	10
Scientists	65	22	13
TV newsreaders	61	27	12
Police	59	31	10
Person in the street	52	33	15

Pollsters	45	32	22
Civil servants	44	43	13
Trade union officials	38	45	17
Business leaders	26	62	11
Govt ministers	22	71	8
Journalists	18	75	7
Politicians	18	76	6

† Top since the poll began in 1983, although in 1993, doctors shared first place with teachers.

The Edelman Trust Barometer 2008 revealed that trust in the media was comparatively low in the UK. When asked 'how much do you trust media to do what is right?', only 38% of those in the UK responded positively, compared to 45% of Americans, 53% of Japanese, and 65% of Indians.

———————————CHILDREN & ALCOHOL———————————

In response to growing concerns about teenagers and alcohol, in May 2008 the government announced proposals to provide parents with guidance on how much alcohol children can safely be given. The plans were created in an effort to encourage teens to drink more responsibly. Research by Ipsos MORI for Ofcom in Nov 2007 revealed that in fact the majority of 11–17-year-olds never or infrequently drink alcohol. Respondents were asked to classify their drinking habits thus:

Never   *I have never drunk alcohol*
Infrequent drinker   *I have only tried alcohol once or twice/I have an alcoholic drink*
                              on special occasions such as birthdays, Christmas or New Year
Occasional drinker   *I sometimes have alcohol but not >2 or 3 times a month*
Regular drinker   *I have an alcoholic drink once or twice a week/I have an alcoholic*
                              drink 3 or 4 times a week/I have an alcoholic drink every day

Age	never		infrequent	occasional	regular
♀11–13	47		46		3 3
♂11–13	45		49		3 4
♀14–17	17	37	23	23	
♂14–17	17	32	26	25	
♀18–21	6	14	21	59	
♂18–21	8	14	12	66	

The locations at which young people had drunk alcohol in the last 6 months:

% by location	age: 11–13	14–17	18–21
With parents	66	44	32
With meal	11	24	48
At home without parents	11	40	49
At a party	4	36	56
In a public place	6	25	18
In a bar, pub, or club	3	25	78

Although alcopops have declined in popularity with teenagers since 2005, more young people are now drinking cider. The most popular brand of alcohol was Fosters – which 36% of respondents mentioned by name. The alcopop WKD was the second most mentioned drink (35%), followed by Carling lager (32%). Alcohol consumption (in the last 6 months, 2005 & 2007), by category and age, is below:

Age	11–13		14–17		18–21	
Drink (%)	2005	2007	2005	2007	2005	2007
Any beer	38	47	55	65	67	71
Any alcopop	53	37	76	62	69	61
Any cider	3	9	14	30	11	31

[Source: Ofcom: Young People and Alcohol Advertising report · November 2007] In a separate 2005 study by Ipsos MORI, 27% of teens said they had put themselves in danger when they were drunk.

———————ALCOHOL & UNITS———————

In May 2008, government statistics revealed that in 2007, 69% of people reported that they had heard of government guidelines on alcohol consumption, but of these, 40% admitted that they did not know what the guidelines were. The government recommends that men should not regularly consume more than 3–4 units of alcohol a day, and women not more than 2–3 units. If larger amounts than this are consumed, it is advisable not to drink alcohol for 48 hours to allow the body to recover. In England in 2006, 12% of men and 7% of women reported drinking every day in the previous week. The Department of Health produced the following list to show the number of units [1 unit = 10ml of pure alcohol] in common drinks:

Drink	example	units
Pint of ordinary strength lager	Carling Black Label, Fosters	2
Pint of strong lager	Stella Artois, Kronenbourg	3
Pint of ordinary bitter	John Smith's, Boddingtons	2
Pint of best bitter	Fuller's ESB, Young's special	3
Pint of ordinary strength cider	Woodpecker	2
Pint of strong cider	Dry Blackthorn, Strongbow	3
175ml glass of wine at 13%	–	2·3
Pub measure of spirits	–	1
Alcopop	Smirnoff Ice, Bacardi Breezer	1·5

———————SMOKING WORLDWIDE———————

There are more than 1 billion smokers in the world, according to a February 2008 report on tobacco usage released by the World Health Organization (WHO). The WHO found that 80% of the world's smokers currently reside in low or middle income countries, and ⅔ of the world's smokers live in one of the 10 countries below:

	% adults who smoke				
	♂	♀		♂	♀
China	57	3	US	28	19
India	33	1	Japan	43	12
Indonesia	63	5	Brazil	20	13
Russian Federation	60†	16†	Bangladesh	41	2
			Germany	33	22
			Turkey	52	17

The report also noted the price of cigarettes in each of the countries listed above:

China	$1·92	Japan	$2·46	[Cost for a pack of 20 of the
India	$7·04	Brazil	$1·29	most popular brand, in inter-
Indonesia	$2·32	Bangladesh	$1·38	national dollars – which have
Russ. Fed.	$1·53	Germany	$5·01	the same purchasing power as
US	$3·89	Turkey	$4·31	a US dollar has domestically.]

The most affordable cigarettes are apparently to be found in Laos, where a pack of 20 costs just 22¢.
† Percentage who smoke daily; other information unavailable. Figures drawn from 2001–06 surveys.

———————————————— DRUGS CLASSIFICATION ————————————————

Home Secretary Jacqui Smith announced in May 2008 that cannabis would be re-reclassified as a Class B drug – a decision which attracted some criticism, since a recent review by the Advisory Council on the Misuse of Drugs recommended that cannabis remain at Class C. The Labour government had downgraded cannabis from Class B to C in 2004, but argued that the mental health problems associated with a stronger form of the drug (skunk) demanded a rethink. The current classes are:

CLASS A	CLASS B	CLASS C
Ecstasy, LSD, heroin, amphetamines (if prepared for injection), magic mushrooms, cocaine, crack	Amphetamines (e.g., speed), Methylphenidate (Ritalin), Pholcodine	Cannabis [sic], Ketamine tranquillisers, some painkillers, Gamma hydroxybutyrate (GHB)
MAXIMUM PENALTIES: *Possession*: Up to 7 years in prison, an unlimited fine, or both. *Dealing*: Up to life in prison, an unlimited fine, or both.	MAXIMUM PENALTIES: *Possession*: up to 5 years in prison, an unlimited fine, or both. *Dealing*: Up to 14 years in prison, an unlimited fine, or both.	MAXIMUM PENALTIES: *Possession*: Up to 2 years in prison, an unlimited fine, or both. *Dealing*: Up to 14 years in prison, an unlimited fine, or both.

———————————————— EXPENDITURE ON BENEFITS ————————————————

Expenditure on social protection benefits in real terms for 2005/06 is below:

Benefit	(£bn[†])	1995/96	2005/06	±
Old age and survivors[‡]		107·8	146·2	+38·4
Sickness, healthcare, & disability		87·4	129·7	+42·3
Family & children		22·3	20·4	–1·9
Housing		17·2	18·1	+0·9
Unemployment		13·9	8·4	–5·5
Other		1·5	2·3	+0·8

† adjusted to 2005/06 prices using the GDP market prices deflator. ‡ Survivors are those whose entitlement derives from their relationship to a deceased person, e.g., widows. [Source: ONS]

Comparative data for expenditure on social protection per head across the EU:

Country	PPS thousand per head[‡]		
Luxembourg	12·2	Italy	6·3
Sweden	8·8	Ireland	5·2
Netherlands	8·1	Spain	4·4
France	7·8	Poland	2·2
Germany	7·2	Latvia	1·2
UK	7·0		

‡ Purchasing power standard per inhabitant
[Source: Eurostat, figures for 2004]

—————————— HOSPITAL EPISODE STATISTICS ——————————

Described below are some common NHS procedures and diagnoses from 2006/07:

Procedure	% emergency	% male	average age	average stay
Cataract	0	40	74·6	1·3 day
Upper digestive tract	11	49	59·3	11·2 days
Heart (CABG†)	3	79	66·9	12·9 days
Heart (PTCA‡)	17	74	63·5	3·0 days
Hip replacement	33	34	73·1	11·3 days
Kidney transplant	56	62	43·1	13·2 days
Diagnosis (primary)				
Cancer & other neoplasms	11	49	60·9	7·8 days
Ischaemic heart disease	51	65	67·9	6·1 days
Influenza, pneumonia, &c.	78	50	56·2	6·8 days
Hernia	11	68	55·6	3·1 days
Head injuries	87	65	40·5	3·1 days

† Coronary artery bypass graft. ‡ Percutaneous transluminal coronary angioplasty.
[Source: Department of Health Hospital Episode Statistics 2006/07, published December 2007]

——————— INTERNATIONAL CLASSIFICATION OF DISEASES ———————

At least one new disease has been identified every year since the 1970s, according to the World Health Organization's 2007 world health report. The International Classification of Diseases (ICD) database provides a globally recognised method of identifying diseases and causes of death, and it facilitates the collection of health and morbidity figures that can be assessed and compared internationally. ❦ A method of classifying causes of death was first suggested in 1891 at the International Statistical Institute conference in Vienna. In 1893, medical statistician Jacques Bertillon presented his *Classification for Causes of Death*, and in 1900 this was expanded to include the classification of diseases. Since then, as medical knowledge has grown, so too has the list; in 2007 the ICD contained 12,420 codes representing a myriad of diseases and causes of death from TB to accidental drowning. ❦ Since 1948, the ICD has been the responsibility of the World Health Organization. The current edition (the 10th, and thus known as ICD-10) was approved by WHO member states in 1994, but is continuously under revision. Every disease or cause of death is given a code or a series of codes to represent each possible variant. For example, neoplasms (cancers) are currently described by codes C00–C97 and D00–D48. These are subdivided by body part or area affected, so that breast cancer is described by the codes C50–C50·9. Finally, an individual code describes the exact nature of each disease; C50·3, for example, relates to breast cancer affecting the lower-inner quadrant of breast. ❦ Additionally, since 1978 the WHO has maintained the International Classification of Health Interventions (ICHI), a system to measure 'the distribution and evolution of health interventions for statistical purposes'; and since 2001, it has maintained the International Classification of Functioning, Disability and Health (ICF), an international standard to measure health and disability.

──────── ACCESS TO NHS DENTISTS ────────

The shortage of NHS dentists is an escalating problem in the UK, according to a survey by the Commission for Patient and Public Involvement in Health (CPPIH) in October 2007. 45% of dentists questioned admitted that their surgery was not currently accepting new NHS patients, and 10% of patients reported that they were not registered with any dentist. The government introduced a new contract for dentists in April 2006, designed to make it easier for patients to access treatment, and understand NHS pricing. Despite this, 84% of dentists reported that they did not believe that the new dental contracts had made it easier for patients to get an NHS dental appointment. Further findings from the survey of dentists included:

Do you believe that NHS patients get the same quality of service as private?	*Do you believe the new dental contracts have affected the quality of care?*
It is better 3%	It is better 2%
It is the same......................45%	It is the same......................40%
It is worse 52%	It is worse 58%

Three standard charges for NHS dental treatment were introduced in April 2007:

Band 1 · £15·90	*covers examination, diagnosis, advice, scale & polish*
Band 2 · £43·60	*band 1 + treatment such as fillings, root canal, & tooth removal*
Band 3 · £194	*band 1 & 2 + crowns, dentures, or bridges*

According to the CPPIH survey, 24% of dentists did not think that this pricing of NHS treatment was easy to understand, and 54% of patients agreed. 73% of dentists reported they were aware of patients declining treatments because of the cost. Only 40% of patients said they thought NHS charges provided value for money. Of the >2,000 people questioned, 65% were existing NHS patients, 25% had a private dentist, and 10% were not registered with a dental surgery. Those not registered were asked why they had left their previous dental surgery:

Previous dentist went private	29%	Never been registered	9%
Recently moved house	25%	Unhappy with treatment received	8%
Previous dentist closed	10%	Other	20%

Respondents were asked why they were not registered with an NHS dentist:

No available dentists in area	35%	On a waiting list	13%
Don't know how to find dentist	22%	Other	30%

6% of those questioned admitted that they had self-medicated because they had been unable to get treatment from a dentist. Of those who had self-medicated, a number admitted they had pulled out their own teeth using pliers, and one revealed that they had filled their teeth using an ingenious (though ill-advised) mixture of Polyfilla and clove oil. One respondent utilised a screwdriver to scrape off troublesome plaque and another admitted they fixed a crown using superglue.

———————————HEALTH & THE GOVERNMENT———————————

Despite reported concerns about the 'nanny state', the majority of Britons would like government to encourage the public to lead a healthier life. 82% of those questioned for a BBC/ICM poll in June 2008 agreed that the government should do more to help people get off illegal drugs. Respondents were asked if they thought the government should become more or less involved with the following health issues:

Getting people to ...	% more	% less	Cut down on drinking	69	28
Give up smoking†	67	28	Eat more healthily	69	29
Lose weight	65	32	Get off illegal drugs	82	15

Despite this apparent desire for government intervention, not all respondents thought the NHS should pay for all treatments. Just 51% agreed that alcoholics should get free treatment, and only 64% thought smokers deserved treatment for lung cancer. However, 85% believed treatment for depression should be free.

† In the months preceding and following the smoking ban of July 2007, the number of people seeking NHS Stop Smoking Services rose by 22% compared with the same period in the previous year. Between April and December 2007, 234,060 people gave up smoking with the help of the NHS. A July 2008 Department of Health report into the impact of the smoking ban also found that 70% thought that creating smoke-free public spaces had had a positive effect on the nation's health.

———————————CLASSIFICATION OF BURNS———————————

Medics assess burns on the severity of damage to the skin, using three categories:

FIRST DEGREE *(superficial)*	SECOND DEGREE *(partial thickness)*	THIRD DEGREE *(full thickness)*
Top layer of skin damaged; skin is red & swollen. This is the most common type of burn; it usually heals in days leaving no scar.	Top & middle layers of skin are damaged; skin is dark red or purple and swollen, blistered, & weeping. Usually heals in 2–3 weeks leaving scarring.	All 3 layers of skin damaged; affected skin burnt away and tissue appears pale/blackened. Skin grafts usually needed to minimise scarring.

The extent of a burn is usually expressed as the proportion of the total body surface area which is affected. There are three methods commonly used to calculate this:

Palmar surface	*Wallace rule of nines*	*Lund & Browder chart*
Burns are assessed in proportion to the size of a palm (including fingers), which is *c*.0·8% of the total body surface area.	The body is divided into nine areas which are assessed individually. This is not accurate in children.	A standardised chart, used in most hospitals, which offers the most accurate assessment of burns in a controlled environment.

[Sources: NHS Direct, *BMJ*] Palmar and Wallace tend to be used for triage assessments in the field.

—————SOME HEALTH STORIES OF NOTE—————

{OCT 2007} · The National Institute for Health and Clinical Excellence (NICE) suggested that pregnant women might be able to drink up to 1·5 units of alcohol per day in the final 6 months of pregnancy without the risk of ill-effects to the foetus. This advice appeared to contradict government advice that pregnant women should avoid all alcohol. In March 2008, NICE recommended that pregnant women drink no alcohol during the first 3 months of pregnancy and, after this, only a maximum of 2 units once or twice a week. ❦ A review of >40 years of international research into the causes of cancer by World Cancer Research Fund indicated that those with a Body Mass Index (BMI) ≥25 were at greater risk of developing cancer; the study also advised against drinking alcohol and eating processed meats such as bacon. {NOV} · Those who mix alcohol and energy-drinks are twice as likely to be injured or come to harm, according to research conducted by Wake Forest University School of Medicine, N Carolina. The researchers suggested that those who combined alcohol with energy-drinks tended to indulge in more risky behaviour, since the latter masked the feelings of drunkenness caused by the former. {DEC} · A common chemical created by frying, roasting, or grilling food may double the risk of cancer in women, a University of Maastricht study found. The EU advised people to avoid eating burnt toast or golden brown chips. ❦ Researchers from Utrecht University suggested that it is possible to die from a broken heart, since the risk of death increases by up to a fifth in the month after the death of a loved one. {JAN 2008} · Moderate drinkers (consuming up to 14 drinks a week) have a lower risk of premature death than teetotallers or heavy drinkers, according to a 20-year study by the University of Southern Denmark. ❦ A Nottingham University study found that people whose index finger was shorter than their ring finger had a higher risk of getting osteoarthritis; the ratio of index to ring finger (known as 2D:4D) has also been associated with hormone levels, athletic prowess, and sexual orientation. ❦ A report by gastroenterology experts at Charité University Hospital, Berlin, warned that too much sugar-free chewing gum can cause severe weight loss and diarrhoea, due to some of the sweeteners used. ❦ The International Scientific Forum on Home Hygiene report found that greeting someone with a kiss on the cheek is more hygienic than a handshake [see p.13]. ❦ A team at the University of Auckland suggested that calcium supplements, often prescribed to older women to counter bone density loss, may increase the likelihood of heart attacks. ❦ A study by London's Institute of Cancer found that black women are more likely to develop breast cancer earlier than their white peers. ❦ A joint US–Swedish study funded by the Mobile Manufacturers Forum suggested that using a mobile phone just before going to bed was bad for your health, affecting sleep quality and causing headaches. ❦ An Oxford University team concluded that the contraceptive pill has prevented at least 100,000 deaths from ovarian cancer in the last 50 years. {FEB} · A study published in the online journal *Hypertension* suggested that drinking 500ml of beetroot juice daily could significantly reduce blood pressure. ❦ A study by

──────── SOME HEALTH STORIES OF NOTE cont. ────────

King's College, London, suggested that black pepper could provide a new treatment for the dermatological condition vitiligo, which causes skin to lose its pigment. Researchers found that piperine, the spicy flavour in black pepper, can stimulate pigmentation. ❧ Taking high doses of vitamin E supplements may increase the risk of lung cancer, according to a joint study published in the *American Journal of Respiratory & Critical Care Medicine*. ❧ A Hungarian study, published in the journal *Sleep*, concluded that heavy snorers were significantly more likely to suffer a stroke or heart attack. ❧ The Royal National Institute for Deaf People warned that young people should wear ear plugs when listening to loud music; 68% of young people reported hearing problems after a gig. ❧ A University of California, Berkeley, study suggested that a diet rich in folates can help produce healthy sperm. The study, published in *Human Reproduction*, found that men who ate a lot of folate (found in leafy green vegetables, fruit and pulses) had sperm with fewer abnormal chromosomes. ❧ A study by academics from the Paris School of Economics and the European Centre for Social Welfare Policy & Research suggested that people who believed in God were more content and more able to cope with setbacks such as divorce or unemployment [see p.294]. {APR} · The *Journal of the American Society of Nephrology* published a review of studies that indicated drinking extra water does not in fact have any notable benefits. ❧ A review of 54 studies by the Cochrane Collaboration indicated that many products designed to cut asthma attacks by eradicating dust mites (e.g.,

specialist vacuum cleaners and mattress covers) do not work. {MAY} · Research published in the *New England Journal of Medicine* concluded that smokers were more likely to give up if friends or family members were also giving up. ❧ French scientists writing in the *BMJ* warned that women taking oral HRT supplements could double their risk of blood clots. ❧ Research by *Which?* suggested some computer keyboards harbour more germs than a toilet seat. Of the 33 keyboards swabbed for the study, 4 were potential health hazards and 1 had 5 times as many germs as a toilet seat. {JUNE} · A study by the University of Buffalo indicated that those who 'bottle up' trauma may cope better than those who talk about it. The researchers studied people affected by 9/11 and found that those who had initially been unwilling to talk about the event were less likely to be adversely affected 2 years on. ❧ Researchers at Imperial College, London, suggested that the popular herbal remedy ginkgo biloba is not an effective treatment for dementia. The herbal extract is said to aid memory, but the study found no difference between those taking ginkgo and those taking a placebo. {JUL} · Research led by the Institute of Psychiatry at King's College London warned that those who smoke the strongest form of cannabis (skunk) may be at greater risk of psychosis. ❧ A study in the journal *Dementia and Geriatric Cognitive Disorders* suggested that eating high levels of soy products, such as tofu, could raise the risk of memory loss in older people. {AUG} · The World Cancer Research Fund reported that eating a fry-up every day raises the risk of contracting bowel cancer by 63%.

─────────────FOREIGN NATIONALS IN JAIL─────────────

In October 2007, the government admitted that two jails (Bullwood Hall and Canterbury) held *only* foreign national prisoners, re-igniting the debate over the repatriation of foreign criminals. Government figures from 2005 indicated that of 9,610 foreign prisoners, only 136 were repatriated. As of March 2008 there were 82,226 prisoners in England & Wales, of whom 11,371 were foreign nationals:

Origin of prisoners by region:		*Origin of prisoners by country:*	
Africa	3,421	Jamaica	1,227
Europe	3,237	Nigeria	1,117
Asia	2,120	Irish Republic	630
West Indies	1,492	Vietnam	462
Middle East	578	Poland	420
Central/South America	348	Somalia	418
North America	123	Pakistan	398
Oceania	51	China	398
Other	2	India	321

[Source: Ministry of Justice · Population in Custody, March 2008 · figures include those held under the Immigration Act 1971 (including those held in immigration removal centres)]

──── YOUNG PEOPLE'S VIEWS ON GUN & KNIFE CRIME────

29% of young people (<25) have been affected by gun and knife crime [see p.22], and 41% knew someone who had been affected, according to a National Children's Homes report published in April 2008. Other results from this survey include:

53% ....*thought giving 17–21-year-olds longer sentences would help reduce crime*
46..............*felt some music and violent computer games were influential in crime*
36...*were worried about gangs in their area*
45......................................*did not feel safe at any time in their community*
28...*felt very safe in their community*

────── PRISONERS RECONVICTED WITHIN 2 YEARS──────

Offence reconvicted within 2 years %		
Theft from vehicles	82	
Theft†	74	
Burglary	73	
Criminal/malicious damage	60	
Robbery	55	
Drugs possession/sml scale supply	48	
Violence		46
Fraud and/or forgery		39
Drink-driving offences		32
Drugs import, export, production, or supply		31
Sexual		18
Other		57

† Includes theft, handling of stolen goods, and theft of vehicles; excludes theft from vehicles. [Source: Ministry of Justice · England & Wales · Reconvicted within 2 years after being released in 2004]

———————WHOLE LIFE SENTENCES———————‡

During one week in February 2008, two men were given 'whole life' prison terms for multiple murders. Steve Wright was convicted of murdering 5 women in Ipswich in 2006, while Levi Bellfield was convicted of murdering 2 young women and the attempted murder of a third in SW London in 2003–04. In 2007, in response to a Freedom of Information request, the Home Office published the names of 31 of the 35 murderers then serving whole life sentences. The following list has been compiled from the Home Office information and a variety of other published sources:

Year of sentence Name	*Conviction*
2008.......Levi Bellfield........	*see above*
2008....... Steve Wright........	*see above*
2007........David Tiley	*2 murders*
2007.......Rahan Arshad	*4 murders*
2007......Kenneth Regan......	*5 murders*
2007....... Michael Smith	*1 murder*
2006...... Stephen McColl	*2 murders*
2006........Mark Martin........	*3 murders*
2006........David Morris.......	*4 murders*
2006....... John McGrady.......	*1 murder*
2006.....Viktor Dembovskis.....	*1 murder*
2006........Stephen Ayre..............	*rape*
2005........Glyn Dix..........	*1 murder*
2005.........Paul Glen ,,.. ..	*1 murder*
2005...... William Horncy	*5 murders*
2005...... Mark Hobson	*4 murders*
2005........Paul Culshaw.......	*1 murder*
2004........David Bieber........	*1 murder*
2004....... Philip Hegarty.......	*1 murder*
2004.....Andrzej Kunowski.....	*1 murder*
1996....... Peter Moore	*4 murders*
1995......Rosemary West....	*10 murders†*

1993.......Colin Ireland.......	*5 murders*
1992....... John Hilton	*2 murders/robbery*
1991......Malcolm Green.......	*1 murder*
1991......Reginald Wilson§.....	*1 murder*
1990.....Victor Castigador.....	*2 murders*
1989.....Anthony Arkwright....	*3 murders*
1988.........John Duffy.	*2 murders/5 rapes*
1988..... Anthony Entwistle.....	*1 murder*
1988.....Victor Miller........	*1 murder*
1986......Jeremy Bamber.......	*5 murders*
1984.....Arthur Hutchinson...	*3 murders*
1983...... Dennis Nilsen......	*6 murders*
1979......Robert Mawdsley....	*4 murders*
1979........John Childs ...,...	*6 murders*
1977.......Trevor Hardy.......	*3 murders*
1976 ....Donald Neilson	*4 murders*
1966.........Ian Brady ,.. ..	*3 murders‡*

The convictions listed above are those for which the whole life term was given; they do not include previous convictions. § Term reduced in May 2008 to 18 years, and increased to 30 years in July 2008. [Home Office, *Guardian*, *Times*, BBC]

† West was convicted with her husband Fred. He admitted to 12 murders but committed suicide while awaiting trial. ‡ Brady was convicted with his lover Myra Hindley, who died in prison in 2002.

———————OWNERSHIP OF HOME SECURITY DEVICES———————

	% owning security device	
British Crime Survey 2006–07	*victims of theft*	*all households*
Window locks	42	79
Double/deadlocks	40	75
Outdoor sensor/timer lights	18	40
Security chains on doors	19	32
Indoor sensor/timer lights	10	24
Window bars/grilles	4	3

———————————THE UK DNA DATABASE———————————

In February 2008, Suffolk serial murderer Steve Wright was captured as a result of Britain's DNA database, which is the largest in the world. Wright's details were on the database after his conviction for theft in 2003. Police found traces of his DNA on the bodies of some of the five women found murdered in Ipswich in 2006, and he was subsequently arrested and convicted [see p.117]. At the end of 2005, the database held over 3·4m DNA profiles, which represent 5·2% of the UK population. The % of the population on the DNA databases of various countries is as follows:

Country	% on database				
UK	5·24	Estonia	0·39	Czech Republic	0·08
EU	1·13	Finland	0·36	Denmark	0·06
Austria	0·98	Slovenia	0·29	Sweden	0·06
Switzerland	0·83	Canada	0·23	Netherlands	0·04
USA	0·50	Croatia	0·21	Belgium	0·03
Germany	0·41	Norway	0·15	Spain	0·01
		France	0·11	[Source: Home Office]	

45,000 crimes were matched to samples on the DNA database in 2005/06, including 422 homicides and 645 rapes. The police can take and retain DNA samples from anyone (over the age of ten) who has been arrested for a recordable offence and held in police custody. The sample can be kept even if the individual is not charged, or is acquitted of the offence. DNA samples are also taken from crime scenes. Below is the age distribution of those whose DNA has been entered into the National DNA Database, and the number of new samples entered each year since 1995:

Age	% of total sample on database	Year	samples added
Under 14	8	1995/96	35,668
15–24	41	1997/98	136,248
25–34	24	1999/2000	227,180
35–44	16	2001/02	507,099
45–54	7	2003/04	475,183
55–64	3	2004/05	508,663
>65	1	2005/06	715,239

80% of those on the DNA database are male; 82% are English; 6% Scottish; 5% Northern Irish; 5% Welsh; and 2% other. 76% are white-skinned Europeans. [Source: Home Office]

———————————SCOTLAND YARD'S MOST WANTED———————————

Fugitive	allegation		
Farouk Abdulhak	murder	Sukhdip Singh Chhina	murder
Ibrahim Adam	terrorism	Hayman Mustafa	murder
Lamine Adam	terrorism	James Walter 'Jimbles' Tomkins	murder
Saifullah 'Saffi' Siddiqi	murder	Youseff Ahmed Wahid	murder
Noel F. Cunningham	armed robbery	Daniel Milic	fraud
Ayub Khan	murder	Magdalena Zajdel	murder
		[Source: Scotland Yard; as at 19/9/2008]	

———————BRITISH CRIME SURVEY 2007/08———————

Overall crime in England and Wales fell by 9–10% between 2006/07–2007/08, though it was revealed that there were 22,151 offences involving knives during the period (knife crime has only been separately counted since April 2007) [see p.22]. ❦ The annual British Crime Survey (BCS) measures crime in England and Wales by interviewing people about crimes they have experienced in the past year, and their fear of crime. The BCS is widely seen as a useful partner to the police's recorded crime figures since, for a number of reasons, certain crimes often go unreported. Charted below are the changes in BCS and reported crimes from 2006/07–2007/08:

British Crime Survey	06/07–07/08	*Police Recorded Crime*	06/07–07/08
ALL BCS CRIME	↓10%	TOTAL RECORDED CRIME	↓9%
Violent crime	↓12%	Violence against the person	↓8%
Domestic burglary	*no change*	Sexual offences	↓7%
Vehicle-related theft	↓11%	Robbery	↓16%
Personal theft	*no change*	Domestic burglary	↓4%
Other household theft	↓12%	Offences against vehicles	↓14%
Vandalism	↓10%	Criminal damage	↓13%
Risk of being victim of crime	↓2%	Drug offences	↑18%

Although BCS crime has fallen since 1995, and people report increased confidence in the police and the criminal justice system, 65% perceive that there is more crime:

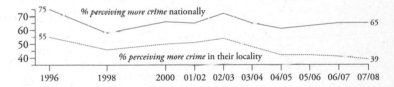

———————ANTI-SOCIAL BEHAVIOUR INDICATORS———————

Anti-social behaviour is defined by the Crime and Disorder Act (1998) as 'acting in a manner that caused or was likely to cause harassment, alarm, or distress to one or more person'. Respondents to the British Crime Survey were asked which of the following anti-social behaviours were a 'very/fairly big problem' in their area:

Anti-social behaviour problem (%)	2001/02	2003/04	2006/07
Teenagers hanging around on the streets	32	27	33
Rubbish or litter lying around	32	29	31
People using or dealing drugs	31	25	28
Vandalism, graffiti, &c.	34	28	28
People being drunk or rowdy in public places	22	19	26
Noisy neighbours or loud parties	10	9	11
Abandoned or burnt-out cars	20	15	9
High level of perceived anti-social behaviour	19	16	18

Media & Celebrity

One of the drawbacks of fame is that one can never escape from it.
— NELLIE MELBA (1861–1931)

HELLO! vs OK! COVER STARS

Date	Hello!	OK!
01·01·08	Wayne Rooney & Coleen McLoughlin	Jordan & Peter Andre
08·01·08	Brian McFadden & Delta Goodrem	Sarah Harding & Tom Crane
15·01·08	New Year Wedding Belles	Kerry Katona & baby
22·01·08	Prince William & Kate Middleton	Britney Spears
29·01·08	Princess Diana	Victoria Beckham
05·02·08	The Spice Girls	Cheryl Cole
12·02·08	Jemima Khan	Jordan
19·02·08	Kimberly & Ruby Stewart	Kian Egan & Jodi Albert
26·02·08	Christina Aguilera & baby	Assorted footballers' WAGs
04·03·08	The Oscars	Jordan & Harvey
11·03·08	Prince Harry	Victoria & David Beckham
18·03·08	Ulrika Jonsson & Brian Monet's wedding	Girls Aloud
25·03·08	Cheryl Cole	Kerry Katona
01·04·08	Suzanne Shaw	J-Lo & her twins, Max & Emme
08·04·08	Carla Sarkozy	Jordan
15·04·08	Brendan Cole & Zoe Hobbs	Sarah Harding & Tom Crane
22·04·08	Prince William & Kate Middleton	V. Beckham & Eva Longoria
29·04·08	Tim Jefferies & Malin Johansson's wedding	Jordan & family
06·05·08	Melinda Messenger	Kerry Katona & children
13·05·08	Peter Phillips & Autumn Kelly	Sheree Murphy & Harry Kewell
20·05·08	Girls Aloud	Mariah Carey & Nick Cannon
27·05·08	Peter Phillips & Autumn Kelly's wedding	Victoria Beckham
03·06·08	Geri Halliwell	Coleen McLoughlin
10·06·08	Prince William	Angelina Jolie
17·06·08	Girls Aloud	Jordan & Peter
24·06·08	Ulrika Jonsson & baby	Wayne Rooney & Coleen's wedding
01·07·08	Autumn Kelly	Wayne & Coleen's wedding party
08·07·08	Summer's hottest couples	Wayne & Coleen's honeymoon
15·07·08	Cheryl & Ashley Cole	Charlotte Church & Gavin Henson
22·07·08	Brad & Angelina	Matt Willis & Emma Griffiths's wedding
29·07·08	Jamie & Louise Redknapp	Victoria Beckham
05·08·08	Kate Middleton	Gareth Gates's wedding
12·08·08	Brad, Angelina & baby twins	Jordan & Princess Tiamii
19·08·08	Geri Halliwell	*Big Brother*'s Dale & Jen
26·08·08	Angelina Jolie	Britney Spears
02·09·08	Victoria Beckham	Coleen Rooney

SOME HATCHED, MATCHED, & DISPATCHED

HATCHED

Ruby Megan *to* .... Charlotte Church & Gavin Henson
James Alexander Philip Theo [Viscount Severn] *to* ..... Earl & Countess of Wessex
Harlow Winter Kate *to* .... Nicole Richie & Joel Madden
Max Liron *to* ....Christina Aguilera & Jordan Bratman
Max & Emme *to* ....Jennifer Lopez & Marc Anthony
Nahla Ariela *to* ....Halle Berry & Gabriel Aubry
Maxwell *to* ....Kerry Katona & Mark Croft
Ignatius Martin *to*................................ Cate Blanchett & Andrew Upton
Maddie Briann *to* .... Jamie Lynn Spears & Casey Aldridge
Sunday Rose *to*..................................... Nicole Kidman & Keith Urban
Knox Leon & Vivienne Marcheline *to* ....Angelina Jolie & Brad Pitt
Zuma Nesta Rock *to*............................. Gwen Stefani & Gavin Rossdale

MATCHED

Pamela Anderson & Rick Salomon .... Mirage Hotel, Las Vegas
Billie Piper & Laurence Fox.............................. Easebourne, West Sussex
Liam Gallagher & Nicole Appleton...........Marylebone Register Office, London
Sean Bean & Georgina Sutcliffe...............Marylebone Register Office, London
Beyoncé Knowles & Jay-Z (aka Shawn Carter)...........................New York
Mariah Carey & Nick Cannon...Bahamas
Wayne Rooney & Coleen McLoughlin ....Santa Margherita Ligure, Italy
Peaches Geldof & Max Drummey.......................................Las Vegas

DISPATCHED

Natalie Imbruglia & Daniel Johns *(married for 4 years)*....................divorcing
Pamela Anderson & Robert Ritchie *aka* 'Kid Rock' *(4 months)*............ divorced
Alecia Moore *aka* 'Pink' & Carey Hart *(2 years)*.........................separating
Kym & Jack Ryder *(5 years)*..separating
Pamela Anderson & Rick Salomon *(2 months)* .... annulled
Michelle Heaton & Andy Scott-Lee *(18 months)*........................separating
Matt Lucas & Kevin McGee *(18 months)*...............................separating

TOP CELEBRITY TOTS

Below is *Forbes* magazine's December 2007 list of the most influential celebrity
infants (aged 5 and under) – as assessed by web presence and press clippings:

1 .... Shiloh Jolie-Pitt	6 .... Sam Alexis Woods†
2 .... Suri Holmes-Cruise	7 = ... David Banda Ritchie
3 .... Zahara Jolie-Pitt	7 = ...Dannielynn Hope‡
4 .... Sean Preston Federline	9 = ...Romeo Beckham
5 .... Pax Jolie-Pitt	9 = ... Cruz Beckham

† Daughter of Tiger Woods & wife Elin. ‡ Daughter of Anna Nicole Smith & Larry Birkhead.

——— IACGMOOH ———

The 7th series of *I'm a Celebrity ... Get Me Out of Here* had a curious start when Malcolm McLaren quit the show before even getting to the jungle. Media interest focused on the romance between Cerys Matthews and Marc Bannerman, but Christopher Biggins was eventually crowned *King of the Jungle*. The 'celebs' left in the following order:

11th	Marc Bannerman
10th	Katie Hopkins
9th	Lynne Franks
8th	John Burton Race
7th	Rodney Marsh
6th	Anna Ryder Richardson
5th	Gemma Atkinson
4th	Cerys Matthews
3rd	Jason 'J' Brown
2nd	Janice Dickinson
WINNER	Christopher Biggins

QUOTES OF NOTE

JOHN BURTON RACE on JANICE DICKINSON · She's a bonkers, mental, outspoken, loud, camera-hogging diva, but I like it a lot. ❦ RODNEY MARSH · (when asked by Ant & Dec if he wanted to stay in the jungle) I'd rather chew on a broken light bulb. ❦ CERYS MATTHEWS · I'm always Jane looking for a Tarzan. ❦ CHRISTOPHER BIGGINS (on winning) · I'm really, really shocked and thrilled. Thank you, Great Britain.

——— BIG BROTHER 9 ———

Viewing figures for *BB9* were down, but the 5·3m who watched the finale ensured it remained one of Channel 4's top-rated shows. Trainee teacher Rachel Rice beat favourite Mikey Hughes to win the £100,000 prize and a few seconds of fame. The housemates were evicted (or ejected) in the following order:

Eviction order		
21	Stephanie	12 .... Luke
20	Alexandra	11 .... Dale
	(ejected)	10 .... Stuart
19	Dennis	9 .... Nicole
	(ejected)	8 .... Lisa
18	Sylvia	7 .... Mohamed
17	Jennifer	6 .... Kathreya
16	Mario	5 .... Darnell
15	Belinda	4 .... Rex
14	Rebecca	3 .... Sara
13. Maysoon (left)		2 .... Mikey
		Winner RACHEL

QUOTES OF NOTE

❦ LISA · I'll get a job as a weather girl when I get out of here! ❦ KATHREYA · There's so much time to think! Outside we got so many things to do, then we turn on TV and forget! ❦ REX · It takes the strongest of housemates to be in hell with no hair straighteners! ❦ SARA · I can't imagine anyone voting for me! ❦ RACHEL · You dream about going into *Big Brother*, that's like a dream! And people say you'll never get in! And then when you win, it's amazing!

——— BRITAIN'S BEST DRESSED MEN ———

The May 2008 edition of *GQ* featured 50 of the nattiest dressers; the top 10 were:

1 .... Daniel Craig	6 .... David Beckham	4 Royal family members were
2 .... Noel Fielding	7 .... Jude Law	in the *GQ* list: Prince Harry at
3 ..... Daniel Day-Lewis	8 .... David Cameron	12, Prince Charles at 25, the
4 .... James McAvoy	9 .. David de Rothschild	Duke of Edinburgh at 33, and
5 .... Tom Ford	10 .... David Furnish	Prince Michael of Kent at 34.

VANITY FAIR'S HOLLYWOOD · 2008

The stars featured on the cover of the 2008 *Vanity Fair* 'Hollywood issue' were:

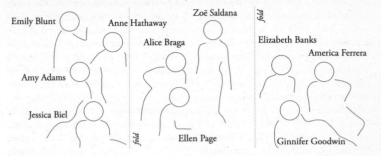

The 2007 cover stars were: Ben Stiller, Owen Wilson, Chris Rock, Jack Black, and some penguins.

THE BRITNEY INDUSTRY

The soap opera that is Britney Spears's life continued to fascinate the media throughout 2008, and in its February issue, *Condé Nast Portfolio* estimated that the annual value of the 'Britney industry' could be as much as $120m (*c.*£60m). Below are some aspects of what *Portfolio* described as the 'Britney Industrial Complex':

Sale of 83m records since her debut album in 1999 .... >$400m
Ticket sales on her tours.. $150m
Fee for a Britney appearance .... $250,000–$400,000
Sales of Britney's 3 perfumes: *Believe*, *Curious*, and *Fantasy* $100m
Paparazzi photos of Britney (average shot fetches $250–$100,000) $4m
Celebrity magazine covers.................................... 33% addition to sales

In January, the Rambert Dance Company premiered *Meltdown*, a ballet about Spears, in London.

SEXIEST MEN & WOMEN 2008

FHM's 'sexiest' women		*Interwomen.co.uk's* 'sexiest' men
Megan Fox	1	Colin Firth
Jessica Alba	2	Jude Law
Keeley Hazell	3	David Tennant
Elisha Cuthbert	4	Brad Pitt
Hayden Panettiere	5	Keanu Reeves
Scarlett Johansson	6	Chris Evans (US actor, not the ginger DJ)
Cheryl Cole	7	Johnny Depp
Hilary Duff	8	Wentworth Miller
Angelina Jolie	9	David Beckham
Keira Knightley	10	John Cusack

─────────── CELEBRITY CAUSES ───────────

Raising money for, and awareness of, various causes has long been an obligatory component of Hollywood celebrity, and the trend showed no sign of abating in 2008. Below are some celebrities of note, and a selection of the causes they support:

Angelina Jolie ...... Goodwill Ambassador for UNHCR; Education Partnership for
       Children of Conflict; Global Action for Children; Daniel Pearl Foundation
Brad Pitt..................Make It Right [rebuilding the Lower Ninth Ward in New Orleans]
Leonardo DiCaprio...........Leonardo DiCaprio Foundation [environmental issues]
Oprah Winfrey...................... Angel Network [awards grants to build schools, &c.]
Madonna....................................Raising Malawi Orphan Care Initiative
George Clooney...................................UN Messenger of Peace for Darfur
Bono.........(RED)[†]; ONE Campaign [AIDS, poverty]; DATA [Debt, AIDS, Trade, Africa]
Michael J. Fox.............The Michael J. Fox Foundation for Parkinson's Research
Tyra Banks .... TZONE Foundation [female self-empowerment]
Denis Leary .... Leary Firefighters Foundation [funding for equipment &c.]
Ellen DeGeneres.......American Society for the Prevention of Cruelty to Animals
Hilary Duff......................Kids With a Cause, Inc. [teaching philanthropy to kids]
Jon Bon Jovi....... Philadelphia Soul Charitable Foundation [poverty & homelessness]
Teri Hatcher...Make a Wish Foundation
Ashley Judd .... Population Services International [HIV/AIDS]
Nicole Kidman........US Committee for the UN Development Fund for Women
Bette Midler... New York Restoration Project
Jessica Simpson .... Operation Smile [corrective facial surgery]
Rosie O'Donnell............................ For All Kids Foundation [children in need]
Kanye West...............Kanye West Foundation [encouraging high school graduation]
Reese Witherspoon .... UN Trust to End Violence Against Women
Salma Hayek .... One Pack = One Vaccine [inoculations against tetanus]

[Sources: Sixdegrees.org, LooktotheStars.org.] † Since January 2006, (RED)-branded products from Gap, Armani, Apple, Motorola, Converse, Hallmark, American Express, and Dell have appeared on store shelves, in TV ads, and splashed on billboards in major cities. The initiative, co-founded by Bono, funnels a portion of the profits from these red-hued products towards the Global Fund to Fight AIDS, Tuberculosis, and Malaria. However, some have expressed concern as to whether the extensive advertising for (RED) products may, in the final analysis, cost more than the project is able to raise.

─────── MOST-HATED & MOST-LOVED CELEBS ───────

The most-loved/hated celebs according to a May '08 survey by *Marketing* magazine:

Most hated celebrity	%	*Most loved celebrity*	%
Heather Mills	28	Paul McCartney	15
Amy Winehouse	11	Lewis Hamilton	11
Victoria Beckham	10	Gary Lineker	11
Kerry Katona	10	Simon Cowell	10
Simon Cowell	5	David Beckham	9

—————— CELEBRITY INTRIGUE ——————

{OCT 2007} · Britney Spears lost shared custody of her 2 young sons to ex-husband Kevin Federline. ❦ Amy Winehouse was arrested and held overnight in Norway for alleged possession of cannabis; she was released after paying a £350 fine. {NOV} · Heather Mills appeared on TV to complain about her treatment by the press; she told GMTV, 'They've called me a whore, a gold-digger, a fantasist, a liar, the most unbelievably hurtful things, and I've stayed quiet for my daughter'. Her PR adviser later stepped down after advising her against 'attacking newspapers'. ❦ After a shambolic performance on the opening night of her tour, Winehouse cancelled her remaining dates on doctor's orders. She said she was unable to perform while her husband Blake Fielder-Civil was in custody charged with attempting to pervert the course of justice. ❦ The RSPCA condemned Madonna for dyeing a flock of sheep on her country estate blue, pink, yellow, and green for a *Vogue* photo-shoot. {DEC} · Kiefer Sutherland, star of the hit TV series *24*, was given a 48-day jail sentence for drink-driving. ❦ Comedian Alan Davies apologised after being accused of biting a homeless man's ear during a scuffle outside the Groucho Club. ❦ Jodie Foster 'came out' as a lesbian, paying tribute to her girlfriend of 14 years at an awards ceremony; it was reported in May 2008 that the couple had split. ❦ Winehouse was arrested in connection with an investigation into perverting the course of justice; the police later said that no further action would be taken. {JAN

Amy Winehouse

> *I've had worse press than a paedophile or a murderer and I've done nothing but charity for 20 years.* – HEATHER MILLS

2008} · Britney Spears was taken into police custody on a stretcher after a dispute involving custody of her 2 sons; her former husband Kevin Federline was later given sole custody. {FEB} · The Spice Girls cut short their reunion world tour blaming 'family and personal commitments', amidst denied rumours of tensions between members of the group. ❦ {MAR} · Michael Jackson refinanced his Neverland ranch a week before it was due to be sold at auction. ❦ Heather Mills was awarded £24·3m in a divorce settlement from Paul McCartney, ending months of public acrimony and speculation. ❦ {APR} · Supermodel Naomi Campbell was arrested on suspicion of assaulting a police officer after a row on a BA flight at Heathrow. ❦ Singer Pete Doherty was sentenced to 14 weeks in jail for using drugs and violating his probation. ❦ Hollywood star Wesley Snipes was jailed for 3 years for $15m tax evasion. {MAY} · 15-year-old Disney star Miley Cyrus attracted numerous negative column inches after appearing semi-topless in a Annie Leibovitz shoot for *Vanity Fair*. Cyrus apologised to her fans saying, 'I took part in a photo shoot that was supposed to be "artistic" ... I feel so embarrassed'. {JUN} · American comedienne Joan Rivers was thrown off the live TV show *Loose Women* after insulting Russell Crowe. ❦ Naomi Campbell was sentenced to 200 hours of community service after assaulting 2 police officers. {AUG} · Ex-Atomic Kitten singer Kerry Katona was made bankrupt after failing to pay £82,000 of a £417,000 tax bill.

CELEBRITY QUOTES

KATHERINE HEIGL (to *Eve*) · I satisfy my vices instead of fighting them. Mostly just the smoking. Well. There's the drinking and cursing. ❦ EVA LONGORIA PARKER (to the *Daily Mail*) · I was very dark, scrawny and the only one in my family with black hair. I hated it. ❦ NICOLE KIDMAN (to *Vogue*) · You're either going to walk through life and experience it fully or you're going to be a voyeur. And I'm not a voyeur. ❦ JAMES MCAVOY (to *Details*) · I think inside all actors there's a kid who secretly yearns to jump off buildings and say 'Yippeekayay, motherfucker!' ❦ ANGELINA

Paris Hilton

JOLIE (to *Vanity Fair*) · It's very easy to get married, but it's not easy to build a family and be parents together. ❦ AMY WINEHOUSE (to *Rolling Stone*) · I'm young, and I'm in love, and I get my nuts off sometimes. ❦ ZAC EFRON (to *Details*) · I don't feel like I deserve any of the attention. There's really nothing but one audition for a Disney Channel movie that separates me from 2,000 other brown-haired, blue-eyed guys in L.A. ❦ JENNIFER LOVE HEWITT (on her blog, after comments on bikini photos) · A size 2 is not fat! Nor will it ever be. And being a size 0 doesn't make you beautiful. ❦ RENÉE ZELLWEGER (to *Harper's Bazaar*) · It's weird to have fame precede you in any situation ... and I'm very proud of myself that I've not been to Betty Ford yet ... never say never! ❦ JANET JACKSON (to *Extra*) · You don't know how many people come up to me and say, 'This child was conceived listening to you'. ❦ CHRISTIAN BALE (to *GQ*) · Quite frequently, I've been talking to somebody, telling a story, and then I realise halfway through, This didn't happen ... After a few years, you can't differentiate between the clarity of something you've played and a real event. ❦ VICTORIA BECKHAM (to *Elle*) · It became very obvious from the start that I was never going to be the best singer or the best dancer or the best actress. I was never a 'natural'... I've never been that good at anything, to be completely honest. ❦ LINDSAY LOHAN (on nude *New York* magazine photos) · I didn't have to put much thought into it. I mean, Bert Stern? Doing a Marilyn shoot? When is that ever going to come up? ❦ PARIS HILTON (in Johannesburg, in *People*) · I love Africa in general: South Africa and West Africa, they are both great countries. ❦ SCARLETT JOHANSSON (to AP) · I am engaged ... to Barack Obama. My heart belongs to Barack! ❦ ANG LEE (to AP) · Working with Heath [Ledger] was one of the purest joys of my life [see p.62]. ❦ MILEY CYRUS (on her controversial *Vanity Fair* photos, to *Good Morning America*) · Anyone who was 15 years old can't say they haven't made a mistake. ❦ GUY RITCHIE (quoted by the *Daily Mirror*) · Think of the calories in sugar. Fat kills more people than anything else. Sugar is responsible for a lot of deaths, arguably more than crack cocaine. ❦ SHARON STONE (in the *Guardian*, on China's Tibet policies [see p.38]) · Then all this earthquake ... happened, and I thought, is that karma? When you're not nice, that the bad things happen to you? ❦ KEIRA KNIGHTLEY (to *Tatler*) · Not going to university did give me an incredible driving force because it leaves you with a slight chip on your shoulder. It makes me feel I am going to read absolutely everything so I can prove I am not stupid. ❦

MOST-DESIRED CELEB FEATURES

Each year, plastic surgeons Toby G. Mayer and Richard W. Fleming poll their *c.*1,500 clients at the Beverly Hills Institute of Aesthetic & Reconstructive Surgery about the celebrity features they consider to be the most desirable. The 2008 list:

Feature	most desirable ♀	most desirable ♂
Nose	*Katherine Heigl, Amy Adams, Nicole Kidman*	*Leonardo DiCaprio, Heath Ledger, Jake Gyllenhaal*
Eyes	*Katie Holmes, Megan Fox, Ellen Pompeo*	*Daniel Craig, Brad Pitt, Justin Timberlake*
Lips	*Angelina Jolie, Jessica Alba, Scarlett Johansson*	*Matt Damon, Nick Lachey, John Mayer*
Jaw/chin	*Carrie Underwood, Tyra Banks, Jennifer Love-Hewitt*	*Christian Bale, Will Smith, Ben Affleck*
Body	*Jessica Biel, Beyoncé, Charlize Theron*	*David Beckham, Hugh Jackman, Matthew McConaughey*

HOLLYWOOD'S WORST-DRESSED WOMEN

Designer Richard Blackwell has compiled a 'Worst Dressed Celebrity List' every year since 1960. In 2007, Victoria Beckham topped the list for wearing 'one skinny-mini monstrosity after another'; Amy Winehouse was described as 'exploding beehives above, tacky polka-dots below'; and Blackwell dismissed actress Mary-Kate Olsen as 'a tattered toothpick trapped in a hurricane'. Below are his worst-dressed of 2007:

1 ..... Victoria Beckham	5 .... Kelly Clarkson	9 .... Lindsay Lohan
2 ...... Amy Winehouse	6 .... Eva Green	10 ...... Alison Arngrim
3 ..... Mary-Kate Olsen	7 .... Avril Lavigne	† The singer, not the former
4 .... Fergic†	8 .... Jessica Simpson	Royal, or Man Utd manager.

CELEBRITY DRUG ABUSE

In a detailed, 120-page 2007 analysis of the global drug trade, the UN's International Narcotics Control Board (INCB) included an unexpected comment on celebrity drug abuse. Noting that 'celebrity drug offenders can profoundly influence public attitudes, values, and behaviour towards drug abuse', the INCB recommended that criminal justice authorities 'should ensure that public celebrities who violate drug laws are made accountable for their offences', arguing that 'cases involving drug-abusing celebrities who are treated more leniently than others breed public cynicism and may lead to youth adopting a more permissive attitude towards illicit drugs'.

In March 2008, Tim Martin, chairman of JD Wetherspoon pubs, suggested that disorderly behaviour in pubs may be linked to 'examples of poor behaviour by a number of celebrities' during events like the Brits and the 2005 Ashes celebrations. Martin noted that the drunken antics of celebrities were 'frequently replicated by the general public during birthday parties, stag and hen parties, and so on'.

RADIO 4 & THE MIDDLE CLASSES

The staid world of Radio 4 was ruffled in February 2008 when the new presenter of *Woman's Hour*, Jane Garvey, suggested that the station had a limited class and age focus. Speaking to the *Guardian*, Garvey said, 'I think there is a massively middle-class bent to every programme on Radio 4. Find me a programme that isn't like that'. And she added, 'The idea of Radio 4 existing in 25, 30 years' time, I don't know. My daughter has no channel loyalty and whether that generation of children will take to radio, God knows'. ❦ Garvey's comments touched a nerve within the media and the BBC. While praising his new presenter, the controller of Radio 4 Mark Damazer said, 'The stereotypes about class may lurk in the collective consciousness – and are applied to Radio 4 by some who don't listen, or for whom Radio 4's wildly eclectic mix is too demanding to describe properly. But, in reality, the middle-class audience to Radio 4 is fabulously varied'. ❦ To the right are the results of a *Schott's Almanac*/Ipsos Mori poll on this subject from March 2008 [see p.102]:

How often do you listen to Radio 4?

%	all or some of the time	rarely or never
All	30	70
Male	33	67
Female	28	72
Age: 16–34	20	80
· 35–54	28	72
· 55+	41	59
Class: working	21	79
· middle	42	58
Read: tabloid	23	77
· broadsheet	54	46
Region: North	27	73
· South	34	66
· Midlands	30	70

Of all those who have ever listened: *To what extent do you agree or disagree that Radio 4 is too middle class?*

%	All	♂	♀
Agree	24	27	23
Neither	11	10	13
Disagree	53	55	50
Don't know	11	9	14

TV LICENCE EVASION

TV Licensing caught more than 413,000 people watching their televisions without a licence in 2007, an increase of more than 20,000 on 2006. Those who fail to buy a licence risk prosecution and a fine of up to £1,000 (plus legal costs). London led the league of most-offending cities; the worst 10 cities in Britain are listed below:

City	2007 evaders
London†	35,191
Glasgow	21,715
Birmingham	10,417
Manchester	8,427
Liverpool	8,168
Edinburgh	7,158
Belfast	6,251
Bristol	5,658
Nottingham	5,428
Hull	5,206

† Some London boroughs have more evaders than entire cities (e.g., Newham *vs* Cardiff).

In April 2008, TV licence fees went up. The fee for a black and white licence (34,700 of which are issued) rose from £45·50 to £47. The price of a colour licence rose from £135·50 to £139·50. Those aged >75 are entitled to a free TV licence. Second homeowners need a licence for each residence.

─────────── THE INFLUENCE OF THE MEDIA ───────────

A January 2008 survey by Ipsos MORI revealed the perceived power of the media. The public were asked: Thinking of what affects and influences society and people's day to day lives in Britain, which of the following has the most powerful influence?

TV/radio broadcasters	34%
Celebrities	25
Newspapers	21
The government	10
Big companies	7
Civil servants	3

─────────── REGULAR MEDIA ACTIVITIES ───────────

The consumption of traditional media (such as newspapers) has declined according to Ofcom's May 2008 Adult Media Literacy Report, and TV is still by far the most dominant medium. Adults were asked which of the following they regularly did:

Media activity (%)	2005	2007	±				
Watch TV	95	97	+2	Watch videos/DVDs	66	63	–3
Use a mobile	73	77	+4	Use the internet	50	56	+6
Read newspapers	78	73	–5	Listen to music, hi-fi	71	56	–15
Listen to radio	77	69	–8	Listen to music, MP3	18	25	+7

Ofcom's May 2008 report into children's 'media literacy' revealed a growth in the use of personal MP3 players. Below is a breakdown of children's media usage:

8–11-year-olds			% using media		12–15-year-olds	
2005	2007	±		±	2005	2007
48	56	+8	mobile phone	+8	82	90
61	65	+4	internet	+7	68	75
87	91	+4	DVD player	+3	91	94
21	46	+25	MP3 player	+43	32	75
30	37	+7	digital camera	+9	45	54
86	83	–3	CD player	–4	93	89
80	66	–14	VCR	–17	82	65

─────────── UPTAKE OF MEDIA PLATFORMS AT HOME ───────────

According to research by Ofcom in May 2008, the new media platform that most people have access to at home is digital radio; below is a breakdown of platforms:

% with access to	2005	2007	±				
Digital radio	77	88	+11	Digital TV	62	82	+20
Mobile phone	82	85	+3	Internet	54	62	+8

[Respondents aged over 16]

———————— UK TELEVISION INDUSTRY OVERVIEW ————————

In August 2008, Ofcom released the following snapshot of the UK's TV industry:

Indicator	2002	2004	2006	2007
Total TV industry revenue (£bn)	8·9	10·1	10·8	11·2
Proportion of revenue from public funds (%)	25	23	23	23
Proportion of revenue from advertising (%)	35	34	32	32
Proportion of revenue from subscription (%)	32	35	37	38
TV as proportion of total advertising spend (%)	30·9	29·6	27·9	26·8
Spend on originated output by 5 main ntwrks (£bn)	3·0	3·0	2·8	2·6
Digital TV (DTV) take-up (% homes in Q1)	38·5	53·0	69·7	86·3
Proportion of DTV homes paying for TV (Q1, %)	86·6	71·7	60·0	55·0
Viewing per head, per day (hours) in all homes	3:34	3:42	3:36	3:38
Share of 5 main networks in all homes (%)	77·7	73·8	66·8	63·5
Number of channels broadcasting in UK	236	379	433	470

[Source: Ofcom, *The Communications Market 2008*]

———————— MOST-COMPLAINED ABOUT ADVERTS ————————

The Advertising Standards Authority's [ASA] 2007 annual report listed the broadcast adverts which drew the most complaints. The 6 most objected to were:

DEPARTMENT OF HEALTH

The NHS anti-cigarette advertisements showed smokers speared by fish hooks through their mouths and cheeks. The ASA ruled that the ads could frighten and distress children.

774 complaints · Upheld

CADBURY'S

Trident Gum adverts depicted people speaking in stereotyped Caribbean accents, which some complained were offensive and racist. The ASA agreed the ads had caused offence.

519 complaints · Upheld

KEPAK UK

The ASA ruled that an ad for *Rustlers* burgers, showing a woman undressing with the slogan '*If only everything was as quick as Rustlers*', should not have been screened during *Bugsy Malone*.

219 complaints · Upheld

MFI RETAIL

The ads featured heated family arguments in MFI stores; the ASA agreed that one, showing a woman slapping her husband for leaving the toilet seat up, could be seen to condone violence.

217 complaints · Upheld

MARLOW FOODS

The ASA did not agree that a TV ad for *Quorn*, which showed a girl threatening her brother with a fork, was irresponsible and could encourage bullying.

181 complaints · Not upheld

COCA-COLA GB

The ASA rejected concerns that the *Oasis* soft drink ad, which involved a crocodile attacking a wildebeest, would cause serious or widespread offence.

180 complaints · Not upheld

[Source: asa.org.uk]

THE HARDING TEST

In March 2008, a music video by the eccentric hip-hop duo Gnarls Barkley (best known for their 2006 hit, *Crazy*) briefly attracted press attention after reportedly failing the Harding Test, which screens for images that can trigger epileptic attacks. Developed in 2001 by Cambridge Research Systems and neuroscientist Graham Harding, the Harding Broadcast Flash and Pattern Analyser analyses TV, film, and video game content frame-by-frame for images that flash, flicker, or appear intermittently, or that include more than five light-and-dark stripes. Such images have been known to produce seizures in those with photosensitive epilepsy, which reportedly affects *c.*1 in 4,000 worldwide. The Gnarls Barkley video, which featured Justin Timberlake as the host of a fictional public access TV show 'City Vibin', was re-edited before being released on MTV.

In June 2007, an animation of the logo for the London 2012 Olympics triggered a number of complaints from viewers with photosensitive epilepsy. OfCom reported that within the animation a sequence of '45 frames (around 2 seconds in length) contained an excessive number of "flashes" that were clearly in breach of the guidelines'. ❦ According to OfCom, since television 'is by nature a flickering medium' it is 'impossible to eliminate the risk of television causing convulsions in viewers with photosensitive epilepsy'. However, OfCom warns of three dangers: *potentially harmful flashes* (an increase in luminance followed by a decrease, or a decrease followed by an increase); *Rapidly changing image sequences* (e.g., fast cuts) where they result in areas of the screen that flash; and *potentially harmful regular patterns* (containing clearly discernible stripes when there are more than five light-dark pairs of stripes in any orientation).

MOST-WATCHED TV PROGRAMMES

The Christmas episodes of *EastEnders* and *Doctor Who*, both on BBC1, were the most-watched television programmes of 2007. The statistics, produced by audience researchers Barb, also revealed that combined prime-time viewing figures for ITV1 and BBC1 dropped below 50% for the first time. 2007's top 10 TV shows were:

Show	channel	viewers (million)
EastEnders Christmas episode	BBC1	14·38
Doctor Who Christmas episode†	BBC1	13·31
Rugby World Cup final	ITV1	13·13
Coronation Street	ITV1	13·08
The Vicar of Dibley	BBC1	13·06
The X Factor Results	ITV1	12·23
Concert for Diana‡	BBC1	12·22
Strictly Come Dancing	BBC1	12·09
Britain's Got Talent	ITV1	11·58
England *vs* Croatia football match	BBC1	11·19

† Featured a special appearance by Kylie Minogue, who shortly afterwards was awarded an OBE [see p.279] ‡ Held on 1 July (which would have been Diana's 46th birthday), featuring Sir Elton John, Rod Stewart, Duran Duran, Kanye West, Lily Allen, &c. The show raised £1·2m for charity.

THE TV BAFTAS · 2008

Best actor	Andrew Garfield · *Boy A* [C4]
Best actress	Eileen Atkins · *Cranford* [BBC1]
Entertainment performance	Harry Hill · *Harry Hill's TV Burp* [ITV1]
Comedy performance	James Corden · *Gavin & Stacey* [BBC3]
Single drama	*The Mark of Cain* [C4]
Drama series	*The Street* [BBC1]
Drama serial	*Britz* [C4]
Continuing drama	*Holby City* [BBC1]
Feature	*Ramsay's Kitchen Nightmares* [C4]
Factual series	*The Tower: A Tale of Two Cities* [BBC1]
Specialist factual	*Andrew Marr's History of Modern Britain* [BBC2]
Flaherty award for single documentary	*Lie of the Land* [C4]
Sport	*F1: Canadian Grand Prix Live* [ITV1]
News coverage	*Sky News – Glasgow Airport Attack* [SKY NEWS]
Current affairs	*China's Stolen Children – A Dispatches Special* [C4]
Best interactivity	*Spooks Interactive* [bbc.co.uk]
Lew Grade award for entertainment	*Harry Hill's TV Burp* [ITV1]
Sitcom	*Peep Show* [C4]
International	*Heroes* [BBC2]
Comedy programme or series	*Fonejacker* [C4]
SKY+ audience award for programme of the year	*Gavin & Stacey* [BBC3]
Special award	Paul Watson
BAFTA Fellowship	Bruce Forsyth

BAFTA IN QUOTES

GRAHAM NORTON [host] · I do love this night. It's sort of like the Oscars, but with less surgery. ❦ DAME JUDI DENCH [after losing to *Cranford* co-star Dame Eileen Atkins] · There'll be a catfight later. ❦ ANDREW MARR · We didn't have any dancing dogs in our series, but we did have the British people. ❦ BRUCE FORSYTH · A few golfing trophies will go and I will put this in their place. ❦ HARRY HILL · Baffy Waff!

MOST-WATCHED TV PRESENTERS

Ant McPartlin and Dec Donnelly (aka Ant & Dec) were the most-watched TV hosts in 2007, according to a report by media agency MPG. They were seen at least once by 51% of the nation while presenting *I'm A Celebrity ... Get Me Out of Here*, *Britain's Got Talent*, and *Saturday Night Takeaway*, all on ITV. The top 10 were:

Ant & Dec	(see above)	Richard Hammond	*Top Gear*;
Dermot O'Leary	*X Factor*;		*Brainiac*
	Big Brother's Little Brother	Bruce Forsyth	*Strictly Come Dancing*
Phillip Schofield	*This Morning*	Jeremy Clarkson	*Top Gear*;
Gary Lineker	*Match of the Day*		*Have I Got News For You*
Tess Daly	*Strictly Come Dancing*;	James May	*Top Gear*
	Just the Two of Us	Jonathan Ross	*Fri. Night*; *Film 2007*

———————— BEST CHILDREN'S TV SHOW ————————

In March 2008, *Grange Hill* was voted the greatest ever children's TV show, a month after the BBC said it would axe the school drama after 30 years. The top 10 were:

Grange Hill [see p.63]	*The Magic Roundabout*	*The Flintstones*
The Muppet Show	*DangerMouse*	*Wacky Races*
Tom & Jerry	*Scooby Doo*	
Bagpuss†	*Inspector Gadget*	[Source: OnePoll.com]

In March 2008, the BBC announced the launch of *Sesame Tree*, a Northern Irish version of the US children's TV series *Sesame Street*. *Sesame Tree* will feature the adventures of Muppets Potto, Hilda, and Claribelle, and include such japes as Irish dancing and preparing for a Boys' Brigade expedition. † Bagpuss triumphed in a CBeebies survey of top children's TV animals in April 2008. Completing the top five were: Tom & Jerry, Winnie-the-Pooh, the Magic Roundabout clan, and DangerMouse.

———————— DAVID BECKHAM & SESAME STREET ————————

In April 2008, David Beckham filmed a slot for the US children's TV show *Sesame Street*. Beckham appeared alongside Elmo and introduced the red monster to his word of choice: *persistence*. Other British stars to have appeared on the show include: Jeremy Irons, who in 1988 sang in a celebrity version of the instructive song *Put Down the Duckie*, in which Ernie is advised that if he wants to be able to play the saxophone he must relinquish his rubber duck; Patrick Stewart, who enacted a soliloquy on the letter 'B' and assisted Count Von Count; and James Blunt, who performed a special version of his hit song *You're Beautiful* entitled *My Triangle*.

———————— THE CHILDREN'S BAFTAS ————————

The 2007 British Academy Children's Awards were presented against a backdrop of concern over falling investment in kids' TV and an increasing reliance on cartoons and US imports†. The BBC had cut its children's programme budget by 10%, while ITV had stopped producing them altogether. Some notable Bafta winners were:

Channel of the year......... CBeebies		Pre-school live action ....
Animation.............. *The Secret Show*		*In the Night Garden*‡
Drama............... *That Summer Day*		Presenter............. Barney Harwood
Entertainment............ *The Slammer*		
Factual.............. *The Wrong Trainers*		‡ A huge hit since its launch on CBeebies in
Feature film .... *Happy Feet*		March 2007, the show features the antics of
International ...*SpongeBob SquarePants*		Igglepiggle, Upsy Daisy, Makka Pakka, the
Pre-school animation .. *Charlie & Lola*		Tombliboos, and the Pontipines.

† In April 2008, the Producers Alliance for Cinema & Television (PACT) gave *The Wombles* an American makeover (with American accents) to highlight its concerns about the high number of imported children's TV shows. PACT claims that only 1% of new programmes are made in the UK.

———————————— TIME-SHIFT TV ————————————

57% of Britons watch >10 hours of recorded or 'time-shift' television a week – reflecting the increasing availability of on-demand TV. The May 2008 survey by Redback Networks revealed that the most common methods for recording television were video recorders (27%); Sky+ (22%); internet catch-up services such as the BBC iPlayer (16%); and on-demand TV (11%). Of those who time-shift their television viewing, roughly one-third reported that they watched at least 3 hours of on-demand television a week. In a separate survey, released in July 2008, Sky collated the viewing habits of a cross-section of Sky+ users across the country. The most popular time-shifted programmes by region 1 Jan–8 Jun 2008 were:

Region	most time-shifted programmes
Scotland	*Heroes, Britain's Got Talent Final, Coronation Street*
London	*The Apprentice, EastEnders, Doctor Who*
Midlands	*The Apprentice, Doctor Who, Britain's Got Talent*
Yorkshire	*Doctor Who, Benidorm, Ashes to Ashes*
East	*Doctor Who, EastEnders, Britain's Got Talent*
Wales & West	*Doctor Who, The Apprentice, Britain's Got Talent*
North-east	*Coronation Street, Doctor Who, Ashes to Ashes*
Lancashire	*Benidorm, Coronation Street, Britain's Got Talent*

The Sky survey also discovered: people in the South-east watch an average of 3 hours 17 minutes of television each day, 79% of it live and 21% time-shifted. London women watch the most time-shifted TV on Friday nights 11pm–12·30am; London men watch most on Sunday mornings 6am–9·30am. In Scotland, men watch the most time-shifted TV from 11pm–12·30am and women watch the most on Wednesday and Friday mornings. Women in Yorkshire watch the most on Wednesday mornings, men on Monday mornings. The Scottish watch the most arts programmes; Londoners record the most soap operas and those in the South-west the least; people from the Midlands watch the most films. In Wales *Gavin & Stacey* was the 8th most popular show to time-shift; Lancashire was the only region to feature *Waterloo Road* in its top ten most recorded shows.

———————————— GLADIATORS ————————————

Sky One revived guilty pleasure *Gladiators* in May 2008, after an eight-year hiatus. Ian Wright and Kirsty Gallagher presented the new show, with legendary referee John Anderson returning to reprise his role (and his catchphrase 'Contender, ready? Gladiator, ready?'). The 13 new gladiators and their predecessors are below:

Original Gladiators†	*New Gladiators*
♀ Flame · Jet · Lightning	♀ Battleaxe · Cyclone · Enigma
Panther · Phoenix · Scorpio	Ice · Inferno · Panther · Tempest
♂ Cobra · Hawk · Saracen	♂ Atlas · Destroyer · Oblivion
Shadow · Warrior · Wolf	Predator‡ · Spartan · Tornado

† From the first ITV series, broadcast in 1992. ‡ Du'aine Ladejo, two-time 400m relay Olympic medallist, described by Sky as 'volatile, quick, and poisonous, hunts down prey and takes no prisoners'.

—————————— PRESS COMPLAINTS ——————————

The number of complaints made to the Press Complaints Committee (PCC) in 2007 increased by 31% since 2006, to 4,340 – although these figures are inflated by a large number of complaints made about just a few articles. For example, 485 people complained about a *Daily Mirror* report criticising the Portuguese investigation into the disappearance of Madeleine McCann. The PCC's annual report revealed that 822 formal investigations took place; these were concluded, on average, in 41 days.

Complaints by type	%
Accuracy	75·4
Privacy	9·2
Intrusion into grief or shock	6·6
Discrimination	1·9
Children	1·8
Harassment	1·6

Opportunity to reply	1·4
Reporting of crime	0·9
Clandestine devices/subterfuge	0·5
Confidential sources	0·4
Hospitals	0·1
Victims of sexual abuse	0·1
Payment to criminals	0·1

The PCC made 1,229 rulings in 2007 (up 20% since 2006); a breakdown is below:

No breach of the PCC code	560	46%
Sufficient remedial action offered by the newspaper	154	13%
Resolved to the satisfaction of the complainant	483	39%
Adjudication upheld	16	1%
Adjudication not upheld	16	1%

In 2007, the PCC made its first ruling concerning audio-video content. After some teenage boys filmed themselves throwing petrol bombs at a freight train and posted the video on YouTube, the *Northwich Guardian* picked up the story and ran the video on its own website. As a result, one of the boys' parents complained that the paper had breached their son's privacy. The PCC rejected the complaint because the story was in the public interest and had been posted in the public domain.

————— THE PULITZER PRIZE · JOURNALISM · 2008 —————

PUBLIC SERVICE AWARD
The Washington Post for '*the work of Dana Priest, Anne Hull, and Michel du Cille in exposing mistreatment of wounded veterans at Walter Reed Hospital, evoking a national outcry and producing reforms by federal officials*'

BREAKING NEWS REPORTING
The Washington Post staff for its '*exceptional, multi-faceted coverage of the deadly shooting rampage at Virginia Tech, telling the developing story in print and online*'

INTERNATIONAL REPORTING
Steve Fainaru of *The Washington Post* for his '*heavily reported series on private security contractors in Iraq that operate outside most of the laws governing American forces*'

EXPLANATORY REPORTING
Amy Harmon of *The New York Times* for her '*striking examination of the dilemmas and ethical issues that accompany DNA testing, using human stories to sharpen her reports*'
[See pulitzer.org for other prizes]

———————————FREEDOM OF THE PRESS———————————

A December 2007 poll released by the BBC World Service asked 11,344 people in 14 countries which of the following statements most closely matched their beliefs:

'Freedom of the press to report the news truthfully is very important to ensure we live in a fair society, even if it sometimes leads to unpleasant debates or social unrest'	*'While freedom of the press to report news truthfully is important, social harmony and peace are more important, which sometimes means controlling what is reported for the greater good'*

Respondents in North America and Western Europe were most likely to value press freedom, while those in India, Singapore, and Russia more often chose harmony:

Country	press freedom	harmony
US	70%	28%
Germany	67	26
UK	67	29
Venezuela	64	36
South Africa	63	34
Kenya	62	37
Nigeria	56	43
Egypt	55	45
Brazil	52	48
Mexico	51	46
UAE	51	48
Singapore	43	48
India	41	48
Russia	39	47
(WORLD	56	40)

Respondents were also asked to assess the freedom of their national press and broadcasters to report the news 'truthfully and without bias'. Respondents were given a 5-point scale, where 5 was 'very free' and 1 was 'not at all free'. Below are the percentages of respondents in each country who rated their press 4 or 5 on this scale:

Kenya	81%	UK	56	South Africa	49
India	72	UAE	56	Russia	46
Nigeria	66	Germany	55	Mexico	41
Egypt	64	US	53	Singapore	36
Venezuela	63	Brazil	52	(WORLD	56)

———————————TOP NEWS SOURCES WORLDWIDE———————————

The world overwhelmingly turns to television as its number-one news source, according to a Pew Global Attitudes survey released in October 2007. However, radio remains the dominant source in several African nations, while the internet has been gaining ground in N America and W Europe. Below are the percentages of those around the world who cite various media as their *first* or *second* news source:

(%)	TV	papers	radio	net		TV	papers	radio	net
Britain	83	58	29	21	Germany	84	62	26	19
Canada	82	51	30	25	Poland	92	45	33	15
Ethiopia	65	25	81	5	Russia	95	51	27	6
France	81	53	34	25	S Africa	86	47	54	3
					US	83	47	22	35

2008 NEWSROOM BAROMETER

The World Editors Forum conducted a survey of >700 newspaper editors and senior news executives from over 120 countries in March 2008, with the aim of gauging opinion on the future of newspapers. One of the key trends was the growth of multimedia newsrooms, where journalists are expected to produce reports not only for print but also for the web – incorporating both audio and video. 86% of editors agreed that multimedia newsrooms would be the norm in five years' time. 56% of editors predicted that the majority of news (print and online) will be free in the future, compared to 48% predicting the same in 2006. Some further results are below:

In 10 years' time, what do you think will be the most common way of reading the news?

%	2006	2008
Print	35	31
Online	41	44
Mobile phone	11	12
e-paper	7	7

In the next 10 years do you think the quality of journalism will:

%	2006	2008
Worsen	27	28
Be about the same	16	22
Improve	50	45

Do you think in future opinion & analysis pages will:

%	2006	2008
Increase	66	67
Be about the same	20	23
Decrease	12	9

What do you view as the greatest threat to the future of your newspaper?

Declining youth readership	58
Internet & digital media	38
Lack of editorial innovation	36
Lack of investment	29
Free newspapers	13
Radio & TV	5
None of the above	6

What do you view as the principal threat to newspapers' editorial independence?

Advertising pressure	23
Shareholder pressure	20
Political pressure	19
PR firms	12

In Western Europe & N America shareholder pressure was 35 & 23 respectively but political pressure was just 3 for both.

BRITISH PRESS AWARDS 2008

Newspaper	*Financial Times*
Journalist of the year	Andrew Gilligan · *London Evening Standard*
Political journalist	Philip Stephens · *Financial Times*
Show business	Sean Hamilton · *Sunday Mirror*
Columnist	Matthew Norman · *The Independent*
Feature writer	A.A. Gill · *Sunday Times*
Interviewer	Chrissy Iley · *Freelance*
Sports journalist	Martin Samuel · *The Times*
Reporter	Tom Newton Dunn · *The Sun*
Scoop	'Friendly fire kills Matty Hull' by Tom Newton Dunn · *The Sun*
Team	Help For Heroes · *The Sun*

——————————— UK RADIO HALL OF FAME ———————————

The Radio Academy, a body that 'exists to celebrate excellence in all aspects of UK radio', oversees the UK Radio Hall of Fame. In 2007, the following were inducted:

Adrian Love · Alan Green · Alan Keith · Alvar Liddell
Brian Hayes · Franklin Engelman · Mike Dickin · Neil Fox
Nick Clarke · Richard 'Dickie' Murdoch

——————————— RADIO LISTENERSHIP BY PLATFORM ———————————

According to Rajar, radio listenership in 2008 was shared across these platforms:

Platform	listenership share %		
AM/FM	72·7	– Internet	2·1
All digital	17·8	– Digital unspecified	1·7
– DAB	10·8	Unspecified	9·5
– DTV	3·2		

[Rajar · 1st Quarter (Q1) March 2008]

The continued growth in DAB radio ownership and the number of adults (aged >15) listening to the radio on their mobile phones in 2008 is also notable:

% of adults who ever listen to radio via a mobile phone:

Q1 2002	0·9%
Q1 2003	2·4%
Q1 2004	4·5%
Q1 2005	5·8%
Q1 2006	6·4%
Q1 2007	8·0%
Q1 2008	11·6%

% of adults who own a DAB radio at home:

Q1 2004	3·9%
Q1 2005	8·1%
Q1 2006	13·6%
Q1 2007	19·5%
Q1 2008	27·3%

Britons now listen 111m hours/week to DAB.

——————————— THE SONY AWARDS · 2008 ———————————

For twenty-five years, the Sony Radio Academy has rewarded excellence in British radio with bronze, silver, or gold awards. Some of the 2008 golds are listed below:

Breakfast show	The Chris Moyles Show [BBC Radio 1]
Music radio personality of the year	Jonathan Ross [BBC Radio 2]
Music broadcaster of the year	Andi Durrant [Galaxy Digital]
Entertainment award	The Russell Brand Show [BBC Radio 2]
Speech broadcaster	Simon Mayo [BBC Radio 5 live]
News journalist	Owen Bennett-Jones [BBC World Service]
Digital station of the year	Planet Rock
Station of the year UK	BBC Radio 4

NOTABLE DESERT ISLAND DISCS · 2008

Castaway	luxury	favourite Desert Island Disc
George Michael	an Aston Martin DB9	Love is a Losing Game (Amy Winehouse)
Alan Johnson	a digital radio	And Your Bird Can Sing (The Beatles)
Nicholas Parsons	a portable radio with endless battery supply	Children Will Listen (Barbra Streisand)
Ronnie Corbett	a hammock	Music Maestro Please (Ann Hart)
Jung Chang	snorkelling gear	The Messiah (Handel)
Eliza Manningham-Buller	a large supply of pencils & pens	String Quintet in C major (Schubert)
Armistead Maupin	a vaporiser	Wicked Little Town (Tommy Gnosis)
Steven Isserlis	photo album of friends	Erbarme Dich from St Matthew Passion (J.S. Bach)
Alec Jeffreys	the world's biggest church organ	Fugue in D minor (J.S. Bach)
Paul Weller	a settee	Tin Soldier (The Small Faces)
Victoria Wood	a bumper book of sudoku & pen	What A Fool Believes (The Doobie Brothers)
Karren Brady	her own pillow	Total Eclipse of the Heart (Bonnie Tyler)
John Humphrys	a cello	Cello Concerto (Elgar)
Simon Rattle	a coffee machine & grinder	Scherza Infida from Ariodante (Handel) sung by Magdalena Kožená
Rory Stewart	an Afghan ceramic bowl	Die Forelle (Schubert)
Natasha Spender	a grand piano	String Quintet in G minor (Mozart)
Beryl Bainbridge	pens & paper	Can I Forget You? (sung by Richard Tauber)
Oleg Gordievsky	good toiletries for his bath	Erbarme Dich from St Matthew Passion (J.S. Bach)
Sir Martin Evans	a microscope	Their Sound is Gone Out into all Lands from Messiah (Handel)
David Dimbleby	drawing books, pencils & varnish	Song That You'd Like (Kate Dimbleby)
Michael Ball	Cloudy Bay Sauvignon Blanc	Sailing By (composed by Ronald Binge)
Liz Smith	an artist's set	Only the Lonely (sung by Roy Orbison)
Tariq Ali	a mini DVD player	Meda Ishq Vi Toon (performed by Pathaney Khan)
Stanley 'Mac' McMurry	a tenor saxophone	Violin Concerto in G minor (Bruch)
Penelope Wilton	an open-air cinema & a selection of films	String Quintet in C major (Schubert)
Richard Ingrams	a grand piano	Mass in B minor (J.S. Bach)

———————————BLOGGING ARRESTS———————————

35 people were arrested for blogging about political issues across the world in 2007, a sharp increase since 2006, when 10 were arrested. The World Information Access (WIA) report released in June 2008 revealed that, since 2003, 64 people have been arrested because of the content of their blog. A summary of these arrests is below:

Blogging activity	*Number of arrests* · 2007	'03–'07
Using blog to organise/cover social protest	Burma (2), China (1) Egypt (4), Iran (1)	15
Violating cultural norms	China (1), Egypt (2), India (1) Hong Kong (1), Philippines (1)	14
Posting comments on public policy	Fiji (1), Malaysia (1) Pakistan (1), Saudi Arabia (1) Thailand (1), Syria (1)	12
Exposing corruption/human rights violations	China (3), Tunisia (1)	9
Posting comments about political figures	Egypt (1), Iran (1) Kuwait (1), Russia (1)	6
Other	China (1), Egypt (1), Fiji (1) Malaysia (1), Thailand (1), USA (2)	8

————TECHNORATI'S STATE OF THE BLOGOSPHERE————

>120,000 new blogs were created each day (1·4 blogs a second) according to blog search engine Technorati's *State of the Blogosphere*. The final report was released in April 2007, after which Technorati founder and author of the reports David Sifry stepped down as CEO; at the time of writing, no further reports had been published. Between Q2 2004 and Q2 2006, the blogosphere doubled in size every 5–7 months (150–220 days). Recently this growth has slowed to a doubling roughly every 320 days. In April 2007, there were approximately 1·5m blog posts each day – about 17 posts a second. Japanese and English are the dominant languages of the blogosphere – accounting for 37% and 36% of all posts respectively. The third most popular blogging language is Chinese, which accounts for 8% of posts.

————MOST POPULAR CELEBRITY MAGAZINES————

Below are the most popular weekly celebrity and gossip magazines for the period July–December 2007, according to February 2008 circulation figures from ABC:

Magazine	*weekly circulation*		
OK!†	683,451	Hello!	405,615
Closer	548,594	Reveal	326,057
Heat	533,034	Star	305,806
Now	470,290		
New!	464,727		

† *OK!* magazine was launched in 1993; it is currently published in 19 countries.

MAJOR BRITISH NEWSPAPERS

Title	editorial address	phone	editor	circulation	readership	cost	owner	founded
Sun	1 Virginia St, Wapping, London E98 1SN	020 7782 4000	Rebekah Wade	3,148,792	8,031,000	30p	N	1911
Daily Mail	Northcliffe Ho., 2 Derry St., London W8 5TT	020 7938 6000	Paul Dacre	2,258,843	5,347,000	50p	A	1896
Daily Mirror	1 Canada Sq., Canary Wharf London E14 5AP	020 7293 3000	Richard Wallace	1,455,270	3,685,000	40p	T	1903
Daily Telegraph	111 Buckingham Palace Rd, London SW1W 0DT	020 7331 2000	Will Lewis	860,298	2,060,000	90p	H	1855
Daily Star	10 Lower Thames St, London EC3R 6EN	0871 434 1010	Dawn Neesom	751,494	1,484,000	35p	S	1978
Daily Express	10 Lower Thames St, London EC3R 6EN	0871 434 1010	Peter Hill	748,664	1,598,000	40p	S	1900
Times	1 Virginia St, Wapping, London E98 1XY	020 7782 5000	James Harding	612,779	1,731,000	80p	N	1785
Financial Times	1 Southwark Bridge, London SE1 9HL	020 7873 3000	Lionel Barber	417,570	377,000	150p	P	1888
Guardian	119 Farringdon Rd, London EC1R 3ER	020 7278 2332	Alan Rusbridger	332,587	1,165,00	80p	G	1821
Evening Standard	Northcliffe Ho., 2 Derry St., London W8 5TT	020 7938 6000	Veronica Wadley	278,889	623,000	50p	A	1827
Independent	191 Marsh Wall, London E14 9RS	020 7005 2000	Roger Alton	230,033	702,000	80p	I	1986
News of the World	1 Virginia St, Wapping, London E98 1SN	020 7782 1001	Colin Myler	3,249,147	7,903,000	95p	N	1843
Mail on Sunday	Northcliffe Ho., 2 Derry St., London W8 5TT	020 7938 6000	Peter Wright	2,177,527	5,884,000	150p	A	1982
Sunday Mirror	1 Canada Sq., Canary Wharf London E14 5AP	020 7293 3000	Tina Weaver	1,311,386	4,108,000	95p	T	1915
Sunday Times	1 Virginia St, Wapping, London E98 1XY	020 7782 5000	John Witherow	1,156,540	3,159,000	200p	N	1821
Sunday Express	10 Lower Thames St, London EC3R 6EN	0871 434 1010	Martin Townsend	655,053	1,790,000	130p	S	1918
People	1 Canada Sq., Canary Wharf London E14 5AP	020 7293 3000	Lloyd Embley	649,420	1,616,000	90p	T	1881
Sunday Telegraph	111 Buckingham Palace Rd, London SW1W 0DT	020 7931 2000	Ian MacGregor	618,772	1,744,000	190p	H	1961
Observer	119 Farringdon Rd, London EC1R 3ER	020 7278 2332	John Mulholland	411,244	1,318,000	190p	G	1791
Daily Star Sunday	10 Lower Thames St, London EC3R 6EN	0871 434 1010	Gareth Morgan	403,753	888,000	90p	S	2002
Independent on Sun.	191 Marsh Wall, London E14 9RS	020 7005 2000	John Mullin	196,752	757,000	180p	I	1990
Scotland on Sunday	108 Holyrood Rd, Edinburgh EH8 8AS	0131 620 8620	Les Snowdon	67,300	226,000	140p	J	1988

Ownership: [N]ews Corporation · Northern & [S]hell Media · [P]earson · Press [H]oldings Ltd · [A]ssociated Newspapers · [G]uardian Media Group · [J]ohnston Press [I]ndependent News & Media · [T]rinity Mirror · Circulation: ABC [Aug 2008] · Readership: NRS [June 2008] · Founded dates relate to the paper's earliest incarnation.

Music & Cinema

Movies are so rarely great art that if we cannot appreciate the
great trash we have very little reason to be interested in them.
— PAULINE KAEL (1919–2001)

UK NUMBER ONES · 2007–08

W/ending	weeks	artist	song
06·10·07	4	Sugababes	*About You Now*
03·11·07	7	Leona Lewis	*Bleeding Love*
22·12·07	1	Eva Cassidy & Katie Melua	*What a Wonderful World*
29·12·07	3	Leon Jackson	*When You Believe*
19·01·08	5	Basshunter featuring DJ Mental Theo	*Now You're Gone*
23·02·08	5	Duffy	*Mercy*
29·03·08	4	Estelle featuring Kanye West	*American Boy*
26·04·08	4	Madonna featuring Justin Timberlake	*4 Minutes*
24·05·08	1	The Ting Tings	*That's Not My Name*
31·05·08	2	Rihanna	*Take a Bow*
14·06·08	2	Mint Royale	*Singin' in the Rain*
28·06·08	1	Coldplay	*Viva La Vida*
05·07·08	1	Ne-Yo	*Closer*
12·07·08	4	Dizzee Rascal/Calvin Harris/Chrome	*Dance Wiv Me*
09·08·08	1	Kid Rock	*All Summer Long*
16·08·08	5	Katy Perry	*I Kissed a Girl*

UK'S MOST-PLAYED SONGS

Bad Day by Canadian one-hit-wonder Daniel Powter was the most-played song in
the UK over the last five years, according to a PRS report in July 2008. Airplay on
radio, TV, websites, and in live music venues were all counted. The top ten were:

[1] Daniel Powter · *Bad Day* [2] Kelly Clarkson · *Because of You*
[3] James Blunt · *You're Beautiful* [4] Scissor Sisters · *I Don't Feel Like Dancing*
[5] Snow Patrol · *Chasing Cars* [6] Maroon 5 · *This Love*
[7] Take That · *Shine* [8] Corinne Bailey Rae · *Put Your Records On*
[9] Will Young · *Leave Right Now* [10] Gwen Stefani · *Sweet Escape*

In an HMV/*Q* magazine poll of the 50 Best Ever British Albums, published in February 2007, Oasis
came top, with *Definitely Maybe*. Oasis also scooped the second spot with *(What's the Story) Morning
Glory?* Making up the rest of the top ten were: Radiohead, *OK Computer*; the Beatles, *Revolver*; The
Stone Roses, *The Stone Roses*; the Beatles, *Sgt Pepper's Lonely Hearts Club Band*; The Clash, *London
Calling*; Keane, *Under the Iron Sea*; Pink Floyd, *Dark Side of the Moon*; and The Verve, *Urban Hymns*.

———————FREE MUSIC & 360 DEGREE DEALS———————

The ease with which people can download music from the internet and share their music collections for free has severely hit record company profits: CD sales in Britain fell by 10% in 2007. In contrast, attendance at rock arena shows has grown (by >10% in 2006), making touring an increasingly profitable endeavour. As a result established bands like Radiohead have embraced the flexibility of downloads, giving away their music for an optional fee, in return for larger paying crowds at their gigs. And record companies, fast seeing their profits slump, have introduced '360 degree' record deals under which they take a slice of a musician's entire portfolio of earnings. 360 degree contracts allow the record company to take a cut not just of music profits but of touring, merchandising, publishing, and other revenue streams. Below are some of the recent developments in these areas:

Free music

{7/07} Prince gave away free copies of his latest album *Planet Earth* with the *Mail on Sunday*, prompting criticism from some music retailers: HMV chief executive Simon Fox called the giveaway 'absolute madness'. {10/07} The Charlatans allowed their tenth studio album to be downloaded for free from Xfm's website. Lead singer Tim Burgess explained 'We want "the people" to own the music and we want the artist, i.e., us, to own the copyright. Why let a record company get in the way of the people getting the music?' {10/07} Radiohead announced that their new album *In Rainbows* would be available to download for whatever fans decided to pay[†]. {5/08} Coldplay made their new single *Violet Hill* available for free from their website for one week only. The single was downloaded by >2m people. {5/08} Nine Inch Nails released *The Slip* for free on their website. {7/08} McFly gave away latest album *Radio:ACTIVE* free with the *Mail on Sunday*; singer Tom Fletcher commented, 'hopefully the 3m people will enjoy the music and they'll decide to see us when we go on tour'.

360 degree deals

{10/07} Madonna signed a revolutionary recording, publishing, and touring contract with Live Nation worth a reported £59m; the first major star to shun a traditional record deal in favour of an all-in-one contract. {3/08} Dance act Groove Armada signed an integrated marketing deal with Bacardi which allowed the drinks company to release a 4-track EP by the band with the option to use the music in its advertising campaigns. The group will also play at a series of Bacardi sponsored live concerts. {3/08} U2 signed a 12-year deal with Live Nation. The band's physical recordings will still be distributed through Universal Music Group, Live Nation will handle digital distribution, branding rights, and merchandising. {5/08} Jay-Z signed a 360 degree deal with Live Nation. Reportedly worth $150m, the deal creates a new joint entertainment venture – Roc Nation plus gives Live Nation a cut of Jay-Z's own recordings and tours for the next ten years. {7/08} Shakira signed a *c.*$100m 360 degree deal with Live Nation. ❦ Nickelback signed a 3-album, 3-tour deal with Live Nation.

[†] Between 1–29 October 2007, 1·2m people visited the *In Rainbows* website; 38% of people worldwide chose to pay something to download the album. According to comScore, 62%, paid nothing, 17% paid <$4 for the album, 6% paid $4·01–$8, 12% paid $8·01–$12, and 4% paid >$12.

THE BRIT AWARDS · 2008

Hosted by the Osbourne clan (Ozzy, Sharon, Jack, & Kelly), the 2008 Brits was a far from polished affair. Sharon clashed with Vic Reeves when he fluffed his lines ('Shut up, you're pissed, piss off you bastard'), and the Arctic Monkeys (dressed as country gents) had their mikes cut when their acceptance speech became tired and emotional. (Ofcom received 43 complaints about bad language.) Paul McCartney closed the proceedings with a medley dedicated to John Lennon and his late wife, Linda.

British male solo artist...Mark Ronson
British female solo artist... Kate Nash
British group...Arctic Monkeys
British album ....Arctic Monkeys · *Favourite Worst Nightmare*
British single[1] ....Take That · *Shine*
British live act[2]...Take That
British breakthrough act[3]... Mika
International male solo artist..Kanye West
International female solo artist... Kylie Minogue
International album.................Foo Fighters · *Echoes, Silence, Patience & Grace*
International group...Foo Fighters
Critics' choice..Adele
Outstanding contribution to music...........................Sir Paul McCartney†

[1] Live public vote that night. [2] Voted for by Radio 2 listeners. [3] Voted for by Radio 1 listeners.

IN QUOTES: VIC REEVES · [on Kylie Minogue] ... all right, a bit of work there and she will be OK. ❦ MARK RONSON · I've never felt so British or male in my entire life. ❦ AMY WINEHOUSE · [addressing the crowd] Make some noise for my husband, my Blake. ❦ KANYE WEST · [in his acceptance video] I'm sure there's someone who deserves this more than me, but I just don't know who they are. ❦ SHARON OSBOURNE · [introducing Jonathan Rhys-Meyers] ... a man who is so gorgeous he needs a good licking, and I think I'm the woman to do it. ❦ SIR PAUL McCARTNEY · I need to get back to what I do best, and that's what I'm going to do.

† Sales of McCartney's album *Memory Almost Full* rose 5× after his performance, according to HMV.

WORST LYRICISTS

Sting's 'mountainous pomposity and cloying spirituality' earned him the number one spot on *Blender* magazine's 2007 list of the Worst Lyricists in Rock. Sting was faulted for abandoning 'new-wave songs about hookers' for lyrics that 'rip off Chaucer, St Augustine, and Shakespeare. The complete top ten list was as follows:

1 .... Sting	5 ....Dan Fogelberg	9 .... Donovan
2 ......Neil Peart (Rush)	6 .Tom Marshall (Phish)	10........Jim Morrison
3 ... Scott Stapp (Creed)	7 .... Paul Stanley (Kiss)	† Songwriter responsible for
4 ..N. Gallagher (Oasis)	8 .... Diane Warren†	'Blame It On the Rain', &c.

———————————— 'SUBSTANCES' IN MUSIC————————————

Popular music is rife with references to substance use, according to a 2008 analysis led by Dr Brian Primack of the University of Pittsburgh Medical School. Based on an assessment of the 279 most popular songs of 2005 (according to the American Billboard charts), researchers concluded that Americans 15–18 years old hear *c.*84 references to drugs, alcohol, tobacco, &c. per day and >30,000 each year. However, some genres of music featured such substances significantly more often than others:

References per song-hour:	*country*	*pop*	*R&B*	*rap*	*rock*	*all*
Tobacco	1	0	0	1	1	1
Alcohol	30	1	9	22	2	14
Marijuana	1	0	3	38	0	11
Any substance (incl. 'other')	34	2	14	105	7	35

———————————— ROCK & ROLL HALL OF FAME————————————

Madonna stole the spotlight at the March 2008 induction ceremony for the *Rock & Roll Hall of Fame*, held at New York City's Waldorf-Astoria Hotel. After being introduced by the pop singer Justin Timberlake, Madonna thanked 'the ones that said I was talentless, that I was chubby, that I couldn't sing, that I was a one-hit wonder', adding she was 'grateful for their resistance'. The 2008 inductees were:

Leonard Cohen · The Dave Clark Five (Dave Clark, Lenny Davidson, Rick Huxley, Denis Payton, Mike Smith) · Kenny Gamble & Leon Huff Madonna · John Mellencamp · The Ventures (Bob Bogle, Nokie Edwards, Gerry McGee, Mel Taylor, Don Wilson) · Little Walter

———————————— CHRISTMAS NUMBER ONE · 2007————————————

For the third year in succession, the winner of ITV's *X Factor* hit the Christmas No. 1, when Leon Jackson's *When You Believe* topped the 2007 festive singles chart. At No. 3, with *Bleeding Love*, was the 2006 *X Factor* winner, Leona Lewis – who also topped the Christmas album chart. The No. 2 spot was claimed by Eva Cassidy and Katie Melua's version of *What a Wonderful World*. The most controversial single in the chart was *Fairytale of New York* by the Pogues and Kirsty MacColl. This 1987 track reached No. 4 after a flurry of publicity caused by Radio 1's decision to censor the words 'slut' and 'faggot'[†] because 'some members of the audience might find [them] offensive'. In the face of widespread derision, Radio 1 backed down.

† In December 2007, Brighton and Hove became the first British city to ban from local venues art and music that incited racist, homophobic, or sectarian violence. The ban was a response to the allegedly homophobic lyrics in the reggae and dancehall songs of artists like Buju Banton and Beenie Man. Banton's song *Boom Bye Bye* is said to advocate shooting, burning, and pouring acid on 'batty boys' [gay men], while the singer Bounty Killer urged listeners to burn 'Mister Fagoty' and make him 'wince under agony'. If any pubs or clubs flout the ban they could be stripped of their licence or closed down.

———————THE EUROVISION SONG CONTEST · 2008———————

In March 2008, the *Eurovision: Your Decision* final was broadcast to allow the public to choose which of these six acts would represent Britain at the May Eurovision:

Michelle Gayle – *Woo (U Make Me)*
Rob McVeigh – *I Owe It All To You* · Simona Armstrong – *Changes*
LoveShy – *Mr Gorgeous* · Andy Abraham – *Even If* · The Revelations – *It's You*

The British public voted for former binman and *X Factor* finalist, Andy Abraham.

Ladbrokes' odds for Eurovision winner
Russia 11/4 · Ukraine 7/2 · Serbia 8/1 · Sweden 8/1 · Greece 9/1 · UK 66/1

THE FINAL · 24·05·08 · BELGRADE, SERBIA

Russian heart-throb Dima Bilan scooped the honours at the 53rd Eurovision in Belgrade. The contest lived up to its reputation for high kitsch with the usual kaleidoscope of novelty acts, perma-tanned lovelies, and power-ballads. However, the festival of Europop was once again overshadowed by Eastern European 'block voting'. Even Sir Terry Wogan, for so long a keen supporter of Eurovision, voiced concerns that it was 'no longer a music contest'. Writing in the *Telegraph*, Wogan went on to suggest that racism may have played a part in the UK's poor showing: 'The elephant in the room was our singer Andy Abraham's colour. East of the Danube, they won't be voting for any black singer any day soon.' The UK's entry garnered just 14 points, finishing in last place. The top three acts were:

Country	artist	song	score
Russia	Dima Bilan	*Believe*	272
Ukraine	Ani Lorak	*Shady Lady*	230
Greece	Kalomira	*Secret Combination*	218

WOGANISMS OF NOTE

'What did they do at Eurovision before the smoke and fireworks?' ❦ 'A pleasing view of the first belly button of the evening.' ❦ 'Of course the statutory three gyrating eejits.' ❦ 'It's not easy to sing in a high wind like that.' ❦ 'The Polish entry is a winsome lovely whose time has not been misspent on the sunbed.' ❦ 'And there is again just the vague hint of the Zorba.' ❦ 'This introduces the Russian entry which is called *Believe*, and if you believe in political voting rather than voting for the song, this must have a very good chance.' ❦ 'Just cling to the wreckage, it will be over soon.'

SONG LYRICS OF MERIT

GREECE · *Boy you have to try it hard, to win a destination in the centre of my heart!* ❦ RUSSIA · *Cause I've got something to believe in, as long as I'm breathing.* ❦ UKRAINE · *Shady Lady I'm gonna strike like thunder, Are you ready I wanna make you wonder.* ❦ AZERBAIJAN · *Our feelings play with us, But you must keep yourself under control, If you're searching for resolves, be ready for the tolls.* ❦ SWEDEN · *Take it or leave it you'd better believe it.* ❦ UK · *Even if my heart was breakin', I could never break your heart too, Even if all words lost their meaning, You would understand I love you.*

OTHER NOTABLE MUSIC AWARDS · 2008

Awards	prize	winner
	Best British band	Bullet For My Valentine
Kerrang!	*Hall of fame*	Rage Against The Machine
	Best live band	Machine Head
	Best British band	Arctic Monkeys
	Best solo artist	Kate Nash
NME	*Best new band*	The Enemy
	God-like genius award	Manic Street Preachers
	Best video	Arctic Monkeys · *Teddy Picker*
	Best female video	Britney Spears · *Piece of Me*
MTV	*Best male video*	Chris Brown · *With You*
	Best pop video	Britney Spears · *Piece of Me*
	Record of the year	Amy Winehouse · *Rehab*
Grammys	*Album of the year*	Herbie Hancock · *River: The Joni Letters*
	Song of the year	Amy Winehouse · *Rehab*
	Best New Age album	Paul Winter Consort · *Crestone*
	Best song	Amy Winehouse · *Love Is a Losing Game*
Ivor Novello	*Songwriter of the year*	Mika
	Most performed work	Take That · *Shine*
	Best contemporary song	Cherry Ghost · *People Help The People*
	Best UK male	Dizzee Rascal
	Best UK female	Amy Winehouse
MOBO [2007]	*Best R&B*	Ne-Yo
	Best hip hop	Kanye West
	Best African act	2Face Idibia
	Icon award	The Sex Pistols
Mojo	*Legend*	Irma Thomas
	Song of the year	Duffy · *Mercy*

THE MERCURY MUSIC PRIZE · 2008

Elbow won the 2008 Nationwide Mercury Prize for their fourth album *The Seldom Seen Kid*. It was the second time the Bury rock band had been nominated; their debut album *Asleep In The Back* missed out in 2001 to PJ Harvey. Accepting the award, frontman Guy Garvey said, 'I know I'm supposed to be cool, and say something coy, but this is quite literally the best thing that has ever happened to us'.

The 2008 Mercury nominees

Adele *19*
British Sea Power ....
          Do You Like Rock Music?
Burial .... *Untrue*
Estelle .... *Shine*
The Last Shadow Puppets ....
          The Age of the Understatement
Laura Marling.... *Alas, I Cannot Swim*
Neon Neon.............. *Stainless Style*
Portico Quartet ....
          Knee-Deep in the North Sea
Rachel Unthank & The Winterset .....
          The Bairns
Radiohead................ *In Rainbows*
Robert Plant/A. Krauss ... *Raising Sand*

———————GLOBAL BEST-SELLING ALBUMS · 2007———————

Album	artist	publisher
High School Musical 2[†]	Cast soundtrack	Disney Music Group
Back to Black	Amy Winehouse	Universal
Noel	Josh Groban	Warner
The Best Damn Thing	Avril Lavigne	SBMG
Long Road Out Of Eden	Eagles	Eagles Recording Co./Universal
Minutes To Midnight	Linkin Park	Warner
As I Am	Alicia Keys	SBMG
Call Me Irresponsible	Michael Bublé	Warner
Life in Cartoon Motion	Mika	Universal
Not Too Late	Norah Jones	EMI

[Sources: IFPI · Physical albums & downloads] † *High School Musical 3* was released in 2008; *HSM 4* is currently being written; a stage version and an ice show of *HSM 1* are currently on tour.

———————THE ECONOMICS OF GLASTONBURY———————

Glastonbury 2007 generated >£73m according to a report by Mendip District Council, released in April 2008. 177,500 people attended the event in Somerset, and the average festival-goer spent £293·24 excluding the price of the ticket (which cost £145) but including transport to the event. 64% of attendees travelled to the event by private car, and 33% used public transport – the majority (46·8%) travelled from London and the South-east. The event cost organisers £21·2m to stage, of which £2·5m was spent on paying performers such as The Arctic Monkeys. Due to heavy rain and the consequent mud, more money than usual was spent on food and drink, with an average on-site spend of £144·11 per person. The report also noted that 39% of firms in Glastonbury suffered a decline in trade during the festival, whereas pubs, restaurants, and a marquee firm all saw their profits increase.

———————WORLD'S GREENEST BAND———————

Radiohead is the world's greenest band, according to a January 2008 list compiled by music magazine *NME*. The ranking was based on an analysis by carbonfootprint. com, which measured the amount of CO_2 produced by some recent tours. On a scale from 0 ('as carbon neutral as Bob Geldof's bathwater') to 10 ('as good for the earth as an oil spill') various bands were rated as 'green' as follows:

Band	CO_2 rank			
Radiohead	2	The Cribs	4	Bands ranked by
Babyshambles	4	Kasabian	7	carbonfootprint.com on
		The Police	7	the basis of their last tour.

MusicMatters, a US marketing firm that helps bands reduce their environmental impact, states that a single stadium concert can produce 500–1,000 tons of CO_2. By comparison, the average medium-sized car produces about 6 tons CO_2 per year (according to renewable energy firm NativeEnergy).

———————————— HOME COPYING ————————————

95% of young people illegally copy music, according to research by British Music Rights (BMR)†. While anti-piracy efforts have focused on illegal swapping of music online, BMR's April 2008 survey of 18–24-year-olds found that far more illegal copying happens 'offline'. Two-thirds of those surveyed copied 5 CDs a month from friends, while 58% had copied the contents of a friend's hard drive. Almost half of the music in the average MP3 player collection is made up of stolen tracks.

† The BMR, established in 1996, speaks on behalf of songwriters, composers and music publishers. Its chief executive, Feargal Sharkey, was formerly lead singer of *The Undertones* and later a solo artist.

———————————— DIGITAL MUSIC WORLDWIDE ————————————

Record company revenue from digital music amounted to $2·9bn in 2007 – 15% of the total music market. Below is the growth in digital music revenue since 2004:

Digital music revenue		*% of total music market*
$0·4bn	2004	2%
$1·1bn	2005	5%
$2·1bn	2006	11%
$2·9bn	2007	15%

South Korea is the only country where digital sales outstrip physical – 60% of all music sold in the country is digital. ❦ The global growth rate of music downloads did not offset the continuing slump in CD sales, and in 2007 the music industry experienced an overall fall in music sales. [Source: IFPI]

———————————— GRACENOTE'S MUSIC MAP ————————————

The Gracenote Media Recognition Service is used by CD players and burners, portable MP3 players, music software, cars, and other devices to recognise and display information on audio CDs, including artist, title, and tracklist. Since 2007, Gracenote has maintained a 'music map' displaying the artists and albums most often accessed in various parts of the world. The top artists as of January 2008 were:

Place	*top artist* (genre)
Afghanistan	Queen (classic hard rock)
Australia	Ministry of Sound (trance)
Canada	The Beatles (rock)
California	The Beatles (rock)
Cuba	Joaquín Sabina (Latin rock)
Egypt	Elissa (Lebanese pop)
France	The Beatles (rock)
Germany	Die Ärzte (punk)
India	Linkin Park (rap metal)
Iran	Pink Floyd (psychedelic rock)
Ireland	U2 (adult alternative rock)
Kenya	Alkaline Trio (emo)
Malaysia	Avril Lavigne (teen rock)
New York	The Beatles (rock)
Russian Fed.	Linkin Park (rap metal)
Pakistan	Jal (rock/pop)
Spain	The Beatles (rock)
South Korea	Bigbang (hip hop)
United Kingdom	The Beatles (rock)
Venezuela	Wisin & Yandel (reggaetón)
	[Genre according to Gracenote, MySpace, &c.]

THE FACH SYSTEM

The Fach System is a German method of categorising opera singers according to the range, colour, and character of their voice, as well as their acting ability and physical appearance. The system was once used to facilitate casting in European repertory opera houses, although it is used less frequently today. Below is an adaptation of the system based on information compiled by the singer and teacher Bard Suverkrop:

	Fach	description	role example
Soprano	Soubrette	mellow, light, supple	Adèle, *Die Fledermaus*
	Lyric Coloratura	flexible, bright	Zerbinetta, *Ariadne auf Naxos*
	Dramatic Coloratura	dramatic, rich	Violetta, *La Traviata*
	Full Lyric Soprano	supple, feminine	Michaela, *Carmen*
	Spinto Soprano	powerful, intense	Desdemona, *Othello*
	Charaktersopran	lyric with dramatic abilities	Tosca, *Tosca*
	Dramatic Soprano	intense, metallic, emotional depth	Aïda, *Aïda*
	Wagnerian Soprano	large, heavy	Brünnhilde, *Die Walküre*
Mezzo/ Alto	Lyric Mezzo	light, expressive	Cherubino, *Le nozze di Figaro*
	Dramatic Mezzo I	flexible, metallic, dark	Carmen, *Carmen*
	Dramatic Mezzo II	flexible, metallic, dramatic	Herodias, *Salome*
	Alto	rich, extended bottom range	Erda, *Das Rheingold*
Tenor	Buffo Tenor	smaller voice, good acting skills	Jacquino, *Fidelio*
	Light Lyric Tenor	mellow, extended top range	Alfredo, *La Traviata*
	Full Lyric Tenor	heavier lyric tenor	Des Grieux, *Manon*
	Charaktertenor	large voice, good characterisation	Herodes, *Salome*
	Spinto Tenor	noble, staying power	Max, *Der Freischütz*
	Dramatic Tenor	full, baritonal ability	Siegfried, *Götterdämmerung*
Baritone	Lyric Baritone	mellow, good actor	Malatesta, *Don Pasquale*
	Kavalierbariton	manly, good looks	Don Juan, *Don Giovanni*
	Verdi Baritone	powerful, nuanced	Scarpia, *Tosca*
	Heldenbariton	heavy, projecting	Kurwenal, *Tristan*
Bass	Buffo Bass	smaller, flexible, expressive	Pasquale, *Don Pasquale*
	Heavy Buffo	large, imposing	Baron Ochs, *Der Rosenkavalier*
	Bass Baritone	refined, good characterisation	Zuniga, *Carmen*
	Basso Cantabile	full, dark, low	Philip, *Don Carlos*

Below are some opera singers, past and present, known for singing in various Fachs:

Soubrette	Dawn Upshaw	Dramatic Mezzo II	Christa Ludwig
Lyric Coloratura	Beverly Sills	Alto	Clara Butt
Dramatic Coloratura	Maria Callas	Light Lyric Tenor	Rockwell Blake
Full Lyric Soprano	Elisabeth Schwarzkopf	Full Lyric Tenor	Fritz Wunderlich
Spinto Soprano	Aprile Millo	Spinto Tenor	Luciano Pavarotti & Plácido Domingo
Dramatic Soprano	Birgit Nilsson	Lyric Baritone	Lawrence Tibbett
Lyric Mezzo	Cecilia Bartoli	Basso Cantabile	Nicolai Ghiaurov

[Sources: Bard Suverkrop & IPASource.com; *The New Grove Dictionary of Opera*; Vocalist.org]

CLASSIC FM HALL OF FAME · 2008

Every year the radio station *Classic FM* compiles a 'Hall of Fame', reflecting its listeners' 300 favourite pieces. In 2008 Vaughan Williams' *The Lark Ascending* topped the chart for the second year running, with another of his pieces, *Fantasia on a Theme of Thomas Tallis*, at number 3. The top 10 (with 2007 places in brackets) were:

```
 1 .... [1] ..... Ralph Vaughan Williams ...................... The Lark Ascending†
 2 .... [3] ..... Sergei Rachmaninov .............. Piano Concerto No. 2 in C minor
 3 .... [10] .... Ralph Vaughan Williams ....... Fantasia on a Theme of Thomas Tallis
 4 .... [5] ..... Ludwig van Beethoven ..... Piano Concerto No. 5 in E flat (Emperor)
 5 .... [8] ..... Ludwig van Beethoven .................. Symphony No. 6 (Pastoral)
 6 .... [4] ..... Wolfgang Amadeus Mozart ................. Clarinet Concerto in A
 7 .... [2] ..... Edward Elgar ...................................... Cello Concerto
 8 .... [7] ..... Max Bruch ................................. Violin Concerto No. 1
 9 .... [6] ..... Edward Elgar ................................. Enigma Variations
10 ... [9] ..... Ludwig van Beethoven .................. Symphony No. 9 (Choral)
```

† Composed in 1914, it was inspired by a poem of the same name by English poet George Meredith.

QUEEN'S MEDAL FOR MUSIC

The Queen's Medal for Music is awarded annually to those who have had 'a major influence on the musical life of the nation'†. The nomination process is overseen by a committee under the chairmanship of the Master of The Queen's Music‡, currently Sir Peter Maxwell Davies. Established in 2005, the first award was presented to the conductor Sir Charles Mackerras; in 2006, Welsh opera singer Bryn Terfel was honoured. The 2007 winner was the composer JUDITH WEIR. ❦ Weir was born in 1954 in Cambridge into a Scottish family. She took up the oboe and played with the National Youth Orchestra of Great Britain. After studying at Cambridge University, Weir worked as a community musician in southern England before moving to Glasgow to teach. Between 1995–2000, Weir was artistic director of the Spitalfields Festival in east London. In 2004, she was the Fromm Foundation Visiting Professor at Harvard University, and she is currently a Research Professor in Composition at Cardiff University. ❦ Weir is best known for her opera and theatre compositions including the full-length operas *The Vanishing Bridegroom*, *Blond Eckbert*, and *A Night at the Chinese Opera*. *The Times* described the latter as 'the wittiest piece of music-theatre written by a British composer in the past 50 years', and praised Weir for having 'a knack for saying something very moving, funny, or deep with a tiny number of notes on a handful of instruments'.

† Her Majesty presents a number of other medals and prizes including the Queen's Gold Medal for Poetry, the Queen's Award for Enterprise, and the Queen's Award for Voluntary Service.
‡ The committee members include composer Michael Berkeley, MD of the Barbican Nicholas Kenyon, retired ambassador Sir Humphrey Maud, and *The Times*' music critic Richard Morrison.

─────────── MUSIC & WINE ───────────

Listening to certain styles of music can enhance the taste of wine, according to psychologists at Heriot-Watt University. The researchers first identified four songs which exemplified certain styles of music: *Carmina Burana* by Orff (which was classified as 'powerful and heavy'), Tchaikovsky's *Waltz of the Flowers* from *The Nutcracker* ('subtle and refined'), *Slow Breakdown* by Michael Brook ('mellow and soft'), and *Just Can't Get Enough* by Nouvelle Vague ('zingy and refreshing'). Then, subjects were given wine to quaff while listening to these tracks and were asked if the music influenced its flavour. White wine was rated as 40% more 'zingy' when supped while listening to Nouvelle Vague, but only 26% more 'mellow and soft' while listening to Michael Brook. Red wine was most enhanced (by 60%) when imbibed during *Carmina Burana*. The Chilean winemaker Aurelio Montes (who admitted he is wont to play hypnotically soothing monastic chants to his wines as they mature) commissioned the research in May 2008, and subsequently recommended the following complementary wine and music combinations:

SYRAH *best drunk with* ...
Nessun Dorma · Puccini
Chariots of Fire · Vangelis
Orinoco Flow · Enya

CABERNET SAUVIGNON
Honky Tonk Woman · Rolling Stones
Won't Get Fooled Again · The Who
Live & Let Die · Paul McCartney

MERLOT
Easy · Lionel Richie
Heartbeats · José González
Over the Rainbow · Eva Cassidy

CHARDONNAY
Atomic · Blondie
Spinning Around · Kylie Minogue
Rock DJ · Robbie Williams

─────────── MUSICAL INSTRUMENTS IN SCHOOLS ───────────

The guitar may soon overtake the violin as the instrument most widely taught in British schools, according to a 2007 report from the Institute of Education:

Instrument (% learning)	2005	2007
Violin	23·9	19·2
Acoustic guitar	17·1	18·3
Keyboard	8·9	8·0
Flute	11·0	7·7
Clarinet	9·2	6·7

Instrument	2005	2007
Recorder	11·5	5·8
Voice	10·1	5·1
Trumpet	3·8	3·7
Cello	3·7	3·4

Only 0·45% of children learn the euphonium.

─────────── THE CLASSICAL BRITS · 2008 ───────────

Best album	Blake · *Blake*
Female artist of the year	Anna Netrebko
Male artist of the year	Sir Colin Davis
Young British classical performer or group	Nicola Benedetti
Outstanding contribution award	Andrew Lloyd Webber

——————————— THE BBC PROMS · 2008 ———————————

The 2008 Proms were the first to be directed by Roger Wright, who succeeded Nicholas Kenyon after 12 years. The programme celebrated the 50th anniversary of the death of Ralph Vaughan Williams, the centenaries of Olivier Messiaen and Elliott Carter, and the 80th anniversary of Karlheinz Stockhausen. There were 20 UK premieres, including 11 BBC commissions, and performances from a galaxy of stars, including Murray Perahia, Daniel Barenboim, and Bernard Haitink. Press and public curiosity was piqued by Prom 13 – a celebration of the music of *Dr Who*.

PROM 76 · THE LAST NIGHT OF THE PROMS · 13·9·2008

Ludwig van Beethoven ....*The Creatures of Prometheus – overture*
Richard Wagner....................*Tannhäuser – 'Wie Todesahnung Dämmrung ...'*
Giacomo Puccini.....................................*Tosca – 'Tre sbirri, Una carrozza'*
Giuseppe Verdi.............................*Falstaff – 'Ehi paggio! ... L'onore Ladri!'*
Beethoven......*Fantasia in C minor for piano, chorus and orchestra, 'Choral Fantasy'*
Luigi Denza (arr. Nikolai Rimsky-Korsakov)......................*Funiculì, funiculà*
Traditional (arr. Chris Hazell)......................................*Folk song medley*
Anna Meredith..*froms* [sic]
Edward Elgar......*Pomp and Circumstance March No. 1 – 'Land of Hope and Glory'*
Vaughan Williams ....*Sea Songs*
Thomas Arne (arr. Malcolm Sargent)...............................*Rule, Britannia!*
Hubert Parry (orch. Edward Elgar) ....*Jerusalem*
Henry Wood (arr.)..*The National Anthem*

BBC Singers, Symphony Chorus, & Symphony Orchestra; Sir Roger Norrington conductor

——————— YOUNG MUSICIAN OF THE YEAR · 2008 ———————

Peter Moore, a 12-year-old trombonist, was named the youngest ever BBC Young Musician of the Year in May 2008. Moore beat guitarist Jadran Duncumb (18), flautist David Smith (18), percussionist Jim Molyneux (17), and pianist Erdem Misirlioglu (18) to take the biennial title at Cardiff's Wales Millennium Centre.

——————— SOME CLASSICAL ANNIVERSARIES · 2009 ———————

2009 marks a number of significant anniversaries for German(ic) composers. It is 200 years since the birth of FELIX MENDELSSOHN-BARTHOLDY (3·2·1809). G.F. HANDEL died 250 years ago (14·4·1759), and 200 years have passed since the death of FRANZ JOSEPH HAYDN (31·5·1809). Other classical anniversaries in 2009 are:

*b.*1659...................... Henry Purcell	*d.*1959............Heitor Villa-Lobos[†]
*b.*1709.................... Franz Benda	*d.*1959.................... Ernest Bloch
*b.*1859.................... Basil Harwood	
*b.*1934..........Peter Maxwell Davies	[†] Brazilian by birth, he is considered to be the
*b.*1934..............Harrison Birtwistle	best-known classical composer from S America.

---------------------MUSIC & NOISE---------------------

In February 2008, the music and entertainment industries became bound by EU regulations requiring employers to protect workers from damaging levels of noise. The *EU Noise at Work Directive 2003/10/EC* established an average weekly workplace sound level of 85 decibels (dB), after which specially designed earplugs, noise-reducing screens, and other measures are required. While rock and pop are more commonly associated with loud noise, the directive also caused some difficulty for classical musicians, since orchestras can produce dangerous decibel levels. The German Federal Industrial Safety Commission noted that the noise produced by orchestral musicians is 'by all means comparable to the strain in main industrial work environments'. While the full consequences of the law were not clear at the time of writing, some musicians immediately described the regulations as unworkable, and critics voiced concern that a number of pieces, such as those by Wagner[†] and Strauss, would be rendered virtually unplayable. Listed below are the average decibel levels of various instruments, with some other noises for comparison:

0 dB .... threshold of hearing	84 dB........................percussion
10 dB......rustling leaves, whispering	86 dB............... flute, double bass
30 dB................ ticking clock	87 dB........................... trumpet
40 dB................ quiet living room	88 dB.......bassoon, horn, trombone
60 dB............normal conversation	90 dB........ heavy truck, lawnmower
70 dB........ cars[†], ringing telephone	100 dB ....dance club
80 dB..... busy street, vacuum cleaner	110 dB .... jackhammer, rock band
82 dB............................. harp	130 dB .....absolute threshold of pain
83 dB............................. violin	140 dB ....jet plane

† During Wagner's *Der Ring des Nibelungen*, trumpets and tubas can reach 110 dB, violins can hit 109 dB, and a deafening 118 dB (louder than a jackhammer) has been measured at the right ear of a flautist. ‡ In the extreme motor sport 'dB drag racing', enthusiasts compete to see who can produce the most noise inside a sealed car using only its motor and various amplifiers. At the time of writing, the loudest recorded car reportedly achieved 180·2 dB, in December 2007. [Sources: Arbeitsinspektion Austria, German health insurance firm Innungskrankenkasse, the German government, termpro.com]

--------ROYAL PHILHARMONIC SOCIETY AWARDS · 2008--------

BBC Radio 3 listeners' award	Christine Brewer
Chamber-scale composition...................... Rebecca Saunders ·	*Stirrings Still*
Concert series and festivals........ RNCM Manchester International Cello Festival
Conductor	Edward Gardner
Education .... Land Sea Sky Trilogy (WNO Max)
Ensemble...................................Orchestra of the Age of Enlightenment
Instrumentalist...	Imogen Cooper
Large-scale composition....................................... Thomas Adès ·	*Tevot*
Opera..James MacMillan ·	*The Sacrifice*
Singer...	John Tomlinson
Young artist	Gustavo Dudamel

———————— UK TOP-GROSSING FILMS · 2007 ————————

Film	UK box office gross (£m)	Director
Harry Potter: Order of the Phoenix	49·4	David Yates
Pirates of the Caribbean: At World's End	40·7	Gore Verbinski
Shrek the Third	38·7	Chris Miller
The Simpsons	38·7	David Silverman
Spider-Man 3	33·6	Sam Raimi
*The Golden Compass**	26·0	Chris Weitz
*I Am Legend**	25·5	Francis Lawrence
Ratatouille	24·8	Brad Bird
The Bourne Ultimatum	23·7	Paul Greengrass
Transformers	23·5	Michael Bay

[Source: Nielsen EDI, RSU · Box office gross as at 2·3·08 · * still being shown 2·3·2008]

———————— BEST FILM COSTUME ————————

The green dress worn by Keira Knightley in *Atonement* was voted best film costume in a January 2008 survey by Sky Movies and *In Style*. The top five costumes were:

Actress & costume	Film
Keira Knightley's emerald green satin evening dress	*Atonement*
Marilyn Monroe's white halterneck dress	*The Seven Year Itch*
Audrey Hepburn's black Givenchy dress†	*Breakfast at Tiffany's*
Olivia Newton-John's skin-tight trousers	*Grease*
Kate Winslet's blue gown	*Titanic*

† In 2006, this dress was sold at auction for £467,200; the proceeds went to a Calcutta-based charity.

———————— TOP PERFORMING UK ACTORS ————————

104 of the top 200 films at the international box office since 2001 have featured a British actor in either the lead role (26 films), or in the supporting cast (78). UK Film Council figures released in July 2008 revealed the top ten British actors by appearances in the top 200 films at the worldwide box office 2001–07; they are:

Actor	No. film appearances	gross box office ($bn)	Actor	No. film appearances	gross box office ($bn)
Orlando Bloom†	8	6·30	Keira Knightley	5	3·13
Ian McKellen	7	4·71	Timothy Spall	6	2·88
Daniel Radcliffe‡	4	4·48	Ewan McGregor	4	1·94
Christopher Lee	5	3·76	Kate Beckinsale	4	1·20
			Brian Cox	4	1·14
			Jude Law	5	1·03

† Bloom appeared in two of the biggest film trilogies of all time – *Lord of the Rings* and *Pirates of the Caribbean*. ‡ The same figure applies to *Harry Potter* co-stars Emma Watson and Rupert Grint.

—80TH ACADEMY AWARD WINNERS · 2008—

The media world breathed a sigh of relief when the Writers' Guild of America strike was settled in time for the 2008 Oscars [see p.163]. Yet for many the show failed to live up to the dazzle of previous years. A gang of bleak Best Picture nominees did nothing to lift a strike-bruised industry, and with little time to prepare the ceremony, host Jon Stewart's presentation was top-heavy with pre-prepared clips. Though no one film dominated, it was a good night for those outside the Hollywood elite – all 4 Best Actor awards went to people without a US passport. And the winners were …

Leading actor	Daniel Day-Lewis · *There Will be Blood*
Leading actress	Marion Cotillard · *La Vie en Rose*
Supporting actor	Javier Bardem · *No Country for Old Men*
Supporting actress	Tilda Swinton · *Michael Clayton*
Best picture	*No Country for Old Men*
Directing	Joel Coen & Ethan Coen · *No Country for Old Men*
Animated feature	Brad Bird · *Ratatouille*
Art direction	Dante Ferretti & Francesca Lo Schiavo · *Sweeney Todd*
Cinematography	Robert Elswit · *There Will be Blood*
Costume design	Alexandra Byrne · *Elizabeth: The Golden Age*
Doc. feature	Alex Gibney & Eva Orner · *Taxi to the Dark Side*
Doc. short subject	Cynthia Wade & Vanessa Roth · *Freeheld*
Film editing	Christopher Rouse · *The Bourne Ultimatum*
Foreign language film	Stefan Ruzowitzky · *The Counterfeiters*
Make-up	Didier Lavergne & Jan Archibald · *La Vie en Rose*
Music (score)	Dario Marianelli · *Atonement*
Music (song)	Glen Hansard & Marketa Irglová *Falling Slowly* · *Once*
Short film (animated)	Suzie Templeton & Hugh Welchman · *Peter & The Wolf*
Short film (live)	Philippe Pollet-Villard · *Le Mozart des Pickpockets*
Sound mixing	Scott Millan, David Parker, & Kirk Francis *The Bourne Ultimatum*
Sound editing	Karen Baker Landers & Per Hallberg · *The Bourne Ultimatum*
Visual effects	Fink, Westenhofer, Morris, & Wood · *The Golden Compass*
Screenplay (adapted)	Joel Coen & Ethan Coen · *No Country for Old Men*
Screenplay (original)	Diablo Cody · *Juno*
Honorary award	Robert Boyle

QUOTES ❦ JON STEWART · Does this town need a hug? What happened? ❦ TILDA SWINTON · I have an American agent who is the spitting image of this. Really, truly the same shaped head and, it has to be said, the buttocks. ❦ MARION COTILLARD · Thank you life. Thank you love. And it is true there are some angels in this city. ❦ JAVIER BARDEM · Thank you to the Coens … [for putting] one of the most horrible haircuts in history over my head. ❦ DANIEL DAY-LEWIS (receiving his award from Dame Helen Mirren) · That's the closest I'll ever come to getting a knighthood. ❦ JOEL COEN · We're very thankful to all of you out there for letting us continue to play in our corner of the sandbox. ❦ HELEN MIRREN · Unfortunately, so often the roles are not good enough for the women, but the roles for the men are always wonderful. ❦ DIABLO CODY (*Juno* screenwriter) · This is for the writers.

OSCAR NIGHT FASHION · 2008

Star	dress	designer
Nicole Kidman	*simple black silk, empire line*	Balenciaga
Hilary Swank	*black, one-shoulder, netting fish-tail skirt*	Versace
Tilda Swinton	*black silk, unstructured, asymmetric*	Lanvin
Ellen Page	*black, vintage flapper-style dress*	Jean Louis Scherrer
Cate Blanchett	*deep purple, empire line, flower details*	Dries Van Noten
Amy Adams	*dark green, corseted strapless, fish-tail*	Proenza Schouler
Anne Hathaway	*bright red draped dress, garland shoulder detail*	Marchesa
Katherine Heigl	*bright red, sleek, one-shoulder*	Escada
Diablo Cody	*leopard print, chiffon*	Dior
Marion Cotillard	*pearl white, sequin encrusted fish-scales*	Jean-Paul Gaultier

OSCAR LOSERS

The Shawshank Redemption is the film that most deserved to win an Oscar but never did – according to a 2008 poll by advertising company Pearl & Dean. Below are the top 10 most deserving films snubbed by the Academy:

#	film	released
1	*The Shawshank Redemption*	1994
2	*The Sixth Sense*	1999
3	*Fight Club*	1999
4	*Blade Runner*	1982
5	*It's a Wonderful Life* [tie]	1946
5	*The Great Escape* [tie]	1963
7	*Taxi Driver* [tie]	1976
7	*Psycho* [tie]	1960
9	*Singin' in the Rain*	1952
10	*Dr Strangelove*	1964

In 2008, *Entertainment Weekly* named Jimmy Stewart's failure to win an Oscar for his 1958 performance in *Vertigo* the worst Oscar snub.

OSCAR ODDS

Oscar-watchers have long suspected that actors who perform in dramas are more likely to be nominated for an Academy Award. In January 2008, a team of Harvard and UCLA sociologists confirmed these suspicions by analysing the Internet Movie Database records for every Oscar-eligible film released from 1927–2005. The researchers discovered that actors who appeared in dramas were 9× as likely to receive an Oscar nomination, when compared to actors who appeared in other genres. Women also had a higher chance of nomination, since there are fewer roles for the fairer sex but the same number of Oscar slots. An actor's chances of nomination were also increased by previous nominations and a higher placing in past movie credits, as well as by having a major distributor. Cast size and industry ties were found to have little effect.

THE OSCARS OF ...

A variety of awards are touted as 'the Oscars of' various industries, including: the Golden Bone Awards, the Oscars of the dog world · the British Archaeological Awards, the Oscars of British archaeology · the Britain in Bloom Awards, the Oscars of community gardening · the Health and Social Care awards, the Oscars of the caring professions · the AVN Adult Movie Awards, the Oscars of porn.

————— THE HOLLYWOOD SIGN —————

The Hollywood sign was erected on the southern slope of Mt Lee in the Santa Monica Mountains in 1923, by property developer Harry Chandler, with the goal of publicising a housing development below. The sign's prominent position soon made it a metonym for both the area and the burgeoning film industry. However, as the chart below illustrates, the fluctuating fortunes of Hollywood have since been reflected in the changing typographical condition of the sign's 50'-tall letters:

HOLLYWOODLAND

The sign cost $21,000 but was only intended to last a year and a half.

OLLYWOODLAND

Two decades of neglect resulted in the H toppling over in the late 1940s.

HOLLYWOOD

In 1949 the Hollywood Chamber of Commerce repaired the sign, removing the LAND.

HOL YWO

During the 1970s the top of the D and the third O fell down,
and an arsonist set fire to the bottom of the second L.

HOLLYWEED

In 1973 a practical joker altered the letters to encourage the loosening of laws on marijuana.

$ HOLLYWOOD $

In 1978 Hugh Hefner hosted a gala fundraiser to restore the sign, with
celebrities sponsoring individual letters. Rocker Alice Cooper
bought an O, and crooner Andy Williams bought the W.

For three months in 1978, while the old sign was removed
and a new one constructed, Hollywood had no sign at all.

HOLLYWOOD

The sign was altered to mark Pope John Paul II's visit in 1987.

In March 2008, a Chicago-based investment group offered 138 acres above and left of the sign for $22m; inevitably, some groups have expressed fears that developing the land would overshadow the landmark. ❦ Hollywood has become so iconic that other entertainment-related locations have adopted names ending in '-wood', including: Bollywood (Bombay-based film industry), Lollywood (Lahore-based Pakistani film industry), Nollywood (Nigerian film industry), and Dollywood (Dolly Parton's Tennessee theme park). Hollywood, California, should not be confused with the Belfast suburb of Holywood, County Down, whose attractions include the Ulster Folk & Transport Museum.

——— MOVIE AWARDS OF NOTE ———

BAFTAs 2008 · *bafta.org*

Best film..*Atonement*
Best British film...*This is England*
Best actor in a leading role.................Daniel Day-Lewis · *There Will be Blood*
Best actress in a leading role..................... Marion Cotillard · *La Vie en Rose*
Best actor in a supporting role..........Javier Bardem · *No Country For Old Men*
Best actress in a supporting role.................. Tilda Swinton · *Michael Clayton*

MTV MOVIE AWARDS 2008 · *mtv.com*

Best male performance ....Will Smith · *I Am Legend*
Best female performance .... Ellen Page · *Juno*
Best movie... *Transformers*
Best villain .... Johnny Depp · *Sweeney Todd*
Best fight ....Sean Faris *vs.* Cam Gigandet · *Never Back Down*

GOLDEN GLOBES 2008 · *hfpa.org*

Best dramatic film ....*Atonement*
Best dramatic actor ....Daniel Day-Lewis · *There Will be Blood*
Best dramatic actress................................. Julie Christie · *Away From Her*
Best director.................... Julian Schnabel · *The Diving Bell and the Butterfly*
Best actor in musical or comedy ....Johnny Depp · *Sweeney Todd*
Best actress in musical or comedy............... Marion Cotillard · *La Vie en Rose*

BRITISH INDEPENDENT FILM AWARDS 2007 · *bifa.org.uk*

Best British independent film ....*Control*
Best actor......................................Viggo Mortensen · *Eastern Promises*
Best actress ....Judi Dench · *Notes on a Scandal*
Richard Harris award for outstanding achievement................. Ray Winstone

GOLDEN RASPBERRIES 2008 · *razzies.com*

Worst picture ....*I Know Who Killed Me*
Worst actor.. Eddie Murphy · *Norbit*
Worst actress .... Lindsay Lohan · *I Know Who Killed Me*

EMPIRE AWARDS 2008 · *empireonline.co.uk*

Best actor..James McAvoy · *Atonement*
Best actress ....Keira Knightley · *Atonement*
Best director...............David Yates · *Harry Potter and the Order of the Phoenix*
Best British film..*Atonement*
Best film.. *The Bourne Ultimatum*

EVENING STANDARD BRITISH FILM AWARDS 2008

Best film...*Control*
Best actor...................................Daniel Day-Lewis · *There Will be Blood*
Best actress ....Helena Bonham-Carter · *Sweeney Todd*
Most promising newcomer....................................John Carney · *Once*

———————————FOREIGN LANGUAGE FILMS———————————

The number of foreign language films shown in UK & Irish cinemas 2002–07:

Year	number	% of all releases	box office (£m)	% of total gross
2002	131	35·5	17·1	2·2
2003	147	34·7	20·4	2·5
2004	169	37·5	38·1	4·6
2005	203	43·5	26·9	3·2
2006	171	33·9	29·8	3·5
2007	170	32·9	32·3	3·5

Films in 34 different languages were shown in UK and Irish cinemas in 2007 (30 in 2006). Listed below are the languages and number of releases in 2007:

Language	No. releases				
Aboriginal	1	Greek	1	Punjabi	2
Arabic	4	Hebrew	2	Romanian	1
Cantonese	2	Hindi	52	Russian	2
Czech	1	Hungarian	1	Spanish	7
Danish	2	Indonesian	1	Swedish	2
Dutch	1	Italian	4	Tamil	12
English	315	Japanese	2	Telugu	2
English with others	30	Korean	3	Thai	2
Finnish	1	Mandarin	5	Turkish	6
Flemish	1	Mayan	1	Urdu	2
French	34	Norwegian	2	Silent	1
German	7	Polish	3		
		Portuguese	1	TOTAL	516

[Source: UK Film Council Statistical Yearbook 2008, Nielsen EDI, BBFC, IMDb, RSU analysis]

———————————DOG WALK OF FAME———————————

In order to give due respect to the legendary dogs of film and TV, the first ever canine 'walk of fame' was established in London's Battersea Park in November 2007. The first 6 dogs to be immortalised with a permanent plaque on the walk were:

Dog	film or TV series	breed
Bullseye	*Oliver!* (1968)	bull terrier
Lassie	*Lassie* (TV 1958–74); *Lassie Come Home* (1943)	collie
Toto	*The Wizard of Oz* (1939)	cairn terrier
Bobby	*Greyfriars Bobby* (1961)	Skye terrier
Gromit	*Wallace & Gromit* (1989–)	cartoon beagle
Chance & Shadow	*Homeward Bound* (1963)	bulldog, golden retriever
Fang	The *Harry Potter* films (2001–)	Neapolitan mastiff

Dogs chosen via an online vote at Skymovies.com, which sponsored the walk with the Kennel Club.

─────── METHOD ACTING ───────

2008 Best Actor Oscar winner Daniel Day-Lewis is famous for his involved preparations before a role. He lived off the land for six months to prepare for *The Last of the Mohicans*, trained in the ring for nearly three years before his turn in *The Boxer*, and while shooting *My Left Foot*, in which he played a character with cerebral palsy, rarely left his wheelchair and was reportedly spoon-fed by crew members. Such measures are a more extreme form of method acting, which emphasises emotional identification with the character one is to portray. The Russian theatre director Konstantin Stanislavsky (1863–1938), usually cited as the father of method acting, urged a move away from the exaggerated, artificial style of theatrical performance towards a naturalistic approach emphasising psychological depth. After founding the Moscow Art Theatre in 1897, he developed the Stanislavsky System, a set of techniques through which actors are trained to become their characters by drawing upon the experiences and emotions of their own life. These techniques were later refined at the Actors Studio in Manhattan, under the auspices of the formidable Lee Strasberg, an immigrant from the Ukraine. Strasberg drew upon Stanislavsky's theories to create a series of physical and psychological exercises that encouraged actors to plumb their own psyche as well as the motivations of their character. While a school of sorts, the Actors Studio (still extant) offers no final degree, and its membership is for life. Notable Actors Studio members include:

James Dean · Marlon Brando · Marilyn Monroe · Dustin Hoffman
Robert De Niro · Al Pacino · Sidney Poitier · Norman Mailer · Geraldine Page
Edward Albee · Montgomery Clift · Shelley Winters · Frank Corsaro

By most accounts, Stanislavsky and Lee Strasberg's ideas are now part of mainstream acting theory, although the 'method' also has its detractors. According to an oft-repeated anecdote, when Dustin Hoffman stayed awake for two days to 'get into' his character during the filming of *Marathon Man*, his co-star Laurence Olivier is said to have quipped, 'Why don't you try acting? It's so much easier'.

─────── BEST FILMS BY GENRE ───────

The American Film Institute (AFI) balloted a host of actors, critics, and film-makers to create a series of lists of the 10 greatest films across 10 different genres, in June 2008. According to AFI members, the top ranking film of each genre is as follows:

Genre	top ranking film
Animation	*Snow White & the Seven Dwarfs* (1937)
Fantasy	*The Wizard of Oz* (1939)
Gangster	*The Godfather* (1972)
Science fiction	*2001: A Space Odyssey* (1968)
Western	*The Searchers* (1956)
Sports	*Raging Bull* (1980)
Mystery	*Vertigo* (1958)
Romantic comedy	*City Lights* (1931)
Courtroom drama	*To Kill a Mockingbird* (1962)
Epic	*Lawrence of Arabia* (1962)

According to the UK Film Council, the most popular genre of film at the UK box office in 2007 was comedy, making up 24·6% of all film releases, and taking 22·1% of the gross box office.

———————— FILM FESTIVAL PRIZES · 2008 ————————

Sundance · World Cinema Dramatic [JAN]... *The King of Ping Pong* · Jens Jonsson
Berlin · Golden Bear [FEB] .... *Elite Squad* · José Padilha
Tribeca · Best Narrative Feature [APR] ..... *Let the Right One In* · Tomas Alfredson
Cannes · Palme d'Or [MAY] .... *The Class* · Laurent Cantet
Moscow · Golden St George [JUN] .... *As Simple as That* · Reza Mir Karimi
Edinburgh · Audience Award [JUN].................... *Man on Wire* · James Marsh
Montreal · Grand Prize of the Americas [AUG]........... *Okuribito* · Yojiro Takita
Venice · Golden Lion [SEP]........................ *The Wrestler* · Darren Aronofsky
Toronto · People's Choice Award [SEP] .... *Slumdog Millionaire* · Danny Boyle
London · Sutherland Trophy [OCT '07].... *Persepolis* · M. Satrapi & V. Paronnaud

———————— SOME MOVIE TAGLINES OF NOTE ————————

Why so serious? ....*The Dark Knight*
Heroes never die ... They just reload ....*Rambo (2008)*
One elephant, one world, one story ....*Horton Hears a Who*
Shoot first. Sightsee later ....*In Bruges*
The last man on earth is not alone....................................*I Am Legend*
Get carried away.. *Sex and the City*
Privilege. Ambition. Desire.. *Brideshead Revisited*
Put this in your pipe and smoke it .... *Pineapple Express*
His karma is huge...*The Love Guru*
Because you were home...*The Strangers*
Saving the world. And loving it ....*Get Smart*
A story of sex, thugs, and rock 'n' roll..................................*RocknRolla*
... Here we go again ....*Mamma Mia!*

According to a 2008 survey released by branding agency Tagline Guru, the top tagline ever is *In space no one can hear you scream* (from *Alien*), followed by *Houston, we have a problem* (*Apollo 13*), *They're back* (*Poltergeist II*), and *We are not alone* (*Close Encounters of the Third Kind*). The survey of 500 ad professionals rated taglines based on humour, attitude, expression, and influence on popular culture.

———————— BEST MOVIE SOUNDTRACKS ————————

In October 2007, *Vanity Fair* produced a one-off magazine *Movies Rock*, in which they asked their editors to create a list of the greatest movie soundtracks of all time:

Movie/soundtrack	*artist*
1 ..*Purple Rain*†	Prince
2 ..*A Hard Day's Night*	The Beatles
3 ..*The Harder They Come*	various
4 ..*Pulp Fiction*	various
5 ..*The Graduate*	Simon & Garfunkel
6 ..*Superfly*	Curtis Mayfield
7 ..*Trainspotting*	various
8 ..*Saturday Night Fever*	various
9 ..*American Graffiti*	various
10.*The Big Chill*	various

† The film (directed by Albert Magnoli) won an Oscar in 1985 for Best Original Song Score.

WRITERS' STRIKE

On 5/11/2007, the Writers Guild of America (WGA) called 'pencils down' in a fight over new-media royalties, DVD residuals, and jurisdiction over reality and animation writers. Scarred by a 1985 deal which gave them only a small cut of home video revenues, WGA members boycotted work for 100 days while their representatives negotiated with the Alliance of Motion Picture & TV Producers (AMPTP). The sticking point proved to be new-media revenues, but eventually a 'precedent-setting deal' was reached to give writers a piece of the action. The strike cost LA's economy *c*.$2·5bn and very nearly cancelled the Oscars. Below is a timeline of events:

{16/7/07} The WGA and AMPTP begin contract negotiations. {18/7} Talks end without progress. {19/9} Talks resume. '*The WGA made clear today that they ... have a total disregard for the true state of the industry and its fundamental economics.*' – Nick Counter, AMPTP President. {5/10} Talks end; no progress. {19/10} 90% of the WGA votes to strike. {25/10} Talks resume. {31/10} Talks end; the WGA contract expires. {2/11} The WGA calls for a strike: '*The studios have not responded to a single one of our important proposals.*' – Patric Verrone, the WGA West President. {5/11} The strike begins; within days several shows suspend production. '*How greedy can you get, they won't even share the net!*' – strike chant. {8/11} 4,000 striking writers picket LA's Avenue of the Stars. {26/11} Talks resume; *Last Call with Carson Daly* resumes production with non-union writers. {7/12} Talks collapse. {11/12} The WGA approves a script waiver for the Screen Actors Guild Awards. {13/12} The WGA claims the AMPTP refused to bargain in good faith. {17/12} The WGA declines script waivers for Academy Award and Golden Globes telecasts. {2/1/08} Jay Leno, Conan O'Brien, and Jimmy Kimmel resume their shows without writers. *The Late Show with David Letterman* resumes with writers after a one-off deal. {6/1} United Artists reaches a deal with the WGA. '*One-off deals do nothing to bring the WGA closer to a permanent solution for working writers.*' – AMPTP statement. {7/1} *The Daily Show with Jon Stewart* and *The Colbert Report* return without writers. {13/1} An ersatz, nominee-free Golden Globes ceremony airs: '*It's like an Irish wake where there's food and drink but somebody is missing.*' – Kevin Jacobsen, security guard. {18/1} The stalemate has ended, the WGA says. {23/1} Talks resume after the WGA agrees to withdraw its demands to organise reality and animation writers. '*Must be present to win.*' – mock Oscar-nomination certificate unveiled by Academy President Sid Ganis. {5/2} *Vanity Fair* cancels its annual Oscar party. {9/2} WGA board announces a tentative deal: '*Our strike has been a success.*' – P. Verrone. {10/2} The WGA East and West boards approve the contract. {12/2} WGA membership approves ending strike, by 92·5%. '*Can anyone remember what we were working on three months ago?*' – Shane Brennan, CBS producer, to writing staff. {24/2} Oscars air [see p.156]. {26/2} The WGA membership ratifies the new contract.

NOTABLE STRIKE CHANTS

Hey, hey, ho, ho, management can't write the show!

No more scripts, no more pages, soon we'll empty all your stages!

They tried to make me do a rewrite, but I said, No! No! No!

Books & Arts

The more minimal the art, the more maximum the explanation.
— HILTON KRAMER (*b.*1928)

NOBEL PRIZE IN LITERATURE

The 2007 Nobel Prize in Literature was awarded to DORIS LESSING (1919–),

that epicist of the female experience, who with scepticism, fire,
and visionary power has subjected a divided civilisation to scrutiny

At 87, Doris Lessing is the oldest person to win the Nobel Prize in Literature – and the 11th woman. Upon learning of the award from a group of reporters on her doorstep, Lessing's response was characteristically sharp: 'Either they were going to give it to me sometime before I popped off, or not at all'. Indeed, many in the press saw the selection as somewhat tardy – coming as it did decades after the release of her most celebrated works. Yet few would deny that Lessing's fearlessness and insight had earned her the prize. ❦ Born in Iran in 1919, Lessing moved with her family to Rhodesia (now Zimbabwe), and her experiences there shaped her interest in racial, social, and sexual conflict. Her first book, *The Grass Is Singing* (1950), described a doomed love affair between a white woman and her African servant, and proved a near-instant bestseller. The *Children of Violence* series (1952–69) traced the intellectual development of heroine Martha Quest through turbulent mid-century Africa and England, furthering Lessing's themes and finding real resonance with readers. Yet it was *The Golden Notebook* (1962) that earned Lessing her highest acclaim. The story of one woman as told through four journals, the book was embraced by the embryonic feminist movement for its intimate portrayal of a 'liberated' woman and her conflicted desires. Lessing never felt comfortable with her position as a feminist pioneer, sometimes calling *The Golden Notebook* her 'albatross', and preferring to see herself as a chronicler of the human condition. She followed *The Golden Notebook* with explorations of both inner and outer space, offering a vision of mental illness with *Briefing for a Descent into Hell* (1971), and turning towards science fiction with the *Canopus in Argos: Archives* series (1979–83). In 1984, she wrote two books under the pseudonym Jane Somers, to prove the difficulty of being published as an unknown writer (her British publisher rejected both). ❦ Lessing's Nobel acceptance speech extolled the value of literature and bemoaned the rise of the internet in today's 'fragmenting culture'. In May 2008, she called her Nobel win 'a bloody disaster', saying the relentless media attention made it near impossible to write a full novel.

—————————— FUTURE OF BOOKS ——————————

The challenges facing the book trade were revealed in a survey of >1,300 publishing professionals from 86 countries at the Frankfurt Book Fair in October 2007:

What is the most important challenge currently facing the book industry? %
Digitisation 53
Globalisation 24
User-generated content 22
Rights issues 15

What is the greatest threat to the publishing industry today? %
Competition from other media 50
Over-publishing 31
Piracy 23
Literacy levels 17
Conglomeration 15
Censorship 7

Which market is likely to commercially dominate in the coming decade? %
Europe 36
North America 32
China 29
Asia 23
India 14
Australasia 2
Africa 2
South America 2
Middle East 1

Who is now driving the industry? %
Publishers 37
Marketeers 31
Customers 22
Retailers 20
Agents 11
Authors 8

Which of the following will be obsolete in fifty years' time? %
High street bookseller 23
The printed book 11
The electronic reader .... 10·5
The editor 6
The publisher 4
None of the above .... 55·5

Which of the following do you see as a major area of future growth? %
E-books 44
Audiobooks 41
Books in translation 27
Educational publishing 27
Graphic novels & comics 18
Children's literature 17
Commercial fiction 15
Literary fiction 10

—————————— MAN BOOKER PRIZES ——————————

Anne Enright won the 2007 (£50,000) Man Booker Prize for her novel *The Gathering* (Jonathan Cape). Enright spoke of her surprise at winning: 'I was ready for anything – possibly anything except that'. In July 2008, to celebrate the Booker's 40th anniversary, the public was asked to vote for the 'Best of the Bookers' from a shortlist of six. The winner (with 36% of the vote) and nominees were:

Salman Rushdie [winner] .... *Midnight's Children* (won Booker in 1981) .... Vintage
Pat Barker .... *The Ghost Road* (1995) .... Penguin
Peter Carey .... *Oscar & Lucinda* (1988) .... Faber & Faber
J.M. Coetzee .... *Disgrace* (1999) .... Vintage
J.G. Farrell .... *The Siege of Krishnapur* (1973) .... Phoenix
Nadine Gordimer .... *The Conservationist* (1974) .... Bloomsbury

————————TEENS' FAVOURITE READS————————

Celebrity mag *Heat* was the most-loved read amongst 11–14-year-olds, according to a March 2008 report commissioned for the National Year of Reading. The most-hated reading matter included 'homework' and Shakespeare. Perversely, Harry Potter novels featured on both lists. Below are the ten most-loved and hated reads:

MOST-LOVED READS	MOST-HATED READS
[1] *Heat* magazine	[1] Homework
[2=] *Bliss* magazine/online song lyrics	[2] Shakespeare
[3] Online computer game cheats	[3] Books of more than 100 pages
[4] My own blog or fan fiction	[4] Articles about skinny celebs
[5] The *Harry Potter* series	[5] Books assigned by school
[6] *The Diary of Anne Frank*	[6] Encyclopedias & dictionaries
[7] Film scripts	[7] The *Beano*
[8] Anthony Horowitz books	[8=] Music scores/*Harry Potter*/maps
[9] *The Lion, the Witch & the Wardrobe*	[9] Facebook
[10=] BBC website	[10=] *The Financial Times*/
Louise Rennison books	anything in a foreign language

——————BAD SEX IN FICTION PRIZE · 2007——————

Each year the *Literary Review* awards its 'Bad Sex in Fiction' prize to a novel featuring the most 'inept, embarrassing, and unnecessary' sex scene. 2007's winner was the late Norman Mailer [see p.61] for this passage in *The Castle in the Forest*:

> *His mouth lathered with her sap, he turned around and embraced*
> *her face with all the passion of his own lips and face, ready at last*
> *to grind into her with the Hound, drive it into her piety.*

——————ODDEST BOOK TITLE OF THE YEAR · 2007——————

The Diagram Group's prize for the Oddest Title of the Year celebrated its 30th anniversary with its 2007 award. Administered by *The Bookseller*, and voted on by members of the book trade, the 'oddest' title of 2007, and the runners-up, were:

If You Want Closure in Your Relationship, Start With Your Legs Big Boom [WINNER]	*How to Write a How to Write Book* Brian Piddock
I Was Tortured by the Pygmy Love Queen Jasper McCutcheon [2ND]	*Are Women Human?* Catharine A. MacKinnon
Cheese Problems Solved ed. P.L.H. McSweeney [3RD]	*People Who Mattered in Southend and Beyond: From King Canute to Dr Feelgood* Dee Gordon

NABOKOV & UNFINISHED MANUSCRIPTS

When Vladimir Nabokov died in 1977, he left behind the unfinished manuscript of a novel tentatively titled *The Original of Laura*. Before his death, Nabokov ordered the remains of the manuscript to be destroyed, but his family chose to disobey this wish. For over 30 years, the manuscript (in the form of 50 index cards) has languished in a Swiss safe deposit box. In March 2008, Dmitri Nabokov, Vladimir's son, hinted that a decision on the fate of *Laura* could be near. A series of press articles followed, focusing on Dmitri's dilemma – whether to burn the manuscript, as his father had requested, or to publish it, satisfying the demands of Nabokov scholars and devotees. In April, Dmitri revealed plans to publish the book, telling Germany's *Der Spiegel* that his father had appeared to him and said, 'You're stuck in a right old mess. Just go ahead and publish'. ❦ *Other unfinished works by authors of note*: Charles Dickens completed only 6 of the 12 planned instalments of *The Mystery of Edwin Drood* before he died in 1870. This meant that the work's central mystery, the disappearance of Mr Drood, was never solved. Notably, Dickens is said to have offered to share the story's denouement with Queen Victoria only months before he died – an offer she declined. ❦ Franz Kafka published very little during the course of his life, and left his 3 major novels (*The Trial*, *The Castle*, and *Amerika*) unfinished at his death in 1924. Before he died, he asked his friend Max Brod to destroy all his work, a request that Brod ignored. ❦ The Latin epic poem the *Aeneid* was unfinished when its author, Virgil, died in 19 BC. However, Emperor Augustus (commissioner of the poem) ignored Virgil's request to burn the manuscript, and asked that it be published with as few changes as possible. ❦ When Mark Twain died in 1910, he left behind 3 unfinished manuscripts on similar themes: *The Chronicle of Young Satan*, *Schoolhouse Hill*, and *No. 44, the Mysterious Stranger*. Albert Bigelow Paine, Twain's biographer, combined the 3 into a single work, released in 1916 as *The Mysterious Stranger*. Today the compilation is seen as badly compromised, and a poor synthesis of Twain's attempt to write a dark social commentary on 'the damned human race'.

BULWER-LYTTON FICTION CONTEST

In 1982, the Department of English and Comparative Literature at San José State University created a literary contest in honour of E.G.E. Bulwer-Lytton (1803–73), who infamously opened his book *Paul Clifford* with 'It was a dark and stormy night'. The contest rewards the best 'bad' opening line to an imaginary novel. The 2008 winner was 41-year-old Garrison Spik from Washington, DC, whose entry was:

> *Theirs was a New York love, a checkered taxi ride burning rubber, and like the city their passion was open 24/7, steam rising from their bodies like slick streets exhaling warm, moist, white breath through manhole covers stamped 'Forged by DeLaney Bros., Piscataway, N.J.'*

——MOST RE-READ BOOKS——

Nearly one-fifth of us read our favourite books more than 5 times, according to a survey to mark the 2007 Costa Book Awards. The books most often re-read are:

Harry Potter series · J.K. Rowling	*Nineteen Eighty-four* · George Orwell
The Lord of the Rings	*The Da Vinci Code* · Dan Brown
J.R.R. Tolkien	*The Lion, The Witch & The Wardrobe*
Pride & Prejudice · Jane Austen	C.S. Lewis
The Hobbit · J.R.R. Tolkien	*Wuthering Heights* · Emily Brontë
Jane Eyre · Charlotte Brontë	*Catch 22* · Joseph Heller

————OTHER BOOK PRIZES OF NOTE · 2008————

Carnegie Medal	Philip Reeve · *Here Lies Arthur*
Kate Greenaway Medal	Emily Gravett · *Little Mouse's Big Book of Fears*
Commonwealth Writers' Prize	Lawrence Hill · *The Book of Negroes*
Forward Prize: best poetry collection [2007]	Sean O'Brien · *The Drowned Book*
Guardian children's fiction [2007]	Jenny Valentine · *Finding Violet Park*
First book award	Dinaw Mengestu · *Children of the Revolution*
Orange prize	Rose Tremain · *The Road Home*
Samuel Johnson Prize for non-fiction	Kate Summerscale · *The Suspicions of Mr Whicher: or The Murder at Road Hill House*
T.S. Eliot Prize for poetry [2007]	Sean O'Brien · *The Drowned Book*
Costa Book of the Year [2007]	A.L. Kennedy · *Day*
Children's prize	Ann Kelley · *The Bower Bird*
Biography	Simon Sebag Montefiore · *Young Stalin*
Poetry	Jean Sprackland · *Tilt*
First Novel	Catherine O'Flynn · *What Was Lost*
Nestlé (formerly Smarties) Prize [2007]:	
5 & under	Sean Taylor & Nick Sharratt · *When a Monster is Born*
6–8	Chris Riddell · *Ottoline and the Yellow Cat*
9–11	Matt Haig · *Shadow Forest*
British Book Awards: Author of the year	Ian McEwan
Book of the year	Ian McEwan · *On Chesil Beach*
Newcomer of the year	Catherine O'Flynn · *What Was Lost*
Crime thriller of the year	Patricia Cornwell · *Book of the Dead*

————COOKBOOKS & PERSONALITY————

Choice of celebrity cookbook can be revealing of the buyer's personality, according to research by Andrea Tonner of the University of Strathclyde in March 2008:

Cookbook author buyer's personality	
Gordon Ramsay..... *smart dresser, show-off*	Delia Smith .... *family-orientated*
Gary Rhodes ...... *likes impressing colleagues*	Nigella Lawson...... *'achievers without fuss'*
	Rose Elliot...................... *'worriers'*

——————— BEST CHILDREN'S BOOK ———————

A February 2008 survey by Booktrust revealed the top 10 children's books were:

*The Lion, the Witch
& the Wardrobe* · C.S. Lewis
The V. Hungry Caterpillar · Eric Carle
The Famous Five series† · Enid Blyton
Winnie-the-Pooh · A.A. Milne
The BFG · Roald Dahl
Harry Potter & the Half Blood Prince
J.K. Rowling

The Faraway Tree · Enid Blyton
The Wind in the Willows
Kenneth Grahame
Alice in Wonderland · Lewis Carroll
The Gruffalo · Julia Donaldson

† 21 books, charting the adventures of Julian,
Dick, Anne, George, and Timmy the dog.

According to the survey, 4 out of 5 parents read their children a bedtime story every night, devoting on average 22 minutes to the task. More than half started reading books to their children when they were 6 months old; 18% claimed to have read stories to their children before they had even been born.

——————— AGE GUIDANCE ON CHILDREN'S BOOKS ———————

In April 2008, the Publisher's Association announced the introduction of age guidance bands on the back of children's books, designed to help adults buy age appropriate books for kids. At the time of writing, it had been agreed that from autumn 2008 age bands (5+, 7+, 9+, 11+ or 13+/teen) would be displayed on the back of *c.*95% of new titles and reprints. Though the majority of children's publishers had signed up to the scheme, many authors were critical, raising concerns that prominent age identification might curb adventurous bookworms or embarrass less proficient readers. An online petition (notoagebanding.org) was signed by a host of authors, librarians, illustrators, and booksellers – including Jacqueline Wilson and children's laureate Michael Morpurgo. Philip Pullman said 'I write books for whoever is interested. When I write a book I don't have an age group in mind'. In July 2008, the Society of Authors published the results of a survey showing that 77% of its members opposed the scheme. The booksellers Borders announced it would initially not use the guidance, adopting instead a policy of 'wait and see'.

——————— FAVOURITE CHILDREN'S AUTHORS ———————

Below are the UK's top children's authors, according to a 2007 survey by ITV3:

1 .... Roald Dahl	5 .... Anthony Horowitz	9 ..... Francesca Simon‡
2 .... C.S. Lewis	6 ..... Jacqueline Wilson	10 .... Enid Blyton
3 .... J.M. Barrie	7 .... Dr Seuss†	† Theodor ('Ted') Seuss Geisel
4 .... J.K. Rowling	8 .... Philip Pullman	‡ Creator of Horrid Henry

45% of 11-year-olds reported they would rather read a book than watch TV, compared to 38% saying the same in 2004. The research by the National Foundation for Educational Research, released in March 2008, also revealed that cartoons were the most popular reading matter for 9–11-year-olds.

————————————— AUTHORS' PAPERS —————————————

The British Library announced at the end of 2007 that it had acquired for the nation the papers of playwright and Nobel prize-winner Harold Pinter, at a cost of £1·1m. Pinter's papers run to 150 boxes of letters, emails, photographs, scrapbooks and manuscripts. 12,000 letters represent correspondence between Pinter and some of the leading theatrical figures of the last half century, including Noël Coward, John Gielgud, Philip Larkin [see below], Arthur Miller, John Osborne, and Tom Stoppard. Below are the locations of the papers of some of Britain's leading writers – although Pinter's will remain in Britain, a significant number of others are now abroad:

Jane Austen...................... *The Morgan Library, New York · The British Library*
Kingsley Amis... *Harry Ransom Center, Texas Uni · Huntington Library, California*
Winston Churchill......... *Churchill Archives Centre, Churchill College, Cambridge*
Arthur Conan Doyle ...... *Harry Ransom Center, Texas Uni · Portsmouth Museums*
George Eliot (Mary Ann Evans) ....*Beinecke Library, Yale · British Library*
Graham Greene........*Lauinger Library, Georgetown Uni · Boston College Libraries*
Rudyard Kipling.. *Sussex University Library*
Philip Larkin.. *Hull University Archives & others*
George Orwell (Eric Blair) .... *University College London Library*
Wilfred Owen......................*Harry Ransom Center, Texas University & others*
Tom Stoppard .... *Harry Ransom Center, Texas University*
Alfred Tennyson .... *Lincolnshire Archives · Houghton Library, Harvard*
Anthony Trollope ....*Illinois University Library & others*
Evelyn Waugh .... *British Library · Harry Ransom Center, Texas University*
P.G. Wodehouse ....*Dulwich College Archive*
Virginia Woolf.. *Sussex University Library*

————————————— MILLS & BOON'S CENTENARY —————————————

In 1908, Gerald Mills and Charles Boon established a publishing company that, a century later, would sell >7m romantic novels a year in the UK alone. Originally a general fiction publisher, Mills & Boon began to specialise in love stories during WWI and, in 1997, 'Mills & Boon' entered the *Oxford English Dictionary* as an almost generic term for a 'romantic story book'. Nowadays, 50 new M&B titles are published every month; these are translated into 26 languages and sold in 109 countries. There are currently 10 different genres in the Mills & Boon collection:

Modern...... *glamorous & sophisticated*
Modern Extra.........*sizzling & stylish*
Romance .... *fresh & tender*
Blaze..........................*hot & sexy*
Medical................ *doctors & nurses*
Historical....... *bringing the past to life*
Desire 2-in-1........ *2 stories in 1 book*
Special Edition............*a longer read*
Super-romance... *realistic & passionate*

Intrigue...... *danger, deception & desire*

In September 2008, Mills & Boon announced it was introducing a more racy 'Spice' range which would feature 'sex for enjoyment'. The first Spice book is entitled *Spies, Lies, and Naked Thighs*. ❦ M&B estimated that during the past 50 years its characters had enjoyed 35,250 hugs, 29,500 kisses, and 10,325 weddings.

THE TURNER PRIZE · 2007

Founded in 1984, the Turner Prize is awarded each year to a British artist (defined, somewhat loosely, as an artist working in Britain or a British artist working abroad) under 50, for an outstanding exhibition or other presentation in the twelve months prior to each May. The winner receives £25,000 – and three runners-up £5,000.

Mark Wallinger won the 2007 Turner Prize for his installation *State Britain*, which replicated veteran campaigner Brian Haw's anti-war protest outside Parliament. The award was presented in Liverpool (the first time the ceremony has taken place outside London), to mark the city's status as 2008 European Capital of Culture [see p.178]. It took 15 people 6 months to make *State Britain*, which recreates in exact detail the banners, flags, and tarpaulin shelter of Haw's iconic camp. Haw had initially rejected Wallinger's proposal (telling him to 'piss off'), but later discovered that the two 'shared the same heart'. Haw even attended the Turner Prize ceremony. ❦ Wallinger presented a different work in Liverpool – the film *Sleeper*, in which he wanders around Berlin's National Gallery dressed in a bear costume. ❦ Born in 1959, Mark Wallinger studied at Goldsmiths College – the alma mater of many other members of the YBA (Young British Artist) movement

Mark Wallinger

which emerged in the late 1980s. Wallinger switched from painting to sculpture to 'steel [himself] to work in other ways'. He is best known for *Ecce Homo* – a statue of Christ, which stood on the fourth plinth in Trafalgar Square in 1999 [see p.185]. ❦ Wallinger, who lost out to Damien Hirst's pickled animals in the 1995 Turner Prize, was the clear favourite to win the 2007 contest. The jury praised his work for its 'immediacy, visceral intensity and historic importance', commenting that it combined 'a bold political statement with art's ability to articulate fundamental human truths'. ❦ The *Daily Telegraph*'s Richard Dorment was enthusiastic about the choice, describing Wallinger as 'one of Britain's most thoughtful and most original artists'. The Stuckists, an anti-conceptual group of artists and self-publicists, failed to picket the ceremony as usual – although their co-founder Charles Thomson predictably described the entries as 'utter bilge'.

Year	winner				
'92	Grenville Davey*	'97	Gillian Wearing*	'03	Grayson Perry
'93	Rachel Whiteread	'98	Chris Ofili	'04	Jeremy Deller
'94	Antony Gormley*	'99	Steve McQueen*	'05	Simon Starling
'95	Damien Hirst	'00	Wolfgang Tillmans	'06	Tomma Abts
'96	Douglas Gordon	'01	Martin Creed		
		'02	Keith Tyson	* Graduate of Goldsmiths	

It was announced in May 2008 that the following four artists were shortlisted for the 2008 Turner Prize, the winner of which will be announced on 1 December:

artist Mark Leckey · *installation artist* Cathy Wilkes
visual artist Runa Islam · *'cultural archaeologist'* Goshka Macuga

─────────────THE ART FUND PRIZE · 2008─────────────

The £100,000 Art Fund Prize (formerly the Gulbenkian Prize) is the UK's richest prize for innovative and challenging museums and galleries. In 2008, the prize was awarded to community museum *The Light Box* in Woking, Surrey, which was described by the judges as 'novel, brave, and full of delights'. The other award finalists were: *'Breaking the Chains'*, *The British Empire & Commonwealth Museum*, Bristol; *Shetland Museum & Archives*, Shetland; and *The Wellcome Collection*, London.

─────────────TOP EXHIBITIONS · 2007─────────────

The *Art Newspaper*'s figures for the most popular art exhibitions in the world illustrate the continuing success of shows in Japan. Below are the most popular art exhibitions of 2007 around the world – and in London – by the number of daily visitors:

GLOBAL TOP FIVE

2007 exhibition	museum	daily attendance
The Mind of Leonardo	Tokyo National	10,071
Monet's Art and its Posterity	National Art Centre Tokyo	9,273
Legacy of the Tokugawa	Tokyo National	9,067
Richard Serra Sculpture: 40 Years	Museum of Modern Art, NY	8,585
Masterpieces of French Painting	Museum of Fine Arts Houston	7,268

LONDON TOP TEN

Manet to Picasso	National Gallery	4,625
Velázquez	National Gallery	3,288
Royal College of Art Summer Show	The Royal College of Art	2,920
Cézanne in Britain	National Gallery	2,456
Summer Exhibition	Royal Academy	2,279
Antony Gormley: Blind Light	Hayward Gallery	2,255
Kylie: the Exhibition	Victoria and Albert Museum	2,204
Holbein in England	Tate Britain	2,165
Hogarth	Tate Britain	2,157
Rodin	Royal Academy of Arts	2,107

─────────MUSEUMS & GALLERIES IN MAJOR CITIES─────────

London compares favourably with other leading world cities in terms of museums and art galleries, according to figures produced by *Museums Journal* in April 2008.

City	population	national museums	other museums	public art galleries
London	7·6m	22	162	92
New York	8·3m	16	85	N/A
Paris	2·2m	19	138	59
Shanghai	9·8m	6	100	6
Tokyo	8·5m	8	71	40

————————— UNUSUAL MUSEUMS OF NOTE —————————

A selection of the many unusual and offbeat museums found around the world:

American International Rattlesnake Museum............ Albuquerque, New Mexico
Atomic Testing Museum...Las Vegas, Nevada
Bakelite Museum .... Williton, Somerset, England
Barometer World & Museum ....Okehampton, Devon, England
Big Daddy Don Garlits Museum of Drag Racing....................... Ocala, Florida
Big Mac Museum................................North Huntingdon, Pennsylvania
Bramah Museum of Tea and Coffee................................. London, England
British Lawnmower Museum.........................Southport, Lancashire, England
Bunny Museum.. Pasadena, California
Burlingame Museum of Pez Memorabilia .... Burlingame, California
Carrot Museum.. Berlotte, Belgium
Cockroach Hall of Fame Museum .... Plano, Texas
Conspiracy Museum (JFK & other assassinations) ....Dallas, Texas
Cumberland Pencil Museum............................Keswick, Cumbria, England
Dutch Cheese Museum.......................Alkmaar, North Holland, Netherlands
Ice Museum...Fairbanks, Alaska
Icelandic Phallological Museum (phallic specimens)................... Húsavík, Iceland
Jesse James Museum.. Stanton, Missouri
Kool-Aid: Discover the Dream (dedicated to Kool-Aid; see p.260) .....Hastings, Nebraska
Leila's Hair Museum.. Independence, Missouri
Le Musée de la Banane (Banana Museum) ....Sainte-Marie, Martinique
Matchbox Museum .... Tomar, Portugal
Mount Horeb Mustard Museum........................... Mount Horeb, Wisconsin
Museo del Jamón-Centro de Interpretación del Cerdo Ibérico
(Cured Ham Museum and Ibérico Pig Interpretation Centre) .... Aracena, Spain
Museum of Brands, Packaging, and Advertising................... London, England
Museum of Broken Relationships............................ travelling (brokenships.com)
Museum of Drinking Water...Taipei, Taiwan
Museum of Questionable Medical Devices........................St Paul, Minnesota
Museum of Roller Skating .... Lincoln, Nebraska
Museum of Temporary Art....................................... Tübingen, Germany
Muzium Padi (National Rice Museum)................................Kedah, Malaysia
National Great Blacks in Wax Museum ....Baltimore, Maryland
Norwegian Canning Museum .... Stavanger, Norway
Owl Art and Craft Museum.....................................Seoul, South Korea
Phosphate Museum .... Mulberry, Florida
Salt Museum..Northwich, Cheshire, England
Shin-Yokohama Ramen Museum ....Yokohama, Japan
Spam Museum (the food, not the email) .... Austin, Minnesota
Sulabh International Museum of Toilets ....New Delhi, India
Telephone Historical Centre (call before visiting) ....Edmonton, Alberta, Canada
US Border Patrol Museum...El Paso, Texas
Williams Hall Museum of Kitsch Art............................Burlington, Vermont
World Brick Museum ....Maizuru City, Japan

ATTACKS ON WORKS OF ART

In October 2007, intruders broke into the Musée d'Orsay in Paris and punched a 4" hole in Claude Monet's *Le Pont d'Argenteuil*. French police later arrested five people, whose motive for attacking the Impressionist masterpiece remains unknown. Some other notable examples of deliberate attacks on works of art are listed below:

The Portland Vase
British Museum, London
In 1845, an 'intemperate vandal' smashed the 1st-century Roman glass vase, causing significant damage.

The Nightwatch · *Rembrandt*
Rijksmuseum, Amsterdam
This painting has been attacked 3 times: in 1911 and 1975 with a knife, and in 1990, when a psychiatric patient sprayed it with sulphuric acid.

The Rokeby Venus · *Velázquez*
National Gallery, London
In 1914, suffragette Mary Richardson slashed the Venus in protest against the imprisonment of Emmeline Pankhurst.

Virgin & Child with St Anne & St John the Baptist · *Leonardo da Vinci*
National Gallery, London
In 1962, a schizophrenic German artist threw ink at the da Vinci; in 1987, it was shot by a former soldier.

The Thinker · *Rodin*
Cleveland Museum of Art, Ohio
In 1970, radical student group the Weathermen dynamited the sculpture.

Pietà · *Michelangelo*
St Peter's, Rome
A geologist smashed the Virgin's forearm and nose in 1972.

Guernica · *Pablo Picasso*
Museo Reina Sofía, Madrid
In 1974, an anti-war protester sprayed *Guernica* with 'Kill Lies All' while it was on loan to MOMA, New York.

Assorted statues
Villa Borghese Gardens, Rome
A biology professor broke the noses off 80 stone statues of historic figures, in 1985. By way of explanation, he reportedly said, 'the KGB are after me'.

Myra · *Marcus Harvey*
Royal Academy, London
Harvey's painting of Myra Hindley was attacked twice during the calculatedly controversial Saatchi-backed show *Sensation* in 1997.

Bamiyan Buddhas
Northern Afghanistan
In 2001, these giant statues (which were at least 1,300 years old) were blown up by the Taliban, who claimed they were un-Islamic idols.

Fountain · *Marcel Duchamp*
Centre Pompidou, Paris
Duchamp's Dadaist artwork (a porcelain urinal) was attacked twice by Pierre Pinoncelli. In 1993, he urinated in it, and 3 years later he cracked it with a hammer. Pinoncelli claimed his attacks were themselves a work of performance art.

[Sources: various] In October 2007, the waters of Rome's Trevi fountain ran red after a man poured in a bucket of dye before fleeing. Leaflets found at the scene said the act was a protest against the expense of the Rome Film Festival, and a reference to the event's red carpet. ❦ In July 2008, a German man was arrested after ripping the head off a wax Adolf Hitler at the newly-opened Berlin Madame Tussauds.

TOP TEN ARTISTS BY REVENUE · 2007

Artprice annually publishes a ranking of artists based on sales generated by their works at auction. 2007 marked the first year in a decade that Picasso was not No. 1:

Rank artist ('06 rank)   2007 sales ($)
1 .... Andy Warhol (2) 420m
2 .... Pablo Picasso (1) 319m
3 .... Francis Bacon (19) 245m
4 .... Mark Rothko (78) 207m
5 .... Claude Monet (14) 165m
6 .... Henri Matisse (9) 114m
7 .... Jean-Michel Basquiat (36) . 102m

8 .... Fernand Léger (26) 92m
9 .... Marc Chagall (6) 89m
10 ... Paul Cézanne (17) 87m

In Sep 2008, Damien Hirst bypassed dealers and galleries, and auctioned parts of his collection at Sotheby's. The 2-day sale earned £111m, and set the record for an auction of one artist's work.

ART DONATIONS

An Israeli shipping magnate's £20m gift to the National Maritime Museum (NMM) in March 2008 was the largest single donation ever made by an individual to a cultural project in Britain. The doner, Sammy Ofer, served in the Navy during WWII and much of his shipping group is based in London. His gift will go towards the NMM's new £35m wing. Below are some other large cultural donations in Britain:

Year	benefactor	recipient	sum (£m)
2008	Julian Blackwell	Bodleian Library, Oxford	5
2008	Randy Lerner	National Portrait Gallery, London	5
2007	John Studzinski	Tate Modern, London	5
2004	Tom Hunter	Kelvingrove, Glasgow	5
2000	Christopher Ondaatje	National Portrait Gallery, London	2·75
1991	Sainsbury brothers	National Gallery, London	35
1985	John Paul Getty Jr	National Gallery, London	50†

† For an endowment fund to purchase works of art, rather than for a specific new development.

MONA LISA'S EYEBROWS

In October 2007, the French engineer Pascal Cotte revealed some fascinating secrets about the world's most famous portrait, Leonardo da Vinci's *Mona Lisa* [1506]. As a member of the *Centre de Recherche et de Restauration des Musées de France* (an arm of the French government devoted to preserving works in the nation's museums), Cotte was permitted to take the first high-resolution multispectral pictures of the painting. These images revealed remnants of one finely painted hair over the Mona Lisa's left brow, as well as an absence of cracks near the eye area – leading Cotte to theorise that her brows and lashes were removed at some point by an overzealous conservator cleaning the eye area. According to Cotte, Mona Lisa's face was also painted over in order to make her appear more slender – which might mean that her smile was originally broader and perhaps somewhat less enigmatic.

THE CRITICAL YEAR · 2007–08

{SEPT 2007} · The *Guardian*'s Jonathan Jones' preconceptions of the Pre-Raphaelites were overturned by Tate Britain's Millais exhibition. Jones admitted, 'the *Blind Girl* is a mawkish, manipulative masterpiece. Seeing it, and others, in Tate Britain's revelatory exhibition of Millais gave me a shock: I've discovered that I like the Pre-Raphaelites'. {OCT} · *The Coronation of Poppea* at the ENO, Coliseum, did not impress *Telegraph* critic Rupert Christiansen, who called the production 'vacuous, vulgar, and ugly'. He went on to criticise the staging: 'Ottavia crouches on what looks like a giant peeled lychee, Nero has his love-nest in a yacht, and some scenes appear to be set under-

Tutankhamun

water. Beyond that, I failed to detect anything approaching a serious interpretation of the text or engagement with the characters.' {NOV} · Benedict Nightingale of *The Times* was enthusiastic about Shakespeare's *Henry V* at the Courtyard, Stratford, commenting on Michael Boyd's 'refreshingly unfashionable direction' in his patriotic interpretation of the play. ❧ *The Times*'s Rachel Campbell-Johnston praised the treasures on view in *Tutankhamun & the Golden Age of the Pharaohs* at O2 London, but was less enthusiastic about the surroundings, describing them as 'tacky … Tutankhamun goes to Hollywood'. In the *Evening Standard*, Brian Sewell was damning: 'the minds behind this exhibition and the Dome deserve each other; between them they offer the most unpleasant "cultural" experience of my life'. ❧ Ian McKellen's interpretation of *King Lear* for the RSC was widely praised. Quentin Letts in the *Daily Mail* described

McKellen as 'the king of Lears'. {DEC} · The Donmar Warehouse's sell-out *Othello* received mixed reviews. Ewan McGregor's Iago was 'assured and scintillating at the off [but] … peters out', according to the *Independent*'s Kate Bassett. The *Telegraph*'s Charles Spencer describes him as 'the weakest link in a mixed production … static and dull'. However Spencer praised Chiwetel Ejiofor's Othello as 'beautifully spoken, massively dignified'. ❧ The Old Vic continued its new tradition of adult Christmas pantos with *Cinderella*, scripted by Stephen Fry and starring Sandi Toksvig as the narrator and Pauline Collins as the Fairy Godmother. Critics were underwhelmed: in the *Independent*, Paul Taylor called it a 'garish, unsympathetic production' with a lot of 'leaden larkiness'. {JAN 2008} · Cirque du Soleil's new show *Varekai* at the Albert Hall did not impress Benedict Nightingale in *The Times*, who felt it 'substituted technical expertise for humanity. Bluntly, it lacks soul'. ❧ Disaster nearly struck the Royal Academy's *From Russia* exhibition when, 2 weeks before opening, the Russian government refused to allow the paintings to travel to England; the British government's last-minute change of indemnity laws saved the day. Tom Lubbock in the *Independent* was unsure if it was worth the diplomatic wrangling: 'the quality of the painting … careers wildly'. {FEB} · Two productions of *The Mikado* opened at the same time in London. *The Times*'s Neil Fisher enjoyed Jonathan Miller's English National Opera revival, with its Art Deco design. He was less complimentary about the Carl Rosa Company production at the Gielgud, which used reproductions of the 1885 designs. Fisher said 'there isn't enough zing to the ensembles, not enough crackle to the wordplay', although he appreciated impressionist Alistair McGowan's Mikado. {MAR}· A power failure on the first night of *God of Carnage*, the new play by Yasmina Reza (of *Art* fame), resulted in most of the stage lights going out. Yet this did not deter some favourable reviews: Michael Billington in the *Guardian* described it as 'rancidly funny'. {APR} · 'We are in the realm of masks, myths and mayhem', with Harrison Birtwistle's new work *The Minotaur* at the Royal Opera House, according to Rupert Christiansen in the *Telegraph*: 'This is a mighty opera that must be taken seriously ... but not one that is easy to enjoy, let alone love.' ❦ *Pop Idol*'s Darius Danesh received a standing ovation for his performance as Rhett Butler on the first night of the musical adaptation of *Gone With the Wind* at the New London Theatre. Reviews, however, were mixed. Paul Callan in the *Daily Express* thought Danesh's performance saved the show 'from crumbling into utter mediocrity... sadly, *Gone With the Wind*, despite its meaty story, just flaps limply in the breeze'. The *Independent*'s Paul Taylor damned with faint praise: 'the show is neither as bad as one feared nor as good as one has a right to expect.' {MAY} · Dominic Maxwell of *The Times* said of the Take That tribute musical *Never Forget*, 'it's terrible old cobblers and it knows it. What's more, it knows we know it, and strongly suspects that we don't mind'. {JUNE} · The first major UK exhibition of Gustav Klimt's work opened at Tate

Chiwetel Ejiofor

Liverpool, but the *Guardian*'s Alfred Hickling was less than impressed: 'though Tate Liverpool has rolled out the red carpet, you are left with the impression of a hyped catwalk show to which too many A-listers declined to attend'. ❦ Much hype surrounded the arrival in London of Damon Albarn's opera *Monkey: Journey to the West*. The *Independent*'s Simon O'Hagan thought the hype deserved: 'Combining both grandeur and intimacy, exquisite melody and thrilling soundscapes, it was Albarn's remarkable score, played by an orchestra using both Western and traditional Chinese instruments, that gave *Monkey* its real emotional depth.' {JUL} · In *The Times*, Benedict Nightingale cautioned those thinking of attending *High School Musical* at the Apollo Hammersmith: 'Anybody hoping to enjoy this stage version of Disney's film should come wearing a cheerleader's top, trailing a child aged 8 or 9 and, above all, harbouring a deep interest in American high-school culture'. {AUG} · With David Tennant and Patrick Stewart in starring roles, the RSC's *Hamlet* was a hot ticket. Critics were impressed; Benedict Nightingale said of Tennant's performance, 'I've seen bolder Hamlets and more moving Hamlets, but few who kept me so riveted throughout'. In the *Telegraph* Charles Spencer wrote 'this is a gripping Hamlet that could become great if Tennant finds the courage to raise the dramatic stakes still further'. {SEP} The much anticipated Francis Bacon retrospective at Tate Britain was slightly overwhelming. Rachel Campbell-Johnston of *The Times* felt there were almost 'too many great paintings'.

EUROPEAN CAPITAL OF CULTURE

Liverpool was one of the two 2008 European Capitals of Culture, sharing the honour with Stavanger, Norway. The EU Capitals of Culture scheme was founded in 1985 with the aim of bringing European peoples closer together. Each EU member state is given the opportunity to host the capital in turn. Liverpool beat Bristol, Birmingham, Cardiff, Newcastle-Gateshead, and Oxford to become the UK's latest choice. Below are the cities that have held the title during the past decade:

1998 . . . . Stockholm, Sweden
1999 . . . . Weimar, Germany
2000† . . . . Avignon, France
    Bergen, Norway; Bologna, Italy;
Brussels, Belgium; Helsinki, Finland;
Krakow, Poland; Prague, Czech Rep.;
    Reykjavik, Iceland; Santiago, Spain
2001 . . . . Porto, Portugal;
    Rotterdam, Netherlands

2002 . . . . Bruges, Belgium;
    Salamanca, Spain
2003 . . . . Graz, Austria
2004 . . . . Lille, France; Genoa, Italy
2005 . . . . Cork, Ireland
2006 . . . . Patras, Greece
2007 . . . . Luxembourg; Sibiu, Romania

† 9 cities were chosen to mark the millennium.

Some of the many events and attractions staged in Liverpool in 2008 included:

Liverpool Sound concert with Sir Paul McCartney, the Zutons, and Kaiser Chiefs
Liverpool Biennial · Tall Ships' Race · Go Superlambananas† · Public lectures by
Richard Dawkins, Robert Winston, Willy Russell, and Jonathan Miller
BBC Sports Personality of the Year [see p.315] · The Art of Doctor Who
Liverpool International Tennis tournament · Community art projects
MTV Europe Music Awards · Arabic Arts Festival

† The original Super Lamb Banana is a 17-foot, yellow, concrete and steel sculpture fusion of a lamb/
banana, created in 1998 by Japanese-based artist Taro Chiezo to illustrate the dangers of GM food.
The sculpture has stood in various different locations in Liverpool, and has become an unlikely symbol of the city. As part of the celebrations for Liverpool 2008, more than 100 6ft superlambananas
were created by local artists, community groups, and celebrities and displayed throughout the city.

ARTS PARTICIPATION

There were 49,140 amateur arts groups in England in 2007, ranging from book clubs to knitting circles, with a combined membership of *c.*5·9m. Below is a breakdown of this membership, according to the Dept for Culture, Media, & Sport:

Artform	group members	Literature	17,000	Visual arts	265,000
Craft	28,000	Media	62,000	Multi-art	2,339,000
Dance	128,000	Music	1,642,000		
Festivals	328,000	Theatre	1,113,000	TOTAL	5,922,000

Amateur music groups are most popular in the South-east (403,000 members), and least popular in
the West Midlands (81,000). Craft is most popular in the North-west (6,000) & South West (6,000).

WEST END THEATRE AUDIENCES

Attendance at West End performances reached its highest point for 20 years in 2007, according to the Society of London Theatre's annual report, released in July 2008. 13·6m people attended plays, musicals, operas, and dance in central London in 2007, bringing in revenues of £469·9m – up nearly £70m on 2006. The success of productions whose stars were chosen by the public via reality TV shows (including *The Sound of Music*, *Joseph and His Amazing Technicolour Dreamcoat*, and *Grease*) were substantially responsible for this fillip, and attendances at musicals boomed. Below is a breakdown of West End theatre attendances in 2007:

| Genre | % attendance | Plays | 22 | Opera | 4 |
| Musicals | 65 | Dance | 6 | Other | 3 |

TOP ARTS EVENTS ATTENDED BY AGE

67% of adults in England attended an arts event in the 12 months prior to being interviewed about their habits in 2005/06. The most popular events were:

Event · % attended by age	16–24	25–44	45–64	>65	All
Theatre performance	29	37	42	31	36
Carnival and street arts	28	31	27	16	26
Live music event	34	29	25	8	24
Art, photography, sculpture	16	23	26	16	22
Craft exhibition	5	14	21	17	15
Classical music performance	3	5	12	12	8
Jazz performance	4	5	7	5	6
Opera or operetta	2	3	6	6	4

[Source: *Taking Part: the National Survey of Culture, Leisure and Sport*, DCMS]

LAURENCE OLIVIER AWARDS OF NOTE · 2008

Best actor	Chiwetel Ejiofor · *Othello*†
Best actress	Kristin Scott Thomas · *The Seagull*
Best newcomer in a play	Tom Hiddleston · *Cymbeline*
Best new play	*A Disappearing Number* · Simon McBurney
Best new musical	*Hairspray*
Best actor (musical)	Michael Ball · *Hairspray*
Best actress (musical)	Leanne Jones · *Hairspray*
Best new comedy	*Rafta Rafta* · Ayub Khan-Din
Best director	Rupert Goold · *Macbeth*
Best revival	*Saint Joan*

† Ejiofor's Othello beat two of Britain's most distinguished actors, Ian McKellen and Patrick Stewart, who were appearing as two other Shakespearian heavyweights, King Lear and Macbeth respectively.

———————————THE MAGIC CIRCLE———————————

The exclusive and mysterious Magic Circle was formed in 1905 by a group of 23 professional magicians at Pinoli's restaurant in London. Celebrated magician David Devant became the society's first president, and he chaired weekly meetings at which fellow conjurors could share their knowledge and skills. Membership is difficult to obtain as candidates must be proposed and seconded by existing members before passing a series of interviews and examinations to prove their prestidigital skills. The Circle has different levels of membership: amateurs may become associate members; professionals full members; and the highest accolade is to become a member of the Inner Magic Circle. Professional members of the club may use the letters MMC after their name. A further examination can be taken to become an associate of the Inner Magic Circle (AIMC), but only the president can select people to join the exclusive Inner Magic Circle (MIMC) – the membership of which never exceeds 300. The society's motto *Indocilis privata loqui* [not apt to disclose secrets] reveals the club's preoccupation with secrecy. Any member discovered revealing the tricks of the magician's trade can be expelled from the club. The Magic Circle currently has >1,500 members, a quarter of whom live overseas. The HQ in London has a library and archive of magic, and a theatre.

Since J.K. Rowling's *Harry Potter* series, membership of the Magic Circle's Young Magicians Club has increased dramatically – at one point 20 new members were joining each week. Apropos of nothing, the Magic Circle is also informally used to describe the top five leading law firms in London – Allen & Overy, Clifford Chance, Freshfields Bruckhaus Deringer, Linklaters, and Slaughter & May.

———————————NATIONAL DANCE AWARDS · 2007———————————

The Critics' Circle National Dance Awards are judged and presented by the critics and journalists involved in reviewing dance productions. The awards aim to celebrate the diversity of dance in Great Britain. The winners in 2007 included:

Outstanding achievement .... Celeste Dandeker · *Candoco* co-founder
Best male dancer .... Jonathan Goddard · *Richard Alston Dance Company*
Best female dancer .... Natalia Osipova · *Bolshoi Ballet*
Dance UK industry award .... Celeste Dandeker
Best choreography: classical .... Wayne McGregor · *Chroma*
– modern .... Michael Keegan-Dolan · *The Bull*
Spotlight Awards: male modern dancer.... Dane Hurst · *Rambert Dance Company*
– female modern dancer........Kialea-Nadine Williams · *Phoenix Dance Company*
– male classical dancer.................................... Ivan Vasiliev · *Bolshoi Ballet*
– female classical dancer............. Carol-Anne Miller · *Birmingham Royal Ballet*
Company prize for outstanding repertoire: classical................... *Scottish Ballet*
– modern...*Henri Oguike Dance Company*
Best foreign dance company.. *The Bolshoi Ballet*
Working Title *Billy Elliot* award................................ Brandon Lawrence
Patron's award..Darcey Bussell

IF.COMEDDIES · 2008

Edinburgh Fringe's comedy awards, the if.comeddies, were presented in August 2008. The £8,000 prize was awarded to Irish comedian David O'Doherty for his show, *Let's Comedy*. Director of the judges Nica Burns said, 'an hour with David O'Doherty fills the world with laughter and charm, and sends you home on a wave of happiness'. Sara Millican was named Best Newcomer for her first solo show.

WINNER & NOMINEES 2008

DAVID O'DOHERTY.. *Let's Comedy*
Kristen Schaal & Kurt Braunohler............................ *Double Down Hearts*
Rhod Gilbert... *The Award Winning Mince Pie*
Russell Kane .... *Gaping Flaws*

Apropos of nothing, in September 2008 it was reported that churchgoers were struggling to find suitable partners as a consequence of shrinking congregations. Online dating agency Christian Connections published a list of Christian chat-up lines, as recommended by their clients, to encourage more churchgoers to get into dating. Examples included: 'Is this pew taken?'; 'You float my ark.'; 'My parents are home, want to come over?'; 'Now I know why Solomon had 700 wives. He never met you!'; 'I didn't believe in predestination until tonight.'; 'Is that a thinline, duo-tone, compact, ESV travel bible in your pocket?'; 'Let me sell you an indulgence – it's a sin to look as good as you.'; 'How many times do I have to walk around you before you fall for me?'; 'The name is Will ... God's Will.'

BRITISH COMEDY AWARDS · 2007

Best TV comedy actor....................................David Mitchell · *Peep Show*
Best TV comedy actress .... Liz Smith · *The Royle Family: The Queen of Sheba*
Best comedy ent. personality........... Simon Amstell · *Never Mind the Buzzcocks*
Best TV comedy ....*Peep Show*
Best comedy entertainment programme..................*Never Mind the Buzzcocks*
Best new comedy entertainment programme.............*Al Murray's Happy Hour*
Best international comedy show ....*Curb Your Enthusiasm*
Best male comedy newcomer..................... James Corden · *Gavin & Stacey*
Best female comedy newcomer........................Ruth Jones · *Gavin & Stacey*
Best new British TV comedy...................................... *Gavin & Stacey*
Best comedy film .... *The Simpsons Movie*
Best live stand-up...Alan Carr
Ronnie Barker writer of the year.......................................Simon Pegg
Lifetime achievement award..Stephen Fry

In May 2008, Ant and Dec returned their 2005 People's Choice prize for *Saturday Night Takeaway* after an audit revealed they did not win the phone vote. The actual winner of the public vote was *The Catherine Tate Show* but there was 'insufficient evidence' to conclude why the award went instead to Ant and Dec. A report by law firm Olswang stated, 'Robbie Williams was invited to present an award. It was understood that he would be happy [to do so] if the recipients were Anthony McPartlin and Declan Donnelly. In order to ensure his attendance, this assurance was given'. There was no suggestion whatsoever that Williams, McPartlin, or Donnelly were aware of any of these issues.

———————HAUTE COUTURE & PRÊT-À-PORTER———————

Haute couture ('high dress-making') is the exclusive design and creation of the finest made-to-measure garments. Englishman Charles Worth[†] became known as the 'father of haute couture' after he established the first elite Parisian couture house in 1858, designing and showing finished couture outfits for the *beau monde*. In 1868, Worth established the *Chambre Syndicale de la Haute Couture Parisienne* to protect couture designs from being copied. Since 1945, the production of haute couture has been protected by law. Originally, fashion houses only qualified to use the title if they met the following rules: couturiers had to produce a minimum of 50 original designs for each collection, show their collections twice a year, and employ at least 20 artisans in their atelier. In 1992, the rules were relaxed to allow new designers to produce couture for a trial 2-year period, during which they need only employ 10 people in their workshop and produce 25 designs per collection (more established houses must still employ 15 technicians and show 35 designs per collection). Costs are so prohibitive (reportedly ≥$150,000 for an evening gown) that it is rumoured that there are only *c.*300 couture clients worldwide. Recently many haute couture houses have closed, preferring to concentrate on their more profitable ready-to-wear (*prêt-à-porter*) lines. In 1946 there were 106 official couture houses, but by 2008 only a handful of these remained – they are:

Adeline André · Anne Valérie Hash · Chanel · Christian Dior
Christian Lacroix · Dominique Sirop · Elie Saab[‡] · Emanuel Ungaro
Franck Sorbier · Givenchy · Maison Martin Margiela[‡] · Giorgio Armani[‡]
Jean Paul Gaultier · Maurizio Galante · Valentino[‡]

† Charles Worth was court dressmaker to Empress Eugénie of France and Empress Elizabeth of Austria. ‡ These non-French designers are allowed to show as 'correspondent' haute couture houses.

———————READY-TO-WEAR FASHION WEEKS———————

NEW YORK
February & September
Who shows: *Ralph Lauren, Vera Wang,
Diane Von Furstenberg, Calvin Klein,
Zac Posen, Oscar de la Renta,
Michael Kors, Donna Karan*

MILAN
February & September/October
Who shows: *Gucci, Armani, Prada,
Dolce & Gabbana, Moschino, Versace,
Roberto Cavalli, Max Mara,
Burberry Prorsum, Fendi*

LONDON
February & September
Who shows: *Aquascutum, Ben de Lisi,
Paul Smith Women, Nicole Farhi,
Jasper Conran, Betty Jackson,
Marios Schwab, Gareth Pugh*

PARIS
February/March & October
Who shows: *Stella McCartney, Chanel,
Vivienne Westwood, Jean Paul Gaultier,
John Galliano, Issey Miyake,
Christian Dior, Chloé, Lanvin*

According to *Vogue*, some key trends for Autumn/Winter 2008/09 include: tunics and trousers; folk; tomato red; black lace; statement coats; embroidery and embellishment; and over-sized checks.

——————— MOST STYLISH KIDS ———————

According to US celebrity magazine *In Touch Weekly*, Gwen Stefani's 21-month-old son Kingston is the 'most stylish kid' in Hollywood. When apprised of the news, Stefani confirmed that her son is indeed a 'chilled-out little guy'. Below are the top five most stylish celebrity tots, according to the list released in February 2008:

#	child	born	parents
1	Kingston Rossdale	26/5/2006	Gwen Stefani & Gavin Rossdale
2	Suri Cruise	18/4/2006	Tom Cruise & Katie Holmes
3	Leni Klum	4/5/2004	Heidi Klum & Flavio Briatore
4	Brooklyn Beckham†	4/3/1999	David & Victoria Beckham
5	Ava Phillippe	9/9/1999	Reese Witherspoon & Ryan Phillippe

† Unsurprisingly, Brooklyn favours football jerseys – but, as *In Touch Weekly* notes, 'very stylish' ones.

——— FASHION INVENTIONS ———

The push-up bra was voted top fashion favourite in a March 2008 poll conducted by Debenhams. The top 20 were:

1 .... *push-up bra*	14 ...... *flip flops*
2 ...*boot-cut jeans*	15. *chicken fillets‡*
3 ... *pull-in pants*	16 .... *pencil skirt*
4 .... *stilettos*	17 ...... *hot pants*
5 .... *LBD†*	18 ...... *boy shorts*
6 ... *hipster jeans*	19 ... *trainer socks*
7 .... *miniskirt*	20. *comfy trainers*
8 .... *strapless bra*	
9 ...*support tights*	† Little Black Dress
10 .... *kitten heels*	‡ Nickname for the
11 ...... *stockings*	silicone bra inserts
12 ...... *sports bra*	that are used to
13 .... *G-string*	enhance the bust.

——— ELLE STYLE AWARDS ———

Best	winner
Actor	James McAvoy
Actress	Keira Knightley
British music act	Kate Nash
British band	The Feeling
Style icon	Kate Hudson
Outstanding achievement	Anya Hindmarch
Woman of the year	Kylie Minogue
Model	Agyness Deyn
British designer	Jonathan Saunders
Int. designer	Luella Bartley
H&M young designer	Richard Nicoll
H&M style visionary	William Baker
TV male	Nicholas Hoult
TV female	Kelly Osbourne
Accessory designer	Pierre Hardy

——————— BRITISH FASHION AWARDS · 2007 ———————

Designer of the year	Stella McCartney
New designer of the year	Christopher Kane
Designer brand	Anya Hindmarch
Red carpet designer	Marchesa
Model of the year	Agyness Deyn†
Outstanding achievement in fashion	Dame Vivienne Westwood

† Deyn's real name is Laura Hollins; her first job was in a fish 'n' chip shop in Stubbins, Lancashire.

―――――――――WORLD'S TALLEST BUILDING―――――――――

In April 2008, Riyadh-based company Kingdom Holding announced plans for the £5bn 'Mile High Tower' in the Saudi Arabian city of Jeddah, which will be taller than the Burj Dubai, currently under construction in Dubai and due for completion in 2009. (Although the Burj Dubai's owners have not revealed its final height, the tower is expected to exceed 800m.) Yet another 'super sky-scraper' is planned for Kuwait. Currently, the world's five tallest buildings are:

Building	year built	location	storeys	metres
Taipei 101	2004	Taipei, Taiwan	101	509
Petronas Towers	1998	Kuala Lumpur, Malaysia	88	452
Sears Tower	1974	Chicago, USA	110	442
Jin Mao	1999	Shanghai, China	88	421
Two Internat. Finance Centre	2003	Hong Kong	88	415

The Council on Tall Buildings and Urban Habitat, which compiled this list, takes as its measurement the distance from the pavement level of the main entrance to the architectural top of the building, which includes spires – but not antennae, signage, or flag poles. A structure qualifies as a building (as opposed to a telecommunications tower) if at least 50% of its height is occupied by usable floor area. The Council, founded in 1969, is based at the Illinois Institute of Technology in Chicago.

―――――――――LEANING TOWER OF SUURHUSEN―――――――――

The small village of Suurhusen in northern Germany caused a minor architectural sensation in November 2007, when *Guinness World Records* declared the community's church steeple the world's 'most tilted tower' – banishing the leaning tower of Pisa to an inglorious second. According to officials who measured both towers, the steeple in Suurhusen reportedly tilts at 5·19°, while the tower of Pisa leans at 3·97°.

―――――――――THE SERPENTINE GALLERY PAVILION―――――――――

Each summer since 2000, the Serpentine Gallery in Kensington Gardens, London, has commissioned an architect (who has yet to build in Britain) to design a temporary pavilion for the Gallery lawn. The Pavilion designers, so far, have been:

Year	Name of Architect	nationality
2008	Frank Gehry	Canadian-born American
2007	Olafur Eliasson & Kjetil Thorsen	Danish & Norwegian
2006	Zaha Hadid	Iraqi-born British
2005	Rem Koolhaas & Cecil Balmond	Dutch & Sri Lankan-born British
2004	Alvaro Siza & Eduardo Souto de Moura	Portuguese
2003	Oscar Niemeyer	Brazilian
2002	Toyo Ito	Japanese
2001	Daniel Libeskind	Polish-born American
2000	Zaha Hadid	Iraqi-born British

PRITZKER ARCHITECTURE PRIZE

The Pritzker Prize honours living architects whose work 'has produced consistent and significant contributions to humanity and the built environment through the art of architecture'. In 2008, the Pritzker was awarded to Jean Nouvel, the bulk of whose work has been in his native France – including the Institut du Monde Arabe (1987) and the Cartier Foundation for Contemporary Art (1994), both in Paris.

TRAFALGAR SQUARE'S FOURTH PLINTH

Sir Charles Barry's 1838 design for Trafalgar Square included a statue plinth at each corner. Statues of King George IV, General Sir Charles Napier, and Major General Sir Henry Havelock[†] occupied three of the plinths – the final north-west plinth remained empty because of disagreements about funding and the choice of subject. In 1998, the Royal Society of Arts initiated a scheme to commission new works to fill the north-west corner and, in 1999, the Fourth Plinth Commissioning Group assumed responsibility for choosing new works. The five commissions to date are:

Ecce Homo
Mark Wallinger · 1999
Sculpture of Christ with his
arms folded behind him [see p.171]

Alison Lapper Pregnant
Marc Quinn · 2005
Marble statue of naked,
pregnant disabled woman

Regardless of History
Bill Woodrow · 2000
Man's head crushed by vast book
bound to plinth by tree roots

Model for a Hotel 2007
Thomas Schütte · 2007
Coloured glass model of
21-storey building

Monument
Rachel Whiteread · 2001
Upside-down cast of the plinth
itself to create mirror image

(During the 2002 Football World Cup,
Madame Tussauds sneakily placed a waxwork
of footballer David Beckham on the plinth.
It was only allowed to stay a few hours.)

† Napier and Havelock were both C19th British military heroes who made their reputations in India. ❦ In June 2008 it was announced that Antony Gormley and Yinka Shonibare had been selected to display their artworks on the fourth plinth. Gormley will present *The One and the Other* in which > 2,400 people will stand on the plinth for one hour at a time. Shonibare's exhibit is entitled *Nelson's Ship in a Bottle*. ❦ In August 2008 it was revealed that the fourth plinth was being reserved for a permanent statue of the Queen riding a horse that will be commissioned after her death.

THE STIRLING PRIZE · 2007

The 12th RIBA £20,000 Stirling Prize was awarded, in October 2007, to David Chipperfield Architects for the Museum of Modern Literature at Marbach am Neckar, Germany. The judges praised the museum as 'a building that is simultaneously rich and restrained … a shrine to the soul of a literate nation'.

——SHIPWRECKS, TREASURE, & HISTORIC VESSELS——

International law governing the ownership and protection of shipwrecks was tested in 2008 when the Spanish government began proceedings against a US salvage company after treasure was found at a site in the N Atlantic. The salvage company announced in May 2007 that it had discovered the world's largest haul of maritime treasure after salvaging 17 tons of gold and silver coins worth >$100m. The Spanish government laid claim to the wreck on the grounds that the coins were Spanish, and suspecting that the ship lay in Spanish waters. The salvagers initially declined to reveal the wreck's location, however in January 2008 a Florida judge ordered them to disclose the details to the Spanish (the location was kept secret to protect the wreck from scavengers). At the time of writing it was suspected the wreck was the C19th galleon *Nuestra Señora de las Mercedes*, which might enable Spain to claim the ship and its booty. ❦ This ongoing dispute highlighted the complexities of maritime treasure salvage. It was hoped that the UNESCO 2001 Draft Convention on the Protection of Underwater Cultural Heritage (created to halt the commercial exploitation of important sites) would clarify disputes in international waters. However, since <20 countries have ratified the convention it has yet to come into force. In the UK, important shipwrecks are preserved under the Protection of Wrecks Act (1973). Designated sites are marked with a yellow buoy inscribed 'Protected Wreck' that prohibits anyone without a licence from tampering with the site, diving or salvaging at the site, or depositing anything (e.g., anchors) which could damage the site. There are currently 60 protected wreck sites in UK waters, including the *Mary Rose* – their locations are marked below:

[Source: English Heritage; positions are approximate]

The National Register of Historic Vessels holds the details of >1,200 vessels of extraordinary maritime importance which were based and operated in UK waters and are at least 50 years old. Some of the Register's most important vessels include:

Vessel	date & function	built	current location
Mary Rose	1509? [fighting vessel]	Portsmouth	Portsmouth
Prince Frederick's Barge	1732 [passenger vessel]	London	Greenwich
HMS *Trincomalee*	1816 [fighting vessel]	Bombay	Hartlepool
HMS *Warrior*	1860 [fighting vessel]	London	Portsmouth
Cutty Sark	1869 [cargo vessel]	Dumbarton	Greenwich
Holland 1	1901 [fighting sub]	Barrow-in-Furness	Gosport
HMS *Belfast*	1938 [fighting vessel]	Belfast	London
Royal Yacht *Britannia*	1952 [passenger vessel]	Glasgow	Leith

———————THE ARCHAEOLOGICAL YEAR 2007–08———————

{OCT 2007} · A report in the *Proceedings of the National Academy of Sciences* suggested that early humans migrated out of Africa *c.*90,000–70,000 years ago, due to climate change. Samples taken from Lake Malawi indicated that water levels during that period had fallen drastically – supporting the theory of a mega-drought. ❦ Scientists from the University of Barcelona reported in *Science* that analysis of Neanderthal DNA indicated that some of them may have been redheads. {NOV} · The mummified face of King Tutankhamun, previously only seen by *c.*50 people, was put on public display. ❦ A royal Anglo-Saxon cemetery, discovered in Teesside, contained some of the finest examples of gold jewellery found in Britain. ❦ The British Museum revealed that 58,290 archaeological objects were found by the public in 2007; the majority were unearthed with metal detectors. {DEC} · A student at Bristol University identified a new species of dinosaur, *Carcharodontosaurus iguidensis* (i.e., shark lizard), from bones discovered in 1997 in Niger; it is one of the largest carnivorous dinosaurs ever found. {JAN 2008} · Palaeontologists in Uruguay unearthed the fossilised skull of a rat (*Josephoartigasia monesi*); at the time of its existence, *c.*4m years ago, the rat would have been the size of a car. {FEB} · The fossil of a giant frog that would have weighed 4kg was discovered in Madagascar; scientists nicknamed the beast *Beelzebufo* – 'frog from hell'. {MAR} · Archaeologists at a site in N Spain discovered the oldest human remains in western Europe; the jawbone and teeth date from between 1·1m and 1·2m years ago. ❦ The first archaeological dig inside Stonehenge for more than four decades began. Archaeologists hoped to date the site more accurately, and explore the significance of the smaller bluestones that stand inside the ring. {APRIL} · A necklace found near Lake Titicaca in Peru, by a team from the University of Arizona, was thought to be the oldest gold artefact from the Americas, dating back >4,000 years. ❦ A task force of archaeologists, climbers, and mountain rescue teams was established in the Alps to prevent the theft of prehistoric treasures that are being revealed as glaciers melt. {MAY} · The first dinosaur footprints to be discovered in the Arabian peninsula were uncovered in Yemen; the trackways were thought to have been made by a herd of 11 sauropods *c.*150m years ago. {JUN} · Archaeologists from University College London unearthed a collection of tools thought to have belonged to Neanderthals. The find, in Beedings, W Sussex, revealed the sophistication of the Neanderthals' hunting technology. ❦ A cannon, musket, and navigational calendar were all raised from a C16th shipwreck discovered off Alderney. It was hoped the objects will give insight into Elizabethan maritime techniques. {AUG} · Forensic scientists examining the skeletons of those who died aboard the *Mary Rose* suggested that the ship may have sunk because the majority of the crew were from southern Europe, and might not have understood the orders of their British captain. ❦ >100 prehistoric rock carvings were identified across N England. The English Heritage project catalogued a number of previously undiscovered, and frequently remote, sites of Neolithic rock art in the countryside around Durham and Northumberland.

Sci, Tech, Net

Men have become tools of their tools.
— HENRY DAVID THOREAU, *Walden*, 1854

─────────────── HONEY ───────────────

In November 2007, Farming Minister Lord Rooker predicted that the English honeybee might be extinct within a decade if more is not done to protect it. In July 2008, the Honey Association warned that stocks of English honey would run dry by Christmas, after which no more would be available until summer 2009. Shortly thereafter, the British Beekeepers' Association (BBKA) reported that *c.*30% of the UK's 240,000 honeybee hives had not survived the winter – a loss BBKA president Tim Lovett called 'deeply worrying'. ❦ The causes of this decline in the bee population (and therefore the honey supply) are unclear. The BBKA has urged the government to increase funding into bee diseases such as the Varroa mite, which entered Britain in 1992 and has ravaged the wild bee population. Honey stocks in other countries have also suffered recently. The vast Argentinian honeybee population has been damaged both by droughts and the conversion of land to the growth of soya beans for biofuel [see p.209]. And, the mysterious 'colony collapse disorder' has been blamed for the death of *c.*36% of American honeybees. ❦ One of the earliest depictions of honey harvesting comes from 15,000-year-old cave paintings found near Valencia, Spain, in which a stick figure climbs a ladder to collect the sweet treat. The ancient

Egyptians revered honey as the food of kings – Tutankhamun was found buried with a pot of honey said still to be edible. Many have surmised that the ambrosia offered to the gods of Ancient Greece was honey, and there are numerous biblical references to honey, most famously the 'land of milk and honey' for which the Israelites searched. ❦ Honey is predominately made up of carbohydrates – fructose (*c.*38%) and glucose (*c.*31%), as well as small quantities of sucrose, maltose, isomaltose, maltulose, turanose, and kojibiose, and traces of various enzymes, vitamins, and minerals. Since fructose tastes slightly sweeter than sucrose, honey tastes, on average, 1·5× sweeter than sugar. Honey also contains traces of hydrogen peroxide, which research suggests might give it some medicinal benefits. Scientists at Aintree Hospital, Liverpool, and the University of Wales have suggested that manuka honey can help prevent MRSA when applied to wounds. ❦ Consumers of honey are not the only ones affected by the honeybee crisis. According to DEFRA, honeybees contribute £165m a year to the British economy by pollinating fruits and vegetables. And a global shortage of honeybees could be devastating. As Albert Einstein apparently prognosticated: 'If the bee disappears off the surface of the globe, then man would only have four years of life left.'

———————— SOME INTERNET MALADIES ————————

Condition	primary symptoms
Blog Streaking	*overexposing oneself via a blog*
MySpace Impersonation	*assuming false (often famous) identities on the net*
Photolurking	*rummaging through online photo albums for private information*
Wikipediholism	*excessive checking and correction of Wikipedia articles*
Egosurfing	*excessively Googling your own name*
Google Stalking	*snooping on friends and enemies via the search engine*
Infornography	*unhealthy addiction to new and current information*
Cyberchondria	*fear of maladies diagnosed on the internet*
YouTube Narcissism	*believing the whole world is waiting for your holiday video*

[Source: *New Scientist*, 2007] In the May 2008 issue of the *American Journal of Psychiatry*, Dr Jerald J. Block argued that internet addiction should be listed in the next edition of the *DSM*, the US classification of psychiatric conditions. According to Block, internet addiction has 3 subtypes (gaming, sexual preoccupations, and email/text messaging), and is characterised by: excessive use; anger or depression when the computer is inaccessible; and negative repercussions, such as social isolation.

———————— LOLCATS & LOLSPEAK ————————

'Lolcats' are photographs of felines in various poses, adorned with weirdly spelled captions designed to appear as if they were spoken by the cats themselves (lol = 'laugh out loud'). This perplexing internet phenomenon became a nearly inescapable part of online culture in 2008. Lolcat captions tend to recycle jokes from the internet, gaming, and elsewhere. They are written in an imagined (and nauseating) feline baby talk – 'kitty pidgin' – which has come to be known as 'Lolspeak'. Like the hacker slang 'Leet speak' (of which it is a relative), Lolspeak is constantly evolving, yet it relies on several established formulas. One of the most popular is '*I'm in ur* [noun], [verb]-*ing your* [noun]', which apparently derives from a posting in an online game forum which read: 'I'm in ur base killing ur d00ds'. Another common formula depicts a cat licking some item and proclaiming: '[noun] *haz a flavor*'. Although the precise origins of lolcats are disputed, the website 'I Can Has Cheezburger?' (the most popular lolcat URL) posted its first lolcat picture in January 2007. Lolcats have given rise to numerous spin-offs, including lolgays, lolruses (walruses), loldogs, lolbees, lolpresidents, lolbrarians, lolgoths, lolmaps, and even lolchairs. Inevitably, in January 2008, a lolcat book project was announced.

Like lolcats, the phrase 'All Your Base Are Belongs to Us' (sometimes AYBABTU or AYB) spread rapidly and inexplicably across the internet. AYB derives from the video game *Zero Wing*, originally released in Japanese in 1989. The English adaptation, released in 1991, featured some unfortunate subtitles, including 'All your base are belongs to us', uttered by the menacing villain 'CATS' during the game's opening sequence. In the late 1990s, this subtitle attracted attention on the 'Zany Video Game Quotes' forum and, in 1998, a Kansas City programmer created a Flash animation in which the AYB phrase takes over the world – appearing on planes, a *Time* cover, and at the UN. The animation was widely forwarded and re-posted, earning mainstream news coverage in 2001. Some attribute AYB's popularity to gamer nostalgia for all things '80s. Like lolcats, AYB has yet to die a natural death.

—————————— NOBEL PRIZES IN SCIENCE · 2007 ——————————

THE NOBEL PRIZE IN PHYSICS

Albert Fert
*Université Paris-Sud; Unité Mixte
de Physique CNRS/Thales, France*

Peter Grünberg
Forschungszentrum Jülich, Germany

'for the discovery of Giant
Magnetoresistance'

Fert and Grünberg independently discovered a method of layering magnetic material and non-magnetic material, allowing tiny magnetic changes to produce large differences in electrical resistance – an effect called Giant Magnetoresistance (GMR). GMR has enabled extremely sensitive read-out heads to be made for devices that register data magnetically, such as hard drives and iPods, in turn allowing these devices to be produced on a minuscule scale. Because GMR depends on structures only a few atoms in size, it is considered one of the first real applications of nanotechnology.

THE NOBEL PRIZE IN CHEMISTRY

Gerhard Ertl
*Fritz-Haber-Institut der Max-Planck-
Gesellschaft, Germany*

'for his studies of chemical
processes on solid surfaces'

By demonstrating how chemical reactions take place on microscopic surfaces, Ertl pioneered a methodology now used in both academic and industrial surface chemistry. Ertl's methods have provided insights into everything from car exhaust emissions and the ozone layer to the Haber-Bosch process. The latter has been used since WWI to produce ammonia for artificial fertilisers, though its mechanism was previously little understood.

THE NOBEL PRIZE IN PHYSIOLOGY OR MEDICINE

Mario R. Capecchi
University of Utah

Sir Martin J. Evans
Cardiff University

Oliver Smithies, *University of
North Carolina at Chapel Hill*

'for their discoveries of principles
for introducing specific gene
modifications in mice by the use
of embryonic stem cells'

The work of Capecchi, Evans, and Smithies led to a technology called 'gene targeting' that allows scientists to study the roles of individual genes in mice. Capecchi and Smithies created a method of pinpointing and manipulating individual genes at the cellular level, while Evans, using embryonic stem cells, discovered a way to transfer the genetic manipulations to the animal – creating so-called knockout mice. Because mice and humans share many genes, 'mouse models' provide insight into human growth, ageing, and disease, and are now used to explore and test gene therapies.

─────ABEL PRIZE─────

The Abel Prize, awarded for outstanding scientific work in the field of mathematics, was presented in 2008 to John Griggs Thompson of the University of Florida and Jacques Tits of the Collège de France. Thompson and Tits won the c.£0·6m prize for their 'profound achievements in algebra and in particular for shaping modern group theory', which is also known as the 'science of symmetries'.

─────COPLEY MEDAL─────

The Copley Medal is presented by the British Royal Society; it is the world's oldest prize for scientific achievement. The 2007 award, worth £5,000, was given to Lord Robert May for his 'seminal studies of interactions within and among biological populations'. The prize has been awarded since 1731, and has previously been won by Charles Darwin, Albert Einstein, Louis Pasteur, and Stephen Hawking.

─────IG NOBEL PRIZES─────

Ig Nobel prizes are awarded for scientific 'achievements that cannot or should not be reproduced'. Below are some notable honours presented at the 2007 ceremony:

AVIATION · Patricia V. Agostino, Santiago A. Plano, and Diego A. Golombek (Universidad Nacional de Quilmes, Argentina) *for their discovery that Viagra assists jet lag recovery in hamsters.*

MEDICINE · Brian Witcombe (Gloucestershire Royal NHS Foundation Trust) and Dan Meyer (Sword Swallowers' Association International) *for their penetrating medical report 'Sword Swallowing and its Side Effects'.*

PHYSICS · L. Mahadevan (Harvard University) and Enrique Cerda Villablanca (Universidad de Santiago de Chile) *for studying how sheets become wrinkled.*

CHEMISTRY · Mayu Yamamoto (Intl Medical Centre of Japan) *for developing a way to extract vanillin (vanilla fragrance & flavouring) from cow dung.*

LINGUISTICS · Juan Manuel Toro, Josep B. Trobalon, and Núria Sebastián-Gallés (Universitat de Barcelona) *for showing that rats sometimes cannot tell the difference between a person speaking Japanese backwards and a person speaking Dutch backwards.*

PEACE · The US Air Force Wright Laboratory *for instigating research and development on a chemical weapon – the so-called gay bomb – that will make enemy soldiers become sexually irresistible to each other.*   [Source: improb.com]

─────DARWIN AWARDS─────

A 58-year-old Texan who died after consuming three litres of sherry via enema won the 2007 Darwin Award, which commemorates '*those who improve our gene pool by accidentally removing themselves from it*'. According to the wife of the deceased, enemas were a favourite mode of intoxication for her husband, named by the awards only as 'Michael'. Toxicology reports found he had a blood alcohol level of 0·47%.

——— UNIVERSAL ETHICAL CODE FOR SCIENTISTS ———

In September 2007, the British government's chief scientific adviser, Sir David King, unveiled a Universal Ethical Code for Scientists. Developed by a government working group over a period of years, the code is in part a response to a series of scandals that have eroded public trust in scientists, such as the Woo Suk Hwang† cloning brouhaha. The code is intended to restore public confidence, remind scientists of their own responsibilities, and provide support for potential whistleblowers. While the code is not mandatory, King has encouraged its adoption by scientists in the UK and across the world. The code's seven commandments are:

[1] *Act with skill and care in all scientific work. Maintain up-to-date skills and assist their development in others.*

[2] *Take steps to prevent corrupt practices and professional misconduct. Declare conflicts of interest.*

[3] *Be alert to the ways in which research derives from and affects the work of other people, and respect the rights and reputations of others.*

[4] *Ensure that your work is lawful and justified.*

[5] *Minimise and justify any adverse effect your work may have on people, animals, and the natural environment.*

[6] *Seek to discuss the issues that science raises for society. Listen to the aspirations and concerns of others.*

[7] *Do not knowingly mislead, or allow others to be misled, about scientific matters. Present and review scientific evidence, theory, or interpretation honestly and accurately.*

[Source: UK Government Office for Science]

† In 2004, Hwang reported that he had successfully created stem cells from cloned human embryos; he was later found to have falsified key data, among other violations. Yet in 2008 there were reports of a Hwang comeback. In July, the *New Scientist* confirmed that Hwang was to begin research on animal cloning at a private lab in Seoul. The California-based BioArts International also announced a partnership with Hwang on a project to clone pet dogs for the highest bidders in 5 online auctions.

——— THE EDGE ANNUAL QUESTION · 2008 ———

Each year, the online science and culture magazine *Edge* invites notable scientists, philosophers, and others to answer an unusual open-ended question. In 2008, the question was, 'What have you changed your mind about? Why?' Some responses:

DAVID MYERS (social psychologist)
*Newborns are not the blank slates
I once presumed.*

NICK BOSTROM (philosopher)
Everything.

SIMON BARON-COHEN (psychologist)
Whilst it is a wonderfully cosy, warm, feel-good idea, I have changed my mind about equality.

LEE M. SILVER (molecular biologist)
'If we could just get people to understand the science, they'd agree with us'. Not.

MARK HENDERSON (science editor)
Consulting the public about science isn't always a waste of time.

RANDOLPH M. NESSE (psychiatrist)
I used to believe that you could find out what is true by relying on experts.

—————GENES OF NOTE————— | ————ANIMAL GENOMES————

Some of the year's notable discoveries in genetic research:

A variant of the *KIF6* gene was found to raise the risk of heart attack and increase the chances of benefiting from intensive statin therapy. ❦ A *BDNF* gene variant was linked to a tendency towards obsessive worry, though with different effects in women and young girls. ❦ 5 different genetic variants, 3 located on chromosome 8, and 2 on chromosome 17, were found to significantly increase the odds of prostate cancer. ❦ 4 *FKBP5* gene variants were found to increase susceptibility to post-traumatic stress disorder in those who have suffered an abusive childhood. ❦ Mutations in the adenomatous polyposis coli (*APC*) gene are known to increase significantly the odds of developing colonic polyps and colorectal cancer. Researchers in Utah demonstrated that two such mutations, not found in the UK, could nonetheless be traced back to an American couple who sailed from England *c*.1630. ❦ Variants of the *GRIK2* and *GRIA3* genes were found to increase the likelihood of suicidal thoughts in patients with major depression treated with certain drugs. ❦ A mutation in the *ASIP* gene was found to increase the likelihood of red hair, freckles, and also skin cancer, even in populations rarely exposed to the sun. ❦ A variant of the *CHRNA5* gene has been linked to a higher chance of developing lung cancer. ❦ A variant of the *FTO* gene in children was linked to increased difficulty recognising satiety. ❦ A variant of the Duffy antigen receptor for chemokines (*DARC*) gene, which confers protection to Africans against some forms of malaria, was shown to increase susceptibility to HIV by *c*.40%, but also to be associated with slower disease progression.

In November 2007, researchers in America announced they had for the first time successfully mapped the entire genetic code of a feline – a four-year-old Abyssinian named Cinnamon. Scientists hope that deciphering an animal's complete set of DNA will provide clues about its evolution and behaviour as well as insights into disease. Other animals and insects whose genomes have been mapped include:

chimpanzee · mouse · rat · dog · platypus
rhesus macaque · orangutan · cow
honeybee · fruit fly · horse · opossum

In September 2007, French and Italian researchers said they were the first to genetically map a fruit: the pinot noir grape. In June 2008, the confectioners Mars announced the Chocolate Genome Project, to map the cacao tree's genome.

—————'DOOMSDAY' VAULT—————

In January 2008, the first shipment of seeds arrived at the Svalbard Global Seed Vault on the remote Arctic island of Spitsbergen, Norway. Maintained by the UN-backed Global Crop Diversity Trust, the seed vault was designed as an 'insurance policy for the world's food supply', in response to the threat of climate change, natural disasters, and global catastrophe. >4·5m seeds, eventually including samples of every major food crop, will be stored at a constant temperature of *c*.−15°C, 390ft deep inside an ice-cold mountain, protected internally by motion detectors and externally by prowling polar bears. Experimental data have shown that some seeds can survive *c*.10,000 years under optimum conditions, though, in practice, scientists plan to 'refresh' seeds in the vault every 20–100 years.

──────── ANTHROPOCENE & GEOLOGICAL TIME ────────

As most schoolchildren learn, the layers of rock on Earth can be divided into eons, eras, periods, and epochs – units of 'geological time' which correspond to various events in the environmental history of the planet. In January 2008, scientists at the Geological Society of London (GSL) proposed that, because of human impact on the environment, the Earth had entered a new geological epoch: the 'Anthropocene'. According to the GSL paper, the Anthropocene epoch [*anthro*: human + *cene*: new] is distinct because of environmental changes that began during the industrial revolution and are likely to leave distinct marks on the planet. As evidence, the paper cites increased erosion and denudation of the continents, higher CO_2 levels and accompanying temperature changes, animal and plant extinctions, rising sea levels, and increasing ocean acidity. Although a final decision on formal adoption of the Anthropocene rests with the International Union of Geological Sciences (IUGS), the term has been used informally by many since it was coined on the spur of the moment by the Nobel laureate Paul Crutzen, at a conference in 2000.

──────────── HUMAN LIMITS ────────────

In 2008, the BBC magazine *Focus* compiled findings on the theoretical and actual limits of human endurance. According to the magazine, the following have been generally established as the 'absolute ceiling of human endeavour' [*do* NOT *attempt!*]:

Blood loss	a loss of ≥50% (3·4–4·9 pints)
Spiciness	5g capsaicin is theoretically the most one could survive; the impact is similar to a severe allergic reaction [see p.227]
Cold	a body temperature <32°F is likely fatal; <86°F produces unconsciousness
Noise	>200 decibels will rupture lungs and is generally fatal
Water consumption	17·5 pints per hour; more will dilute electrolytes to the point of seizure or death
Bee stings	the greatest number of stings survived is 2,243; >600 bee stings gives a 50% chance of death
Electrical shock	a sustained current of 200 milliamps can stop the human heart

──────────── VIAGRA'S OTHER USES ────────────

In recent years, scientists have discovered numerous alternative uses for Viagra, which is used by *c.*30m men around the world to treat erectile dysfunction. Some of Viagra's other benefits include: A protective effect on heart tissue deprived of oxygen before and after heart surgery [*Journal of Molecular and Cellular Cardiology*, 2007]. ❦ Lowering blood pressure in the lungs of patients with chronic bronchitis and emphysema [American College of Chest Physicians, 2006]. ❦ A reduction in attacks of Raynaud's phenomenon, which interrupts blood flow to extremities [*Circulation*, 2005]. ❦ An increase in blood flow to the uterus, which may help women become pregnant [*Human Reproduction*, 2000]. ❦ A freshener for cut flowers, which last *c.*1 week longer when 1mg Viagra is added to their water. [*Plant Physiology & Biochemistry*, 1998].

—————————— STN SIGNIFICA ——————————

Some (in)significa(nt) Sci, Tech, Net footnotes to the year. ❦ Google Trends showed that between 2004–07, internet users in Chile, Mexico, and Colombia were the most likely to search for the word 'gay'; users in Ireland, the UK, and the US for 'hangover'; and those in Philippines, Australia, and the US for 'love'. ❦ Britain's Royal Astronomical Society scrapped plans to report that 'minor planet 2007 VN84' looked set to miss Earth by just 3,500 miles, after scientists discovered that the 'planet' was in fact the European space probe Rosetta. ❦ Dutch police arrested a teenager for allegedly stealing €4,000 (£2,900) worth of virtual furniture in the virtual online game *Habbo Hotel*. ❦ Activists installed a virtual Guantánamo Bay inside *Second Life*, as a means of illustrating the predicament of detainees. ❦ A 26-year-old Moroccan engineer was arrested in Casablanca for 'villainous activities', after he created a fake Facebook profile for Prince Moulay Rachid, who is second in line to the Moroccan throne. ❦ A British survey by electronics retailer Comet found that 47% of UK men said they would forego sex for 6 months in return for a 50" plasma TV. ❦ S Korea developed a special 'space kimchi' for the country's first astronaut to take into space, using radiation to limit bacteria and reducing the smell by 'one-third or by half'. ❦ As part of a recruitment drive, the notoriously secretive Israeli spy agency Shin Bet launched a blog on which 4 agents described their work. ❦ Parents in Europe complained about the online game *Miss Bimbo*, in which girls 9–16 are encouraged to buy their virtual 'bimbos' diet pills and fake breasts. ❦ Scientists who created a synthe-

sized genome of the bacterium *Mycoplasma genitalium* left a 'watermark' on their creation by including a series of amino acids with the same initials as lead researchers. The researchers added the mark to brand the bacteria as man-made. ❦ NASA celebrated the 40th anniversary of the Beatles' song *Across the Universe* (as well as NASA's own 50th birthday) by beaming the tune at the North Star Polaris, 431 lightyears away. ❦ An E Carolina University biologist who discovered a new species of trapdoor spider honoured his rock idol, Neil Young, by naming the arachnid *Myrmekiaphila neilyoungi*. ❦ Bhutan's national assembly banned lawmakers from bringing laptops into House chambers, for fear they would spend government sessions playing computer games. ❦ Bioengineers at MIT created a wintergreen-scented version of *E. coli*, after growing tired of hours in the lab with the 'poopy'-smelling organism. ❦ Two children were admitted to a mental health institution in Spain to be treated for cell phone addiction. ❦ Brazil banned sales of computer games *Counter-Strike* and *EverQuest*, saying they encouraged 'the subversion of public order'. ❦ The Internet Corporation for Assigned Names & Numbers relaxed rules on the net's address system, opening the way for URL endings beyond .com, .org, .net, and country-based addresses. ❦ Brazilian researchers photographed one of the world's last uncontacted tribes, in the Amazon rainforest; *c*.100 are said to still exist. ❦ Honda's Asimo robot led the Detroit Symphony in 'Impossible Dream' from *Man of La Mancha*. It was the first time a robot had conducted a live symphony performance.

——SOME NOTABLE SCIENTIFIC RESEARCH · 2007–08——

{OCT 2007} · An analysis in *Evolution & Human Behaviour* found that mothers with more fat around their hips tend to have children who achieve higher scores on cognition tests, leading scientists to theorise that the polyunsaturated fatty acids deposited around the hips may contribute to brain development *in utero*. ❦ Researchers at Yale and the University of California found that subjects given a set of nearly identical pictures were more likely to notice the difference between the pictures when they involved an animal. This finding led scientists to suggest that ancient predator-detection mechanisms are still at work in the brain. ❦ Researchers at Indiana University helped explain why people often respond with an eerie sensation to robots that are too life-like. After monitoring the emotions of 140 subjects shown lifelike robots, the scientists found that the emotions subjects experienced (fear, nervousness, disgust) were similar to those provoked by images of diseased human bodies. {NOV} · Research presented to the American Society of Plastic Surgeons suggested no correlation between breast-feeding and mammary ptosis (sagging breasts). However, pregnancy in general, smoking, age, and the failure to wear proper bras were all found to contribute to a decline in breast elasticity. ❦ Scientists at Case Western Reserve University, Ohio created a genetically modified 'supermouse' that could run twice as far as a normal mouse. The rodents were bred to aid study into the biochemistry of metabolism. {DEC} · Research from Yale and University of California psychologists found that those whose first names began with a C or D earned lower

grades than those whose names began with an A or B. Researchers attributed the finding to a psychological process called the 'name letter effect', whereby people favour things that remind them of their own name. {JAN 2008} · Swedish researchers suggested that those who were short at birth were more likely to commit suicide as adults. The research published in the *Journal of Epidemiology and Community Health* indicated that poor foetal growth may have damaging long-term effects on brain chemistry. ❦ Scientists at the University of Minnesota created a beating rat's heart by injecting cells from a newborn rat into the hollowed-out structure of a dead one. Scientists suggested that human hearts might one day be created in a similar fashion. ❦ California Institute of Technology economists used brain scans to show that people enjoyed wine more when they were told it was expensive, regardless of its actual quality or price. ❦ A team of researchers at the J. Craig Venter Institute created the largest man-made DNA structure to date, by assembling the entire genome of the bacterium *Mycoplasma genitalium* from its synthesised components. {FEB} · University of Utah scientists proposed a method of tracking where people have lived by analysing their hair for traces of drinking water. The model is based on the discovery that oxygen and hydrogen isotopes found in drinking water vary geographically, and that these isotopes remain in hair even after it has been cut. It is hoped that the discovery will assist forensic analysis. ❦ After analysing data from mental health studies in 72 countries, researchers from the University of Warwick and Dartmouth

—— NOTABLE SCIENTIFIC RESEARCH · 2007–08 cont. ——

College proposed that levels of happiness follow a 'U' shape throughout life, rising in the 20s and 70s but dipping significantly during middle age. ❧ Italian researchers refuted the theory that Napoleon died of arsenic poisoning, after analysing 4 hairs taken from his head during various stages of his life. While the hairs showed levels of arsenic high by modern standards, the researchers found no marked rise during the course of Napoleon's life. {MAR} · A team from the University of Ulster and UAE University found that the skin of the S American paradoxical frog (*Pseudis paradoxa*) contains a substance that can stimulate the release of insulin. ❧ Astronomers at the California Institute of Technology's jet propulsion laboratory reported the first discovery of an organic molecule in the atmosphere of a planet outside Earth's solar system. A molecule of methane was found on the planet Vulpecula, where scientists also confirmed the presence of water. {APR} · A University of St Andrews study proposed that successful cricketers live longer. The research, published in the *British Journal of Sports Medicine*, showed that the more Test matches a cricketer played in, the longer he was likely to live – suggesting that career success could boost health and longevity. ❧ Swedish researchers proposed a link between rhythm and intelligence, after men who performed best on a drumming test were shown to have higher IQs. ❧ US scientists writing in *Science* described a new drug derived from salmonella that can protect cells exposed to radiation, without diminishing the effectiveness of cancer treatment. {MAY} · Scientists from the University of Pittsburgh and Carn-

egie Mellon reported in *Nature* that monkeys fitted with small brain sensors had learned to control a mechanical arm using only their thoughts. ❧ Scientists at St Andrews and Dundee University identified key enzymes that control an anti-tumour gene. Faults in the P53 gene contribute to many cases of cancer, but the scientists discovered a way to 'reboot' the gene, leading to hopes that new cancer drugs could be developed. {JUN} · Psychologists at the University of Plymouth found that students asked to estimate the steepness of a slope assessed it as 10–15% less steep if they had a friend helping them make the judgement. ❧ Researchers at Northwestern University found that the gap between boys and girls on maths test scores narrowed or disappeared altogether in countries with higher standards of gender equality [see p.84]. ❧ Australian researchers who conducted high-resolution brain scans on 15 heavy marijuana users (>5 joints per day for >10 years) found that their hippocampi were 12% smaller, and amygdalae 7·1% smaller, when compared to non-users. {JUL} · A trial of the drug Abiraterone on 21 patients with advanced prostate cancer found significant tumour shrinkage and other major improvements. ❧ German scientists discovered that seven types of small mammal living in western Malaysia regularly drink fermented palm nectar, which has an alcohol level similar to beer. {AUG} · A study published in the *BMJ* indicated that clumsy children were more likely to be obese as adults. Researchers suggested that clumsy or uncoordinated children were more likely to shy away from participation in sport.

────────────── ASTEROID COLLISION THREAT ──────────────

A team of US engineers won a £25,000 Planetary Society prize in February 2008 for designing a space probe capable of tracking an asteroid that threatens to collide with Earth. The asteroid – 99942 Apophis[†] – will pass close enough to Earth in 2029 to be seen by the naked eye, and there is a slim chance it might collide with us in 2036. (NASA estimates there is a <1 in 45,000 chance that Apophis will strike Earth on 13 April, 2036). ❦ The contestants were asked to design a craft capable of planting a tracking device on Apophis which could collect sufficient data about the asteroid's trajectory to enable governments to decide by 2017 if action is required to drive it off course. At present the winning design, the spacecraft Foresight, is only a concept, but Bruce Betts of the Planetary Society said, 'We hope the winning entries will catalyse the world's space agencies to move ahead with designs and missions to protect Earth from potentially dangerous asteroids'.

† In Ancient Egyptian mythology, Apophis (also known as Apep) was the spirit of evil and darkness.

────────────── PLANETARY EVENTS 2009 ──────────────

4 January..................... Perihelion: Earth is at orbital position closest to Sun
26 January....Annular solar eclipse: visible across Indian Ocean and W Indonesia
9 February... Penumbral lunar eclipse: visible in Alaska, Hawaii, Australia, E Asia
20 March............Equinox: Sun passes northward over Equator at 11:43 GMT
21 June.................Solstice: Sun directly above Tropic of Cancer at 5:45 GMT
4 July.....................Aphelion: Earth is at orbital position farthest from Sun
7 July............................Penumbral lunar eclipse: not visible to naked eye
22 July.....Total solar eclipse: visible in India, China, parts of Japan and S Pacific
6 August.........................Penumbral lunar eclipse: not visible to naked eye
22 September........Equinox: Sun passes southward over Equator at 21:18 GMT
21 December......Solstice: Sun directly above Tropic of Capricorn at 17:47 GMT
31 December...................Partial lunar eclipse: visible in Eastern Hemisphere

────────────── NEW SUNSPOT CYCLE ──────────────

On 4 January, 2008, sunspot AR10981 appeared on the N hemisphere of the Sun. While this event may have gone unnoticed by the public, it was of crucial importance to astronomers, since AR10981 heralded a new solar cycle – Cycle 24. Sunspots are regions of lower temperature and heightened magnetic activity that appear as dark patches on the Sun's surface; they have been found to wax and wane in a 'solar cycle' of approximately 11 years. As the number of sunspots increases, so too does other solar activity, such as solar flares. Tracking the evolution of solar cycles is not simply of academic interest, since periods of intense solar activity can impede aeronautic and military communications, disable satellites, and threaten the stability of power grids. Periods of intense solar activity generally take place towards the middle of each solar cycle, which is next expected during 2011 or 2012. (The previous cycle peaked between 2000 and 2002, when there were major solar storms.)

---------------------------- KEY SPACE MISSIONS OF 2008 ----------------------------

JULES VERNE · In April 2008, the European Space Agency's (ESA) automated transfer vehicle (ATV), known as Jules Verne, became the first unmanned, fully automated space vehicle to dock successfully with the International Space Station. The huge ATV transported *c.*5 tons of vital supplies to the ISS, including air, food, and water. The ESA has agreed to build and launch 5 ATVs between 2008–15, in lieu of payment to become part of the ISS project.

JASON-2 · A joint venture between the French space agency CNES and NASA, the Jason-2 satellite was launched in June 2008. The mission aims to measure the effects of climate change by minutely mapping the oceans. It is hoped that images from Jason-2 will allow scientists to measure the extent of rising sea levels.

COLUMBUS · In February 2008, ESA's space lab Columbus docked with the ISS. Columbus will enable astronauts aboard the ISS to carry out hundreds of experiments, including research into the effects of gravity on plant growth.

PHOENIX · NASA's Phoenix lander arrived on Mars in May 2008 with a mission to use a robotic arm to gather samples of water ice. Despite initial problems caused by the surprisingly sticky soil on the Red Planet, Phoenix did eventually retrieve samples of water in July 2008. Although water ice had previously been identified by the Mars Odyssey orbiter, this was the first time samples of Martian water had been collected and analysed. It is hoped that this breakthrough will allow researchers to explore whether Mars might one day be habitable.

GLAST · In June 2008, the Glast space telescope was launched on a five-year mission to examine some of the most dramatic events in space. The NASA project will photograph gamma rays – the highest-energy form of light – that are created in explosive situations such as when neutron stars merge or where supermassive black holes exist. It is hoped that, through the study of these 'energetic objects', fundamental questions about the nature of the universe might be answered.

THE KAVLI PRIZES

The Kavli Prizes in astrophysics, nanoscience, and neuroscience were awarded for the first time in May 2008. The $1m awards, which are to be presented every other year, are a joint venture of the Norwegian Academy of Science and Letters, the Norwegian Ministry of Education and Research, and the California-based Kavli Foundation, which was established in 2000 by the Norwegian-born physicist, entrepreneur, and philanthropist Fred Kavli. The inaugural set of awards went to:

ASTROPHYSICS · Maarten Schmidt of the California Institute of Technology
and Donald Lynden-Bell of Cambridge University
NANOSCIENCE · Louis E. Brus of Columbia University
and Sumio Iijima of Meijo University (Japan)
NEUROSCIENCE · Pasko Rakic of the Yale School of Medicine, Thomas Jessell
of Columbia University, and Sten Grillner of the Karolinska Institute (Sweden)

---————— SOME INVENTIONS OF NOTE · 2007–08 ————————

{OCT 2007} · Legend Technologies began marketing the PistolCam, a lightweight digital camera that attaches to a handgun's barrel and begins recording automatically whenever the gun is drawn. ❧ Japan's Kaneko Sangyo Co. developed a portable toilet for cars, equipped with a privacy curtain and bag for waste, for use in traffic jams and emergencies. ❧ A University of California team unveiled a device only a few atoms large that is able to receive radio waves and transmit them as sound – paving the way for nano-sized radios &c. ❧ Researchers at Queen's University Belfast won £½m for developing a 'bone cement' that can help repair fractures. {NOV} · A team from Hokkaido Industrial Research in Japan built 3 'melody roads' engraved with grooves that emit tones when cars drive over them. {DEC} · Research from the Air Force Institute of Technology demonstrated software that can be used to identify potential office saboteurs or industry spies, by scanning emails both for communication on sensitive topics and for lack of communication on 'normal' or social activities. According to researchers, people flagged as both socially alienated and communicating on sensitive topics are likely to pose a risk. {JAN 2008} · ❧ TN Games designed a USB-enabled 'gaming vest', using special air pockets to mimic the sensation of G-force, bullet wounds, &c. {FEB} · Scientists at Simon Fraser University in Canada unveiled a knee-mounted electrical generator that harvests the power produced by walking. The device, which engages at the end of each stride, can produce *c.*5 watts of power if worn on each knee – enough to run 10 cell phones. ❧

Scientists at the Marine Biological Laboratory in Massachusetts reported that they had trained black sea bass to associate a specific musical tone with being fed. The scientists hope the bass will eventually remember the tone long enough to be raised in the open ocean, then follow the tone to a cage. ❧ The finalists of Microsoft's NextGen PC Design competition included a neck-mounted camera called Momenta, which records everything in front of the viewer and logs the footage whenever it detects a spike in heart rate. {MAR} · A company called ThruVision developed a new kind of body-scanning technology for use in airports, arenas, &c. The technology is based on terahertz rays, which are normally used to study dying stars and are said to be less damaging than X-rays. ❧ A scientist at the USDA created a biodegradable packaging film containing the antimicrobial agent nisin, which kills bacteria that cause food poisoning. {MAY} · A Swiss pilot developed his own set of jet-powered wings, using 4 turbines strapped to his back. The wings allowed him to fly at 186mph and perform tricks, after jumping out of a plane 7,500ft above the Alps. {JUN} · Israeli researchers developed a gesture-recognition system that allows surgeons to access images on a computer during surgery, simply by gesticulating. The system uses a video camera hooked up to a PC, which recognises a basic vocabulary of gestures and translates them into computer commands [see p.13]. {JUL} · NASA announced plans to develop a GPS-like system for use on the moon, using beacons linked to space suits and other devices to help astronauts traverse the lunar surface.

––––––––––––––– STANDBY ('VAMPIRE') POWER –––––––––––––––

Many electronic appliances have a 'standby mode' in which the device is neither in use nor fully switched off. These 'lopomos' (LOw POwer MOdes) range from computer 'sleep' functions to the default mode of power adapters, cell phone chargers, and the like. While devices on standby may appear to be off, they continue to draw electricity as long as they remain plugged in and, since these drains are continuous and take place while devices are 'asleep', they have been nicknamed 'vampire loads'. Below are the average amounts of electricity consumed by appliances on standby:

Device	watts				
Cable box	10·8	DVD player	4·2	Computer	1·7
VCR	6·0	Answering machine	3·0	When in use, the average TV	
Inkjet printer	5·0	Microwave oven	2·9	consumes 210 watts.	
TV	5·0	Portable stereo	2·2	[Source: Lawrence Berkeley	
		Clock radio	1·7	National Laboratory]	

The proliferation of electronic devices with lopomos has made vampire loads an increasing cause of concern. The International Energy Agency (IEA) estimates that a typical European or North American home now contains 20 devices constantly on standby, which together account for 5–10% of residential electricity, and ultimately 1% of global CO_2 emissions. The table below illustrates the average use of standby power in the homes of various OECD countries, according to the IEA:

Av. residential standby power use (watts)		% annual resid. electricity			
87	Australia	12	37	Netherlands	10
27	France	7	100	New Zealand	11
44	Germany	10	19	Switzerland	3
46	Japan	9	32	UK	8
			50	US	5

[Estimates based on a variety of studies]

––––––––––––––– X-PRIZES &c. –––––––––––––––

In 1996 the X-Prize Foundation offered $10m to the first team able to build a privately funded passenger spaceship that could fly into space and back twice in two weeks. The success of the prize led to a new wave of scientific contests, including:

ARCHON X-PRIZE FOR GENOMICS · *Goal*: Sequence 100 human genomes within 10 days · *Purse*: $10m

PETA IN VITRO MEAT PRIZE · *Goal*: Produce in vitro chicken meat & sell it to public by 30/6/2012 · *Purse*: $1m

VIRGIN EARTH CHALLENGE · *Goal*: Design a viable technology to remove anthropogenic greenhouse gases from the atmosphere · *Purse*: $25m

NETFLIX PRIZE · *Goal*: Develop a movie-recommendation algorithm that performs 10% better than Netflix's current system · *Purse*: $1m

In June 2008, John McCain said that, if elected President, he would offer a $300m prize ('$1 for every man, woman, and child in the US') to anyone who could build a more efficient car battery.

——————— SCI, TECH, NET WORDS OF NOTE ———————

SAVIOUR SIBLINGS · children born (or bred) specifically to provide transplant material for extant children. *Also* SPARE PART BABIES.

CYBRIDS · human-animal embryos used to grow stem cells; a controversial practice banned in some countries but allowed by UK authorities in September 2007.

SOCIAL NOTWORKING · avoidance of work through social networking.

HOT PRODUCT THEFT · purloinment (often from children) of high value electronics (e.g., iPods, mobiles, &c.).

EXABYTE · a billion gigabytes – previously an unthinkably large quantity of data, but now, thanks to data mining &c., increasingly common.

OFF-GRID · existing independently from the 'grid' of power, water, phones, &c. *Also* living below the radar of state or corporate surveillance.

G-PHONE · a mobile phone supposedly being developed by Google; superseded in November 2007 by ANDROID – a Google suite of open-source mobile phone software.

QWERTY TUMMY · illness caught from dirty computer keyboards [see p.189].

METAVERSE · online 3-D social environments such as *Second Life* &c.; coined in Neal Stephenson's *Snow Crash*.

SHUFFLE SHAME · to be embarrassed by a poor song on a random playlist.

SEXTING · sending naked photos by text message, or flirting via SMS.

FACESLAMMING · to deny a Facebook friend request. *Also* FACEBOOK SUICIDE · to delete one's online profile.

RHYTHM GAMES · a genre of video games involving music (e.g., *Guitar Hero*) that are increasingly a feature of school physical education classes. *Also* WiiHABILITATION · the use of Wii consoles in physical therapy.

NETHOOD · Internet communities based on real-life proximity, in which users share services and information relevant to their location.

COPYFRAUD · false copyright claims, such as on public domain materials, that demand licence fees when none are required.

KAVOSHGAR-1 · reportedly the first rocket successfully launched into space by Iran (in February 2008).

NANO-GENERATORS · tiny fibres, embedded in fabric &c., that convert mechanical energy (i.e., movement) into electricity.

NERDIC · the language of geeks.

GRIEFERS · online gamers who disrupt, harass, and annoy fellow players; the most famous are the Patriotic Nigras, whose misanthropic slogan is 'Ruining *Second Life* Since 2006'.

RICKROLLING · the practice of duping people into viewing Rick Astley's 1980s classic 'Never Gonna Give You Up', by sending them a supposedly vital URL.

GOOGLEGÄNGER · a namesake who shares the same Google search listings. *Also* GOOGLE TWINS.

———————— SCI, TECH, NET WORDS OF NOTE cont. ————————

GEEK DEFENCE · *Wired*'s term for the US legal strategy of presenting highly intelligent (geeky) defendants as weird misfits who should not be judged by society's norms.

EVIL METER · term used by Google CEO Eric Schmidt, who said of the company's mission statement, '*"Don't be evil" is misunderstood. We don't have an evil meter … the rule allows for conversation. I thought when I joined the company this was crap … it must be a joke. I was sitting in a room in the first six months … talking about some advertising … and someone said that it is evil. It stopped the product. It's a cultural rule, a way of forcing the conversation, especially in areas that are ambiguous*'.

TWEETS · short status updates sent from cell phones or instant messaging services through the website Twitter.

FAIL-GREEN · fail-safe mechanisms that fail in an eco-friendly way.

CYBERCHONDRIACS · those people who (obsessively) search the internet for medical information.

ECO FATIGUE · ennui or annoyance brought on by sanctimonious peddling of 'green' alternatives.

UNBOXING · the unlikely YouTube trend of uploading videos of people unpacking newly purchased technology products. An offshoot of TECHPORN.

E-VENGERS · those (exes) who wreak revenge online.

UPCYCLING · where recycling materials increases their value (e.g., when packing materials are reformed into insulation).

JAILBREAK · to escape from Apple's supposed iPhone iSLAVERY.

NSFW · website or email content that is Not Safe For Work; often used as a warning to others.

MULLET SITES · websites that (like the '70s haircut) have a professional frontend but user-generated content within. *Similarly* POOPULAR · popular on the outside, poopy on the inside.

FAT TV · a non-flat-screen television.

WEBLEBRITY · an internet-only celeb.

SNIPES · informational and advertising graphics overlaid across TV shows.

FANBOY · a fanatical fan, usually of one niche [splendidly, the term dates from 1919].

EARLY-NERD SPECIAL · midnight screenings of cult films (*Star Wars* &c.) designed especially for fanboys &c.

NOTOX · using radio waves, rather than chemicals, to reduce the signs of ageing.

PLUTOID · International Astronomical Union's new designation for all 'dwarf planets lying beyond Neptune' [see p.81].

SPORN · porn created in the game *Spore*.

PASSWORD FATIGUE · the annoyance of having to remember a plethora of passwords. *Also* PASSZHEIMER'S · the inability to remember one's passwords.

TELEPUTING · using a TV to view computer content (games, photos, &c.).

JOURNOSAUR · a journalist who rails against online media.

COMPUTER USAGE AROUND THE WORLD

While computer usage is widespread in the US and Canada and across W Europe, the number of people who use a computer at least some of the time varies widely elsewhere in Europe, Latin America, and Africa. Below, according to 2007 data from the Pew Research Centre, are the countries with the highest and lowest percent of residents who said they used a computer 'at least occasionally' at home or work:

Most computer use	%	Least computer use	%	Biggest gainers			%
					'02	'07	±
Sweden	82	Bangladesh	5				
South Korea	81	Tanzania	6	Brazil	22	44	+22
US	80	Pakistan	9	Slovakia	52	73	+21
Canada	76	Uganda	11	Bulgaria	19	38	+19
UK	76	Indonesia	11	UK	59	76	+17

CHILDREN'S INTERNET USE

63% of children aged 12–15, and 39% of 8–11-year-olds, use the internet almost every day. Online activities carried out at least once a week by children include:

Activity (age)	8–11	12–15			
School work	55%	75%	Social networking	19	55
Look for info	54	63	Download/play music	16	48
Play online games	50	44	Email	18	40
Instant messaging	26	62	TV prog. websites	26	20
			Listen to radio	3	9

83% of parents of 8–11-year-olds, and 93% of parents of 12–15-year-olds, said they trusted their child to use the internet safely. 51% of parents of 8–11-year-olds, and 43% of parents of 12–15-year-olds, had installed parental controls on their computer. [Source: Ofcom, Media Literacy Audit, May 2008]

NET POPULATIONS

Population of		comparable to
MySpace	230m[†]	Indonesia
Google	121m[§]	Japan
Yahoo!	116m[§]	Mexico
AOL	91m[§]	Philippines
eBay	83m[§]	Germany
Facebook	70m[†]	Turkey
Friendster	65m[†]	Iran
Wikipedia	56m[§]	Italy
Second Life	13m[†]	Guatemala
W. of Warcraft	10m[‡]	Hungary

† Users as of 5/08; § Unique visitors in 4/08
‡ Subscribers as of 1/08

2008 WEBBY AWARDS

Activism	loveisrespect.org
Best homepage	lafilm.com
Best writing	wired.com
Blog – political	huffingtonpost.com
Community	flickr.com
Education	earth.columbia.edu
Fashion	journeys.louisvuitton.com
Humour	theonion.com
Lifestyle	cinchouse.com
Magazine	ngm.com
Music	bbc.co.uk/radio1/djs
News	nytimes.com
Politics	factcheck.org
Sports	sports.yahoo.com

———————VIDEO GAME RATING SYSTEM———————

The way video games are rated in the UK came under scrutiny in July 2008 when the government launched a consultation into whether the ratings for games should replicate those of films. Most video games currently use the pan-European Pegi rating system. Only games deemed to have a significant level of adult content are classified by the British Board of Film Classification (BBFC) – currently just 3% of all games. In March 2008, Dr Tanya Byron published an independent review, *Safer Children in a Digital World*, in which she recommended the schemes be used in tandem – BBFC ratings on the front of video game boxes and Pegi ratings on the back. The most widely used Pegi age rating system for video games is detailed below:

$3+$ · may show violence in a comical context.

$7+$ · may include: nudity in a non-sexual context; pictures or sounds that may be frightening to young children; occasional violence to non-realistic fantasy characters.

$12+$ · may include: graphic violence towards fantasy characters; non-graphic violence towards humans or animals; explicit sexual description or images; mild swearing.

$16+$ · may include: graphic, detailed and sustained violence towards unrealistic humans or animals; graphic detailed depictions of death or injury to unrealistic humans or animals; sexual intercourse without displaying genitals; erotic or sexual nudity; sexual expletives or blasphemy; use of tobacco or alcohol; use of illegal drugs; glamorisation of crime.

$18+$ · may include: gross violence (massive blood and gore, dismemberment, torture, sadism &c.) towards realistic humans or animals; graphic, detailed and sustained violence towards realistic humans or animals; violence towards vulnerable or defenceless humans; sexual activity with visible genital organs; sexual violence or threat (including rape); detailed descriptions of techniques that could be used in criminal offences; glamorisation of the use of illegal drugs; ethnic, religious, nationalistic or other stereotypes likely to encourage hatred.

Additional symbols show levels of violence, swearing, nudity, drugs, fear, gambling, & discrimination.

———————VIDEO GAME LANGUAGE———————

Partly as a response to public concern over video game violence, Microsoft maintains a section of its Xbox website devoted to educational materials for parents. Included on the site is a guide to video gaming lingo; a selection appears below:

BUTTON MASHING – pressing all the buttons on a controller at once
CAMPING – staying in one place
EASTER EGG – hidden item in a game
FRAG – to defeat an opponent

KICK – to remove a player from a server · OWNED – defeated soundly
PATCH – addition developed after a game is released · POWER-UP – item that gives a player temporary powers

──────────────ONLINE SHOPPING──────────────

875m people (*c.*85% of the world's online population) have purchased something over the internet, according to 2008 data from Nielsen Online. S Korea had the highest percentage of internet shoppers (99% of the country's online population), followed by Germany, Japan, and the UK (all at 97% of those online). Below are the percentage of internet users who have shopped online, by region of the world:

Region	shopped online (%)	never shopped online (%)
Europe	93	7
N America	92	8
Asia Pacific	84	16
Latin America	79	21
Middle East	67	33

In all the countries surveyed, books were the items most commonly purchased:

Item	% who bought in past 3 months[†]		
Books	41	Airline tickets	24
Clothing/accessories/shoes	36	Electronic equipment	23
Videos/DVDs/games	24		[†] % of global internet users

──────────────SOCIAL NETWORKING──────────────

57% of all internet users belonged to a social networking site in 2008, according to Universal McCann, allowing them to meet, poke, and spy on an ever-increasing number of 'friends'. Below is a breakdown of popular sites around the world.

Canada	USA	Germany
Facebook .. 15·5m *users*[†]	MySpace.... 60·4m *users*	Class Onl. ...... 3m *users*
Blogger .... 8·6m	Facebook 25m	Blogger .... 2·8m
Wind. LiveSp...... 6·3m	Class Onl. .... 13·6m	MySpace........... 2·4m

UK	France	China
Facebook .... 9·9m *users*	Skyrock........ .7m *users*	YeeYoo.......... .6m *users*
Blogger .... 5·6m	Overblog 6m	9158.com .... 5·9m
MySpace........... 5·6m	Blogger .... 5·2m	Zhiji.com.......... 3·1m

Percentage of internet users	Canada 53%	USA 34%
who belong to a social net-	China.............. 42%	France 17%
working site, by country:	UK................. 39%	Germany 12%

[†] Users for all sites are unique users per month, March 2008. Other social networking sites include: Bebo (popular in Ireland and NZ), Orkut (popular in Brazil), LinkedIn (business networking, popular in the US), hi5 (popular in Central America), Together We Served (US military), BlackPlanet. com (mainly US African Americans), Sagazone (mainly UK >50s), FaithBase (mainly US Christians), and MyHeritage (networking through genealogy). [Sources: OfCom; Datamonitor; Ipsos]

FIRST COMPUTER SPAM

Computer 'spam' turned 30 in 2008, though birthday celebrations were probably few and far between. The first piece of spam is said to have been sent on 3/5/1978, by an employee of the computer maker Digital Equipment Corporation (DEC). The message was sent via Arpanet, the US government-run antecedent of the internet, and invited 393 people to view 'the newest members of DECSYSTEM-20 family' at product demonstrations in California. The reaction was almost universally negative, and DEC was chastised by the US Defense Communications Agency, the Arpanet overseer. Today, the security firm Sophos estimates that 95% of all email is spam. The following dozen countries were responsible for sending the most spam in 2007:

% of global spam sent		
United States......22·5	Russia..............4·7	Spam ....2·7
South Korea........6·5	Brazil.................3·8	Italy..................2·7
China...............6·0	France................3·5	India.................2·6
Poland..............4·9	Germany............3·5	
	Turkey..............3·1	[Source: Sophos, 2008]

Spam ('spiced' + 'ham') is a proprietary Hormel brand name. According to the BBC, the first person to use the term with regard to junk email (in 1993) was Joel Furr, an active early member of the Usenet online discussion system. Furr was reportedly inspired by the famous Monty Python sketch in which Eric Idle (as Mr Bun) and Graham Chapman (as Mrs Bun) are thwarted in their attempts to order a restaurant meal that does not include the delicious meat product [see *Schott's Almanac 2007*].

SPAM CATEGORIES

The most common spam categories detected by Symantec (July–Dec 2007):

Commercial products.............	27%
Internet (spam toolkits &c.)	20
Finance	13
Scams................................	10
Health...............................	10
Adult	7
Fraud	7
Leisure...............................	6

SPAM PER CAPITA

The countries that relay the highest number of spam messages per capita, according to IT security firm Sophos:

1 ....Pitcairn Islands (in S Pacific)
2 .... Niue (island in S Pacific)
3 ....Tokelau Islands (3 atolls in S Pacific)
4 ....Anguilla (islands in Caribbean)
5 ....Faroe Islands (in N Europe)
6 ....Monaco
7 ....Bermuda

SPOETRY

Dubbed 'spoetry' in a 2006 *Guardian* article by Eva Wiseman, the seemingly random juxtaposition of words found in many spam messages (a device to foil anti-spam filters) can occasionally provide brief flashes of beauty. Over the past several years a variety of websites and contests devoted to 'spoems' have blossomed on the internet. An entry titled 'Almagest' on one such website, spampoetry.org, reads:
Machinery, and quiet vassily/marvelous, his magician!/have, cervix, dealt the blow.

REDEFINING THE BASE UNITS

Seven base units are used to measure the physical properties of the universe. These units form the fundamental building blocks of the *Système International d'Unités* (SI units), which are the legal standard of measurement for science and trade in most countries. However, in recent years a number of scientists have voiced concerns over one of the most widely used base units – the kilogram – which remains the only base unit defined by reference to a physical artefact. Since 1889, the mass of a kilogram has been fixed to a lump of platinum and iridium alloy held in a vault at the International Bureau of Weights and Measures in Sèvres, France. Unfortunately, the mass of this lump – which is too precious for routine measurement – changes slightly over time. Thus, in November 2007, the General Conference on Weights and Measures resolved to encourage experiments redefining the kilogram in terms of an invariable property of nature (such as the mass of a certain number of photons). The conference also encouraged experiments regarding the redefinition of other base units, since the demands of modern research call for increasingly precise measurements. Below are the SI base units with some of their proposed redefinitions:

METRE · *Measures*: length. *Definition*: length of the path travelled by light in a vacuum during 1/299,792,458 of a second. *Proposed redefinition*: none.

KILOGRAM · *Measures*: mass. *Definition*: mass of the prototype in Sèvres, France. *Proposed redefinition*: mass of a body whose energy is equal to that of a number of photons whose frequencies add up to a particular total (tied to the Planck constant).

SECOND · *Measures*: time. *Definition*: time taken for 9,192,631,770 periods of vibrations of the electromagnetic radiation emitted by a caesium-133 atom. *Proposed redefinition*: none.

AMPERE · *Measures*: electric current. *Definition*: the current in a pair of straight, parallel conductors of infinite length 1 metre apart in a vacuum that produces a force of 2×10^{-7} newtons per metre in their length. *Proposed redefinition*: the electric current in the direction of the flow of a certain number of elementary charges per second.

KELVIN · *Measures*: thermodynamic temperature. *Definition*: the fraction 1/273·16 of the thermodynamic temperature of the triple point of water (the temperature and pressure at which ice, liquid water, and water vapour exist). *Proposed redefinition*: the change of thermodynamic temperature that results in a change of thermal energy by a specific amount (tied to the Boltzmann constant).

CANDELA · *Measures*: luminous intensity. *Definition*: the luminous intensity of a source of frequency 540×10^{12} hertz whose radiant intensity is 1/683 watts per steradian. *Proposed redefinition*: none.

MOLE · *Measures*: substance (used in chemistry). *Definition*: amount of substance that contains as many elementary units as there are atoms in 0·012 kgs of carbon-12. *Proposed redefinition*: such that the Avogadro constant is $6·0221415 \times 10^{23}$ per mole.

[Sources: *New Scientist*; NIST]

Final decisions are expected at the 2011 meeting of the General Conference on Weights & Measures.

Travel & Leisure

One half of the world cannot understand the pleasures of the other.
— JANE AUSTEN (1775–1817)

THE BIOFUEL DEBATE

In July 2008, the government-commissioned Gallagher Review called for the introduction of biofuels in Britain to be slowed, to curtail the transfer of land from food crops to fuel: 'We have concluded that there is a future for a sustainable biofuels industry but that feedstock production *must* avoid agricultural land that would otherwise be used for food.' Gallagher warned that current policies could cause oil seed prices in the EU to rise by 50%, grain by 15%, and sugar by 7%. ❦ Until recently, some had regarded biofuels as a 'magic bullet' against our dependence on oil, which is both polluting and, in terms of the security of its supply, problematic. The majority of biofuels currently come from agricultural crops: in Europe, predominantly from sugar beet, rapeseed, and wheat; in the US, from corn and soybeans; and in Brazil, from sugar cane. To meet rising demand, the global production of ethanol doubled between 2000–05. ❦ Biofuels are not new. In 1925, Henry Ford told the *New York Times* that 'the fuel of the future is going to come from fruit like that sumac out by the road, or from apples, weeds, sawdust – almost anything'. However an abundance of oil meant that biofuel was of minority interest until the oil spikes of the 1970s. Over the last decade, concerns over global warming have been matched by soaring oil prices and the next wave of industrialisation and mass consumption in the BRIC countries [see p.271] and beyond. Together, these forces have accelerated the pace of biofuel production – but at a cost, which is only now being addressed. ❦ The Gallagher Review was not alone in sounding a note of caution in 2008. The Royal Society warned of the impact of biofuels on 'biological diversity and natural ecosystems'. A study in *Science* suggested that US-grown ethanol had not cut greenhouse emissions by 20%, but rather had doubled them, as farmers in the developing world destroyed grassland and rainforest in order to grow food. And a range of groups, including the UN, the IMF, and the World Bank, highlighted the disturbing link between biofuels and agflation [see p.16]. ❦ It will clearly take time to balance ecological concerns and food security with the need for biofuels and an entrenched biofuel lobby. And it is possible that the solution lies in a 'second generation' of biofuels – straw, grass, wood-chip, pulp, &c. – which have a far smaller ecological footprint. Recognising the need for swift action, a number of governments have already modified their ambitious biofuel targets since, as Oxfam noted, 'it takes the same amount of grain to fill an SUV with ethanol as it does to feed a person'.

———————————————— ROAD TAX ————————————————

9·4m motorists will pay more road tax in 2010–11, after the government introduced measures to target the most polluting vehicles. Controversy was sparked in July 2008 when – contrary to Gordon Brown's assertion that 'the majority of drivers will benefit' – it became clear that vehicle excise duty would in fact only fall for 18%. In calculations released by the House of Commons, Treasury minister Angela Eagle revealed that, in 2010–11, 18% (3·9m people) will see their car tax fall, 39% (8·5m people) will see no difference, and 43% (9·4m people) will pay more under the new measures. In response to the furore, Chancellor Alistair Darling indicated that he may introduce measures to ease the transition. The Exchequer would receive >£1bn in extra revenue from the tax by 2011. Below is a table, released by the House of Commons, showing the impact of the tax in 2010–11:

Band	CO_2 (g/km)	standard rate 2010 (£)	% paying less tax	% paying same tax	% paying more tax
A	≤100	0	–	100	–
B	101–110	20	100	–	–
C	111–120	35	20	80	–
D	121–130	95	100	–	–
E	131–140	115	100	–	–
F	141–150	125	–	100	–
G	151–160	155	–	40	60
H	161–170	180	–	–	100
I	171–180	210	–	–	100
J	181–200	270	–	–	100
K	201–225	310	–	–	100
L	226–255	430	–	–	100
M	>255	455	–	–	100

The government stated that only 5 of the 30 most popular cars in Britain would cost more to tax. The most popular car in the UK, according to 2007 sales, was the Ford Fiesta 1·2 P Zetec Climate.

———————————— BUMPER STICKERS & ROAD RAGE ————————————

While bumper stickers may offer a temporary source of amusement during traffic jams, in 2008 Colorado State University scientists uncovered a darker side to the garish plastic rectangles. In three separate studies on car adornment and driving behaviour, the researchers discovered that the more bumper stickers, window decals, and mirror hangings students displayed on their vehicle, the more likely they were to report aggressive road behaviour or 'road rage'. Interestingly, drivers with more car adornments also reported greater feelings of attachment to their vehicles, and the researchers explained that drivers who decorate their cars may be more prone to confusing the social norms of private property protection with the norms of sharing a public space – i.e., a road. Intriguingly, the researchers found no relationship between the content of the bumper stickers (whether religious, sport-related, political, ironic, or other) and reports of a tendency towards aggressive driving.

———————————— NEW PARKING LAWS ————————————

New parking regulations came into force across England and Wales, as of 31 March 2008, in an attempt to make the penalty system both uniform and transparent. Councils have been assigned one of five bands which will set the level of fine†:

OUTSIDE LONDON				LONDON	*minor*	*serious*
Band	*(fines £)*	*minor*	*serious*	A	£80	£120
A		£50	£70	B	£60	£100
B		£40	£60	C	£40	£80

Other changes include: traffic wardens to be re-branded as 'civil enforcement officers'; evidence collection via CCTV with fines issued by post; drivers to be given 21 days (not 14) to pay fines; and fines to be forwarded by post if a vehicle is driven away before the ticket has been completed. Below are some examples of offences:

Serious offences	*Minor offences*
Parking on a taxi rank	Parking for longer than permitted
Parking on a cycle path	Parking beyond parking bay markers
Parking in a permit space without a valid permit	Parking in a closed car park
Parking in a disabled bay without showing a valid disabled badge	Parking without clearly displaying valid pay & display ticket
	Parking with the engine running

† For more information on banding contact your local council. The National Parking Adjudication Service admitted they expected the number of parking fines to soar as people adjust to the new rules.

———————— ACCIDENTS CAUSED BY FOREIGN DRIVERS ————————

The number of accidents on British roads caused by foreign drivers in foreign vehicles increased by 47% between 2001–06, according to a 2007 study by the Association of British Insurers (ABI). Notably, foreign lorries were 3× more likely (per mile) to be involved in collisions on British roads than domestic lorries. The ABI highlighted weaker road safety rules in continental Europe, citing 45 key differences in legislation and safety testing. Lithuanian drivers were responsible for the largest percentage rise in collisions on British roads between 2001–06, as below:

Country (collisions)	*2001*	*2006*			
Lithuania	1	745	Hungary	192	655
Slovak Republic	22	462	Czech Republic	250	870
Latvia	11	96	Irish Republic	128	413
Poland	361	3,132	Slovenia	68	206
Estonia	28	99	Romania	76	227
			[Source: UK Green Card Bureau]		

Of course, driving on different sides of the road does not help. In 2005, 20% of collisions involving foreign-registered lorries involved 'sideswiping', where a vehicle pulls out and hits another vehicle in the driver's blind spot. Only 7% of accidents involving British-registered lorries involved sideswiping.

—— LEAST & MOST DANGEROUS CITIES FOR CARS ——

The safest and riskiest British cities for motor thefts and accidents were revealed in a December 2007 report by Endsleigh Insurance; Swindon and Belfast were safest.

Safest & riskiest cities for car theft		*Safest & riskiest cities for car* accidents	
City	*± national average (%)*	*City*	*± national average (%)*
Swindon	–42·9	Belfast	–47·0
Norwich	–42·3	Swansea	–29·9
Dundee	–38·9	Aberdeen	–20·6
Solihull	–36·7	Chester	–20·1
Exeter	–36·4	Cambridge	–19·4
Hull	143·9	Slough	35·7
Nottingham	82·9	Ilford	35·5
Leeds	77·8	Birmingham	32·9
Ilford	77·7	Bradford	27·3
Bradford	68·1	London	27·1

———————— LONDON CONGESTION CHARGE ————————

GENERAL INFORMATION		HOW TO PAY	
Current price	£8 per day	Online	cclondon.com
Operating times	7am–6pm	Phone	0845 900 1234
Days of operation	Mon–Fri	Text message (SMS)	81099

TfL reports that since congestion charging was introduced in 2003, traffic in the zone has reduced by 21%. In 2006/07, £123m was raised from the charge to spend on improving London's transport.

———————— EMBASSIES & THE CONGESTION CHARGE ————————

The US embassy topped the list of London's embassies and high commissions with unpaid congestion charge payments and other traffic penalties†. Many embassies refuse to pay the congestion charge as a matter of legal principle, arguing that it is a *tax* from which they have diplomatic exemption. The 10 worst offenders were:

Embassy/high commission	*sum owed*		
US	£2,087,945	Sudan	£712,900
Japan	£1,003,300	Kenya	£435,250
Nigeria†	£982,350	Tanzania	£409,120
Russian Federation	£912,360	South Africa	£362,500
Germany	£828,170	Sierra Leone	£320,120
		[Source: Transport for London, March 2008]	

† The same report revealed that Nigeria was the second worst offender in relation to unpaid parking fines; Saudi Arabia was first, and Guinea was third, followed by the UEA, Egypt, Qatar, and Brunei.

———HOUSEHOLD EXPENDITURE ON TRANSPORT———

Some UK household expenditures on transport per week between '97/'98–'05/'06:

Purchase of £/week	'97/'98	'99/'00	'01/'02	'03/'04	'05/'06
New cars and vans	5·80	7·90	10·70	11·40	9·60
Second-hand cars and vans	13·40	14·30	14·40	16·00	14·00
Motorcycles and scooters	0·60	0·50	0·50	0·60	–
Petrol	11·30	12·80	12·70	12·40	14·30
Diesel	1·20	1·40	2·00	2·50	3·10
All motoring & bicycle costs	40·90	45·70	49·40	51·90	51·80
Rail & tube fares	1·40	1·80	1·90	1·90	2·10
Bus & coach fares	1·30	1·40	1·50	1·40	1·50
Air fares	1·30	1·00	1·20	1·90	2·50
All transport	48·00	53·80	57·80	60·70	61·70
All household expenditure	328·80	359·40	398·30	418·10	443·40
% house. exp. on transport	14·6%	15·0%	14·5%	14·5%	13·9%

[Source: Expenditure and Food Survey · ONS]

———FAVOURITE DRIVING SONGS———

Drivers who listen to Blues music are most likely to get caught speeding, according to a May 2008 survey by Saga Motor Insurance. Country music fans are second most likely to speed, followed by reggae devotees. The most popular driving songs:

Bat Out of Hell – Meatloaf · *Bohemian Rhapsody* – Queen · *Born To Be Wild* – Steppenwolf · *Don't Stop Me Now* – Queen · *Hotel California* – The Eagles

———ROAD REPAIRS———

Councils in England and Wales spent more on compensation for injuries and vehicle damage caused by potholes than they did on mending the potholes themselves, according to the 13th Annual Local Authority Road Maintenance (ALARM) survey, published in April 2008. The total compensation bill for pothole injuries and damage was £65m (£53m in claims + £12m on staff and processing), whereas councils spent just £52·3m on actually filling the holes. The ALARM survey also revealed:

Number of road works by utility companies[†] .... *c*.2·5m (*c*.2m in 2006)
Backlog of maintenance work.. 11 years
Shortfall in highway maintenance budgets .... >£1bn
Average wait for road re-surfacing .... 65 years[‡]
Average cost to fill one pothole £69
Total number of potholes reported filled during 2006/7 862,267

† Estimated to reduce road life by *c*.30%. ‡ Urban roads are resurfaced twice as often as rural ones.

———————— PROXIMITY TO LOCAL FACILITIES ————————

Below is a breakdown of how long it takes Britons to reach various local facilities†:

Time taken (mins)	GP	grocery shop	hospital	post office	primary school
<15	78%	92	23	87	91
16–20	10	3	13	7	4
21–30	6	2	23	4	3
31–40	1	0	9	1	0
41–60	2	1	23	1	1
>60	1	1	9	1	0

† On foot or using public transport; % of households. [Source: National Travel Survey 2006, DoT]

———————————— BUSES: WALK vs WAIT ————————————

Three American mathematicians finally proved that it is nearly always worth waiting at a bus stop for the next bus, rather than beginning to walk towards your destination. This vital conclusion was drawn by Scott Kominers and Robert Sinnott of Harvard, and Justin Chen of the California Institute of Technology in their paper *Walk Versus Wait: The Lazy Mathematician Wins* – featured in the *New Scientist* in January 2008†. Only when a bus is not due for more than an hour, or your destination is less than 1km away, should you risk walking.

† In the same month, Stagecoach, which runs *c*.7,000 buses nationwide, produced a guide to getting on and off a bus. The company said its research demonstrated that many members of the public were scared of buses, and that its step-by-step guide was intended to encourage use of public transport.

———————— ACCOMPANYING CHILDREN TO SCHOOL ————————

61% of all children (7–13) are accompanied to school by an adult; the most common reason for so doing was concern about traffic. Below are National Travel Survey figures for the percentage of children accompanied to school, and the reason:

%	age 7–10		11–13		All 7–13	
	2002	2006	2002	2006	2002	2006
Usually accompanied by an adult	78	85	27	31	55	61
Usually unaccompanied	15	12	64	62	37	34
Accompanied part of the way	1	0	3	1	2	1
REASONS · traffic danger	57	59	27	32	51	53
– fear of assault/molestation	47	36	29	25	43	34
– school too far away	25	20	34	25	27	21
– child might not arrive on time	12	16	14	12	12	15
– child might get lost	11	14	6	3	10	12
– fear of bullying	7	8	9	10	8	8
– other	22	13	32	17	24	14

MOTORCYCLES

There are currently only *c*.1·22m licensed motorcycles in Great Britain, and Britons own fewer motorcycles per head than any other major European Union country, except Ireland. Less than 3% of British households owned a motorbike in 2005/06 – though the rate of motorcycle ownership was highest in the South-west and lowest in Scotland. That said, motorcycle traffic has increased by *c*.37% since 1996; most motorbike journeys are made during the summer, and July is the peak month. As might be expected, motorcycles are by far the riskiest mode of travel; in 2006, the relative risk of a motorcyclist being killed or seriously injured per kilometre travelled was 51 times higher than it was for car drivers. Tabulated below are motorcyclist casualties in 2006, by type of vehicle, and age of driver:

2006	Numbers killed or seriously injured		
Age	*moped*	*motorcycle <125cc*	*motorcycle >125cc*
<16	39	36	19
16–19	502	491	220
20–29	84	455	930
30–39	58	240	1,199
40–49	44	113	1,171
50–59	27	52	485
60–69	5	28	140
≥70	6	12	30
TOTAL (inc. age unknown)	775	1,451	4,259

[Source: Road Accident Statistics, DfT. Figures for Great Britain, 2006]

CARAVANNING

The traditional British caravan holiday made a comeback in 2007–08 as concerns over the economy, the environment, and the cost of foreign travel encouraged 'staycations' [see p.221]. National Caravan Council (NCC) data revealed that camp-site bookings for July and August 2008 had risen by 20%, and sales of caravans and motorhomes were buoyant. The UK is by far the largest European market for caravans; the British buy 50% more mobile homes than their nearest rivals, the Germans. Below are the number of units recently manufactured by NCC members:

Type of caravan	*2004*	*2005*	*2006*
Touring caravans	32,370	29,060	29,290
Motorhomes	10,131	10,849	11,069
Caravan holiday homes	32,280	23,605	23,515
Park homes	3,350	2,535	2,270

According to the NCC, 90% of all caravans sold in the UK were manufactured domestically. The NCC reported in June 2008 that a family of 4 could travel with a medium-sized car and caravan to one of >1,000 UK caravan parks for less than the cost of the airline fuel surcharge (£128 (£32×4)). Britain's most famous caravanner is arguably the former Foreign Secretary, Margaret Beckett MP.

———————————— WORLD'S WORST AIRPORTS ————————————

The US magazine *Foreign Policy* published its five worst airports in October 2007:

Name & location   explanation
Léopold Sédar Senghor, Dakar, Senegal ....*3-hour immigration queues, no seats*
Indira Gandhi, New Delhi, India........*filthy toilets, used syringes on terminal floor*
Mineralnye Vody, SW Russia................*snow, ice, and feral cats inside terminal*
Baghdad, Iraq............*pilots employ terrifying landing techniques to avoid missiles*
Charles de Gaulle, Paris, France ....*rude staff, dirty terminals, overpriced food*

A March 2008 Skytrax survey of 7·8m air passengers ranked Hong Kong International as the world's best airport. Heathrow fell 58 places from the previous year's ranking, coming in 103rd out of 162 airports. Heathrow's worst feature was its transit facilities; its best was the duty-free shopping.

———————————————— AIR ACCIDENTS ————————————————

2007 saw the lowest number of air accidents for more than 40 years, according to the Aircraft Crashes Record Office (ACRO) in Geneva. (An accident is defined as any event where the aircraft is so badly damaged it cannot be used and is removed from service; the number of victims is not taken into consideration.) ACRO recorded 136 accidents internationally, with North America accounting for the highest number (32% of the total). Europe was the safest, recording no significant accidents in 2007. The worst accidents in 2007, ranked in terms of fatalities, were:

Deaths	date	location	airline (plane)
187	17/07	São Paulo, Brazil	TAM (Airbus A320-233)
114	05/05	Douala, Cameroon	Kenya Airways (Boeing 737-8AL)
102	01/01	off Ujung Pandang, Indonesia	Adam Air (Boeing 737-4Q8)
90	16/09	Phuket, Thailand	One-Two-Go (McDonnell Douglas MD-82)
57	30/11	Isparta, Turkey	Atlasjet (McDonnell Douglas MD-83)

———————————————————— AIR RAGE ————————————————————

There were 2,219 reports of air rage on British planes in 2007, up from 1,359 in the previous year, according to the Civil Aviation Authority (CAA). In 42 cases the disruption was so serious that passengers had to be restrained. Air rage is most commonly blamed on alcohol consuption or passengers being prevented from smoking, but many disputes involve bickering couples, or are caused by minor irritations such as seat allocation or annoyance at people reclining. Passengers were ordered off planes in 235 cases; police or security were forced to intervene 345 times; take-off was prevented on 19 occasions; and planes were diverted 14 times. CAA statistics indicate that males in their 30s are most likely to suffer from air rage, although roughly a quarter of all disruptive incidents involved women. Although alcohol is a common factor in air rage, it is thought that onboard irritations can be exacerbated by anxiety, flight delays, a lack of oxygen, and feelings of helplessness.

———————————— BEST BUSINESS CLASS ————————————

The Times ranked the top 10 business class aircraft seats, in a February 2007 report:

1 .... Air Canada	5 .... Jet Airways	9 .... United Airlines
2 .... British Airways	6 .....Singapore Airlines	10 ...... Virgin Atlantic
3 ...Eos Airlines (defunct)	7 ...... Silverjet (defunct)	
4 ...... Etihad Airways†	8 .... S African Airways	† Based in Abu Dhabi

———————— BUSIEST INTERNATIONAL AIRLINES ————————

Rank	country	airline	passengers (m)	passenger km (bn)
1	USA	American	98·1	224·3
2	USA	Delta	73·5	158·9
3	USA	United	69·3	188·7
4	USA	Northwest	54·8	116·8
5	Germany	Lufthansa	51·2	114·7
6	France	Air France	49·4	128·7
7	Japan	All Nippon Airways	49·2	58·0
8	Japan	JAL	48·9	89·3
9	USA	Continental	46·7	122·7
10	China	China Southern Airline	40·8	59·6
11	Ireland	Ryanair	40·5	39·8
...				
14	UK	British Airways	32·7	112·6
16	UK	easyJet	28·0	27·6

The busiest airport in the world is Hartsfield-Jackson International Airport in Atlanta, USA; 84·8m passengers passed through its terminals in 2006. Chicago's O'Hare International is the second busiest, with 76·2m passengers; London Heathrow is third with 67·3m. [Source: ICAO, 2006]

———————————— AIRLINE LOST LUGGAGE ————————————

Air Portugal and British Airways were the European carriers most likely to lose their passengers' luggage, according to February 2007 figures from the Association of European Airlines. 61% of lost bags went missing during flight transfers and, while most were returned within 48 hours, 1 in 2,000 bags were lost for good. The table below shows the number of bags lost by each carrier, per 1,000 passengers:

Airline	2006	2007
TAP Air Portugal	21·0	27·8
British Airways	23·0	26·5
KLM	16·4	19·7
Alitalia	16·5	19·7
Air France	16·6	17·6
Luxair	16·4	17·2

Airline	2006	2007
BMI	–	17·0
Finnair	14·2	15·8
Lufthansa	18·1	15·8
Spanair	9·5	15·4

The AEA does not represent budget operators (e.g., easyJet and Ryanair) which are excluded.

——————TRAIN INCIDENTS & MALICIOUS ACTION——————

The number of incidents on the railways caused by vandalism and malicious action is falling, according to the Office of Rail Regulation's 2007 rail safety report, viz:

Malicious action	2003	2004	2005	2006	2007
Collisions	25	12	1	0	0
Derailments	4	6	3	0	1
Running into obstructions	107	128	98	108	99
Fires in trains	141	188	96	67	51
Missile damage	334	308	254	263	224
TOTAL	611	642	452	438	375

In 2007, there were 52 confirmed suicides on the railways and 129 suspected suicides.

——————RAILWAYS & COMPLAINTS——————

According to the Office of Rail Regulation, 89·9% of trains were on time in 2007–08. Roughly 1·2bn passenger journeys were made in 2007–08, an increase of 7·1% from the previous year; this generated £5·6bn in revenue. 57 complaints are currently made per 100,000 passenger journeys; the reasons are listed below:

Reason for complaint	% 2007–08
Train service performance	42
Fares, retailing, refunds	18
Quality on train	12
Staff conduct/availability	6
Information at stations/on trains	5
Complaints handling	4
Station quality	4
Praise comments	2
Timetable/connection issue	1
Safety and security	1
Special needs	1
Other complaints	1

[Source: Office of Rail Regulation, National Rail trends yearbook, 2007–08]

——————LONDON STATION DESTINATION GUIDE——————

Charing Cross . . . . *serves* South & South-east
Euston . . . . Midlands, North-west of England & Scotland
King's Cross . . . . Midlands, North of England & Scotland
Liverpool Street . . . . East of England & East Anglia · Stansted Express
Marylebone . . . . .Chilterns
Paddington . . . . West of England & Wales · Heathrow Express
St Pancras[†] . . . . .East Midlands & Yorkshire · Eurostar
Victoria . . . . .South & South-east · Gatwick Express
Waterloo . . . . South & South-west

† In November 2007, the Queen formally opened the new £800m St Pancras station. The station replaces Waterloo as the hub of the Eurostar, providing a high-speed rail link that cuts 20 minutes off the journey time to Paris. The original neo-Gothic frontage will re-open in 2010 as a five-star hotel.

SUBWAYS OF THE WORLD

System	est. annual ridership	no. stations	single fare	single fare GBP
Tokyo Subway	2·9bn	282	160–300¥	78p–£1·48
Moscow Metro	2·6bn	172	17 roubles	37p
NYC Subway	1·5bn	468	$2	£1·02
Seoul Metropolitan Subway	1·5bn	263	900 won	44p
Mexico City Metro	1·4bn	175	2 pesos	10p
Paris Metro	1·4bn	380	€1·40	£1·12
London Underground	976m	275	£4·00	£4·00
Osaka Municipal Subway	880m	123	≥200¥	≥99p
Hong Kong MTR	867m	53	$4–26	26p–£1·70
St Petersburg Metro	810m	58	14 roubles	30p

Below are the metro fares for some other cities of note, in GBP as of March 2008:

City	single metro fare (£)		
Athens	64p	Montreal	1·42
Boston	1·02	Philadelphia	1·02
Helsinki, Finland	1·61	Rome	80p
Lisbon, Portugal	60p–84p	São Paulo	74p
Los Angeles	64p	Stockholm	1·72–5·17
		Washington, DC	84p–2·29

[Sources: NYC MTA, Hong Kong MTR, Transport for London, City of St Petersburg, Virgin Atlantic, Metro International. Currency conversions are approximate guides and current at time of writing.]

WORLD'S BEST PUBLIC TRANSPORT

London's public transport system was voted the world's best by travellers polled by TripAdvisor in October 2007. 83% said that they used public transport while on holiday; 43% said that the most important factor for a public transport system was that it goes everywhere they want to go. Further results from this poll are below:

World's best [1] London [2] NY [3] Paris [4] Washington DC [5] Hong Kong
World's cleanest [1] Washington DC [2] Tokyo [3] Paris [4] London [5] Montreal
World's safest [1] London [2] Washington DC [3] Paris [4=] New York & Tokyo

---
PAINTING THE FORTH RAIL BRIDGE

For decades, the never-ending painting of the Forth Rail Bridge has served as a simile for any interminable task, but perhaps not for much longer. In February 2008, Network Rail announced that by 2012 the bridge's entire cantilevered span will have a fresh coat of paint, originally developed for oil rigs, that will last for 30 years. ❦ The 2·5km bridge spans the Firth of Forth, 14 km west of Edinburgh. It was completed in 1890 and was the world's first major steel bridge. The bridge, now Scotland's largest listed structure, is traversed by up to 200 trains each day.

—————————— TRENDS IN TRAVEL ——————————

For some years the terminally ill have travelled to countries like the Netherlands, Belgium, and Switzerland where euthanasia is legal or tolerated, and it seems that this trend of SUICIDE TRAVEL (or TRAVELCIDE) may be growing. In June, Reuters reported that elderly tourists from around the world were travelling to Mexico to buy liquid pentobarbital, a drug used by vets to euthanise animals. Apparently this 'Mexico option' is popular because 'pentobarbital is one of the few drugs that produces a reliable and tranquil death by sending a person to sleep before shutting down breathing'. ❦ One of the curious trends of travelcide is LANDMARK SUICIDE where people travel to iconic locations (e.g., the Eiffel Tower or the Golden Gate Bridge) to end their lives. In 2007, the NY Academy of Medicine reported that >1 in 10 of those who killed themselves in Manhattan between 1990–2004 were 'suicide tourists' who had travelled to die in the city that never sleeps.

The illegality of same-sex unions in many jurisdictions has resulted in a new and lucrative strand of GAY MARRIAGE TOURISM. Just before California legalised same-sex marriages in June 2008, a study estimated that 67,500 gay couples would travel to the state in the following three years, contributing more than $683·6 million to the economy.

Travel and debauchery have long been hand in glove, from the licentious behaviour of medieval pilgrims to the British 'grand tour' travellers accused of importing venereal diseases. Yet, the ease and cheapness of modern travel has resulted in an entire industry of DEBAUCHERY TOURISM, aimed at those with inhibitions as relaxed as

their purse strings. ❦ The success of the zeitgeist-capturing slogan 'What happens in Vegas stays in Vegas' proves that 'morality-free' bubbles still have the power to enchant: in 2007, 39 million visitors to The Strip spent $8·4 billion on gambling alone. ❦ A host of cities blessed by the advent of budget flights have been cursed by the blight of DEBAUCHERISM – not least from British stag and hen parties. Riga, Tallinn, Bratislava, Wroclaw, Budapest, &c. have all suffered from drunken hordes taking advantage of flights that are often cheaper than the now ubiquitous 'lads on tour' T-shirts. ❦ At the opposite end of this spectrum is HALAL TOURISM – holidays that comply with Islamic law and tradition designed especially for observant Muslims. Such tours ensure that Halal food is served, alcohol is prohibited, times for prayer are accommodated, &c.

The idea of travelling in order to participate in or influence the politics of another country is hardly new. (Famously, and fatally, in 1823 Byron travelled to Greece to fight for Greek independence against the Turks.) However, the trend of ACTIVACATIONS has grown in line with the globalisation of politics and economics. Major summits (e.g., the G8) regularly attract a motley crew of activists, peaceful and otherwise, from around the globe, and protesters frequently travel to demonstrate at the AGMs of controversial companies like Halliburton or Shell. (It could be argued that those who travel abroad to study radical ideologies or be trained in terror tactics are participating in an extreme form of activacation.) Both the US presidential election and the Beijing Olympics attracted activacationers keen to make their voices heard.

—————————— TRENDS IN TRAVEL cont. ——————————

In June it was reported that tourists were visiting the house where Josef Fritzl imprisoned and abused members of his family – making the Austrian town of Amstetten the latest attraction in DARK TOURISM. ❦ Other sites of dark tourism include *prisons* (Robben Island); *cemeteries* (Père Lachaise); *battlefields* (the Somme); *concentration camps* (Bergen–Belsen); *scenes of natural disaster* (New Orleans), and *human disaster* (Hiroshima); and locations associated with *specific tragedies* (Ground Zero). ❦ However, dark tourism can play a pedagogical role. In February, the British government announced proposals to send two 6th-form students from every school in England to Auschwitz to learn about the Holocaust.

PILGRIMAGES to religious sites have grown in popularity in recent years, facilitated by cheap travel and specialist tour operators [see p.292]. In 2008, Lourdes celebrates the 150th anniversary of the 18 apparitions of the Blessed Virgin Mary. As a result, the tally of pilgrims is expected to exceed the usual total of 6m. The number of pilgrims visiting Mecca has grown from *c*.250,000 in 1930 to over 2·5m in 2007. ❦ Recent years have seen the rise of PAGAN PILGRIM AGES to alternative events gatherings, from *music festivals* (Glastonbury) to *lifestyle happenings* (Burning Man), and *extreme events* (the Pamplona bull run).

The chance to sample foreign food has always been one of the lures of travel. But as certain restaurants (El Bulli, Spain) and culinary centres (Napa, California) achieve international fame, so GASTROTOURISM has developed. Allied to this is the trend of EXTREME DINING, where fugu in Japan or fried tarantula in Cambodia is justification

enough for a journey. Recently, food guides and websites have become influential on travel choices, as Japanese chefs discovered after the publication of the 2008 Tokyo Michelin Guide [see p.229].

An offshoot of the slow food movement, SLOW TRAVEL eschews jet-set buzz in favour of eco-friendly and culturally sensitive holidays. Slow travellers aim to spend longer periods of time in fewer locations in order to develop relationships with the local community and the environment. Low-impact methods of travel (e.g., trains, buses, bikes, and walking) are preferred, as are locally sourced food, products, and services. ❦ Allied to slow travel is the trend of AGRITOURISM where (urban) holidaymakers stay on farms and work on the land to learn about agriculture and animal husbandry.

FRONTIER VACATIONS are based on a desire to be the first to travel somewhere new, before it is ruined by the hoi polloi. As the tentacles of travel creep ever further, finding the new frontier is ever harder. Which may explain the demand for SPACE TOURISM.

Many of these trends are likely to be threatened by the price of oil and its impact on travel costs and geopolitical insecurity [see p.37]. As a result, the STAYCATION or DAYCATION has become more popular, as travellers stay closer to home and explore previously overlooked local sights. Some hotels have created staycation packages for locals, and some far-flung resorts have offered airfare refunds to persuade people back aboard long-haul flights.

[Sources: JWT Intelligence, World Travel Market, slowplanet.com, cpabroad.co.uk, &c.]

——————————————TWIN TOWNS——————————————

Coventry was the first British town to link formally with another, when in 1944 it twinned with Stalingrad (Volgograd) in recognition of their similar wartime experiences. Twinning continued in earnest after WWII in an effort to foster international friendship and cooperation. Nowadays, towns and cities have any number of twins; in the UK, this process is instigated and maintained by local councils.

UK town/city	*(some) twins*
Aberdeen	Bulawayo, Zimbabwe; Clermont-Ferrand, France; Gomel, Belarus
Barnsley	Gorlovka, Ukraine; Fuxin, China; Schwäbisch Gmünd, Germany
Belfast	Nashville, USA
Cambridge	Heidelberg, Germany; Szeged, Hungary
Cardiff	Hordaland, Norway; Lugansk, Ukraine; Nantes, France
Colchester	Avignon, France; Colchester, USA; Imola, Italy; Wetzlar, Germany
Doncaster	Dandong, China; Doncaster, Australia; Gliwice, Poland
Edinburgh	Dunedin, NZ; Florence, Italy; Kiev, Ukraine; Vancouver, Canada
Liverpool	Shanghai, China; Corinto, Nicaragua; Liverpool, Australia
London	Berlin, Germany; Moscow, Russia; New York, USA; Paris, France
Truro	Truro, USA; Truro, Canada
Swansea	Arhus Amter, Denmark; Cork, Ireland; Ferrara, Italy; Pau, France
Whitby	Anchorage, USA; Nuku'Alofa, Tonga; Port Stanley, Falkland Islands

——— NEWLY INSCRIBED WORLD HERITAGE SITES · 2008 ———

Cultural sites: Kuk Early Agricultural Site, Papua New Guinea
Melaka and George Town, historic cities of the Straits of Malacca, Malaysia
Stari Grad Plain, Croatia · Fortifications of Vauban, France
Berlin Modernism Housing Estates, Germany
Mantua and Sabbioneta, Italy · The Mijikenda Kaya Forests, Kenya
Historic Centres of Berat and Gjirokastra, Albania
San Marino Historic Centre and Mount Titano, San Marino
Historic Centre of Camagüey, Cuba
The Wooden Churches of the Slovak part of Carpathian Mountain Area, Slovakia
Preah Vihear Temple, Cambodia · Armenian Monastic Ensembles in Iran, Iran
Rhaetian Railway in the Albula/Bernina Landscapes, Switzerland/Italy
Bahá'i Holy Places in Haifa and Western Galilee, Israel
Chief Roi Mata's Domain, Vanuatu
San Miguel and the Sanctuary of Jesús de Nazareno de Atotonilco, Mexico
Archaeological Site of Al-Hijr (Madâin Sâlih), Saudi Arabia
Le Morne Cultural Landscape, Mauritius
Natural properties: The Joggins Fossil Cliffs, Canada
Mount Sanqingshan National Park, China
The Lagoons of New Caledonia: Reef Diversity and Assoc. Ecosystems, France
Surtsey, Iceland · Saryarka – Steppe and Lakes of Northern Kazakhstan
Monarch Butterfly Biosphere Reserve, Mexico
The Swiss Tectonic Arena Sardona, Switzerland · Socotra Archipelago, Yemen

CITY STATUS

Cities in Britain were traditionally large towns with an Anglican cathedral. Yet, over time this definition became increasingly inaccurate as many large towns without cathedrals were granted city status, and many towns with cathedrals were not. (At present there are 18 cities in the United Kingdom with no cathedral and 16 towns with an Anglican cathedral but without city status.) City status is awarded by the Queen (on Ministerial advice) and conferred by Letters Patent; the Department of Constitutional Affairs (DCA) calls it 'a rare mark of distinction'. City status is granted rarely and only ever in years of celebration chosen by the Sovereign. ❧ No formal criteria exist to be granted city status, in part to prevent a town from claiming the honour as a right. However, towns applying to become cities are advised by the DCA that the following factors are taken into account: notable features, regional significance, historical (and Royal) considerations, and a 'forward-looking attitude'. City status is purely honorific and it does not confer any special rights or privileges; there is no right of appeal against the Sovereign's decision. There are currently 66 cities in the UK, 50 of which are in England, 6 in Scotland, 5 in Wales, and 5 in N Ireland. Most recently, the Queen granted 3 city statuses for the millennium, and 5 in 2002 for her Golden Jubilee (39 towns applied for the honour). Below is a list of the UK's cities and the year in which they so became.

City	year granted	location
Preston	2002	ENG
Newport	2002	WAL
Stirling	2002	SCO
Lisburn	2002	NI
Newry	2002	NI
Brighton & Hove	2000	ENG
Inverness	2000	SCO
Wolverhampton	2000	ENG
Armagh	1994	NI
St David's	1994	WAL
Sunderland	1992	ENG
Derby	1977	ENG
Swansea	1969	WAL
Southampton	1964	ENG
Cambridge	1951	ENG
Lancaster	1937	ENG
Plymouth	1928	ENG
Portsmouth	1926	ENG
Salford	1926	ENG
Stoke-on-Trent	1925	ENG
Leicester	1919	ENG
Cardiff	1905	WAL
Hull	1897	ENG
Bradford	1897	ENG
Nottingham	1897	ENG
Leeds	1893	ENG
Sheffield	1893	ENG
Dundee	1889	SCO
Belfast	1888	NI
Birmingham	1888	ENG
Wakefield	1888	ENG
Newcastle	1882	ENG
Liverpool	1880	ENG
St Albans	1877	ENG
Truro	1877	ENG
Ripon	1865	ENG
Manchester	1853	ENG
Derry	1613	NI
Bristol	1542	ENG
Oxford	1542	ENG
Chester	1541	ENG
Gloucester	1541	ENG
Peterborough	1541	ENG
Westminster	1540	ENG

The following cities have all traditionally held the title by Ancient Prescriptive Usage: [ENG] Bath, Canterbury, Carlisle, Chichester, Coventry, Durham, Ely, Exeter, Hereford, Lichfield, Lincoln, London, Norwich, Salisbury, Wells, Winchester, Worcester, York; [SCO] Aberdeen, Glasgow, Edinburgh; [WAL] Bangor. [Sources: DCA, lovemytown.co.uk]

TOURISM SLOGANS

In September 2007, the *Daily Mail* reported that Gordon Brown sought a national motto to capture 'Britishness' in a pithy phrase. Although the government later played down the story, this didn't stop the press encouraging its readers to submit suggestions. Below are some of the best 5-word phrases from readers of *The Times*.

Dipso, Fatso, Bingo, Asbo, Tesco	*Sorry, is this the queue?*
Britain, a terribly nice place	*At least we're not French*
Less stuffy than we sound	*Once mighty empire, slightly used*
Turned out nice again	*Americans who missed the boat*

Below are some (actual) mottoes used by British regions, counties, and cities:

Aberdeen	*Energy capital of Europe*
Cornwall	*Kernow Bys Vykken (Cornwall for ever)*
Dumfries & Galloway	*A touch of the exotic*
Eastbourne	*The sunshine coast*
Hampshire	*Jane Austen country*
Lincolnshire	*Big county, big skies, big future*
London	*Totally LondON*
Peterborough	*A city to surprise & delight you*
Poole	*Surf, rest, and play*
Nottinghamshire	*N* [sic]
Skegness	*Skegness is SO bracing*
Southport	*Day time, night time, great time*
Warwickshire	*Shakespeare's county*

In November 2007, the Scottish Executive unveiled a new £125,000 slogan for their country: *Welcome to Scotland*. It replaced Scotland's previous slogan *The Best Small Country in the World*.

LEAST RECOGNISABLE UK LANDMARKS

83% of Britons were able to identify Antony Gormley's Angel of the North when shown an image of the iconic sculpture, whereas only 38% recognised St Paul's Cathedral, suggesting that longevity is not necessarily the key to recognition. The survey, carried out by Travelodge in April 2008, revealed that many Britons were confused as to the location of many of the UK's top attractions – 61% thought St Paul's was St Peter's Basilica in the Vatican; 32% mistook Hadrian's Wall for the Great Wall of China; and 67% thought the Royal Brighton Pavilion was the Taj Mahal in India. The least recognised landmarks in the UK are listed below:

Landmark	% failed to recognise		
Royal Pavilion, Brighton	78	Edinburgh Castle	62
Canary Wharf	76	St Paul's Cathedral	61
Oxford's 'dreaming spires'	73	Tyne Bridge	54
Spinaker Tower	64	Trafalgar Square	51
		Ben Nevis	52

———————THE COST OF CULTURE———————

London is one of the world's most expensive cities for cultural experiences, according to a May 2008 survey by the Post Office, which compared the price of a range of equivalent cultural activities (museums; classical music concerts; visits to opera and ballet; and heritage sites) across ten major tourist destinations. The total cost for each city was: Warsaw (£75·28) · Prague (£103·52) · Lisbon (£108·15) · Amsterdam (£165·53) · Rome (£208·80) · Berlin (£210·86) · Paris (£246·22) · Barcelona (£259·31) · New York (£260·64) · London (£308·30). Detailed findings for some cities are below:

WARSAW Total: £75·28	BERLIN Total: £210·86	NEW YORK Total: £260·64	LONDON Total: £308·30
National Museum £1·52	Pergamon Museum £6·65	Guggenheim £9·79	Tate Modern *free*
Warsaw Rising £1·02	Checkpoint Charlie £10·40	MOMA £10·88	Natural History Museum *free*
Zacheta Nat. Gallery of Art £2·54	Natural History Museum £4·99	Museum of Natural History £8·16	V&A *free*
Warsaw Phil. Symphony Orch. £10·28	Berlin Philharmonic £58·23	NY Philharmonic £41·36	London Philharmonic £32·00
Polish Nat. Opera £24·12	Berlin State Opera £56·56	Metropolitan Opera £119·71	Royal Opera £137·00
Polish Nat. Ballet £24·12	Berlin State Ballet £56·56	NY City Ballet £46·80	Royal Ballet £81·00
Wilanow Palace £4·06	Berlin Cathedral £4·16	Empire State £10·34	Buckingham Palace £28·50
Royal Castle £4·57	Reichstag *free*	Statue of Liberty *free*	Hampton Court £13·30
Palace on the Water £3·05	Charlottenburg Palace £13·31	Harlem Renaissance Tour £13·60	Tower of London £16·50

———————TOP BRITISH ATTRACTIONS———————

Site	*visits*
Blackpool Pleasure Beach (F)	5·5m
British Museum (F/C)	5·4m
Tate Modern (F)	5·2m
The National Gallery (F)	4·2m
Natural History Museum (F)	3·6m
Science Museum (F)	2·7m
V&A Museum (F)	2·4m
Tower of London (C)	2·1m
National Maritime Museum (F)	1·7m
St Paul's Cathedral (F/C)	1·6m
National Portrait Gallery (F)	1·6m
Tate Britain (F)	1·6m
Kew Gardens (F/C)	1·4m
British Library (F)	1·4m

Admissions: (F)ree/(C)harged

[Source: Association of Leading Visitor Attractions, 2007] In January 2008, ALVA announced that visitor figures made a strong recovery towards the end of 2007, despite the unusually wet summer.

———————————————— SCOUTS' BADGES ————————————————

In January 2008, the Scout Association announced the introduction of forty new badges in the largest-ever overhaul of its activities. The Scouts aim to encourage young people to achieve 'their full physical, intellectual, social, and spiritual potential, as individuals, as responsible citizens, and as members of their local, national, and international communities'. The movement was founded in 1907 by Boer War hero Lord Baden-Powell who set up an experimental camp for 20 boys on Brownsea Island, Dorset. The following year Baden-Powell published *Scouting for Boys*, which has since sold in numbers second only to the Bible. There are now 400,000 Scouts in Britain (10% are female)†, and *c*.28m scouts in 218 countries worldwide. The Scout motto is 'Be Prepared', and the Chief Scout is former *Blue Peter* presenter Peter Duncan. Some of the new activity badges are below:

Beaver Scouts	Cub Scouts	Scouts	Explorer Scouts
(6–8 yrs)	*(8–10 yrs)*	*(10½–14 yrs)*	*(14–18 yrs)*
Emergency aid	Astronomer	Astronautics	Canoeing · Caving
Health & fitness	Emergency aid	Communicator	Motor sport
Healthy eating	Hikes away (hiking)	Parascending	Public relations
Imagination	Map reader	Street sports	Snowboarding

† Nearly 30,000 young people currently have their names on waiting lists to join the Scouts; this is partly due to a lack of individuals willing to join the 100,000 voluntary adult Scout leaders.

———————————————— TOY OF THE YEAR ————————————————

Since 1965, the Toy of the Year Award has been presented by the Toy Retailers Association to celebrate top market performers. The overall 2007 winner was 'In The Night Garden Blanket Time Igglepiggle'. Other notable winners included:

Category	*winner*	
Outdoor.......	Flashing Storm scooter	Creative .... Moon Sand sandcastle set
Puzzle..........	Rubik's Cube original†	Pre-school range ....Peppa Pig
Game... *High School*	DVD board game	† 43,252,003,274,489,856,000 combinations.

———————————————— CHRISTMAS SPENDING ON TOYS ————————————————

Below is the average spend on Christmas toys and games per child in 2006 according to the annual Europe-wide 2007 Duracell Toy Survey. 52% of British parents admitted to spending more on their children at Christmas than they intended.

Country	*spend (€)*				
Belgium	83	Netherlands	105	Europe average	146
France	174	Portugal	128		
Germany	82	Spain	232	The survey also revealed that
Italy	149	Sweden	82	the average UK child attends
		UK	277	8 birthday parties a year.

───────ANGELS COSTUMIERS & FANCY DRESS───────

The family firm of Angels (formerly Angels & Bermans) is the world's longest-established costume supplier to film, television, and theatre – and of fancy dress outfits to the public. (The firm has >2·5m costumes which can be hired from its central London shop.) Angels has provided the clothing for 30 films which have received Oscars for Best Costume, including *Lawrence of Arabia, Star Wars, Titanic,* and *Gladiator†*. Although emerging trends in fancy dress-hire include dog costumes and themed weddings, some of Angels' most popular current rentals are below:

Halloween ♂ . . . . *Ghostbusters; body bag; banana; grim reaper; bloody doctor*
Halloween ♀ . *Wizard Wanda; Batgirl; prom nightmare; Enchantra; Midnight Witch*
Top themes. . . . . *pirates; the 70s; Elvis; Moulin Rouge; 18th century*

† In the early 1970s, Angels created a special blue Santa Claus costume for PM Edward Heath, after he declined to wear the traditional red garb because of the colour's left-wing political connotations.

───────────THE WORLD'S TOP TABLES───────────

The top 5 in *Restaurant Magazine*'s 2008 list of the world's best restaurants were:

El Bulli [1]. . . . . Girona, Spain	*The French Laundry* [4]. .California, US
The Fat Duck [2]. . . . . .Bray, UK	*Per Se* [9]. . . . . .New York, US
Pierre Gagnaire [3]. . . . . . . .Paris, France	[2007 positions in brackets]

───────────────THE GHOST CHILLI───────────────

The Bhut Jolokia – or 'Ghost Chilli', as it is known in its native land of India – was pronounced the world's hottest chilli pepper by Guinness World Records in October 2007. The Ghost Chilli yields 1m Scoville Heat Units (SHU), almost twice the amount contained in former chilli champion the Red Savina. Scientists at New Mexico State University discovered the pepper after being alerted to its existence by the Indian Defence Research Laboratory. Researchers are said to be excited about its commercial possibilities, since a minute amount of the dehydrated pepper can provide extremely potent spice. ❧ In 1912, American chemist Wilbur Scoville created a method of measuring the amount of spice in a chilli pep-per, by progressively mixing its extract with sugar water until a panel of tasters could no longer discern any heat. The more sugar water necessary, the higher the number of Scoville Heat Units assigned. Although the method used to arrive at SHUs has since evolved, the rating system remains in use. Tabulated below are the SHUs for some chillis (and chilli products) of note:

Pure capsaicin . . . . . .SHU =	16,000,000
Pepper spray (commercial) .	2,000,000
Bhut Jolokia.	1,000,000
Red Savina	577,000
Habanero.	200,000
Thai.	100,000
Cayenne	50,000
Jalapeño	5,000

————————— SUPERMARKETS & CLASS —————————

Waitrose is the poshest supermarket, according to a March 2008 *Schott's Almanac/*
Ipsos Mori poll [see p.102]; 30% of us think the chain is most likely to be used by
the upper class, and 5% by the working class. In comparison, Tesco's success may
be linked to its broad appeal: 36% think any class would shop there. Jean Anthelme
Brillat-Savarin's promise, 'Tell me what you eat, and I will tell you what you are',
could be rephrased: 'Tell me where you shop for food, and I will tell you your class.'

Class most likely to use	% Working	Middle	Upper	Any	d/k
ASDA	50	18	1	28	3
Iceland	63	12	<½	18	7
LIDL	70	7	1	14	8
Morrisons/Safeway	40	26	1	29	4
Sainsbury's	8	53	10	27	2
Somerfield	45	22	1	24	8
Tesco	31	30	1	36	2
Waitrose	5	39	30	15	11

————————— ORGANIC FOOD & EGGS —————————

Organic food sales slumped in spring 2008, according to figures released in August
by TNS. The organic food market had been growing steadily and significantly since
the late 1990s, but the credit crunch and rampant agflation forced families to
balance organic ideology with economic necessity. This downturn came as a further
blow to beleaguered British farmers who, in September 2008, warned that wet
weather had ruined the wheat harvest and that high fuel prices had made it the most
expensive crop ever. The rise and fall in sales of organic food and eggs are below:

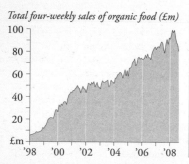

Total four-weekly sales of organic food (£m)

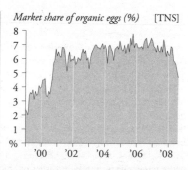

Market share of organic eggs (%)   [TNS]

Sales of free-range eggs and chickens were given a boost in 2008; 35% more free-range poultry was
sold in January 2008 than in January 2007, and in March 2008, sales of free-range eggs overtook
those from battery farms for the first time ever. This shift away from factory farming followed a high-
profile Channel 4 series in which celebrity chefs Jamie Oliver and Hugh Fearnley-Whittingstall pub-
licised the often horrific realities of industrial factory farming. It remains to be seen if this trend for
free-range is sustainable or whether it will also fall victim to credit-crunch-tightened purse-strings.

─────────── NEW UK MICHELIN STARS · 2008 ───────────

The 2008 Michelin Guide gave 13 new 1-star awards to restaurants in the UK, but no new 2- or 3-star awards. Below are the UK restaurants that won stars in 2008:

* *Apicius*	Cranbrook, Kent	modern British
* *Ballachulish House*	Ballachulish, Argyll	international
* *Champany Inn*	Linlithgow, West Lothian	traditional British
* *The Goose*	Britwell Salome, Oxfordshire	modern British
* *Hibiscus*	Maddox Street, London W1	French
* *La Trompette*	Chiswick, London W4	French
* *Nathan Outlaw*	Fowey, Cornwall	modern British
* *Quilon*	Buckingham Gate, London SW1	southern Indian
* *Rhodes W1 Restaurant*	Great Cumberland Place, London W1	French
* *Tean*	St Martin's, Isles of Scilly	modern European
* *The Sportsman*	Whitstable, Kent	modern British
* *West Stoke House*	Chichester, West Sussex	modern European
* *Wild Honey*	St George Street, London W1	modern British

An anonymous Michelin inspector interviewed in the guide revealed how gruelling the job is: each inspector eats out 5 times a week, and sleeps in *c.*150 hotels annually; inspectors write >1,000 reports and drive on average 18,640 miles each year. Recognising the health impact of consuming so much rich food, Michelin provides its inspectors with health checks and cholesterol tests every six months. ❦ Tokyo now boasts the largest number of Michelin stars of any city in the world, with 191 in total (awarded to 150 restaurants); Paris has 97; and New York, 54. Tokyo now enjoys eight 3-star establishments, three of which serve French food, and all but one of which has a Japanese head chef. The Michelin guide sold well in Japan, but leading figures in the Tokyo culinary world, as well as the governor of the city, have questioned the guide's choice of restaurants and ratings.

─────────────── WATER SOMMELIERS ───────────────

'Water sommeliers' have infested certain fine dining establishments since *c.*2002, charged with understanding the characteristics of various waters and recommending harmonious water pairings for food and wine. In 2007, two Nestlé waters, San Pellegrino and Acqua Panna, and L'Association de la Sommellerie Internationale, released the Water Codex II – a guide to water tasting and service for sommeliers and others. According to this Codex, waters can be divided into 2 categories: HEAVY-BODIED (sparkling, mildly acidic, stimulates salivation) and LIGHT-BODIED (still, low acid, velvety). The Codex suggests that heavy-bodied waters should be paired with red wines, rich food, and meats, whereas light-bodied waters are best with white wine, salads, and light dishes of chicken or fish. Those who wish to perform their own water tasting are advised by the Codex to adopt the following five steps:

[1] *Pour* water into the appropriate glass; [2] *Taste* a sip of *c.*15ml, allow it to linger on the tongue, then distribute throughout the mouth; [3] *Observe* the water at eye level, then lower the glass and view from above; [4] *Smell* the water, breathing deeply at regular intervals; and [5] *Taste* again, allowing the water to rest on the tongue.

CRUFTS BEST IN SHOW · 2008

The 2008 Crufts Best in Show was won by the giant schnauzer *Ch Jafrak Philippe Oliver*†, owned by Kevin Cullen from St Leonards-on-Sea. 22,964 dogs competed in more than 2,000 individual classes at Crufts, which attracted 160,000 people to the NEC in Birmingham. In an attempt to modernise the 117-year-old event, organisers the Kennel Club introduced innovations which included a new dancing to heel competition with music and flashing lights, dubbed 'Strictly Come Barking'.

† Judge Clare Coxall commented that Best in Show Ch Jafrak Philippe Oliver had 'the pair of jettest black eyes. I looked into his eyes and he sold himself to me and he knew he was doing it.'

DOWNSIZING DOGS

Sales of smaller dog breeds (miniature schnauzers, pugs, &c.) are rising in Britain while those of larger breeds (alsatians, Rottweilers, &c.) are declining, according to data from the Kennel Club. This may be because smaller dogs are more suitable to apartment living and modern lifestyles – but it has also been suggested that the popularity of handbag-sized pooches amongst celebrities such as Paris Hilton may be influencing public demand. Below are the top 20 breeds from 2006 and 2007:

Breed · sales	2007	2006
Retriever (lab)	45,079	45,700
Spaniel (cocker)	20,883	20,459
Spaniel (springer)	14,702	15,133
Staffs. bull terrier	12,167	12,729
Alsatian	12,116	12,857
King Chrls spaniel	11,422	11,411
Retriever (golden)	9,557	9,373
Border terrier	8,814	8,916
W. Highland terrier	8,309	9,300
Boxer	8,191	9,006
Miniature schnauzer	5,152	4,396
Shih Tzu	5,147	4,436
Lhasa Apso†	4,713	4,154
Rottweiler	4,257	6,575
Yorkshire terrier	4,055	4,042
Bulldog	3,979	3,522
Pug	3,547	2,681
Bull terrier	3,335	3,361
Whippet	3,043	2,672
Weimaraner	2,724	2,744

† A small, heavy-coated dog originally bred in Tibet to guard monasteries.

THE SUPREME CAT SHOW · 2007

The annual Supreme Cat Show is organised by the Governing Council of the Cat Fancy (GCCF). To be eligible, a cat must first have qualified by winning a certificate at an ordinary GCCF championship show. All breeds recognised by the GCCF may take part in the Supreme shows – and there is a special category for non-pedigree cats. A knock-out competition selects the Supreme Kitten, the Supreme Adult, and the Supreme Neuter, who then battle it out to be crowned the Supreme Exhibit. The 2007 Supreme Cat Show was held at Birmingham's NEC on 17 November where 1,365 cats competed for honours. The Supreme Exhibit was awarded to Supreme UK & Imperial Grand Premier TIANLEX FULL MONTY, a male neutered Cream Point Siamese owned by Dr J.H. Muir-Taylor, and bred by Mrs P. Cook.

———————— APPROVED PETS ————————

After a review of the Dangerous Wild Animals Act (1976) in October 2007, Defra announced that ownership of the following animals will now require a licence. Experts consulted by Defra asserted the beasts posed a 'genuine risk to the public':

Argentine black-headed snake · Peruvian racer · South American green racer
Amazon false viper · Middle Eastern thin-tailed scorpion · Dingo[†]

Defra removed from the list 33 species which are no longer considered a threat. Britons may now own any of the following animals without obtaining a licence:

Woolly lemur · Tamarin · Night (or Owl) monkey · Titis monkey
Squirrel monkey · Sloth · North American porcupine · Capybara
Crested porcupine · Cat hybrids · Wild cat · Pallas cat · Little spotted cat
Geoffroy's cat · Kodkod · Bay cat · Sand cat · Black-footed cat
Rusty-spotted cat · Cacomistles · Raccoon · Coati · Olingo
Little coatimundi · Kinkajou[‡] · Binturong · Hyraxes · Guanaco
Vicugna · Emu · Sand snake · Mangrove snake · Brazilian wolf spider

† Dingoes are currently classified as 'vulnerable' on the IUCN Red List [see p.75] · ‡ Kinkajous are members of the raccoon family native to South America. The tree-dwelling beasts came to prominence in 2006 when socialite and self-professed animal lover Paris Hilton acquired one. The unfortunately named Baby Luv was later reported to have bitten Hilton after becoming over-excited.

———————— WILDLIFE CRIME ————————

The issue of 'wildlife crime' was highlighted in 2008 by the conviction of Richard Pearson, who in April was sentenced to 23 weeks in prison for illegally collecting >7,000 birds' eggs. A Scottish Executive inquiry in the same month found that police and prosecutors were failing to tackle wildlife crime through mismanagement and a lack of resources[†]. The Partnership for Action Against Wildlife Crime (PAW), which coordinates the police, government departments, and voluntary bodies involved in wildlife law enforcement, categorises three broad types of wildlife crime:

Illegal trade in endangered species	*Crimes involving endangered native species*	*Cruelty to and persecution of wildlife species*
Import/export of the 2,500 animal & 25,000 plant species in the Convention on International Trade in Endangered Species of Wild Fauna and Flora (CITES).	Including killing or extracting these species (e.g., birds of prey, plants, &c.) from the wild, collecting or trading eggs or skins, and destroying nests or breeding sites.	Including badger baiting, illegal snaring, poaching, poisoning, hunting, &c. Certain species (e.g., badgers and deer) are protected with specific legislation.

† The inquiry was launched after a female golden eagle was poisoned on a grouse moor near Peebles in August 2007. The female was half of the only breeding pair of golden eagles in the Borders.

ANIMALS IN THE NEWS · 2007

Some of the year's more unusual animal stories. ❧ Philippines customs officials at a mail processing centre were unsettled to discover in a package marked 'personal clothing' 300 live scorpions and tarantulas. ❧ According to *The Times*, there were only two sightings of the Loch Ness monster in 2007 (as of the end of September) – a marked decline from previous years that could spell doom for regional tourism. ❧ New York and Houston are the cities most at risk from rat infestation, according to poison maker d-CON. ❧ An Indian man married a dog in the hope it would lift the curse he claims he has been under since stoning to death two other dogs. ❧ A man was questioned by police at LaGuardia Airport in New York after smuggling a monkey under his hat on a flight from Peru, with a stopover in Florida. ❧ A jellyfish invasion wiped out the only salmon farm in Northern Ireland, killing more than 100,000 fish. ❧ In New Zealand, the Christmas song 'A Very Silent Night' was recorded at a frequency only audible to dogs, and released to raise money for an animal charity. ❧ Newquay Zoo in Cornwall, England, was condemned by conservation groups for euthanising two Sulawesi crested black macaques because the monkeys would not stop fighting. ❧ The long-eared jerboa, a tiny, nocturnal desert creature with one of the biggest ear-to-body ratios of any mammal, was caught on camera for the first time in the Gobi Desert. ❧ Male monkeys 'pay' for sex by grooming female monkeys, according to a study of macaques in Kalimantan Tengah, Indonesia, reported in the *New Scientist*. In areas where there are fewer females, males are forced to groom their partners for up to twice as long before they are able to have sex with them. ❧ A female orangutan called Nonja, thought to be the oldest in captivity, died at the Miami Metro Zoo at the age of 55, a decade past the age to which most orangutans survive. ❧ Scientists from a university in Hungary developed a computer program that 'translates' dog barks, and can classify them with 'reasonable' accuracy. ❧ Hamster prices tripled in China after the Year of the Rat began on 7 February, 2008; wary parents deemed the cuddly creatures an acceptable rodent substitute. ❧ An octopus at an aquarium in Newquay, England, became so possessive of his new Mr Potato Head toy that he began to attack anyone who tried to take it from him. ❧ A man who was seized by a crocodile in N Australia was accidentally shot by a colleague who came to his rescue; the croc dropped his victim, who was then flown to the hospital to be treated for bite and bullet wounds. ❧ A team at the University of Melbourne in Australia concluded that chameleons first evolved the ability to change colour to make themselves more noticeable to other chameleons, rather than to blend in to their background. ❧ Animal rights campaigners welcomed an announcement by the British Ministry of Defence that the military will no longer use live goats in experiments to measure the risks of 'the bends' for crews trapped in submarines. ❧ A New Zealand man was charged with assault after using a hedgehog as a weapon; the animal left a large welt and several puncture wounds. ❧ A British study found that human yawns are contagious for dogs; 72% of 29 dogs tested yawned after watching humans do so.

Money

Money can't buy friends, but you can get a better class of enemy.
— SPIKE MILLIGAN (1918–2002)

―――――――――――――― FUEL POVERTY ――――――――――――――

'Fuel poor' households are those that have to spend >10% of their income on fuel to maintain a satisfactory level of domestic heat: 21ºC for main living areas; 18ºC for other occupied rooms. According to the Department for Business, Enterprise, and Regulatory Reform (BERR), three factors influence the prevalence of fuel poverty: the energy efficiency of a property; household income; and the cost of energy. ❦ BERR estimates that every 1% rise in energy prices pushes *c.*40,000 households into fuel poverty; the Welsh Assembly estimates that a 10% increase in energy prices pushes a further 48,000 Welsh households into fuel poverty; and Communities Scotland estimates that for every 5% increase in fuel prices a further 30,000 households are pushed into fuel poverty. ❦ During 2007–08, as oil prices rocketed and household incomes were squeezed, fuel poverty became an urgent political and economic issue. In April 2008, while the government estimated 2·5m households were fuel poor, the consumer group Energywatch stated that 'Energy has become unaffordable for 4·5m households'. In May, the National Housing Federation reported that those using prepayment meters for their gas or electricity (usually the poorest families) can pay up to £400 more per year for their fuel than other customers, and that 14% of gas and 9% of electricity prepayment customers 'self disconnected' in 2007 because they could not afford to 'top up' their meters. Energywatch reported that, in 2008, prepayment fuel meters were being installed at the rate of >1,000 each day. ❦ Charted below are the increases in domestic gas and electricity bills from January 2008, as compiled by the BBC:

Date	company	(+%)	gas	elec.	Date	company	gas	elec.
04/01	Npower		17·2	12·7	05/07	EDF Energy	22·0	17·0
15/01	EDF Energy		12·9	7·9	30/07	British Gas	35·0	9·0
18/01	British Gas		15·0	15·0	21/08	E.ON	26·0	16·0
01/02	Scottish Power		15·0	14·0	21/08	Scottish & Sth.	29·2	19·2
07/02	E.ON		15·0	9·7	21/08	Scottish Power	34·0	9·0
19/03	Scottish & Sth.		15·8	14·2	21/08	Npower	26·0	14·0
						All figures are announced % increases		

As winter drew near, the government was urged to help the poor, and pressure groups joined with *c.*120 Labour MPs to demand a 'windfall tax' on the profits of energy companies. However, Gordon Brown was reluctant to agree, fearing these companies might raise their prices or move abroad. Instead, in September, Brown announced a range of measures, including free or cut-price insulation and a boost in cold weather payments. Help the Aged was not alone in calling Brown's plan 'nothing more than a half-defrosted package of inadequate intentions and initiatives'.

OIL PRICES & TRADING SIGNALS

On 2/1/2008, the price of oil hit a (psychologically) significant milestone when a trader on the New York Mercantile Exchange (NYMEX) bid $100 for a single barrel of crude oil futures. Although some dismissed this as a headline-grabbing 'vanity trade', in the months that followed, the price of oil has yo-yoed up and down [see p.37], influenced by a host of complex dynamics including: the anaemic US dollar, post-subprime credit illiquidity, booming demand from China and India, and supply-side tensions in Iran, Iraq, Nigeria, &c. The effect of such turbulence on public confidence (as well as on prices at the pump) has sparked increased interest in oil brokerage. And, perhaps because they are more photogenic than numbers on a screen, the bizarre gesticulations of the remaining 'open outcry' oil traders have, for the media, become a metonym for the market. Demonstrated below are the signals used on the floor of the NYMEX.

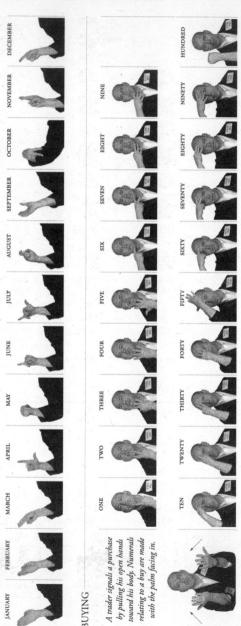

MONTHS OF THE YEAR

JANUARY · FEBRUARY · MARCH · APRIL · MAY · JUNE · JULY · AUGUST · SEPTEMBER · OCTOBER · NOVEMBER · DECEMBER

ONE · TWO · THREE · FOUR · FIVE · SIX · SEVEN · EIGHT · NINE

TEN · TWENTY · THIRTY · FORTY · FIFTY · SIXTY · SEVENTY · EIGHTY · NINETY · HUNDRED

BUYING

A trader signals a purchase by pulling his open hands toward his body. Numerals relating to a buy are made with the palm facing in.

——OIL PRICES & TRADING SIGNALS cont.——

SELLING

A trader signals a sale by pushing his open hands away from his body. Numerals relating to a sell are made with the palm facing out.

ONE · TWO · THREE · FOUR · FIVE · SIX · SEVEN · EIGHT · NINE

TEN · TWENTY · THIRTY · FORTY · FIFTY · SIXTY · SEVENTY · EIGHTY · NINETY · HUNDRED

OTHER SIGNALS

GASOLINE · HEATING OIL · PUT · CALL · STRANGLE · HOW MANY? · FILL [ORDER] · WORKING · I'M OUT · CHECK/O.K.

RAYMOND CARBONE

Raymond Carbone has been trading on the floor of the New York Mercantile Exchange for over 20 years.

A PUT option is the right to sell a set quantity of an asset, at a set price, on or before a set date. A CALL option is a similar right to buy.
A STRANGLE combines the two, using the same expiration date but with different strike prices for each trade.

Some suggest that these open outcry signals are an arcane and dying art, threatened by electronic systems and supported by a dwindling number of exchanges around the world. However, Raymond Carbone [pictured above] who trades energy options on the floor of the NYMEX for his company, Paramount Options, is upbeat about open outcry: "People have been saying that these signals will only be around for another couple of years. But they've been saying that for a decade." And, he notes, 'I can signal a trade faster than you can type it'.

BUDGET 2008 · KEY POINTS

Alistair Darling delivered his first Budget on 12 March 2008, somewhat in the shadow of the longest-serving Chancellor since 1823, PM Gordon Brown. In what the Tories called the 'bad news Budget', Darling marked No Smoking Day by adding 11p to the cost of a packet of cigarettes. Some of the other key measures presented in the Budget are below (further ones are detailed elsewhere in this section):

Income tax	[announced in 2007] basic rate to 20%; 10% band scrapped [see p.237]
Corporation tax	will fall from 30% to 28% by April
	simpler taxes for smaller companies
National Insurance	upper earnings limit goes up by £100 to £770 a week
Female entrepreneurs	to be encouraged with a £12·5m capital fund
Housing	sites for 70,000 new homes identified
	£26m to make homes greener
Stamp duty	on shared ownership homes not required until 80% owned
Education	£200m for schools to raise GCSE results
	a new £30m fund to improve science teaching
Capital gains	help for small businesses
ISAs	cash limit raised to £3,600 a year from April
'Non doms'	new annual charge from April, expected to be £30,000
Transport	2p increase in fuel duty deferred until Oct 08
	from 2010 lowest-polluting new cars will pay no road tax in 1st year
	from 2010 highest-polluting new cars will pay £950
Airports	new measures to speed up security checks
Child benefit	for first-born up to £20 a week
Families	£17 more per week for poor families with one child
	a further £125m to be spent over next 3 years to help families
Incapacity benefit	all 2·6 m recipients to be re-assessed
Plastic bags	tax will be introduced by 2009 if shops do not begin to charge
Defence	an extra £2bn for frontline troops, including £900m in equipment
Pensioner heating	winter fuel help for over 60s raised from £200 to £250
	winter fuel help for over 80s raised from £300 to £400 [see p.233]
Government departments	spending must be matched by reform
NHS	focus for the next decade on creating 'world-class services'
Air passenger duty	to be replaced with a per-plane duty from November 2009

BUDGET 2008 BOOZE 'n' FAGS

Typical unit	*Budget*		
Pack 20 cigarettes	+11p	75cl bottle wine	+14p
Pack 5 cigars	+4p	75cl sparkling wine	+18p
Pint beer	+4p	Spirits	+55p
		Litre cider	+3p

Darling made himself unpopular in his homeland of Scotland: whisky distillers did not appreciate the end of a decade-long freeze on spirit duty, while the chief executive of the Scottish Chambers of Commerce complained that Darling did not mention Scotland once in his speech.

─────────── BUDGET 2008 · REACTION & MISC. ───────────

David Cameron *'In the years of plenty they put nothing aside. They didn't fix the roof when the sun was shining'* · Nick Clegg *'an act of political ventriloquism'*
SNP MP Stewart Hosie *'a sub-prime Budget from a sub-prime Chancellor'*
Guardian *'Darling: the hesitant debutant'* · Sun *'Drinkers get well hammered'*

Darling's speech lasted 50 minutes; he talked at a rate of 154 words per minute, slightly faster than Gordon Brown in 2007, who averaged 147wpm. When Darling's speech (7,711 words) is entered into the Auto Summarise feature of *Microsoft Word* and reduced to *c.*1% of the original (7 sentences), the result is:

With low inflation, Mr Deputy Speaker, our fiscal policy, like our monetary policy is designed to support stability. Mr Deputy Speaker, public spending grew by 3·6% a year in real terms between 1997 and 2007. Transport spending is now 90% higher. Mr Deputy Speaker, this has been an exceptional commitment to improving public services. Increased spending on education has benefited children across the UK. Long-term growth must be sustainable.

Both Darling and Cameron wore purple ties. Lord (Geoffrey) Howe, Chancellor for 4 years under Thatcher, gave his own verdict on Darling's debut by appearing, to some, to snooze in the gallery.

─────────── THE 10p TAX DEBACLE ───────────

Gordon Brown's reputation as PM and Chancellor was further dented in 2008 when the headline measure of his 2007 Budget was exposed as significantly inequitable. In a dramatic flourish at the end of his 11th and final Budget, Brown cut the basic rate of income tax by 2p (from 22% to 20%) and abolished the 10p starter rate. However, during 2008 it became clear that these moves would *increase* the taxes paid by *c.*5·3m of the poorest in Britain, while benefiting some of the better-off. The resulting political storm almost engulfed the PM and his Chancellor Alistair Darling – who faced the derision of the Tories, the scorn of the media, and the outrage of the Labour Party. (The latter was led by ex-minister Frank Field, who threatened to table an amendment to the Finance Bill calling for compensation.) In a series of political contortions, Brown and Darling initially denied there was a problem; then they admitted the problem but queried its significance; then they said that the Budget could not be rewritten; and finally – after weeks of political and electoral damage – they produced a mini 'emergency Budget' to remedy the situation. On 13 May 2008, Darling announced a temporary (1-year) backdated increase to the personal tax allowance of £600, so that those earning ≤£40,835 would gain £120 in the 2008–09 tax year. (The higher rate threshold would be cut by £600 so that the better-off did not benefit.) Darling proposed to pay for this unfunded and highly unusual tax cut by borrowing an extra £2·7bn. Although Darling's U-turn placated some of his colleagues, it damaged New Labour's reputation for fiscal prudence. The Tories called the move 'cynical', and the *Financial Times* damned it as 'a last-ditch effort to avert a backbench rebellion over the finance bill and avoid humiliation in the Crewe and Nantwich by-election' [see p.28].

———————————— INCOME TAX · 2008–09 ————————————

Income tax was first levied in 1799 by Pitt the Younger as a 'temporary measure' to finance the French Revolutionary War. The initial rate was 2 shillings in the pound. The tax was abolished in 1816, only to be re-imposed in 1842 by Robert Peel (again temporarily) to balance a fall in customs duties. By the end of the C19th, income tax was a permanent feature of the British economy. The current rates are:

Income tax allowances	2007–08	2008–09
Personal allowance	5,225	6,035
Personal allowance (65–74)	7,550	9,030
Personal allowance (>75)	7,690	9,180
Income limit for age-related allowances	20,900	21,800
Married couple's allowance (born before 6·4·1935)	6,285	6,535
Married couple's allowance (aged ≥75)	6,365	6,625
Minimum amount of married couple's allowance	2,440	2,540
Blind person's allowance	1,730	1,800

The rate of relief for the continuing married couple's allowance, maintenance relief for people born before 6 April 1935, and for the children's tax credit, remains 10%.

Income tax rates	*threshold*	%
Basic rate†	£0–£36,000	20
Higher rate	>£36,000	40

† The 10% starting rate for income tax was abolished in 2007; see p.237.

There will be a new 10% starting rate for savings income only, with a limit of £2,320. Where an individual has non-savings income in excess of this limit, the 10% savings rate will not be applicable. The tax rates for dividends remain unchanged at 10% for income up to the basic rate limit, and 32·5% thereafter.

———————————— STAMP DUTY ————————————

The thresholds below (in £) represent the 'total value of consideration' of the deal. The rate that applies to any given transfer applies to the whole value of that deal.

rate %	*Residential* not *in a* disadvantaged area	*Residential in a* disadvantaged area	*Non-* residential
0†	0–125,000	0–150,000	0–150,000
1	125,001–250,000	150,001–250,000	150,001–250,000
3	250,001–500,000	250,001–500,000	250,001–500,000
4	>500,001	>500,001	>500,001

The rate of stamp duty on the transfer of SHARES and SECURITIES is set at 0·5%.
† In September 2008, the government announced that buyers will pay no stamp duty on properties less than £175,000 for a temporary 12-month period [see p.21].

––––––––– NATIONAL INSURANCE · 2008–09 –––––––––

Although National Insurance dates from 1911, modern funding of social security was proposed by Beveridge and established by the National Insurance Act (1946).

Lower earnings limit, primary Class 1	£90/w
Upper earnings limit, primary Class 1	£770/w
Primary threshold	£105/w
Secondary threshold	£105/w
Employees' primary Class 1 rate	11% of £105–£770/w · 1% >£770/w
Employees' contracted-out rebate	1·6%
Married women's reduced rate	4·85% of £105–£770/w · 1% >£770/w
Employers' secondary Class 1 rate	12·8% on earnings above £105/w
Employers' contracted-out rebate, salary-related schemes	3·7%
Employers' contracted-out rebate, money-purchase schemes	1·4%
Class 2 rate	£2·30/w
Class 2 small earnings exception	£4,825/y
Special Class 2 rate for share fishermen	£2·95/w
Special Class 2 rate for volunteer development workers	£4·50/w
Class 3 rate	£8·10/w
Class 4 lower profits limit	£5,435/y
Class 4 upper profits limit	£40,040/y
Class 4 rate	8% of £5,435–£40,040/y · 1% >£40,040/y

––––––––– CAPITAL GAINS TAX –––––––––

Annual exemptions 2008–09   Individuals &c. = £9,600 · Other trustees = £4,800

Capital Gains Tax is charged at 18%. This flat rate replaces a complicated system of taper relief and indexation allowance, under which CGT payments were calculated on the basis of how long an asset had been held; the charges were banded, according to income, at 10%, 20%, and 40%. The revisions, announced in the October 2007 Pre-Budget Report, were criticised by small businesses, who argued that they would be worst affected by the changes, and by industry groups, who suggested that entrepreneurs would be put off by the flat rate. In response, the Chancellor introduced an 'entrepreneurs' relief' rate of 10% for cumulative lifetime gains of up to £1m. The move was valued at £200m annually, and is expected to benefit *c*.80,000 people.

Capital gains arising on disposal of a 'principal private residence' remain exempt.

––––––––– CORPORATION TAX ON PROFITS –––––––––

2008–09	£ per year
Small companies' rate: 21%	0–300,000
Marginal small companies' relief	300,001–1,500,000
Main rate: 28%	>1,500,001

—— BANK OF ENGLAND INTEREST RATES & THE MPC——

Since 1997, the Monetary Policy Committee (MPC) has been responsible for setting UK interest rates. Charted below are the base rate changes since June 2004:

Date	change	rate						
10·04·08	−0·25	5·00%	05·07·07	+0·25	5·75%	03·08·06	+0·25	4·75%
07·02·08	−0·25	5·25%	10·05·07	+0·25	5·50%	04·08·05	−0·25	4·50%
06·12·07	−0·25	5·50%	11·01·07	+0·25	5·25%	05·08·04	+0·25	4·75%
			09·11·06	+0·25	5·00%	10·06·04	+0·25	4·50%

———— INCOME TAX PAYABLE · 2007–08————

Annual income (£)	No. of taxpayers (000s)	Total tax liability (£m)	Average rate of tax (%)	Average amount of tax (£)
5,225–7,499	2,460	263	1·7	107
7,500–9,999	3,630	1,330	4·2	365
10,000–14,999	6,380	7,000	8·8	1,100
15,000–19,999	4,890	10,500	12·4	2,150
20,000–29,999	6,670	24,400	14·9	3,660
30,000–49,999	5,220	33,700	17·1	6,460
50,000–99,999	1,750	28,200	24·5	16,200
100,000–199,999	418	17,200	30·8	41,200
200,000–499,999	123	12,000	34·0	98,200
500,000–999,999	22	5,230	35·6	241,000
≥1,000,000	8	6,370	35·8	782,000
ALL INCOMES	31,600	146,000	18·1	4,630

————UK TAX RECEIPTS 2007–08————

In 2007–08 Her Majesty's Revenue & Customs (HMRC) estimates it will receive £450,400,000,000 in revenue. Below is a breakdown of the sources of this income:

Receipt (2007–08 forecast)	% *of total*		
Income tax	33·21	Wine duties	0·58
National Insurance	21·43	Insurance premium tax	0·53
VAT	18·07	Customs duties & levies	0·52
Corporation tax	10·27	Spirit duty	0·51
Fuel duties	5·52	Air passenger duty	0·45
Stamp duties	3·36	Petroleum revenue tax	0·34
Tobacco duties	1·80	Betting & gaming duties	0·32
Capital gains tax	1·06	Landfill tax	0·20
Inheritance tax	0·86	Climate change levy	0·15
Beer duties	0·68	Aggregates levy	0·08
		Cider & perry duties	0·05

--------------------------- THE SUNDAY TIMES RICH LIST · 2008 ---------------------------

No.	Billionaire (UK)	£ billion	activity	'07
1	Lakshmi Mittal and family	27·7	steel	1
2	Roman Abramovich	11·7	oil, industry	2
3	The Duke of Westminster	7·0	property	3
4	Sri and Gopi Hinduja	6·2	industry, finance	4
5	Alisher Usmanov	5·7	steel, mining	–
6	Ernesto and Kirsty Bertarelli	5·7	pharmaceuticals	–
7	Hans Rausing and family	5·4	packaging	6
8	John Fredriksen	4·7	shipping	8
9	Sir Philip and Lady Green	4·3	retailing	7
10	David and Simon Reuben	4·3	property	9

--------------------------------- PAY COMPARISONS ---------------------------------

The 2008 BBC2 programme *What Britain Earns* divided Britain's workers into 10 different pay brackets, which allowed for curious and unexpected comparisons:

Less than £10,000 cleaners · hairdressers *£10,000–£20,000* checkout staff · farmers mortuary assistants	*£20,000–£30,000*† dustbin men vicars nurses · rabbis carpenters MI5 agents	*£30,000–£40,000* RAF pilots · vets pole-dancers · bishops police constables black cab drivers paramedics

† The average UK salary is £24,907, but two-thirds of the population earn below the national average.

--------------------------- FORBES MAGAZINE RICH LIST · 2008 ---------------------------

After 13 years as the world's richest man, (now ex) Microsoft chairman Bill Gates slipped to number 3 in *Forbes*'s 2008 rich list; Warren Buffett assumed Bill's place.

No.	Billionaire	nationality	$ billion	business	marital status (kids)
1	Warren Buffett	American	62·0	investing	married (3)
2	Carlos Slim Helu	Mexican	60·0	telecoms	widowed (6)
3	William Gates III	American	58·0	software	married (3)
4	Lakshmi Mittal	Indian	45·0	manufacturing	married (2)
5	Mukesh Ambani	Indian	43·0	manufacturing	married (3)
6	Anil Ambani	Indian	42·0	various	married (2)
7	Ingvar Kamprad & family	Swedish	31·0	retail (IKEA)	married (4)
8	K.P. Singh	Indian	30·0	real estate	married (3)
9	Oleg Deripaska	Russian	28·0	various	married (2)
10	Karl Albrecht	German	27·0	retail (Aldi)	married (2)

† The list revealed that Russia now has more billionaires than any other country, apart from America.

————————— FEAR, UNCERTAINTY, & DOUBT —————————

In July 2008, *Schott's Almanac* and Ipsos MORI investigated some of the trends associated with financial, political, and sociological 'fear, uncertainty, and doubt'.

74% think it is likely there will
be a SERIOUS AND PROLONGED
ECONOMIC DOWNTURN

All	74%	*Age:* 16–24	72%
Male	73%	· 25–54	78%
Female	74%	· 55+	68%

28% think it is likely that they will
not be able to HEAT THEIR
HOME ADEQUATELY [see p.233]

All	28%	*Age:* 16–24	25%
Male	24%	· 25–54	28%
Female	32%	· 55+	30%

23% sometimes feel anxious about
OPENING THEIR POST in case it
contains bills they cannot pay

All	23%	*Age:* 16–24	21%
Male	21%	· 25–54	25%
Female	25%	· 55+	21%

18% think it is likely that they will
not be able to BUY ENOUGH FOOD
for themselves or their family

All	18%	*Class:* AB	11%
Male	16%	· C1/C2	16%
Female	20%	· DE	31%

51% have started buying more
OWN-BRAND GENERIC PRODUCTS

All	51%	*Age:* 16–24	49%
Male	45%	· 25–54	55%
Female	56%	· 55+	46%

21% of those with mortgages think it
likely they will not be able to keep up
with their MORTGAGE PAYMENTS

All	21%	*Age:* 16–24	36%
Male	18%	· 25–54	21%
Female	25%	· 55+	15%

20% REGRET PURCHASES they made
over the past few years because of
their current economic position

All	20%	*Age:* 16–24	36%
Male	21%	· 25–54	22%
Female	20%	· 55+	11%

81% ON OCCASION FEEL ANXIOUS
about their non-mortgage debts:

Always	11%
Most of the time	14%
Sometimes	33%
Rarely/Never	42%

36% think they will *not* be able
to AFFORD THEIR CURRENT
LIFESTYLE in five years' time

All	36%	*Age:* 16–24	32%
Male	30%	· 25–54	36%
Female	41%	· 55+	36%

69% worry about NOT HAVING
ENOUGH MONEY

All	69%	*Age:* 16–24	79%
Male	67%	· 25–54	76%
Female	71%	· 55+	54%

—————— FEAR, UNCERTAINTY, & DOUBT cont. ——————

66% think *Britain as a whole* is a
LESS SAFE PLACE TO LIVE
than it was 10 years ago

More safe	6%
Less safe	66%
No change	26%

29% think *the area they live in* is a
LESS SAFE PLACE TO LIVE
than it was 10 years ago

More safe	7%
Less safe	29%
No change	56%

65% think it is likely that there will be FURTHER TERRORIST
ATTACKS IN BRITAIN in the next 12 months

%	All	♂	♀	Con	Lab	LD	16–24	25–54	>55+
Likely	65	62	67	72	54	61	59	59	75
Unlikely	29	32	26	22	40	37	38	34	18

59% think it likely INDUSTRIAL
ACTION will affect their daily life
in the next 12 months

All	59%	*Vote:* Con	62%
Male	58%	· Lab	53%
Female	61%	· Lib D	63%

36% think it likely that someone
they know will be the VICTIM OF
VIOLENT CRIME within 12 months

All	36%	*Age:* 16–24	50%
Male	35%	· 25–54	34%
Female	37%	· 55+	33%

19% think it likely that *they* will be the VIC-
TIM OF VIOLENT CRIME within 12 months

25% KEEP EXTRA RESERVES at
home in case of an emergency, viz:

Food	21%	Batteries	1%
Water	9%	Medicines	1%
Candles &c.	4%	Clothes &c.	1%
Cash	2%	Other	3%
Petrol &c.	1%	Nothing	75%

47% worry about their PERSONAL
FREEDOM or CIVIL LIBERTY

All	47%	*Vote:* Con	50%
Male	47%	· Lab	39%
Female	46%	· Lib D	56%

61% worry about TROUBLE
BETWEEN PEOPLE OF
DIFFERENT RACES OR RELIGIONS

All	61%	*Age:* 16–24	58%
Male	57%	· 25–54	61%
Female	66%	· 55+	64%

83% worry about CRIME OR
DISORDER BY YOUNG PEOPLE

All	83%	*Age:* 16–24	84%
Male	81%	· 25–54	82%
Female	84%	· 55+	84%

When asked which leader would make them and their family feel most secure as PM, 28% said
Margaret Thatcher, 18% Tony Blair, 12% David Cameron, & 8% Gordon Brown. See ipsos-mori.com

———— FINANCIAL SNAP-SCHOTT · 2008 ————

Item (£)	09·2007	09·2008
Church of England · marriage service (excluding certificate)	240·00	247·00
– funeral service (excluding burial and certificate)	93·00	96·00
Season ticket · Arsenal FC (2007/8; centre, E & W upper tiers)	1,825·00	1,825·00
– Grimsby Football Club (2007/8; Upper Carlsberg)	342·00	323·00
Annual membership · MCC (full London member)	344·00	358·00
– Stringfellows, London	600·00	600·00
– Groucho Club, London (+35; London member)	550·00	550·00
– Trimdon Colliery & Deaf Hill Workmen's Club	3·50	4·50
– The Conservative Party (>22)	25·00	25·00
– The Labour Party (those in work)	36·00	36·00
– The Liberal Democrats (minimum required)	9·00	10·00
– UK Independence Party	20·00	20·00
– Royal Society for the Protection of Birds (adult)	32·00	34·00
Annual television licence† · colour	135·50	139·50
– black & white	45·50	47·00
Subscription, annual · *Private Eye*	28·00	28·00
– *Vogue*	39·00	29·90
– *Saga Magazine*	19·95	17·95
New British Telecom line installation	124·99	124·99
Entrance fee · Thorpe Park (12+ 'thrill seeker' purchased on the day)	32·00	33·00
– Buckingham Palace State Rooms (adult)	15·00	15·50
– Eden Project, Cornwall (adult, day)	14·00	15·00
'Pint of best bitter' · Railway Inn, Yelverton, Devon	2·50	2·50
– Railway Inn, Banff, Scotland	2·50	2·60
– Railway Inn, Trafford, Manchester	1·80	1·90
– Railway Inn, Coleshill, Birmingham	2·40	2·50
– Railway Tavern, Globe St, London, E2	2·00	2·40
Fishing rod licence · Salmon and Sea Trout (full season)	66·50	68·00
List price of the cheapest new Ford (Ford Ka 1·3i 'on the road')	7,095·00	7,645·00
British Naturalisation (includes ceremony fee)	655·00	655·00
Manchester United home shirt (2007/8 season)	39·99	39·99
Tea at the Ritz, London (afternoon, per person)	36·00	37·00
Kissing the Blarney Stone (admission to Blarney Castle) [€10]	5·00	7·30
Hampton Court Maze (adult)	3·50	3·50
Ordinary London adult single bus ticket (cash)	2·00	2·00
Mersey Ferry (adult return)	2·20	2·30
Passport · new, renewal, or amendment (3-week postal service)	66·00	72·00
Driving test (practical + theory; cars, weekday)	77·00	86·50
Driving licence (first · car, motorcycle, moped)	45·00	50·00
NHS dental examination (standard)	15·90	16·20
NHS prescription charge (per item)	6·85	7·10
Moss Bros three-piece morning suit hire (weekend, basic 'Lombard')	45·00	45·00
FedEx Envelope (≤0·5kg) UK–USA	52·55	74·40

† The blind concession is 50%. Those ≥75 may apply for a free licence.

———————— INFLATION ————————

The spectre of inflation haunted much of 2008, exacerbated by a range of forces including the global credit crunch, the spike in oil [see p.37] and fuel prices [see p.233], and the pressures of agflation [see p.16]. Critics of the official inflation rates claimed that lower prices for 'one-offs' (e.g., clothing and electronics) were masking the escalating 'everyday' costs (e.g., food and fuel), and that neither the CPI nor the RPI reflected the real costs of those on low or fixed incomes. In response, a number of organisations made their own inflation calculations, including the *Daily Mail*, which established a 'Cost of Living Index' designed 'to chart the burden of "must pay" bills as families struggle to keep afloat in the midst of an uncertain economic period'. As conditions worsened, a number of trade unionists put pressure on the government to increase public sector pay, threatening to strike to protect their members' interests, and leading some to predict a new 'winter of discontent'.

Some 2008 changes to the RPI basket:

items removed · frozen vegetarian ready meals; lager stubbies [a size]; washable carpets; microwave ovens; TV repairs; steering lock devices; 35mm camera film; top-40 CD singles

items added · pure fruit smoothies; peppers; small-type oranges (e.g., clementines, mandarins); muffins; 20 bottles lager (alcohol 4·3–7·5%); flower bouquet with next day delivery†; non-chart CD albums; portable digital storage devices (e.g, camera memory cards, USB keys); livery charges (i.e., for horses)

† Replaces the traditional measure which was the cost of sending a 'red rose to Watford'.

CPI & RPI % change over 12 months:

Year	month	CPI	RPI
2008	Aug	4·7	4·8
	Jul	4·4	5·0
	Jun	3·8	4·6
	May	3·3	4·3
	Apr	3·0	4·2
	Mar	2·5	3·8
	Feb	2·5	4·1
	Jan	2·2	4·1
2007	Dec	2·1	4·0
	Nov	2·1	4·3
	Oct	2·1	4·2
	Sep	1·8	3·9
	Aug	1·8	4·1
	Jul	1·9	3·8
	Jun	2·4	4·4
	May	2·5	4·3
	Apr	2·8	4·5
	Mar	3·1	4·8

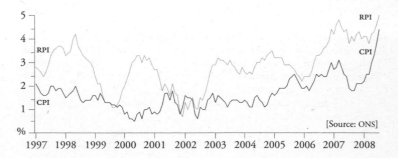

[Source: ONS]

—CONSUMER DURABLES—

Below are the UK rates of ownership of a selection of consumer durables [ONS]:

% households owning	'97	'06	±
Tumble dryer	51	59	+8
Dishwasher	22	38	+16
Microwave oven	77	91	+14
CD player	63	88	+25
Home computer	29	67	+38
Mobile phone	20	80	+60

—THE END OF CHEQUES—

According to APACS, the UK payments association, *c*.4·9m cheques were issued each day in 2006, compared to 11m in 1990 – the peak year for cheque volume. By 2016, APACS states that only 2·5m cheques will be issued per day.

——UNSECURED DEBT——

19% of British adults had unsecured credit card debt in 2006 – owing on average £2,284. Below are the various forms of unsecured debt by % of the GB population and the average sum owed:

% of adults	debt type	av. debt £
19	Credit card	2,284
16	Personal loan	7,751
9	Car loan	5,769
6	Catalogue	220
5	Student loan company	6,973
3	Family & friends	2,875
3	Storecard	471
2	Social fund loan	484
1	Money lender	1,336
1	Store loan	1,201
1	Rent arrears	682

[Source: ONS, FSA; Aug–Sep 2006 data]

————UK HOUSEHOLD EXPENDITURE————

ONS data show that, in 2006, UK households spent £761bn more than in 1971 – shedding light on the shifting patterns of domestic spending, not least the dramatic decline in the proportion of expenditure spent on food [though see p.16].

Household expenditure by purpose (%)	1971 %	2006 %	± %
Food and non-alcoholic drinks	21	9	–12
Alcoholic drinks and tobacco	7	4	–3
Clothing and footwear	9	6	–3
Housing, water and fuel	15	20	+5
Household goods and services	7	6	–1
Health	1	2	+1
Transport	12	15	+3
Communication	1	2	+1
Recreation and culture	9	12	+3
Education	1	1	0
Restaurants and hotels	10	12	+2
Miscellaneous goods and services	7	11	+4
TOTAL HOUSEHOLD EXPENDITURE	100	98	–2
– of which goods	65	48	–17
– of which services	35	51	+16
ALL HOUSEHOLD EXPENDITURE (£bn)	34	795	+761

POSTAL PRICING IN PROPORTION

Category	size (mm)	thickness (mm)	weight (g)	1st	2nd
Letter	≤240×165	≤5	0–100	36p	27p
Large Letter	≤353×250	≤25	0–100	52p	42p
			101–250	78p	66p
			251–500	108p	90p
			501–750	157p	131p
Packet	>353 long or >250 wide	or >25	0–100	114p	95p
			101–250	145p	124p
			251–500	194p	163p
			501–750	251p	208p
			751–1,000	308p	249p
			1,001–1,250	430p	—

Items >1,250g cost an extra 70p for each additional 250g or part thereof, up to 2,000g.

Recorded Signed For = postage + 72p · Special Delivery (9am) = £10·30 for up to 100g

AIRMAIL RATES

AIRMAIL	Letters Europe	Rest of World	Small packets		Printed papers	
			Europe	RoW	Europe	RoW
Postcards	0·50	0·56				
≤10g	0·50	0·56				
≤20	0·50	0·81				
≤40	0·72	1·22				
≤60	0·94	1·64				
≤80	1·14	2·08				
≤100	1·36	2·52	1·24	1·64	1·07	1·56
≤120	1·58	2·94	1·36	1·87	1·16	1·79
≤140	1·80	3·38	1·50	2·10	1·28	2·03

To find a postcode call
08456 039 038
For further information see
royalmail.com

A universal stamp can be used to send letters up to 40g to Europe (60p), or worldwide (£1·12).

ROYAL MAIL STAMPS OF 2008

8 Jan........ Ian Fleming's James Bond	18 Sep................. RAF Uniforms
5 Feb .... Working Dogs	29 Sep...............50th Anniversary
28 Feb.............House of Lancaster	of County Definitives
11 Mar . Celebrating Northern Ireland	14 Oct.........Women of Distinction
13 Mar ....Mayday Rescue at Sea	4 Nov.................Christmas 2008
15 Apr............................Insects	6 Nov.................. Lest We Forget
13 May......................Cathedrals	
10 Jun ... Carry On & Hammer Films	As the pioneer of the philatelic system, the
17 Jul......................Air Displays	UK is the only country exempt from having to
22 Aug................Olympic Games	display its name on its international stamps.

———————SAVING · 1957, 2007, 2057———————

In 2007, to mark its 50th anniversary, National Savings & Investments (NS&I) commissioned the Future Foundation to assess past, present, and future trends in saving. Among the many predictions made in the NS&I report were: a shift towards 'remote' mobile and internet transactions; the rise of biometric and encrypted security systems; better-qualified women out-earning men in 'pre-family life stages'; an increase in individual (rather than joint) asset-holding within relationships and a possible 'return to secrecy' about personal savings; the decline in cash and the demise of the cheque; a growth in 'peer-to-peer' lending[†], and in the popularity of savings linked to brands, sports teams, celebrities, &c. Below are some other trends:

Issue	1957	2007	2057
% of disposable income saved	1·5%	5%	7%
Total UK savings[‡]	<£1bn	£43bn	c.£150bn
Average annual household savings[‡]	£59	£633	£1,767
% of households saving weekly	37%	7%	>7%
% of households saving regularly	37%	43%	50%
% of all transactions using cash	>98%	59%	<10%
% of savers using online banking	0%	28%	98%
Average years spent in retirement · ♂	7·6	15	19
Average years spent in retirement · ♀	13·9	22	23

† Peer-to-peer lending (aka P2P, person-to-person, or social lending) allows money to be loaned and borrowed outside of the traditional banking sphere, often at rates more advantageous for all parties. In its simplest form, P2P lending takes place within families or amongst friends, but a number of websites (e.g., zopa.com) allow individuals to invest and borrow sums from a general pool of money.
‡ Constant 2003 prices. [Source: NS&I/Future Fdtn *50 Years of Saving: Yesterday, Today, & Tomorrow*]

———————PRICIEST CONSUMER GOODS———————

Londoners pay c.38% more for popular consumer goods, compared to those in 28 other major cities, according to a 2007 PriceRunner.com report – though this was nothing compared to the prices paid by those in Oslo. 26 products (e.g., digital cameras) were checked to create an average against which cities were judged.

MOST EXPENSIVE	% *costlier*	LEAST EXPENSIVE	% *cheaper*
Oslo	83	Beijing	47
London	38	Vilnius, Lithuania	40
Stockholm	34	Shanghai	38
Paris	31	Warsaw, Poland	23
Copenhagen	30	Prague, Czech Republic	23

Among the cities surveyed, Tokyo was the cheapest place to buy a 700ml bottle of Absolut vodka (£5·28) while Oslo was the most expensive (£23·97). Unsurprisingly, Tokyo was also the cheapest place to purchase electronic gadgets such as a Nintendo Wii (£107·22) and an iPod (£121·44). Hungary was the least expensive place for cinema tickets (£3·14), and London the costliest (£8·90).

ECONOMIC INDICATORS OF NOTE

Indicator	2007	2006	2005	2004	2003	2002	2001	2000	1999	1998	1997
FTSE 100 share index	6,425	5,941	5,168	4,520	4,030	4,566	5,541	6,348	6,313	5,667	4,695
Dow Jones Industrial Average	13,170	11,409	10,548	10,317	8,994	9,226	10,189	10,735	10,465	8,626	7,441
CBI business optimism survey	-1.5	-8.0	-18.5	6.5	-7.5	-3.2	-27.0	-3.0	-7.0	-33.8	0.0
RPI inflation (% year-on-year)	4.3	3.2	2.8	3.0	2.9	1.6	1.8	2.9	1.6	3.4	3.1
Real GDP (% year-on-year)	3.1	2.9	1.8	3.3	2.8	2.1	2.4	3.8	3.0	3.4	3.1
Average mortgage rate (%)	7.44	6.51	6.53	6.15	5.47	5.65	6.81	7.58	6.97	8.64	7.79
Number of taxpayers (million)	31.4	31.1	30.3	28.5	28.9	28.6	29.3	27.2	26.9	26.2	25.7
Highest rate of income tax (%)	40	40	40	40	40	40	40	40	40	40	40
Employment rate (%)	74.5	74.6	74.7	74.7	74.6	74.5	74.4	74.4	74.0	73.4	72.8
Unemployed (millions)	1.65	1.67	1.47	1.42	1.49	1.53	1.49	1.59	1.73	1.79	1.99
Unemployment rate (%)	5.4	5.4	4.9	4.8	5.1	5.2	5.1	5.4	6.0	6.3	6.9
Growth in consumer credit (% year-on-year)	6.1	7.6	12.5	14.2	14.9	15.9	13.4	14.5	15.8	17.2	17.1
Credit cards in issue (millions)	68.4	67.7	70.6	71.4	66.4	60.4	53.9	49.7	43.5	40.1	36.6
Outstanding credit card balance (£bn)	65.3	66.4	67.5	63.8	54.2	47.5	40.7	35.6	29.7	24.6	19.3
Mortgage loan approvals (thousands)	1,246	1,223	1,196	1,262	1,363	1,425	1,260	1,125	1,146	1,036	1,190
Housing transactions (thousands)	1,686	1,647	1,531	1,793	1,345	1,588	1,458	1,431	1,470	1,347	1,440
Halifax house price (% change year-on-year)	9.4	8.3	5.7	18.3	22.4	17.4	8.5	9.8	7.2	5.4	6.3
Change in average earnings (%)	3.9	4.1	4.1	4.3	3.4	3.5	4.5	4.5	4.8	5.2	4.3
Lending secured on houses (£bn)	363.8	345.2	288.4	291.4	277.4	220.8	160.1	119.8	114.7	89.4	77.2
Properties repossessed (%)	0.22	0.18	0.13	0.07	0.07	0.11	0.16	0.20	0.27	0.31	0.31
New car registrations (thousands)	2,390	2,340	2,444	2,599	2,646	2,682	2,578	2,337	2,242	2,262	2,157
US Dollar/GB Pound ($/£)	2.00	1.84	1.82	1.83	1.63	1.50	1.44	1.51	1.62	1.66	1.64
Euro/GB Pound (€/£) [pre-1999 estimated]	1.46	1.47	1.46	1.47	1.44	1.59	1.61	1.64	1.52	(1.48)	(1.45)
Gold price per Troy ounce (£)	347	328	245	223	222	206	188	184	172	177	202
Oil US Dollar/barrel (Brent futures close)	72.7	66.1	55.2	38.0	28.5	25.0	24.9	28.5	18.0	13.3	19.3

[Sources: Bank of England; ONS; Halifax Building Society; Council of Mortgage Lenders; HM Treasury; British Bankers' Association · Many figures have been rounded]

Parliament & Politics

At Downing Street upon the stair, I met a man who wasn't Blair.
He wasn't Blair again today, Oh how I wish he'd go away.

In March 2008, as Gordon Brown's grip on power was whitening at the knuckles, Matthew Parris reported in *The Times* that a Labour MP had passed him this ditty. According to Parris, 'this variation on the nursery doggerel is from a Labour backbencher, via another Labour backbencher – but composed by a Cabinet minister who must not be named'. The author remains unknown, but he or she is clearly a fan of the poet Hughes Mearns, upon whose poem, *Antigonish*, this rhyme is based.

THE HOUSE OF COMMONS

House of Commons, London, SW1A 0AA · parliament.uk

STATE OF THE PARTIES · as at 16 September 2008

Labour	349	Independent Conservative	1
Conservative	193	Independent Labour	1
Liberal Democrat	63	Ulster Unionist	1
Scottish National Party	7	Respect	1
Plaid Cymru	3	Speaker (Michael Martin)	1
Democratic Unionist	9	Deputy Speakers	3
Sinn Féin [seats not taken]	5	Vacant [Glenrothes by-election due Oct '08]	1
Social Democratic & Labour	3	TOTAL	646
Independent	4	GOVERNMENT MAJORITY	62

TOP POLITICAL BLOGS

The rise in the range and impact of British political blogging has been notable. And although these blogs may not yet have achieved the power of American sites such as Drudge or the Huffington Post, a range of British bloggers wield considerable influence, both by disseminating gossip and innuendo and by pursuing stories with a fearlessness that the 'mainstream media' or 'dead tree press' on occasion eschew. In 2008, the blogger Guido Fawkes (aka Paul Staines) could claim at least some part both in the Cabinet resignation of Peter Hain and the Charity Commission's formal investigation of the Smith Institute think tank. Below are the top 15 political blogs as voted for in an (admittedly unscientific) survey by TotalPolitics.com:

1 .... *Guido Fawkes*	6 .... *Devil's Kitchen*	11 .... *EU Referendum*
2 .... *Iain Dale*	7 . *Spectator Coffee House*	12 .... *Tim Worstall*
3 .... *Conservative Home*	8 .... *Burning our Money*	13 ...... *Tom Harris MP*
4 .... *Dizzy Thinks*	9 .... *John Redwood*	14 .. *Archbishop Cranmer*
5 .... *Political Betting*	10 .... *Ben Brogan*	15 .... *LibDem Voice*

─────── GRAZIA WOMEN & POLITICS SURVEY · 2008 ───────

Grazia explored the political opinions of British women in a May 2008 survey:

Who did you vote for in the last General Election?	%
Didn't vote	36
Labour (Tony Blair)	27
Conservative (Michael Howard)	18
Lib Dem (Charles Kennedy)	13
Other	6

If there was an election tomorrow, who would you vote for?	%
Undecided – could be swayed	33
Conservative (David Cameron)	33
Labour (Gordon Brown)	14
Wouldn't vote	9
Lib Dem (Nick Clegg)	7
Other	4

What concerns you most about Britain right now?	%
Yob culture/violent crime	79
The cost of living	66
The state of the NHS	65
The environment	53
Immigration	50
Amount of tax you pay	49
The property ladder	44
The threat of terrorism	43

Is it important for male politicians to have sex appeal/charisma?	%
Very much so	4
Reasonably so	49
Not at all	47

To which political wife do you most relate?	%
Samantha Cameron	42
Sarah Brown	19
Other	17
Cherie Blair	14
Miriam Gonzalez Durantez [Mrs Clegg]	8

When judging politicians, which qualities turn you on or off?		
% turn on		turn off %
97	Admitting mistakes	3
95	A strong moral code	5
94	Sense of humour	6
93	Proud to be British	7
86	Green credentials	14
83	A modern image	17
72	Showing emotion	28
39	Having a blog	61
25	Being religious	75
6	Hanging out with stars	94

The *Grazia* survey also revealed: Anne Widdecombe was the favourite British female politician with 26% of the vote; 73% of respondents thought things would improve if there were more female politicians. The word most associated with Gordon Brown was 'boring' (50%); the word most associated with David Cameron was 'modern thinking' (53%). When asked which female politicians were the most stylish, 79% said they didn't find any of them stylish. 35% thought the ideal age for a Prime Minister was 41–45. If able to vote in the US presidential elections, 51% said they would vote for Barack Obama; 52% of respondents said that if a British politician supported George W. Bush it would turn them off. The most acceptable number of sexual partners for a party leader to have had was 6–10 (35%) [see p.254]. If they had to, 63% of respondents would marry David Cameron; 49% would call Gordon Brown in a crisis; 52% would ask David Cameron for relationship advice.

─────── POLITICAL LEADERS & THE BEATLES ───────

When asked for their favourite Beatles' song, Gordon Brown chose *All My Loving*, David Cameron, *The Long and Winding Road*, and Nick Clegg, *A Day in the Life*.

BRITISH PRIME MINISTERS

Prime Minister	date of birth	star sign	position in family	siblings	child of MP	at Eton	at Harrow	at Oxbridge	in the forces	party as PM	age when first PM	time as PM	Admins.	date of death	age at death
Gordon Brown	20-02-1951	♓	2nd of 3	2b						Lab	56y 129d	—	—	—	—
Tony Blair	06-05-1953	♉	2nd of 3	1b 1s				○		Lab	43y 361d	10y c.55d	3	—	—
John Major	29-03-1943	♈	4th of 4	2b 1s						Con	47y 245d	6y 154d	2	—	—
Margaret Thatcher	13-10-1925	♎	2nd of 2	1s				○		Con	53y 204d	11y 209d	3	—	—
James Callaghan	27-03-1912	♈	2nd of 2	1s					◆	Lab	64y 9d	3y 29d	1	26-03-2005	92
Edward Heath	09-07-1916	♋	1st of 2	1b				○	◆	Con	53y 335d	3y 259d	1	17-07-2005	89
Harold Wilson	11-03-1916	♓	2nd of 2	1s				○		Lab	48y 219d	7y 279d	4	24-05-1995	79
Alec Douglas-Home	02-07-1903	♋	1st of 7	4b 2s		◆		○		Con	60y 109d	363d	1	09-10-1995	92
Harold Macmillan	10-02-1894	♒	3rd of 3	2b		◆		○	◆	Con	62y 335d	6y 281d	2	29-12-1986	92
Anthony Eden	12-06-1897	♊	4th of 5	3b 1s		◆		○	◆	Con	57y 299d	1y 279d	1	14-01-1977	79
Clement Attlee	03-01-1883	♑	7th of 8	4b 3s				○	◆	Lab	63y 205d	6y 92d	2	08-10-1967	84
Winston Churchill	30-11-1874	♐	1st of 2	1b	◆		◆		◆	Con	65y 163d	8y 240d	3	24-01-1965	90
Neville Chamberlain	18-03-1869	♓	3rd of 6	1b 4s	◆					Con	68y 71d	2y 348d	1	09-11-1940	71
Ramsay MacDonald	12-10-1866	♎	only child	0						Lab	57y 102d	6y 289d	4	09-11-1937	71
Stanley Baldwin	03-08-1867	♌	only child	0			◆	C		Con	55y 292d	7y 82d	4	13-12-1947	80
Andrew Bonar Law	16-09-1858	♍	4th of 7	3b 3s						Con	64y 37d	209d	1	30-10-1923	65
David Lloyd George	17-01-1863	♑	3rd of 4	1b 2s						Lib	53y 325d	5y 317d	2	26-03-1945	82
Herbert Henry Asquith	12-09-1852	♍	2nd of 5	1b 3s				○		Lib	55y 198d	8y 244d	4	15-02-1928	75
Henry Campbell-Bannerman	07-09-1836	♍	6th of 6	1b 4s				C		Lib	69y 89d	3y 122d	1	22-04-1908	71
Arthur James Balfour	25-07-1848	♌	3rd of 8	4b 3s		◆		C		Con	53y 352d	3y 145d	1	19-03-1930	81
Earl of Rosebery	07-05-1847	♉	3rd of 4	1b 2s	◆	◆		○		Lib	46y 302d	1y 109d	1	21-05-1929	82
Marquess of Salisbury	03-02-1830	♒	5th of 6	3b 2s	◆	◆		○		Con	55y 144d	13y 252d	4	22-08-1903	73
William Ewart Gladstone	29-12-1809	♑	5th of 6	3b 2s	◆	◆		○		Lib	58y 340d	12y 126d	4	19-05-1898	88
Benjamin Disraeli	21-12-1804	♐	2nd of 5	3b 1s						Con	63y 68d	6y 339d	2	19-04-1881	76
Viscount Palmerston	20-10-1784	♎	1st of 5	1b 3s			◆	C		Lib	71y 109d	9y 141d	2	18-10-1865	81
Earl of Aberdeen	28-01-1784	♒	1st of 7	5b 1s	◆		◆	C		Con	68y 326d	2y 42d	1	14-12-1860	76

——— BRITISH PRIME MINISTERS cont. ———

Prime Minister	date of birth	star sign	position in family	siblings	child of MP	at Eton	at Harrow	at Oxbridge	in the forces	party as PM	age when first PM	time as PM	Admins.	date of death	age at death
Earl of Derby	29-03-1799	♈	1st of 7	2b 4s	◈	◈	·	O	·	Con	52y 331d	3y 280d	3	23-10-1869	70
Lord John Russell	18-08-1792	♌	3rd of 7	6b	◈	·	·	C	◈	Lib	53y 316d	6y 11d	2	28-05-1878	85
Robert Peel	05-02-1788	♒	3rd of 11	5b 5s	◈	·	◈	O	·	Con	46y 308d	5y 57d	2	02-07-1850	62
Lord Melbourne	15-03-1779	♓	2nd of 6	3b 2s	·	◈	·	C	·	Whig	55y 123d	6y 255d	2	24-11-1848	69
Earl Grey	13-03-1764	♓	2nd of 9	6b 2s	·	◈	·	C	·	Whig	66y 254d	3y 229d	1	17-07-1845	81
Duke of Wellington	01-05-1769	♉	6th of 9	6b 2s	◈	◈	·	·	◈	Tory	58y 266d	2y 320d	2	14-09-1852	83
Viscount Goderich	01-11-1782	♏	2nd of 3	2b	·	·	◈	O	·	Tory	44y 305d	130d	1	28-01-1859	76
George Canning	11-04-1770	♈	2nd of 13	7b 5s	·	◈	·	O	◈	Tory	57y 1d	119d	1	08-08-1827	57
Earl of Liverpool	07-06-1770	♊	1st of 3	1b 1s	◈	·	·	O	·	Tory	42y 1d	14y 305d	1	04-12-1828	58
Spencer Perceval	01-11-1762	♏	5th of 9	2b 6s	◈	·	◈	C	·	Tory	46y 338d	2y 221d	1	11-05-1812	49
Lord Grenville	24-10-1759	♏	6th of 9	3b 5s	◈	◈	·	O	·	Whig	46y 110d	1y 42d	1	12-01-1834	74
Henry Addington	30-05-1757	♊	4th of 6	1b 4s	◈	·	·	O	·	Tory	43y 291d	3y 54d	1	15-02-1844	86
William Pitt	28-05-1759	♊	4th of 5	2b 2s	◈	·	·	C	◈	Tory	24y 205d	18y 343d	2	23-01-1806	46
Duke of Portland	14-04-1738	♈	3rd of 6	1b 4s	·	◈	·	O	·	Whig	44y 335d	3y 82d	2	30-10-1809	71
Earl of Shelburne	02-05-1737	♉	1st of 5	1b 3s	·	·	·	O	◈	Whig	45y 63d	266d	1	07-05-1805	68
Lord North	13-04-1732	♈	1st of 6	1b 4s	◈	◈	·	O	·	Tory	37y 290d	12y 58d	1	05-08-1792	60
Duke of Grafton	28-09-1735	♎	2nd of 3	2b	·	◈	·	C	·	Whig	33y 16d	1y 106d	1	14-03-1811	75
Earl of Chatham	15-11-1708	♏	4th of 7	1b 5s	◈	◈	·	O	·	Whig	57y 257d	2y 76d	1	11-05-1778	69
Marquess of Rockingham	13-05-1730	♉	8th of 10	4b 5s	◈	·	·	O	·	Whig	35y 61d	1y 113d	2	01-07-1782	52
George Grenville	14-10-1712	♎	2nd of 7	5b 1s	◈	◈	·	·	·	Whig	50y 184d	2y 85d	1	13-11-1770	58
Earl of Bute	25-05-1713	♊	2nd of 8	2b 5s	·	◈	·	O	·	Tory	49y 1d	317d	1	10-03-1792	78
Duke of Devonshire	1720	?	2nd of 7	3b 3s	◈	·	·	·	·	Whig	c.36	225d	1	02-10-1764	c.44
Duke of Newcastle	21-07-1693	♋	8th of 11	2b 8s	◈	·	·	C	◈	Whig	60y 238d	7y 205d	2	17-11-1768	75
Henry Pelham	26-09-1694	♎	9th of 11	2b 8s	◈	·	·	·	·	Whig	48y 336d	10y 191d	1	06-03-1754	59
Earl of Wilmington	?1673	?	5th of 5	3b 1s	·	·	·	O	·	Whig	c.69	1y 136d	1	02-07-1743	c.70
Robert Walpole	26-08-1676	♍	5th of 17	9b 7s	◈	·	·	C	◈	Whig	44y 107d	20y 314d	1	18-03-1745	60

──────── LIB DEM LEADERSHIP ELECTION 2007 ────────

The resignation of Sir Menzies 'Ming' Campbell, on 15/10/2007, after <2 years as Lib Dem leader was one of the consequences of Gordon Brown's decision not to seek an electoral mandate. With Brown secure (if beleaguered) in Downing Street and David Cameron's Tories ascendent, Campbell knew that attacks on him would redouble. As he said, 'it has become clear that following the PM's decision not to hold an election, questions about leadership are getting in the way of further progress by the party'. Campbell, who was 64 when he became leader, failed to shake off the impression of being a 'caretaker', and his authority was further weakened by lacklustre performances at PMQs, and almost continual speculation over his position. Ming's reputation was not helped by the unexpectedly stellar performance of his temporary successor, deputy party leader Vince Cable. In a series of attacks on the accident-prone PM, Cable drew blood and laughter – famously noting Brown's 'remarkable transformation in the past few weeks from Stalin to Mr Bean'. ❦ After many senior candidates (including Cable) ruled themselves out, the contest to replace Campbell was between 40-year-old Nick Clegg and 53-year-old Chris Huhne. Despite a certain amount of internecine nastiness, the contest sparked little public interest, and was characterised by the *Guardian* as 'a rather small-minded affair, with each candidate wary of allowing any sign of ideological difference'. On 18/12/2007, Clegg was declared the 3rd Lib Dem leader in 2 years, winning by just 511 votes (1·2%):

Candidate	votes	%
Nick Clegg	20,988	50·6
Chris Huhne	20,477	49·4
Turnout	*41,465*	*64·1*

In victory, Clegg was quick to praise Huhne (whom he appointed to home affairs), and eager to explain his vision: 'I have one simple ambition: to change Britain to make it the liberal country I believe the British people want it to be. I want a new politics, a people's politics. I want to live in a country where rights, freedoms and privacy are not the playthings of politicians, but safeguarded for everyone. Where political life is not a Westminster village freak show, but open, accessible, and helpful in people's everyday lives'. At his first PMQs, Clegg played it safe, challenging Brown on energy prices. In response Brown said his door was 'always open' to Clegg – an indication that although Lib Dem leadership did not arouse much public excitement, the third party may prove to be decisive in the event of a hung parliament. ❦ Clegg's honeymoon was short-lived. A series of poor parliamentary performances were compounded by a *GQ* interview in which he confided that he had bedded 'no more than 30' women. Inevitably, the press dubbed him 'Cleggover'. The Lib Dems' unremarkable showing in the 2008 local elections [see p.26] led some to ask whether they had erred in dumping Ming and passing over Cable.

──────── THINK TANK OF THE YEAR · 2007 ────────

In 2007, *Prospect* magazine gave its 'Think Tank of the Year' award to the Institute for Public Policy Research, whose slogan is 'Changing ideas, Challenging policy'.

——————————— PORK BARREL POLITICS ———————————

In US politics, 'pork barrel spending' refers to the distribution of federal funds for lo-cal projects by congressmen hoping to curry favour with their electorate. Generally, politicians 'bring home the bacon' by inserting requests for specific projects (e.g., museums or roads) into federal spending bills. In the UK, in June 2008, Nick Clegg said of the government's win over 42-day detention [see p.29], 'It is a victory for pork barrel politics, and nothing to do with principle'. ❦ It seems that pork barrels (in which pig flesh was stored in brine) have long had connotations of prosperity or security; in James Fenimore Cooper's 1845 classic *The Chain Bearer*, one character notes: 'I hold a family to be in a desperate way, when the mother can see the bot-tom of the pork barrel'. Yet pork barrels are also associated with fat and grease, and some maintain that the term's current usage dates from when slave owners would set out barrels of salted pork for their captives. During the 2008 US elections, the term gained particular prominence, thanks to John McCain's staunch opposition to such spending. McCain's running mate Sarah Palin is Governor of Alaska, a state notorious for its pork barrel appetite, not least for the infamous $398m 'Bridge to Nowhere', which would have connected Gravina Island with Ketchikan airport.

——————— WESTMINSTER DOG OF THE YEAR · 2007 ———————

The Westminster Dog of the Year contest is organised jointly by the Kennel Club and the Dogs Trust; it is open to all MPs, Lords, and, for the last two years, parlia-mentary journalists. In October 2007, 12 political pooches were up for the prize (4 Tory, 4 Labour, no Lib Dems, 3 journalists, and Black Rod's dog, Sugar). The win-ner was rescue dog Max the mongrel, owned by Mike Hall, Labour MP for Weaver Vale. The runners up were Myrtle the cocker spaniel, owned by Gabriel Milland of the *Daily Express*, and Michael the labrador, hound of Tory MP David Amess.

In a survey to mark Gordon Brown's first year as PM, the *Mail on Sunday* found that the dog with which he was most associated by voters was a St Bernard, 'known chiefly for its loyalty (and large Gordon Brown-type jowls)'. David Cameron was seen as a Labrador, 'middle England's favourite four-legged friend', and Nick Clegg was 'humiliatingly seen as a cross between a poodle and a chihuahua'.

——————— TOP TEN MOST FANCIABLE MPs ———————

Below are the 'most fanciable' MPs, according to *Sky News* political editor Adam Boulton, who canvassed members themselves for his annual Valentine's Day poll:

Name (Age)	Party
1 .. Jeremy Hunt (41)	Con
2 .. Julie Kirkbride (47)	Con
3 .. Julia Goldsworthy (29)	Lib Dem
4 .. Jenny Willott (33)	Lib Dem
5 .. Lynne Featherstone (56)	Lib Dem
6 .. Edward Garnier (55)	Con
7 .. Angela E. Smith (49)†	Labour
8 .. Nick Clegg (40)	Lib Dem
9 .. Jo Swinson (28)	Lib Dem
10. Shahid Malik (40)	Labour

† MP for Basildon, never to be confused with Angela Smith, MP for Sheffield Hillsborough.

THE SCOTTISH PARLIAMENT

The current state of parties (as at 16 September 2008)

Number of MSPs	Constituency	Regional	Total
Scottish National Party	21	26	47
Scottish Labour	37	9	46
Scottish Conservative	3	13	16
Scottish Liberal Democrat	11	5	16
Scottish Green Party	0	2	2
Independent	0	1	1
Presiding Officer (Alex Fergusson)	1	0	1

THE NATIONAL ASSEMBLY FOR WALES

The current state of parties (as at 16 September 2008)

Number of AMs	Constituency	Regional	Total
Labour	24	2	26
Plaid Cymru	7	8	15
Conservative	5	7	12
Liberal Democrat	3	3	6
Independent	1	0	1
Presiding Officer (Lord Dafydd Elis-Thomas)	1	0	1

THE NORTHERN IRELAND ASSEMBLY

The current state of parties (as at 16 September 2008)

DUP..................36	SDLP................16	Green Party 1
Sinn Féin.............28	Alliance...............7	Independent...........1
Ulster Unionists......18	PUP 1	Speaker: William Hay

On 4 March 2008, Ian Paisley announced that he would stand down as Northern Ireland's first minister; he also said he would resign as leader of the DUP. Peter Robinson replaced him in both roles.

THE LONDON ASSEMBLY

The current state of parties (as at 16 September 2008)

Conservative 11	Liberal Democrat 3	British Nat. Party 1
Labour................8	Green..................2	(May 2008 turnout, 45·3%)

Mayoral and Assembly elections were held on 1 May 2008. Conservative candidate Boris Johnson ended Ken Livingstone's eight-year reign at City Hall, winning with 1,168,738 votes; see p.26.

―――――――――― THE HOUSE OF LORDS ――――――――――

State of the parties (as at 1 July 2008) | Bishops 26
Conservative . . . . 202 | Other 13
Labour. . . . . 215 | Total 735
Liberal Democrat 76
Crossbench. . . . . 203 | 11 Peers on leave of absence are excluded.

Archbishops and Bishops. . . . . .26 [0]
Life Peers under the Appellate Jurisdiction Act 1876 . . . . .23 [1]
Life Peers under the Life Peerages Act 1958. . . . . .605 [144]
Peers under the House of Lords Act 1999. . . . . .92 [2]
[Numbers within brackets indicate the number of women included in the figure.]

―――――――――― 'FREE & FAIR' ELECTIONS ――――――――――

According to the US State Dept, 'free and fair elections increase the likelihood of a peaceful transfer of power. They help to ensure that losing candidates will accept the validity of the election's results and cede power to the new government'. However, in a warning that chimes with Zimbabwe's 2008 elections [see p.33], the State Dept cautions that 'elections alone do not assure democracy since dictators can use the resources of the state to tamper with the election process'. Listed below are the State Dept's prerequisites for elections to be considered free and fair:

Universal suffrage for all eligible men and women to vote. ❦ Freedom to register as a voter or run for public office. ❦ Freedom of speech for candidates and political parties. ❦ Numerous opportunities for the electorate to receive objective information from a free press. ❦ Freedom to assemble for political rallies and campaigns. ❦ Rules that require party representatives to maintain a distance from polling places on election day; election officials, volunteer poll workers, and international monitors may assist voters with the voting process but not the voting choice. ❦ An impartial or balanced system of conducting elections and verifying election results; trained election officials must either be politically independent or those overseeing elections should be representative of the parties in the election. ❦ Accessible polling places, private voting space, secure ballot boxes, and transparent ballot counting. ❦ Secret ballots. ❦ Legal prohibitions against election fraud, and enforceable laws to prevent vote tampering (e.g., double counting, ghost voting). ❦ Recount and contestation procedures. ❦ Voting methods should include: paper ballots; ballots with pictures of candidates or party symbols so that illiterate citizens may cast the correct vote; electronic systems with touchscreen or push-button machines; and absentee ballots, allowing those who will not be able to vote on election day to cast their ballots prior to the election.

See also p.13 for the use of ink stains in election monitoring. ❦ In April 2007, Nigerian elections were monitored using text messages. The Network of Mobile Election Monitors asked voters to send SMS reports of electoral irregularities, which were then passed on to official election monitors.

———— PARLIAMENTARY SALARY & ALLOWANCES ————

Members of Parliament

Members' Parliamentary salary.................................. £61,820 (from 1-4-2008)
Staffing allowance†...£100,205
Incidental Expenses Provision (IEP).. £22,193
IT equipment (centrally provided)................................... worth *c*.£3,000
London supplement (for inner London seats)............................... £2,916
Additional costs allowance (for those with seats outside London).........£24,006
Winding Up Allowance (maximum)..£40,799
Car mileage, first 10,000 miles..40p per mile
– thereafter...25p per mile
Motorcycle allowance...24p per mile
Bicycle allowance ....20p per mile

† This figure reflects a decision to allow for an increase of staff from 3 to 3·5. At the time of writing, it had not been decided whether to provide additional funds to cover staff employed in London.

Position

Prime Minister†.....................................£128,174 (from 1-11-2007)
Cabinet Minister†..£76,904
Cabinet Minister (Lords)..£104,386
Minister of State†..£39,893
Minister of State (Lords) £81,504
Parliamentary Under Secretary†...£30,280
Parliamentary Under Secretary (Lords) £70,986
Government Chief Whip†...£76,904
Government Deputy Chief Whip†..£39,893
Government Whip†...£25,673
Leader of the Opposition†...£70,497
Leader of the Opposition (Lords)..£70,986
Opposition Chief Whip†...£39,893
Speaker†...£76,904
Attorney General £109,201
Lord Chancellor £232,900

[† Ministers in the Commons additionally receive their salaries as MPs (as above).]

Backbench Peers

Subsistence.......................................Day £82·50 · Overnight £165·50
Office secretarial allowance........£71·50 per sitting day and <40 additional days
Travel..as for MPs
Spouses/children's expenses........................... 6 return journeys per year

Lords Ministers and paid office holders

Ministers' night subsistence allowance......£36,410 for those with a second home in London
London supplement ....£1,833 except those with official residence &c.
Secretarial allowance...£5,389
Spouses/children's expenses...........................15 return journeys per year

——SALARIES FOR DEVOLVED LEGISLATURES &c.——

Scottish Parliament (from 1·11·2007) — *total salary*
Member of the Scottish Parliament (MSP) £54,093
First Minister..£132,452
Scottish Minister...£94,743
Junior Scottish Minister...£79,555
Presiding Officer...£94,743
Solicitor General...£92,495

National Assembly for Wales (from 1·4·2008) — *total salary*
Assembly Member (AM)...£50,692
Assembly First Minister £129,047
Assembly Minister...£91,337
Presiding Officer...£91,337
Leader of the largest non-cabinet party.................................£91,337
AMs who are also MPs or MEPs...£16,897

Northern Ireland Assembly — *total salary*
Members of the Legislative Assembly (MLA) £43,101
Presiding Officer...£43,901
These salaries have applied since the Assembly was restored on 8/5/2007 (it had been suspended since 14/10/2002). Prior to this, MLAs were paid only for the work carried out in their constituency.

European Parliament (from 1·4·2008) — *total salary*
UK Members of the European Parliament ....as MPs

Members of Parliament who are also members of a devolved legislature receive their full parliamentary salary [see above] and one-third of the salary due to them for their other role. Since 2004, Westminster MPs are ineligible to serve additionally as MEPs. The devolved legislatures control their own expenses and allowances.

London Assembly (from 6·4·2008) — *total salary*
Member of the London Assembly (MLA)..................................£50,582
Mayor of London..£137,579
Deputy Mayor..£90,954

————BROKEN LIGHT BULBS IN PARLIAMENT————

In December 2007, to the amusement of the press, MPs were issued with a 10-point guide on how to deal with a broken light bulb in the Palace of Westminster, viz:

1 .... Put on protective gloves	6......... Clean area with damp cloth
2............... Put on protective mask	7...... Place splinters and cloth in box
3......................Open sturdy box	8.................... Seal box with tape
4......... Place large fragments in box	9 ... Label box with details of contents
5...... Collect splinters using stiff card	10......... Take to waste removal area

DRINKING THE KOOL-AID

To 'drink the Kool-Aid' is to give unthinking, quasi-brainwashed support to a cause or individual. The construction has long been a media cliché; during the interminable 2007–08 US primaries, supporters of almost every contender were accused at one time or another of drinking their candidate's Kool-Aid. The popular use of the phrase seems to date to two events. In 1968, Tom Wolfe published *The Electric Kool-Aid Acid Test*, a pioneering work of 'new journalism' that described the trans-American travels of Ken Kesey, the 'Pied Piper of the psychedelic era' (according to the *New York Times*) and author of *One Flew Over the Cuckoo's Nest*. Of all Kesey's hedonistic excesses, the act that captured the public's attention (and gave Wolfe his title) was the 'Acid Test', where Kesey and his followers challenged members of the public to drink Kool-Aid laced with LSD to see if they 'freaked out'. Ten years later, on 18 November 1978, in Jonestown, Guyana, the maverick preacher Jim Jones induced 913 members of his People's Temple cult (including 276 children) to commit suicide by drinking fruit juice spiked with cyanide. Although there is some debate about what type of juice this was (a 1979 FBI report refers variously to 'a flavored water drink', 'flavor aid', and 'Kool-Aid'), the tragically submissive Jonestown murder-suicides have ever since been associated with 'drinking the Kool-Aid'.

Kool-Aid was first marketed in *c.*1915 as a soft drink syrup called Fruit Smack by Perkins Products Co. of Nebraska. In 1927, the syrup was concentrated into a powder (in cherry, grape, lemon-lime, orange, strawberry, and raspberry flavours) and renamed Kool-Aid. Kool-Aid is now made by Kraft. ❦ Apropos of nothing, in July 2008, the Association of Licensed Multiple Retailers (ALMR) issued a press release that claimed the House of Commons Refreshment Dept enjoyed a £5·5m subsidy in 2007/08. This allows MPs to quaff pints of Foster's for just £2·10 and glasses of Pimm's for £1·65.

POLITICAL PLAYING CARDS

In 2003, US forces in Iraq were given 'Most Wanted' playing cards to assist in their hunt for Saddam Hussein and his cronies. Playing cards are now being used for purposes beyond games of snap or identifying possible war criminals, for example:

Archaeology cards	*Criminal cases cards*	*Foxhunting cards*
In July 2007, the US Dept of Defense issued cards depicting Iraqi & Afghan archaeological sites and artefacts, in an attempt to educate their troops about the places to which they were deployed.	Since July 2007, inmates of Florida state jails have had access to cards which show 'cold cases' – in an attempt to crack unsolved crimes. A resulting tip has led to two men being charged with a 2004 murder.	In October 2004, in advance of the vote on the anti-hunting bill, the Countryside Alliance produced cards featuring MPs it believed were most opposed to foxhunting and other blood sports.[†]

† Saddam Hussein's place as ace of spades in the 'Most Wanted' cards was taken by Gordon Prentice, Labour MP for Pendle, in the anti-foxhunting pack. Pendle was a leading advocate of the hunting ban. ❦ In July 2008, a controversial pack of 'happy family'-esque cards was launched in Germany. 'Das Führer-Quartett' features 32 tyrants, including Hitler, Stalin, Mussolini, Idi Amin, and Papa Doc.

——————STANDING ORDER NO. 46——————

Under Standing Order No. 46, in a situation of 'grave disorder', the Speaker of the House of Commons has the power to halt proceedings until a time they judge fitting. The Speaker may temporarily SUSPEND the Commons (usually for 10–30 minutes), or ADJOURN the business altogether. Below are some recent examples:

Date	reason for suspension/adjournment
May 1976	Michael Heseltine brandished the Mace[†] during a heated debate
Mar 1988	'uproar' during Nigel Lawson's Budget speech
May 1994	the death of Labour leader John Smith
Oct 2001	a package containing white power prompted fears of an anthrax attack
Feb 2004	heckles of 'whitewash'[‡] from anti-war campaigners in the gallery
May 2004	'Fathers for Justice' threw a condom full of purple flour at Tony Blair
Sep 2004	an intrusion by pro-hunting campaigners
July 2005	the terrorist attacks on London's transport system

Until November 2004, the Commons could be suspended by an MP who, wishing to disrupt or delay the House's proceedings, would declare 'I spy Strangers' (strangers being non-members of the House). The Speaker would then suspend all debate until the Public and Press Galleries had been cleared. This procedure was abolished and replaced with a simpler, and less easily abused, system whereby an MP proposes a motion 'that the House sit in private'. † The Mace is a silver gilt ornamental club, dating from the era of Charles II, that represents Royal authority in the House. It is carried at the head of the Speaker's procession by the Serjeant-at-Arms each day the House sits, and is laid by him upon the Table of the House. The House cannot debate if the Mace is not present. Any interference with the Mace constitutes 'gross disorderly conduct', and is considered contempt of the House. When Oliver Cromwell dismissed the Rump Parliament on 20 April 1653, he referred to the Mace as 'that fool's bauble' – a bauble being a traditional jester's cane. In 1976, Heseltine seized the Mace and swung it mightily over his head, when Welsh Labour MPs began to sing their party's anthem ('The Red Flag) after winning a vote on aircraft and shipbuilding. ‡ Whitewash is a liquid composite of lime and water used for covering architectural faults and blemishes. According to the *OED*, the term was first applied to a political 'cover up' by George Colman in *Prose on Several Occasions* (1787), when he wrote 'such as are blackened in the North Briton are ... white-washed in the Auditor'.

——THE SPECTATOR PARLIAMENTARIAN AWARDS '07——

Newcomer of the year	Nick Clegg [Lib Dem]
Minister to watch	Liam Byrne [Lab]
Speech of the year[†]	William Hague [Con]
Inquisitor of the year	Michael Connarty [Lab]
Peer of the year	Baroness Thatcher [Con]
Resignation of the year	Tony Blair [Lab]
Campaigner of the year	Iain Duncan Smith [Con]
Politician of the year	George Osborne [Con]
Parliamentarian of the year	Alex Salmond [SNP]

† Hague's winning speech was on the bicentenary of the abolition of the slave trade.

──────GENERAL ELECTION BREAKDOWN 1979–2005──────

Date	3·5·79	9·6·83	11·6·87	9·4·92	1·5·97	7·6·01	5·5·05
Winning party	Con	Con	Con	Con	Lab	Lab	Lab
Seat majority	43	144	102	21	179	167	67
PM	Thatcher	Thatcher	Thatcher	Major	Blair	Blair	Blair
Leader of Op.	Callaghan	Foot	Kinnock	Kinnock	Major	Hague	Howard
Lib (Dem) leader	Steel	Steel	Steel	Ashdown	Ashdown	Kennedy	Kennedy

Conservative

Seats	339	397	375	336	165	166	198
Votes (m)	13·70	13·01	13·74	14·09	9·60	8·36	8·78
Share of votes (%)	43·9	42·4	42·2	41·9	30·7	31·7	32·4
% of seats	53·4	61·1	57·8	51·6	25·0	25·2	30·5

Labour

Seats	268	209	229	271	418	412	355
Votes (m)	11·51	8·46	10·03	11·56	13·52	10·72	9·55
Share of votes (%)	36·9	27·6	30·8	34·4	43·2	40·7	35·2
% of seats	42·4	32·2	35·2	41·6	63·6	62·7	55·2

Liberal Democrat (&c.)

Seats	11	23	22	20	46	52	62
Votes (m)	4·31	7·78	7·34	6·00	5·24	4·81	5·99
Share of votes (%)	13·8	25·4	22·6	17·8	16·8	18·3	22·0
% of seats	1·7	3·5	3·4	3·1	7·0	7·9	9·6

Monster Raving Loony

Candidates	–	11	5	22	24	15	19
Average vote (%)	–	0·7	0·7	0·6	0·7	1·0	–
Lost deposits	–	11	5	22	24	15	19

Women MPs	19	23	41	60	120	118	127
– as %	3·0	3·5	6·3	9·2	18·2	17·9	19·7

Turnout (%)	76·0	72·7	75·3	77·7	71·4	59·4	61·4
– England (%)	75·9	72·5	75·4	78·0	71·4	59·2	61·3
– Wales (%)	79·4	76·1	78·9	79·7	73·5	61·6	62·6
– Scotland (%)	76·8	72·7	75·1	75·5	71·3	58·2	60·8
– N. Ireland (%)	67·7	72·9	67·0	69·8	67·1	68·0	62·9

Postal vote (%)	2·2	2·0	2·4	2·0	2·3	5·2	14·6
Spoilt ballots (%)	0·38	0·17	0·11	0·12	0·30	0·38	0·7
– av./constituency	186	79	57	61	142	152	291
Deposit to stand	£150	£150	£500	£500	£500	£500	£500
– threshold (%)	12½	12½	5	5	5	5	5

Some figures (e.g., that of a winning party's majority) are disputed. Source: House of Commons.

COLOUR REVOLUTIONS

In recent years, popular protest movements have led to bloodless coups in several former Soviet nations. These revolutions have come to be called the 'Colour Revolutions'. They are said to be inspired by the 1989 Velvet Revolution, when massive protests and a general strike led to the renouncement of power by the Communist regime in the former Czechoslovakia. The Colour Revolutions include:

Rose Revolution · A 2003 coup in the former Soviet state of Georgia. Eduard Shevardnadze sparked mass protests after he claimed to have won a parliamentary election which many denounced as fraudulent. Protesters stormed Parliament, with leader Mikhail Saakashvili holding a long-stemmed rose. The crowd forced Shevardnadze to flee, and Saakashvili was elected president [see p.23].

Orange Revolution · After official reports showed that Moscow-backed Viktor Yanukovych had won Ukraine's 2004 presidential election, thousands of protesters took to the streets wearing orange, the colour of opposition leader Viktor Yushchenko's party. The protesters claimed massive election fraud and other abuses; Yushchenko claimed he had been poisoned. The protests were successful, and a new presidential election was ordered by the Supreme Court, which Yushchenko subsequently won.

Tulip Revolution · In 2005, after weeks of protests in Kyrgyzstan following a disputed parliamentary election, protesters stormed the presidential palace. President Askar Akayev was forced to flee, and later signed a resignation letter from Moscow. The revolution was reportedly named for the country's rich assortment of tulips.

Some in the press saw fit to label the September 2007 Burmese protests the *Saffron Revolution*, after the saffron sashes worn by the Buddhist monks leading the demonstrations.

Other revolutions that have come to be associated with specific colours or symbols:

Carnation Revolution	largely peaceful spring 1974 military coup in Portugal
Cedar Revolution	2005 revolt in Lebanon after the assassination of former PM Rafik Hariri; protesters called for Syrian withdrawal
Denim Revolution	unsuccessful revolt in Belarus after the 2006 presidential election; jeans were reportedly waved as a symbol of freedom
Green Revolution	controversial change in Third World agriculture methods beginning in the 1940s; credited with increasing cereal yields
Purple Revolution	term used by George W. Bush to praise the 2005 Iraq elections; named for the ink used to stain voters' fingers [see p.13]
White Revolution	programme of reforms enacted by the Shah of Iran in 1963

The Carnation Revolution was so named because those flowers were then in bloom; the cedar is a Lebanese emblem. ❦ The Cedar and Denim revolutions are also sometimes called Colour Revolutions by those who wish to emphasise their peaceful tactics and popular support. Bush's use of the term 'Purple Revolution' sought to associate Iraq with a peaceful transition to democracy. ❦ The Tulip Revolution has been called the Lemon Revolution, since yellow was the colour of the opposition. One Kyrgi leader said that yellow was viewed as a colour of change because of its use on traffic lights.

─────────── THE CABINET & SHADOW CABINET ───────────

On 21/1/08, Brown reshuffled his Cabinet after Peter Hain quit. Although rumours of a further reshuffle circulated, at the time of writing his Cabinet was as follows:

Prime Minister; First Lord of the Treasury .... Gordon Brown
Chancellor of the Exchequer .... Alistair Darling
SoS Foreign & Commonwealth Affairs .... David Miliband
SoS Justice; Lord Chancellor .... Jack Straw
SoS the Home Department .... Jacqui Smith
SoS Defence; SoS Scotland .... Des Browne
SoS Health .... Alan Johnson
SoS Environment, Food, & Rural Affairs .... Hilary Benn
SoS International Development .... Douglas Alexander
SoS Business, Enterprise, & Regulatory Reform .... John Hutton
Leader of the Commons; Minister for Women & Equalities ...... Harriet Harman
SoS Work & Pensions .... James Purnell
SoS Transport .... Ruth Kelly
SoS Communities & Local Government .... Hazel Blears
SoS Children, Schools, & Families .... Ed Balls
Minister for Cabinet Office; Chancellor of the Duchy of Lancaster ... Ed Miliband
SoS Culture, Media, & Sport .... Andy Burnham
SoS Northern Ireland .... Shaun Woodward [unpaid]
Leader of the House of Lords; Lord President of the Council ..... Baroness Ashton
Chief Secretary to the Treasury .... Yvette Cooper
Parliamentary Secretary to the Treasury; Chief Whip .... Geoff Hoon
SoS Innovation, Universities, & Skills .... John Denham
SoS Wales .... Paul Murphy
Also attending · Chief Whip (House of Lords) .... Baroness Royall
   Minister for the North West .... Beverley Hughes
   Minister for the Olympics & London (Paymaster General) .... Tessa Jowell
   Attorney General .... Baroness Scotland
   Minister for Housing .... Caroline Flint
   Minister for Africa, Asia, & the UN .... Lord Malloch-Brown

The Shadow Cabinet & their portfolios: David Cameron, Leader of the Opposition; Peter Ainsworth, Environment, Food, & Rural Affairs; Baroness Anelay, Opposition Lord's Chief Whip; Alan Duncan, Business, Enterprise, & Regulatory Reform; Liam Fox, Defence; Cheryl Gillan, Wales; Michael Gove, Children, Schools, & Families; Chris Grayling, Work & Pensions; Dominic Grieve, Home Secretary; William Hague, Foreign Sec.; Philip Hammond, Chief Sec. to the Treasury; Nick Herbert, Justice; Jeremy Hunt, Culture, Media & Sport; Andrew Lansley, Health; Oliver Letwin, Policy Review &c.; David Lidington, Foreign Office &c.; Francis Maude, Cabinet Office &c.; Theresa May, Leader of the Commons, & Women; Patrick McLoughlin, Commons Chief Whip; Andrew Mitchell, International Development; David Mundell, Scotland; Baroness Neville-Jones, Security, &c.; George Osborne, Chancellor; Owen Paterson, Northern Ireland; Eric Pickles, Communities & Local Government; Grant Shapps, Housing; Caroline Spelman, Chairman of the Conservative Party; Lord Strathclyde, Leader of the Opposition in the Lords; Theresa Villiers, Transport; Baroness Warsi, Community Cohesion & Social Action; David Willetts, Innovation, Universities & Skills.

MPs' EXPENSES & THE 'JOHN LEWIS LIST'

In January, the Standards & Privileges Cmte ruled that Tory MP Derek Conway should be suspended from the Commons for 10 days after it emerged that he paid his son Frederick c.£40,000 for part-time research work while he was a full-time student in Newcastle. (The Cmte noted that Freddy 'seems to have been all but invisible during the period of his employment'.) Conway apologised to the House and said he would step down at the next election. Although >100 MPs employ members of their family in various positions (most quite properly), all parties, fearful of further scandal, rushed to clarify their internal rules. Speaker Martin announced a 'root and branch' inquiry into the use of public funds, not least the Additional Costs Allowance (ACA). [Under the ACA, MPs can claim up to £22,110 a year for costs incurred while staying away from their main home; receipts are not required on items ≤£250 (£25 from April), or food bills worth ≤£400 a month.] ❦ A swathe of allegations followed, including the inappropriate use of allowances to pay off mortgages, claiming unjustifiable travel expenses, using Air Miles for personal travel, and the refurbishment of homes and gardens at the taxpayer's expense. In March, the Commons was forced to release details of the 'John Lewis list' – an undisclosed table of maximum prices against which MPs' ACA claims were judged. ❦ On 25 June, the Members Estimate Cmte recommended a series of reforms, including ending the ACA and the 'John Lewis list' and introducing external audits, in return for a new annual allowance of £23,800. To some anger, on 3 July, MPs voted (172 votes to 144) to reject these reforms and maintain the status quo – although they did show some restraint, settling for a non-inflation-busting pay rise of 2·5%.

'JOHN LEWIS LIST'	*maximum* £
Air conditioning unit	299·99
Bed	1,000
Bedside cabinet	100
Bookcase/shelf	200
Bookcase/cabinet	500
Carpet	35/m²
Carpet fitting	6·50/m²
Coffee maker/machine	100
Coffee table	250
Dining armchairs (each)	150
Dining chairs (each)	90
Dining table	600
Dishwasher	375
Drawer chest (five)	500
Dressing table	500
Food mixer	200
Freestanding mirror	300
Fridge/freezer combi	550
Gas cooker	650
Hi-fi/stereo	750
New bathroom installation	6,335
New kitchen installation	10,000
Lamp table	200
Nest of tables	200
Recordable DVD	270
Rugs (each)	300
Shredder	50
Sideboard	795
Suite of furniture	2,000
Television set	750
Tumble dryer	250
Underlay (basic)	6·99/m²
Wardrobe	700
Washer dryer	500
Washing machine	350
Wooden flooring/carpets	35/m²
Workstation	150

Personal items (e.g., toiletries) are not claimable, nor is mortgage payment protection or illness cover; to claim mortgage interest, an MP's name must appear on the mortgage; garden furniture such as patio sets and BBQs are not allowed, nor are plants, or other decorations; however, basic garden maintenance is allowed.

──PROSCRIBED TERRORIST GROUPS──

The organisations below are currently proscribed under UK legislation, and are consequently outlawed within the UK. 44 international terrorist organisations are proscribed under the Terrorism Act 2000, of which 2 are proscribed as glorifying terrorism under powers introduced in the Terrorism Act 2006. Additionally, 14 organisations in Northern Ireland are proscribed under previous legislation.

17 November Revolutionary Org. [N17] · formed in 1974 to oppose the Greek military Junta, its stance was initially anti-Junta and anti-US.

Abu Nidal Org. [ANO] · aims to destroy Israel; hostile to states supporting Israel.

Abu Sayyaf Group [ASG] · aims appear to include the establishment of an Islamic state in the S Philippine island of Mindanao.

Al-Gama'at al-Islamiya [GI] · aims to replace the Egyptian government with an Islamic state.

Al Gurabaa · splinter group of Al-Muajiroon that glorifies acts of terrorism.

Al Ittihad Al Islamia [AIAI] · aims to establish a radical Sunni Islamic state in Somalia, and to regain the Ogaden region of Ethiopia as Somalian; suspected of aiding al-Qaeda.

Al-Qaeda · inspired and led by Osama Bin Laden; aims to expel Western forces from Saudi Arabia, destroy Israel, and end Western influence in the Muslim world.

Ansar Al Islam [AI] · opposes the influence of the US in Iraqi Kurdistan and the relationship of the KDP and PUK to Washington.

Ansar Al Sunna [AS] · aims to expel all foreign influences from Iraq and create a fundamentalist Islamic state.

Armed Islamic Group (Groupe Islamique Armée) [GIA] · aims to create an Islamic state in Algeria.

Asbat Al-Ansar (League of Partisans or Band of Helpers) · aims to enforce strict Islamic law within Lebanon and elsewhere.

Babbar Khalsa [BK] · a Sikh movement that aims to establish an independent Khalistan within the Punjab region of India.

Baluchistan Liberation Army [BLA] · seeks an independent nation encompassing the Baluch areas of Pakistan, Afghanistan, and Iran.

Egyptian Islamic Jihad [EIJ] · aims to replace Egyptian government with an Islamic state. Now, also allied to Osama Bin Laden.

Euskadi ta Askatasuna (Basque Homeland and Liberty) [ETA] · seeks the creation of an independent state comprising the Basque regions of both Spain and France.

Groupe Islamique Combattant Marocain [GICM] · aims to replace the governing Moroccan monarchy with a caliphate.

Hamas Izz al-Din al-Qassem Brigades · aims to end Israeli occupation in Palestine.

Harakat-Ul-Jihad-Ul-Islami [HUJI] · fights for accession of Kashmir to Pakistan and aims to spread terror throughout India.

Harakat-Ul-Jihad-Ul-Islami (Bangladesh) [HUJI-B] · aims to create an Islamic regime in Bangladesh.

Harakat-Ul-Mujahideen/Alami [HUM/A] & *Jundallah* · reject all forms of democracy; aim for a caliphate based on Sharia law and accession of all Kashmir to Pakistan.

—————— PROSCRIBED TERRORIST GROUPS cont. ——————

Harakat Mujahideen (HM) · seeks independence for Indian-administered Kashmir.

Hizballah External Security Org. · committed to the 'liberation' of Palestinian territories.

Hezb-E Islami Gulbuddin [HIG] · aims to make Afghanistan an Islamic state.

International Sikh Youth Federation [ISYF] · aims to create an independent state of Khalistan for Sikhs within India.

Islamic Army of Aden [IAA] · aims to replace the Yemeni government with an Islamic state following Sharia law.

Islamic Jihad Union [IJU] · aims to replace the Uzbek regime with an Islamic democracy.

Islamic Movement of Uzbekistan [IMU] · aims to establish an Islamic state in Uzbekistan.

Jaish e Mohammed [JEM] · seeks to remove Indian control of Kashmir.

Jeemah Islamiyah [JI] · aims to create a unified Islamic state in Singapore, Malaysia, Indonesia, and the Southern Philippines.

Khuddam Ul-Islam [KUL] & *Jamaat Ul-Furquan* [JUF] · aim for Pakistani control of Kashmir, an Islamist state in Pakistan; the destruction of India and the USA, &c.

Kongra Gele Kurdistan [PKK] · seeks an independent Kurdish state in SE Turkey.

Lashkar e Tayyaba [LT] · seeks independent Islamic Kashmir.

Liberation Tigers of Tamil Eelam [LTTE] · aims for a separate Tamil state in Sri Lanka.

Tehrik Nefaz-e Shari'at Muhammadi [TNSM] · anti-coalition forces in Afghanistan.

Palestinian Islamic Jihad – Shaqaqi [PIJ] · aims to create an independent Islamic Palestine.

Revolutionary Peoples' Liberation Party – Front (Devrimci Halk Kurtulus Partisi – Cephesi) (DHKP–C) · aims to establish a Marxist–Leninist regime in Turkey.

Teyre Azadiye Kurdistan [TAK] · Kurdish terrorist group operating in Turkey.

Salafist Group for Call and Combat (Groupe Salafiste pour la Prédication et le Combat) [GSPC] · aims to create an Islamic state in Algeria.

Saved Sect or *Saviour Sect* · Al-Muajiroon splinter that glorifies acts of terrorism.

Sipah-E Sahaba Pakistan [SSP], aka *Millat-E Islami Pakistan (MIP), Lashkar-E Jhangvi* [LEJ] · aims to turn Pakistan into a Sunni state under Sharia law.

Libyan Islamic Fighting Group [LIFG] · aims to create an Islamic state in Libya.

Jammat-ul Mujahideen Bangladesh [JMB] · Bangladeshi terror group.

[Removed, June 2008] *Mujaheddin e Khalq* [MEK] · Iranian dissidents based in Iraq.

PROSCRIBED IRISH GROUPS
Continuity Army Council · Cumann na mBan · Fianna na hEireann Irish National Liberation Army Irish People's Liberation Organisation Irish Republican Army · Loyalist Volunteer Force · Orange Volunteers Red Hand Commando · Red Hand Defenders · Saor Eire · Ulster Defence Association · Ulster Freedom Fighters Ulster Volunteer Force

[Source & descriptions: Home Office]

———————————— THE EUROPEAN UNION ————————————

The European Union (EU) has its roots in the European Coal & Steel Community (ECSC), formed in 1951 between Belgium, France, Germany, Italy, Luxembourg, and the Netherlands, who united to co-operate over production of coal and steel: the two key components of war. Since then, through a series of treaties, Europe as an economic and political entity has developed in size, harmonisation, and power. For some, the expansion in EU membership [see below] and the introduction of the euro (in 2002) are welcome developments in securing co-operation and peace; for others, the growth of the EU is a threat to the sovereignty of member nations.

MAJOR EU INSTITUTIONS

European Parliament · the democratic voice of the people of Europe, the EP approves the EU budget; oversees the other EU institutions; assents to key treaties and agreements on accession; and, alongside the Council of Ministers, examines and approves EU legislation. The EP sits in Strasbourg and Brussels, and its members are directly elected every 5 years.

Council of the EU · the pre-eminent decision-making body, the Council is made up of ministers from each national government. The Council meets regularly in Brussels to decide EU policy and approve laws, and every three months Presidents and PMs meet at European Councils to make major policy decisions.

European Commission · proposes new laws for the Council and Parliament to consider, and undertakes much of the EU's day-to-day work, such as overseeing the implementation of EU rules. Commissioners are nominated by each member state, and the President of the Commission is chosen by the national governments. It is based in Brussels.

European Court · ensures EU law is observed and applied fairly, and settles any disputes arising. Each state sends a judge to the Court in Luxembourg.

EU MEMBERSHIP

Country	entry	members
Belgium		
France		
Germany	1952	6
Italy		
Luxembourg		
Netherlands		
Denmark		
Ireland	1973	9
UK		
Greece	1981	10
Portugal	1986	12
Spain		
Austria		
Finland	1995	15
Sweden		
Cyprus		
Czech Rep.		
Estonia		
Hungary		
Latvia		
Lithuania	2004	25
Malta		
Poland		
Slovakia		
Slovenia		
Romania		
Bulgaria	2007	27
Turkey		
Croatia	*in accession talks*	
Serbia		
Bosnia-Hercegovina		
Montenegro	*potential candidates*	
Albania		
Macedonia		

—————————— UK OPINION ON THE EU ——————————

The latest Eurobarometer Survey (Spring 2008) shows just how Eurosceptic the UK is. Charted below are some UK opinions and comparisons with the EU27 average:

Generally speaking, do you think that (our country's) membership of the EU is

%	EU	UK
A good thing	52	30
A bad thing	14	32
Neither good nor bad	29	30
Don't know	5	8

In general, what kind of image does the EU conjure up for you?

%	EU	UK
Very positive	7	4
Fairly positive	41	25
Neutral	35	32
Fairly negative	12	22
Very negative	3	12
Don't know	2	5

Taking everything into account, would you say that (our country) has on balance benefited from being in the EU?

%	EU	UK
Benefited	54	36
Not benefited	31	50
Don't know	15	14

Do you trust these EU institutions?

% who tend to trust	EU	UK
European Parliament	52	27
European Commission	47	24
Council of the EU	43	20

What are the 2 most important issues facing (our country) at the moment?

Issue (%)	EU	UK
Rising prices/inflation	37	19
Unemployment	24	7
Crime	20	38
Economic situation	20	13
Healthcare system	19	15
Pensions	12	9
Immigration	11	35
Taxation	10	12
Housing	9	15
The educational system	8	6
Terrorism	7	13
The environment	5	6
Energy related issues	5	6
Defence/foreign affairs	2	2
Other	2	1

Which of these institutions do you trust?

% who tend to trust	EU	UK
The army	70	82[†]
The police	63	67
Radio	61	55
The United Nations	54	54
Television	53	51
Legal system	46	49
European Union	50	29
Internet	36	28
National parliament	34	27
National government	32	24
Press	44	19
Political parties	18	13

† Only the Finns trust their army more: 92%.

39% of UK citizens claimed to know how the EU works – that said, 39% of those in the UK did not know how many countries were in the EU, and 22% thought that Switzerland was a member (it isn't). These high levels of UK scepticism and ignorance may be explained by the fact that 68% of UK citizens believe the EU imposes its views on their country, compared with the EU27 average of 27%.

─────────────── THE EURO ───────────────

CURRENT CIRCULATION OF THE EURO

OFFICIAL CURRENCY	SPECIAL ARRANGEMENTS
Austria, Belgium, Cyprus, Finland, France, Germany, Greece, Ireland, Italy, Luxembourg, Malta, the Netherlands, Portugal, Spain, Slovenia, Slovakia†	Monaco, Vatican City, San Marino
	OVERSEAS TERRITORIES
	Guadeloupe, French Guiana, Martinique, Mayotte, Réunion,
DE FACTO CURRENCY	Saint Pierre and Miquelon, French
Andorra, Kosovo, Montenegro	Southern & Antarctic Territories

† On 1 January 2009, the euro will become legal tender in Slovakia, replacing the
Slovak koruna (SKK) at the irrevocably fixed exchange rate of €1=SKK 30·1260.
Bulgaria, Czech Republic, Denmark, Estonia, Latvia, Lithuania, Hungary, Poland, Romania,
Slovakia, Sweden and the United Kingdom are EU Member States but do not currently use euros.

Charted below is the value of the euro against the pound and dollar, since 1999:

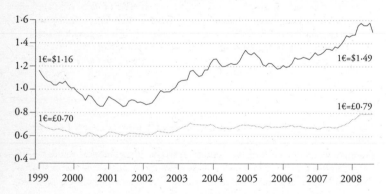

According to the European Central Bank, national central banks in the euro area
will exchange their old national notes 'free of charge either for a very long period of
time (at least ten years) or indefinitely', but 'national coins can only be exchanged,
in most cases, for a few years'. A breakdown of this timetable for exchange is below:

Bank	notes	coins		Bank	notes	coins
Belgium	unlimited	31/12/04		Cyprus	31/12/17	31/12/09
Germany	unlimited	unlimited		Luxembourg	unlimited	31/12/04
Greece	1/3/12	1/3/04		Malta	31/12/18	1/2/10
Spain	unlimited	unlimited		Netherlands	1/1/32	1/1/07
France	17/2/12	17/2/05		Austria	unlimited	unlimited
Ireland	unlimited	unlimited		Portugal	28/2/22	31/12/02
Italy	29/2/12	29/2/12		Slovenia	unlimited	31/12/16
				Finland	29/2/12	29/2/12

———————— NEW COUNTRY GROUPINGS ————————

A profusion of formal country groupings exist across the world – from the UN, the G8, and NATO to OPEC, the Paris Club, and the African Union [see *Schott's Almanac* 2008]. Recently, however, a range of informal terms have been popularised to describe emerging spheres of economic, political, or military influence and power:

BRIC
Brazil, Russia, India, China
*from this group, a number
of terms have developed*
BRIMC = BRIC + Mexico
BRICS = BRIC + South Africa
BRICA = BRIC + the Arab Gulf
Cooperation Council (GCC) states:
Saudi Arabia, Kuwait, UAE,
Oman, Bahrain, and Qatar
BRICET = BRIC + Eastern Europe
and Turkey

G8+5
G8 nations (Canada, France, Germany,
Italy, Japan, Russia, UK, & US)
+ Brazil, China, India, Mexico,
and South Africa

CHINDIA
China and India

FOUR ASIAN TIGERS
Hong Kong, Singapore,
South Korea, and Taiwan

EU8+2
recent EU members [see p.268]
Czech Republic, Estonia, Hungary,
Latvia, Lithuania, Poland, Slovakia,
and Slovenia + Bulgaria and Romania

NEXT ELEVEN (N-11)
Bangladesh, Egypt, Indonesia,
Iran, Mexico, Nigeria, Pakistan,
Philippines, Turkey,
Vietnam, and South Korea

———————— THE COMMONWEALTH ————————

The Commonwealth of Nations is a voluntary association of 53 sovereign states – all of which, excepting Mozambique, have experienced British rule. The Commonwealth has no formal constitution; its goal is to promote 'democracy and good governance, respect for human rights and gender equality, the rule of law, and sustainable economic and social development'. The Commonwealth Nations are:

Antigua & Barbuda* · Australia* · Bahamas* · Bangladesh · Barbados*
Belize* · Botswana · Brunei Darussalam · Cameroon · Canada* · Cyprus
Dominica · Fiji Islands† · The Gambia · Ghana · Grenada* · Guyana · India
Jamaica* · Kenya · Kiribati · Lesotho · Malawi · Malaysia · Maldives · Malta
Mauritius · Mozambique · Namibia · Nauru · New Zealand* · Nigeria · Pakistan
Papua New Guinea* · St Kitts & Nevis* · St Lucia* · St Vincent* · Samoa
Seychelles · Sierra Leone · Singapore · Solomon Islands* · South Africa
Sri Lanka · Swaziland · Tanzania · Tonga · Trinidad & Tobago
Tuvalu* · Uganda · United Kingdom · Vanuatu · Zambia

In December 2003, Zimbabwe withdrew its membership after its suspension was not lifted.
* The Queen is not only Queen of the UK and its overseas territories, but also of these realms.
† Fiji's military regime was suspended from the Councils of the Commonwealth on 8·12·06.

Establishment & Faith

A king is a thing men have made for their own sakes, for quietness' sake.
Just as in a family one man is appointed to buy the meat.
— JOHN SELDEN (1584–1654)

THE SOVEREIGN

ELIZABETH II
by the Grace of God, of the United Kingdom of Great Britain
and Northern Ireland and of her other Realms and Territories Queen,
Head of the Commonwealth, Defender of the Faith

Born at 17 Bruton Street, London W1, on 21 April 1926, at *c.*2·40am
Ascended the throne, 6 February 1952 · Crowned, 2 June 1953

OLDEST & LONGEST REIGNING BRITISH MONARCHS

At 5pm on 22/12/07, Elizabeth II became Britain's oldest reigning monarch, surpassing her great-great-grandmother. Britain's three oldest reigning monarchs are:

Monarch	born	died	longevity
Elizabeth II	21/4/1926	—	currently 82y
Victoria	24/5/1819	22·01·1901	81y 7m 29d
George III	04/6/1738	29·01·1820	81y 7m 25d

On 5 March 2008, Queen Elizabeth II overtook Henry III (who reigned for 56 years, 1216–72) to become the third longest reigning monarch in 1,000 years of British history. In 2012, Elizabeth II will surpass George III (who reigned for 59 years, 1760–1820), and on 9 September 2015 she could become Britain's longest reigning monarch by overtaking Queen Victoria, who reigned for nearly 64 years (1837–1901).

ORDER OF SUCCESSION

The Prince of Wales · Prince William of Wales · Prince Henry of Wales
The Duke of York · Princess Beatrice of York · Princess Eugenie of York
The Earl of Wessex · The Lady Louise Windsor · The Princess Royal
Mr Peter Phillips · Miss Zara Phillips · Viscount Linley [&c...]

The eldest son of the monarch is heir to the throne followed by his heirs. After whom come any other sons of the monarch and their heirs, followed by any daughters of the monarch and their heirs. Roman Catholics are barred from succession under the Act of Settlement (1701).

PRINCE HARRY IN AFGHANISTAN

From the time Prince Harry joined the army in May 2005, and especially after he graduated from Sandhurst in April 2006, intense speculation surrounded whether he would see active service. In May 2007, Chief of the General Staff General Sir Richard Dannatt ordered that Harry would not serve in S Iraq, saying, 'There have been a number of specific threats, some reported and some not reported. These threats exposed him and those around him to a degree of risk I considered unacceptable'. Some of the reported threats included rumours that the insurgency considered Harry 'the mother of all targets', and that he had been nicknamed 'the bullet magnet' because of the threat his presence posed to his fellow soldiers. Dannatt also hinted at the role that media speculation had played: 'I have to add that a contributing factor ... has been the widespread knowledge and discussion of his deployment'. However, on 28 February 2008 it emerged that Harry had been serving for 10 weeks in the S Afghan province of Helmand.

To the chagrin of Buckingham Palace and the British media, who had negotiated a strict embargo, the story was broken by the US news website Drudge Report, after which it hit front pages across the world. (It later emerged that an Australian magazine had first printed the scoop.) The press then rushed to report that since late December, Harry had served as a battlefield air controller, coordinating air attacks on the Taliban. 'Widow Six Seven', as he was known to pilots, was the first Royal to take part in military action since Prince Andrew served in the Falklands War. Within hours of the news breaking, Harry had been withdrawn back to Britain, expressing disappointment that his service had ended. ❦ Prince William was slightly embarrassed by a series of helicopter escapades in 2008, including landing his Chinook on the lawn of his girlfriend Kate Middleton. In June, William began a 2-month Royal Navy deployment aboard HMS *Iron Duke* in the W Indies on hurricane-relief duty and counter-narcotics patrol. In July, the *Iron Duke*'s crew seized a haul of cocaine in the West Indies valued at *c*.£40m.

THE UNION FLAG

Government buildings are obliged to fly the Union Flag on these days:

BD Countess of Wessex	20 Jan
Queen's Accession	6 Feb
BD Duke of York	19 Feb
St David's Day (Wales)	1 Mar
Commonwealth Day	13 Mar
BD Earl of Wessex	10 Mar
BD The Queen	21 Apr
St George's Day (England)	23 Apr
Europe Day	9 May
Coronation Day	2 Jun
BD Duke of Edinburgh	10 Jun
Official BD The Queen	13 Jun
BD Duchess of Cornwall	17 Jul
BD The Princess Royal	15 Aug
Remembrance Day	11 Nov
BD Prince of Wales	14 Nov
Queen's Wedding Day	20 Nov
St Andrew's Day (Scotland)	30 Nov

Also, the Opening & Prorogation of Parliament

On the days listed above, the Union Flag should be flown from 8am to sunset.

─────────── ROYAL FAMILY ENGAGEMENTS · 2007 ───────────

Mr Tim O'Donovan annually compiles a list of official engagements undertaken by the Royal family during the year – as reported in the pages of the Court Circular – which is subsequently published as a letter to *The Times*. Below is 2007's listing:

	Official visits, openings, &c	Receptions, lunches, dinners, &c	Other, e.g., investitures, meetings	Total official engagements UK	Total official engagements abroad
The Queen	97	63	233	393	47
Duke of Edinburgh	147	137	50	334	46
Prince of Wales	161	84	164	409	89
Duchess of Cornwall	76	33	16	125	68
Duke of York	104	84	76	264	292
Earl of Wessex	140	58	25	223	139
Countess of Wessex	74	38	27	139	8
Princess Royal	285	89	88	462	151
Duke of Gloucester	156	41	30	227	102
Duchess of Gloucester	79	31	15	125	21
Duke of Kent	136	27	15	178	47
Princess Alexandra	67	27	19	113	7

─────────────── ROYAL CONGRATULATIONS ───────────────

The tradition of sending messages of royal congratulations to subjects on certain auspicious days was inaugurated in 1917 by George V, who sent telegrams to those celebrating their 60th wedding anniversary or 100th birthday. Nowadays, on request, the Queen sends congratulatory cards, via the Royal Mail, to citizens of her Realms or UK Overseas Territories, on the following celebratory occasions:

WEDDING ANNIVERSARIES	BIRTHDAYS
60th, 65th, & 70th anniversaries and then every year thereafter	100th & 105th birthdays and then every year thereafter

─────────────── HOTTEST YOUNG ROYALS ───────────────

Forbes magazine placed Prince William at the top of its 'Hottest Young Royals' list in May 2008. Only unmarried royals under 35 were considered; they were rated on 'winning combinations of looks, money, and popularity on the web'. The top ten:

1	Prince William	6	Sheikh Hamdam (UAE)
2	Prince Harry	7	Princess Victoria (Sweden)
3	Zara Phillips	8	Prince Azim (Brunei)
4	Princess Beatrice	9	Prince Carl Philip (Sweden)
5	Charlotte Casiraghi (Monaco)	10	Andrea Casiraghi (Monaco)

─────── MAUNDY THURSDAY & MAUNDY MONEY───────

In the Christian liturgical calendar, Maundy Thursday is the day in Holy Week prior to Good Friday; its name derives from the Latin *mandatum* [command] and from Jesus' exhortation to his disciples at the Last Supper, after he had washed their feet:

Mandatum novum do vobis ut diligatis invicem sicut dilexi vos (John xiii. 34)
A new commandment I give unto you, That ye love one another

The charitable (and self-abasing) ritual of foot washing – often accompanied by more practical alms of clothing, food, or money – was adopted by ecclesiastics, aristocrats, and monarchs from at least AD 700. It seems that the first English sovereign to perform Maundy charity (including foot washing) was King John (1199–1216) after he was excommunicated by Pope Innocent III in 1209. English monarchs have dispensed largesse to the poor since then, although the nitty-gritty of foot washing fell out of royal favour in *c.*1730. Since Henry IV, the number of recipients has matched the sovereign's age (under John the number was always 13; Edward III linked it to the length of his reign). And, until the C18th, all recipients had to be the same sex as the sovereign. Nowadays, the Queen distributes (essentially symbolic) charity to men and women who have given distinguished service to Church and community. Her gift is presented in two leather purses: a red one that holds an allowance in ordinary money in lieu of food &c.; and a white one that holds specially minted silver Maundy coins [1p, 2p, 3p, 4p] to the value of the Queen's age. (The coins are legal tender, but are usually kept or sold to collectors.) ❦ In 2008, the Queen deviated from tradition by attending the first Royal Maundy service held outside England or Wales. To mark the end of her three-day visit to Northern Ireland, the Queen dispensed 328 Maundy purses [i.e., (82×2)×2] at St Patrick's Church of Ireland Cathedral, in Armagh.

─────────── ROYAL FINANCES ───────────

The Queen receives income from public funds to meet expenditure that relates to her duties as Head of State and the Commonwealth. This derives from 4 sources:

Source (year ending 31 March)	2007	2008
The Queen's Civil List	£12·2m	£12·7m
Parliamentary Annuities	£0·4m	£0·4m
Grants-in-Aid	£20·6m	£22·0m
Expenditure met directly by Government Departments and the Crown Estate	£4·8m	£4·9m
TOTAL	£38·0m	£40·0m

The cost of the monarchy to the UK taxpayer in 2008 was the equivalent of 66p per person, an increase of 4p since 2007. It was revealed in 2008 that there were insufficient funds in the Royal coffers to cover the £32m needed to carry out essential works on Royal palaces. The budget for maintaining Buckingham Palace, Windsor Castle, &c. has been frozen at £15m for the next three years.

—————— THE QUEEN'S CHRISTMAS BROADCAST · 2007 ——————

'One of the features of growing old is a heightened awareness of change. To remember what happened 50 years ago means that it is possible to appreciate what has changed in the meantime. It also makes you aware of what has remained constant. In my experience, the positive value of a happy family is one of the factors of human existence that has not changed. The immediate family of grandparents, parents and children, together with their extended family, is still the core of a thriving community. ... Now today, of course, marks the birth of Jesus Christ. Among other things, it is a reminder that it is the story of a family; but of a family in very distressed circumstances. Mary and Joseph found no room at the inn; they had to make do in a stable, and the new-born Jesus had to be laid in a manger. This was a family which had been shut out. ... The Christmas story also draws attention to all those people who are on the edge of society – people who feel cut off and disadvantaged; people who, for one reason or another, are not able to enjoy the full benefits of living in a civilised and law-abiding community. For these people the modern world can seem a distant and hostile place. It is all too easy to 'turn a blind eye', 'to pass by on the other side', and leave it to experts and professionals. All the great religious teachings of the world press home the message that everyone has a responsibility to care for the vulnerable. Fortunately, there are many groups and individuals, often unsung and unrewarded, who are dedicated to ensuring that the 'outsiders' are given a chance to be recognised and respected. However, each one of us can also help by offering a little time, a talent or a possession, and taking a share in the responsibility for the well-being of those who feel excluded. ... We have all been conscious of those who have given their lives, or who have been severely wounded, while serving with the Armed Forces in Iraq and Afghanistan. The dedication of the National Armed Forces Memorial was also an occasion to remember those who have suffered while serving in these and every other place of unrest since the end of the Second World War. For their families, Christmas will bring back sad memories, and I pray that all of you, who are missing those who are dear to you, will find strength and comfort in your families and friends. ... Wherever these words find you, and in whatever circumstances, I want to wish you all a blessed Christmas.'

The Christmas story also draws attention to all those people who are on the edge of society

[The message was made available online via the Royal family's channel on YouTube.]

When the Queen's Christmas broadcast is entered into Microsoft Word's 'Auto Summarise' feature and is condensed down to two sentences, the result is:

The immediate family of grandparents, parents and children, together with their extended family, is still the core of a thriving community. Among other things, it is a reminder that it is the story of a family; but of a family in very distressed circumstances.

GREAT BRITISH ICONS

Below are some of the icons that have been used over the years to represent or personify Great Britain:

BRITANNIA · The figure of Britannia was first used as the eponymous heroine of Roman Britain; her earliest known images are found on Roman coins struck in the time of Hadrian (AD 117–138). In 1672, Charles II reintroduced Britannia onto copper coins; as in Roman times, she was pictured sitting on a rock, wearing a helmet, with an olive branch in her right hand, a spear (later a trident) in her left, and a shield adorned with the Union Flag beside her – this became the enduring image of Britannia. Since the success of Thomas Arne's rousing song *Rule, Britannia* (first performed in 1740), Britannia is frequently shown looking out across the seas. Currently she can be found on 50 pence pieces styled traditionally but with a lion at her side.

JOHN BULL · The political satirist Dr John Arbuthnot (1667–1735) created this personification of England in his 1712 pamphlet, *The History of John Bull*. Arbuthnot described his character as 'ruddy and plump, with a pair of cheeks like a trumpeter'. Cartoonists soon adopted the honest but irascible Bull as the typical Englishman, and he was regularly depicted as a stout country man, in a Union Jack waistcoat.

THE BRITISH BULLDOG · Originally bred for bull-baiting, these squat and sturdy dogs later came to represent the Churchillian spirit of Britain. In a 1914 speech, Churchill famously compared the British Navy to a bulldog: 'the nose of the bulldog has been turned backwards so that he can breathe without letting go'. The cussed,

loyal, and stubborn bulldog buttoned in a Union Jack coat was often used in WWII propaganda, forever linking the canine to British patriotism.

MR PUNCH · The genealogy of this anarchic puppet dates to C16th Italian *commedia dell'arte* in which the 'lord of misrule' was Pulcinella – later Anglicised as Mr Punch. (Samuel Pepys diarised seeing an early Punch & Judy show in Covent Garden on 9 May 1662, a date that has since been celebrated as the birth of the British Punch.) The long-nosed, black-masked Italian character soon evolved into the recognisably more British Mr Punch, with his still large but now hooked nose, hunched back, squeaky voice, and predilection for violence. Most often associated with seaside puppet shows, Mr Punch (despite his murderous, wife-beating, police-assaulting ways) came to represent a caricature of the British working class.

THE LION · Richard the Lionheart was the first English king to place on his banner the Angevin symbol of the three lions. By 1603, when James VI united the crowns of England and Scotland, the three lions became the emblem for the United Kingdom. Since then, the lion has most commonly been used in a sporting context: three lions adorn the badges of the England football team and the England and Wales Cricket Board. The brave spirit of the British lion is also used to represent the British & Irish combined Rugby Union side.

A host of characters have been used to represent nations around the world. Some notable icons include: Uncle Sam, USA · Mother Russia, Russia · Athena, Greece · Germania, Germany.

———————— WHO'S NEW IN WHO'S WHO ————————

Published annually since 1849, *Who's Who* is one of the world's most respected biographical reference books. Below are some of the 1,200 new entries in the 2008 *Who's Who* (those who have died during the year enter the companion *Who Was Who*):

Yasmin Alibhai-Brown.......*journalist*
Lisa Armstrong.......*fashion journalist*
Nihal Arthanayake.....*DJ & journalist*
Alison Balsom................*trumpeter*
Muhammad Bari.......................
   Secretary General, Muslim Council
Samantha Bond ....*actress*
William Burdett-Coutts.....*impresario*
John Burton Race...................*chef*
Reeta Chakrabarti.......*BBC journalist*
Alina Cojocaru............*ballet dancer*
Sarah Connolly ....*opera singer*
Ray Dolan.................*neuroscientist*
Domenico Dolce.......*fashion designer*
Marcus du Sautoy.......*mathematician*
Jonathan Evans..*Director General, MI5*
Stefano Gabbana.......*fashion designer*
Fiona Glover ....*BBC journalist*
Jacqueline Gold.................*retailer*
Oleg Gordievsky.................*writer*
Richard Hammond.......*TV presenter*
Ann Henderson-Sellers...*meteorologist*
Eamonn Holmes..........*TV presenter*
Armando Iannucci. *writer & comedian*
Dylan Jones ....*GQ editor*
Bernard Kouchner ....
  French Foreign Secretary, MSF founder
Damian Lewis.....................*actor*
Ottoline Leyser ....*plant biologist*
Giorgio Locatelli....................*chef*
Nicholas 'Rodney' Lyndhurst ....*actor*

Robert Lindsay (Stevenson) ......*actor*
Emily Maitlis............*BBC journalist*
Stella McCartney ......*fashion designer*
Patrick McGrath ....*novelist*
William McGuire.......................
   geophysical hazard expert
Angela Merkel......*German Chancellor*
Kate Moss........................*model*
Pervez Musharraf.. *Pakistani politician*
Rufus Norris ....*theatre director*
Nigel (Sam) Neill ....*actor*
Ehud Olmert................*Israeli PM*
Michael Owen ....*footballer*
Jane Packer........................*florist*
Miuccia Prada..........*fashion designer*
James Reynolds ....*journalist*
David Rowan .. *Jewish Chronicle editor*
Dominic Rudd.........*Chief Executive,*
   The Samaritans
Mortimer Sackler ....*philanthropist*
Emma Sergeant ....*painter*
László Sólyom.....*Hungarian President*
Mario Testino ....*photographer*
Luc Tuymans...................*painter*
Donatella Versace ......*fashion designer*
David Wark ....*particle physicist*
(Susan) Sigourney Weaver.......*actress*
Kevin '*Lewis!*' Whately ....*actor*
Geoffrey Wheatcroft.........*journalist*
Tom Wilkinson ....*actor*
Toby Young ....*journalist*

A few recreations – LISA ARMSTRONG 'reading, riding, needlepoint, finding places to put finished needlepoint' · PROFESSOR BRIAN AVERY 'cursing inefficiency of the National Health Service' · CHRISTOPHER BILSLAND 'taking credit for children's achievements' · STEPHEN DYSON 'drinking real ale, eating pork scratchings, learning from mistakes' · MARK FRITH 'finding things to read in other people's recycling bins, Dostoyevsky (not really!)' · CLAIRE HICKMAN 'literature, music, finding silver linings' · MARK LEVER 'negotiating peace settlements and behaviour-related pay with my four sons' · JOHN MOORE 'plankton wrangling' · RUFUS NORRIS 'talking incessantly to myself in extreme dialects' · DAVID TUFFIN 'concocting out of office auto-reply messages for my email'

SOME HONOURS OF NOTE · 2008

New Year Honours

CH
Sir Ian McKellen.................actor

KNIGHT BACHELOR
Michael Parkinson........broadcaster
Stuart Rose.........Chief Exec. M&S
Professor Ian Wilmut.........scientist

DBE
Jacqueline Wilson...............writer

CBE
Brendan Foster............. sportsman
Hanif Kureishi.....playwright, author
Leslie Phillips.....................actor
Charles Saumarez Smith..Nat. Gallery
Stanley Tracey.......pianist, composer
Julie Walters......................actor

OBE
John Akomfrah ....director
George Alagiah............broadcaster
Jazzie B........................musician
Barbara Broccoli.........film producer
Jasper Conran..................designer
Roy Dotrice......................actor
Romy Fraser................ Neal's Yard
Rachael Heyhoe-Flint.........cricketer
Richard Griffiths.................actor
Des Lynam.........sports broadcaster
Karen Millen....................retailer
Kylie Minogue...................singer
Jason Robinson ....rugby player
Gordon Taylor ....footballer
Peter Vansittart.................author
Alison Watt ....artist

MBE
Ian Anderson........ singer, songwriter
Brian Ashton.............. rugby coach
Antoni Burakowski............designer
Debjani Chatterjee........poet, author
Errol Douglas ....hairdresser
John Higgins...........snooker player

Queen's Birthday Honours

CH
Lord Richard Rogers.........architect

CMG
Michael Apted............film director

KNIGHT BACHELOR
Mark Elder............Hallé Orchestra
Paul Stephenson ....Met. Police

DBE
Joan Bakewell..............broadcaster
Clara Furse.Chief Exec. Ldn Stk Exch
Margaret Drabble.................writer

CBE
Bill Beaumont.............rugby player
Jo Calzaghe.......................boxer
Lynda La Plante..................writer
Michael Nyman..............composer
Des O'Connor.............broadcaster
Gerald Scarfe.................cartoonist
Victoria Wood ....comedian

OBE
Malorie Blackman ....writer
Lawrence Dallaglio ....rugby player
Russell T. Davies..........screenwriter
Chiwetel Ejiofor ....actor
Eve Pollard ....broadcaster
Janet McTeer......................actor
Don Paterson ....poet
John Surtees............... motorsport
Anna Wintour ......fashion journalist

MBE
Wale Adeyemi..................designer
June Brown.......................actor
Justin Fletcher............TV presenter
David Healy..................footballer
Neil Mantle .... conductor
Paul O'Grady ....comedian
Saleem Arif Quadri..............artist
Kelly Smith ....footballer

─────────── ON FORMS OF DIPLOMACY ───────────

MADMAN DIPLOMACY involves deliberately presenting oneself as irrational, unstable and dangerous in order to intimidate one's opponents and/or conceal a weak position. It was famously used by Richard Nixon, who attempted to persuade the N Vietnamese and Russians that he would 'do anything', including using nukes, to halt the war. Since then, Nikita Khrushchev, Saddam Hussein, Fidel Castro, Vladimir Putin, Mahmoud Ahmadinejad, Kim Jong-il, and even George W. Bush have been accused of madman diplomacy.

BLADDER DIPLOMACY was a tactic of President Assad of Syria, who would speak to foreign politicians and diplomats at inordinate length while relentlessly plying them with drinks.

DOLLAR DIPLOMACY (or ECONOMIC IMPERIALISM) involves the imposition of economic influence over other countries and the use of political influence (and ultimately force) to protect overseas investments. Although a host of powers through history have exercised such influence (and still do), the phrase is usually associated with William Taft's presidency (1909–13), when the US sought control over Latin America and E Asia by guaranteeing loans.

MEGAPHONE DIPLOMACY involves the public statement of demands in place of actual negotiation. Usually these demands are not backed by a credible threat of force – either because no capability for force exists, or because there is insufficient desire to exercise it.

MORAL DIPLOMACY is premised either on a (self-defined) moral code, or the moral authority of an individual. The former was somewhat unsuccessfully advocated by Woodrow Wilson, who declared 'no nation is fit to sit in judgement upon any other nation'. Examples of *personal* moral diplomacy include a host of intercessions by various popes, and the Elders – a group of freelance moral diplomats whose members include Desmond Tutu, Kofi Annan, Nelson Mandela, Mary Robinson, and Aung San Suu Kyi.

CULINARY DIPLOMACY is the use of food and drink to lubricate negotiations and to disseminate information about a culture through its cuisine. It is no accident that state banquets are opulent and lavish, nor that they invariably showcase national dishes and indigenous produce. (When George W. Bush hosted a dinner for Queen Elizabeth II in May 2007, much was made of the President foregoing his Tex-Mex favourites for a banquet featuring US caviar and Napa Valley wines.) ❦ At its most brutal, culinary diplomacy involves halting food exports, blockading food imports, or supplying food by force (e.g., the Berlin airlift or the Iraqi oil for food programme). Recent agflation suggests that states with excess food may see their diplomatic stock rise. And, as Cyclone Nargis has shown, the importance of food in the wake of disasters cannot be overestimated [see p.32].

The essence of PANDA DIPLOMACY is twofold: [a] giant pandas are adored universally; and [b] China has a giant panda monopoly. Since the Tang dynasty (618–907), when Japan was presented with 2 of the species, China has been using *Ailuropoda melanoleuca* to spread goodwill. The zenith of modern panda diplomacy was 1972, when the Sino-American summit was sealed by China's gift of 2 pandas to the US; similar gifts followed to Japan,

———————— ON FORMS OF DIPLOMACY cont. ————————

France, Britain, Mexico, Spain, and Germany. However, in 2006, Taiwan rejected China's offer of 2 pandas, citing 'ecological concerns' – but it seems that Taiwan was fearful that accepting a *transfer* of these 'Trojan pandas' would strengthen China's claim to the island.

In 2003, George W. Bush identified the BUSH DOCTRINE as one 'defined by action, as opposed to by words'. In 2006, *Time* concluded that Bush's post-9/11 stance on geopolitics ('Either you are with us, or you are with the terrorists') was dead, and declared 'the end of COWBOY DIPLOMACY'.

PING PONG DIPLOMACY dates to 1971, when the US table tennis team became the first Americans to enter China since 1949. Nixon capitalised on this sporting encounter to facilitate his historic visit to the country in 1972. Examples of SPORTING DIPLOMACY have been seen throughout history, from the jousting and archery on the Field of the Cloth of Gold in 1520 to the part a sports boycott of South Africa played in the collapse of apartheid. The diplomacy that preceded Beijing's hosting of the Olympics was often fraught – with some calling for a boycott, comparing the Chinese games to 'Hitler's Olympics' in 1936.

MEDICAL DIPLOMACY seeks to exploit a superiority in medical resources for political gain. The US Surgeon General boasted, 'America's compassion and generosity to use our medical expertise and financial resources can be a powerful instrument in spreading hope, health, dignity, *and democracy* to many nations around the world' [emphasis added]. Yet, medical diplomacy is not a tool exclusive to major powers. Since

the 1959 revolution, Cuba has punched above its weight with a programme of DOCTOR DIPLOMACY. By exporting medical personnel to at least 68 countries, Castro has ameliorated relations with foreign governments and drawn political and economic assistance into Cuba. Recently, Hugo Chávez has emulated Castro's policy by offering free eye surgery to Latin America's poor.

The NY Philharmonic Orchestra's 2008 performance in Pyongyang was hailed as a landmark in relations with N Korea, and decried as a 'disgrace'. Either way, it was a fine illustration of CULTURAL DIPLOMACY which, through the years, has also been described variously as CONCERT, ART, MUSICAL, VIOLIN, or ORCHESTRA DIPLOMACY. ❦ Like its culinary counterpart, CULTURAL DIPLOMACY seeks to soften the hard edges of geopolitics, using the creative arts as a way of spanning international divides – from reciprocal gift-giving between sovereigns to state-sponsored cultural programmes. (Bona fide cultural diplomacy is often not helped by the tendency of governments to use it as cover for espionage; often the diplomatic title 'Cultural Attaché' is so transparent a cover for intelligence gathering as to be risible.) ❦ Cultural diplomacy can easily slip into cultural imperialism – or worse. After the 2003 invasion of Iraq, many questioned why Allied troops literally stood by while the country's treasures were looted. Donald Rumsfeld famously dismissed the episode with two words: 'Stuff happens'. But not everyone was convinced that the failure to protect Iraq's antiquities was an oversight. If a country is defined by its cultural identity, then allowing that identity to be sacked may be useful. As Simon Jenkins observed, 'Even the Nazis protected the Louvre'.

—— AN ELEMENTARY GUIDE TO FORMS OF ADDRESS ——

Personage	envelope	start of letter	verbal address
The Queen	The Queen's Most Excellent Majesty†	Madam/May it please your Majesty	Your Majesty/Ma'am
The Duke of Edinburgh	HRH The Duke of Edinburgh†	Sir	Your Royal Highness/Sir
The Queen Mother	Her Majesty Queen —— The Queen Mother†	Madam	Your Majesty/Ma'am
Royal Prince	HRH The Prince —— (The Prince of ——)†	Sir	Your Royal Highness/Sir
Royal Princess	HRH The Princess (of) ——†	Your Royal Highness	Your Royal Highness/Madam
Royal Duke	HRH The Duke of ——†	Your Royal Highness	Your Royal Highness/Sir
Royal Duchess	HRH The Duchess of ——†	Your Royal Highness	Your Royal Highness/Madam
Duke	His Grace the Duke of ——	My Lord Duke/Dear Duke	Your Grace/Duke
Duchess	Her Grace the Duchess of ——	Dear Madam/Dear Duchess	Your Grace/Duchess
Marquess	The Most Honourable The Marquess of ——	My Lord/Dear Lord	My Lord/Lord
Marchioness	The Most Honourable The Marchioness of ——	Madam/Dear Lady	Madam/Lady
Earl	The Rt Hon. The Earl of ——	My Lord/Dear Lord	My Lord/Lord
Earl's wife	The Rt Hon. The Countess of ——	Madam/Dear Lady	Madam/Lady
Countess	The Rt Hon. The Countess of ——	Madam/Dear Lady	Madam/Lady
Viscount	The Rt Hon. The Viscount ——	My Lord/Dear Lord	Lord
Viscount's wife	The Rt Hon. The Viscountess ——	Madam/Dear Lady	Lady
Baron	The Rt Hon. Lord ——	My Lord/Dear Lord	Lord
Baron's wife	The Rt Hon. Lady ——	My Lady/Dear Lady	Lady
Baroness	The Rt Hon. The Lady (*or* The Baroness) ——	My Lady/Dear Lady	Madam/Lady
Baronet	Sir Bertie Wooster Bt (*or* Bart) ——	Dear Sir Bertie	Sir Bertie
Baronet's wife	Lady ——	Dear Madam/Dear Lady	Lady
Knight of an Order	Sir Bertie Wooster (*and order*) ——	Dear Sir Bertie	Sir Bertie
Knight Bachelor	Sir Bertie Wooster ——	Dear Sir Bertie	Sir Bertie
Knight's wife	Lady ——	Dear Madam/Dear Lady	Lady
Dame	Dame ——	Dear Madam/Dear Dame	Dame

— AN ELEMENTARY GUIDE TO FORMS OF ADDRESS cont. —

Personage	envelope	start of letter	verbal address
Life Peer	The Rt Hon. Lord —— (of ——)	My Lord/Dear Lord ——	Lord ——
Life Peeress	The Rt Hon. The Lady (or Baroness) —— (of ——)	My Lady/Dear Lady ——	Lady ——
Archbishop	The Most Rev. & Rt Hon. the Lord Archbishop of ——	Dear Archbishop	Your Grace/Archbishop
Bishop	((The Rt Rev.) (and Right Hon.)) The Bishop of ——	Dear Bishop	Bishop
Lord Chancellor	The Rt Hon. The Lord Chancellor	by rank	by rank
Prime Minister	The Rt Hon. The Prime Minister PC MP	Dear Prime Minister	Prime Minister/Sir
Deputy PM	The Rt Hon. The Deputy Prime Minister PC MP	Dear Deputy Prime Minister	Deputy Prime Minister/Sir
Chancellor of the Exchequer	The Rt Hon. The Chancellor of the Exchequer PC MP	Dear Chancellor	Chancellor/Sir
Foreign Secretary	The Rt Hon. The SoS for Foreign & Comwth Affairs	Dear Foreign Secretary	Foreign Secretary/by rank
Home Secretary	The Rt Hon. The SoS for the Home Department	Dear Home Secretary	Home Secretary/by rank
Secretary of State	The Rt Hon. The SoS for ——	Dear Secretary of State	Secretary of State/by rank
Minister	(The Rt Hon.) Bertie Wooster Esq. (PC) MP	Dear Minister	Minister/by rank
MP†	Bertie Wooster Esq MP	Dear Mr Wooster	Mr Wooster
MP Privy Councillor	The Rt Hon. Bertie Wooster PC MP	Dear Mr Wooster	Mr Wooster
Privy Councillor	The Rt Hon. Bertie Wooster PC	Dear Mr Wooster	Mr Wooster
High Court Judge	The Hon. Mr Justice ——	Dear Sir —— /Dear Judge	Sir/My Lord/Your Lordship
Ambassador (British)	His Excellency —— HM Ambassador to ——	by rank	Your Excellency
Lord Mayor	The Rt Hon. the Lord Mayor of ——	My (Dear) Lord Mayor	Lord Mayor
Mayor	The Worshipful Mayor of ——	(Dear) Mr Mayor	Mr Mayor

It is hard to overstate the complexity of 'correct' form which (especially in the legal and clerical fields, as well as chivalry) can become extremely rococo, and is the subject of considerable dispute between sources. Consequently, the above tabulation can only hope to provide a very elementary guide. ❦ Readers interested in the correct formal styling of the wives of younger sons of earls, for example, are advised to consult specialist texts on the subject. † It is usual to address correspondence to members of the Royal family in the first instance to their Private Secretary. ‡ A similar styling is used for Members of the European Parliament [MEP]; Scottish Parliament [MSP]; National Assembly for Wales [AM]; and Northern Ireland Assembly [MLA]. From the moment Parliament is dissolved there are no Members of Parliament, and consequently the letters MP should not be used. By convention medical doctors are styled Dr ——, whereas surgeons use the title Mr ——; many gynaecologists, although surgeons, are styled Dr ——.

—— JURY SUMMONS FOR CROWN & CIVIL COURTS——

Crown & civil courts, England & Wales	*2002/03*	*2006/07*
Total number of summons issued	486,890	393,880
Total number of jurors who served	197,340	181,100
Deferred to serve at a later date	74,470	71,730
Refused deferral	296	162
Excused by right of having served in past 2 yrs	29,250	4,410
Excused for other reasons†	134,120	97,460
Refused excusal	2,010	1,840
Disqualified – residency, mental disorders, criminality	101,710	87,260
Disqualified – aged >70 at selection	59,010	54,170
Disqualified – failed police national computer check	151	190
Failed to reply to summons	47,990	38,360
Summons undelivered	23,620	18,950
Postponed by Jury Central Summoning Bureau	12,300	5,640

† Including childcare, work commitments, medical, language difficulty, being a student, having moved from area, travel difficulties, financial hardship, &c. [Source: HM Courts Service, 2008]

—————— JURY SERVICE ——————

To be ELIGIBLE for jury service you must be: older than 18 and younger than 70 on the day your service is to start; a registered parliamentary or local government elector; and you must have lived in the United Kingdom, the Channel Islands, or the Isle of Man for any period of at least 5 years since you were 13 years old.

INELIGIBLE individuals include: those on bail or involved in criminal proceedings; those sentenced to life imprisonment; those who have in the previous 10 years served any part of a sentence of imprisonment or had passed on them a suspended sentence of imprisonment; and those with mental disorders.

Individuals may request DEFERRAL of service to another date within 12 months (if, for example, the date clashes with an examination), or EXCUSAL from the summons (if, for example, they do not speak English). Jurors may claim for loss of earnings, travel costs, and daily subsistence, based upon these current rates:

Loss of earnings (max.).....£61·28 for first 10 days; £122·57 for subsequent days
General subsistence rate...£5·39 per day

—————— LAW TERMS · 2009 ——————

The legal year is traditionally divided into four terms. The law terms in 2009 are:

HILARY.................12 Jan – 8 Apr	TRINITY.................2 Jul – 31 Jul
EASTER..............21 Apr – 22 May	MICHAELMAS ....1 Oct – 21 Dec

MAGNA CARTA

In December 2007, the only copy of the Magna Carta still in private hands was sold for $21·32m (£10·6m)[†] at Sotheby's in New York. The document was purchased by David Rubenstein, founder of the Carlyle Group, who pledged that it would go back on public display at the National Archives in Washington. ❦ The Magna Carta is often regarded as the original bill of rights and a cornerstone of English liberty – though its name ('Great Charter') refers only to its unusual length and not its political significance at the time. The charter's preamble and 63 clauses were an attempt by a group of medieval noblemen to impose limits on the feudal powers of their king, John, whose disastrous foreign policy, unremitting demands for money, and failure properly to administer justice had made him unpopular. John was forced to accept the charter at Runnymede, on the River Thames, in 1215. ❦ Although it was never intended to be a constitutional pillar, the Magna Carta has been employed repeatedly over the last 800 years as a defence against unjust rule. Three of its clauses

remain incorporated in English statute law – one protects the rights of the English Church; one defends the liberties of towns such as London; and one, famously, asserts the rights of citizens:

No free man shall be seized or imprisoned, or stripped of his rights or possessions, or outlawed or exiled · nor will we proceed with force against him · except by the lawful judgement of his equals or by the law of the land. To no one will we sell, to no one deny or delay right or justice

Two of the Magna Carta's clauses became the 5th and 6th amendments to the American Constitution. ❦ Four copies of the original 1215 grant survive, two at the British Library, and the others at Salisbury and Lincoln cathedrals. There are 13 additional copies issued by John's royal successors. Only two of these are outside the UK: David Rubenstein's, and one other purchased by the Australian government in 1952, now displayed in Canberra.

† The Magna Carta is 2,500 words long, so Mr Rubenstein paid $8,528 (£4,240) per word.

MOST RIDICULOUS BRITISH LAWS

The public were asked to vote on the most absurd legislation in Britain in a UKTV Gold survey undertaken in November 2007. The six most laughable laws were:

It is illegal to die in the Houses of Parliament
....
It is treasonous to stick on a postage stamp with the Queen's head upside down
....
In Liverpool, it is illegal for a woman to be topless unless she works in a tropical fish store[†]
....
Mince pies cannot be eaten on Christmas Day
....
In Scotland, if someone knocks at your door you must let them use your lavatory
....
It is illegal not to tell the tax man anything you do not want him to know, but legal not to tell him information you don't mind him knowing

† Liverpool Council denied this law ever existed, and, clearly, many of these laws are probably tosh.

——————————FIRST WORLD WAR VETERANS——————————

The last known German, French, Austrian, and Turkish veterans of WWI (1914–18) all died during 2008. Below is a very brief biography of each of these veterans:

Erich Kästner[†]
10·3·1900–1·1·2008
(died aged 107)
In 1918, Kästner served in the German army for 4 months and was sent to the Western Front. During WWII he was in the Luftwaffe, stationed predominantly in France.

Franz Künstler
24·7·1900–27·5·2008
(died aged 107)
Künstler was born into the German minority in the (then) Hungarian town of Soos; he was drafted into the Austrian army in February 1918, where he served as a gunner in Italy.

Lazare Ponticelli
7·12·1897–12·3·2008
(died aged 110)
Born in Italy, Ponticelli moved to France as a boy. In 1914, he joined the French Foreign Legion and the following year, when Italy joined the Allies, the Italian army.

Yakup Satar
11·3·1898–2·4·2008
(died aged 110)
Satar joined the Ottoman army in 1915 and fought in the 1917 Mesopotamian campaign against the British. Captured by them at Kut, he was a POW for over a year.

† Verification of Kästner's status is problematic since Germany keeps no records of its war veterans. ☙ There are 3 surviving British WWI veterans: *Bill Stone* (*b.* 23·9·1900, joined the Royal Navy 2 months before the end of WWI. He did not see action, but remained in the Navy and fought in WWII); *Harry Patch* (*b.* 17·6·1898, joined the Duke of Cornwall's Light Infantry, served on the Western Front and survived the Battle of Passchendaele); and *Henry Allingham* (*b.* 6·6·1896, joined the Royal Naval Air Service and witnessed the Battle of Jutland). Mr Allingham is Britain's oldest man. The oldest person in the world is Edna Parker from Indiana, USA, who was 115 on 20 April 2008.

——————————MILITARY CODENAMES——————————

Codenames are assigned to military operations to simplify communications and ensure security – though it is noticeable that UK and US forces favour very different nomenclatures. Not only are British codenames usually single words (the Yanks are more verbose), but the Brits tend towards an ideological neutrality that the Americans eschew in favour of bold statements of purpose – as shown below:

Operation	US codename	British codename
Invasion of Iraq (2003–)	*Iraqi Freedom*	*Telic*
Response to 9/11 (2001–)	*Enduring Freedom*[†]	*Veritas*
The First Gulf War (1990–91)	*Desert Shield & Storm*	*Granby*[‡]
Berlin Airlift (1948–49)	*Vittles*	*Plainfare*

† Changed from *Infinite Justice* after concerns the name might offend Muslims; Islam teaches that only Allah can provide infinite justice. ‡ Named after the Marquis of Granby, C18th British general.

UK SERVICE RANKS

service	ROYAL NAVY	ROYAL MARINES†	ARMY	ROYAL AIR FORCE	NATO
OFFICERS	Admiral of the Fleet	—	Field Marshal	Marshal of the RAF	OF-10
	Admiral	General	General	Air Chief Marshal	OF-9
	Vice-Admiral	Lieutenant General	Lieutenant General	Air Marshal	OF-8
	Rear Admiral	Major General	Major General	Air Vice-Marshal	OF-7
	Commodore	Brigadier	Brigadier	Air Commodore	OF-6
	Captain	Colonel	Colonel	Group Captain	OF-5
	Commander	Lieutenant Colonel	Lieutenant Colonel	Wing Commander	OF-4
	Lieutenant Commander	Major	Major	Squadron Leader	OF-3
	Lieutenant	Captain	Captain	Flight Lieutenant	OF-2
	Sub-Lieutenant	Lieutenant/2nd Lieutenant	Lieutenant/2nd Lieutenant	Flying Officer/Pilot Officer	OF-1
	Midshipman	—	Officer Cadet	Officer Designate	OF-(D)
OTHER RANKS	Warrant Officer Class 1	Warrant Officer Class 1	Warrant Officer Class 1	Warrant Officer	OR-9
	Warrant Officer Class 2	Warrant Officer Class 2	Warrant Officer Class 2	—	OR-8
	Chief Petty Officer	Colour Sergeant	Staff Sergeant	Flight Sergeant/Chief Technician	OR-7
	Petty Officer	Sergeant	Sergeant	Sergeant	OR-6
	Leading Rate	Corporal	Corporal	Corporal	OR-4
		—	Lance Corporal	—	OR-3
	Able Rating	Marine	Private (Class 1–3)	Junior Technician/Leading & Senior Aircraftman	OR-2
		—	Private (Class 4)/Junior	Aircraftman	OR-1

[Source: DASA] The Naval rank of Warrant Officer Class 2 was introduced in 2004. † The Royal Marines were established in 1664 as a corps of sea soldiers to be raised and disbanded as required. In 1755, they became a permanent part of the Navy, trained as soldiers and seamen to fight and to maintain discipline on ships. The Royal Marines gained their tough fighting reputation during the capture of Gibraltar in 1704, and have since played a decisive role in military deployments across the world.

THE VICTORIA CROSS

Instituted in 1856 by Queen Victoria, the Victoria Cross is the highest military award for gallantry. The medal has been awarded 1,356 times, and can be given posthumously. The legend that VC medals were all struck from the bronze of Russian guns captured at Sebastopol during the Crimean War has recently been challenged, but the same London firm, Hancocks & Co. (Jewellers) Ltd, has cast every VC since 1856. 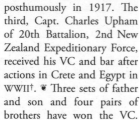 ❦ The most VCs awarded for actions in a single day was 24 – on 16 November 1857, at the Relief of Lucknow during the Indian Mutiny (the First War of Indian Independence). The largest number of VCs awarded to a regiment for a single action was 7 – to the 24th Foot for the defence of Rorke's Drift in 1879 (immortalised by the 1964 film *Zulu*). In 1921, the VC was awarded to the American Unknown Warrior, in return for the Americans bestowing the US Congressional Medal of Honor on the British Unknown Warrior. ❦ Only three people have won the VC twice (in which event the original medal is augmented with a metal bar). Two were members of the Royal Army Medical Corps – Lt-Col Arthur Martin-Leake who received his for actions in the Boer War and WWI, and Capt. Noel Chavasse who received his VC in 1916 and his bar posthumously in 1917. The third, Capt. Charles Upham of 20th Battalion, 2nd New Zealand Expeditionary Force, received his VC and bar after actions in Crete and Egypt in WWII[†]. ❦ Three sets of father and son and four pairs of brothers have won the VC. (Women are eligible for the medal, but to date no woman has been so honoured.) ❦ The most recent recipients are Cpl Bryan Budd[‡] of the 3rd Battalion, The Parachute Regiment, who was awarded a posthumous VC for acts of 'inspirational leadership and the greatest valour' in southern Afghanistan in 2006, and Pte Johnson Beharry from 1st Battalion, The Princess of Wales's Royal Regiment, whose two separate acts of outstanding gallantry in Al Amarah, Iraq, resulted in his 2004 VC. ❦ Each VC is inscribed 'For Valour' on the obverse; the reverse is inscribed with the date of the act for which it was awarded. The recipient's name, rank, number, and unit are inscribed on the reverse of the suspension bar.

[†] In December 2007, Charles Upham's VC was stolen from the Army Museum, Waiouru, on New Zealand's North Island, along with 8 other VCs and 90 additional medals. [‡] An inquest into Cpl Budd's death in December 2007 concluded that he was almost certainly killed by 'friendly fire'.

TOP WORLDWIDE MILITARY SPENDERS

Country	spending $bn	world share %
USA	528·7	46
UK	59·2	5
France	53·1	5
China	49·5	4
Japan	43·7	4
Germany	37·0	3
Russia	34·7	3

[US$ billions at constant 2005 prices and exchange rates. Source: Stockholm International Peace Research Institute, 2006]

——————————LAND ARMY GIRLS & BEVIN BOYS——————————

In 2008, after decades of campaigning, the contribution of 3 wartime groups was formally recognised by the British government. In January, it was announced that members of the Women's Land Army (WLA) and the Women's Timber Corps (WTC) could apply for an official badge, and in March, Gordon Brown awarded commemorative badges to 27 'Bevin Boys' who worked as miners during the war.

Land Army & *Timber Corps* · The Land Girls numbered 80,000 at their peak in 1943 and were involved in a range of agricultural tasks. The 6,000-strong Women's Timber Corps (nicknamed 'Lumberjills') felled trees and ran sawmills. *Bevin Boys* · Men who were conscripted or volunteered to work as miners during the war were known as 'Bevin Boys', after Ernest Bevin, wartime Minister of Labour. From 1943–48, 48,000 men were recruited.

——————————UK FORCES CAUSES OF DEATHS · 2006——————————

Cause of death [Source: DASA]	*All*	*Navy*	*Army*	*RAF*
Disease-related conditions	40	9	14	17
Accidental and violent deaths	146	23	93	30
deaths due to accidents	*95*	*15*	*53*	*27*
land transport accident	*59*	*10*	*37*	*12*
other	*36*	*5*	*16*	*15*
deaths due to violence	*49*	*8*	*38*	*3*
killed in action	*33*	*6*	*27*	*0*
died of wounds	*14*	*2*	*10*	*2*
other	*2*	*0*	*1*	*1*
suicide	*2*	*0*	*2*	*0*
Cause not currently available	4	1	2	1
ALL DEATHS	190	33	109	48

——————————MILITARY SEARCH & RESCUE——————————

2007 saw the highest level of activity for military search & rescue (SAR) units since 1996. Royal Navy and RAF helicopters, Nimrod aircraft, and mountain rescue teams were called out 2,065 times to a total of 1,877 UK and overseas incidents[†]. SAR's primary role is to rescue military crew after aircraft accidents, but nearly all its callouts are to help civilians. Below is a breakdown of SAR activity in 2007:

Medrescue [moving injured from a hostile environment to hospital] 946
Rescue [moving uninjured from a hostile to a benign environment] 582
Medtransfer [moving a sick person, or occasionally transplant organs, between hospitals] ... 198
Recovery [moving people declared dead at the scene or confirmed dead on arrival] 24
Transfer [moving military personnel, or their families, on compassionate grounds].......... 17

† One incident may result in more than one callout, e.g., a helicopter and mountain rescue team.

———————— ON BELIEF, SUPERSTITION, &c. ————————

In October 2007, *Schott's Almanac* and Ipsos Mori polled British attitudes on belief:

Most people (40%) believe in neither heaven nor hell. Optimistically, 16% believe in the former and not the latter. Below are those believing in:

%	heaven but not hell	hell but not heaven	heaven and hell	neither
All	16	1	34	40
Men	9	1	31	52
Women	22	1	37	28
Age: 16–34	14	1	37	40
· 35–54	15	2	31	42
· 55+	18	1	34	36
· 65+	23	1	36	29
Christian	20	1	43	26
· other religion	10	3	41	39
· none	5	1	7	78
Ethnicity: white	16	1	32	41
· other	8	1	55	24
Read: tabloid	16	1	39	36
· broadsheet	15	1	28	47

Below are those who believe in: reincarnation; life after death; that it is possible to receive communications from the dead:

% believing	reincarnation	life after death	speak w/dead
All	23	47	32
Men	18	40	21
Women	27	54	42
Age: 16–34	25	54	36
· 35–54	22	42	31
· 55+	22	47	30
· 65+	19	49	26
Ethnicity: white	22	46	32
· other	35	69	29

Do you ever cross your fingers to bring good luck?

%	Yes	No	?
All	39	60	1
Men	30	70	0
Women	48	51	1
Religion: Christian	44	56	0
· other	28	72	0
· none	31	69	0
Read horoscope	62	38	0

Do you believe 13 to be unlucky?

%	Yes	No	?
All	15	85	0
Men	12	88	0
Women	17	82	1
Religion: Christian	18	81	1
· other	5	95	0
· none	9	91	0
Read horoscope	28	71	1

Do you ever literally 'touch wood' in order to avoid bad luck?

%	Yes	No	?
All	51	48	1
Men	40	60	0
Women	62	38	0
Ethnicity: white	53	47	0
· other	33	66	1
Religion: Christian	56	44	0
· other	35	65	0
· none	44	55	1
Read horoscope	70	29	1

Do you believe that certain magical words, or spells, can have real effects?

%	Yes	No	?
All	12	83	5
Ethnicity: white	11	85	4
· other	27	65	8

─────── ON BELIEF, SUPERSTITION, &c. cont. ───────

Below are those who do or think something special if – when alone – they:

%	See a magpie	Break a mirror	Spill salt
All	26	7	22
Men	18	4	11
Women	34	10	33
Newspaper: tabloid	29	8	26
· broadsheet	21	6	20
Ethnicity: white	28	7	24
· other	12	4	6
Religion: Christian	30	8	27
· other	12	8	6
· none	23	5	18
Age: 16–34	31	5	14
· 35–54	31	9	24
· 55+	18	6	28
· 65+	20	7	31

% men	differences in belief & superstition by sex	women %
34	Believe in telepathy	47
47	Believe in premonitions	68
53	Believe in fate	70
54	Believe humans have souls	69
11	Carry or wear a lucky charm	22
26	Believe in guardian angels	50
31	Believe in ghosts	44
11	Have consulted a fortune-teller, medium, &c.	36
14	Read their horoscope regularly	31
29	Believe that dreams can predict the future	40

42% of those who claim *not* to be superstitious say they still touch wood for luck:

Say they are superstitious %		Claim not to be superstitious %			
64	believe in ghosts	31	44	visited fortune-teller &c.	18
38	carry lucky charm	10	21	believe in spells &c.	10
55	believe in telepathy	37	50	read horoscope	15
76	believe in premonitions	53	51	dreams predict future	30
76	believe we have souls	58	40	believe 13 to be unlucky	8
82	believe in fate	56	59	believe in guardian angels	33
19	believe in witches &c.	11	37	believe in reincarnation	19
			59	believe in life after death	44
			71	cross fingers for luck	30
			82	touch wood for luck	42

[See ipsos-mori.com for full details; some 'don't knows' have been excluded for reasons of space.]

PILGRIMAGE SITES

By some accounts, every major world religion, apart from Protestant Christianity, has a tradition of travel to holy sites. The following sites have been places of pilgrimage in the major monotheistic religions since ancient times:

JERUSALEM · For early Jews, pilgrimage to Jerusalem several times a year was a duty undertaken to perform sacrifices at the Temple. When Titus's army destroyed the second Temple in AD 70, these sacrifices ceased forever, and with them obligatory pilgrimages. However, Jews with the means so to do are still encouraged to visit Jerusalem, particularly the Western Wall (the last remaining section of the Second Temple), though now for nationalist as well as religious reasons. ❦ Jerusalem is significant to Christians as the home of Jesus Christ, and pilgrims have been visiting the city since the C4th. Fewer visited after AD 638, when the city was surrendered to the caliph Omar, but numbers increased again with the Crusades, whose earliest members saw themselves as pilgrims with a divine mission to retake Jerusalem. Today many Christians make pilgrimages to the Church of the Holy Sepulchre, considered the likely site of Jesus's crucifixion. ❦ Jerusalem (*Al-Quds* in Arabic) is the third holiest site in Islam, after Mecca and Medina. The Dome of the Rock is where Muhammad ascended to heaven.

ROME · Christians began making pilgrimages to Rome under Constantine (AD 274–337) to visit the graves of the apostles and martyrs, see the holy relics throughout the city, and visit the Pope. Penitential pilgrims also came to seek absolution, and pilgrimages to Rome were sometimes imposed as punishments for sin. Rome assumed a further importance for pilgrims in 1300, which Pope Boniface VIII declared a 'Jubilee Year' – a period in which believers could be granted a full pardon for all sins if they visited the major shrines of Rome and made their confession. The concept of Jubilee Years has continued within the Catholic Church, although the rites and requirements have evolved; the next is scheduled in 2025.

MECCA · Originally a trading route oasis, Mecca (in Saudi Arabia) is now the holiest city in Islam. All adult Muslims with the means and ability are commanded to make the *hajj* (the pilgrimage to Mecca), and *c.*2·5m currently do so each year. Islam is the only religion that explicitly commands its followers to perform a pilgrimage, and the rites of the *hajj* are considerably more formal and elaborate than those of other traditions. Central in these rites is the Ka'bah, a shrine built by Adam, rebuilt by Abraham, and dedicated to Allah by Muhammad. The *hajj* is undertaken during the 12th month of the Muslim calendar, *Dhu-ul-Hijja*, and involves days of travel between Mecca, Arafat, and Medina, performing rituals based on the lives of Abraham and Muhammad. Those who have performed the *hajj* are entitled to call themselves *hajji*, a title that carries with it great esteem. [See *Schott's Almanac 2007* for an analysis of the *hajj*.]

Buddhist pilgrims travel to Lumbini, Nepal, as well as Bodh Gaya, Sarnath, and Kusinagara in India; all are key sites in the life of the Gautama Buddha. Hindus take pilgrimages to wash in the River Ganges, the water of which is considered spiritually purifying. Japanese pilgrims scale Mount Fuji, revered in both Shintoism and Buddhism. For Sikhs, Amritsar, India, is the main centre of pilgrimage.

SEVEN NEW DEADLY SINS

In March 2008, the Vatican added to the traditional enumeration of deadly sins seven new sins for the modern era. Bishop Gianfranco Girotti, head of the Apostolic Penitentiary (which grants absolutions and rules on matters of conscience), said 'while sin used to concern mostly the individual, today it has mainly a social resonance, due to the phenomenon of globalisation'. The new 'seven social sins' are:

Taking or dealing in drugs	*Causing poverty*
Genetic manipulation	*Accumulating excessive wealth*
'Morally debatable' scientific experiments	
Environmental pollution	The original 7, laid down in the C6th, are anger,
Social inequalities & injustice	envy, gluttony, greed, lust, pride, and sloth.

TEMPLETON PRIZE

The *Templeton Prize for Progress Toward Research or Discoveries about Spiritual Realities* was awarded in 2008 to Michael Heller, a Polish theologian, cosmologist, and philosopher. Heller's work has sought to answer some of the most fundamental and abstract questions of the universe (e.g., 'why is there something rather than nothing?') by drawing on knowledge from both science and religion. Interviewed by *The New York Times* soon after his win, Heller noted the necessity of reconciling the two fields, saying that 'Science gives us knowledge, and religion gives us meaning. Both are prerequisites of the decent existence'. ✹ Sir John Templeton founded his eponymous prize in 1972, 'to encourage and honour the advancement of knowledge in spiritual matters'. The £820,000 prize (currently valued at >$1·6m) is said to be the richest annual monetary prize of any kind given to an individual. Templeton stipulated its value always be greater than the Nobel Prize, to 'underscore that research and advances in spiritual discoveries can be quantifiably more significant than disciplines recognised' by the Nobels. He died on 8 July 2008.

THE VATICAN & ALIENS

In an interview with the Vatican's newspaper *L'Osservatore Romano* in May 2008, the director of the Vatican Observatory, Father José Gabriel Funes, said that belief in aliens does not contradict a belief in God. In the article entitled 'Aliens Are My Brother', Funes went on to say that the existence of aliens cannot be ruled out: 'Just as there is a multiplicity of creatures over the Earth, so there could be other beings, even intelligent [beings], created by God. This is not in contradiction with our faith, because we cannot establish limits to God's creative freedom. To agree with St Francis, if we can consider some earthly creatures as "brothers" or "sisters", why could we not speak of a "brother alien"? He would also belong to the creation'.

The Ministry of Defence made previously classified files on UFO sightings available for the first time in May 2008. The 1978–87 files can now be downloaded from the National Archives website.

———————————— EINSTEIN ON RELIGION ————————————

A letter in which Albert Einstein discussed his religious views was bought for £170,000 at a London auction in May 2008. The recipient of the letter (posted 3/1/1954) was philosopher Eric Gutkind who had sent Einstein his book *Choose Life: The Biblical Call to Revolt.* The extract below gives a flavour of Einstein's belief:

> *The word God is for me nothing more than the expression and product of human weaknesses, the Bible a collection of honourable, but still primitive legends which are nevertheless pretty childish. No interpretation no matter how subtle can (for me) change this. These subtilised interpretations are highly manifold according to their nature and have almost nothing to do with the original text. For me the Jewish religion like all other religions is an incarnation of the most childish superstitions.*

———————————— WORLD RELIGIONS & LANGUAGES ————————————

Religion	%	Language	%
Christian	33·32	Mandarin Chinese	13·22
Roman Catholic	16·99	Spanish	4·88
Protestant	5·78	English	4·68
Orthodox	3·53	Arabic	3·12
Anglican	1·25	Hindi	2·74
Muslim	21·01	Portuguese	2·69
Hindu	13·26	Bengali	2·59
Buddhist	5·84	Russian	2·2
Sikh	0·35	Japanese	1·85
Jewish	0·23	Standard German	1·44
Other religions	11·9	Wu Chinese	1·17

[In % of world population · Only first language speakers · Source: CIA World Factbook, 2008]

———————————— RELIGION AS AN INSURANCE FOR HAPPINESS ————————————

Religious believers enjoy higher levels of 'life satisfaction', according to research amongst Europeans by Andrew Clark and Orsolya Lelkes presented to the Royal Economic Society in March 2008. In their paper *Deliver Us From Evil: Religion as Insurance*, Clark and Lelkes also asserted that religion 'insure[s] against some of life's adverse events' (e.g., unemployment and divorce), and that people seem to become happier the more often they attend church or pray. The authors also claimed that religious people tend to conservatism, in that they are 'both anti-divorce and anti-job creation programmes for the unemployed'. And, while Catholics and Protestants are less hurt by marital separation than the non-religious, Protestants suffer less than Catholics do. The authors conclude: 'Over and above denomination, churchgoing and prayer are also associated with greater satisfaction. Religion tempers the impact of adverse life events: it has current as opposed to after-life rewards.'

THE 2008 LAMBETH CONFERENCE

The Lambeth Conference is a meeting of all the archbishops and bishops of the Anglican Communion. It was first convened in 1867 at the Archbishop of Canterbury's London seat, Lambeth Palace; since then, the conference has been held every *c.*10 years. ❦ The 2008 (and 14th) conference was destined to be controversial. The Anglican communion remained divided over a range of issues, including the ordination of women bishops [see p.35], the conversion of other faiths, and, most controversially, the church's stance on homosexuality, same-sex union, and gay clergy. The latter has been a source of worsening dissent since the US ordination of the gay Bishop of New Hampshire, the Right Rev Gene Robinson, in 2003. So intractable were some of the divisions, that *c.*250 more 'traditionalist' bishops boycotted the Lambeth Conference, attending instead a 'rival' meeting in Jerusalem. ❦ After 20 days of reflection and debate, it was clear that no instant solutions to the divisions in Anglicanism had been found. A *Times* survey of those at the conference found >90% felt there was still value in the Communion, despite its problems – yet this did not include the voices of those who felt so strongly that they had stayed away.

BELIEF IN GOD

Below is the % of inhabitants across Europe who stated that they believed in God:

believe in God %			
Malta	95	Italy	74	Netherlands	34
Romania	90	Ireland	73	France	34
Portugal	81	Spain	59	Sweden	23
Greece	81	Germany	47	Estonia	16
		UK	38	[Source: Eurobarometer 05]

CROP CIRCLES & EXTRATERRESTRIALS

Belief in crop circles and ETs was explored in a *Schott's Almanac*/Ipsos Mori poll:

Do you believe that some crop circles are the work of extraterrestrial forces?			
%	Yes	No	?
ALL	9	84	7
Men	11	82	7
Women	7	85	8
Religion: Christian	7	84	9
· other	21	69	10
· none	9	87	4
Read: tabloid	10	81	9
· broadsheet	5	90	5
Ethnicity: white	7	85	8
· other	23	62	15

Do you believe that some governments around the world are concealing evidence of extraterrestrial beings?			
%	Yes	No	?
ALL	31	60	9
Men	34	59	7
Women	28	61	11
Social class: ABC1	26	65	9
· C2DE	38	54	8
Read: tabloid	37	55	8
· broadsheet	21	72	7

[October 2007; see ipsos-mori.com for all data.]

Sport

*It's the desire to rekindle that feeling of what it is to be Olympic champion,
it wouldn't matter if it was in the team sprint, or the keirin, table tennis,
volleyball. I'd do any sport for that.* — CHRIS HOY

TEAM GB AT THE OLYMPICS · BEIJING 2008

Team GB achieved the nation's best Olympic performance since 1908, bringing home from Beijing 19 golds and claiming 4th place in the medals table. The unexpected depth and breadth of British success took the media by surprise, and coverage which had been sniffy and sceptical rapidly became proud and patriotic as the 'great haul of China' rolled in. ❦ It was fitting that Britain's first gold came from road cyclist Nicole Cooke, since the cycling team went on to dominate the Laoshan Velodrome, winning 14 medals, of which 8 were gold. Scottish cyclist Chris Hoy achieved superstar status after winning 3 golds, with a talent neatly summed up by Dutch rival Theo Bos: 'It's like he has swallowed a motorbike'. ❦ At the Water Cube, 19-year-old Rebecca Adlington won gold in both the 400m and the 800m freestyle, setting a new world record for the latter (the previous 800m record was set in 1989, the year of Adlington's birth). Elsewhere in the pool, 14-year-old Tom Daley, Britain's youngest competitor, had to contend with the media spotlight as well as difficulties with his team mate. But Daley and Aldridge finished respectably in the synchronised diving, raising medal hopes for London 2012. ❦ Britain's sailors were second only to the cyclists, taking 6 medals – 4 golds, a silver, and

Au 19
Ag 13
Cu 15

[*The bronze medals were mainly copper.*]

a bronze. Ben Ainslie led the way, winning his 3rd gold in consecutive games. ❦ Adversity dogged some athletic stars – notably, Paula Radcliffe struggled injured through the marathon. But Christine Ohuruogu put a year-long ban for missing three drugs tests behind her and stormed to gold in the 400m. ❦ The sustained excellence of Team GB upset the traditional image of plucky but doomed British sportsmen. Emerging in its place was a picture of supremely confident and highly trained athletes, who had clearly benefited from the dramatic increase in funding from the National Lottery. ❦ Inevitably there were some who sneered that Britain excelled in 'elite' sports (sailing, equestrianism), or sports that could be undertaken sitting down (cycling, rowing). And the Australians found it especially tough to be beaten by their old adversary, as one Aussie sportswriter moaned: 'Frankly I don't care where we sit on the tally as long as it's somewhere in front of those gappy toothed sock and sandal wearing bastards.' ❦ Prior to Beijing, UK Sport had set a bullish target of 41 medals and 8th in the medals table. That Team GB exceeded this with 47 medals, 19 golds, and 4th place in the table provided a dramatic boost to British sport and a (much-needed) fillip to preparations for London 2012.

──────── BEIJING 2008 · MISCELLANY ────────

CONSTRUCTION AND COST · China spent *c*.$43bn on the 2008 games and constructed 12 spectacular new venues, notably the National Stadium (called the 'Bird's Nest' after its lattice-work structure), and the National Aquatics Centre (aptly called the 'Water Cube'). The Bird's Nest, which hosted the opening and closing ceremonies, has 91,000 seats, uses 2·8m square feet of space, and cost *c*.$500m.

MASCOTS · The 2008 Olympic mascots were five fanciful creatures inspired by the colours of the Olympic rings: *Beibei* [a fish], *Jingjing* [a panda], *Huanhuan* [the Olympic flame], *Yingying* [a Tibetan antelope], and *Nini* [a swallow]. Together, they were known as the *Fuwa*, which equates to 'the friendlies'. When combined, their names spell out *Bei Jing Huan Ying Ni* – 'Welcome to Beijing'.

TORCH RELAY · The Olympic torch relay was disrupted by pro-Tibet protests in a number of countries [see *Chronicle*]. It was noted that the idea of lighting the Olympic torch in Greece and running it through different countries was first conceived by the Nazis as a propaganda stunt before the 1936 Berlin games.

BBC & VIEWERSHIP · 40m people watched at least 15 minutes of the BBC's Olympic coverage, of which 2,750 hours were broadcast. (The 7-hour time difference from Beijing gave a significant boost to the usually modest daytime viewing figures.) 5·8m tuned in to watch Usain Bolt take gold in the 100m. The closing ceremony garnered the largest audience of the games, with a peak of 6·8m viewers.

PROTESTS · In response to criticism of China's human rights record, Beijing designated 3 'protest zones' for demonstrations during the games (Purple Bamboo Park, Ritan Park, and World Park). However, the city said that only 77 applications to protest had been received, all of which were 'withdrawn' or rejected. The press reported that Chinese citizens applying for permission to demonstrate were detained, and some were sentenced to 're-education through labour'. Additionally, a number of foreign protesters were arrested and deported.

TEAM GB · 311 British athletes (168 ♂, 143 ♀) competed in 20 of the 26 Olympic sports. (236 Team GB officials accompanied the athletes to Beijing.) The British Airways plane that flew Team GB home was repainted with a gold nose cone and renamed *Pride*.

CLOSING CEREMONY & LONDON 2012 · Beijing's closing ceremony was almost as spectacular as that which opened the games. London had an 8-minute slot to preview 2012; Leona Lewis and Jimmy Page performed *Whole Lotta Love* atop a curiously dismantled red double-decker, and David Beckham hoofed a football into the crowd. London's new mayor, Boris Johnson, accepted the Olympic flag from the IOC chairman, Jacques Rogge.

PARALYMPICS · The 'ParalympicsGB' team turned in a series of spectacular performances, hauling home 102 medals, 42 of which were gold. In the medal table, Britain came second to China. Swimmer David Roberts won 4 golds, bringing his career tally to 11; Darren Kenny led the cycling team's haul of 20 medals; and 13-year-old Eleanor Simmonds won 2 swimming golds to become GB's youngest-ever champion. The paralympics also proved more popular than ever, in what organisers hoped would be but a preview for 2012.

———— TEAM GB · MEDALS TABLE · BEIJING 2008 ————

Discipline · event	winner	medal
Aquatics · ♀ 400m freestyle final	Rebecca Adlington	G
♀ 800m freestyle final	Rebecca Adlington	G
♀ Marathon 10km final	Keri–Anne Payne	S
♂ Marathon 10km final	David Davies	S
♀ 400m freestyle final	Joanne Jackson	B
♀ Marathon 10km final	Cassandra Patten	B
Athletics · ♀ 400m final	Christine Ohuruogu	G
♂ High jump final	Germaine Mason	S
♂ Triple jump final	Phillips Idowu	S
♀ 400m hurdles final	Tasha Danvers	B
Boxing · 69–75kg final ranking	James DeGale	G
75–81kg final ranking	Tony Jeffries	B
Over 91kg final ranking	David Price	B
Canoeing and kayaking · ♂ K–1 1000m final ranking	Tim Brabants	G
♂ C–1 final ranking	David Florence	S
♂ K–1 500m final ranking	Tim Brabants	B
Cycling · ♀ Individual pursuit final ranking	Rebecca Romero	G
♂ Individual pursuit final ranking	Bradley Wiggins	G
♂ Keirin final ranking	Chris Hoy	G
♀ Road race	Nicole Cooke	G
♀ Sprint final ranking	Victoria Pendleton	G
♂ Sprint final ranking	Chris Hoy	G
♂ Team pursuit final ranking	Team GB	G
♂ Team sprint final ranking	Team GB	G
♀ Individual pursuit final ranking	Wendy Houvenaghel	S
♀ Individual time trial	Emma Pooley	S
♂ Keirin final ranking	Ross Edgar	S
♂ Sprint final ranking	Jason Kenny	S
♂ Individual pursuit final ranking	Steven Burke	B
♂ Points race final	Chris Newton	B
Equestrian · Individual – ranking after jumping qualifier	Kristina Cook	B
Team ranking	Team GB	B
Gymnastics · ♂ Pommel horse final ranking	Louis Smith	B
Modern pentathlon · ♀ Modern pentathlon standings	Heather Fell	S
Rowing · ♂ Double sculls (lightweight) final ranking	Team GB	G
♂ Four without coxswain (heavyweight) final ranking	Team GB	G
♂ Eight with coxswain final ranking	Team GB	S
♀ Quadruple sculls without coxswain final ranking	Team GB	S
♀ Double sculls (heavyweight) final ranking	Team GB	B
♂ Double sculls (heavyweight) final ranking	Team GB	B
Sailing · ♂ Laser – one person dinghy – through nine races	Paul Goodison	G
Mixed finn – heavyweight dinghy – through seven races	Ben Ainslie	G
♂ Star – keelboat final	Team GB	G
♀ Yngling – keelboat – through seven races	Team GB	G
♂ 470 – two person dinghy – through seven races	Team GB	S
♀ RS:X – windsurfer – through nine races	Bryony Shaw	B
Taekwondo · ♀ >67 kg final ranking	Sarah Stevenson	B

—— EURO 2008 ——

On 29 June 2008, Spain beat serial finalists Germany in a thrilling final, fulfilling years of promise to take their first international title since 1964. In a tournament with no domestic interest due to the home nations' failed qualifying campaigns, there was a danger that the avalanche of media coverage and hours of televised matches would be wasted on an uninterested audience. However, the excitement created by the new guard of European soccer – Croatia, Turkey, Russia, and the Czech Rep. – soon caught the imagination of British football fans. Hosted by Switzerland and Austria, the tournament got off to a lively start as the young pretenders played attacking football, leaving old guard teams such as France and world champions Italy looking staid. The group stages provided a number of upsets: France failed to progress and neither host reached the quarter-finals.

GROUP A	*points*	GROUP B	*points*	GROUP C	*points*	GROUP D	*points*
Portugal	6	Croatia	9	Holland	9	Spain	9
Turkey	6	Germany	6	Italy	4	Russia	6
Czech R	3	Austria	1	Romania	2	Sweden	3
Switzerland	3	Poland	1	France	1	Greece	0

THE QUARTER-FINALS

Germany	3–2		Portugal	Russia	3–1		Holland
Turkey	1–1	(*pens* 3–1)	Croatia	Spain	0–0	(*pens* 4–2)	Italy

THE SEMI-FINALS

GERMANY	3–2	TURKEY	SPAIN	3–0	RUSSIA
Schweinsteiger 26,		Ugur 22,	Xavi 50,		
Klose 79,		Semih 86	Guiza 73,		
Lahm 90			Silva 82		

Turkey had battled through to the semis with a thrilling last-minute goal against Croatia, and looked set to challenge Germany for a place in the final in the same way, when Semih levelled the score at 2–2 in the 86th minute. But against the flow of play, the Germans beat the plucky Turks at their own game with a 90th minute goal from Lahm that ended an exciting match.

Spain swarmed all over the Russians in a one-sided match. The Spaniards were forced to adapt after tournament-leading goal scorer Villa limped off injured. The resulting 5-man midfield, anchored by Senna, nullified the danger of Russian star striker Arshavin. A young Spanish squad played flowing, passing football, achieving a deserved place in the final.

– THE FINAL –

29·06·08 – Ernst Happel Stadion, Vienna
GERMANY 0–1 SPAIN (Torres 33)
Player of the tournament – Xavi [ESP] · Golden Boot – David Villa [ESP]

There was relief from sports fans around Europe as Spain laid to rest the ghosts of past failures and excelled to beat the characteristically efficient Germans. Aragonés's young squad were widely considered the team of the tournament and the worthy winners of a final, the scoreline of which failed to reflect Spain's true superiority.

THE PREMIERSHIP · 2007/08

Team	won	drew	lost	goals for	goals against	goal difference	points
Manchester Utd	27	6	5	80	22	58	87
Chelsea	25	10	3	65	26	39	85
Arsenal	24	11	3	74	31	43	83
Liverpool	21	13	4	67	28	39	76
↑ CHAMPIONS LEAGUE ↑							
Everton	19	8	11	55	33	22	65
↑ UEFA CUP ↑							
Aston Villa	16	12	10	71	51	20	60
Blackburn	15	13	10	50	48	2	58
Portsmouth	16	9	13	48	40	8	57
Manchester City	15	10	13	45	53	−8	55
West Ham	13	10	15	42	50	−8	49
Tottenham	11	13	14	66	61	5	46
Newcastle	11	10	17	45	65	−20	43
Middlesbrough	10	12	16	43	53	−10	42
Wigan Athletic	10	10	18	34	51	−17	40
Sunderland	11	6	21	36	59	−23	39
Bolton	9	10	19	36	54	−18	37
Fulham	8	12	18	38	60	−22	36
↓ RELEGATION ↓							
Reading	10	6	22	41	66	−25	36
Birmingham	8	11	19	46	62	−16	35
Derby County	1	8	29	20	89	−69	11

OTHER DIVISIONS – UP & DOWN

Up	*2007/08*	*Down*
West Bromwich Albion Stoke City, Hull City†	*Championship*	Leicester City, Scunthorpe Colchester
Swansea City, Nottingham Forest, Doncaster	*League One*	Bournemouth, Gillingham Port Vale, Luton Town
MK Dons, Peterborough Hereford, Stockport	*League Two*	Mansfield Town Wrexham
Aldershot Town Exeter City	*Blue Square Premier*	Altrincham‡, Farsley Celtic Stafford Rangers, Droylsden

† The first time Hull had reached the top flight of English football since they were founded in 1904. ‡ Altrincham were saved from relegation for an unprecedented third season in a row. Despite repeatedly finishing in the relegation zone, the club kept gaining a reprieve as other teams suffered points penalties. In 2007/08, Altrincham stayed up because Halifax Town were forced into liquidation and out of the league. ❦ From 2007/08, the Conference was renamed the Blue Square Premier.

―――――FA CUP――――― ―CHAMPIONS LEAGUE―

18/5/2008 · Wembley Stadium
Attendance: 89,874
PORTSMOUTH 1–0 CARDIFF CITY
Referee: Mike Dean

21/5/2008 · Luzhniki Stad., Moscow
Attendance: 69,552
MAN U 1–1 (6–5 *pens*) CHELSEA
Referee: Lubos Michel [SLO]

THE KEY MOMENTS

13........Parry shot blocked by James
15............ Pompey free kick cleared
22.. Kanu hit post after promising run
34...Enkelmann saved 2 goal attempts
37........Kanu GOAL for Portsmouth
39.. McNaughton counter-attack wide
45.....Hreidersson booked for arguing
45.Loovens goal disallowed – handball
51............Kanu shot deflected wide
53.................... Kranjcar booked
56.......... Muntari shot over the bar
80.......Loovens header missed target
84..great Distin run ended by Johnson
93.....last-minute free kick to Cardiff,
R. Johnson shot blocked

THE KEY MOMENTS

20......Scholes nose bloodied in fracas
Scholes & Makelele booked
26............Ronaldo headed in GOAL
45....Lampard GOAL evened the score
77..... Malouda penalty appeal denied
115 Drogba sent off for slapping Vidić
PENALTIES
Tevez scored......Man U 1–0 Chelsea
Ballack scored....Man U 1–1 Chelsea
Carrick scored....Man U 2 –1 Chelsea
Belletti scored.....Man U 2–2 Chelsea
Ronaldo missed...Man U 2–2 Chelsea
Lampard scored...Man U 2–3 Chelsea
Hargreaves scored.Man U 3–3 Chelsea
A. Cole scored.....Man U 3–4 Chelsea
Nani scored ......Man U 4–4 Chelsea
Terry missed......Man U 4–4 Chelsea
Anderson scored ..Man U 5–4 Chelsea
Kalou scored .....Man U 5–5 Chelsea
Giggs scored......Man U 6–5 Chelsea
Anelka missed....Man U 6–5 Chelsea

Portsmouth's victory was their first FA Cup Final win since 1939 · Two Portsmouth players had their winning medals stolen from the hotel where they were staying · *c.*200,000 Pompey fans turned out to watch a victory parade.

―――― ENGLISH PLAYERS IN THE PREMIER LEAGUE ――――

Just 170 of the 498 footballers who started matches in the Premiership in 2007/08 were English, according to research by BBC Sport – a dearth of home talent that could signal trouble for the national squad. One solution championed by FIFA president Sepp Blatter would be to restrict to five the number of foreign players in each team, an idea that might contravene EU employment laws and is unlikely to be introduced. Below are the English players in the Premier League from 2000–08:

Season	*No. English*				
2000/01	207	2002/03	179	2005/06	186
2001/02	199	2003/04	182	2006/07	191
		2004/05	184	2007/08	170

On average, just 4 players from each club were English in 2007/08. West Ham had the most English players in its starting line-up with an average of 6·61, followed by Aston Villa with 6·42. Arsenal had by far the fewest English players, with an average of just 0·34 making the starting line-up. Scotland fared slightly better with an average of 6·27 Scottish players starting in the Scottish Premier league.

──────────── RICHEST FOOTBALL CLUBS ────────────

For the third year running, Real Madrid was the world's wealthiest club (although Manchester Utd is predicted to overtake it within a year), according to Deloitte's annual Football Money League, published in February 2008. For the first time, three British clubs featured in the top five. Below are the top 20 richest clubs, based on total revenue generated from tickets, broadcasting, and commercial activities:

Club	£m
Real Madrid	236·2
Manchester Utd	212·1
Barcelona	195·3
Chelsea	190·5
Arsenal	177·6
AC Milan	153·0
Bayern Munich	150·3
Liverpool	133·9
Inter Milan	131·3
AS Roma	106·1
Tottenham	103·1
Juventus	97·7
Lyon	94·6
Newcastle Utd	87·1
SV Hamburg	81·0
Schalke 04	76·9
Celtic	75·2
Valencia	72·4
Marseille	66·6
Werder Bremen	65·5

† Based in NW Germany, founded on 4 May, 1904.

On 1/9/08, Abu Dhabi United Group bought Manchester City. ❦ According to *Formula Money*, Formula 1 is the world's richest sport, with each of the 17 Grand Prix generating on average £66m.

──────────── SOME FOOTBALL AWARDS OF NOTE · 2007/08 ────────────

FIFA world player of the year..................................Kaka [AC Milan/Brazil]
European footballer of the year ....Kaka [AC Milan]
Prof. Footballers' Assoc. player of the year............Cristiano Ronaldo [Man. Utd]
PFA young player award ....Cesc Fabregas [Arsenal]
PFA special merit award .... Jimmy Armfield [BBC commentator, former England player]
Football Writers' Assoc. player of the year............Cristiano Ronaldo [Man. Utd]
FA women's football awards: players' player of the year...........Jill Scott [Everton]
LMA manager of the year...............................Sir Alex Ferguson [Man. Utd]

──────────── AFRICA CUP OF NATIONS ────────────

The 2008 Africa Cup of Nations football tournament was hosted by Ghana and won by defending champions Egypt, who beat Cameroon 1–0 in the final in Accra. Many of the competing teams have nicknames, often with animal connections:

Angola	*The Palancas Negras*†	Namibia	*Brave Warriors*
Benin	*The Squirrels*	Nigeria	*The Super Eagles*
Cameroon	*The Indomitable Lions*	Senegal	*The Teranga Lions*
Egypt	*The Pharaohs*	South Africa	*Bafana Bafana*‡
Ghana	*Black Stars*	Sudan	*The Nile Crocodiles*
Guinea	*Syli Nationale*	Tunisia	*The Carthage Eagles*
Ivory Coast	*The Elephants*	Zambia	*The Chipolopolo*
Mali	*The Eagles*		
Morocco	*The Atlas Lions*		

† Black Antelopes ‡ 'The Boys' [BBC Sport]

RUGBY WORLD CUP · 2007

The 2007 Rugby World Cup Finals in France provided plenty of surprises. Many rugby minnows flourished, while some of the big fish (most notably favourites New Zealand) floundered. Argentina revealed themselves to be a formidable team, taking a number of scalps and third place from a gutsy French side. Wales, Scotland, and Ireland all had a disappointing competition – only Scotland reached the quarters before being defeated by the Argentines. Low English expectations were compounded by an uncertain start. Yet game after game their confidence grew and England dispatched first Australia and then France to reach their second final in a row. South Africa played superbly throughout the tournament, helped by the metronomic kicking of Percy Montgomery and the try-scoring guile of Bryan Habana. Despite a 36–0 drubbing at the hands of the Springboks earlier in the tournament, England began to hope. Tickets began changing hands for vastly inflated sums as hordes of English fans descended on Paris, hoping to witness their boys retain the William Webb Ellis trophy. England played bravely but ultimately could not overcome the South African defence, and most agreed the Boks were the worthy winners. Below are some key moments from the 2007 Rugby World Cup final:

ENGLAND 6–15 SOUTH AFRICA
20·10·07 · Stade de France, Paris · Att: 80,430 · Ref: A. Rolland [IRE]

THE KEY MOMENTS

2 min......... SA win first line-out, but possession returns to ENG after knock-on
6 .... SA awarded a PENALTY. Matthew Tait penalised for not releasing the ball
7 ....Percy Montgomery sends ball between the posts. ENG 0–3 SA
10..... Habana tackles Sackey to ground, PENALTY to ENG as SA go over the top
11..................Jonny Wilkinson successfully kicks tricky penalty. ENG 3–3 SA
14.........Lewis Moody's needless trip of Butch James gifts SA another PENALTY
15........................ Percy Montgomery effortlessly scores again. ENG 3–6 SA
17....................................Jonny Wilkinson fluffs a drop-goal opportunity
21.........................Phil Vickery caught offside to give SA another PENALTY
22............ François Steyn's long-range effort just misses the mark. ENG 3–6 SA
25......SA charge dangerously into ENG's 22, but messy moves cost SA possession
35. Steyn leads marauding attack, Smit stopped just inches short of ENG's try line
38............ SA repeatedly scrum at 5m, Rossouw goes for try but is well tackled
40.... ENG kill the ball to hand SA a PENALTY, Montgomery scores. ENG 3–9 SA
42...............break by Tait who beats 4 men to allow Cueto to dive for the line
44..... after agonising wait, video referee declares 'no try' as Cueto's foot in touch
44..Wilkinson scores PENALTY awarded for earlier SA infringement. ENG 6–9 SA
45.................Jason Robinson goes off injured to be replaced by Dan Hipkiss
50................ Corry gives away PENALTY, Montgomery scores. ENG 6–12 SA
58.........Flood chases kick into SA's 22 & knocks Montgomery into TV camera
61.....ENG give away silly PENALTY, Steyn scores long-range kick. ENG 6–15 SA
69...Wilkinson penalty into SA's 22, but ENG lose another line-out and initiative
72..Wilkinson miss-kicks a potential drop goal
78..................dogged attacks by ENG backs cannot break down SA's defence
80...Full-time. ENG 6–15 SA

————————— RUGBY UNION SIX NATIONS · 2008 —————————

Date		result		venue
02·02·08	Ireland	16–11	Italy	Croke Park
02·02·08	England	19–26	Wales	Twickenham
03·02·08	Scotland	6–27	France	Murrayfield
09·02·08	Wales	30–15	Scotland	Millennium Stadium
09·02·08	France	26–21	Ireland	Stade de France
10·02·08	Italy	19–23	England	Stadio Flaminio
23·02·08	Wales	47–8	Italy	Millennium Stadium
23·02·08	Ireland	34–13	Scotland	Croke Park
23·02·08	France	13–24	England	Stade de France
08·03·08	Ireland	12–16	Wales	Croke Park
08·03·08	Scotland	15–9	England	Murrayfield
09·03·08	France	25–13	Italy	Stade de France
15·03·08	Italy	23–20	Scotland	Stadio Flaminio
15·03·08	England	33–10	Ireland	Twickenham
15·03·08	Wales	29–12	France	Millennium Stadium

FINAL TABLE 2007						TOTAL HONOURS EVER		
points	w	d	l	pd	country	triple crowns	grand slams	titles
10	5	0	0	82	Wales	19	10	24
6	3	0	2	25	England	23	12	25
6	3	0	2	10	France	n/a	8	16
4	2	0	3	-6	Ireland	9	1	10
2	1	0	4	-54	Scotland	10	3	14
2	1	0	4	-57	Italy	n/a	0	0

————————— HEINEKEN EUROPEAN CUP FINAL · 2008 —————————

MUNSTER 16–13 TOULOUSE
24·05·08 · Millennium Stadium, Cardiff

Munster – *tries*: Leamy; *penalty goals*: O'Gara (3); *cons*: O'Gara · Toulouse – *tries*:
Donguy; *penalty goals*: Elissalde; *dropped goal*: Elissalde; *cons*: Elissalde

Munster secured their second European title in three years in a close match against
French side Toulouse. The two teams had appeared in seven of the last nine finals.

————————— INTERNATIONAL RUGBY BOARD AWARDS · 2007 —————————

International player of the year .... Bryan Habana [RSA]
International team of the year... South Africa
International coach of the year...................................... Jake White [RSA]
International sevens team of the year................................. New Zealand
International sevens player of the year........................ Afeleke Pelenise [NZL]
International women's personality of the year....................... Sarah Corrigan

RUGBY LEAGUE CHALLENGE CUP · 2008

ST HELENS 28–16 HULL
30·8·08 · WEMBLEY STADIUM

St Helens – *tries*: Gidley, Meli (2), Wilkin, Pryce · *goals*: Long (4)
Hull – *tries*: Yeaman (2), Raynor · *goals*: Tickle (2)

St Helens survived a scare from plucky Hull to win their third Challenge Cup final in a row. With 15 minutes to play, Hull were leading 12–10 after two tries by Kirk Yeaman (both converted by Danny Tickle). But the Saints were not to be thwarted and produced three more tries to turn the match around and seal a historic win. St Helens' Paul Wellens was awarded the Lance Todd Man of the Match Trophy.

MAN OF STEEL · 2007

St Helens hooker James Roby was presented with the 2007 Man of Steel prize, awarded by sports journalists to the most outstanding player in Rugby League's Super League. Roby is the third St Helens player in a row to win the accolade.

RYDER CUP · 2008

At Valhalla, Kentucky, in September 2008, the US brought to an end Europe's hat trick of consecutive Ryder Cup wins, with a 16½–11½ victory. Even the absence of world number one Tiger Woods[†] did not hamper a youthful US side that, under the captaincy of Paul Azinger, finally found its team spirit. Europe's captain Nick Faldo was criticised both for his team selection and its order, but his players accepted their share of the blame for Europe's worst performance since 1981.

† In June 2008, Woods secured his 14th Major title at the US Open – playing through the pain of recent arthroscopic knee surgery. Those who expressed scepticism that Woods was injured were discomfited when it was announced he would miss the rest of the season to undergo further treatment.

GOLF MAJORS · 2008

♂	course	winner	score
MASTERS	Augusta, Georgia	Trevor Immelman [RSA]	+3
US OPEN	Torrey Pines, California	Tiger Woods [USA]	−1
THE OPEN	Royal Birkdale, England	Padraig Harrington [IRE]	+3
USPGA	Oakland Hills, Michigan	Padraig Harrington [IRE]	−3
♀			
KRAFT NABISCO	Mission Hills, California	Lorena Ochoa [MEX]	−11
LPGA	Havre de Grace, Maryland	Yani Tseng [TAI]	−12
US OPEN	Interlachen, Minnesota	Inbee Park [KOR]	−9
BRITISH OPEN	Sunningdale, England	Ji Yai Shin [KOR]	−18

—————————— TOUR DE FRANCE · 2008 ——————————

As Spain's Carlos Sastre crossed the Paris finish line to win the 2008 Tour de France, there were hopes that the tour might be emerging from years darkened by doping scandals. 33-year-old Sastre, nicknamed Don Limpio (Mr Clean), became the third successive Spaniard to win the tour in what was arguably Spain's greatest sporting year (victory in Euro 2008 [see p.299], and Nadal's triumph at Wimbledon [see p.312]). The spectre of doping still haunted the event (three competitors were expelled early in the tour), but race commentators praised the return of more fallible riders – a fact that seemed to indicate an absence of drug abuse. Sastre laid the foundations for his win with a daring sprint away from the pack at the bottom of the Alpe-d'Huez, creating a 1min 34s lead over Cadel Evans. Pre-race favourite Evans had the chance to reclaim the yellow jersey in a decisive time-trial, but despite his much-vaunted speed he failed to trim enough seconds off Sastre's lead. Australian Evans was runner-up in the 2007 tour, but was not able to translate that promise into victory in 2008, again coming in second place. ❦ For Britain the focus was on the amazing performance of 23-year-old Manxman Mark Cavendish, who sealed his reputation as one of the world's best sprinters by taking an impressive 4 stage victories. Cavendish claimed emphatic victories in stages 5, 8, 12, and 13 before retiring from the tour to prepare for the Olympics. The final standings were:

1	Carlos Sastre [ESP]	Team CSC	87 hours 52 mins 52s
2	Cadel Evans [AUS]	Silence – Lotto	+58s
3	Bernhard Kohl [AUT]	Gerolsteiner	+ 1min 13s

Lance Armstrong announced in September 2008 that he would return to competitive cycling in 2009 to try and capture a record eighth Tour de France victory. Armstrong, who retired in 2005, said of his decision to launch a comeback, 'It is in order to raise awareness of the global cancer burden'.

—————— CYCLING WORLD TRACK CHAMPIONSHIP · 2008 ——————

Great Britain continued their domination of the World Track Championships in Manchester in March 2008, beating 2007's record haul of seven gold medals with nine gold and two silver in 2008. The British medallists are listed below:

	Event	name	medal
♂	Men's sprint	Chris Hoy	G
♂	Individual pursuit	Bradley Wiggins	G
♂	Team pursuit	Great Britain	G
♂	Team sprint	Great Britain	S
♂	Keirin	Chris Hoy	G
♂	Madison	Mark Cavendish & Bradley Wiggins	G
♀	Women's sprint	Victoria Pendleton	G
♀	Individual pursuit	Rebecca Romero	G
♀	Team pursuit	Great Britain	G
♀	Team sprint	Great Britain	G
♀	Keirin	Victoria Pendleton	S

───────FORMULA ONE TEAMS & DRIVERS · 2008───────

McLaren Mercedes.............. Lewis Hamilton [GBR] & Heikki Kovalainen [FIN]
Renault............................Fernando Alonso [ESP] & Nelsinho Piquet [BRA]
Ferrari .... Felipe Massa [BRA] & Kimi Räikkönen [FIN]
Honda............................ Rubens Barrichello [BRA] & Jenson Button [GBR]
BMW Sauber ....Nick Heidfeld [GER] & Robert Kubica [POL]
Toyota...Timo Glock [GER] & Jarno Trulli [ITA]
Red Bull.............................David Coulthard [GBR] & Mark Webber [AUS]
Williams...............................Kazuki Nakajima [JAP] & Nico Rosberg [GER]
Toro Rosso ....Sebastien Bourdais [FRA] & Sebastian Vettel [GER]
Force India (formerly Spyker).......Giancarlo Fisichella [ITA] & Adrian Sutil [GER]
Super Aguri .... forced out of F1 in May 2008 due to lack of finance

─────FORMULA ONE WORLD CHAMPIONSHIP · 2008─────

Date	Grand Prix	track	winning driver	team
16·03·08	Australian	Albert Park	Lewis Hamilton	McLaren
23·03·08	Malaysian	Sepang	Kimi Räikkönen	Ferrari
06·04·08	Bahrain	Sakhir	Felipe Massa	Ferrari
27·04·08	Spanish	Catalunya	Kimi Räikkönen	Ferrari
11·05·08	Turkish	Istanbul Park	Felipe Massa	Ferrari
25·05·08	Monaco	Monte Carlo	Lewis Hamilton	McLaren
08·06·08	Canada	Gilles-Villeneuve	Robert Kubica	BMW
22·06·08	French	Magny-Cours	Felipe Massa	Ferrari
06·07·08	British	Silverstone	Lewis Hamilton	McLaren
20·07·08	German	Hockenheim	Lewis Hamilton	McLaren
03·08·08	Hungarian	Hungaroring	Heikki Kovalainen	McLaren
24·08·08	European	Valencia	Felipe Massa	Ferrari
07·09·08	Belgian	Spa	Felipe Massa	Ferrari
14·09·08	Italian	Monza	Sebastian Vettel	Toro Rosso
28·09·08	Singaporean	Singapore		
12·10·08	Japanese	Fuji Speedway		
19·10·08	Chinese	Shanghai Int. Circuit		
02·11·08	Brazilian	Interlagos		

───────SUPERBIKES, RALLY & MOTORSPORT───────

Isle of Man TT (Senior) [2008]............................ John McGuinness (Honda)
Isle of Man TT (Supersport Junior) [2008]....................Bruce Anstey (Suzuki)
Moto GP [2007] ....Casey Stoner (Ducati)
British Superbikes [2007]................................. Ryuichi Kiyonari (Honda)
World Superbikes [2007] ....James Toseland (Honda)
World Rally [2007] ....Sébastien Loeb (Citroën)
Le Mans [2008] .... Rinaldo Capello, Tom Kristensen, Allan McNish (Audi)
Indie 500 [2008].. Scott Dixon (Dallara-Honda)

─────────────── TWENTY20 WORLD CUP ───────────────

India triumphed at the inaugural Twenty20 World Cup in South Africa in September 2007. Twelve teams contested the cup, and the first round of matches mostly followed the form book (only the West Indies suffered a shock after they were edged out of the competition by Bangladesh). England disappointed in the Super Eight stage by failing to win any matches. The semi-final results were:

SEMI-FINAL 1	SEMI-FINAL 2
New Zealand *vs* Pakistan	India *vs* Australia
New Zealand.....................143/8	India..............................188/5
Pakistan 147/4	Australia.........................173/7
Pakistan won by 6 wickets	India won by 15 runs

THE FINAL – 24·09·07
India won the toss and elected to bat
India 157/5 · Pakistan 152/10 · India won by 5 runs
Man of the Match: Irfan Pathan · Man of the Series: Shahid Afridi

The final was close-run. India started well, Gautam Ghabir scored a distinguished 75, and R. Sharma made 30 runs off 16 balls. Pakistan's Imran Nazir impressed by scoring 33 off 14 balls before being run out by Uthappa. Misbah-ul-Haq scored 4 sixes as he powered his way to 43 while wickets fell around him. In the final over, Misbah brought Pakistan within an inch of the title but was caught out trying to hit another boundary. India won with 3 balls remaining, securing their first major victory since 1983, in what many saw as a fitting end to an exciting World Cup.

─────────────── INDIAN PREMIER LEAGUE ───────────────

The Rajasthan Royals, captained by Shane Warne, won the Indian Premier League's opening season in June 2008. The Twenty20 league was created by the Board of Control for Cricket in India (BCCI) to cater for the huge numbers of ardent Indian cricket fans with money to spend. The league will run for 6 weeks each summer, and represents a significant pay day for the players and for the BCCI (the auction for the 8 team franchises raised $723m, and the television rights sold for $1bn). The England and Wales Cricket Board (ECB), concerned that centrally contracted players might be tempted away from international and county duties, refused to sign the requisite 'No Objection Certificates'. As a consequence, Dimitri Mascarenhas was the only English cricketer to play in the inaugural season. Prior to the opening season, players were auctioned to the highest bidding team. The top bids were:

Player	*team*	*cost* ($)			
M. Dhoni [IND]	Chennai	1·5m	I. Pathan [IND]	Mohali	925,000
A. Symonds [AUS]	Hyderabad	1·35m	B. Lee [AUS]	Mohali	900,000
S. Jayasuriya [SRI]	Mumbai	975,000	J. Kallis [RSA]	Bangalore	900,000
			H. Singh [IND]	Mumbai	850,000

After a successful first season, two further teams will join the IPL in 2010, Ahmedabad & Kanpur.

—————————— WISDEN CRICKETER OF THE YEAR ——————————

In 2008, the *Wisden* Cricketers of the Year (awards for the players who exerted the greatest influence on the English season in 2007) were Ian Bell [ENG], Ryan Sidebottom [ENG], Shivnarine Chanderpaul [WI], Ottis Gibson [WI], and Zaheer Khan [IND]. The *Wisden* Leading Cricketer in the World was Jacques Kallis [RSA].

—————————— TWENTY20 CUP FINAL DAY · 2008 ——————————

Middlesex won their first trophy since the 1993 County Championship when they triumphed in the Twenty20 Cup in July 2008. They fought their way to the final by using spin bowlers Murali Kartik and Shaun Udal to limit their opponents' run rates. Middlesex's Owais Shah was Man of the Match for his 75 off 35 balls.

Semi-final 1	Kent (173–7) *bt* Essex (159–8) by 14 runs
Semi-final 2	Middlesex (141–2) *bt* Durham (138–6) by 8 wickets
Cup Final	Middlesex (187–6) *bt* Kent (184–5) by 3 runs

—————————— WORLD BOXING CHAMPIONS · AT 19·9·2008 ——————————

Weight	WBC	WBA	IBF	WBO
Heavy	Peter [NGR]	Valuev [RUS]	Klitschko [UKR]	Klitschko [UKR]
Cruiser	*vacant*	Arslan [GER]	Cunningham [USA]	*vacant*
Light heavy	Diaconu [ROM]	Garay [ARG]	Tarver [USA]	Erdei [HUN]
Super middle	*vacant*	Kessler [DEN]	Bute [ROM]	Calzaghe [GBR]
Middle	Pavlik [USA]	Sturm [GER]	Abraham [GER]	Pavlik [USA]
Light middle	Mora [USA]	Santos [PUR]	Phillips [USA]	Dzinziruk [UKR]
Welter	Berto [USA]	Margarito [MEX]	Clottey [GHA]	Williams [USA]
Light welter	Bradley [USA]	Kotelnik [UKR]	Malignaggi [USA]	Holt [USA]
Light	Pacquiao [PHI]	Campbell [USA]	Campbell [USA]	Campbell [USA]
Super feather	*vacant*	Valero [PAN]	Baloyi [RSA]	Cook [GBR]
Feather	Larios [MEX]	John [INA]	Guerrero [USA]	Luevano [USA]
Super bantam	Vazquez [MEX]	Caballero [PAN]	Molitor [CAN]	Lopez [PUR]
Bantam	Hasegawa [JAP]	Moreno [PAN]	Agbeko [GHA]	Peñalosa [PHI]
Super fly	Mijares [MEX]	Mijares [MEX]	Darchinyan [AUS]	Montiel [MEX]
Fly	Naito [JAP]	Sakata [JAP]	Donaire [PHI]	Narvaez [ARG]
Light fly	Sosa [MEX]	Asloum [FRA]	Solis [MEX]	Calderon [PUR]
Straw	Sithsamerchai [THA]	González [NIC]	Garcia [MEX]	Nietes [PHI]

The Ring magazine, the self-proclaimed 'bible of boxing', creates a ranking of the best boxers across all weight divisions, which many fans regard as an authoritative source of the best 'pound-for-pound' boxers in the world. At 15/9/2008, *The Ring* top 10 were: [1] Manny Pacquiao (Super Featherweight); [2] Juan Manuel Marquez (Super Featherweight); [3] Joe Calzaghe (Super Middleweight/Light Heavyweight); [4] Bernard Hopkins (Light Heavyweight); [5] Israel Vazquez (Super Bantamweight); [6] Antonio Margarito (Welterweight); [7] Kelly Pavlik (Middleweight); [8] Christian Mijares (Super Fly); [9] Rafael Marquez (Super Bantamweight); [10] Miguel Cotto (Welterweight).

---------------- LONDON MARATHON · 2008 ----------------

On Sunday 13 April 2008, *c.*35,000 took part in the 28th London Marathon.

♂ *race results*
M. Lel [KEN].................2h 5m 15s
S. Wanjiru [KEN] ....02·05·24
A. Goumri [KEN] ....02·05·30

♂ *wheelchair race results*
D. Weir [GBR] ....01·33·56
K. Fearnley [AUS].............01·34·00
S. Lemeunier [FRA]...........01·34·01

♀ *race results*
I. Mikitenko [GER] ....02·24·14
S. Zakharova [RUS] ....02·24·39
G. Wami [ETH] ....02·25·37

♀ *wheelchair race results*
S. Graf [SUI] ....01·48·04
A. McGrory [USA]............01·51·58
S. Woods [GBR]...............02·01·59

– OTHER MARATHONS OF NOTE · 2007/08 –

BERLIN.................*first run* 1974
2007 · Sep 30 ....mild, cloudy
♂ .....H. Gebrselassie [ETH] · 2:04:26
♀.............G. Wami [ETH] · 2:23:17
Purse.......................*c.*€265,000

NEW YORK.............*first run* 1970
2007 · Nov 4...............dry, sunny
♂ ....M. Lel [KEN] · 2:09:04
♀...........P. Radcliffe [GBR] · 2:23:09
Purse........................>$600,000

CHICAGO...............*first run* 1977
2007 · Oct 7 ....hot, humid
♂ ....P. Ivuti [KEN] · 2:11:11
♀............. B. Adere [ETH] · 2:33:49
Purse.......................$579,000

BOSTON ....*first run* 1897
2008 · Apr 21 ....cool, cloudy
♂ .....R. K. Cheruiyot [KEN] · 2:07:46
♀.............D. Tune [ETH] · 2:25:25
Purse.......................$796,000

---------------- UK MARATHONS & RUNS ----------------

The Flora London Marathon is Britain's best-known race, but a host of other runs and marathons take place throughout the year. Some 2008 events are listed below:

Race	date	location	miles	terrain
Cornwall Coastal Marathon...	15/03...	N Cornish coast	26........	off-road
Belfast City Marathon........	05/05...	Belfast	26.............	road
Neolithic Marathon...........	05/05...	Wiltshire.............	26........	off-road
Edinburgh Marathon.........	25/05...	Edinburgh	26†	road
Dartmoor Discovery...........	07/06...	Princetown, Devon...	32.......	moorland
Great North Run	05/10...	Gateshead	13...........	road
Loch Ness Marathon	05/10...	Loch Ness	26.......	moorland
Beachy Head Marathon	25/10...	East Sussex...........	26..	off-road/cliffs
Snowdonia Marathon.........	25/10...	Wales.................	26...	mountainous
Great South Run.............	26/10...	Portsmouth	10...........	road
Sodbury Slog.................	09/11...	Chipping Sodbury....	9½ ...multi-terrain

† Runners can form a 'Hairy Haggis' relay team and divide this distance up between four people.

—————————— DWAIN CHAMBERS vs BY-LAW 25 ——————————

In July 2008, Dwain Chambers failed in his bid to suspend the British Olympic Association's (BOA) 'by-law 25', which prohibits athletes found guilty of doping offences from competing at the Olympics. Chambers argued that the BOA's ban represented an unfair restraint of trade, and that his winning 100m time (10·0s) at the GB Olympic trials in Birmingham days earlier had earned him the right to be considered for Beijing. Yet, while Justice Sir Colin Mackay agreed that 'people both inside and outside sport would see this by-law as unlawful', he ruled against Chambers, citing the weakness of his case and the imminence of the games: 'In my judgement it would take a much better case than the claimant has presented to persuade me to overturn the status quo at this stage and compel his selection for the games.' ❦ Chambers was caught using steroids in 2003 and went on to admit taking a range of banned substances. He was stripped of his 2002 European Championship 100m gold and his 2003 World Championship 4×100m relay silver; asked to return his prize money from that period; and banned from athletics for two years. During that time, Chambers attempted a variety of careers – including American football, rugby league, and reality TV – but with his sprinting talent undiminished, his goal was Beijing 2008. ❦ Welcoming the judgement, the BOA's chairman Lord Moynihan said that 'nobody found guilty of serious drug-cheating offences should have the honour of wearing GB vests at the Olympic Games'. Yet the Judge's ruling indicated that the BOA's 'by-law 25' might not stand forever.

—————————— THE EUROPEAN ATHLETICS CUP · 2008 ——————————

In a welcome boost for British athletics, in June 2008 in Annecy, France, the Great Britain men's team won the European cup – the last ever before a re-branding[†]. After securing promotion back to the top flight of competition in 2007, Britain's women went on to take bronze. The cup has been contested annually by national teams – each fielding one representative per event, who accumulates points for their team (8 points for 1st to 1 point for 8th). The 2008 results were as follows:

♂ country	points	♀ country	points
1 ... Great Britain & NI	112	1 ... Russia	122
2 ... Poland	98	2 ... Ukraine	108·5
3 ... France	96	3 ... Great Britain & NI	89
4 ... Germany	95	4 ... Poland	86
5 ... Russia	84	5 ... France	81
6 ... Italy	82	6 ... Italy	79·5
7 ... Spain	81	7 ... Belarus	78
8 ... Greece	68	8 ... Germany	74

† In 2009 the competition will be re-branded as the European Team Championships in an effort to make the competition more exciting and media-friendly. 12 teams will contest for honours; the winner will be decided by a combination of the men's and women's scores. In a further concession to impatient television audiences, the three slowest athletes will be eliminated from the 3,000m, 3,000m steeplechase, and 5,000m, in the hope that athletes will desist from running slow tactical races.

—————————— WIMBLEDON WINNERS · 2008 ——————————

Rafael Nadal finally beat his nemesis Roger Federer in an epic rain-delayed final, as the king of clay took on the king of grass, and won. The longest Wimbledon men's final in history (4 hours 48 minutes) was watched by 12·7m awestruck viewers amazed at a supreme battle that rivalled the classic 1981 final between Borg and McEnroe. Venus Williams took the women's title for a fifth time. The results were:

MEN'S SINGLES
Rafael Nadal [ESP]
bt Roger Federer [SUI]
6–4, 6–4, 6–7 (5–7), 6–7 (8–10), 9–7
———
'It is a dream to play on this court,
my favourite tournament,
but to win I never imagined.'
RAFAEL NADAL

LADIES' SINGLES
Venus Williams [USA]
bt Serena Williams [USA]
7–5, 6–4
———
'It's monumental.' – VENUS WILLIAMS

MEN'S DOUBLES
Daniel Nestor [CAN]
& Nenad Zimonjic [SRB]
bt Jonas Bjorkman [SWE]
& Kevin Ullyett [ZIM]
7–6 (14–12), 6–7 (3–7), 6–3, 6–3

LADIES' DOUBLES
Venus Williams [USA]
& Serena Williams [USA]
bt Lisa Raymond [USA]
& Samantha Stosur [AUS]
6–2, 6–2

MIXED DOUBLES
Bob Bryan [USA]
& Samantha Stosur [AUS]
bt Mike Bryan [USA]
& Katarina Srebotnik [SLO]
7–5, 6–4

BOYS' SINGLES
Grigor Dimitrov [BUL]
bt Henri Kontinen [FIN]
7–5, 6–3

GIRLS' SINGLES
Laura Robson [GBR]
bt Noppawan Lertcheewakarn [THA]
6–3, 3–6, 6–1

BOYS' DOUBLES
Cheng-Peng Hsieh [TPE]
& Tsung-Hua Yang [TPE]
bt Matt Reid [AUS]
& Bernard Tomic [AUS]
6–4, 2–6, 12–10

GIRLS' DOUBLES
Polona Hercog [SLO]
& Jessica Moore [AUS]
bt Isabella Holland [AUS]
& Sally Peers [AUS]
6–3, 1–6, 6–2

———————— WIMBLEDON 2008 PRIZE MONEY ————————

Round (No. prizes)	singles[†]
Winner (1)	£750,000
Runner-up (1)	£375,000
Semi-final (2)	£187,500
Quarter-final (4)	£93,750
4th round (8)	£50,000
3rd round (16)	£28,125
2nd round (32)	£17,000
1st round (64)	£10,250

† Winnings for doubles differ. Total prize money for the entire championship was £11·8m.

———————————— THE DAVIS CUP ————————————

The Davis Cup began in 1900 and now involves 134 countries, of which only 16 qualify to play in the World Group. The rest fight it out in continental leagues in an effort to gain promotion into the elite World Group – from which, after losing to Austria in September, Britain was relegated. Below are Britain's 2008 results:

8–10 February · World Group, round 1
Estadio Parque Roca, Buenos Aires (surface: clay)
Argentina *bt* Great Britain 4–1

David Nalbandian [ARG] *bt* Jamie Baker [GBR] 6–1, 6–3, 6–3
Agustin Calleri [ARG] *bt* Alex Bogdanovic [GBR] 6–3, 6–1, 6–1
Jose Acasuso & David Nalbandian [ARG]
bt Jamie Murray & Ross Hutchins [GBR] 6–2, 7–6 (13–11), 6–0
Jose Acasuso [ARG] *bt* Alex Bogdanovic [GBR] 7–5, 7–5
Jamie Baker [GBR] *bt* Agustin Calleri [ARG] 7–6 (7–4), 6–4

———————

19–21 Sept · World Group Play-offs
All England Lawn Tennis Club, London (surface: grass)
Austria *bt* Great Britain 3–2 (GBR relegated to Euro-African Group one)

Jurgen Melzer [AUT] *bt* Alex Bogdanovic [GBR] 3–6, 7–6, 6–2, 6–1
Andy Murray [GBR] *bt* Alexander Peya [AUT] 6–4, 6–1, 6–3
Julian Knowle & Jurgen Melzer [AUT]
bt Jamie Murray & Ross Hutchins [GBR] 6–4, 6–3, 6–1
Andy Murray [GBR] *bt* Jurgen Melzer [AUT] 6–4, 5–7, 6–4, 6–1
Alexander Peya [AUT] *bt* Alex Bogdanovic [GBR] 2–6, 6–4, 6–4, 6–2

——— TENNIS GRAND SLAM TOURNAMENTS · 2008 ———

Event	month	surface	♂ winner	♀
Australian Open	Jan	Plexicushion†	Novak Djokovic	Maria Sharapova
French Open	May/Jun	clay	Rafael Nadal	Ana Ivanovic
Wimbledon	Jun/Jul	grass	Rafael Nadal	Venus Williams
US Open	Aug/Sep	DecoTurf	Roger Federer‡	Serena Williams

† In 2008 the surface was switched from Rebound Ace to Plexicushion Prestige. It was hoped that the new acrylic surface would react better to the sometimes extreme heat at the Australian Open. Plexicushion Prestige is classified by the International Tennis Federation (ITF) as a Category 3 (medium) speed court. ‡ Roger Federer claimed his fifth consecutive US Open in 2008, becoming the first man to win five successive titles at two Grand Slam events (Wimbledon and the US Open). Federer beat Britain's Andy Murray 6–2, 7–5, 6–2. Previously, Murray had never got beyond the quarter-finals in a Grand Slam competition – however, an impressive victory over world number one Rafael Nadal in the semi-finals set up his first Grand Slam final. Murray reflected: 'There are so many things I can improve on, and that's exciting. I hope this will be the start of big things for me.'

─────────── SPORTS PARTICIPATION ───────────

Data released by the Department of Culture, Media & Sport in August 2008 revealed the type of people who took part in moderate-intensity sport once a week:

Characteristic	% participating in sport
Age · 16–24	32·1
25–44	26·0
45–64	19·4
65–74	13·5
>75	5·0
Gender · ♂	25·0
♀	18·3
Disability · limiting disability	9·4
Non-limiting disability	21·4
No disability	25·2
Ethnicity · White	21·8
Mixed race	30·0
Asian	17·6
Black	19·3
Other	16·6
Religion · no religion	26·4
Christian	20·1
Buddhist	30·3
Hindu	17·8
Muslim	17·9
Sikh	22·8
Other religion	12·2

60% of those questioned for the survey had not taken part in any moderate-intensity sport at all in the preceding week. [Source: DCMS · Taking Part 2006/07 · data refer to England only]

─────── THE ROYAL ENCLOSURE AT ROYAL ASCOT ───────

In January 2008, a stricter dress code was issued for the Royal Enclosure at Ascot Racecourse. The Queen's Representative, the Duke of Devonshire, clarified the code in response to criticisms of the revealing attire of some racegoers in recent years. Anyone who flouts the dress code, below, will be asked to leave the Royal Enclosure.

WOMEN
'Her Majesty's Representative wishes to point out that only formal day dress with a hat or substantial fascinator will be acceptable. Off the shoulder, halter neck, spaghetti straps and dresses with a strap of less than one inch and/or mini skirts are considered unsuitable. Midriffs must be covered and trouser suits must be full length and of matching material and colour.'

GENTLEMEN
'...either black or grey morning dress, including a waistcoat, with a top hat.'

CHILDREN (OVER 10)
'Girls must wear a dress or skirt, boys a suit or jacket ...with a tie.'

OVERSEAS VISITORS
'...are welcome to wear the formal national dress of their country.'

Royal Ascot takes place every year in June. For further information on obtaining a badge for the Royal Enclosure, contact The Royal Enclosure Office at Ascot Racecourse. First-time applicants need to be sponsored by an individual who has attended the Royal Enclosure for 4 years. ❦ 18-year-old Princess Eugenie caused a stir by wearing a short white studded Collette Dinnigan dress that many thought broke the new dress code. Eugenie was not excluded from the Royal Enclosure. ❦ In May 2008 the first new British racecourse in 80 years opened in Great Leighs, Essex. The floodlit all-weather track will host 70–80 race meetings a year. Another new track, Ffos Las in Wales, is due to open in July 2009; this will bring the total number of racecourses in Britain to 61.

———BBC SPORTS PERSONALITY OF THE YEAR · 2007———

Sports personality of the year ....Joe Calzaghe
Team of the year.......................................England Rugby Union team
Overseas personality .... Roger Federer
Coach of the year..Enzo Calzaghe
Lifetime achievement...Sir Bobby Robson
Young personality ....Tom Daley (Olympic diver)
Unsung hero ....Margaret Simons (Bardwell Football founder)
Helen Rollason award 'for courage and achievement in the face of adversity' ...... Oscar Pistorius

———————— CORDON ROUGE CLUB ————————

Seventeen adventurers and explorers were inducted as founding members of the
Cordon Rouge Club in April 2008. The club – sponsored by Mumm Champagne
– will meet once a year to celebrate the collective achievements of its members and
nominate suitably inspiring new blood. The inaugural members of the club were:

Bear Grylls – *adventurer & club Chair*
Tom Avery – *Polar adventurer* · Charley Boorman – *motorcyclist & adventurer*
Dee Caffari MBE – *round-the-world yachtswoman*
Ben Fogle – *Trans-Atlantic rower & adventurer*
Mike Golding MBE – *round-the-world yachtsman*
David Hempleman-Adams MBE OBE – *Polar balloonist & adventurer*
Sir Robin Knox-Johnston – *round-the-world yachtsman*
Neil Laughton – *Everest mountaineer & adventurer*
Dame Ellen MacArthur – *round-the-world yachtswoman*
Ewan McGregor – *motorcyclist & adventurer*
Olly & Suzi – *expedition adventurer artists* · Ben Saunders – *Polar adventurer*
Oliver Steeds – *tribal expert & adventurer*
Brian Thompson – *round-the-world yachtsman*
Patrick Woodhead – *Antarctic adventurer*

———————— SKIING & SNOWBOARDING INJURIES ————————

Skiiers and snowboarders are increasingly putting themselves at risk of serious
injury or death, according to a review of 24 studies by Charles Tator of Toronto
Western Hospital. The research, published in *Injury Prevention* in December 2007,
found that the incidence of spinal cord and traumatic brain injury was increasing
amongst winter sport devotees – with snowboarders and young males most at risk.
The review suggested that the need for speed and a growing trend for performing
acrobatic jumps could both be causal factors. One of the studies reviewed suggested that snowboarders were 50% more likely to sustain head and neck injuries than
skiers, while another indicated that male skiers and snowboarders were 2·2 times
more likely to sustain head injury than females. The report's authors noted that
helmets were found to reduce the risk of head injury by between 22–60 per cent.

---------- DARTS · PDC ----------

Canadian John 'Darth Maple' Part clinched his second PDC World title in January 2008, beating plucky qualifier Kirk 'Karate Kid' Shepherd 7–2. Part started with great flair, taking the first set in 14 darts and powering on to a 4–0 lead. Shepherd mustered something of a rally to pull back a set with an 108 check-out, but Part was not to be stopped and after six attempts finally took the sixth set to lead 5–1. Shepherd bravely responded with a 12-dart finish and a 160 check-out to snatch another set. Part was not rattled, and confidently took the last two sets and with them the £100,000 title. Although it was Part who took victory, it was Shepherd who gained most plaudits. The 21-year-old factory worker from Kent started the competition as a 500–1 outsider, beat five seeds to reach the final, and improved his ranking by 118 places to reach No. 22 in the world.

---------- DARTS · BDO ----------

World number one Mark Webster beat qualifier Simon 'The Wizard' Whitlock 7–5 in a thrilling final at Lakeside to become 2008 BDO World Champion. The quality of darts was high, with Webster and Whitlock throwing 28 180s between them as they fought for the title. Welshman Webster started with great class, winning nine of the first eleven legs to hold a 3–0 lead. But mullet-sporting Whitlock was not to be thwarted and the Australian pulled the score back to 3–2. Webster won the next set, but Whitlock stayed perilously close, refusing to let Webster run away with victory before proving his mettle by taking the seventh set to zero. Webster ultimately triumphed, securing the £85,000 title with his first attempt at a double ten. 24-year-old Webster became just the third Welshman and the second left-handed player to lift the trophy.

---------- THE LAUREUS AWARDS · 2008 ----------

The Laureus World Sporting Academy encourages the 'positive and worthwhile in sport', presenting awards to athletes in all disciplines. Some 2008 winners were:

World sportsman of the year .... Roger Federer (tennis)
World sportswoman of the year .... Justine Henin† (tennis)
World team of the year .... South African rugby team
World breakthrough of the year .... Lewis Hamilton (Formula One)
Comeback of the year .... Paula Radcliffe (running)
World Sportsperson of the Year with a Disability .... Esther Vergeer (tennis)
World Action Sportsperson of the Year .... Shaun White (snow/skateboarding)
Spirit of Sport Award .... Dick Pound (World Anti-Doping Agency)
Sport for Good Award ..... Brendan and Sean Tuohey (PeacePlayers International)
Lifetime Achievement Award .... Sergey Bubka (pole vault)

† On 14 May 2008, Justine Henin surprised the tennis world by announcing her immediate retirement. At 25 years old and ranked number one in the world (for 177 weeks), Henin was at her peak, but explained, 'I've been playing tennis for 20 years and it's been my whole life but as a woman, as you get older, you need to think about the future.' Henin won four French Open titles (2003, 2005, 2006, 2007), two US Opens (2003, 2007), one Australian Open, and 41 WTA singles titles.

——888.COM WORLD SNOOKER CHAMPIONSHIP · 2008——

Ronnie O'Sullivan took his third world title in 2008, beating Ali 'The Captain' Carter 18–8 at the Crucible. The Rocket was rarely challenged in the final, and he displayed only glimpses of the effortless skill he used to defeat seven-times Crucible champion Stephen Hendry 17–6 in the semis. Carter failed to capitalise on O'Sullivan's lack of sparkle, but did manage a break of 84 in the 21st to fend off the ignominy of being beaten in just three sessions. As the evening session resumed, the tension was broken by an exuberant streaker who lay spread-eagled under the table. O'Sullivan, who led 11–5 overnight, was not distracted and produced a break of 69 in the 25th frame, before seizing victory in the 26th after Carter missed a blue.

THE FINAL · FRAME-BY-FRAME
Ronnie O'Sullivan [ENG] 18–8 Ali Carter [ENG]

DAY ONE			
Frame *tally*	65–18............5–2	77–32 (57) 10–5	85–0 (71)......14–6
81–56............1–0	73–0............6–2	110–5 (106)...11–5	0–84 (84)......14–7
127–0 (88) 2–0	78–0 (78)........7–2		62–42.........15–7
99–4 (99)........3–0	36–60............7–3	DAY TWO	1–89 (71)......15–8
0–104 (104).....3–1	86–8 (86)........8–3	*Frame* *tally*	72–39..........16–8
86–4 (74)........4–1	28 93 (76) 8–4	76–48 (52) 12–5	73–32 (69) 17–8
62–76...........4–2	45–80 (80) 8–5	74–0...........13–5	62–16..........18–8
	126–0 (86) 9–5	25–64.........13–6	

The 2008 championship was the first to feature two 147s. O'Sullivan made his maximum against Mark Williams, and he pledged to splurge the £147,000 prize on a new Bentley. However, Ali Carter's 147 against Peter Ebdon forced The Rocket to share the purse, and perhaps downgrade his car selection.

—WORLD SCRABBLE CHAMPIONSHIPS & SCRABULOUS—

The biannual 2007 World Scrabble Championship, held in Mumbai, India, was won by Nigel Richards of New Zealand who trousered the $15,000 prize. The 2007 competition was the first to be played under the World English-language Scrabble Players Association (WESPA) rules. The official dictionary was the *Collins Scrabble Tournament & Club Word List*. ❦ Scrabble was invented sometime in the 1930s by American Alfred Butts, an unemployed architect, with the help of entrepreneur James Brunot. They registered the name 'Scrabble' in 1948, and 100 million sets have since been sold worldwide. ❦ In January 2008, to the consternation of millions of players, Facebook was asked to remove its hugely popular game 'Scrabulous'. Scrabble's owners, Hasbro and Mattel, claimed that Scrabulous infringed their copyright. By July 2008 the developers behind Scrabulous had remodelled the game and it returned to Facebook. Round tiles, custom-designed boards and a new name, 'Wordscraper', were introduced in an effort to foil possible legal action.

500 participants from 20 French-speaking countries attended the Francophone World Scrabble Championship in Dakar, Senegal, in July 2008. 32-year-old Elysée Poka of the Ivory Coast won the classic title after travelling by bus for five days to compete in the prestigious 37th championship.

—— READY RECKONER OF OTHER RESULTS · 2007/08——

AMERICAN FOOTBALL · Superbowl	New York Giants 17–14 New England Patriots
ANGLING · National Coarse Ch. Div.1	Richard Lattimer 31·8kg
BADMINTON · English Nat. Ch.	♀ Elizabeth Cann *bt* Tracey Hallam 21–15, 21–19
	♂ Rajiv Ouseph *bt* Aamir Ghaffar 21–15, 12–21, 21–11
BASEBALL · World Series [2007]	Boston Red Sox 4–0 Colorado Rockies
BASKETBALL · NBA finals	Boston Celtics 4–2 Los Angeles Lakers
BBL Trophy final	Guildford Heat 86–79 Newcastle Eagles
THE BOAT RACE	Oxford *bt* Cambridge [by 6 lengths, in 20m, 53s]
BOG SNORKELLING · World Championships	Conor Murphy [NI] 1min 38·9s
BOWLS · World Indoor Cup	Alison Merrien *bt* Val Smith 17–3, 1–10 (4–0)
World Indoor Champion	Alex Marshall [SCO] *bt* Ian Bond [ENG] 10–2, 11–5
CHEESE ROLLING · Cooper's Hill	♂ Christopher Anderson [ENG] ♀ Flo Early [ENG]
CHESS · British Championship	GM Stuart Conquest
FIDE World Championship [2007]	Vishwanathan Anand
COMPETITIVE EATING · Int. Hot Dog Eating	Joey 'Jaws' Chestnut [USA] [59 in 10 mins]
World Nettle Eating Championship	Paul Collins [ENG] 64 ft of raw leaves
CRICKET · Test series – England *vs* New Zealand (in NZ)	England *bt* NZ 2–1
One day series	NZ *bt* England 3–1
Test Series – England *vs* New Zealand (in England)	England *bt* NZ 2–0
One day series	NZ *bt* England 3–1
Test Series – England *vs* South Africa (in England)	South Africa *bt* England 2–1
One day series	England *bt* South Africa 4–0
Women's one day series	England *bt* South Africa 4–0
Friends Provident Trophy	Essex *bt* Kent by 5 wickets
County Championship [2007]	Sussex
CROQUET · British Open	Robert Fulford
CYCLING · Tour de France	Carlos Sastre [ESP] [see p.306]
Tour of Britain	Geoffroy Lequatre (Agritubel)
DARTS · Ladbrokes W. Ch. [PDC]	John Part *bt* Kirk Shepherd [see p.316]
Lakeside World Championship [BDO]	Mark Webster *bt* Simon Whitlock [see p.316]
ELEPHANT POLO · World Championships	Chopard 7–4 Chivas Regal Scotland
ENDURANCE RACES · Marathon des Sables	♂ Mohamad Ahansal [MAR] 19:27·46
	♀ Touda Didi [MAR] 28:38·11
Devil o' the Highlands	♂ Jez Bragg 5:22·54 · ♀ Sharon Lawless 7:12·55
EQUESTRIANISM · Badminton	Hildago de L'ile *ridden by* N. Touzaint [FRA] 48·4 pen
Burghley	Tamarillo *ridden by* William Fox-Pitt [GBR] 47·8 pen
FOOTBALL · FA Cup Women's	Arsenal Ladies 4–1 Leeds United Ladies
UEFA Cup	Zenit St. Petersburg 2–0 Rangers
Community Shield	Manchester United 0–0 Portsmouth (AET; 3–1 penalties)
Carling Cup	Tottenham Hotspur 2–1 Chelsea
Johnstone's Paint Trophy	Milton Keynes Dons 2–0 Grimsby Town
Premier League	Manchester United
Championship	West Bromwich Albion
League 1	Swansea City
League 2	Milton Keynes Dons
Scottish Premier League	Celtic

—READY RECKONER OF OTHER RESULTS · 2007/08 cont.—

Scottish Cup	Rangers 3–2 Queen of the South
Euro 2008	Spain 1–0 Germany
Africa Cup of Nations	Egypt 1–0 Cameroon
FORMULA ONE · World Drivers' Champion [2007]	Kimi Räikkönen [FIN] · Ferrari
World Constructors' Championship [2007]	Ferrari [ITA]
GOLF · Women's World Cup of Golf	Philippines
Mission Hills World Cup	Scotland
GREYHOUND RACING · Blue Square Greyhound Derby	Loyal Honcho
HOCKEY · World Hockey Champions Trophy	Australia *bt* Spain 4–1
HORSE RACING	
Grand National	Comply Or Die *trained by* David Pipe *ridden by* Timmy Murphy
Vodafone Epsom Derby	New Approach *trained by* Jim Bolger *ridden by* Kevin Manning
Cheltenham Gold Cup	Denman *trained by* Paul Nicholls *ridden by* Sam Thomas
1,000 Guineas	Natagora *trained by* Pascal Bary *ridden by* Christophe Lemaire
2,000 Guineas	Henrythenavigator *trained by* Aidan O'Brien *ridden by* Johnny Murtagh
The Oaks	Lush Lashes *trained by* Jim Bolger *ridden by* Kevin Manning
St Leger	Conduit *trained by* Sir Michael Stoute *ridden by* Frankie Dettori
ICE HOCKEY · Stanley Cup	Detroit Red Wings *bt* Pittsburgh Penguins, 4–2
MOBILE PHONE THROWING · World Champ. [2007]	Tommi Huotari [FIN] 294'
NETBALL · World Championship [2007]	Australia 42–38 New Zealand
RUGBY LEAGUE · Super League [2007]	Leeds Rhinos
Challenge Cup	St Helens 28–16 Hull
League Leaders' Shield	St Helens
World Club Challenge	Leeds Rhinos 11–4 Melbourne Storm
RUGBY UNION · Guinness Premiership	Gloucester [top of table]
Guinness Premiership Championship	London Wasps 26–16 Leicester Tigers
EDF Energy Anglo-Welsh Cup	Ospreys 23–6 Leicester Tigers
Magners Celtic League	Leinster
Heineken Cup	Munster 16–13 Toulouse
European Challenge Cup	Bath 24–16 Worcester Warriors
Varsity Match [2007]	Cambridge 22–16 Oxford
RUNNING · Great North Run [2007]	♂ Martin Lel [KEN] 1:00·08
	♀ Kara Goucher [USA] 1:06·57
SQUASH · British Open	Nicol David [MAS] *bt* Jenny Duncalf [GBR] 9–1, 10–8, 9–0
SUDOKU · World Sudoku Championship	Thomas Snyder [USA]
TENNIS · Australian Op.	N. Djokovic [SRB] *bt* J. Tsonga [FRA] 4–6, 6–4, 6–3, 7–6 (7–2)
	Maria Sharapova [RUS] *bt* Ana Ivanovic [SRB] 7–5, 6–3
French Open	Rafael Nadal [ESP] *bt* Roger Federer [SUI] 6–1, 6–3, 6–0
	Ana Ivanovic [SRB] *bt* Dinara Safina [RUS] 6–4, 6–3
US Open	Roger Federer [SUI] *bt* Andy Murray [GBR] 6–2, 7–5, 6–2
	Serena Williams [USA] *bt* Jelena Jankovic [SRB] 6–4, 7–5
Fed Cup	Russia *bt* Spain 4–0
Davis Cup [2007]	USA *bt* Russia 4–1
TRIATHLON · Triathlon World Championship	♂ Javier Gomez [ESP] 1:49·48
	♀ Helen Tucker [GBR] 2:01·37
British Champion	♂ Will Clarke · ♀ Hollie Avil

Ephemerides

By the help of good astronomical tables, or ephemerides,
the construction of almanacks is extremely easy.
– ANON, *The Mirror of Literature, Amusement, & Instruction*, 1824

―――――――――――――――2009―――――――――――――――

Roman numerals.............. MMIX	Indian (Saka) year......1931 (22 Mar)
English Regnal year[1] .....57th (6 Feb)	Sikh year ... 541 Nanakshahi Era (14 Mar)
Dominical Letter[2]...................D	Jewish year ....5770 (18 Sep)
Epact[3] III	Roman year [AUC] ......2762 (21 Apr)
Golden Number (Lunar Cycle)[4] ...XV	Masonic year.................6009 AL[5]
Chinese New Year...Ox 4707 (26 Jan)	Knights Templar year........ 891 AO[6]
Hindu New Year.......2065 (27 Mar)	Baha'i year................166 (21 Mar)
Islamic year............ 1431 (18 Dec)	Queen bee colour................ green

[1] The number of years from the accession of a monarch; traditionally, legislation was dated by the Regnal year of the reigning monarch. [2] A way of categorising years to facilitate the calculation of Easter. If January 1 is a Sunday, the Dominical Letter for the year will be A; if January 2 is a Sunday, it will be B; and so on. [3] The number of days by which the solar year exceeds the lunar year. [4] The number of the year (1–19) in the 19-year Metonic cycle; it is used in the calculation of Easter, and is found by adding 1 to the remainder left after dividing the number of the year by 19. [5] Anno Lucis, the 'Year of Light' when the world was formed. [6] Anno Ordinis, the 'Year of the Order'.

―――――――――――――――THE WEEK―――――――――――――――

Wash on MONDAY, *Iron* on TUESDAY,
Bake on WEDNESDAY, *Brew* on THURSDAY,
Churn on FRIDAY, *Mend* on SATURDAY, *Church* on SUNDAY.

―――――――――A CURATE'S WEEK OF CONFESSION―――――――――

In his 1854 book *Table Traits*, John Doran recounted the story of a curate at Basse-Bretagne, noted for his wit, who found that his duty at the confessional interfered with a number of invitations to dine. Seeking to indulge his stomach, the curate declared from the pulpit: 'In order to avoid confusion, my brethren, I have to announce that tomorrow, Monday, I will receive at confession the *liars* only; on Tuesday, the *misers*; on Wednesday, the *slanderers*; on Thursday, the *thieves*; Friday, the *libertines*; and Saturday, the *women of evil life*'. Doran noted 'that the priest was left during that week to enjoy himself without let or hindrance'.

─────── RED-LETTER DAYS ───────

Red-letter days are those days of civil and ecclesiastical importance – so named because they were marked out in red ink on early religious calendars. (The Romans marked unlucky days with black chalk, and auspicious days with white.) When these days fall within law sittings, the judges of the Queen's Bench Division sit wearing elegant scarlet robes. The Red-letter days in Great Britain are tabulated below:

Conversion of St Paul	25 Jan	St Barnabas	11 Jun
Purification	2 Feb	Official BD HM the Queen†	13 Jun
Accession of HM the Queen	6 Feb	St John the Baptist	24 Jun
Ash Wednesday	25 Feb	St Peter	29 Jun
St David's Day	1 Mar	St Thomas	3 Jul
Annunciation	25 Mar	St James	25 Jul
BD HM the Queen	21 Apr	St Luke	18 Oct
St Mark	25 Apr	SS Simon & Jude	28 Oct
SS Philip & James	1 May	All Saints	1 Nov
St Matthias	14 May	Lord Mayor's Day†	14 Nov
Ascension	21 May	BD HRH the Prince of Wales	14 Nov
Coronation of HM the Queen	2 Jun	St Andrew's Day	30 Nov
BD HRH Duke of Edinburgh	10 Jun	(† *indicates the date varies by year*)	

─ ──TABULATION OF OCCULT CORRESPONDENCES───

Archangel	Angel	Planet	Body part	Animal	Bird	Stone
Raphael	Michael	Sun	heart	lion	swan	carbuncle
Gabriel	Gabriel	Moon	left foot	cat	owl	crystal
Camael	Zamael	Mars	right hand	wolf	vulture	diamond
Michael	Raphael	Mercury	left hand	ape	stork	agate
Zadikel	Sachiel	Jupiter	head	hart	eagle	sapphire
Haniel	Anael	Venus	generative organs	goat	dove	emerald
Zaphkiel	Cassiel	Saturn	right foot	mole	hoopoe	onyx

— H. STANLEY REDGROVE, *Bygone Beliefs*, 1919

─────── KEY TO SYMBOLS USED OVERLEAF ───────

[★ BH]	UK Bank Holiday	[§ *patronage*]	Saint's Day
[●]	Clocks change (UK)	[WA 1900]	Wedding Anniversary
[➹]	Hunting season (traditional)	[AD 1900]	Admission Day [US States]
[ND]	National Day	●/☺	New/Full Moon [GMT]
[NH]	National Holiday	[✦]	Annual meteor shower
[ID 1900]	Independence Day	[UN]	United Nations Day
[BD 1900]	Birthday	[◉]	Eclipse [see p.198]
[†1900]	Anniversary of death	[£]	Union Flag to be flown (UK)

Certain dates are subject to change, estimated, or tentative at the time of printing.

--------------------------------- JANUARY ---------------------------------

Capricorn [♑] · *Birthstone* · GARNET · *Aquarius* [♒]
(Dec 22–Jan 20) · *Flower* · CARNATION · (Jan 21–Feb 19)

1★.................New Year's Day [★BH] · E.M. Forster [BD1879].................Th
2.........[★BH Scotland] · St Munchin [§ *Limerick*] · David Bailey [BD1938]......... F
3................Clement Attlee [BD1883] · Mel Gibson [BD1956]................ Sa
4....................Quadrantids [♄] · Louis Braille [BD1809]...................Su
5............... Twelfth Night · St Edward the Confessor [†1066] .... M
6..................... Epiphany · Rowan Atkinson [BD1955] ....Tu
7............Gerald Durrell [BD1925] · Hirohito [†1989]..................... W
8..... Dame Shirley Bassey [BD1937] · Professor Stephen Hawking [BD1942] ....Th
9............................Joan Baez [BD1941] .... F
10........Grigori Rasputin [BD1872] · Dame Barbara Hepworth [BD1903] .... Sa
11..... ☺ · Nepal – National Unity Day [NH] · Francis Scott Key [†1843]......Su
12........................Dame Agatha Christie [†1976] .... M
13.............St Hilary of Poitiers [§ *snake-bites*] · James Joyce [†1941].............Tu
14.............Humphrey Bogart [†1957] · Anthony Eden [†1977].............. W
15..........Martin Luther King Jr's Birthday · Ivor Novello [BD1893]..........Th
16.................Carole Lombard [†1942] · Kate Moss [BD1974]................. F
17...........St Anthony of Egypt [§ *basket-makers*] · Al Capone [BD1899] .... Sa
18.....................Rudyard Kipling [†1936] ....Su
19.............USA – Martin Luther King Day · Dolly Parton [BD1946]............ M
20... Presidential Inauguration Day, USA · St Sebastian [§ *archers, soldiers, & athletes*] ... Tu
21...............Christian Dior [BD1905] · George Orwell [†1950] .... W
22.....................Lord Byron [BD1788] ....Th
23....... St John the Almsgiver · Edouard Manet [BD1832]............... F
24................ St Francis de Sales [§ *journalists*] .... Sa
25...... Scotland – Burns Night · Conversion of St Paul · St Dwyn [§ *lovers*]......Su
26.......[◉] · ☻ · Australia – Australia Day [NH] · Edward Jenner [†1823] ...... M
27.......Holocaust Memorial Day · Wolfgang Amadeus Mozart [BD1756].......Tu
28...............Charlemagne [† 814] · King Henry VIII [†1547] .... W
29.........................George III [†1820].............................Th
30.................... Mahatma Gandhi [†1948 *assassinated*] .... F
31............ Guy Fawkes [†1606 *executed*] · Franz Schubert [BD1797] .... Sa

French Rev. calendar......*Nivôse* (snow)	Dutch month ......*Lauwmaand* (frosty)
Angelic governor................*Gabriel*	Saxon month.......*Wulf-monath* (wolf)
Epicurean calendar..... *Marronglaçaire*	Talismanic stone ....*Onyx*

❦ The Latin month *Ianuarius* derives from *ianua* ('door'), since it was the opening of the year. It was also associated with *Janus* – the two-faced Roman god of doors and openings who guarded the gates of heaven. Janus could simultaneously face the year just past and the year to come. ❦ *If January Calends be summerly gay, 'Twill be winterly weather till the calends of May.* ❦ *Janiveer – Freeze the pot upon the fier.* ❦ *He that will live another year, Must eat a hen in Januvere.* ❦ On the stock market, the *January effect* is the trend of stocks performing especially well that month. ❦

FEBRUARY

Aquarius [♒]   **Birthstone** · AMETHYST   **Pisces** [♓]
(Jan 21–Feb 19)   **Flower** · PRIMROSE   (Feb 20–Mar 20)

1 . . . . . . .National Freedom Day, USA · Partridge shooting season ends [❦] . . . . . . Su
2 . . . . .Candlemas · Groundhog Day, USA. . . . . M
3 . . . . .St Blaise [§ *sore throats*] · Val Doonican [BD1927]. . . . . .Tu
4 . . . . Norman Wisdom [BD1915] · Liberace [†1987] . . . . W
5 . . . . St Agatha [§ *bell founders*] . . . . .Th
6 . . .Accession of HM Queen Elizabeth II [£] · New Zealand – Waitangi Day . . . F
7 . . . . Charles Dickens [BD1812] · Eddie Izzard [BD1962]. . . . . Sa
8 . . . . .St Jerome Emiliani [§ *abandoned children and orphans*] . . . . Su
9 . . . .[◉] · ☺ · St Apollonia [§ *dentists*] · Mia Farrow [BD1945] . . . . M
10 . . . . .St Scholastica [§ *convulsive children*] · Bertolt Brecht [BD1898]. . . . . .Tu
11 . . . . .Scottish salmon fishing season opens [❦] . . . . W
12 . . . . *Traditionally considered the day on which birds begin to sing* . . . . .Th
13 . . . . St Modomnoc [§ *bee-keepers*] · Catherine Howard [†1542 *beheaded*]. . . . . F
14 . . . . St Valentine [§ *lovers*] · P.G. Wodehouse [†1975] . . . . Sa
15 . . . . .Susan B. Anthony Day, USA · Sir Ernest Shackleton [BD1874]. . . . . Su
16 . . . . .Lithuania [ID 1918] · June 'Dot Cotton' Brown [BD1927]. . . . . M
17 . . . . Molière [†1673] · Ruth Rendell [BD1930] . . . . .Tu
18 . . . . .Count Alessandro Volta [BD1745] · John Travolta [BD1954] . . . . W
19 . . . . Prince Andrew [BD1960] [£] · Saparmurat Niyazov [BD1940]. . . . . Th
20 . . . . Sidney Poitier [BD1927] . . . . F
21 . . . . .Int. Mother Language Day [UN] · Sir Douglas Bader [BD1910] . . . . Sa
22 . . . . .Feast of Chair of St Peter · Andy Warhol [†1987] . . . . Su
23 . . . . Samuel Pepys [BD1633] · John Keats [†1821] . . . . M
24 . . . . .George Harrison [BD1943] · Alain Prost [BD1955]. . . . . .Tu
25 . . . . ☻ · Ash Wednesday · Tennessee Williams [†1983]. . . . . W
26 . . . . .Levi Strauss [BD1829] · Johnny Cash [BD1932] . . . . .Th
27 . . . . Dominican Republic [ID 1844] · Spike Milligan [†2002] . . . . F
28 . . . . .Hind stalking season closes [❦] · Henry James [†1916] . . . . Sa

---

French Rev. calendar. . . . . *Pluviôse* (rain)	Dutch month *Sprokelmaand* (vegetation)
Angelic governor. . . . .*Barchiel*	Saxon month. . . . .*Solmonath* (Sun)
Epicurean calendar. . . . *Harrengsauridor*	Talismanic stone . . . . *Jasper*

❦ Much mythology and folklore considers February to have the most bitter weather: *February is seldom warm.* ❦ *February, if ye be fair, The sheep will mend, and nothing mair; February, if ye be foul, The sheep will die in every pool.* ❦ As the day lengthens, the cold strengthens. ❦ That said, a foul February is thought to predict a fine year: *All the months in the year, Curse a fair Februeer.* ❦ The word *February* derives from the Latin *februum* – which means cleansing, and reflects the rituals undertaken by the Romans before spring. ❦ Having only 28 days in non-leap years, February was known in Welsh as *y mis bach* – the little month. ❦ February is traditionally personified in pictures either by an old man warming himself by the fireside, or as 'a sturdy maiden, with a tinge of the red hard winter apple on her hardy cheek'. ❦

—MARCH—

 Pisces [♓]
(Feb 20–Mar 20)

Birthstone · BLOODSTONE
Flower · JONQUIL

Aries [♈]
(Mar 21–Apr 20)

1 .... St David [§ *Wales*] · Trout fishing season begins [❧] .... Su
2 .... Mikhail Gorbachev [BD1931] · John Irving [BD1942] .... M
3 .... Doll's Festival, Japan · Jean Harlow [BD1911] .... Tu
4 .... Ronald Reagan & Nancy Davis [WA 1952] .... W
5 .... St Piran [§ *tin-miners*] · Patsy Cline [†1963] .... Th
6 .... Ghana [ID 1957] · Davy Crockett [†1836] .... F
7 .... St Felicity & St Perpetua of Carthage [§ *mothers separated from their children*] ...... Sa
8 .... Women's Rights & Int. Peace Day [UN] .... Su
9 .... Napoleon Bonaparte & Joséphine de Beauharnais [WA 1796] .... M
10 .... Prince Edward [BD1964] [£] · Sharon Stone [BD1958] .... Tu
11 .... ☺ · Sir Alexander Fleming [†1955] .... W
12 .... Thomas Augustine Arne [BD1710] · Liza Minelli [BD1946] .... Th
13 .... Earl Grey [BD1764] · Czar Alexander II [†1881 *assassinated*] .... F
14 .... St Matilda [§ *parents with large families*] .... Sa
15 .... Hungary [ND] · Eduard Strauss [BD1835] .... Su
16 .... St Urho [§ *Finnish immigrants in America*] · Aubrey Beardsley [†1898] .... M
17 .... St Patrick [§ *Ireland*] · World Maritime Day [UN] .... Tu
18 .... Fra Angelico [†1455] · Ivan the Terrible [†1584] .... W
19 .... St Joseph [§ *fathers and carpenters*] · Bruce Willis [BD1955] .... Th
20 .... First Day of Spring · Sir Isaac Newton [†1727] .... F
21 .... Gary Oldman [BD1958] · Ayrton Senna [BD1960] .... Sa
22 .... World Day for Water [UN] · William Shatner [BD1931] .... Su
23 .... World Meteorological Day [UN] · Roger Bannister [BD1929] .... M
24 .... St Dunchad [§ *Irish sailors*] · Queen Elizabeth I [†1603] .... Tu
25 .... Annunciation Day · Elton John [BD1947] .... W
26 .... ● · Ludwig van Beethoven [†1827] · Cecil Rhodes [†1902] .... Th
27 .... Quentin Tarantino [BD1963] .... F
28 .... Sergei Rachmaninov [†1943] · Virginia Woolf [†1941 *suicide*] .... Sa
29 .... Robert Falcon Scott [†1912] · Elle Macpherson [BD1964] .... Su
30 .... Vincent van Gogh [BD1853] · Piers Morgan [BD1965] .... M
31 .... John Constable [†1837] · Charlotte Brontë [†1855] .... Tu

French Rev. calendar ..... *Ventôse* (wind)	Dutch month .. *Lentmaand* (lengthening)
Angelic governor .... *Machidiel*	Saxon month ..... *Hrèth-monath* (rough)
Epicurean calendar .... *Oeufalacoquidor*	Talismanic stone .... *Ruby*

❧ The first month of the Roman year, March is named for Mars, the god of war but also an agricultural deity. ❧ The unpredictability of March weather leads to some confusion (*March has many weathers*), though it is generally agreed that March *comes in like a lion, and goes out like a lamb*. Yet, because March is often too wet for crops to flourish, many considered *a bushel of Marche dust* [a dry March] *is worth a ransom of gold*. ❧ March hares are 'mad' with nothing more than lust, since it is their mating season. ❧ The *Mars* bar is named after its creator, Frank Mars. ❧

-------------------------------- APRIL --------------------------------

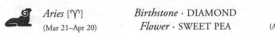

Aries [♈] | *Birthstone* · DIAMOND | *Taurus* [♉]
(Mar 21–Apr 20) | *Flower* · SWEET PEA | (Apr 21–May 21)

1 ....April Fool's Day [except in Scotland] · Roebuck season opens [♥] .... W
2 ....St Urban of Langres [§ *vine dressers*] · Georges Pompidou [†1974]........Th
3 ....Jesse James [†1882] · Graham Greene [†1991]................... F
4 ....Senegal [ID 1960] · Martin Luther King [†1968 *assassinated*] .... Sa
5 ...... Palm Sunday · St Vincent Ferrer [§ *builders*] · Howard Hughes [†1976] ..... Su
6 ....Harry Houdini [BD1874] · Gustave Moreau [BD1826] .... M
7 ....World Health Day [UN] · W.K. Kellogg [BD1860] ....Tu
8 ....Japan – Flower Festival · Pablo Picasso [†1973]................. W
9 .... ☉ · Passover · Isambard Kingdom Brunel [BD1806].............Th
10.....................Good Friday · Omar Sharif [BD1932]...................... F
11....St Stanislaw of Krakow [§ *Poland*] · Queen Margaret of Navarre [BD1492] ... Sa
12.......Easter Day · St Zeno [§ *Verona*] · Franklin D. Roosevelt [†1945].........Su
13 ★ .....[★BH] Easter Monday · Chad [ND] · Garry Kasparov [BD1963].........M
14................Abraham Lincoln [†1865 *assassinated; he died the next day*].................Tu
15.........Leonardo da Vinci [BD1452] · Jean Paul Sartre [†1980]..............W
16................St Drogo [§ *shepherds*] · Charlie Chaplin [BD1889]................Th
17......................... Benjamin Franklin [†1790] .... F
18...............Zimbabwe [ID 1980] · Albert Einstein [†1955]................. Sa
19.............Benjamin Disraeli [†1881] · Dudley Moore [BD1935]..............Su
20................. Bram Stoker [†1912] · Leslie Phillips [BD1924] .... M
21................. Queen Elizabeth II [BD1926] [£] · Lyrids [☄] ....Tu
22......................Jack Nicholson [BD1937] .... W
23..........St George [§ *England*] · World Book & Copyright Day [UN].........Th
24............ William I of Orange [BD1533] · Daniel Defoe [†1731]............ F
25........ ● · Australia & New Zealand – Anzac Day · St Mark [§ *notaries*]........ Sa
26............................Lucille Ball [†1989] ....Su
27........ ,,...... Sierra Leone [ID 1961] · St Zita [§ *bakers*] .... M
28...........Benito Mussolini [†1945 *executed*] · Francis Bacon [†1992]...........Tu
29...................Japan [ND] · Andre Agassi [BD1970]......... ,,......... W
30..........Stag stalking season closes [♥] · Édouard Manet [†1883]...........Th

French Rev. cal. ..... *Germinal* (budding) | Dutch month .... *Grasmaand* (grass)
Angelic governor...............*Asmodel* | Saxon month............ *Eastre-monath*
Epicurean calendar........*Petitpoisidor* | Talismanic stone .... *Topaz*

❦ April, T.S. Eliot's 'cruellest month', heralds the start of spring and is associated with new growth and sudden bursts of rain. ❦ Its etymology might derive from the Latin *aperire* ('to open') – although in Old English it was known simply as the *Eastre-monath*. ❦ *April with his hack and his bill, Plants a flower on every hill.* ❦ The custom of performing pranks and hoaxes on April Fool's Day (or *poisson d'avril*, as it is known in France) is long established, although its origins are much disputed. ❦ *If it thunders on All Fools' day, it brings good crops of corn and hay.* ❦ Cuckoos used to appear in letters to *The Times* c.8 April; the last was on 25 April, 1940. ❦

——————————————MAY——————————————

🐂   *Taurus* [♉]   *Birthstone* · EMERALD   *Gemini* [♊] 🧒🧒
     (Apr 21–May 21)   *Flower* · LILY OF THE VALLEY   (May 22–Jun 21)

1 ....May Day · Antonin Dvořák [†1904] .... F
2 ....Engelbert Humperdinck [BD1936] · David Beckham [BD1975] .... Sa
3 .... World Press Freedom Day [UN] · Bing Crosby [BD1904]............ Su
4 ★....[★BH] · St Florian [§ *invoked against fire & water*]· Audrey Hepburn [BD1929]..... M
5 .... Eta Aquarids [☄] · Napoleon Bonaparte [†1821]................Tu
6 .... Robert Edwin Peary [BD1856] · Sigmund Freud [BD1856] .... W
7 .... Robert Browning [BD1812].........................Th
8 ....VE Day · Sir David Attenborough [BD1926]................... F
9 .....☺ · Europe Day – European Union · Tenzing Norgay [†1986] [see p.61] ... Sa
10 ....St Catald [§ *invoked against plagues, drought & storms*] · Bono [BD1960] .... Su
11 ....Jeremy Paxman [BD1950] · Bob Marley [†1981]................ M
12 ....Florence Nightingale [BD1820] · Katharine Hepburn [BD1907] ...Tu
13 ....Garland Day – Dorset · Daphne du Maurier [BD1907] .... W
14 ....Paraguay [ND] · George Lucas [BD1944].................Th
15 ....International Day of Families [UN] · St Isidore [§ *rural life*]............. F
16 ....Sammy Davis Jr [†1990]........................... Sa
17 .... Sandro Botticelli [†1510] · Edward Jenner [BD1749] .... Su
18 ....:............International Museum Day · Gustav Mahler [†1911] .... M
19 ....St Yves [§ *lawyers & Brittany*] · Anne Boleyn [†1536 *executed*] ....Tu
20 ....St Bernardino of Siena [§ *advertising*].......................... W
21 ..... St Eugene de Mazenod [§ *dysfunctional families*] · Sir John Gielgud [†2000].....Th
22 .... International Day for Biological Diversity [UN] .... F
23 ....Henrik Ibsen [†1906] · Joan Collins [BD1933]................ Sa
24 .... ● · Nicolaus Copernicus [†1543] · Queen Victoria [BD1819] .... Su
25★ ....[★BH] Spring Bank Holiday · Venerable Bede [† 735].............. M
26 ....Samuel Pepys [†1703] · John Wayne [BD1907] ....Tu
27 .... Isadora Duncan [BD1878]......................... W
28 .... Azerbaijan [ND] · Anne Brontë [†1849]....................Th
29 ....International Day of United Nations Peacekeepers [UN]............ F
30 .... St Walstan [§ *agriculture*] · Peter Fabergé [BD1846]................. Sa
31...The Visitation of the Blessed Virgin Mary · Franz Joseph Haydn [†1809]... Su

French Rev. calendar... *Floréal* (blossom)	Dutch month ...... *Blowmaand* (flower)
Angelic governor...............*Ambriel*	Saxon month....... *Trimilchi* [see below]
Epicurean calendar...........*Aspergial*	Talismanic stone .... *Garnet*

❦ Named after *Maia*, the goddess of growth, May is considered a joyous month, as Milton wrote: 'Hail bounteous May that dost inspire Mirth and youth, and warm desire'. ❦ However, May has long been thought a bad month in which to marry: *who weds in May throws it all away.* ❦ Anglo-Saxons called May *Trimilchi*, since in May cows could be milked three times a day. ❦ May was thought a time of danger for the sick; so to have *climbed May hill* was to have survived the month. ❦ Kittens born in May were thought weak, and were often drowned. ❦

———————————— JUNE ————————————

Gemini [Ⅱ]   **Birthstone · PEARL**   **Cancer [♋]**
(May 22–Jun 21)   **Flower · ROSE**   (Jun 22–Jul 22)

1	Marilyn Monroe [BD1926]	M
2	Coronation of Elizabeth II [1953] [£] · Edward Elgar [BD1857]	Tu
3	St Kevin [§ *blackbirds*] · Tony Curtis [BD1925]	W
4	Socrates [BD 470 BC] · Sir Christopher Cockerell [BD1910]	Th
5	World Environment Day [UN] · Denmark [ND]	F
6	D-Day · Björn Borg [BD1956]	Sa
7	☿ · Malta [ND] · Charles Rennie Mackintosh [BD1868]	Su
8	St Medard [§ *good weather, prisoners & toothache*] · Francis Crick [BD1916]	M
9	Peter the Great [BD1672] · Cole Porter [BD1893]	Tu
10	HRH Prince Philip [BD1921] [£] · Spencer Tracy [†1967]	W
11	John Constable [BD1776] · Jacques Cousteau [BD1910]	Th
12	Russia [ID 1990] · The Philippines [ND]	F
13	St Anthony of Padua [§ *horses, mules, & donkeys*] · William Butler Yeats [BD1865]	Sa
14	Che Guevara [BD1928] · Steffi Graf [BD1969]	Su
15	Edvard Grieg [BD1843] · Ella Fitzgerald [†1996]	M
16	Freshwater fishing season opens [✺] · Stan Laurel [BD1890]	Tu
17	St Botulph [§ *agricultural workers*] · Venus Williams [BD1980]	W
18	Seychelles [ND] · Paul McCartney [BD1942]	Th
19	St Juliana Falconieri [§ *bodily ills*] · J.M. Barrie [†1937]	F
20	William IV [†1837] · Errol Flynn [BD1909]	Sa
21	Summer Solstice · Niccolò Machiavelli [†1527]	Su
22	● · St Thomas More [§ *lawyers*] · Fred Astaire [†1987]	M
23	Midsummer's Eve · Alan Turing [BD1912]	Tu
24	Midsummer's Day · Lucrezia Borgia [†1519]	W
25	Slovenia [ID 1991] · George Custer [†1876]	Th
26	International Day for Victims of Torture [UN]	F
27	Helen Keller [BD1880] · Jack Lemmon [†2001]	Sa
28	King Henry VIII [BD1491] · Peter Paul Rubens [BD1577]	Su
29	St Paul [§ *authors*] · Elizabeth Barrett Browning [†1861]	M
30	St Theobald [§ *bachelors*] · Mike Tyson [BD1966]	Tu

French Rev. calendar.. *Prairial* (meadow)	Dutch month ...*Zomermaand* (Summer)
Angelic governor.............. *Muriel*	Saxon month......... *Sere-monath* (dry)
Epicurean calendar....... *Concombrial*	Talismanic stone .... *Emerald*

❧ *June* is probably derived from *iuvenis* ('young'), but it is also linked to the goddess *Juno*, who personifies young women. In Scots Gaelic, the month is known as *Ian t-òg-mbìos*, the 'young month'; and in Welsh, as *Mehefin*, the 'middle'. ❧ According to weather lore, *Calm weather in June, Sets corn in tune*. ❧ To 'june' a herd of animals is to drive them in a brisk or lively manner. ❧ Wilfred Gowers-Round asserts that 'June is the reality of the Poetic's claims for May'. ❧ In parts of South Africa the verb 'to june-july' is slang for shaking or shivering with fear – because these months, while summer in the north, are mid-winter in the south. ❧

——————— JULY ———————

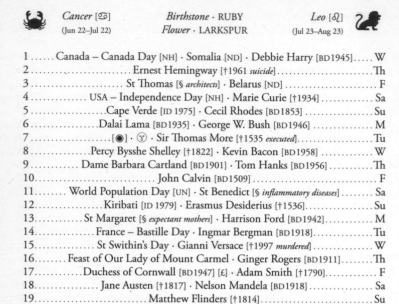

Cancer [♋]	Birthstone · RUBY	Leo [♌]
(Jun 22–Jul 22)	Flower · LARKSPUR	(Jul 23–Aug 23)

1 ...... Canada – Canada Day [NH] · Somalia [ND] · Debbie Harry [BD1945]..... W
2 .... Ernest Hemingway [†1961 *suicide*]......................... Th
3 .... St Thomas [§ *architects*] · Belarus [ND] .... F
4 .... USA – Independence Day [NH] · Marie Curie [†1934] .... Sa
5 .... Cape Verde [ID 1975] · Cecil Rhodes [BD1853] .... Su
6 .... Dalai Lama [BD1935] · George W. Bush [BD1946] .... M
7 .... [◉] · ☿ · Sir Thomas More [†1535 *executed*].................. Tu
8 .... Percy Bysshe Shelley [†1822] · Kevin Bacon [BD1958] .... W
9 .... Dame Barbara Cartland [BD1901] · Tom Hanks [BD1956] .... Th
10 .... John Calvin [BD1509] .... F
11 .... World Population Day [UN] · St Benedict [§ *inflammatory diseases*] .... Sa
12 .... Kiribati [ID 1979] · Erasmus Desiderius [†1536]............... Su
13 .... St Margaret [§ *expectant mothers*] · Harrison Ford [BD1942]............ M
14 .... France – Bastille Day · Ingmar Bergman [BD1918]............... Tu
15 .... St Swithin's Day · Gianni Versace [†1997 *murdered*] .... W
16 .... Feast of Our Lady of Mount Carmel · Ginger Rogers [BD1911]........ Th
17 .... Duchess of Cornwall [BD1947] [£] · Adam Smith [†1790]............. F
18 .... Jane Austen [†1817] · Nelson Mandela [BD1918]................. Sa
19 .... Matthew Flinders [†1814] .... Su
20 .... St Wilgefortis [§ *difficult marriages*] · Bruce Lee [†1973] .... M
21 .... Belgium [ND] · Robert Burns [†1796]...................... Tu
22 .... [◉] · ● · St Mary Magdalene [§ *hairdressers & repentant women*]............ W
23 .... Prince Andrew & Sarah Ferguson [WA 1986] .... Th
24 ...... Simón Bolívar Day – Venezuela & Ecuador · Peter Sellers [†1980] .... F
25 .... St James [§ *labourers*] · Samuel Taylor Coleridge [†1834] .... Sa
26 .... St Ann [§ *women in labour*] · Stanley Kubrick [BD1928]............... Su
27 .... St Aurelius [§ *orphans*] · Hilaire Belloc [BD1870]................... M
28 .... Delta Aquarids (South) [♐] · Johann S. Bach [†1750]............. Tu
29 .... St Martha [§ *cooks*] · Vincent van Gogh [†1890 *suicide*] .... W
30 .... Henry Ford [BD1863] · Arnold Schwarzenegger [BD1947] .... Th
31 ...... St Ignatius of Loyola [§ *those on spiritual exercises*] · J.K. Rowling [BD1965] .... F

French Rev. calendar.. *Messidor* (harvest)	Dutch month ....*Hooymaand* (hay)
Angelic governor............... *Verchiel*	Saxon month....*Mæd-monath* (meadow)
Epicurean calendar........... *Melonial*	Talismanic stone .... *Sapphire*

❦ July was originally called *Quintilis* (from *Quintus* – meaning 'fifth'), but it was renamed by Mark Antony to honour the murdered Julius Caesar, who was born on 12 July. ❦ *A swarm of bees in May is worth a load of Hay; A swarm of bees in June is worth a silver spoon; But a swarm of bees in July is not worth a fly.* ❦ *If the first of July be rainy weather, 'Twill rain mair or less for forty days together.* ❦ *Bow-wow, dandy fly – Brew no beer in July.* ❦ July used to be known as the thunder month, and some churches rang their bells in the hope of driving away thunder and lightning. ❦

—————————————— AUGUST ——————————————

 Leo [♌]   *Birthstone* · PERIDOT   *Virgo* [♍]
   (Jul 23–Aug 23)   *Flower* · GLADIOLUS   (Aug 24–Sep 23)

1 ... Stag & buck stalking seasons begin [❦] · St Alphonsus [§ *confessors, theologians*] .. Sa
2 ....Alexander Graham Bell [†1922] · Wes Craven [BD1939] ....Su
3 ....[★ BH Scotland] · Joseph Conrad [†1924] ....M
4 ....Queen Mother [BD1900] · Hans Christian Andersen [†1875] ....Tu
5 ....Oyster Day, UK · Marilyn Monroe [†1962]..................W
6 ....[◉] · ☺ · Delta Aquarids (North) [✷] · Sir Alexander Fleming [BD1881]...Th
7 ....Labour Day – Western Samoa · St Cajetan [§ *the unemployed*] ....F
8 ....St Dominic [§ *astronomers*] · Dustin Hoffman [BD1937].......... Sa
9 ....International Day of the World's Indigenous People [UN]...........Su
10 ....St Lawrence [§ *cooks*] · Ecuador [ID 1822].....................M
11 ....St Clare [§ *television & sore eyes*] · Enid Blyton [BD1897] ....Tu
12 .... Glorious Twelfth – grouse season begins [❦] · Perseids [✷] ....W
13 ....John Logie Baird [BD1888] · Florence Nightingale [†1910]...........Th
14 ....Pakistan [ID 1947] · William Randolph Hearst [†1951]..............F
15 ....VJ Day · Assumption Day · Princess Anne [BD1950] [£].......... Sa
16 ....St Stephen the Great [§ *bricklayers*] · Elvis Presley [†1977]..............Su
17 ....Gabon [ND] · Mae West [BD1892].......................M
18 ....Genghis Khan [†1227] · Patrick Swayze [BD1952]..............Tu
19 ....Afghanistan [ID 1919] · Blaise Pascal [†1662] ....W
20 ....● · St Oswin [§ *the betrayed*] · Leon Trotsky [†1940 *assassinated*]........Th
21 ....Hawaii [AD1959] · Princess Margaret [BD1930] ....F
22 ....Ramadan · Claude Debussy [BD1862] · Dorothy Parker [BD1893].......Sa
23 ....Gene Kelly [BD1912] · Rudolph Valentino [†1926] ....Su
24 ....Ukraine [ID 1991] · St Bartholomew [§ *tanners*] ....M
25 ....Michael Faraday [†1867] · Friedrich Nietzsche [†1900].............Tu
26 ....St Adrian of Nicomedia [§ *arms dealers, soldiers, & plague*] ....W
27 ....Titian [†1576] · Mother Teresa [BD1910] ....Th
28 ....Donald O'Connor [BD1925] ....F
29 .... St John the Baptist [§ *convulsive children*] · Ingrid Bergman [BD1915] [†1982].... Sa
30 ....Cleopatra [†30BC *suicide*] · Mary Wollstonecraft Shelley [BD1797]........ Su
31 ★ ....[★ BH] · Malaysia [ND] · Diana, Princess of Wales [†1997]............M

French Rev. calendar... *Thermidor* (heat)	Dutch month ..... *Oogstmaand* (harvest)
Angelic governor.............*Hamaliel*	Saxon month...... *Weod-monath* (weed)
Epicurean calendar...........*Raisinose*	Talismanic stone .... *Diamond*

❦ Previously called *Sextilis* (as the sixth month of the old calendar), August was renamed in 8BC, in honour of the first Roman Emperor, Augustus, who claimed this month to be lucky, as it was the month in which he began his consulship, conquered Egypt, and had many other triumphs. ❦ *Greengrocers rise at dawn of sun, August the fifth – come haste away, To Billingsgate the thousands run, Tis Oyster Day! Tis Oyster Day!* ❦ *Dry August and warme, Dothe harvest no harme.* ❦ *Take heed of sudden cold after heat.* ❦ *Gather not garden seeds near the full moon.* ❦ *Sow herbs.* ❦

SEPTEMBER

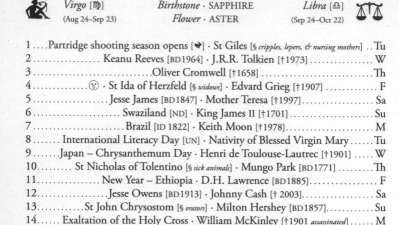

Virgo [♍]
(Aug 24–Sep 23)

Birthstone · SAPPHIRE
Flower · ASTER

Libra [♎]
(Sep 24–Oct 22)

1 ....Partridge shooting season opens [❦] · St Giles [§ *cripples, lepers, & nursing mothers*] .. Tu
2 .... Keanu Reeves [BD1964] · J.R.R. Tolkien [†1973] .... W
3 ....Oliver Cromwell [†1658] .... Th
4 ....☺ · St Ida of Herzfeld [§ *widows*] · Edvard Grieg [†1907] .... F
5 .... Jesse James [BD1847] · Mother Teresa [†1997].................. Sa
6 .... Swaziland [ND] · King James II [†1701]..................... Su
7 .... Brazil [ID 1822] · Keith Moon [†1978]...................... M
8 ...... International Literacy Day [UN] · Nativity of Blessed Virgin Mary ...... Tu
9 ......Japan – Chrysanthemum Day · Henri de Toulouse-Lautrec [†1901] ..... W
10 .... St Nicholas of Tolentino [§ *sick animals*] · Mungo Park [BD1771] ....Th
11 ....New Year – Ethiopia · D.H. Lawrence [BD1885]................ F
12 ....Jesse Owens [BD1913] · Johnny Cash [† 2003]................. Sa
13 ....St John Chrysostom [§ *orators*] · Milton Hershey [BD1857]........... Su
14 ...... Exaltation of the Holy Cross · William McKinley [†1901 *assassinated*] ...... M
15 ....Battle of Britain Day · Guatemala [ND]..................... Tu
16 ....International Day for the Preservation of the Ozone Layer [UN] .... W
17 ....Baz Luhrmann [BD1962]............................. Th
18 .... ☻ · Chile [ND] · Lance Armstrong [BD1971].................. F
19 .... Rosh Hashanah · St Januarius [§ *blood banks*] · William Golding [BD1911].... Sa
20 ....Jakob Grimm [†1863] · Sophia Loren [BD1934]................. Su
21 .... International Day of Peace [UN] · Stephen King [BD1947]........... M
22 .... First Day of Autumn · Mali [ND]....................... Tu
23 .... Wilkie Collins [†1889] · Ray Charles [BD1930]................. W
24 .... Guinea-Bissau [ID 1973] · F. Scott Fitzgerald [BD1896] .... Th
25 .... St Cadoc of Llancarvan [§ *cramps*] · Mark Rothko [BD1903]............ F
26 .... St Cosmas & St Damian [§ *pharmacists & doctors*] · T.S. Eliot [BD1888] .... Sa
27 .... St Vincent de Paul [§ *charitable societies*] · Edgar Degas [†1917]........... Su
28 ......Yom Kippur · Louis Pasteur [†1895] · Arthur 'Harpo' Marx [†1964]...... M
29 .... Michaelmas Day · Miguel de Cervantes [BD1547] ....Tu
30 .... Botswana [ND] · Truman Capote [BD1924] .... W

French Rev. calendar....*Fructidor* (fruit)	Dutch month .... *Herstmaand* (Autumn)
Angelic governor..................*Uriel*	Saxon month......*Gerst-monath* (barley)
Epicurean calendar............*Huîtrose*	Talismanic stone ....*Zircon*

❦ September is so named as it was the seventh month in the Roman calendar. ❦ *September blows soft, Till the fruit's in the loft. Forgotten, month past, Doe now at the last.* ❦ *Eat and drink less, And buy a knife at Michaelmas.* ❦ To be 'Septembered' is to be multihued in autumnal colours, as Blackmore wrote: 'His honest face was Septembered with many a vintage'. ❦ *Poor Robin's Almanack* (1666) states: 'now *Libra* weighs the days and nights in an equal balance, so that there is not an hairs breadth difference betwixt them in length; this moneth having an R in it, Oysters come again in season'. ❦ The Irish name *Meán Fómhair* means 'mid-autumn'. ❦

———————— OCTOBER ————————

♎ *Libra* [♎]   *Birthstone* · OPAL   *Scorpio* [♏] ♏
(Sep 24–Oct 22)   *Flower* · CALENDULA   (Oct 23–Nov 22)

1......Int. Day of Older Persons [UN] · Pheasant shooting season opens [☙] ....Th
2............. Mahatma Gandhi [BD1869] · Graham Greene [BD1904] .... F
3................... Germany [ND] · William Morris [†1896] .... Sa
4........ ☺ · St Francis of Assisi [§ *animals & birds*] · Jackie Collins [BD1937]........ Su
5.............International Teacher's Day [UN] · Bob Geldof [BD1951]............ M
6....................Habitat Day [UN] · Britt Ekland [BD1942] ....Tu
7....................St Sergius [§ *Syria*] · Edgar Allan Poe [†1849]............... W
8.............................Chevy Chase [BD1943].............................Th
9...................Jacques Tati [BD1908] · Che Guevara [†1967].................. F
10.........................Fiji [ND] · Orson Welles [†1985]........................ Sa
11.............. St Gummarus [§ *glove-makers*] · Ulrich Zwingli [†1531] ....Su
12.................Spain [ND] · Luciano Pavarotti [BD1935]................. M
13......Rudolf Virchow [BD1821] · Margaret Thatcher [BD1925]............Tu
14............Dwight D. Eisenhower [BD1890] · Ralph Lauren [BD1939] ....W
15.......St Teresa of Avila [§ *headache sufferers*] · Friedrich Nietzsche [BD1844] ....Th
16...................World Food Day [UN] · St Hedwig [§ *brides*]..................... F
17..... Int. Day for the Eradication of Poverty [UN] · Evel Knievel [BD1938]..... Sa
18......... ● · Alaska Day, USA · Jean-Claude Van Damme [BD1960]..........Su
19............Jonathan Swift [†1745] · John le Carré [BD1931]................ M
20.............. St Acca [§ *learning*] · Sir Christopher Wren [BD1632]...............Tu
21.................. St Hilarion [§ *hermits*] · Orionids [✷]....................... W
22..................Vatican [ND] · Kingsley Amis [†1995]..................Th
23........St John of Capistrano [§ *jurors*] · Al Jolson [†1950]............. F
24.................United Nations Day [UN] · Zambia [ND]................. Sa
25...........Kazakhstan [ND] · Geoffrey Chaucer [†1400].................Su
26................. Domenico Scarlatti [BD1685] .... M
27........ , Turkmenistan [ND] · Captain James Cook [BD1728].............Tu
28.............St Simon the Zealot [§ *rangers*] · Bill Gates [BD1955].............. W
29.............Turkey [ND] · Sir Walter Raleigh [†1618 *executed*].... ,,......Th
30.....St Marcellus the Centurion [§ *conscientious objectors*] · Ezra Pound [BD1885]..... F
31....................Hallowe'en · Harry Houdini [†1926]..................... Sa

French Rev. cal. ... *Vendémiaire* (vintage)	Dutch month .... *Wynmaand* (wine)
Angelic governor.................*Barbiel*	Saxon month....... *Win-monath* (wine)
Epicurean calendar.......... *Bécassinose*	Talismanic stone ....*Agate*

☙ October was originally the eighth month of the calendar. ☙ *Dry your barley land in October, Or you'll always be sober.* ☙ October was a time for brewing, and the month gave its name to a 'heady and ripe' ale: 'five Quarters of Malt to three Hogsheads, and twenty-four Pounds of Hops'. Consequently, *often drunk and seldom sober falls like the leaves in October.* ☙ In American politics, an *October surprise* is an event thought to have been engineered to garner political support just before an election. ☙ Roman Catholics traditionally dedicated October to the devotion of the rosary. ☙

─────────────── NOVEMBER ───────────────

Scorpio [♏]   *Birthstone* · TOPAZ   *Sagittarius* [♐]
(Oct 23–Nov 22)   *Flower* · CHRYSANTHEMUM   (Nov 23–Dec 21)

1 . . . . All Saints' Day · Hind and doe stalking season opens [❦] . . . . Su
2 . . . . ☽ · All Souls' Day · St Eustachius [§ *firefighters*] . . . . M
3 . . . . St Martin de Porres [§ *barbers*] · Henri Matisse [†1954] . . . . Tu
4 . . . . St Charles Borromeo [§ *learning and the arts*] · Felix Mendelssohn [†1847] . . . . . W
5 . . . . Guy Fawkes Night · Taurids [✦] · Art Garfunkel [BD1941] . . . . Th
6 . . . . St Leonard of Noblac [§ *against burglars*] . . . . F
7 . . . . Albert Camus [BD1913] · Steve McQueen [†1980] . . . . Sa
8 . . Remembrance Sunday [£] · Edmond Halley [BD1656] · John Milton [†1674] . Su
9 . . . . Neville Chamberlain [†1940] · Charles de Gaulle [†1970] . . . . M
10 . . . . St Tryphon [§ *gardeners*] · Martin Luther [BD1483] . . . . Tu
11 . . . . Remembrance Day · USA – Veterans Day · Angola [ID 1975] . . . . W
12 . . . . Roland Barthes [BD1915] · Grace Kelly [BD1929] . . . . Th
13 . . . . Camille Pissarro [†1903] · Whoopi Goldberg [BD1955] . . . . F
14 . . . . Prince Charles [BD1948] [£] · Claude Monet [BD1840] . . . . Sa
15 . . . . St Albert the Great [§ *scientists*] · J.G. Ballard [BD1930] . . . . Su
16 . . . ● · Int. Day for Tolerance [UN] · St Gertrude the Great [§ *souls in purgatory*] . . . M
17 . . . . Leonids [✦] · Auguste Rodin [†1917] . . . . Tu
18 . . . . St Odo of Cluny [§ *rain*] · Man Ray [†1976] . . . . W
19 . . . . Monaco [ND] · Indira Gandhi [BD1917] . . . . Th
20 . . . . Queen Elizabeth II & Prince Philip [WA 1947] [£] . . . . F
21 . . . . Presentation of the Blessed Virgin Mary in the Temple . . . . Sa
22 . . . . Aldous Huxley [†1963] · Boris Becker [BD1967] . . . . Su
23 . . . . St Felicity [§ *martyrs*] · Boris Karloff [BD1887] . . . . M
24 . . . . Henri de Toulouse-Lautrec [BD1864] · Freddie Mercury [†1991] . . . . Tu
25 . . . . St Catherine of Alexandria [§ *philosophers*] . . . . W
26 . . . . USA – Thanksgiving · St John Berchmans [§ *altar boys & girls*] . . . . Th
27 . . . . Anders Celsius [BD1701] · Jimi Hendrix [BD1942] . . . . F
28 . . . . East Timor [ND] · William Blake [BD1757] . . . . Sa
29 . . . . C.S. Lewis [BD1898] · Cary Grant [†1986] . . . . Su
30 . . . . St Andrew [§ *Scotland & Russia*] · Winston Churchill [BD1874] . . . . M

French Rev. calendar . . . . . *Brumaire* (fog)	Dutch month . . *Slaghtmaand* [see below]
Angelic governor . . . . *Advachiel*	Saxon month . . . . . . *Wind-monath* (wind)
Epicurean calendar . . . . . . *Pommedetaire*	Talismanic stone . . . . *Amethyst*

❦ Originally the ninth (*novem*) month, November has long been associated with slaughter, hence the Dutch *Slaghtmaand* ('slaughter month'). The Anglo-Saxon was *Blotmonath* ('blood' or 'sacrifice month'). ❦ A dismal month, November has been the subject of many writers' ire, as J.B. Burges wrote: 'November leads her wintry train, And stretches o'er the firmament her veil Charg'd with foul vapours, fogs and drizzly rain'. ❦ Famously, Thomas Hood's poem *No!* contains the lines 'No warmth, no cheerfulness, no healthful ease … No shade, no shine, no butterflies, no bees, No fruits, no flowers, no leaves, no birds —— November!' ❦

——— DECEMBER ———

 Sagittarius [♐]   *Birthstone* · TURQUOISE   *Capricorn* [♑]
(Nov 23–Dec 21)   *Flower* · NARCISSUS   (Dec 22–Jan 20)

1 ....World AIDS Day [UN] · Woody Allen [BD1935]................Tu
2 ....☽ · Kyrgyzstan [ND] · Britney Spears [BD1981]................W
3 ....International Day of Disabled Persons [UN] · Ozzy Osbourne [BD1948] ...Th
4 ....St Ada [§ *nuns*] · Wassily Kandinsky [BD1866]..................F
5 ....Thailand [ND] · Walt Disney [BD1901] ....Sa
6 .... St Nicholas [§ *bakers & pawnbrokers*] · Roy Orbison [†1988].............Su
7 .... USA – Pearl Harbor Day · St Ambrose [§ *protector of bees & domestic animals*] ......M
8 .... The Immaculate Conception · Sammy Davis Jr [BD1925].........Tu
9 .... Clarence Birdseye [BD1886] · Dame Judi Dench [BD1934].........W
10................Nobel Prizes awarded · Human Rights Day [UN] ....Th
11................St Damasus [§ *archaeologists*] · Burkina Faso [ND].................F
12........Chanukah · Pennsylvania [AD1787] · Robert Browning [†1889] ....Sa
13............ Japan – Soot Sweeping Day · Dick Van Dyke [BD1925]............Su
14................ Geminids [☄] · St Agnellus [§ *invoked against invaders*] ....M
15........... USA – National Bill of Rights Day · Walt Disney [†1966] ....Tu
16..............● · Kazakhstan [ID 1991] · Sir Noël Coward [BD1899].............W
17................. Sow Day – Orkney · Simón Bolívar [†1830] ....Th
18........International Migrants Day [UN] · Antonio Stradivari [†1737]..........F
19.................Emily Brontë [†1848] · Edith Piaf [BD1915].................Sa
20.... St Ursucinus of Saint-Ursanne [§ *against stiff neck*] · John Steinbeck [†1968]....Su
21..........Shortest Day · First Day of Winter · Jane Fonda [BD1937] ....M
22............ George Eliot [†1880] · Beatrix Potter [†1943].................Tu
23.................................... Ursids [☄] · Japan [ND] ....W
24................. Christmas Eve · Vasco da Gama [†1524] ....Th
25 ....Christmas Day [NH] · Dean Martin [†1995].................F
26 ....Boxing Day [NH] · St Stephen [§ *stonemasons & horses*]................Sa
27................St John [§ *Asia Minor*] · Johannes Kepler [BD1571]................Su
28................Childermass · Denzel Washington [BD1954]................M
29.......Percy Bysshe Shelley & Mary Wollstonecraft Godwin [WA 1816] ....Tu
30........ Our Lady of Bethlehem · L.P. Hartley [BD1895]..............W
31....[◉] · New Year's Eve · Scotland – Hogmanay · Henri Matisse [BD1869] ...Th

French Rev. calendar.... *Frimaire* (frost)	Dutch month ... *Wintermaand* (Winter)
Angelic governor.................Hanael	Saxon month......*Mid-Winter-monath*
Epicurean calendar.........*Boudinaire*	Talismanic stone ....*Beryl*

❦ *If the ice will bear a goose before Christmas, it will not bear a duck afterwards.* ❦
Originally the tenth month, December now closes the year. ❦ *If Christmas Day be
bright and clear there'll be two winters in the year.* ❦ The writer Saunders warned in
1679, 'In December, Melancholy and Phlegm much increase, which are heavy,
dull, and close, and therefore it behoves all that will consider their healths, to keep
their heads and bodies very well from cold'. ❦ Robert Burns splendidly wrote in
1795 – 'As I am in a complete Decemberish humour, gloomy, sullen, stupid'. ❦

TYPES OF CUCKOLD

The *patient* cuckold he is first,
The *grumbling* cuckold one oth' worst,
The *loving* cuckold he is best,
The *patient* cuckold lives at rest,
The *frenzied* cuckold giveth blows,
The *ignorant* cuckold nothing knows,
The *jealous* cuckold double twang'd,
The *pimping* cuckold would be hang'd

— *Poor Robin's Almanack*, 1699

ON FRIENDSHIP

In time of PROSPERITY
friends will be *plenty*;
In time of ADVERSITY
one out of *twenty*.

ON MEN & SHOES

How much a man is like his shoes!
For instance, both a soul may lose;
Both have been tanned; both are made
By cobblers; both get left and right.
Both need a mate to be complete;
And both are made to go on feet.
They both need healing; oft are sold,
And both in time will turn to mould
With shoes the last is first; with men
The first shall be the last; and when
The shoes wear out they're
mended tight new;
When men wear out they're
men dead too!
They both are trod upon, and both
Will tread on others, nothing loath.
Both have their ties, and both incline,
When polished, in the world to shine;
And both peg out.
Now, would you choose
To be a man or be his shoes?

— Anonymous
The Boston Courier, c.1899

ON SLEEP

On the order of going to bed
Go to bed first,
A golden purse;
Go to bed second,
A golden pheasant;
Go to bed third,
A golden bird.

On the position in bed
He that lies at the stock,
Shall have the gold rook;
He that lies at the wall,
Shall have the gold ball;
He that lies in the middle,
Shall have the gold fiddle.

On when to sleep
To rise at five, And dine at nine;
To sup at five, And bed at nine,
Will make a man live ninety-nine.

Prayers before sleep
Matthew, Mark, Luke, and John,
Bless the bed that I lay on.

Four corners to my bed,
Four angels round my head,
One at head and one at feet,
And two to keep my soul asleep.

On dreaming
Friday night's dream
On the Saturday told,
Is sure to come true,
Be it never so old.

Dreams at night
are the devil's delight,
Dreams in the morning
are the angel's warning.

To dream of things out of season,
Is trouble without reason.

Friday night's dream mark well,
Saturday night's dreams never tell.

————————ON SLEEP · STATISTICS————————

In August 2007, *Schott's Almanac* and Ipsos MORI polled the British on sleep(ing):

<table>
<tr><th colspan="3">*What time do you usually wake up on a typical day?*</th><th colspan="3">*What time do you usually go to sleep on a typical day?*</th></tr>
<tr><th>% Weekday</th><th>Time</th><th>Weekend %</th><th>% Weekday</th><th>Time</th><th>Weekend %</th></tr>
<tr><td>6</td><td>Before 5am</td><td>3</td><td>1</td><td>Before 9pm</td><td>1</td></tr>
<tr><td>19</td><td>5am–6am</td><td>10</td><td>6</td><td>9pm–10pm</td><td>3</td></tr>
<tr><td>37</td><td>6am–7am</td><td>21</td><td>36</td><td>10pm–11pm</td><td>20</td></tr>
<tr><td>25</td><td>7am–8am</td><td>23</td><td>36</td><td>11pm–midnight</td><td>34</td></tr>
<tr><td>7</td><td>8am–9am</td><td>21</td><td>20</td><td>After midnight</td><td>40</td></tr>
<tr><td>3</td><td>9am–10am</td><td>11</td><td>2</td><td>Don't know/refused</td><td>2</td></tr>
<tr><td>3</td><td>After 10am</td><td>9</td><td colspan="3"></td></tr>
<tr><td>1</td><td>Don't know/refused</td><td>1</td><td colspan="3"></td></tr>
</table>

(25% of those who sleep for more than 9 hours on a weekday claim they do not get enough sleep.)

It used to be said, in regard to the number of hours' sleep needed:
Nature requires six; *Custom* requires seven; *Laziness*, nine; and *Wickedness*, eleven.
In reality, most get 6–8 hours' sleep both on weekdays and at weekends:

% Weekday			Hours of sleep	Weekend %		
All	♂	♀		All	♂	♀
5	6	4	≤4 hours	3	2	3
13	17	10	4–6 hours	11	11	10
62	59	65	6–8 hours	48	47	48
18	17	20	8–10 hours	35	35	34
4	5	3	>10 hours	10	13	8

On which side of the bed do you usually sleep?

Side	%
Right	36
Left	32
Middle	7
No preference	22
It depends/varies/DK	2

Political affiliation does not seem to extend to choice of bed side:

Side	Con	Lab	Lib	Other
Right	39	37	44	34
Left	33	32	33	29
Middle	10	6	2	8
No pref.	14	23	19	26
Varies/DK	5	3	2	3

Do you usually sleep with some garments on, or in the nude?

Group	Sleep nude %
All	27
Men	36
Women	18
16–44s	27
45–64s	36
≥65s	12
Single	16
With partner/married	32
Widowed/divorced/separated	23
Conservative voter	28
Labour voter	26
Lib Dem voter	28
Other voter	32

[See ipsos-mori.com for additional data]

ANNIVERSARIES OF 2009

25th Anniversary (1984)
Torvill & Dean won gold at the
Winter Olympics with their Bolero
❦ The Bank of England replaced
£1 notes with coins

50th Anniversary (1959)
Fidel Castro was sworn in as Cuban
Prime Minister ❦ Lunik III took the
first photos of the far side of the Moon

75th Anniversary (1934)
Driving tests were introduced in
Britain ❦ Bonnie Parker and Clyde
Barrow were killed in an ambush ❦
Donald Duck made his screen debut
in *The Wise Little Hen*

100th Anniversary (1909)
Louis Blériot became the first person
to fly across the Channel ❦ Selfridges
in London first opened its doors ❦
The Crystal Palace hosted the world's
first Boy Scout rally ❦
Robert Peary became the first
man to reach the North Pole

150th Anniversary (1859)
Charles Blondin became the first
person to cross Niagara Falls on a
tightrope ❦ Charles Darwin's
Origin of Species was published ❦
The clock known as Big Ben was
wound up for the first time
and it started ticking

200th Anniversary (1809)
Ecuador declared independence from
Spain ❦ The first Two Thousand
Guineas Stakes was run at Newmarket

250th Anniversary (1759)
The British Museum opened ❦
England's first board game, *A Journey
Through Europe*, went on sale

500th Anniversary (1509)
Henry VIII married the first of
his six wives, Catherine of Aragon

800th Anniversary (1209)
The Albigensian Crusade was
launched against the Cathars

THE FLORAL YEAR

In 1761, the Swedish taxonomist and botanist Carl Linnæus (1707–78) published
The Calendar of Flora in which he delineated his personal twelve months of the year:

Reviving Winter	22 Dec–19 Mar	Ripening	12 Jul–4 Aug
Thawing	19 Mar–12 Apr	Reaping	4 Aug–28 Aug
Budding	12 Apr–9 May	Sowing	28 Aug–22 Sep
Leafing	9 May–25 May	Shedding	22 Sep–28 Oct
Flowering	25 May–20 Jun	Freezing	28 Oct–5 Nov
Fruiting	20 Jun–12 Jul	Dead Winter	5 Nov–22 Dec

BRITISH SUMMER TIME

BST starts and ends at 1am on these Sundays (*'spring forward – fall back'*):
2009 .... clocks forward 1 hour, 29 March · clocks back 1 hour, 25 October
2010 .... clocks forward 1 hour, 28 March · clocks back 1 hour, 31 October

NOTABLE CHRISTIAN DATES · 2009

Epiphany · *manifestation of the Christ to the Magi*.......................................6 Jan
Presentation of Christ in the Temple (Candlemas)...........................2 Feb
Ash Wednesday · *1st day of Lent*...25 Feb
The Annunciation · *when Gabriel told Mary she would bear Christ*.................25 Mar
Good Friday · *Friday before Easter; commemorating the Crucifixion*...................10 Apr
Easter Day (Western churches) · *commemorating the Resurrection*.....................12 Apr
Easter Day (Eastern Orthodox) · *commemorating the Resurrection*.....................19 Apr
Ascension Day · *commemorating the ascent of Christ to heaven*........................21 Apr
Rogation Sunday · *the Sunday before Ascension Day*...............................17 May
Pentecost (Whit Sunday) · *commemorating the descent of the Holy Spirit*............31 May
Trinity Sunday · *observed in honour of the Trinity*.......................................7 Jun
Corpus Christi · *commemorating the institution of the Holy Eucharist*.................11 Jun
All Saints' Day · *commemorating all the Church's saints collectively*.....................1 Nov
Advent Sunday · *marking the start of Advent*..29 Nov
Christmas Day · *celebrating the birth of Christ*.....................................25 Dec

A few other terms from the Christian Calendar:

Bible Sunday.................2nd in Advent
Black/Easter Monday..... the day after Easter
Collop/Egg Monday........ first before Lent
Egg Saturday..... day prior to Quinquagesima
Fig/Yew Sunday................Palm Sunday
Holy Saturday..................before Easter
Holy Week.....................before Easter
Low Sunday.............. Sunday after Easter
Maundy Thursday................[see p.275]
Mothering Sunday............... 4th in Lent

Palm Sunday...................before Easter
Passion Sunday.................. 5th in Lent
Plough Monday.............. after Epiphany
Quadragesima............1st Sunday in Lent
Quinquagesima.......... Sunday before Lent
Refreshment........ ...., 4th Sunday in Lent
Septuagesima........ 3rd Sunday before Lent
Sexagesima ....2nd Sunday before Lent
Shrove Tuesday ('pancake day').... before Lent
Shrovetide.............period preceding Lent
St Martin's Lent......................Advent
Tenebrae .... last 3 days of Holy Week

CHRISTIAN CALENDAR MOVEABLE FEASTS

Year	Ash Wednesday	Easter Day	Ascension	Pentecost	Advent Sunday
2009	25 Feb	12 Apr	21 May	31 May	29 Nov
2010	17 Feb	4 Apr	13 May	23 May	28 Nov
2011	9 Mar	24 Apr	2 Jun	12 Jun	27 Nov
2012	22 Feb	8 Apr	17 May	27 May	2 Dec
2013	13 Feb	31 Mar	9 May	19 May	1 Dec
2014	5 Mar	20 Apr	29 May	8 Jun	30 Nov
2015	18 Feb	5 Apr	14 May	24 May	29 Nov
2016	10 Feb	27 Mar	5 May	15 May	27 Nov
2017	1 Mar	16 Apr	25 May	4 Jun	3 Dec
2018	14 Feb	1 Apr	10 May	20 May	2 Dec
2019	6 Mar	21 Apr	30 May	9 Jun	1 Dec
2020	26 Feb	12 Apr	21 May	31 May	29 Nov

NOTABLE RELIGIOUS DATES FOR 2009

HINDU

Makar Sankrant · *Winter festival* ....14 Jan
Vasant Panchami · *dedicated to Saraswati and learning* ....31 Jan
Maha Shivaratri · *dedicated to Shiva* ....23 Feb
Holi · *spring festival of colours dedicated to Krishna* ....11/12 Mar
Varsha Pratipada (Chaitra) · *Spring New Year* ....22 Mar
Hindu New Year & Ramayana Week ....27 Mar
Rama Navami · *birthday of Lord Rama* ....3 Apr
Hanuman Jayanti · *birthday of Hanuman, the Monkey God.* ....9 Apr
Raksha Bandhan · *festival of brotherhood and love.* ....5 Aug
Janmashtami · *birthday of Lord Rama* ....14 Aug
Ganesh Chaturthi · *birthday of Lord Ganesh.* ....23 Aug
Navarati & Durga-puja · *celebrating triumph of good over evil.* .... *starts* 19 Sep
Saraswati-puja · *dedicated to Saraswati and learning* .... *starts* 25 Sep
Dassera (Vijay Dashami) · *celebrating triumph of good over evil* ....28 Sep
Diwali (Deepvali) · *New Year festival of lights* ....17 Oct
New Year ....18 Oct

JEWISH

Purim (Feast of Lots) · *commemorating defeat of Haman.* ....10 Mar
Pesach (Passover) · *commemorating exodus from Egypt.* ....9 Apr
Shavuot (Pentecost) · *commemorating revelation of the Torah* ....29 May
Tisha B'Av · *day of mourning* ....30 Jul
Rosh Hashanah (New Year) ....19 Sep
Yom Kippur (Day of Atonement) · *fasting and prayer for forgiveness* ....28 Sep
Sukkoth (Feast of Tabernacles) · *marking the time in wilderness.* ....3 Oct
Simchat Torah · *9th day of Sukkoth* ....11 Oct
Chanukah · *commemorating re-dedication of Jerusalem Temple* ....12 Dec

ISLAMIC

Ashura · *celebrating Noah leaving the Ark, and the saving of Moses* ....7 Jan
Milad Al-Nabi · *birthday of Muhammad* ....9 Mar
Ramadan · *the month in which the Koran was revealed* .... *starts* 22 Aug
Eid al-Fitr · *marks end of Ramadan* ....21 Sep
Eid al-Adha · *celebrating the faith of Abraham.* ....28 Nov
Al Hijra (New Year). ....17 Dec

SIKH

Birthday of Guru Gobind Singh · *founder of the Khalsa.* ....5 Jan
Sikh New Year (Nanakshahi calendar). ....14 Mar
Hola Mahalla · *festival of martial arts.* ....11 Mar
Vaisakhi (Baisakhi) · *founding of the Khalsa* ....13 Apr
Birthday of Guru Nanak (founder of Sikhism) ....14 Apr
Martyrdom of Guru Arjan ....16 Jun
Diwali · *festival of light.* ....17 Oct
Martyrdom of Guru Tegh Bahadur ....24 Nov

─────── NOTABLE RELIGIOUS DATES FOR 2009 cont. ───────

BAHA'I

Nawruz (New Year)............	21 Mar	Day of the Covenant..........	26 Nov
Ridvan...........................	21 Apr	Ascension of Abdu'l-Baha	28 Nov
Declaration of the Báb........	23 May	*World Religion Day*..............	18 Jan
Ascension of Baha'u'llah	29 May	*Race Unity Day*..................	14 Jun
Martyrdom of the Báb..........	9 July	*World Peace Day*.................	21 Sep
Birth of the Báb.................	20 Oct	*In addition, the eve of each of the*	
Birth of Baha'u'llah	12 Nov	*nineteen Baha'i months is celebrated.*	

JAIN

Mahavira Jayanti · *celebrates the day of Mahavira's birth* .... 7 Apr
Paryushan · *time of reflection and repentance*... 17 Aug
Diwali · *celebrated when Mahavira gave his last teachings and attained ultimate liberation* . . 17 Oct
New Year .... 18 Oct
Kartak Purnima · *time of pilgrimage* .... Oct/Nov

BUDDHIST

Losar · *Tibetan New Year*.. 27 Jan
Parinivana Day · *marks the death of the Buddha* .... 8 Feb
Sangha Day (Magha Puja Day) · *celebration of Buddhist community* .... 11 Mar
Wesak (Vesak) · *marks the birth, death, & enlightenment of the Buddha* .... 9 May
Dharma Day · *marks the start of the Buddha's teaching* .... 7 Jul

RASTAFARIAN

Ethiopian Christmas....	......7 Jan	Birthday of Marcus Garvey.....	17 Aug
Ethiopian Constitution..........	16 Jul	Ethiopian New Year's Day......	11 Sep
Haile Selassie birthday..........	23 Jul	Crowning of Haile Selassie	2 Nov

PAGAN

Imbolc · *fire festival anticipating the new farming season* .... 2 Feb
Spring Equinox · *celebrating the renewal of life* .... 20 Mar
Beltane · *fire festival celebrating Summer and fertility*................................ 1 May
Summer Solstice (Midsummer; Litha) · *celebrating the sun's power*................. 21 Jun
Lughnasadh · *harvest festival*.. 1 Aug
Autumn Equinox (Harvest Home; Mabon) · *reflection on the past season*........ 22 Sep
Samhain (Halloween; All Hallows Eve) · *Pagan New Year*...................... 31 Oct
Winter Solstice (Yule) · *celebrating Winter*....................................... 21 Dec

CHINESE LUNAR NEW YEAR · 26 Jan

[Every effort has been taken to validate these dates. However, readers should be aware that there is a surprising degree of debate and dispute. This is caused by the interplay of: regional variations; differing interpretations between religious authorities; seemingly arbitrary changes in dates when holidays conflict; avoidance of days considered for one or other reason inauspicious; as well as the inherent unpredictability of the lunar cycle. Many festivals, especially Jewish holidays, start at sundown on the preceding day.]

———————— PUBLIC & BANK HOLIDAYS ————————

England, Wales, & N. Ireland	2009	2010	2011
New Year's Day	1 Jan	1 Jan	3 Jan
[NI *only*] St Patrick's Day	17 Mar	17 Mar	17 Mar
Good Friday	10 Apr	2 Apr	22 April
Easter Monday	13 Apr	5 Apr	25 April
Early May Bank Holiday	4 May	3 May	2 May
Spring Bank Holiday	25 May	31 May	30 May
[NI *only*] Battle of the Boyne	13 Jul	12 Jul	12 Jul
Summer Bank Holiday	31 Aug	30 Aug	29 Aug
Christmas Day	25 Dec	27 Dec	27 Dec
Boxing Day	28 Dec	28 Dec	26 Dec

Scotland	2009	2010	2011
New Year's Day	1 Jan	1 Jan	*not confirmed*
2nd January	2 Jan	4 Jan	*not confirmed*
Good Friday	10 Apr	2 Apr	*not confirmed*
Early May Bank Holiday	4 May	4 May	*not confirmed*
Spring Bank Holiday	25 May	31 May	*not confirmed*
Summer Bank Holiday	3 Aug	2 Aug	*not confirmed*
Christmas Day	25 Dec	28 Dec	*not confirmed*
Boxing Day	28 Dec	27 Dec	*not confirmed*

These are the expected dates of holidays; some are subject to proclamation by the Queen.

———————— ON BELIEF & GOD ————————

TRANSCENDENTALISM sinks God and nature in man.
MATERIALISM sinks God and nature in the universe.
ATHEISM sinks the will of God and man in the movement of destiny.
PANTHEISM sinks man and nature in God.

—WILLIAM B. GREENE

—— TRADITIONAL WEDDING ANNIVERSARY SYMBOLS ——

1st	Cotton	10th	Tin	35th	Coral
2nd	Paper	11th	Steel	40th	Ruby
3rd	Leather	12th	Silk, Linen	45th	Sapphire
4th	Fruit, Flowers	13th	Lace	50th	Gold
5th	Wood	14th	Ivory	55th	Emerald
6th	Sugar	15th	Crystal	60th	Diamond
7th	Wool, Copper	20th	China	70th	Platinum
8th	Pottery	25th	Silver	75th	Diamond
9th	Willow	30th	Pearl	*American symbols differ.*	

PHASES OF THE MOON · MMIX

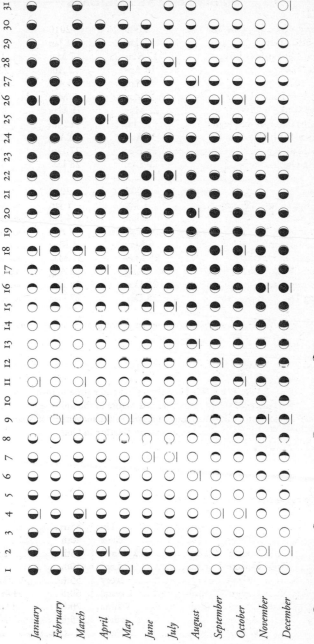

Key: ● New Moon · ◐ First Quarter · ○ Full Moon · ◑ Last Quarter · Dates are based on Universal Time (Greenwich Mean Time)

BENJAMIN FRANKLIN'S VIRTUOUS WEEK

In his autobiography, Benjamin Franklin (1706–90) tells how, aged 27, he 'conceived the bold and arduous project of arriving at moral perfection' by attempting 'to live without committing any fault at any time'. Surprised that this proved harder than he had imagined, Franklin decided to 'acquire the habitude' of the following virtues:

TEMPERANCE	*Eat not to dullness; drink not to elevation*
SILENCE	*Speak not but what may benefit others or yourself; avoid trifling conversation*
ORDER	*Let all your things have their places; let each part of your business have its time* [see p.343]
RESOLUTION	*Resolve to perform what you ought; perform without fail what you resolve*
FRUGALITY	*Make no expense but to do good to others or yourself; i.e., waste nothing*
INDUSTRY	*Lose no time; be always employed in something useful; cut off all unnecessary action*
SINCERITY	*Use no hurtful deceit; think innocently and justly; and, if you speak, speak accordingly*
JUSTICE	*Wrong none by doing injuries or omitting the benefits that are your duty*
MODERATION	*Avoid extremes; forbear resenting injuries so much as you think they deserve*
CLEANLINESS	*Tolerate no uncleanliness in body, clothes, or habitation*
TRANQUILLITY	*Be not disturbed at trifles, or at accidents common or unavoidable*
CHASTITY	[Franklin presumably thought this was self-explanatory]
HUMILITY	*Imitate Jesus and Socrates*

Imitating Pythagoras, Franklin decided that daily examination was required. So, on July 1, 1733, he began a 'little book' in which each virtue was allocated a page, thus:

TEMPERANCE							
Eat not to dullness; drink not to elevation.							
	S.	M.	T.	W.	T.	F.	S.
T[emperance]							
S[ilence]	O	O		O		O	
O[rder]	O O	O	O		O	O	O
R[esolution]			O		O		
F[rugality]		O		O			
I[ndustry]		O					
S[incerity]							
J[ustice]							
M[oderation]							
C[leanliness]							
T[ranquillity]							
C[hastity]							
H[umility]							

Comparing himself to a gardener who does not attempt to eradicate all his weeds in one fell swoop, Franklin attended to one virtue each week, leaving the others 'to their ordinary chance'. He marked each day's transgressions, hoping to keep that week's virtue unsullied and to wean himself from his other faults. One 'course' of virtues would take thirteen weeks; four courses would cover a year. Franklin's initial dedication was such that he acquired a more durable notebook, but later, as his travels became more extensive, his enthusiasm flagged and he abandoned the project – though he always carried an annotated notebook with him. At the age of 79, Franklin wrote that he owed to 'this little artifice' the 'constant felicity' of his life.

—BENJAMIN FRANKLIN'S ORDERED DAY—

Benjamin Franklin was a sworn enemy of idling and the idle. 'Trouble springs from idleness, and grievous toil from needless ease', he wrote, asserting that 'sloth, like rust, consumes faster than labour wears, while the used key is always bright'. In an attempt to employ his time fruitfully and attain the virtue of Order, he devised this 'scheme of employment for the twenty-four hours of a natural day', which he copied into the diary of virtues that he carried with him everywhere [see p.342].

MORNING *Question: What good shall I do this day?*	5 6 7	*Rise, wash and address Powerful Goodness! Contrive day's business, and take the resolution of the day; prosecute the present study, & breakfast.*
	8 9 10 11	**WORK**
NOON	12 1	*Read, or overlook my accounts, & dine.*
	2 3 4 5	**WORK**
EVENING *Question: What good have I done this day?*	6 7 8 9	*Put things in their places. Supper. Music or diversion or conversation. Examination of the day.*
NIGHT	10 11 12 1 2 3 4	**SLEEP**

Of all the virtues to which Franklin aspired, this 'scheme of Order' proved the most problematic, since 'those who must mix with the world' cannot always be masters of their own time. Franklin was so troubled by his failure to adhere to his timetable that he admitted to being 'almost ready to give up the attempt, and content [himself] with a faulty character in that respect'. Citing the parable of the man who prides himself on a 'speckled' ax having failed to sharpen it completely, Franklin confessed to pretending that perfection would have made him 'envied and hated', and that 'a benevolent man should allow a few faults in himself, to keep his friends in countenance'. In reality, however, he found himself 'incorrigible with respect to order'. That said, though he 'never arrived at the perfection [he] had been so ambitious of obtaining', he was 'by the endeavour, a better and a happier man'.

CHÁVEZ TIME, MECCA TIME, &c.

Venezuelan President Hugo Chávez turned his country's clocks back by ½ an hour on Sunday 9 December 2007, in what the government called 'a public health measure' designed to improve the 'metabolism' of the people. ['Chávez Time'=GMT–4½.] Many viewed this idiosyncratic time-shift in the context of a series of economic, constitutional, and symbolic reforms designed in part to imprint Chávez's personality on Venezuela and move the country towards a 'Chávismo' vision of socialism. Some noted that Venezuela was joining a curious club of countries that have adopted 'fractional time zones' outside GMT and the 24 meridians, including Afghanistan, Myanmar, India, Iran, and Sri Lanka. (That said, parts of Canada and Australia also operate in fractional time zones.

The Chatham Islands, east of New Zealand, are, uniquely, GMT+12¾.) Despite international scepticism, Chávez was unrepentant: 'I don't care if they call me crazy, the new time will go ahead.' ❦ A conference of Islamic scholars, meeting in Doha, Qatar, in April 2008, called for the world to abandon GMT in favour of Mecca Time (MT). [MT=GMT+3]. This call was based upon their assertion that the holy city of Mecca – the birthplace of Muhammad – was the true centre of the Earth, and that the international use of GMT was a throwback to colonial time(s). ❦ In March 2008, responding to a serious energy crisis, the S African government raised the possibility of dividing the country into two time zones in order to even out demand for electricity.

THREE TYPES OF MARRIAGE · JACOB COHEN c.1899

If a man marries for	LOVE	CONVENIENCE & COMFORT	A DOWRY
He gets	a wife	a mistress	a madam
Who will	love him	honour him	suffer him
He has her for	himself	his house & friend	society
She will	agree with him	oblige him	dictate to him
When he is ill she will	nurse him	visit him	inquire after him
When he dies she will	shed tears	sigh	wear mourning

LUCKY DAYS ON WHICH TO MARRY

January	2 ~ 4 ~ 11 ~ 19 ~ 21	August	2 ~ 11 ~ 18 ~ 20 ~ 30
February	1 ~ 3 ~ 10 ~ 19 ~ 21	September	1 ~ 9 ~ 16 ~ 18 ~ 28
March	3 ~ 5 ~ 12 ~ 20 ~ 23	October	1 ~ 8 ~ 15 ~ 17 ~ 27 ~ 29
April	2 ~ 4 ~ 12 ~ 20 ~ 22	November	5 ~ 11 ~ 13 ~ 22 ~ 25
May	2 ~ 4 ~ 12 ~ 20 ~ 23	December	1 ~ 8 ~ 10 ~ 19 ~ 23 ~ 29
June	1 ~ 3 ~ 11 ~ 19 ~ 21		
July	1 ~ 3 ~ 12 ~ 19 ~ 21 ~ 31	[A. Cielo, *Signs, Omens & Superstitions*, 1918]

Index

'Make a long arm, Watson, and see what V has to say'. I leaned back and took down the great index volume to which he referred. Holmes balanced it on his knee, and his eyes moved slowly and lovingly over the record of old cases, mixed with the accumulated information of a lifetime. 'Voyage of the *Gloria Scott*', he read ... 'Victor Lynch, the forger. Venomous lizard or gila ... Vittoria, the circus belle. Vanderbilt and the Yeggman ... Vipers. Vigor, the Hammersmith wonder. Hullo! Hullo! Good old index. You can't beat it. Listen to this, Watson, Vampirism in Hungary. And again, Vampires in Transylvania'.

— ARTHUR CONAN DOYLE, *The Adventure of the Sussex Vampire*, 1924

10p TAX DEBACLE – AWARDS, WEBBY

——— GOD, BELIEF & – MATCHED, DISPATCHED, &c. ———

—— MAUNDY THURSDAY &c. – POPULATION, URBAN ——

—————————— ERRATA, CORRIGENDA, &c. ——————————

In keeping with many newspapers and journals, *Schott's Almanac* will publish in this section any significant corrections from the previous year. Below are some errata from *Schott's Almanac 2008* – many of which were kindly noted by readers.

[p.8 *of the 2008 edition*] There was some ambiguity as to who was the least admired man, according to an *Esquire* survey. In fact, Pete Doherty was the least admired, Russell Brand and David Beckham were slightly more admired. [p.70] The 75,000 species of 'marine mammal' should have read 'marine species', and the hairy crab *Kiwa hirsuta* deserved a capital 'k'. [p.76] A number of superlatives have been amended, updated, or clarified, see p.82. [p.216] The introductory text to the chart on most-visited attractions was slightly misleading, since the chart illustrated the ratio of adult to child visits, not the actual number. [p.226] The story of Japanese people being gulled into buying lambs disguised as poodles seemed too unlikely to be true; it was. [p.298] The 1936 Olympics were, of course, held in Berlin, not Munich. [p.308] The IBF World Champion Arthur Abrahams is German, not Australian; and Edwin Valero, the WBA junior lightweight champion, is from Venezuela. [pp. 322–33] Some of the monthly calendrical markers in the Ephemerides section (e.g., the French Revolutionary months) have been shifted, though their positions remain the subject of some debate. [p.341] The symbols of the moon phases (again on p.341) have been switched this year, so that New Moons are dark and Full Moons are light; this seemed more logical.

—————————— ACKNOWLEDGMENTS ——————————

The author would like to thank:

Pavia Rosati · Jonathan, Judith, Geoffrey, & Oscar Schott, Anette Schrag
Benjamin Adams, Richard Album, Joanna Begent, Catherine Best,
Michael Binyon, Keith Blackmore, Martin Birchall, Ray Carbone, Julia Clark,
Andrew Cock-Starkey, James Coleman, Helen Coombs, Aster Crawshaw,
Jody & Liz Davies, Peter DeGiglio, Colin Dickerman, Will Douglas,
Stephanie Duncan, Jennifer Epworth, Sabrina Farber, Kathleen Farrar, Minna Fry,
Alona Fryman, Catherine Gough, Mark & Sharon Hubbard, Nick Humphrey,
Max Jones, Amy King, Robert Klaber, Maureen Klier, Amelia Knight,
Alison Lang, James Ledbetter, Annik Le Farge, John Lloyd, Ruth Logan,
Chris Lyon, Jess Manson, Michael Manson, Susannah McFarlane, Sara Mercurio,
Alice L. Miller, David Miller, Peter Miller, Polly Napper, Nigel Newton,
Sarah Norton, Alex O'Connell, Ben Page, Cally Poplak, Dave Powell,
Alexandra Pringle, Todd Pruzan, Brian Rea, Karen Rinaldi, Natalie Sandison,
David Shipley, Bill Swainson, Caroline Turner, & Greg Villepique